# MODERN MILITARY
## AIRCRAFT ANATOMY
### TECHNICAL DRAWINGS OF 118 AIRCRAFT, 1945 TO THE PRESENT DAY

GENERAL EDITORS: PAUL E. EDEN AND SOPH MOENG

*amber*
BOOKS

This edition first published in 2007

Published by
Amber Books Ltd
Bradley's Close
74–77 White Lion Street
London N1 9PF
United Kingdom
www.amberbooks.co.uk

ISBN-13: 978-1-905704-77-4

Artwork © Mike Badrocke/Aviagraphica

Printed in Thailand

# MODERN MILITARY
## AIRCRAFT ANATOMY

# Contents

# Attack Aircraft

# Dassault Etendard/Super Etendard

*Although the spotlight has been focused on the Super Etendard's precision attack operations, the type has always had a respectable conventional attack capability. This Flottille 14F aircraft totes four MATRA 155 rocket pods, each able to carry 18 2.70-in (68-mm) SNEB rockets.*

## Super Etendard

### Cutaway key

1 Radome
2 Scanner housing
3 Flat plate radar scanner
4 Scanner tracking mechanism
5 Thomson-CSF/ESD Agave multi-mode radar equipment package
6 Refuelling probe housing
7 Retractable inflight refuelling probe
8 Nav/attack avionics equipment
9 UHF aerial
10 Pitot head
11 Temperature probe
12 Refuelling probe retraction link and jack
13 Cockpit front pressure bulkhead
14 Instrument panel shroud
15 Windscreen panels
16 Head-up display
17 Control column
18 Rudder pedals
19 Cockpit section framing
20 Pressure floor level
21 Side console panel
22 Engine throttle lever
23 Radar hand controller
24 Nose undercarriage pivot fixing
25 Carrier deck approach lights
26 Nosewheel leg doors
27 Hydraulic steering jacks
28 Nosewheel forks

29 Nosewheel, aft retracting
30 Nose undercarriage leg strut
31 Rear breaker strut
32 Hydraulic retraction jack
33 Port engine air intake
34 Boundary layer splitter plate
35 Air-conditioning system ram air intake
36 Cockpit sloping rear pressure bulkhead
37 Boundary layer spill duct
38 Hispano-SEMMB built Martin-Baker CM4A ejection seat
39 Starboard engine air intake
40 Ejection seat headrest
41 Face blind firing handle
42 Cockpit canopy cover, upward hinging
43 Canopy hinge point
44 Canopy emergency release
45 Air-conditioning plant
46 Intake duct framing
47 Ventral cannon blast trough
48 Cannon barrel
49 Oxygen bottles (two)
50 Navigation and communications avionics equipment racks

51 Martin Pescador air-to-surface missile (Argentine aircraft only)
52 Martin Pescador guidance pod
53 Starboard external fuel tank
54 Equipment bay dorsal access panels
55 Fuel system inverted flight accumulator
56 Intake suction relief door
57 DEFA 552A 30-mm cannon (two)
58 Ground power and intercom sockets
59 Ventral cannon pack access door
60 Ammunition magazine, 125 rounds per gun
61 Air system pre-cooler, avionics cooling air
62 Forward fuselage bag-type fuel tanks, total internal capacity 719 Imp gal (3270 litres)
63 Fuel tank access panels
64 Wing spar attachment main frames
65 Fuselage dorsal systems ducting

66 Avionics cooling air exit louvres
67 IFF aerial
68 Starboard wing integral fuel tank
69 Pylon attachment points
70 MATRA 155 rocket launcher pack, 18 x 2.70-in (68-mm) rockets
71 Leading-edge dog-tooth
72 Leading-edge flap control rod and links
73 Starboard leading-edge flap, lowered
74 Aileron hydraulic actuator
75 Wing fold hydraulic jack
76 Outboard, folding wing tip panel
77 Strobe identification light
78 Starboard navigation light
79 Starboard wingtip folded position
80 Fixed portion of trailing edge

81 Starboard aileron
82 Aileron hinge control
83 Aileron/spoiler interconnecting link
84 Spoiler hydraulic actuator
85 Starboard spoiler, open
86 Double-slotted Fowler-type flap, down position
87 Rear fuselage bag-type fuel tanks
88 Rudder control cables
89 Engine starter housing
90 Compressor intake
91 Forward engine mounting bulkhead
92 Accessory gearbox drive shaft
93 Gearbox driven generators (two)
94 Engine accessory equipment

95 SNECMA Atar 8K50 non-afterburning turbojet engine
96 Engine bleed air duct to air conditioning system
97 Rudder control cable quadrant
98 Fin spar attachment joint
99 Leading-edge access panel to control runs
100 All-moving tailplane pitch trim control electric motor
101 Tailplane root leading-edge aerodynamic notch
102 Elevator hydraulic actuator
103 Upper/lower fin segment joint

104 Tailplane sealing plate
105 Rudder hydraulic actuator
106 Tailfin construction
107 Starboard all-moving tailplane
108 Forward radar-warning antenna
109 VOR aerial (Argentine aircraft only)
110 VHF aerial

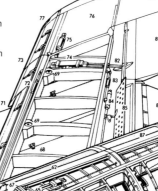

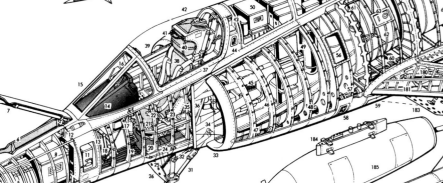

With the F-8P Crusaders of Flottille 12F having retired in December 1999, and the Etendard IVPMs of 16F and Alizés of 6F in 2000, the Super Etendard is the last survivor of the 'old' generation of Aéronavale aircraft. However, it will serve for the first decade of the 21st century alongside the Aéronavale's 'new' generation, in the shape of the Northrop Grumman Hawkeye and Dassault Rafale M. This particular 'SEM', seen during one of the last cruises of the F-8P 'Crouze', is a Standard 3 aircraft carrying an ATLIS II designator pod.

## SPECIFICATION

### Super Etendard

#### Dimensions

**Length:** 46 ft 11½ in (14.31 m)
**Height:** 12 ft 8 in (3.86 m)
**Wingspan:** 31 ft 6 in (9.60 m)
**Wingspan (folded):** 25 ft 7 in (7.80 m)
**Wing area:** 305.71 sq ft (28.40 m²)
**Wing aspect ratio:** 3.23
**Wheel track:** 11 ft 6 in (3.50 m)
**Wheelbase:** 15 ft 9 in (4.80 m)

#### Powerplant

One SNECMA Atar 8K50 turbojet rated at 11,023 lb (49.05 kN) thrust

#### Weights

**Empty equipped:** 14,330 lb (6500 kg)
**Maximum take-off:** 26,455 lb (12000 kg)

#### Fuel and load

**Internal fuel:** 719 Imp gal (3270 litres)
**External fuel:** 616 Imp gal (2800 litres)
**Maximum ordnance:** 4,630 lb (2100 kg)

#### Performance

**Maximum level speed at 36,090 ft (11000 m):** 744 kt (857 mph; 1380 km/h)
**Maximum level speed at sea level:** 637 kt (733 mph; 1180 km/h)
**Maximum rate of climb at sea level:** 19,685 ft (6000 m) per minute
**Service ceiling:** 44,950 ft (13700 m)
**Operational radius:** 459 nm (528 miles; 850 km) on hi-lo-hi anti-ship mission carrying two drop tanks and one AM39 Exocet

#### Armament

Two 30-mm DEFA 552A cannon each with 125 rounds. Four underwing and one centreline hardpoint for drop tanks and various weapons including bombs up to 881 lb (400-kg), rocket pods, BAP100 anti-runway bombs, BAT120 area-denial weapons, EU4/Paveway II LGBs, AS30L laser-guided missile, AM39 Exocet, ASMP tactical nuclear missile or Magic 2 short-range AAMs

The ATLIS II laser designation pod, introduced by the Super Etendard Modernisé Standard 3, is normally carried on the centreline pylon. It provides daylight-only capability.

111 Fintip aerial fairing
112 Command telemetry aerial
113 Rudder
114 Rudder rib construction
115 Brake parachute housing, ground based operations only
116 Tailcone parachute door
117 Tail navigation and anti-collision lights
118 Rear radar warning antenna
119 Port elevator
120 Elevator rib construction
121 Elevator damper
122 Port all-moving tailplane construction
123 Engine exhaust nozzle
124 Jetpipe
125 Inflight-refuelling drogue, extended
126 Refuelling hose
127 Deck arrester hook, lowered
128 Arrester hook stowage fairing
129 Detachable tailcone frame and stringer construction
130 Rear fuselage break point, engine removal

131 Sloping fin spar attachment bulkhead
132 Engine bay heat shroud
133 Engine turbine section
134 Radar warning power amplifier
135 Fin spar and engine mounting bulkhead
136 Main engine mounting spigot
137 Aft avionics equipment bays, port and starboard
138 Port double-slotted Fowler-type flap
139 Flap rib construction
140 Flap shroud ribs
141 Inboard flap guide rail
142 Main undercarriage wheel bay
143 Main undercarriage leg pivot fixing
144 Flap hydraulic jack
145 Port spoiler
146 Spoiler hydraulic jack and control links
147 Outboard flap guide rail
148 Aileron rib construction
149 Port aileron
150 Port wingtip, folded position
151 Wingtip panel construction
152 Wingtip fairing
153 Port navigation light
154 Strobe identification light
155 Wing fold hydraulic jack
156 Wing fold hinge joints
157 Outboard leading-edge flap segment
158 MATRA 550 Magic air-to-air missile
159 Missile launch rail
160 MATRA 155 18 x 2.70-in (68-mm) rocket pod
161 Aileron hydraulic actuator
162 Outboard pylon attachment joint
163 Outboard stores pylon
164 Leading-edge dog-tooth
165 Machined wing skin/stringer panel
166 Wing rib construction
167 Inboard pylon attachment joint
168 Inboard stores pylon
169 External fuel tank, 242 Imp gal (1100 litres)
170 Port mainwheel
171 Hydraulic multi-plate disc brake
172 Torque scissor links
173 Main undercarriage leg strut
174 Hydraulic retraction jack
175 Port wing integral fuel tank bays
176 Inboard leading-edge flap segment
177 Leading-edge flap rib construction
178 Ventral catapult strop hook
179 Wingroot bolted attachment joint
180 Leading-edge flap hydraulic jack
181 Extended chord wingroot leading-edge
182 Airbrake hydraulic jack
183 Ventral airbrake, port and starboard
184 Fuselage centreline pylon
185 Inflight refuelling 'buddy' pack
186 AM39 Exocet AShM

# Dassault Mirage III

*The most far-reaching upgrade proposed for the Mirage III was a conversion to relaxed stability configuration with the installation of an FBW system borrowed from the Mirage 2000. The Mirage 3NG (Nouvelle Génération) first flew on 21 December 1982 wearing a smart blue and white colour scheme and was fitted with foreplanes. Marketed as a 'poor man's' Mirage 2000, the 3NG was demonstrated at Farnborough and Paris, but export orders did not materialise.*

## Mirage IIIE

### Cutaway key

1 Glass-fibre fintip aerial fairing
2 VHF aerial
3 Tail navigation and anti-collision lights
4 Tail radar warning antenna
5 Rudder construction
6 Fin main spar
7 Passive radar antenna
8 UHF aerial
9 Rudder hydraulic actuator
10 Magnetic detector
11 Parachute release link
12 Brake parachute housing
13 Parachute fairing
14 Exhaust nozzle shroud
15 Variable-area exhaust nozzle flaps
16 Nozzle jacks
17 Cooling air louvres
18 Jet pipe
19 Rear fuselage frame and stringer construction
20 Wingroot trailing-edge fillet
21 Fin attachment main frame
22 Fin spar attachment joint
23 Control cable runs
24 Engine bay/jet pipe thermal lining
25 Afterburner duct
26 Elevon compensator hydraulic jack
27 Ventral fuel tank
28 Main engine mounting
29 Wing spar/fuselage main frame
30 Main spar joint
31 Engine gearbox driven generator
32 Engine accessory compartment
33 SNECMA Atar 9C afterburning turbojet
34 Cooling system air intakes
35 Heat exchanger
36 Engine oil tank
37 IFF aerial
38 Port wing integral fuel tank, total internal capacity 733 Imp gal (3330 litres)
39 Inboard elevon
40 Outboard elevon
41 Port navigation light
42 Cambered leading-edge ribs
43 Port wing pylon fixing
44 Leading-edge notch
45 Port leading-edge fuel tank
46 Main undercarriage pivot fixing
47 Fuselage dorsal systems ducting
48 Air system piping
49 Turbojet intake
50 Engine starter housing
51 Fuselage fuel tanks
52 Equipment cooling system air filter
53 Computer system voltage regulator
54 Oxygen bottles
55 Inverted flight fuel system accumulator
56 Intake ducting
57 Matra 530 missile computer
58 VHF radio transmitter/receiver
59 Gyro platform multiplier
60 Doppler transceiver
61 Navigation system computer
62 Air data computer
63 Nord missile encoding supply
64 Radio altimeter transceiver
65 Heading and inertial correction computer
66 Armament junction box
67 Radar programme controller
68 Canopy external release
69 Canopy hinge
70 Radio and electronics bay access fairing
71 Fuel tank stabilising fins
72 286-Imp gal (1300-litre) auxiliary fuel tank (374-Imp gal/1700-litre alternative)
73 137-Imp gal (625-litre) drop tank
74 Cockpit canopy cover
75 Canopy hydraulic jack
76 Ejection seat headrest
77 Face blind firing handle
78 Martin-Baker (Hispano licence) RM4 ejection seat
79 Port side console panel
80 Canopy framing
81 Pilot's head-up display
82 Windscreen panels
83 Instrument panel shroud
84 Instrument pressure sensors
85 Thomson-CSF Cyrano II fire control radar
86 Radar scanner dish
87 Glass-fibre radome
88 Pitot tube
89 Matra 530 air-to-air missile
90 Doppler radar
91 Thomson-CSF Doppler navigation radar antenna
92 Cockpit front pressure bulkhead
93 Rudder pedals
94 Radar scope (head-down display)
95 Control column
96 Cockpit floor level
97 Starboard side console panel
98 Nosewheel leg doors
99 Nose undercarriage leg strut
100 Landing/taxiing lamps
101 Levered suspension axle unit
102 Nosewheel
103 Shimmy damper
104 Hydraulic retraction strut
105 Cockpit rear pressure bulkhead
106 Air-conditioning ram air intake
107 Moveable intake half-cone centre-body
108 Starboard air intake

*During the Six-Day war, the air forces of the Arab nations surrounding Israel continued their attacks, but were met with swift resistance from the IDF/AF's fighter units. The Israeli Shahaks (local name for the Mirage III) were at the forefront of the defensive operations. The top-scoring Shahak was 59 (above), which was credited with scoring 13 kills in the hands of a number of different pilots during its Israeli service career. During the Six-Day War the aircraft downed an Egyptian Il-14 on 5 June 1967 and a MiG-19 the next day. Its finest hour was on 10 July 1970 when, piloted by Israeli Baharav, it downed a pair of Egyptian MiG-21s.*

## SPECIFICATION

### Mirage IIIE

### Dimensions

**Length:** 49 ft 3½ in (15.03 m)
**Height:** 14 ft 9 in (4.50 m)
**Wingspan:** 26 ft 11⅗ in (8.22 m)
**Wing area:** 376.75 sq ft (35.00 m²)
**Aspect ratio:** 1.94
**Wheel track:** 10 ft 4 in (3.15 m)
**Wheel base:** 15 ft 11¾ in (4.87 m)

### Powerplant

One SNECMA Atar 9C-3 rated at 9,436 lb st (41.97 kN) dry and 13,668 lb st (60.80 kN) with afterburning, and provision for one jettisonable SEPR 84 rocket booster rated at 3,307 lb st (14.71 kN)

### Weights

**Empty:** 15,542 lb (7050 kg)
**Normal take-off:** 21,164 lb (9600 kg)
**Maximum take-off:** 30,203 lb (13700 kg)

### Fuel and load

**Internal fuel:** 631.4 US gal (2390 litres)
**External fuel:** Up to two 449-, 343-, 291- or 165-US gal (1700-, 1300-, 1100- or 625-litre) drop tanks, or two 132-US gal (500-litre) non-jettisonable supersonic tanks, or two 66-US gal (250-litre) JL-100 combined drop tanks/rocket launchers, or two 291-US gal (1100-litre) fuel/electronic equipment tanks
**Maximum ordnance:** 8,818 lb (4000 kg)

### Performance

**Maximum level speed 'clean' at 39,370 ft (12000 m):** 1,268 kt

(1,460 mph; 2350 km/h)
**Cruising speed at 36,090 ft (11000 m):** 516 kt (594 mph; 956 km/h)
**Ferry range with three drop tanks:** 2,152 nm (2,486 miles; 4000 km)
**Combat radius:** 647 nm (746 miles; 1200 km)
**Maximum rate of climb at sea level:** More than 16,405 ft (5000 m) per minute
**Climb to 36,090 ft (11000 m):** 3 minutes
**Service ceiling:** 55,775 ft (17000 m) or 75,460 ft (23000 m) with rocket pack
**Take-off run:** Between 2,297 and 5,249 ft (700 and 1600 m), depending on mission-related maximum weight
**Landing run:** 2,297 ft (700 m) with brake chute
**g limits:** +4.83 in a sustained turn at Mach 0.9 at 16,405 ft (5000 m)

### Armament

Cannon armament of two 30-mm DEFA 552 cannon with 125 rounds per gun. Basic IIIC interceptor version with centreline pylon for one radar-guided missile, initially Nord 5103 or MATRA R.511, subsequently MATRA R530 (Hughes AIM-26 Falcon on Swiss aircraft). Two wing pylons for infra-red guided missile, either AIM-9B/P Sidewinder or MATRA R550 Magic. Attack capability in form of JL-100 fuel tank/rocket pod. Mirage IIIE multi-role aircraft introduced a maximum of five pylons with a maximum weaponload of 8,818 lb (4000 kg) including most free-fall bombs and rocket pods. Attack missiles include Aérospatiale AS30 and MATRA AS37 Martel. French aircraft wired for 15-kT yield AN52 tactical nuclear free-fall bomb

**109** Nosewheel well door (open position)
**110** Intake centre-body screw jack
**111** Air-conditioning plant
**112** Boundary layer bleed air duct
**113** Centre fuselage bomb rack
**114** 882-lb (400-kg) HE bombs
**115** Cannon barrels
**116** 30-mm DEFA cannon (2), 250 rounds per gun
**117** Ventral gun pack

**118** Auxiliary air intake door
**119** Electrical system servicing panel
**120** Starboard 30-mm DEFA cannon
**121** Front spar attachment joint
**122** Fuel system piping
**123** Airbrake hydraulic jack
**124** Starboard airbrake, upper and lower surfaces (open position)
**125** Airbrake housing
**126** Starboard leading-edge fuel tank
**127** AS37 Martel, radar-guided air-to-ground missile
**128** Nord AS30 air-to-air missile

**129** Starboard mainwheel
**130** Mainwheel leg door
**131** Torque scissor links
**132** Shock absorber leg strut
**133** Starboard main undercarriage pivot fixing
**134** Hydraulic retraction jack
**135** Main undercarriage hydraulic accumulator
**136** Wing main spar
**137** Fuel system piping
**138** Inboard pylon fixing
**139** Leading-edge notch
**140** Starboard inner stores pylon

**141** Control rod runs
**142** Missile launch rail
**143** AIM-9 Sidewinder air-to-air missile
**144** JL-100 fuel and rocket pack, 55 Imp gal (250 litres) of fuel plus 18 x 68-mm unguided rockets
**145** Outboard wing pylon
**146** Outboard pylon fixing
**147** Front spar
**148** Starboard navigation light
**149** Outboard elevon hydraulic jack
**150** Starboard wing integral fuel tank
**151** Inboard elevon hydraulic actuator
**152** Wing multi-spar and rib construction

**153** Rear spar
**154** Outboard elevon construction
**155** Inboard elevon construction
**156** Elevon compensator
**157** 110-Imp gal (500-litre) auxiliary fuel tanks

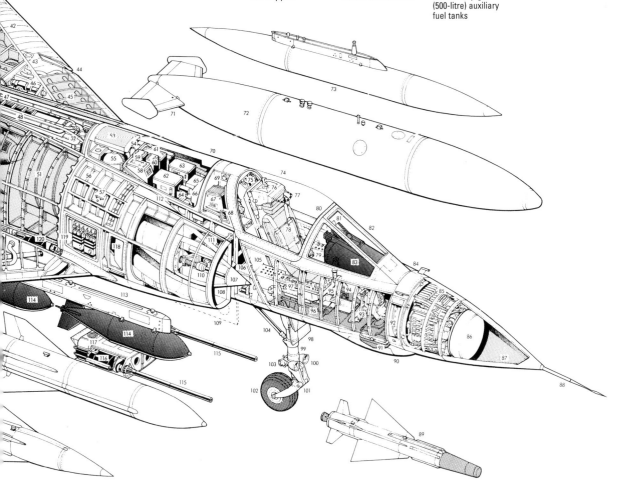

# Dassault Mirage 5/50

Seen here accompanying an RAF Buccane (wearing Desert Storm 'pink') is a Mirage 5 from the Belgian air force's No. 8 Escadrille. T nearest the Belgian Mirage came to combat w on 6 January 1991 when 15 aircraft were deploy to Erhac, Turkey to boost offensive forces in t event that Iraq attacked Turkey (during imminent UN operation to liberate Kuwa

## Mirage 50

**Cutaway key**
1 Pitot head
2 Radome
3 Scanner housing
4 Flat plate radar scanner
5 Scanner tracking mechanism
6 Thomson-CSF/EMID Agave lightweight multi-mode radar (Cyrano IV alternative fit)
7 Nose compartment construction
8 Fixed inflight-refuelling probe (optional)
9 Nose compartment access door
10 Avionics equipment compartment
11 Ventral radar altimeter aerials
12 IFF aerial
13 Instrument system total pressure head
14 Front pressure bulkhead
15 Incidence probe
16 Ventral Doppler aerial (optional equipment)
17 Cockpit pressure floor level
18 Rudder pedals
19 Radar scope (head-down display)
20 Control column
21 Instrument panel shroud
22 Windscreen panels
23 Pilot's head-up display
24 CC 420 30-mm cannon pod
25 Reconnaissance variant nose profile
26 Forward oblique OMERA 53 long-range camera
27 Lateral OMRAF 100 cameras, port and starboard
28 Camera mounting frame
29 Lateral oblique OMERA F 200 cameras, port and starboard

30 Cannon pod ammunition magazine, 250 rounds
31 Cockpit canopy cover, upward-hinging
32 Ejector seat headrest
33 Face blind-firing handle
34 Martin-Baker (Hispano licence-built) RM.4 ejector seat
35 Safety harness
36 Starboard side console panel
37 Engine throttle lever
38 Cockpit section framing
39 Port side console panel
40 Nose landing gear

41 Nosewheel leg doors
42 Nose landing-gear leg strut
43 Landing/taxiing lamps
44 Levered suspension axle beam
45 Nosewheel, aft-retracting
46 Hydraulic retraction jack/lock strut
47 Cockpit rear pressure bulkhead
48 Elevon artificial feel unit
49 Port engine air inlet
50 Movable inlet half-cone centrebody
51 Air-conditioning ram air intake
52 Battery

53 Canopy emergency release
54 Canopy hydraulic jack
55 Radar programme controller
56 Canopy hinge point
57 374-Imp gal (1700-litre) external fuel tank; 110-Imp gal (500-litre) alternative
58 Dorsal spine fairing
59 Forward fuselage fuel lank, total internal capacity 750 Imp gal (3410 litres)
60 Boundary layer spill duct
61 Air-conditioning plant
62 Inlet centrebody screw jack
63 Inlet duct

64 Ventral cannon muzzle blast trough
65 Cannon barrel
66 Intake suction relief door, spring-loaded
67 Electrical system equipment
68 Weapons system control units
69 Oxygen bottles (two)
70 Inverted flight fuel system accumulator
71 Voltage regulator
72 Leading-edge fuel tank
73 Starboard main landing-gear pivot fixing
74 Equipment cooling system air filter
75 Fuselage dorsal systems ducting

76 Bleed air and fuel system piping
77 Fuselage fuel tanks
78 Bifurcated intake trunking
79 Port 30-mm DEFA cannon
80 Front spar attachment joint
81 Engine accessory equipment drive shaft
82 Accessory equipment cooling air duct
83 Engine starter housing
84 Turbojet intake
85 Hydraulic fluid reservoir
86 Gearbox-driven generator
87 Main spar attachment joint
88 Wing spar/fuselage main frame

89 Engine compressor section
90 Bleed air pre-cooler ram air intake
91 Engine oil tank
92 VHF aerial
93 Starboard wing integral fuel tank
94 Elevon control rods
95 Leading-edge notch
96 MATRA R.550 Magic air-to-air missile
97 Missile launch rail
98 Cambered leading-edge ribs
99 Starboard navigation light
100 Outboard elevon

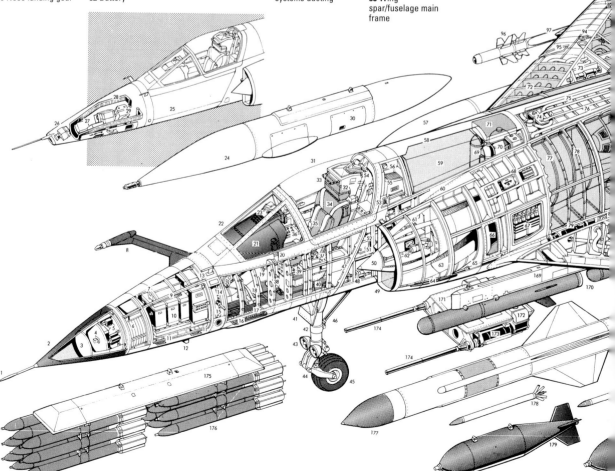

*Improvements in low-speed handling and short field performance were sought through the Milan (Kite) programme undertaken in collaboration with Switzerland. Actual production did not go ahead but the enhanced flying characteristics led to the fitment of canards to Israeli Kfirs.*

## SPECIFICATION

### Mirage 50M

### Dimensions

**Length:** 51 ft ½ in (15.56 m)
**Height:** 14 ft 9 in (4.50 m)
**Wingspan:** 26 ft 11½ in (8.22 m)
**Aspect ratio:** 1.94
**Area:** 376.75 sq ft (35.00 m²)
**Optional canard foreplane area:** 10.76 sq ft (1.00 m²)
**Wheel track:** 10 ft 4 in (3.15 m)
**Wheel base:** 15 ft 11¾ in (4.87 m)

### Powerplant

One SNECMA Atar 09K-50 rated at 11,055 lb st (49.20 kN) dry and 15,873 lb st (70.60 kN) with afterburning

### Weights

**Empty equipped:** 15,763 lb (7150 kg)
**Normal take-off:** 22,046 lb (10000 kg)
**Maximum take-off:** 32,407 lb (14700 kg)

### Fuel and load

**Internal fuel for Mirage III conversions:** 5,044 lb (2288 kg)
**Internal fuel for Mirage 5 conversions:** 5,974 lb (2710 kg)
**External fuel:** Up to two 449-, 343-, 291- or 165-US gal (1700-, 1300-, 1100- or 625-litre) drop tanks, or two 132-US gal (500-litre) non-jettisonable supersonic tanks, or two 66-US gal (250-litre) JL-100 combined drop tanks/rocket launchers, or two 291-US gal (1100-litre) non-jettisonable Bidon Cyclope fuel/electronic equipment tanks
**Maximum ordnance:** 8,818 lb (4000 kg)

### Performance

**Maximum level speed 'clean' at 39,370 ft (12000 m):** 1,262 kt (1,453 mph; 2338 km/h)
**Cruising speed at 36,090 ft (11000 m):** 516 kt (594 mph; 956 km/h)
**Combat radius:** 817 miles (1315 km)
**Maximum rate of climb at sea level:** 36,614 ft (11160 m) per minute
**Climb to 45,000 ft (13715 m):** 4 minutes 42 seconds
**Service ceiling:** 59,055 ft (18000 m)
**Take-off run at maximum take-off weight:** 2,625 ft (800 m)

### Armament

Similar to that of Mirage III family, although not nuclear-capable. Some aircraft designated Mirage 5 have Cyrano fire-control radar and are, in effect, Mirage IIIs. These can launch radar-guided air-to-air missiles, but other Mirage 5 family members cannot. Egypt's Mirage 5s employ US weapons, including the Rockeye cluster bomb. Venezuelan and some Pakistani aircraft (5PA3) have Cyrano IVM3 or Agave radar and the ability to launch the AM39 Exocet anti-ship missile

**101** Elevon hydraulic actuators
**102** Inboard elevon
**103** Rudder control cable runs
**104** SNECMA Atar 09K-50 afterburning turbojet engine
**105** Main engine mounting trunnion
**106** Fuselage ventral fuel tank
**107** Elevon compensator hydraulic actuator
**108** Engine turbine section
**109** Engine bay internal heat shield
**110** Fin spar attachment joints
**111** Rudder control quadrant
**112** Rudder hydraulic actuator
**113** Remote compass transmitter
**114** Fin main spar
**115** UHF aerial

**116** Fin leading-edge rib construction
**117** Forward radar warning antenna
**118** VHF aerial
**119** Glassfibre fintip aerial fairing
**120** Tail navigation and anti-collision lights
**121** Aft radar warning antenna
**122** Rudder
**123** Mass balance weights
**124** Rudder rib construction
**125** Hinge control link
**126** Parachute release link
**127** Brake parachute housing
**128** Conic fairing brake parachute door
**129** Exhaust nozzle shroud
**130** Variable-area exhaust nozzle flaps
**131** Nozzle control jacks
**132** Afterburner ducting
**133** Rear fuselage frame and stringer construction
**134** Wingroot trailing-edge fillet
**135** Elevon inboard compensator panel
**136** 110-Imp gal (500-litre) auxiliary ventral fuel tank
**137** Inboard elevon
**138** Elevon rib construction
**139** Outboard elevon
**140** Cambered wingtip
**141** Port navigation light
**142** Outboard elevon hydraulic actuator
**143** Rearspar
**144** Inboard elevon hydraulic actuator
**145** Port wing integral fuel tank
**146** Front spar
**147** Cambered leading-edge ribs
**148** Outboard missile pylon
**149** Missile launch rail
**150** MATRA R.550 Magic air-to-air missile
**151** JL.100 combined fuel and rocket pack, 56 Imp gal (250 litres) of fuel plus 18 x 68-mm FFAR
**152** Inboard stores pylon
**153** Leading-edge notch
**154** Wing pylon attachment joint
**155** Fuel system piping
**156** Wing rib and multi-spar construction
**157** Main spar
**158** Landing-gear hydraulic accumulator
**159** Hydraulic retraction jack/lock strut
**160** Main landing-gear leg pivot fixing
**161** Mainwheel leg door
**162** Torque scissor links
**163** Port mainwheel
**164** Shock absorber leg strut
**165** Port leading-edge fuel tank
**166** Airbrake housing
**167** Port airbrake, upper and lower surfaces, open position
**168** Airbrake hydraulic jack
**169** Fuselage centreline stores pylon
**170** MATRA Durandal penetration bombs (10)
**171** Ventral cannon pack, lowered
**172** Ammunition feed chute, 125-rounds per gun
**173** DEFA 30-mm cannon (two)
**174** Cannon barrels
**175** Centreline pylon bomb adaptor
**176** BA-100 runway-cratering retarded bombs (18)
**177** AM39 Exocet air-to-surface missile
**178** 68-mm folding fin aircraft rockets (FFAR)
**179** 551-lb (250-kg) general-purpose HE bomb
**180** 882-lb (400-kg) general-purpose HE bomb
**181** C4 rocket launcher
**182** 100-mm unguided FFAR

M. Badrocke

# Dassault Mirage F1

*Possibly one of the most aesthetically pleasing combat aircraft yet designed, the Mirage F1 has demonstrated its considerable combat capability in conflicts ranging from anti-guerrilla strikes in South Africa to Desert Storm.*

## Mirage F1CT

**Cutaway key**

1 Pitot head
2 Glass-fibre radome
3 Radar scanner housing
4 Inflight-refuelling probe
5 Dynamic pressure sensor
6 Thomson-CSF Cyrano IVMR radar equipment module
7 Incidence probe
8 TMV 630A laser rangefinder
9 Rudder pedals
10 Control column
11 Instrument panel shroud
12 Windscreen panels
13 Thomson VE120 head-up display
14 Upward-hinging cockpit canopy cover
15 Martin-Baker F10M zero-zero ejection seat
16 Engine throttle lever
17 Side console panel
18 Nose undercarriage hydraulic retraction jack
19 Twin nosewheels, aft-retracting
20 Hydraulic steering mechanism
21 TACAN aerial
22 Cockpit sloping rear pressure bulkhead
23 Canopy jack
24 Canopy emergency release
25 Central intake control actuator
26 Moveable half-cone intake centre-body
27 Port air intake
28 Air-conditioning equipment bay
29 Intake centre-body screw jack
30 Intake suction relief door

31 Pressure refuelling connection
32 Port airbrake panel
33 Airbrake hydraulic jack
34 Retractable landing lamp
35 Forward fuselage integral fuel tank
36 Boundary layer spill duct
37 Avionics equipment bay
38 Power amplifier
39 Strobe light (white) and anti-collision beacon (red)
40 Fuel system inverted flight accumulator
41 30-mm DEFA cannon, starboard side only
42 Ammunition magazine, 135 rounds
43 External fuel tank
44 Starboard wing integral fuel tank
45 Forged steel wing attachment fitting
46 Inboard pylon attachment hardpoint
47 MATRA-Philips Phimat chaff/flare pod
48 Leading-edge flap
49 Starboard navigation light
50 Wingtip missile launch rail
51 MATRA Magic air-to-air missile
52 Starboard aileron
53 Two-segment double-slotted flaps
54 Spoiler panel (open)
55 Wing panel attachment machined fuselage main frame

56 Fuel system filters
57 Engine intake centre-body/starter housing
58 Wing panel attachment pin joints
59 Engine accessory equipment gearbox
60 SNECMA Atar 9K-50 afterburning engine
61 Engine bleed air pre-cooler
62 Rear spar attachment joint
63 Rear fuselage integral fuel tank
64 Engine turbine section
65 Engine bay thermal lining
66 Fin spar attachment joint
67 Starboard all-moving tailplane
68 Forward SHERLOC ECM antenna fairing
69 UHF antenna
70 VOR aerial
71 Fin-tip aerial fairing
72 IFF/VHF 1 aerial
73 Rear navigation light and anti-collision beacon
74 Aft SHERLOC ECM antenna
75 Rudder
76 Rudder hydraulic actuator
77 Rudder trim actuator
78 VHF 2 aerial
79 Brake parachute housing

80 Variable-area afterburner nozzle
81 Nozzle control jacks
82 Port all-moving tailplane
83 Honeycomb trailing-edge panel
84 Multi-spar tailplane construction
85 Tailplane pivot fitting
86 Tailplane hydraulic actuator
87 Autopilot controller
88 Port ventral fin
89 Inboard double-slotted flap segment
90 Flap hydraulic jack
91 Spoiler hydraulic jack
92 Port spoiler housing and actuating linkage
93 Port aileron hydraulic actuator
94 Outboard double-slotted flap segment
95 Port aileron
96 Wingtip missile interface unit
97 Port navigation light
98 Leading-edge flap
99 Port MATRA Magic air-to-air missile
100 68-mm rocket projectile
101 MATRA 18-round rocket launcher

102 Thomson-CSF ECM pod
103 Outer pylon attachment hardpoint
104 Wing panel multi-spar construction
105 Port wing integral fuel tank
106 Main undercarriage hydraulic retraction jack
107 Shock absorber strut
108 Twin mainwheels
109 Levered suspension axle
110 Mainwheel leg strut and leg rotating linkage
111 Leading-edge flap hydraulic jack
112 Main undercarriage wheel bay
113 Port ammunition bay, unused
114 Centre fuselage weapon pylon
115 881-lb (400-kg) HE bombs
116 Underwing MATRA-Corral conformal chaff/flare dispenser

117 Multiple bomb-carrier
118 Thomson-Brandt BAP-100 runway-cratering bomb or BAT-120 area denial/anti-armour munition
119 MATRA Belouga submunition dispenser
120 MATRA Durandal retarded concrete-piercing bomb

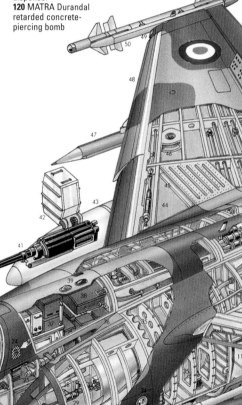

*Libya ordered 38 F1s, including 16 F1EDs. The aircraft are tasked mainly with air defence, but have a limited ground-attack capability. This was practised against Chad in the 1980s, the Libyan Mirages declining to engage French F1s based in the area.*

## SPECIFICATION

### Mirage F1C
(unless otherwise noted)

### Dimensions

**Wingspan without tip stores:** 27 ft 6¾ in (8.40 m)
**Mirage F1B:** 27 ft 8⅓ in (8.44 m)
**Wingspan with tip-mounted Magic AAMs:** 30 ft 6¾ in (9.32 m)
**Wing aspect ratio:** 2.82
**Wing area:** 269.11 sq ft (25.00 m²)
**Length:** 50 ft 2½ in (15.30 m)
**Mirage F1B:** 51 ft ⅙ in (15.55 m)
**Wheel track:** 8 ft 2½ in (2.50 m)
**Wheel base:** 16 ft 4¾ in (5.00 m)
**Height:** 14 ft 9 in (4.50 m)
**Mirage F1B:** 14 ft 8⅚ in (4.49 m)

### Powerplant

One SNECMA Atar 9K-50 turbojet rated at 11,023 lb st (49.03 kN) dry and 15,785 lb st (70.21 kN) with afterburning

### Weights

**Empty:** 16,314 lb (7400 kg)
**Operating empty (Mirage F1B including pilots):** 18,078 lb (8200 kg)
**Normal take-off:** 24,030 lb (10900 kg)
**Mirage F1B:** 24,691 lb (11200 kg)
**Maximum take-off:** 35,715 lb (16200 kg)

### Fuel and load

**Internal fuel capacity:** 1,134 Imp gal (4300 litres)
**Mirage F1B:** 1,017 Imp gal (3850 litres).
**External fuel capacity:** Provision for one 581-Imp gal (2200-litre) tank on centreline and two 299-Imp gal (1130-litre) tanks under the wings
**Maximum weaponload:** 13,889 lb (6300 kg)

### Performance

**Maximum level speed 'clean' at 36,090 ft (11000 m):** 1,453 mph (2338 km/h)
**Maximum rate of climb at sea level:** 41,930 ft (12780 m) per minute
**Mirage F1B (without afterburning):** 13,780 ft (4200 m) per minute
**Service ceiling:** 65,615 ft (20000 m)
**Mirage F1B (stabilised supersonic ceiling):** 52,495 ft (16000 m)
**Take-off run at 25,353-lb (11500-kg) weight:** 1,969 ft (600 m)
**Landing run at 18,739-lb (8500-kg) weight:** 2,198 ft (670 m)

### Range

**Combat radius:** 264 miles (425 km) on a hi-lo-hi attack mission with 14 551-lb (250-kg) bombs, or 373 miles (600 km) on a lo-lo-lo attack mission with six 551-lb (250-kg) bombs and two drop tanks, or 863 miles (1390 km) on a hi-lo-hi attack mission with two 551-lb (250-kg) bombs and three drop tanks
**Endurance:** 2 hours 15 minutes on a CAP with two Super 530 AAMs and one drop tank
**Mirage F1B normal training mission endurance:** 2 hours

### Armament

Two fixed internal DEFA 553 30-mm cannon with 135 rounds per gun; standard air-to-air load of two MATRA Magic or AIM-9 Sidewinder missiles on wingtip rails and either one MATRA R.530 on the centreline station or two Super 530Fs underwing. A limited ground-attack capability is available using various unguided bombs, cluster munitions and rockets.

Mike Badrocke

*With second-hand ex-USAF F-16s complementing the F1 in Jordanian service, a number of Mirages have been sold to Spain. The F1 is a potent multi-role aircraft and it is unlikely that Jordan would wish to relinquish its entire fleet.*

# Dassault Mirage 2000

*The various models within the Mirage 2000 family are, between them, capable of carrying a wide range of contemporary French weaponry. Early production aircraft were optimised for air-to-air operations, but did feature a limited ground-attack capability. This ability was enhanced in the Mirage 2000-5 which, while primarily a long-range interceptor has an expanded air-to-ground capability; the 2000N nuclear attack variant; and the 2000D, which is a dedicated conventional attack variant of the 2000N.*

## Mirage 2000C

**Cutaway key**
1 Pitot tube
2 Glass fibre radome
3 Flat-plate radar scanner
4 Thomson-CSF RDM multi-role radar unit (initial production aircraft)
5 Cassegrain monopulse planar antenna
6 Thomson-CSF RDI pulse-Doppler radar unit (later production aircraft)
7 Radar altimeter aerial
8 Angle-of-attack probe
9 Front pressure bulkhead
10 Instrument pitot heads
11 Temperature probe
12 Fixed inflight refuelling probe
13 Frameless windscreen panel
14 Instrument panel shroud
15 Static ports
16 Rudder pedals
17 Low-voltage formation light strip
18 VHF aerial
19 Nosewheel jack door
20 Hydraulic retraction jack
21 Nose landing gear leg strut
22 Twin nosewheels
23 Towing bracket
24 Torque scissor links
25 Landing/taxiing lamps
26 Nosewheel steering jacks
27 Nose landing gear leg doors
28 Cockpit flooring
29 Centre instrument console
30 Control column
31 Pilot's head-up display (HUD)
32 Canopy arch
33 Cockpit canopy cover
34 Starboard air intake
35 Ejection seat headrest
36 Safety harness
37 Martin-Baker Mk 10 zero-zero ejection seat
38 Engine throttle control and airbrake switch
39 Port side console panel
40 Nosewheel bay
41 Cannon muzzle blast trough
42 Electrical equipment bay
43 Port air intake
44 Intake half-cone centre body
45 Air-conditioning system ram air intake
46 Cockpit rear pressure bulkhead
47 Canopy emergency release handle
48 Hydraulic canopy jack
49 Canopy hinge point
50 Starboard intake strake
51 IFF aerial
52 Radio and electronics bay
53 Boundary layer bleed air duct
54 Air-conditioning plant
55 Intake centre-body screw jack
56 Cannon muzzle
57 Pressure refuelling connection
58 Port intake strake
59 Intake suction relief doors (above and below)
60 DEFA 554 30-mm cannon
61 Cannon ammunition box
62 Forward fuselage integral fuel tanks
63 Radio and electronics equipment
64 Fuel system equipment
65 Anti-collision light
66 Air system pre-cooler
67 Air exit louvres
68 Starboard wing integral fuel tank, total internal fuel capacity 836 Imp gal (3800 litres)
69 Wing pylon attachment hardpoints
70 Leading-edge slat hydraulic drive motor and control shaft
71 Slat screw jacks
72 Slat guide rails
73 Starboard wing automatic leading-edge slats
74 Matra 550 Magic 'dogfight' AAM
75 Missile launch rail
76 Outboard wing pylon
77 Radar warning antenna
78 Starboard navigation light

*The Mirage 2000-01 first flew on 10 March 1978 from Istres in France and was piloted by Jean Coureau. During its first flight, basic handling and performance of the new fighter were validated, and the aircraft was pushed to Mach 1.3 in afterburner. While the Mirage 2000 is externally similar to its predecessor, the Mirage III, it is the adoption of technologies under the skin, such as its 'fly-by-wire' controls, that made it such an advancement over previous Mirages.*

## SPECIFICATION

### Mirage 2000C

#### Dimensions

**Fuselage length:** 47 ft 1¼ in (14.36 m)
**Wingspan:** 29 ft 11½ in (9.13 m)
**Wing area:** 441.33 sq ft (41.00 m²)
**Wing aspect ratio:** 2.03
**Height:** 17 ft ¾ in (5.20 m)
**Wheel track:** 11 ft 1¾ in (3.40 m)
**Wheel base:** 16 ft 4¾ in (5.00 m)

#### Powerplant

One SNECMA M53-P2 turbofan rated at 14,462 lb st (64.33 kN) dry and 21,384 lb st (95.12 kN) with afterburning

#### Weights

**Empty:** 16,534 lb (7500 kg)
**Normal take-off:** 23,534 lb (10680 kg)
**Maximum take-off:** 37,478 lb (17000 kg)

#### Fuel and load

**Internal fuel:** 6,966 lb (3160 kg)
**External fuel:** 8,201 lb (3720 kg) in one 343-US gal (1300-litre) drop tank and two 449 US-gal (1700-litre) drop tanks.
**Maximum ordnance:** 13,889 lb (6300 kg)

#### Performance

**Maximum speed at high level:** Mach 2.2
**Maximum speed at sea level:** Mach 1.2

**Minimum speed in stable flight:** 100 kts (115 mph; 185 km/h)
**Range:** Over 850 nm (979 miles; 1575 km) with 4,409 lb (2000 kg) of underwing ordnance and external fuel tanks
**Service ceiling:** 54,000 ft (16460 m)
**Reaction time:** Under five minutes, from brakes-off to interception of Mach 3 target at 80,000 ft (24400 m)

#### Armament

Two internal DEFA 554 30-mm cannon with 125 rounds per gun. Total of 13,889 lb (6300 kg) of stores carried on five underfuselage and four underwing hardpoints. Standard air defence load is two MATRA Magic 2 infra-red missiles and two Super 530D radar-guided missiles. Early aircraft were only equipped to fire the Super 530F. In the ground-attack role, up to 18 551-lb (250-kg) bombs or BAP 100 anti-runway bombs, two 1,984-lb (900-kg) BGL 1000 laser-guided bombs, six Belouga cluster bombs, two AS30L laser-guided air-to-surface missiles, two ARMAT anti-radiation missiles or two AM39 Exocet anti-ship missiles are options.
**Mirage 2000D/N/S:** The N is dedicated to the carriage of the 1,874-lb (850-kg) ASMP stand-off nuclear missile (150 kT or 300 kT yield). The 2000D/S has provision for the MATRA APACHE, Durandal, F4 rocket pod or Dassault CC630 gun pod.

---

**79** Outboard elevon
**80** Elevon ventral hinge fairings
**81** Flight control system access panels
**82** Elevon hydraulic jacks
**83** Engine intake by-pass air spill duct
**84** Engine compressor face
**85** Hydraulic accumulator
**86** Micro turbo auxiliary power unit
**87** Main landing gear wheel bay
**88** Hydraulic pump
**89** Alternator, port and starboard
**90** Accessory gearbox
**91** Engine transmission unit and drive shaft
**92** Machined fuselage main frames
**93** SNECMA M53-5 afterburning turbofan
**94** Engine igniter unit
**95** Electronic engine control unit
**96** Bleed air ducting
**97** Engine bleed air blow-off valve spill duct
**98** Fin root fillet construction
**99** Leading-edge ribs
**100** Boron/epoxy/ carbon honeycomb sandwich fin skin panels
**101** Tail low-voltage formation light strip
**102** ECM aerial fairing
**103** VOR aerial
**104** Dielectric fin tip fairing
**105** VHF aerial
**106** Tail navigation light
**107** Tail radar warning antenna
**108** Honeycomb rudder construction
**109** Rudder hinge
**110** Fin spar attachment joints
**111** Rudder hydraulic jack
**112** Engine bay thermal lining
**113** ECM equipment housing
**114** Variable-area afterburner exhaust nozzle
**115** Tailpipe sealing flaps
**116** Fueldraulic nozzle control jacks
**117** Afterburner tailpipe
**118** Engine withdrawal rail
**119** Wing root extended trailing-edge fillet
**120** Ventral brake parachute housing
**121** Rear engine mounting main frame
**122** Runway emergency arrestor hook
**123** Port inboard elevon
**124** Elevon honeycomb construction
**125** CArbon fibre skin panels
**126** Elevon hydraulic control jacks
**127** Fly-by wire electronic system command units
**128** Outboard elevon
**129** Elevon tip construction
**130** Port navigation light
**131** Radar warning antenna
**132** Outboard automatic leading-edge slat
**133** Outboard wing pylon attachment hardpoints
**134** Machined upper-and lower-wing skin/stringer panels
**135** Port wing integral fuel tank
**136** Wing rib construction
**137** Rear fuselage/ wingroot fairing integral fuel tank
**138** Wing spar attachment joints
**139** Main spars
**140** Landing gear hydraulic retraction jack
**141** Main landing gear leg pivot fixing
**142** Inboard pylon attachment hardpoints
**143** Port airbrakes (open) above and beneath wing
**144** Airbrake hydraulic jack
**145** Main landing gear leg strut
**146** Leading-edge slat hydraulic drive motor
**147** Mainwheel leg door
**148** Port mainwheel
**149** Slat guide rails
**150** Screw jacks
**151** Auxiliary spar
**152** Wing front spar
**153** Front spar attachment joint
**154** Inboard automatic leading edge slat rib construction
**155** 3,741-Imp gal (1700-litre) auxiliary fuel tank (fuselage centreline or wing inboard stations)
**156** MATRA Super 530 medium-range AAM
**157** Missile launch rail
**158** Inboard wing pylon

# Dassault Ouragan/Mystère

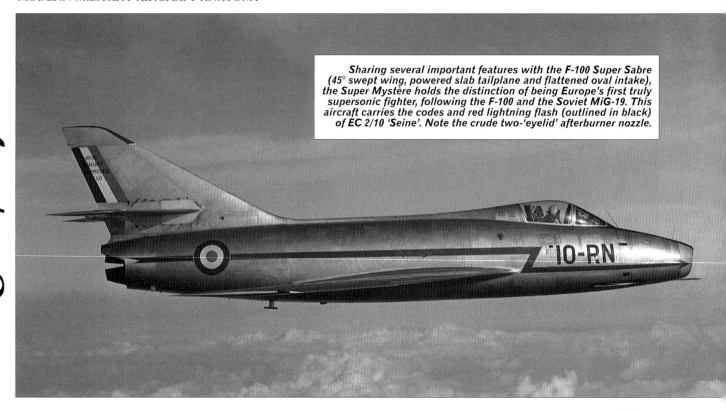

Sharing several important features with the F-100 Super Sabre (45° swept wing, powered slab tailplane and flattened oval intake), the Super Mystère holds the distinction of being Europe's first truly supersonic fighter, following the F-100 and the Soviet MiG-19. This aircraft carries the codes and red lightning flash (outlined in black) of EC 2/10 'Seine'. Note the crude two-'eyelid' afterburner nozzle.

## Mystère IVA

### Cutaway key

1 Engine air intake
2 Radar rangefinder antenna
3 Intake divider
4 Gun camera
5 Nose electronics compartment access door
6 Radar transmitter
7 Radar receiver
8 Nose undercarriage wheel bay
9 Hydraulic retraction jack
10 Battery
11 Cockpit front pressure bulkhead
12 Rudder pedals
13 Cockpit floor level
14 Nose undercarriage pivot fixing
15 Cannon blast trough
16 Cannon muzzle
17 Nosewheel leg door
18 Landing/taxiing lamp
19 Nose undercarriage leg strut
20 Nosewheel
21 Torque scissor links
22 Bifurcated intake duct framing
23 Control column
24 Cockpit coaming
25 Instrument panel shroud
26 Gyro gunsight
27 Windscreen panels
28 Cockpit canopy cover
29 Ejection seat face blind firing handle
30 Headrest
31 Pilot's ejection seat
32 Canopy emergency release lever
33 Engine throttle lever
34 Port side console panel
35 Cockpit pressurised enclosure
36 Cannon mounting
37 DEFA 30-mm cannon
38 Spent cartridge case collector box
39 Gun bay access panel
40 Ammunition feed chute
41 Ammunition box (150 rounds per gun)

42 Control rod runs
43 Cockpit armoured rear pressure bulkhead
44 Sliding canopy rail
45 Oxygen bottle
46 Forward fuselage fuel tank (total internal capacity 396 Imp gal/ 1800 litres)
47 Wing root fillet
48 Aileron hydraulic booster
49 Intake duct framing
50 Radio and electronics equipment bay
51 UHF aerial
52 Starboard wing fuel cells
53 Aileron push-pull control rods
54 Pitot tube
55 Starboard navigation light
56 Wing tip fairing
57 Starboard aileron
58 Aileron hinge control
59 Split trailing-edge flap
60 Flap torque shaft actuator
61 Fuel tank access door
62 Fuel filler cap
63 Control rod duct
64 Centre fuselage fuel tank
65 Wing front spar/ fuselage main frame

66 Wing centre-section carry-through
67 Wing skin bolted root joint
68 Rear spar/fuselage main frame
69 Main undercarriage wheel bay
70 Hydraulic reservoir
71 Engine accessory compartment
72 Fuel system piping
73 Control rod runs
74 Dorsal spine fairing
75 Engine bay access door
76 Generator
77 Compressor intake filter screens
78 Intake plenum chamber
79 Main engine mounting
80 Hispano Suiza Verdon 350 centrifugal-flow turbojet

81 Rear fuselage break point (engine removal)
82 Engine flame cans
83 Fin root fillet
84 Engine turbine section
85 Tailplane control rods
86 Trimming tailplane electric screwjack
87 Tailplane sealing plate
88 Elevator control linkage
89 Rudder push-pull control rod
90 Starboard tailplane

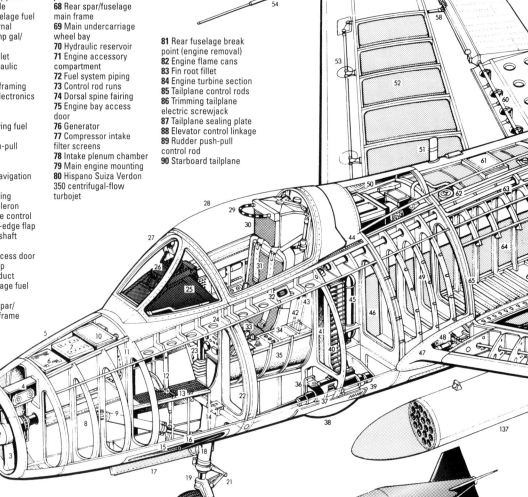

## SPECIFICATION

### Super Mystère B2

#### Dimensions
**Length:** 46 ft 4¼ in (14.13 m)
**Height:** 14 ft 11 in (4.55 m)
**Wingspan:** 34 ft 6 in (10.52 m)
**Wing area:** 376.75 sq ft (35.00 m²)
**Wheelbase:** 14 ft 11½ in (4.56 m)

#### Powerplant
One SNECMA Atar 101-G-2/-3 turbojet rated at 9,833 lb (43.76 kN) thrust with afterburning

#### Weights
**Empty equipped:** 15,282 lb (6932 kg)
**Maximum take-off:** 22,046 lb (10000 kg)

#### Performance
**Maximum speed:** 646 mph (1040 km/h) at sea level and 743 mph (1195 km/h) at 39,370 ft (12000 m)
**Initial climb rate:** 17,505 ft (5335 m) per minute
**Service ceiling:** 55,775 ft (17000 m)
**Normal range:** 540 miles (870 km)

#### Armament
Two 30-mm DEFA 551 cannon plus 35 68-mm SNEB rockets in retractable pack; plus up to 2,205 lb (1000 kg) of stores on four underwing hardpoints, including bombs up to 1,102-lb (500-kg); some aircraft later upgraded to carry AIM-9 Sidewinder or Shafrir AAMs

*Israel's Super Mystères were re-engined to provide greater dry thrust (the new J52 did not have an afterburner) and better fuel consumption. This Sa'ar, as the upgraded aircraft were known, carries two Shafrir air-to-air missiles*

**91** Starboard elevator
**92** IFF aerial
**93** Tailfin construction
**94** VHF aerial
**95** Fin tip aerial fairing
**96** Rudder construction
**97** Tail navigation light
**98** Port elevator construction
**99** All-moving tailplane construction
**100** Engine exhaust nozzle
**101** Jet pipe
**102** Jet pipe heat shroud
**103** Airbrake housing
**104** Hydraulic jack
**105** Port airbrake, open
**106** Wing root trailing-edge fillet
**107** Port split trailing-edge flap

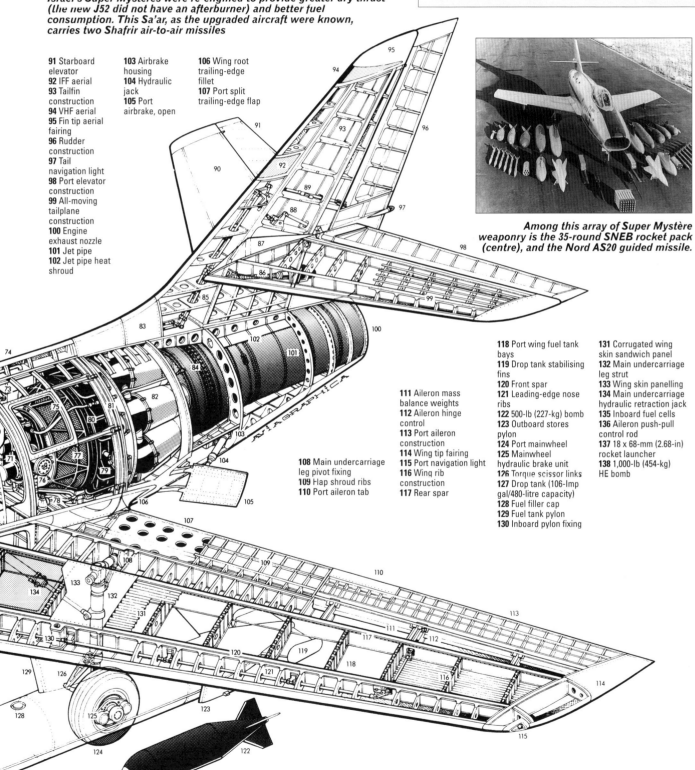

*Among this array of Super Mystère weaponry is the 35-round SNEB rocket pack (centre), and the Nord AS20 guided missile.*

**108** Main undercarriage leg pivot fixing
**109** Flap shroud ribs
**110** Port aileron tab
**111** Aileron mass balance weights
**112** Aileron hinge control
**113** Port aileron construction
**114** Wing tip fairing
**115** Port navigation light
**116** Wing rib construction
**117** Rear spar
**118** Port wing fuel tank bays
**119** Drop tank stabilising fins
**120** Front spar
**121** Leading-edge nose ribs
**122** 500-lb (227-kg) bomb
**123** Outboard stores pylon
**124** Port mainwheel
**125** Mainwheel hydraulic brake unit
**126** Torque scissor links
**127** Drop tank (106-Imp gal/480-litre capacity)
**128** Fuel filler cap
**129** Fuel tank pylon
**130** Inboard pylon fixing
**131** Corrugated wing skin sandwich panel
**132** Main undercarriage leg strut
**133** Wing skin panelling
**134** Main undercarriage hydraulic retraction jack
**135** Inboard fuel cells
**136** Aileron push-pull control rod
**137** 18 x 68-mm (2.68-in) rocket launcher
**138** 1,000-lb (454-kg) HE bomb

# de Havilland D.H. 100 Vampire

*The first pre-production Vampire trainer for the Royal Navy, WW458 was delivered for evaluation in January 1952. Following trials with Nos 759 and 781 Squadrons, Fleet Air Arm it was withdrawn from flying duties and, in early 1954, became an instructional airframe.*

## Vampire FB.Mk 5

### Cutaway key

1 Ciné camera port
2 Cockpit fresh air intake
3 Nosewheel leg door
4 Pivoted axle nosewheel suspension
5 Anti-shimmy nosewheel tyre
6 Nose undercarriage leg strut
7 Nosewheel door
8 Cannon muzzle blast trough
9 Nosewheel hydraulic jack
10 Nose undercarriage pivot fixing
11 Radio
12 Gun camera
13 Windscreen fluid de-icing reservoir
14 Armoured instrument access panel
15 Cockpit front bulkhead
16 Rudder pedals
17 Cockpit floor level
18 Nosewheel housing
19 Instrument panel
20 Reflector gunsight
21 Windscreen panels
22 Side console switch panel
23 Control column
24 Engine throttle
25 Tailplane trim handwheel
26 Undercarriage and flap selector levers
27 Control linkage
28 Cannon barrels beneath cockpit floor
29 Pull-out boarding step
30 Control system cable compensator
31 Emergency hydraulic handpump
32 Pilot's seat
33 Safety harness
34 Sliding canopy rails
35 Cockpit heater
36 Cockpit canopy cover
37 Pilot's head and back armour
38 Hydraulic system reservoir
39 Radio equipment bay
40 Ammunition tanks (150 rounds per gun)
41 Plywood/balsa/plywood fuselage skinning
42 Boundary layer splitter
43 Port engine air intake
44 Ventral gun bay (4 x 20-mm Hispano cannon)
45 Spent cartridge case and link ejector chute
46 Cannon bay access panel
47 Cockpit heating and pressurising intake
48 Intake ducting
49 Fuselage/front spar attachment joint
50 Fuselage/main spar attachment joint
51 Engine bay fire wall
52 Fuselage fuel tank (total internal system capacity 400 Imp gal/1818 litres)
53 Fuel filler cap
54 Wooden skin section fabric covering
55 Cockpit air heat exchanger
56 Engine bearer struts
57 de Havilland Goblin DGn 2 centrifugal-flow turbojet
58 Cabin blower
59 Engine accessories
60 Engine bay access panels
61 Starboard wingroot fuel tank
62 Starboard main undercarriage, retracted position
63 Leading-edge fuel tank
64 Starboard drop tank (112 Imp gal/509 litres)
65 Drop tank pylon
66 Starboard wing fuel tanks
67 Fuel filler cap
68 Gyrosyn compass remote transmitter
69 Starboard navigation light
70 Wingtip fairing
71 Starboard aileron
72 Aileron mass balance weights
73 Trim tab
74 Aileron hinge control
75 Starboard trailing-edge airbrake segment (open)
76 Airbrake hydraulic jack
77 Starboard outer split trailing-edge flap

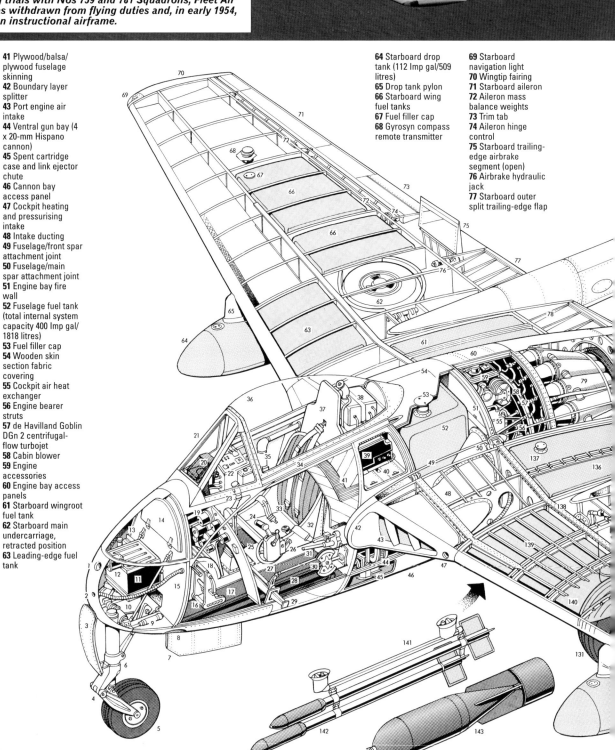

No. 601 (County of London) Squadron, Royal Auxiliary Air Force, received the Vampire F.Mk 3 in December 1949. Based at North Weald, the squadron took its Vampires on summer armament training camps from 1950-52. Here, the Vampires bask in the hot Mediterranean sun on the island of Malta during the summer camp of 1951. No. 601 displayed the unit's red/black triangular insignia on the tailbooms and the squadron's winged sword badge on the nose.

## SPECIFICATION

### Vampire F.Mk 3

**Dimensions**

**Length:** 30 ft 9 in (9.37 m)
**Height:** 8 ft 10 in (2.69 m)
**Wingspan:** 40 ft (12.19 m)
**Wing area:** 266 sq ft (24.71 m²)
**Wing loading:** 39.4 lb/sq ft (192 kg/m²)

**Powerplant**

One de Havilland Goblin 2 centrifugal-flow turbojet rated at 3,100 lb st (14 kN)

**Weights**

**Empty:** 7,134 lb (3236 kg)
**Maximum take-off:** 12,170 lb (5520 kg)

**Fuel**

**Internal fuel:** 530 Imp gal (2409 litres)
**External fuel:** 200 Imp gal (909 litres) in drop tanks

**Performance**

**Maximum level speed at sea level:** 531 mph (855 km/h)
**Maximum level speed at 17,500 ft (5334 m):** 525 mph (845 km/h)

**Maximum level speed at 30,000 ft (9144 m):** 505 mph (813 km/h)
**Rate of climb at sea level:** 4,375 ft (1334 m) per minute
**Rate of climb at 20,000 ft (6096 m):** 2,500 ft (762 m) per minute
**Rate of climb at 40,000 ft (12192 m):** 990 ft (302 m) per minute
**Service ceiling:** 43,500 ft (13259 m)
**Take-off run to 50 ft (15.24 m) at maximum weight:** 3,540 ft (1079 m)
**Landing run from 50 ft (15.24 m):** 3,300 ft (1006 m)

**Range and endurance**

**Range at sea level:** 590 miles (949 km) at 350 mph (463 km/h)
**Range at 30,000 ft (9144 m):** 1,145 miles (1843 km) at 350 mph (463 km/h)
**Patrol duration at sea level:** 2 hours at 220 mph (354 km/h)
**Patrol duration at 30,000 ft (9144 m):** 2 hours 35 mins at 220 mph (354 km/h)

**Armament**

Four 20-mm Hispano cannon mounted in the front of the lower fuselage. Ammunition of 150 rounds per gun, giving a total of 600 rounds

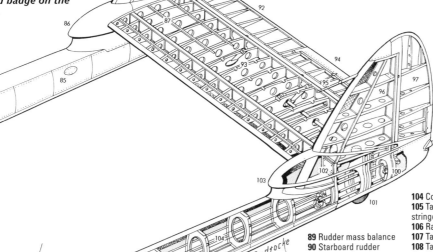

Mike Badrocke

78 Inboard split trailing-edge flap
79 Engine flame tubes
80 Jet pipe heat shroud
81 Gun heater duct
82 Tailcone framing
83 Jet exhaust nozzle
84 Starboard tail boom
85 Control cable access panels
86 Tailplane bullet fairing
87 Tailplane construction
88 Starboard fin
89 Rudder mass balance
90 Starboard rudder
91 Rudder trim tab
92 Elevator construction
93 Ventral elevator mass balance weights
94 Elevator tab
95 Pitot tube
96 Port fin construction
97 Port rudder
98 Rudder trim tab
99 Tail navigation light
100 Rudder and elevator hinge controls
101 Tail bumper
102 Fin/tailplane attachment joint
103 Tailplane bullet fairing

104 Control cable runs
105 Tailboom frame and stringer construction
106 Radio aerial mast
107 Tailboom skinning
108 Tailboom attachment ring joint
109 Trailing-edge root fillet
110 Port inboard split trailing-edge flap
111 Flap interconnection
112 Hydraulic flap jack
113 False rear spar
114 Flap shroud ribs
115 Port outboard split trailing-edge flap
116 Rotating trailing-edge segment airbrake, open
117 Aileron tab
118 Port aileron construction
119 Aileron mass balance weights

120 Retractable landing/taxiing lamp
121 Wingrib and stringer construction
122 Wingtip fairing
123 Port navigation light
124 Leading-edge nose ribs
125 Fuel filler cap
126 Port wing main fuel tanks
127 Fuel tank interconnection
128 Pylon attachment rib
129 Port 112-Imp gal (509-litre) drop tank
130 Drop tank pylon
131 Port mainwheel
132 Mainwheel door actuating linkage
133 Port mainwheel bay
134 Retraction linkages and locks
135 Main undercarriage leg strut pivot fixing
136 Wingroot fuel tank
137 Fuel filler cap
138 Main spar
139 Wing stringers
140 Leading-edge fuel tank
141 Rocket launcher rail
142 60-lb (27-kg) unguided ground attack rocket
143 500-lb (227-kg) HE bomb

A pair of Swiss Vampires (a T.Mk 55 and an FB.Mk 6 with a recce nose) formates with a Venom (foreground). Some Swiss officials originally argued that the Hawker Sea Fury was more suited to Swiss requirements than the Vampire.

# English Electric Lightning

*Designers and engineers from English Electric (and later from its successor BAC) can be justifiably proud of the Lightning. Wholly conceived and developed in Britain, it was the first British aircraft to exceed Mach 2, and was also an unofficial world speed record holder.*

## Lightning F.Mk 6

### Cutaway key

1 Pitot head boom
2 Intake bullet fairing
3 Ferranti AIRPASS radar antenna/scanner
4 Engine air intake lip
5 Hot-air de-icing
6 Bullet lower spacer
7 G 90 camera
8 Radar pack
9 Bullet upper spacer (electrical leads)
10 Forward equipment bay
11 Forward fuse box
12 Capacitor box
13 LOX container
14 Light fighter sight control unit
15 De-icing/demister air
16 Radar ground cooling air coupling
17 Nosewheel door mechanism torque shaft and operating rods
18 Nosewheel bay
19 Nosewheel doors
20 Nosewheel strut
21 Roller guide bracket
22 Forward-retracting nosewheel
23 Castor auto-disconnect
24 Shimmy damper and centring unit
25 Aft door (linked to leg)
26 Flight refuelling probe (detachable)
27 Nosewheel strut pivot pin
28 Heat exchanger
29 Nosewheel hydraulic jack
30 Intake ducting
31 Cockpit canted floor
32 Engine power control panel
33 Control column

34 Instrument panel shroud
35 Rudder pedal assembly
36 Canopy column
37 Rain dispersal duct
38 Windscreen (electro- thermal)
39 CRT display unit (starboard)
40 Airpass (light fighter) attack sight
41 Standby magnetic compass
42 Canopy top panel demisting ducts
43 Magnesium-forged canopy top frame
44 IFF aerial
45 Chemical air driers
46 Starboard (armaments) console
47 Ejection seat face-blind/firing-handle
48 Air conditioning duct
49 Rear pressure bulkhead
50 Martin-Baker ejection seat
51 Port instrument panels
52 Cockpit ladder attachment
53 Cockpit emergency ram air intake
54 Lower (No. 1) engine intake duct frames
55 Firestreak weapons pack
56 Launch sequence units
57 Control units
58 Port missile pylon
59 Firestreak missile
60 Fuse 'windows'
61 Armament safety break panel

62 Aileron accumulator pressure gauges
63 Accumulator group bay
64 Plessey LTSA starter in lower (No. 1) engine nosecone
65 Lower (No. 1) engine intake
66 Wingroot inboard fairing
67 Main equipment bay
68 Selector address unit
69 Electronic unit
70 Air data computer
71 Converter signal unit (datalink)
72 Communications T/R (two)
73 Canopy hinge
74 Dorsal spine bays
75 AC fuse and relay box (cold-air unit and water boiler to starboard)
76 28-Volt battery
77 Upper (No. 2) engine intake duct
78 Fuselage frames
79 Water heater tank and extractor
80 Wing/fuselage main attachment point
81 Aileron idler lever
82 Aileron control push-pull tubes
83 Tube attachment brackets
84 Fuselage multi-bolt forward/centre-section join

85 ADEN gun muzzle
86 Leading-edge integral fuel
87 Muzzle blast tube
88 Aileron tube triple-roller guides
89 Access
90 Fuel lines
91 Non-return valve
92 Detachable leading-edge sections
93 Shuttle valve
94 Undercarriage strut fixed fairing
95 Shock-absorber strut
96 Port mainwheel
97 Brake unit
98 Tubeless tyre
99 Torque links
100 Red Top missile
101 Aft fairing flap
102 Undercarriage pivot
103 Radius rod (inward- breaking)
104 Undercarriage retraction jack
105 Door jack sequence valve
106 Door master locking mechanism
107 Collector tank and booster pumps (two)
108 Aerodynamic leading-edge slot

109 Tank pressurising intake/vent (in slot)
110 Mainwheel door
111 Undercarriage jack sequence valve
112 Door latch linkage
113 Port mainwheel well
114 Aileron control push-pull tubes
115 Aileron movement restrictor
116 Aileron autostabiliser actuator
117 Aileron control linkage
118 Aileron hydraulic runs
119 Cambered leading-edge extension
120 Localiser aerial
121 Port navigation light
122 Port wingtip
123 Port aileron
124 Aileron powered flying-control units
125 Control linkage
126 Wing outer structure
127 Aileron mass balance
128 Wing outer fixed section

129 Flap outer actuator jack
130 Flap sections
131 Flap integral tank
132 Angled aft spar
133 Undercarriage attachment
134 Refuelling/defuelling valve
135 Flap inner actuator jack
136 Three-way cock (manual)
137 DC transfer pump
138 Gate valves
139 Wing/fuselage rear main attachment point
140 Lower (No. 1) engine intermediate jet pipe forward face
141 Wing inboard structure
142 Wing integral fuel
143 Intermediate spar booms (T-section)
144 Port ADEN cannon (forward ventral pack)
145 Wing rib stations
146 Fuel vent pipe

147 Multi-bolt wing attachment plate
148 Access panels
149 Upper (No. 2) engine duct frames
150 Fuselage break frame
151 Voltage regulators
152 Start tank
153 Engine pump units
154 Solenoid valves
155 Communications antenna
156 Starter control unit
157 HF igniter units
158 Fuselage frame
159 Main wing box upper skin
160 Forged centre rib (multi-bolt attachment)
161 Upper (No. 2) engine nosecone
162 Upper (No. 2) engine nosecone
163 Generator cooling ram-air intake

*Lack of funds led to the protracted development of a multi-role Lightning targeted for export, and this prevented the fighter from achieving its full potential on the export market. Sales were made to just one major overseas operator, the Royal Saudi Air Force (RSAF). Shown lifting off smartly at the 1966 Farnborough air show, XR770 was an RAF F.Mk 6 painted in RSAF markings for demonstration purposes.*

**164** Stand-by generator
**165** Anti-icing bleed air
**166** Upper (No. 2) Avon 301 turbojet engine and reheat units
**167** Airpass recorder unit
**168** Engine front mounting point
**169** Engine accessories
**170** No. 2 engine bleed-air turbopump (reheat fuel)
**171** Engine bay firewalls
**172** Integral pumps (two)
**173** HE ignition units
**174** Voltage regulator
**175** Current sensing unit
**176** Rubber spring feel mechanism
**177** Auxiliary intake
**178** Main mounting trunnion
**179** Aft (port) equipment bays
**180** Electronic unit
**181** IFF coder
**182** Tailplane controls
**183** Tailplane trim actuator and feel unit
**184** Ventral fuel tank (aft section)
**185** Fin
**186** Reheat cooling lower intake
**187** Tailplane autostabiliser actuator
**188** Gearbox oil filler
**189** AC generator
**190** Glide-path receiver
**191** IFF transmit/receive unit
**192** Outlet
**193** No. 2 engine intermediate jet pipe
**194** Refrasil heat shrouds
**195** Stress-bearing upper (No. 2) engine hatch
**196** Port airbrake
**197** Airbrake hydraulic actuator jack
**198** DC generator
**199** Main accessory-drive unit
**200** Airbrake lower frame
**201** Turbine exhaust (from 199)
**202** Tailplane accumulator and nitrogen bottle
**203** Reheat 'hotshot' igniter box
**204** Tailplane drive triangular unit
**205** Tailplane powered flying-control unit
**206** Tailplane spigot
**207** Pivot spar
**208** All-moving tailplane
**209** Light alloy honeycomb structure

**210** Braking parachute box internally-retracting doors
**211** Cable operating assembly
**212** Fuselage aft frame
**213** Lower (No. 1) engine reheat jet pipe
**214** Trunnion access panel
**215** AMCU air pipes
**216** Reheat cooling upper intake
**217** Rudder feel unit
**218** Rudder trim actuator
**219** Rudder autostabiliser actuator
**220** Rudder linkage
**221** Fin spar/fuselage bolts
**222** Fuselage frame formers
**223** Rudder powered flying-control unit
**224** Reheat jet pipe mounting rail
**225** Upper (No. 2) engine reheat jet pipe
**226** Rear rollers
**227** Air-driven nozzle actuator
**228** Jet pipe trunnion access panel
**229** Variable propelling nozzles
**230** Streamer cable around rear lip (spring-clipped)
**231** Parachute streaming anchor and jettison unit
**232** Rudder light-alloy honeycomb structure
**233** Flutter damper
**234** Communications antenna
**235** Dielectric tip
**236** Compass unit
**237** Angled aft spars
**238** Main fin structure
**239** Fin leading-edge panels
**240** Accessory drive cooling air
**241** Starboard aileron
**242** Aileron powered flying-control units
**243** Control linkage
**244** Starboard flap outer actuator jack
**245** Starboard flap
**246** Wing panels
**247** Wing skinning
**248** Wing integral fuel
**249** Aileron control push-pull tubes
**250** Aileron movement restrictor
**251** Aileron autostabiliser actuator
**252** Starboard navigation light
**253** Glide-slope aerial

## SPECIFICATION

### Lightning F.Mk 53

### Dimensions

**Length overall (including probe):** 55 ft 3 in (16.84 m)
**Wing span:** 34 ft 10 in (10.62 m)
**Wing aspect ratio:** 2.65
**Wing sweepback angle:** 60° on leading edge and 52° on trailing edge
**Tailplane span:** 14 ft 6 in (4.42 m)
**Wing area:** 458.50 sq ft (42.60 m²)
**Overall height:** 19 ft 7 in (5.97 m)
**Undercarriage track:** 12 ft 9 in (3.89 m)
**Wheel base:** 18 ft 1½ in (5.52 m)
**Maximum wing loading:** 90.9 lb/sq ft (444.0 kg/m²)

### Powerplant

Two Rolls-Royce Avon RA.24 Mk 302C turbojets each rated at 11,000 lb (48.92kN) static military thrust and 16,300 lb (72.49kN) with afterburning

### Weights

**Empty operating:** 28,040 lb (12719 kg), 29,600 lb (13426 kg) with gun pack and missiles
**Maximum take-off (fully armed):** 41,700 lb (18915 kg)

### Fuel and load

**Maximum internal fuel:** 10,608 lb (4812 kg); pressure refuelling of wing tanks via adaptor under port wing trailing edge, provision for detachable fixed inflight-refuelling probe projecting forward from port wing
**Maximum internal fuel capacity:** 1277 Imp gal (5805 litres)
**Wing tank capacity:** 690 Imp gal (3137 litres)
**Ventral tank capacity:** 587 Imp gal (2668 litres), or 515 Imp gal (2342 litres) with 30-mm cannon pack fitted
**Total external fuel capacity:** 520 Imp gal (2364 litres) in two overwing tanks
**Maximum weapon load:** 6,000 lb (2722 kg)

### Performance

**Maximum level speed at high altitude:** 1,320 kt (1,520 mph; 2446 km/h) at 40,000 ft (12190 m) or Mach 2.3
**Maximum level speed at low altitude:** approximately 723 kt (834 mph; 1340 km/h) or Mach 1.1
**Cruising speed for optimum range:** 517 kt (595 mph; 958 km/h)
**Initial rate of climb:** 50,000 ft (15240 m) per minute
**Actual ceiling:** in excess of 60,000 ft (18290 m)
**Service ceiling:** 60,000 ft (18290 m)
**Time to climb:** 150 seconds from brakes release to Mach 0.9 at 40,000 ft (12190 m)
**Acceleration:** 210 seconds from Mach 1 to over Mach 2
**Landing speed:** 160 kt (183mph; 295km/h)
**Crosswind limits:** 25 kts (29 mph; 46 km/h) in dry conditions and 15 kts (17 mph; 28 km/h) in wet conditions
**Take-off run:** 3,300 ft (1006 m) at 38,500 lb (17464 kg) with afterburnor
**Landing run:** 3,600 ft (1097 m) with parachute at 29,000 lb (17237 kg), 4,500 ft (1371 m) at 38,000 lb (17237 kg)

### Range

**Maximum range on internal fuel:** 800 miles (1287 km)
**Combat radius on internal fuel:** 373 miles (600 km)

### Armament

**Fixed:** two 30-mm ADEN Mk 4 cannon, each with 120 rounds, in gun pack forward of ventral fuel tank
**Forward external stores:** standard intercept load of two Red Top or Firestreak infra-red-homing short-range air-to-air missiles; in place of missile pack, alternative loads of pack containing twin retractable launchers for total of 44 2-in (51-mm) MicroCell spin-stabilised rockets, reconnaissance pack containing five Vinten Type 360 70-mm cameras, or night reconnaissance pack containing optical cameras and linescan equipment
**Wing-mounted stores:** single hardpoint under outer wing capable of carrying two 1,000-lb (454-kg) high-explosive, retarded or fire bombs, two MATRA Type 155 launchers containing total of 36 2.68-in (68-mm) SNEB rockets, two flare pods or two machine-gun pods; single hardpoint above inner wing capable of carrying single 1,000-lb (454-kg) bomb, one MATRA Type 155 rocket launcher, two MATRA Type 100 combined fuel/rocket launchers each containing 18 2.68-in (68-mm) SNEB rockets and 50 Imp gal (227 litre) of fuel, or one 260-Imp gal (1182-litre) fuel tank.

# Fairchild A-10 Thunderbolt II

*The A-10 at its peak formed the backbone of the USAF's close air support force, a position it has now lost to the ubiquitous F-16. Nevertheless, the type continues to provide excellent service, although in reduced numbers, notably in the forward air control role. This 'decorated' example served with the now-deactivated 91st TFS based at RAF Woodbridge, England.*

## A-10A Thunderbolt II

### Cutaway key

1 Cannon muzzles
2 Nose cap
3 ILS aerial
4 Air-to-air refuelling receptacle (open)
5 Nosewheel bay (offset to starboard)
6 Cannon barrels
7 Rotary cannon barrel bearing
8 Gun compartment ventilating intake
9 L-band radar warning aerial
10 Electrical system relay switches
11 Windscreen rain dispersal airduct
12 Pave Penny laser receiver and tracking pod
13 Windscreen panel
14 Head-up display symbol generator
15 Pilot's head-up display screen
16 Instrument panel shroud
17 Air-to air refuelling pipe
18 Titanium armour cockpit enclosure
19 Rudder pedals
20 Battery
21 General Electric GAU-8/A 30-mm seven-barrelled rotary cannon
22 Ammunition feed ducts
23 Steering cylinder
24 Nose undercarriage leg strut
25 Nosewheel
26 Nosewheel scissor links
27 Retractable boarding ladder
28 Ventilating air outlets
29 Ladder stowage box
30 Pilot's side console panel
31 Engine throttles
32 Control column
33 McDonnell Douglas ACES 2 ejection seat
34 Headrest canopy breakers
35 Cockpit canopy cover

36 Canopy hinge mechanism
37 Space provision for additional avionics
38 Angle of attack probe
39 Emergency canopy release handle
40 Ventral access panels to gun compartment
41 Ammunition drum (1,174 rounds)
42 Ammunition drum armour plating
43 Electrical system servicing panel
44 Ventral fin
45 Spent cartridge-case return chute
46 Control cable runs
47 Avionics compartments
48 Forward/centre fuselage joint bulkhead
49 Aerial selector switches
50 FF aerial
51 Anti-collision light
52 UHF TACAN aerial
53 Starboard wing integral fuel tank
54 Wing skin plating
55 Outerwing panel attachment joint strap
56 Starboard fixed-wing pylons
57 ALE-37A chaff dispenser pod
58 ALQ-119 electronic countermeasures pod
59 Pitot tube
60 Starboard drooped wingtip fairing
61 Split aileron/deceleron mass balance
62 Deceleron open position
63 Starboard aileron/deceleron
64 Deceleron hydraulic jack
65 Aileron hydraulic jack
66 Control linkages
67 Aileron tab
68 Tab balance weight
69 Slotted trailing-edge flaps
70 Outboard flap jack
71 Flap synchronising shafts

72 Fuselage self-sealing fuel cells (maximum internal fuel capacity 10,700 lb/4853 kg)
73 Fuselage main longeron
74 Longitudinal control and services duct
75 Air-conditioning supply duct
76 Wing attachment fuselage main frames
77 Gravity fuel fillercaps
78 Engine pylon fairing
79 Pylon attachment joint
80 Starboard intake
81 Intake centre cone
82 Engine fan blades
83 Night/adverse weather two-seater variant
84 Radar pod (forward-looking infra-red in starboard pod)
85 Engine mounting struts
86 Nacelle construction
87 Oil tank
88 General Electric TF34-GE-100 turbofan
89 Rear engine mounting
90 Pylon trailing-edge fillet
91 Engine exhaust duct
92 Fan air duct
93 Rudder hydraulic jack
94 Starboard tailfin
95 X-band aerial
96 Rudder mass balance weight

97 Starboard rudder
98 Elevator tab
99 Tab control rod
100 Starboard elevator
101 Starboard tailplane
102 Tailplane attachment frames

103 Elevator hydraulic jacks
104 Tailcone
105 Tail navigation light
106 Rear radar warning receiver aerial

107 Honeycomb elevator construction
108 Port vertical tailfin construction
109 Honeycomb rudder panel
110 Rudder hydraulic jack
111 Formation light
112 Vertical fin ventral fairing
113 Tailplane construction

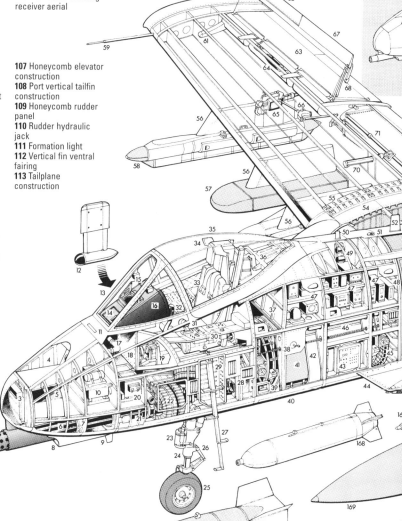

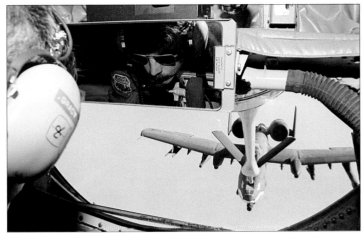

*Placing the refuelling receptacle immediately in front of the pilot allowed easy alignment for rendezvous, as seen here with a KC-135 Stratotanker. During Desert Storm, A-10s were able to loiter over the battlefield for far longer than expected, allowing pilots to remain on station until the best target became available.*

## SPECIFICATION

### A-10 Thunderbolt II

### Dimensions

**Length overall:** 53 ft 6 in (17.53 m)
**Height:** 14 ft 8 in (4.47 m)
**Wingspan:** 57 ft 6 in (17.53 m)
**Aspect ratio:** 6.54
**Wing area:** 506.00 sq ft (47.01 m²)
**Tailplane span:** 18 ft 10 in (5.74 m)
**Wheel track:** 17 ft 2½ in (5.25 m)

### Powerplant

Two General Electric TF34-GE-100 turbofans each rated at 9,065 lb st (40.32 kN) dry

### Weights

**Basic empty:** 21,541 lb (9771 kg)
**Operating empty:** 24,959 lb (11321 kg)
**Maximum take-off:** 50,000 lb (22680 kg)

### Fuel and load

**Internal fuel:** 10, 700 lb (4853 kg)
**External fuel:** three 600-US gal (2271-litre) drop tanks
**Maximum ordnance:** 16,000 lb (7258 kg)

### Performance

**Maximum level speed 'clean' at sea level:** 381 kt (439 mph; 706 km/h)
**Maximum cruising speed at 5,000 ft (1525 m):** 337 kt (387 mph; 623 km/h)
**Maximum rate of climb at sea level:** about 6,000 ft (1828 m) per minute
**Take-off run:** 4,000 ft (1220 m) at maximum take-off weight or 1,450 ft (442 m) at forward strip weight
**Landing run:** 2,000 ft (610 m) at maximum landing weight or 1,300 ft (396 m) at forward strip weight

### Range

**Ferry range with two drop tanks:** 2,131 nm (2,454 miles; 3949 km)
**Combat radius:** 540 nm (620 miles; 1000 km) on a deep strike mission or 250 nm (288 miles; 463 km) on a close air support mission with a 1.7-hour loiter

### Armament

One GAU-8/A 30-mm cannon with 1,350 rounds, plus up to 16,000 lb (7258 kg) of mixed ordnance (including laser-guided bombs, rockets, CBUs and Maverick missiles) on 11 external store stations

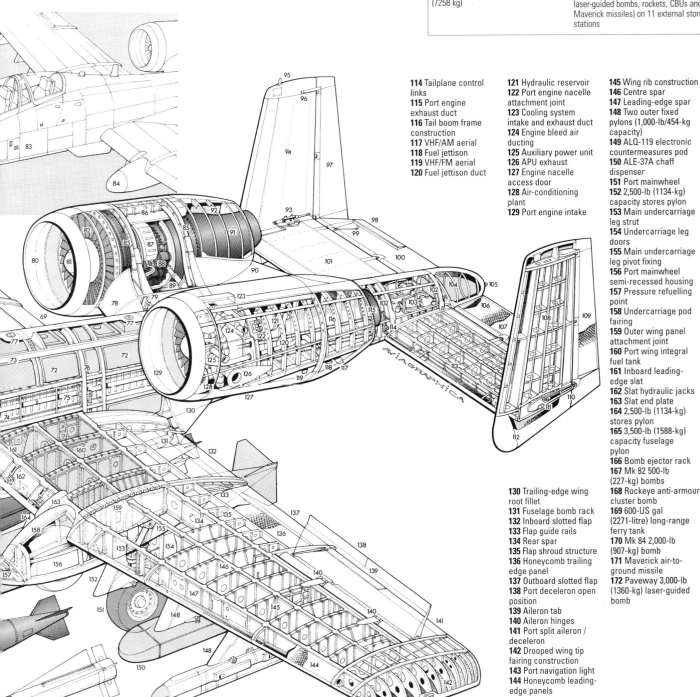

114 Tailplane control links
115 Port engine exhaust duct
116 Tail boom frame construction
117 VHF/AM aerial
118 Fuel jettison
119 VHF/FM aerial
120 Fuel jettison duct
121 Hydraulic reservoir
122 Port engine nacelle attachment joint
123 Cooling system intake and exhaust duct
124 Engine bleed air ducting
125 Auxiliary power unit
126 APU exhaust
127 Engine nacelle access door
128 Air-conditioning plant
129 Port engine intake
130 Trailing-edge wing root fillet
131 Fuselage bomb rack
132 Inboard slotted flap
133 Flap guide rails
134 Rear spar
135 Flap shroud structure
136 Honeycomb trailing edge panel
137 Outboard slotted flap
138 Port deceleron open position
139 Aileron tab
140 Aileron hinges
141 Port split aileron / deceleron
142 Drooped wing tip fairing construction
143 Port navigation light
144 Honeycomb leading-edge panels
145 Wing rib construction
146 Centre spar
147 Leading-edge spar
148 Two outer fixed pylons (1,000-lb/454-kg capacity)
149 ALQ-119 electronic countermeasures pod
150 ALE-37A chaff dispenser
151 Port mainwheel
152 2,500-lb (1134-kg) capacity stores pylon
153 Main undercarriage leg strut
154 Undercarriage leg doors
155 Main undercarriage leg pivot fixing
156 Port mainwheel semi-recessed housing
157 Pressure refuelling point
158 Undercarriage pod fairing
159 Outer wing panel attachment joint
160 Port wing integral fuel tank
161 Inboard leading-edge slat
162 Slat hydraulic jacks
163 Slat end plate
164 2,500-lb (1134-kg) stores pylon
165 3,500-lb (1588-kg) capacity fuselage pylon
166 Bomb ejector rack
167 Mk 82 500-lb (227-kg) bombs
168 Rockeye anti-armour cluster bomb
169 600-US gal (2271-litre) long-range ferry tank
170 Mk 84 2,000-lb (907-kg) bomb
171 Maverick air-to-ground missile
172 Paveway 3,000-lb (1360-kg) laser-guided bomb

# General Dynamics F-111

The three-tone *T.O. 1-1-4 Southeast Asia camouflage,* as applied to this *F-111, proved highly effective. On daylight missions in Vietnam, the F-111 was used for hitting tactical or strategic targets, but was occasionally used as a bomb leader, taking less sophisticated aircraft on bombing missions and supplying drop commands to increase their accuracy.*

## F-111F Aardvark

**Cutaway key**

1 Pitot head
2 Glass-fibre radome
3 AN/APQ-161 navigation and attack radar
4 AN/APQ-146 terrain-following radar
5 Radar equipment module
6 Avionics equipment bay
7 Flight control computers
8 Lower UHF/TACAN antenna
9 Twin nosewheels, forward-retracting
10 Electro-luminescent formation lighting strip
11 Liquid oxygen converter
12 Pressurised escape capsule joint frame
13 Rudder pedals
14 Control column
15 Engine throttle levers and wing sweep control
16 Pilot's head-up display
17 Single curvature windscreen panels
18 Upward-hinged cockpit canopy covers
19 Tactical navigator's seat
20 Rear bulkhead consoles
21 Pilot's seat
22 Escape capsule recovery parachute stowage
23 Self-righting air bag (two)
24 UHF/IFF aerial
25 Stabilising and brake parachute stowage
26 Leading-edge flush ECM antennas
27 Forward fuselage fuel tank
28 Tank floor/weapons bay roof
29 Electrical system equipment
30 Pressure refuelling connection and control panel
31 Port navigation light
32 Escape capsule rear flotation bag
33 Flight-refuelling receptacle
34 Machined fuselage bulkheads
35 Fuselage integral fuel tankage
36 Movable intake centre-body 'spike' (Triple Plow 2 intake)
37 Port engine intake
38 Glove vane lower fairing
39 Wing root rotating glove vane
40 Wing sweep screw jack actuator
41 Upper UHF/TACAN aerial
42 Anti-collision beacon
43 Wing pivot box integral fuel tank
44 Rear fuselage upper longerons
45 Flap and slat drive electrohydraulic motor
46 Formation lighting strip
47 Intake boundary layer spill air louvres
48 Starboard wing pivot point
49 Starboard glove vane
50 GBU-10 2,000-lb (907-kg) laser-guided bomb
51 GBU-24 'Paveway III' laser-guided bomb
52 Swivelling stores pylons
53 Pylon pivot mountings
54 Pylon actuating mechanical link
55 Starboard wing integral fuel tank
56 Leading-edge slats
57 Starboard position light
58 Wingtip formation light
59 Starboard wing fully-forward (16° sweep) position
60 Spoiler panels, open
61 Double-slotted flaps, down position
62 Wing root auxiliary flap
63 Wing glove housing
64 Engine intake ducting
65 Dorsal cable and systems duct
66 HF aerial spine fairing
67 Starboard engine bay
68 Rear fuselage dorsal fuel tank
69 Starboard all-moving tailplane
70 Starboard wing, fully-swept (72.5° sweep) position
71 Radar warning receiver
72 Fin leading-edge honeycomb panel
73 HF aerial shunt
74 Multi-spar tailfin
75 Fin integral fuel tank
76 Formation lighting strip
77 Fin-tip infra-red warning receiver
78 Rudder honeycomb core construction

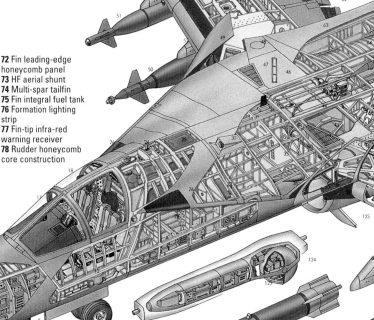

## SPECIFICATION

### F-111F Aardvark

### Dimensions

**Length overall:** 73 ft 6 in (22.40 m)
**Height:** 17 ft 1½ in (5.22 m)
**Wingspan (spread):** 63 ft (19.20 m)
**Wingspan (swept):** 31 ft 11½ in (9.74 m)
**Aspect ratio (spread):** 7.56
**Aspect ratio (swept):** 1.55
**Wing area (spread):** 657.07 sq ft (61.07m²)
**Wing area (swept):** 525 sq ft (48.77m²)

### Powerplant

Two Pratt & Whitney TF30-P-100 turbofans, each rated at 25,000 lb st (111.65 kN) with afterburning

### Weights

**Operating empty:** 47,481 lb (21537 kg)
**Maximum take-off:** 100,000 lb (45360 kg)

### Fuel and load

**Internal fuel:** 5,025 US gal (19021 litres)
**External fuel:** up to four 600-US gal (2271-litre) drop tanks
**Maximum ordnance:** 31,500 lb (14228 kg)

### Performance

**Maximum level clean speed at 36,000 ft (10975 m):** 1,433 kt (1,650 mph; 2655 km/h)

**Cruising speed at high altitude:** 496 kt (571 mph; 919 km/h)
**Service ceiling:** 60,000 ft (18290 m)
**Take-off distance to 50 ft (15 m):** 3,120 ft (951 m)
**Landing run:** less than 3,000 ft (915 m) at normal landing weight

### Range

**Range with maximum internal fuel:** 2,540 nm (2,925 miles; 4707 km)

### Armament

One M61 multi-barreled 20-mm cannon and two B43 bombs in the internal weapon bay. The external stores were carried on three attachments under each wing. Primary weapons included the 500-lb (227-kg) GBU-12 Paveway II, 2,000-lb (907-kg) GBU-10 Paveway II and 2,000-lb (907-kg) GBU-24 Paveway III. Both 2,000-lb (907-kg) weapons were available with either a standard Mk 84 warhead or BLU-109 penetration warhead. The GBU-28 'Deep Throat' was a 4,800-lb (2177-kg) Paveway III hastily developed for Desert Storm. 'Dumb' ordnance such as iron bombs, cluster weapons and the BLU-107 Durandal runway-cratering munition cuold also be carried. An F-111F speciality was the GBU-15 2,000-lb (907-kg) EO-guided bomb. This had either a Mk 84 or BLU-109 warhead, and a TV- or IR-seeker adapted from those fitted to Maverick missiles. For defence, the F-111F routinely carried the AIM-9P-3 Sidewinder

*F-111s can carry a formidable and varied amount of offensive weaponry, though the picture above shows practice bombs. Weapons are placed on a trolley which can be lowered or raised accordingly, and greatly increases the speed and ease of reloading. F-111Fs equipped with GBU-12D/Bs were used to attack Iraqi armoured and motorised formations during the Gulf War and scored 10 times as many tank kills as the F-16 during the conflict.*

**79** Rudder hydraulic actuator
**80** Afterburner nozzle control jacks
**81** Translating primary iris afterburner nozzle
**82** Afterburner duct air mixing intakes
**83** Chaff dispenser
**84** Variable area exhaust nozzle
**85** Rear ECM antenna fairing

**86** Port all-moving tailplane
**87** Static dischargers
**88** Port wing, fully-swept position
**89** Control surface honeycomb core leading and trailing edges
**90** Tailplane pivot fixing
**91** Tailplane hydraulic actuator
**92** Port engine bay
**93** Port ventral fin

**94** AN/AXQ-14 two-way datalink weapon control and guidance pod, carried beneath rear fuselage
**95** Engine bay access doors
**96** Formation lighting strip
**97** Engine accessory equipment compartment
**98** Fuselage flank fuel tank
**99** Wing root pneumatic seal
**100** Pratt & Whitney TF30- P-100 afterburner turbofan
**101** Conical engine intake centrebody
**102** Hydraulic reservoir
**103** Main undercarriage wheel bay
**104** Retraction breaker strut and shock absorbers
**105** Wing pivot bearing
**106** Flap drive shaft and screw jacks
**107** Wing root auxiliary flap
**108** Ventral flap sealing plate
**109** Flap honeycomb core construction
**110** Port double-slotted flap
**111** Port spoiler panels
**112** Multi-spar wing panel construction
**113** Static dischargers
**114** Wingtip formation light
**115** Port position light
**116** Port leading-edge slat
**117** Slat guide rails
**118** Port wing integral fuel tank
**119** Pylon pivot mountings
**120** Port swivelling stores pylons
**121** Leading-edge slat drive shaft and transfer gearbox
**122** Port mainwheel

**123** Ventral airbrake/mainwheel door
**124** AN/AVQ-26 Pave Tack laser designator pod, carried in weapons bay
**125** Swivelling and rotating sighting unit
**126** Pave Tack rotary housing
**127** GBU-28 'Deep Throat' laser-guided bomb
**128** GBU-15 2,000-lb (907-kg) EO-guided bomb

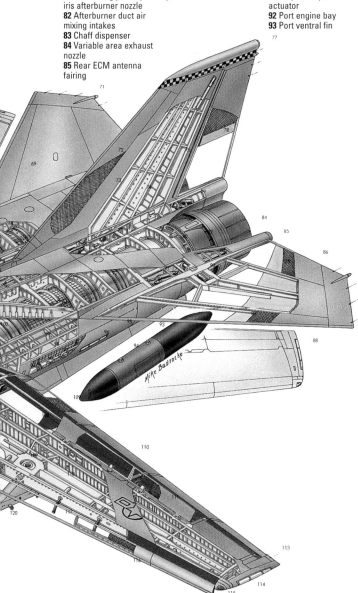

# Gloster Javelin

*Although plagued by serviceability and structural problems,
Javelin was a highly capable bomber-interceptor, equipped as it w
with four 30-mm ADEN cannon and, later, with the addition of fe
IR-seeking missiles. XH881 was an example of the ultimate varia
the FAW.Mk 9. It was built as an FAW.Mk 7, but retained by Glos
for conversion to Mk 9 standard before delivery to No. 25 S*

### Javelin FAW.Mk 9R

**Cutaway key**

1 Detachable flight refuelling probe, used for overseas deployment
2 Glass-fibre radome
3 AI.Mk 22 radar scanner dish (American AN/APQ-43)
4 Scanner tracking mechanism
5 Radar transmitter/ receiver
6 Radar mounting bulkhead
7 Instrument venturi
8 Aft-retracting nosewheel
9 Mudguard
10 Torque scissor links
11 Lower IFF antenna
12 Nose equipment bay access door
13 Additional (long-range) oxygen bottles
14 Radar modulator
15 Upper IFF antenna
16 Front pressure bulkhead
17 Rudder pedals
18 Standard oxygen bottle stowage, port and starboard
19 Side console panel
20 Engine throttle levers
21 Control column
22 Pilot's instrument panel
23 Instrument panel shroud
24 Windscreen rain dispersal air duct
25 Starboard engine intake
26 Windscreen panels
27 Pilot's gyro gunsight
28 Rearward-sliding cockpit canopy
29 Ejection seat faceblind firing handle
30 Pilot's Martin-Baker Mk 4 ejection seat
31 Seat mounting rails
32 Port engine air intake
33 Intake lip bleed air de-icing

34 Intake duct framing
35 Rebecca homing antenna
36 Radar altimeter transmitting antenna
37 Missile cooling system heat exchanger
38 Cold air unit and compressor
39 Port intake duct
40 Radar operator's instrument console
41 Radar indicator
42 Fixed canopy centre section
43 Missile cooling system air bottles
44 Radar operator's rearward-sliding canopy
45 Radar operator's Martin-Baker ejection seat
46 Cockpit pressure shell framing
47 Missile control system equipment
48 Engine compressor intake
49 IPN engine starter fuel tank
50 Central equipment bay
51 Engine-driven gearbox with generators and hydraulic pumps
52 Cabin air system heat exchanger
53 Flight control rods
54 Gee antenna
55 Canopy tail fairing with heat exchanger outlet duct
56 Wing spar attachment fuselage main frame
57 Starboard main undercarriage wheel bay
58 Gun heating system air reservoirs
59 Starboard leading edge fuel tanks Nos 1, 2 and 3. Total internal capacity 950 Imp gal (4319 litres)
60 100-Imp gal (454-litre) external pylon tanks
61 Starboard wing pylons
62 Pylon aerodynamic fairings

63 Cannon muzzle blast fairings with frangible caps
64 Cannon barrel blast tubes
65 30-mm ADEN cannon, four carried for Far Eastern deployment, two only for European operations
66 Link collector boxes
67 Gun camera
68 Aileron control rod and pitch stabiliser
69 Aileron servodyne
70 Vortex generators, three rows
71 Starboard pitot head
72 Starboard navigation light
73 Formation light
74 Starboard aileron
75 Aileron spar
76 Fixed portion of trailing edge
77 Starboard airbrake, upper and lower surfaces
78 Airbrake hydraulic jack (2)
79 Flap hydraulic jack (2)
80 Ventral flap panel
81 Ammunition magazines, 100 rounds per gun
82 Rear fuel tanks, Nos 4 and 5
83 Engine exhaust, zone-3, cooling air intake
84 Artificial feel simulator pressure heads
85 Starboard engine bay
86 Fuselage centre keel structure
87 Rudder feel simulator
88 Port Armstrong Siddeley Sapphire Sa.7R turbojet with 12 per cent limited reheat

89 Engine bay firewall
90 Turbine section
91 Central fuel system collector tanks
92 Engine exhaust duct
93 Fin-mounted bulkhead
94 Fin spar attachment joint
95 Servomotor
96 Rudder servodyne
97 Fin rib structure
98 Leading-edge ribs and control runs
99 Hydraulic accumulators
100 Tailplane hydraulic power control unit
101 Tailplane operating beam
102 Fixed tailplane centre section
103 Tailplane spar bearing
104 Tubular tailplane spar
105 Starboard trimming tailplane
106 Starboard elevator
107 UHF antenna
108 Tail navigation light
109 Tail warning radar antenna
110 Elevator operating linkage
111 Port elevator rib structure
112 Tailplane single spar and rib structure
113 Rudder rib structure
114 Afterburner nozzles
115 Detachable fuselage tail section, engine removal
116 Afterburner duct

117 Tail section joint frame
118 Wing rear spar attachment joint
119 Port flap housing
120 Flap hydraulic jacks
121 Airbrake hydraulic jacks
122 Semi-span rear spar
123 Port airbrake panel, upper and lower surfaces

124 Fixed trailing-edge rib structure
125 Cartridge case ejection chutes
126 Port aileron
127 Aileron rib structure

128 Aileron servodyne
129 Formation light
130 Wingtip member structure
131 Port navigation light

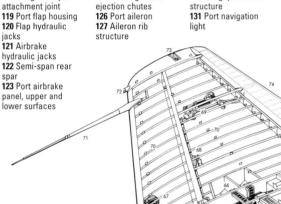

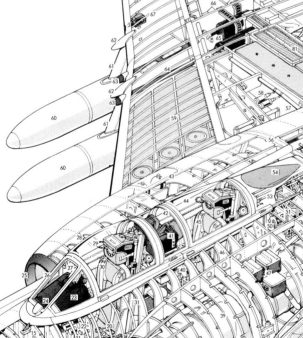

*Javelin FAW.Mk 7 XH712 never entered squadron service in its original mark, spending its early career as a trials airframe. It was initially engaged in handling trials with the Aircraft and Armament Experimental Establishment, before passing to de Havilland as a testbed for both Firestreak (illustrated above) and Red Top AAM trials. In 1959 it was converted to FAW.Mk 9 standard and passed into storage. It was once more modified, this time to Mk 9R standard, before passing to No. 23 Sqn late in 1962. It saw out its service with No. 29 Sqn, before being scrapped on 30 June 1967.*

## SPECIFICATION

### Javelin FAW.Mk 7/8/9/9R

#### Dimensions

**Length, Mk 7/9/9R:** 56 ft 4 in (17.17 m)
**Length, Mk 8:** 55 ft 2½ in (16.83 m)
**Height:** 16 ft (4.88 m)
**Wingspan:** 52 ft (15.85 m)
**Wing area:** 927 sq ft (86.12 m²)
**Wheel track:** 23 ft 4 in (7.11 m)

#### Powerplant

**Mk 7:** Two Armstrong Siddeley Sapphire Sa.7 turbojets rated at 11,000 lb st (48.92 kN) dry
**Mk 8/9/9R:** Two Armstrong Siddeley Sapphire Sa.7R turbojets rated at 11,000 lb st (48.92 kN) dry and 12,300 lb st (54.70 kN) with 12 per cent afterburning at 20,000 ft (6096 m)

#### Weights

**Take-off, 'clean', Mk 7:** 35,690 lb (16188 kg)
**Take-off, 'clean', Mk 8:** 37,410 lb (16968 kg)
**Take-off, 'clean', Mk 9:** 38,100 lb (17272 kg)
**Overload, with two ventral tanks, Mk 7:** 40,270 lb (18266 kg)
**Overload, with two ventral tanks Mk 8:** 42,510 lb (19282 kg)
**Overload, with two ventral tanks Mk 9:** 43,165 lb (19578 kg)

#### Fuel and load

**Internal fuel, Mk 7:** 915 Imp gal (4158 litres)
**Internal fuel, Mk 8/9/9R:** 950 Imp gal (4319 litres)
**External fuel:** All variants could carry up two 250-Imp gal (1137-litre) conformal ventral tanks
**Drop tanks, Mk 7/8/9:** ventral tanks plus up to four 100-Imp gal (454-litre) tanks
**Drop tanks, Mk 9R:** ventral tanks plus up to four 230-Imp gal (1046-litre) tanks

#### Performance

**Maximum level speed 'clean' at sea level, Mk 7:** 708 mph (1141 km/h)
**Maximum level speed 'clean' at sea level, Mk 8/9:** 702 mph (1130 km/h)
**Climb to 45,000 ft (13716 m), Mk 7:** 6 minutes 36 seconds
**Climb to 50,000 ft (15240 m), Mk 8/9:** 9 minutes 15 seconds
**Service ceiling, Mk 7:** 52,800 ft (16039 m)
**Service ceiling, Mk 8/9:** 52,000 ft (15849 m)
**Absolute ceiling, Mk 7:** 54,100 ft (16489 m)
**Absolute ceiling, Mk 8/9:** 54,000 ft (16459 m)

#### Armament

Up to four 30-mm ADEN cannon in the outer wing panels, each with 100 rounds, plus up to four de Havilland Propellers Firestreak IR-homing air-to-air missiles

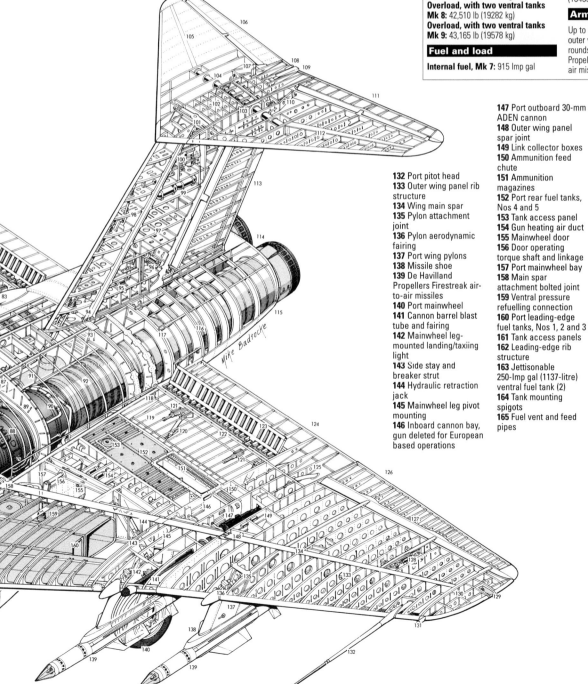

**132** Port pitot head
**133** Outer wing panel rib structure
**134** Wing main spar
**135** Pylon attachment joint
**136** Pylon aerodynamic fairing
**137** Port wing pylons
**138** Missile shoe
**139** De Havilland Propellers Firestreak air-to-air missiles
**140** Port mainwheel
**141** Cannon barrel blast tube and fairing
**142** Mainwheel leg-mounted landing/taxiing light
**143** Side stay and breaker strut
**144** Hydraulic retraction jack
**145** Mainwheel leg pivot mounting
**146** Inboard cannon bay, gun deleted for European based operations

**147** Port outboard 30-mm ADEN cannon
**148** Outer wing panel spar joint
**149** Link collector boxes
**150** Ammunition feed chute
**151** Ammunition magazines
**152** Port rear fuel tanks, Nos 4 and 5
**153** Tank access panel
**154** Gun heating air duct
**155** Mainwheel door
**156** Door operating torque shaft and linkage
**157** Port mainwheel bay
**158** Main spar attachment bolted joint
**159** Ventral pressure refuelling connection
**160** Port leading-edge fuel tanks, Nos 1, 2 and 3
**161** Tank access panels
**162** Leading-edge rib structure
**163** Jettisonable 250-Imp gal (1137-litre) ventral fuel tank (2)
**164** Tank mounting spigots
**165** Fuel vent and feed pipes

# Hawker Hunter

*India was one of the most important export customers for the Hunter in both single-and two-seat form. A total of 252 new-build and refurbished examples were delivered between 1957 and 1973.*

## Hunter FGA.Mk 9

**Cutaway key**

1 Radome
2 Radar scanner dish
3 Ram air intake
4 Camera port
5 Radar ranging equipment
6 Camera access panel
7 Gun camera
8 Ground pressurisation connection
9 Nosewheel door
10 Oxygen bottles
11 IFF aerial
12 Electronics equipment
13 Nosewheel bay
14 De-icing fluid tank
15 Pressurisation control valves
16 Cockpit front bulkhead
17 Nose landing gear leg
18 Nosewheel forks
19 Forward retracting nosewheel
20 Nosewheel leg door
21 Cannon muzzle port
22 Gun blast cascade deflectors
23 Rudder pedals
24 Bullet proof windscreen
25 Cockpit canopy framing
26 Reflector gunsight
27 Instrument panel shroud
28 Control column
29 Cockpit section fuselage frames
30 Rearward sliding cockpit canopy cover
31 Pilot's starboard side console
32 Martin Baker Mk 3H ejector seat
33 Throttle control
34 Pilot's port side console
35 Cannon barrel tubes
36 Pneumatic system airbottles
37 Cockpit canopy emergency release
38 Cockpit rear pressure bulkhead
39 Air conditioning valve
40 Ejector seat headrest
41 Firing handle
42 Air louvres
43 Ammunition tanks
44 Ammunition link collector box
45 Cartridge case ejectors
46 Batteries
47 Port air inlet
48 Boundary layer splitter plate

49 Inlet lip construction
50 Radio and electronics equipment bay
51 Sliding canopy rail
52 Air conditioning supply pipes
53 Control rod linkages
54 Communications aerial
55 Fuselage double frame bulkhead
56 Boundary layer air outlet
57 Secondary air inlet door spring loaded
58 Inlet duct construction
59 Forward fuselage fuel tank
60 Starboard inlet duct
61 Starboard wing fuel tank
62 230 Imp gal (1046 litre) drop tank
63 Inboard pylon mounting
64 Leading edge dog tooth
65 100-Imp gal (455-litre) drop tank
66 Outboard pylon mounting
67 Wing fence
68 Leading edge extension
69 Starboard navigation light
70 Starboard wingtip
71 Whip aerial
72 Fairey hydraulic aileron booster jack
73 Starboard aileron
74 Aileron control rod linkage

75 Flap cut out section for drop tank clearance
76 Starboard flap construction
77 Flap hydraulic jack

78 Flap synchronising jack
79 Starboard main landing gear mounting
80 Retraction jack
81 Starboard landing gear bay
82 Dorsal spine fairing
83 Main wing attachment frames
84 Main spar attachment joint
85 Engine starter fuel tank
86 Air conditioning system
87 Engine inlet compressor face
88 Air conditioning pre-cooler
89 Cooling air outlet louvres
90 Rear spar attachment
91 Aileron control rods
92 Front engine mountings
93 Rolls Royce Avon 207 engine
94 Bleed air duct

95 Engine bay cooling flush air Intake
96 Rear engine mounting
97 Rear fuselage joint ring
98 Joint ring attachment bolts
99 Tailplane control rods
100 Fuel piping from rear tank

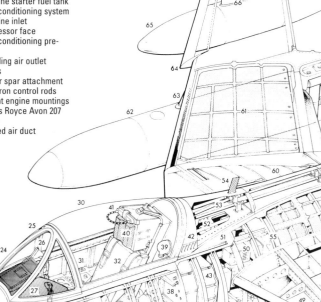

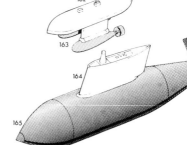

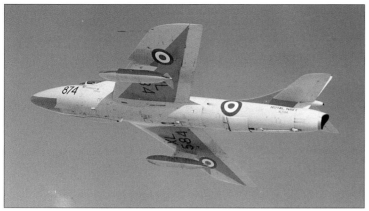

*One of ten new-build **T.Mk 8s** constructed for the Royal Navy at Hawker's Kingston-upon-Thames site, XL584 was delivered in October 1958 for service with No. 764 Sqn, FAA. This aircraft, along with two other examples, subsequently returned to Hawker for preparation in high-gloss epoxy dark blue and white paint for use by the Flag Officer (Flying Training) at Yeovilton, then becoming known as 'the Admiral's barges'. By 1975, like most FAA Hunters, XL584 had been reallocated to the Fleet Requirement and Air Direction Unit (FRADU) and had adopted this high visibility colour scheme.*

**101** Rear fuselage fuel tank
**102** Fuel collector tank
**103** Jetpipe mounting rail
**104** Fin root fairing
**105** Hydraulic accumulator
**106** Tailplane trim jack
**107** Fairey hydraulic elevator booster
**108** Tailplane mounting pivot
**109** Rudder hinge control rods
**110** Starboard tailplane
**111** Starboard elevator
**112** Tailfin construction
**113** Fin tip aerial fairing
**114** Rudder construction
**115** Rudder trim tab
**116** Trim tab control jack
**117** Tailplane anti buffet fairing
**118** Tail navigation light
**119** Brake parachute housing
**120** Tailpipe fairing

**121** Port elevator construction
**122** Tailplane construction
**123** Detachable tailcone
**124** Tailplane spar mounting frames
**125** Jetpipe
**126** Jetpipe access doors
**127** Rear fuselage frame and stringer construction
**128** Airbrake jack housing
**129** Airbrake retracted position
**130** Airbrake operating jack
**131** Airbrake open position
**132** Engine bearing cool air outlet
**133** Wing root trailing edge fillet
**134** Flap housing construction
**135** Port main landing gear bay
**136** Main wheel door
**137** Port main landing gear retraction jack

**138** Main landing gear leg pivot mounting
**139** Flap synchronising jack
**140** Hydraulic flap jack
**141** Port flap
**142** Rear spar
**143** Aileron control rods
**144** Aileron trim tab
**145** Port aileron construction
**146** Fairey hydraulic aileron booster
**147** Wing tip construction
**148** Port navigation light
**149** Pitot tube
**150** 3 in (7.62 cm) rocket projectiles
**151** Leading edge extension ribs
**152** Wing rib construction
**153** Main spar
**154** Dowty main landing gear leg
**155** Shock absorber torque links

**156** Leading-edge dogtooth
**157** Mainwheel doors
**158** Dunlop-Maxaret anti-skid wheel brakes
**159** Port mainwheel
**160** Port wing fuel tank: total internal fuel capacity 392 Imp gal (1782 litres)
**161** Leading edge pin joint
**162** ML twin stores carrier
**163** 9-kg (20-lb) practice bombs
**164** Inboard wing pylon
**165** 1000 lb (454 kg) bomb
**166** Four 30-mm ADEN gun pack
**167** Ammunition boxes, 150 rounds per gun
**168** Link collector box
**169** Gun gas purging air duct
**170** Cannon barrels remaining in aircraft when gun pack is withdrawn

## SPECIFICATION

### Hunter FGA.Mk 9

**Dimensions**

**Length overall:** 45 ft 10½ in (13.98 m)
**Height:** 13 ft 2 in (4.01 m)
**Wingspan:** 33 ft 8 in (10.26 m)
**Aspect ratio:** 3.25
**Wing area:** 349 sq ft (32.42 m²)
**Tailplane span:** 11 ft 10 in (3.61 m)
**Wheel track:** 14 ft 9 in (4.50 m)
**Wheel base:** 15 ft 9 in (4.80 m)

**Powerplant**

One Rolls-Royce Avon RA.28 Mk 207 turbojet rated at 10,150 lb st (45.15 kN)

**Weights**

**Empty equipped:** 14,400 lb (6532 kg)
**Normal take-off:** 18,000 lb (8165 kg)
**Maximum take-off:** 24,600 lb (11158 kg)

**Fuel and load**

**Internal fuel:** 3,144 lb (1426 kg)
**External fuel:** two 230- or 100-Imp gal (1045- or 455-litre) drop tanks
**Maximum ordnance:** 7,400 lb (3357 kg)

**Performance**

**Maximum level speed 'clean' at 36,000 ft (10975 m):** 538 kt (620 mph; 978 km/h)
**Maximum level speed 'clean' at sea level:** 616 kt (710 mph; 1144 km/h)

**Maximum cruising speed at 36,000 ft (10975 m):** 481 kt (554 mph; 892 km/h)
**Economical cruising speed at optimum altitude:** 399 kt (460 mph; 740 km/h)
**Service ceiling:** 50,000 ft (15240 m)
**Maximum rate of climb at sea level:** about 8,000 ft (2438 m) per minute
**Take-off run:** 2,100 ft (640 m) at normal take-off weight
**Take-off distance to 50 ft (15 m):** 3,450 ft (1052 m) at normal take-off weight
**Landing run:** 3,150 ft (960 m) at normal landing weight

**Range**

**Ferry range with two drop tanks:** 1,595 nm (1,840 miles; 2961 km)
**Combat radius:** 385 nm (443 miles; 713 km) on hi-lo-hi attack mission with typical warload and two drop tanks

**Armament**

Four 30-mm ADEN cannon mounted in a pack beneath the forward fuselage with up to 150 rounds of ammunition per gun. Inboard pylons could carry either British or foreign bombs of up to 1000 lb (454 kg), 2-in (5.08-cm) multiple rocket batteries, 100-Imp gal (455-litre) Napalm bombs, practice bomb carriers and a variety of other stores. Outboard pylons could carry launchers for 24 3-in (7.62-cm) rocket projectiles with various warheads or other types of rocket projectile

# Hawker Siddeley Harrier

*Several of No. IV (AC) Squadron's Harrier GR.Mk 3s gained a colourful fin during their last couple of years of service. Initially, the colours were applied to the commanding officer's aircraft for the squadron's 75th anniversary celebrations. Coloured fins were also tested in a bid to avoid collisions during low-level training by increasing conspicuity.*

## Harrier GR.Mk 3

**Cutaway key**
1 Pitot tube
2 Laser window protective 'eyelids'
3 Ferranti Laser Ranger and Marked-Target Seeker (LRMTS) unit
4 Cooling air duct
5 Oblique camera
6 Camera port
7 Windshield washer reservoir
8 Inertial platform
9 Nose pitch reaction control air duct
10 Pitch feel and trim actuator
11 IFF aerial
12 Cockpit ram air intake
13 Yaw vane
14 Cockpit air discharge valve
15 Front pressure bulkhead
16 Rudder pedals
17 Nav/attack 'head-down' display unit
18 Underfloor control linkages
19 Canopy external handle
20 Control column
21 Instrument panel shroud
22 Windscreen wiper
23 Birdproof windscreen panels
24 Head-up display
25 Starboard side console panel
26 Nozzle angle control lever
27 Engine throttle lever
28 Ejection seat rocket pack
29 Fuel cock
30 Cockpit pressurisation relief valve
31 Canopy emergency release
32 Pilot's Martin-Baker Type 9D, zero-zero ejection seat

33 Sliding canopy rail
34 Miniature detonating cord (MDC) canopy breaker

35 Starboard air intake
36 Ejection seat headrest
37 Cockpit rear pressure bulkhead
38 Nose undercarriage wheel well
39 Boundary layer bleed air duct
40 Port air intake
41 Pre-closing nosewheel door
42 Landing/taxiing lamp
43 Nosewheel forks
44 Nosewheel
45 Supplementary air intake doors (fully floating)
46 Intake ducting
47 Hydraulic accumulator
48 Nosewheel retraction jack
49 Intake centrebody
50 Ram air discharge to engine intake
51 Cockpit air-conditioning plant
52 Air-conditioning system ram air intakes
53 Boundary layer bleed air discharge ducts
54 Starboard supplementary air intake doors
55 UHF aerial
56 Engine intake compressor face
57 Air refuelling probe connection
58 Forward fuselage integral fuel tank, port and starboard
59 Engine bay venting air scoop
60 Hydraulic ground connections
61 Engine monitoring and recording equipment

62 Forward nozzle fairing
63 Fan air (cold stream) swivelling nozzle
64 Nozzle bearing
65 Venting air intake

66 Alternator cooling air ducts
67 Twin alternators
68 Engine accessory gearbox
69 Alternator cooling air exhausts
70 Engine bay access doors
71 Gas turbine starter/auxiliary power unit, GTS/APU
72 APU exhaust duct
73 Aileron control rods
74 Wing front spar carry-through
75 Nozzle bearing cooling air duct
76 Engine turbine section

77 Rolls-Royce Pegasus Mk 103 vectored thrust turbofan engine
78 Wing panel centreline joint rib
79 APU intake

80 Centre-section fairing panels
81 Starboard wing integral fuel tank, total internal fuel capacity 630 Imp gal (2865 litres)
82 Fuel system piping
83 Pylon attachment hardpoint
84 Aileron control rod
85 Reaction control air duct
86 Leading-edge dogtooth
87 Starboard inner stores pylon

88 Jettisonable combat fuel tank, capacity 100 Imp gal (454 litres)
89 1000-lb (454-kg) HE bomb
90 BL775 600-lb (272-kg) cluster bomb

91 Starboard outer stores pylon
92 Wing fences
93 Outer pylon hardpoint
94 Hydraulic power control unit
95 Roll control reaction air valve
96 Starboard navigation light

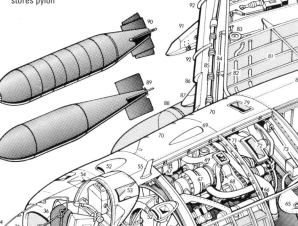

## SPECIFICATION

### Harrier GR.Mk 3

#### Dimensions

**Length:** 46 ft 10 in (14.27 m)
**Height:** 11 ft 11 in (3.63 m)
**Wingspan:** 25 ft 3 in (7.70 m) with combat tips or 29 ft 8 in (9.04 m) with ferry tips
**Wing area:** 201.10 sq ft (18.68 m²) with combat tips or 216.00 sq ft (20.07 m²) with ferry tips
**Wing aspect ratio:** 3.18 with combat tips or 4.08 with ferry tips
**Tailplane span:** 13 ft 11 in (4.24 m)
**Outrigger track:** 22 ft 2 in (6.76 m)

#### Powerplant

One Rolls-Royce Pegasus Mk 103 rated at 21,500 lb st (95.94 kN)

#### Weights

**Empty equipped:** 12,300 lb (5579 kg)
**Operating empty:** 13,535 lb (6139 kg)
**Normal take-off:** 23,500 lb (10660 kg)
**Maximum take-off:** 25,200 lb (11431 kg)

#### Fuel and loadd

**Internal fuel:** 5,060 lb (2295 kg)
**External fuel:** up to two 330-Imp gal (1500-litre) ferry tanks or two 190- or 100-Imp gal (864- or 455-litre) drop tanks
**Maximum ordnance:** 5,000 lb (2268 kg) authorised or 8,000 lb (3269 kg) demonstrated

#### Performance

**Maximum level speed 'clean' at sea level:** 635 kt (730 mph; 1176 km/h)
**Maximum rate of climb at sea level:** 29,000 ft (8840 m) per minute
**Climb to 40,000 ft (12190 m) after VTO:** 2 minutes 23 seconds
**Service ceiling:** 51,200 ft (15605 m)
**Take-off run at maximum take-off weight:** 1,000 ft (305 m)
**Landing run at normal landing weight:** 0 ft (0 m)

#### Armament

One or two 30-mm ADEN cannon plus a wide variety of laser-guided and dumb bombs, cluster bombs and rocket pods plus two AIM-9L air-to-air missiles

*RAF Harrier GR.Mk 3s and Royal Navy Sea Harrier FRS.Mk 1s share the flight deck of HMS Hermes during the Falklands conflict of 1982. With the Sea Harrier's adoption of the air defence role, the GR.Mk 3s were heavily involved in the close air support (CAS) tasking and suffered a number of casualties.*

97 Wingtip fairing
98 Profile of extended-span ferry tip
99 Starboard outrigger fairing
100 Wheel, retracted position
101 Starboard aileron
102 Fuel jettison pipe

103 Starboard plain flap
104 Trailing-edge root fairing
105 Water-methanol filler cap
106 Anti-collision light
107 Water-methanol injection system tank
108 Fire extinguisher bottle
109 Flap hydraulic jack
110 Fuel contents transmitters
111 Rear fuselage integral fuel tank
112 Ram air turbine housing

113 Turbine doors
114 Ram air turbine (extended position)
115 Rear fuselage frames
116 Ram air turbine jack
117 Cooling air ram air intake
118 HF tuner
119 HF notch aerial
120 Rudder control rod linkages

121 Starboard all-moving tailplane
122 Temperature sensor
123 Tailfin construction
124 Forward radar warning receiver
125 VHF aerial
126 Fintip aerial fairing
127 Rudder upper hinge
128 Honeycomb rudder construction
129 Rudder trim jack
130 Rudder tab
131 Tail reaction control air ducting
132 Yaw control port
133 Aft radar warning receiver
134 Rear position light
135 Pitch reaction control valve
136 Tailplane honeycomb trailing edge
137 Extended tailplane tip
138 Tailplane construction
139 Tail bumper
140 IFF notch aerial
141 Tailplane sealing plate
142 Fin spar attachment
143 Tailplane centre section/carry-through

144 All-moving tailplane control jack
145 Ram air exhaust duct
146 UHF standby aerial
147 Equipment air-conditioning plant
148 Ground power supply socket
149 Twin batteries
150 Ventral equipment bay access door
151 Radio and electronics equipment racks
152 Electronics bay access door
153 Ventral airbrake
154 Airbrake hydraulic jack
155 Nitrogen pressurising bottles for hydraulic system
156 Flap drive torque shaft
157 Rear spar/fuselage attachment joint
158 Nozzle blast shield
159 Rear (hot stream) swivelling exhaust nozzle
160 Wing rear spar
161 Port flap honeycomb construction
162 Fuel jettison valve
163 Fuel jettison pipe

164 Aileron honeycomb construction
165 Outrigger wheel fairing
166 Wingtip fairing
167 Profile of extended ferry tip
168 Hydraulic retraction jack
169 Shock absorber leg strut
170 Port outrigger wheel
171 Torque scissor links
172 Outrigger wheel leg fairings
173 Port navigation light
174 Roll control reaction valve
175 Wing rib construction
176 Outer pylon hardpoint
177 Machined wing skin/stringer panel
178 Aileron power control unit
179 Front spar
180 Leading-edge nose ribs
181 Reaction control air ducting
182 Port outer stores pylon
183 Leading-edge fences
184 Twin mainwheels
185 Port inner stores pylon
186 Fuel and air connections to pylon
187 Inboard pylon hardpoint
188 Port wing fuel tank end rib
189 Pressure refuelling connection
190 Wing bottom skin panel/fuselage attachment joint
191 No. 1 hydraulic system reservoir (No. 12 to starboard)
192 Centre fuselage integral fuel tank, port and starboard
193 Nozzle fairing construction
194 Leading-edge dogtooth

195 Cushion augmentation strake (fitted in place of gun pod)
196 Centreline stores pylon
197 Reconnaissance pod
198 Forward F.135 camera
199 Port F.95 Mk 7 oblique cameras
200 Starboard F.95 Mk 7 oblique cameras
201 Signal data converter (SDC) unit
202 Cannon pod
203 Frangible nose cap
204 Cannon barrel
205 Blast suppression ports
206 ADEN 30-mm revolver-type cannon
207 Ammunition feed chute
208 Link ejector chute
209 Ammunition box, 130 rounds
210 ML twin stores carrier
211 Matra 155 rocket launchers, 18 x 2.68-in (68-mm) rockets
212 MATRA 116M rocket launcher, 19 x 2.68-in (68-mm) rockets
213 LEPUS flare
214 Twin light stores carrier
215 28-lb (13-kg) practice bomb

# IAI Kfir

*Although its has now passed from regular front-line Israeli service, the Kfir remains a potent warplane with three operators, including Ecuador. The type proved supremely capable in combat over the Lebanon, scoring air-to-air kills as well as flying its primary attack mission.*

## Kfir-C2

**Cutaway key**
1 Fintip UHF antenna
2 Rear navigation light
3 ECM antenna
4 Fin construction
5 Rudder construction
6 Rudder bellcrank
7 Rudder control rods
8 Fin spar
9 Rudderjack
10 Anti-collision beacon
11 Brake parachute fairing
12 Parachute
13 Release mechanism
14 Tail cone fairing
15 Airflow guide vanes
16 Variable exhaust nozzle
17 Tailcone attachment frame
18 Cooling air outlet
19 Jetpipe inner ducting
20 Tail bumper
21 Tail avionics boxes
22 Fin attachment
23 Fin attachment frame
24 Rear fuselage construction
25 Compensator jack
26 Belly fuel tank
27 Engine mounting attachment
28 Cooling air outlet
29 Finroot intake fairing
30 Cooling air intakes
31 Main fuselage frame
32 Oil tank
33 General Electric J79-GE-17 engine
34 Cooling air ducts
35 Engine front mounting cover
36 Port inboard elevon
37 Aileron
38 Port navigation light

39 Wing main fuel tank
40 Missile launch rail
41 Shafrir 2 air-to-air missile
42 Leading-edge fuel tank
43 Fuel supply piping
44 Fuselage fuel tanks
45 Port constant-speed drive unit
46 Engine starter
47 Port constant-speed drive unit
48 Intake ducting
49 Fuselage frame construction
50 Pressure sensor
51 Inverted flight accumulator
52 Dorsal fairing
53 Oxygen bottles
54 Forward fuselage fuel tank
55 Fuel filler
56 Canard foreplane construction
57 Canopy hinge attachment
58 Canopy external release handle
59 Ejection seat mounting
60 Avionics units
61 Martin Baker MJ6 ejection seat
62 Jettisonable canopy cover
63 Ejection seat firing handles
64 Pilot's control console
65 Instrument panel
66 Reflector sight
67 Windscreen
68 Instrument pitot
69 Nose construction
70 Radar ranging unit
71 Radome
72 Pitot boom
73 Nose strake
74 Yaw sensing vein
75 Autopilot controller
76 Radio and electronics equipment
77 Inertial platform
78 Static inverter
79 UHF aerial

80 Rudder pedal
81 Radar console
82 Control column
83 Ejection seat adjusting handle
84 Control rod linkage
85 Nosewheel leg doors
86 Nosewheel leg
87 Landing lights
88 Nosewheel suspension
89 Steerable nosewheel
90 Shimmy damper
91 Nosewheel leg pivot mounting
92 Locking cylinder
93 Air-conditioning plant
94 Nosewheel door
95 Air intake centre-body half-cone
96 Starboard air intake
97 Intake half-cone operating jack
98 Boundary layer duct
99 Cannon muzzle blast shield
100 Air intake duct
101 Auxiliary intake
102 Canard foreplane root fairing
103 Electrical control unit
104 Electrical servicing panel

105 Cannon barrel
106 DEFA 30-mm cannon
107 Ammunition feed chute
108 Front spar attachment
109 Leading-edge fuel tank

110 Leading-edge construction
111 Starboard constant speed drive unit
112 Mainwheel well
113 Main undercarriage jack
114 Upper surface airbrake

115 Airbrake jack
116 Lower surface airbrake
117 Main undercarriage leg pivot
118 Damper strut
119 Main leg door
120 Shock absorber strut

This Kfir-C7 has a typical air-to-air loadout consisting of four AIM-9 AAMs and a centreline fuel tank. The missiles, in combination with the DEFA cannon, give the Kfir a formidable close-in capability, although during the type's heyday in IDF/AF service the air-to-air role was mostly taken by the F-4 Phantom II and latterly by the even more capable F-15 and F-16. Also evident in this view is the truncated fairing beneath the jet pipe. At its rear, this houses an aft-facing strike camera.

## SPECIFICATION

### Kfir-C7

**Dimensions**

**Length:** 51 ft 4¼ in (15.65 m)
**Wingspan:** 26 ft 11⅔ in (8.22 m)
**Wing aspect ratio:** 1.94
**Wing area:** 374.60 sq ft (34.80 m²)
**Canard foreplane span:** 12 ft 3 in (3.73 m)
**Canard foreplane area:** 17.87 sq ft (1.66 m²)
**Height:** 14 ft 11¼ in (4.55 m)
**Wheel track:** 10 ft 6 in (3.20 m)
**Wheel base:** 15 ft 11⅔ in (4.87 m)

**Powerplant**

One IAI Bedek Division-built General Electric J79-J1E turbojet rated at 11,890 lb st (52.89 kN) dry and 18,750 lb st (83.41 kN) with afterburning

**Weights**

**Empty:** about 16,060 lb (7285 kg)
**Normal take-off:** 22,961 lb (10415 kg)
**Maximum take-off:** 36,376 lb (16500 kg)

**Fuel and load**

**Internal fuel:** 5,670 lb (2572 kg)
**External fuel:** up to 8,216 lb (3727 kg) in three 449-, 343-, 218-, 159- or 132-US gal (1700-, 1300-, 825-, 600- or 500-litre) drop tanks
**Maximum ordnance:** 13,415 lb (6085 kg)

**Performance**

**Maximum level speed 'clean' at sea level:** 750 kt (863 mph; 1389 km/h)
**Maximum level speed 'clean' at 36,000 ft (10975 m):** more than 1,317 kt (1,516 mph; 2440 km/h)
**Maximum rate of climb at sea level:** 45,930 ft (14000 m) per minute
**Climb to 50,000 ft (15240 m) with full internal fuel and two Shafrir AAMs:** 5 minutes 10 seconds

**Zoom climb ceiling:** 75,000 ft (22860 m)
**Service ceiling:** more than 50,000 ft (15240 m)
**Stabilised supersonic ceiling:** 58,000 ft (17680 m)
**Take-off run at maximum take-off weight:** 4,757 ft (1450 m)
**Landing distance from 50 ft (15 m) at 25,500 lb (11566 kg):** 5,102 ft (1555 m)
**Landing run at 25,500 lb (11566 kg):** 4,200 ft (1280 m)
**Ferry range:** 1,744 nm (2,000 miles; 3232 km) with one 343-US gal (1300-litre) and two 449-US gal (1700-litre) drop tanks
**Combat radius on a hi-hi-hi interception mission with two Shafrir AAMs, one 218-US gal (825-litre) and two 343-US gal (1300-litre) drop tanks:** 419 nm (482 miles; 776 km)
**Combat radius on a 1-hour CAP with two Shafrir AAMs, one 449-US gal (1700-litre) and two 343-US gal (1300-litre) drop tanks:** 476 nm (548 miles; 882 km)
**Combat radius on a hi-lo-hi attack mission with two 800-lb (363-kg) and two 400-lb (181-kg) bombs, two Shafrir AAMs, and one 343-US gal (1300-litre) and two 449-US gal (1700-litre) drop tanks:** 640 nm (737 miles; 1186 km)

**g limits**

+7.5

**Armament**

Two internal 30-mm IAI-built DEFA 552 cannon with 140 rounds per gun, plus a range of stores including M117, M118, Mk 82, Mk 83, Mk 84 and Israeli-designed/derived bombs; CBU-52/58 and Israeli-built TAL-1/2 cluster bombs, LAU-3A, LAU-10A and LAU-32A rocket pods, Python 3 and Shafrir 2 AAMs, and the Elta EL/L-8202 ECM pod

121 Undercarriage scissors link
122 Mainwheel
123 Main spar
124 Main spar attachment
125 Fuel system piping
126 Main wing fuel tank
127 Leading-edge spar
128 Leading-edge dogtooth
129 Leading-edge construction

134 Elevon compensator
135 Outboard elevon
136 Outboard elevon jack
137 Wingtip profile
138 Navigation light
139 Missile launcher
140 Shafrir 2 air to-air missile
141 Fuel tank pylon attachment
142 Fuel tank fins
143 Tank pylon
144 Fuel tank (110-Imp gal/500-litre capacity)

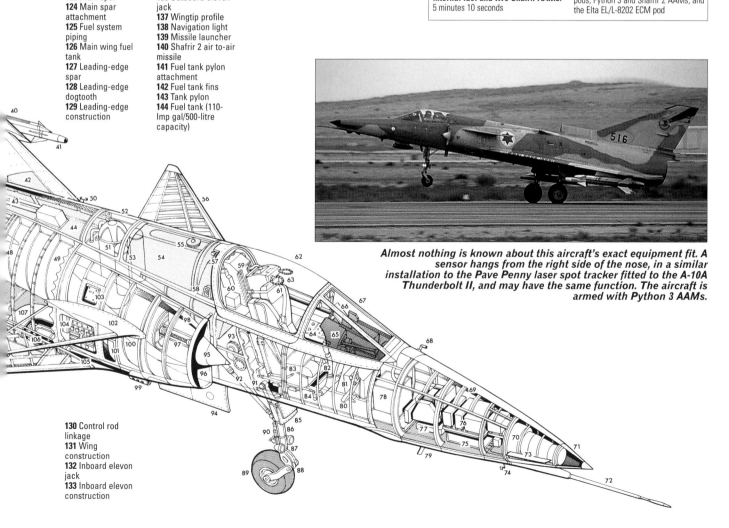

Almost nothing is known about this aircraft's exact equipment fit. A sensor hangs from the right side of the nose, in a similar installation to the Pave Penny laser spot tracker fitted to the A-10A Thunderbolt II, and may have the same function. The aircraft is armed with Python 3 AAMs.

130 Control rod linkage
131 Wing construction
132 Inboard elevon jack
133 Inboard elevon construction

# Lockheed P-80 Shooting Star

*Conceived in the shortest possible time, the Lockheed P-80 Shooting Star first flew in January 1944 and, in an enlarged and more powerful form, entered service in 1946. This weatherbeaten P-80A (later F-80) operated with the 56th Fighter Group at Selfridge AFB, Michigan. Of particular note is the fact that this aircraft carries Pearl Gray tip tanks and flaps. As this finish was applied only to very early aircraft, it seems likely that this aircraft's tip tanks and flaps were borrowed from another machine.*

## F-80C Shooting Star

### Cutaway key

1 Nose antenna fairing
2 D/F loop aerial
3 Machine-gun muzzles
4 Oxygen tank
5 Nose compartment access panel
6 Port and starboard ammunition boxes, 300 rounds per gun
7 0.5-in (12.7-mm) machine-guns
8 Spent cartridge case and link ejector chutes
9 Landing and taxiing lamps
10 Nosewheel leg torque scissors
11 Nosewheel
12 Steering linkage
13 Nosewheel doors
14 Retraction strut
15 Radio and electrical equipment bay
16 External canopy-release handle
17 Cockpit front bulkhead
18 Windscreen heater duct
19 Bulletproof windscreen panel
20 Reflector gunsight
21 Instrument panel shroud
22 Instrument panel
23 Rudder pedals
24 Cockpit floor level
25 Nosewheel bay
26 Intake lip fairing
27 Port air intake
28 Boundary layer bleed air duct
29 Intake ducting
30 Boundary layer air exit louvres
31 Engine throttle control
32 Safety harness
33 Pilot's ejection seat
34 Cockpit rear bulkhead
35 Starboard side console panel
36 Sliding cockpit canopy cover
37 Ejection seat headrest
38 Canopy aft decking
39 D/F sense antenna
40 Starboard wing fuel tanks
41 Fuel filler caps
42 Leading-edge tank
43 Fletcher-type tip tank, capacity 265 US gal (1003 litres)
44 Tip tank, capacity 165 US gal (625 litres)
45 Tip tank filler cap
46 Starboard navigation light
47 Aileron balance weights
48 Starboard aileron
49 Aileron hinge control
50 Trailing-edge fuel tank
51 Starboard split trailing-edge flap
52 Flap control links
53 Fuselage fuel tank, total internal capacity 657 US gal (2487 litres)
54 Fuselage main longeron
55 Centre fuselage frames
56 Intake trunking
57 Main undercarriage wheel well
58 Wing spar attachment joints
59 Pneumatic reservoir
60 Hydraulic accumulator
61 Control access panel
62 Spring-loaded intake pressure relief doors
63 Allison J33-A-23 centrifugal-flow turbojet engine
64 Rear fuselage break point
65 Rear fuselage attachment bolts (three)
66 Elevator control rods
67 Jet pipe bracing cable
68 Fin-root fillet
69 Elevator control link
70 Starboard tailplane
71 Starboard elevator
72 Fin construction
73 Pitot tube
74 Fintip communications antenna fairing
75 Rudder mass balance
76 Rudder construction
77 Fixed tab
78 Elevator and rudder hinge control
79 Tail navigation light
80 Jet pipe nozzle
81 Elevator tabs
82 Port elevator construction
83 Elevator mass balance
84 Tailplane construction

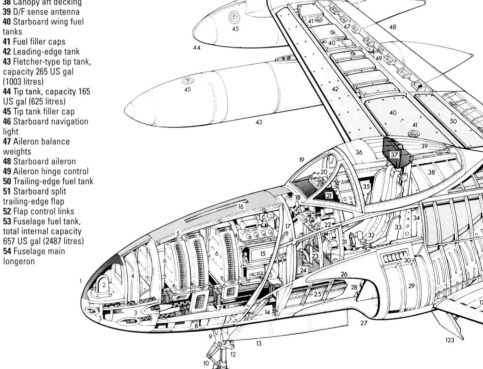

## SPECIFICATION

### F-80C Shooting Star (early)

### Dimensions

**Length:** 34 ft 5 in (10.49 m)
**Height:** 11 ft 3 in (3.42 m)
**Wingspan:** 38 ft 9 in (11.81 m)
**Wing area:** 237.5 sq ft (22.07 m²)

### Powerplant

One Allison J33-A-23/35 turbojet rated at 4,600 lb st (20.7 kN) dry, and 5,200 lb st (23.4 kN) with water injection

### Weights

**Empty:** 8,420 lb (3819 kg)
**Gross:** 12,200 lb (5534 kg)
**Maximum take-off:** 16,856 lb (7646 kg)

### Fuel

**Fuel (normal):** 425 US gal (1609 litres)
**Fuel (maximum):** 755 US gal (2858 litres) including drop tanks

### Performance

**Maximum level speed at sea level:** 594 mph (956 km/h)
**Maximum level speed at 25,000 ft (7620 m):** 543 mph (874 km/h)
**Cruising speed:** 439 mph (707 km/h)
**Landing speed:** 122 mph (196 km/h)
**Climb to altitude:** climb to 25,000 ft (7620 m) in 7 minutes
**Rate of climb:** 6,870 ft (2094 m) per minute
**Service ceiling:** 46,800 ft (14265 m)

### Range

**Range:** 825 miles (1328 km)
**Maximum range:** 1,380 miles (2221 km)

### Armament

Four 0.50-in (12.7-mm) Colt-Browning M3 machine-guns each with 300 rounds, plus ten 5-in (127-mm) HVARs or two 1,000-lb (454-kg) bombs

*This flight of **P-80Cs** from the 94th 'Hat-in-the-Ring' squadron was based at Ladd Field, Fairbanks, Alaska, for six months of training. During this time the aircraft had their wingtips and tails painted red so that they could be easily spotted from the air in the event of an emergency landing in the snow. Lockheed 'winterised' the aircraft by incorporating new greases and hydraulic units to allow the aircraft to operate below -65°C (-85°F).*

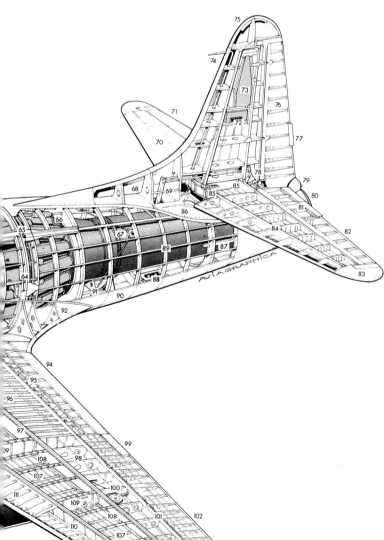

85 Fin/tailplane attachment joints
86 Tailplane fillet fairing
87 Jet pipe mounting rail
88 Rear fuselage frame and stringer construction
89 Gyrosyn radio compass flux valve
90 Fuselage skin plating
91 Jet pipe support frame
92 Trailing-edge wingroot fillet
93 Flap drive motor
94 Port split trailing-edge flap
95 Flap shroud ribs
96 Trailing-edge fuel tank bay
97 Rear spar
98 Trailing-edge ribs
99 Port aileron tab
100 Aileron hinge control

101 Upper-skin panel aileron hinge line
102 Aileron construction
103 Wingtip fairing construction
104 Tip tank
105 Port navigation light
106 Tip tank mounting and jettison control
107 Detachable lower wing skin panels
108 Port wing fuel tank bays
109 Inter tank bay ribs
110 Front spar
111 Corrugated leading-edge inner skin
112 Port stores pylon
113 1,000-lb (454-kg) HE bomb
114 5-in (127-mm) HVAR ground attack rockets (10 rockets maximum load)

115 HVAR mountings
116 Port mainwheel
117 Mainwheel doors
118 Wheel brake pad
119 Main undercarriage leg strut
120 Retraction jack
121 Upper skin panel wing stringers
122 Wingroot leading-edge extension
123 Port ventral airbrake

*Having force-landed on a frozen lake 75 miles (120 km) from its base, this 65th **FIS F-80C** was resurrected over a three-week period, in which **USAF** ground crew fitted it with specially made aluminium skis. The take-off, the first successful jet-ski **JATO** take-off, was accomplished by Lt Col William F. Benedict. This method was used on a number of occasions to salvage stricken fighters throughout the area.*

# Lockheed AC-130 Hercules

*An AC-130A from the 711th SOS lets fly with a 40-mm round during live-fire exercises. The gunship concept calls for the aircraft to fly in a smooth left-hand orbit with the guns trained on a central point at all times. Fine-tuning the aim is accomplished using roll and yaw inputs.*

## AC-130U

**Cutaway key**
1 Air data boom
2 Radome
3 AN/APG-80 radar scanner
4 Radar equipment racks
5 Front pressure bulkhead
6 Downward vision windows
7 Pilot's head-up-display
8 Cockpit radar repeater
9 Windscreen panels and wipers
10 Radar warning receivers
11 Overhead systems switch panels
12 Inflight-refuelling receptacle
13 Dual flight engineer's stations
14 Two-pilot cockpit with observer's seat
15 Control column
16 Rudder pedals
17 Side console panel
18 Pitot heads
19 Battery compartment
20 AN/AAQ-117 FLIR turret
21 Twin nosewheel undercarriage, forward-retracting
22 Nosewheel door
23 Avionics equipment racks
24 Crew entry door and airstairs
25 Access ladder to flight deck
26 Galley unit
27 Crew closet
28 Escape hatch access ladder
29 Cockpit roof escape hatch
30 Aerial cable lead-in
31 Crew rest compartment
32 Radar warning antennas and ECM transmitter fairing
33 Flexible gun seal
34 GAU-12U 25-mm five-barrelled rotary cannon

35 Ball Aerospace ALLTV turret
36 Cannon ammunition magazine, 3,000 rounds
37 Port-side equipment racks
38 Spare crew seats
39 Starboard side observer's seat
40 Observation hatch
41 UHF aerial
42 ADF loop antennas
43 Battle management centre
44 IR, TV, fire control, radar/nav and EW operators' seats and consoles
45 Hydraulic system equipment
46 Conditioned air delivery ducting
47 Wing spar attachment fuselage main frame
48 Engine fire extinguisher bottles
49 Wing centre-section integral fuel tank
50 Sigint antenna
51 Centre wing panel rib construction
52 Wing stringers
53 Starboard engine nacelles
54 External fuel tank
55 Hamilton Standard four-bladed constant-speed propellers
56 Starboard outer wing panel

57 Leading-edge flush aerial panel
58 Starboard navigation light
59 Starboard aileron
60 Single-slotted flaps
61 Flap shroud ribs
62 Life raft stowage
63 Satcom antenna
64 Aileron hydraulic booster
65 Mid-cabin escape hatch
66 Emergency equipment stowage
67 Rear fuselage air ducting
68 VHF/UHF aerial
69 Fin-root fillet construction

70 ELT antenna
71 AN/ALQ-172 EW equipment packs
72 Starboard tailplane
73 Fin spar box construction
74 VOR aerial
75 Anti-collision light
76 Rudder
77 Rudder tab
78 Tail radar warning and ECM transmitter fairing
79 Rudder and elevator hinge controls

80 Elevator tab
81 Port elevator
82 Tailplane rib construction
83 Elevator hydraulic booster unit
84 Rear ramp door hydraulic jack
85 Rear escape hatch
86 Ventral observation hatch
87 Observer's prone position
88 Ramp hydraulic jack
89 Rear loading ramp
90 Central flap drive hydraulic motor
91 105-mm Howitzer

92 Port single-slotted flaps
93 Flap rib construction
94 Aileron mass balance weights
95 Aileron tab
96 Port aileron
97 Static dischargers
98 Fuel jettison
99 Port navigation light
100 Leading-edge flush aerial panel
101 Outer wing panel integral fuel tank
102 Leading-edge ribs
103 Exhaust infra-red suppression mixing air duct
104 Allison T56-A-15 turboprop engine

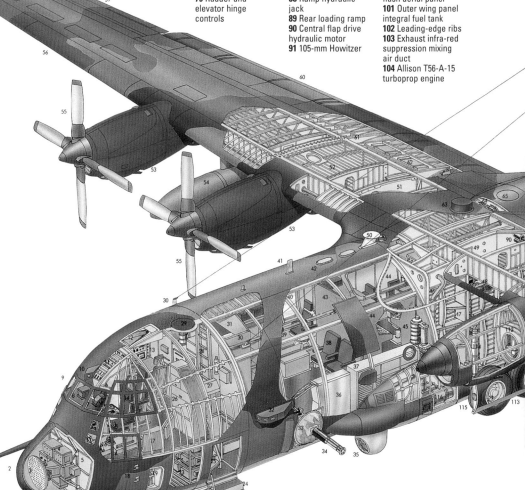

*The gunship concept was developed for the war in Southeast Asia. AC-130s were the most powerful and best-equipped of the gunship types, and were used principally on night interdiction sorties over the Ho Chi Minh Trail.*

## SPECIFICATION

### C-130H (AC-130H/U similar)

#### Dimensions

**Wingspan:** 132 ft 7 in (40.41 m)
**Wing aspect ratio:** 10.07
**Wing area:** 1,745 sq ft (162.12 m²)
**Tailplane span:** 52 ft 8 in (16.05 m)
**Tailplane area:** 381 sq ft (35.40 m²)
**Length overall:** 97 ft 9 in (29.79 m)
**Height overall:** 38 ft 3 in (11.66 m)
**Wheelbase:** 32 ft 1 in (9.77 m)
**Wheel track:** 14 ft 3 in (4.35 m)

#### Powerplant

Four Allison T56-A-15 turboprops, each rated at 4,508 shp (3362 kW), driving a Hamilton Standard 54H60 four-bladed constant-speed, reversible-pitch, fully-feathering propeller

#### Weights

**Operating empty (C-130H):** 76,469 lb (34686 kg)
**Maximum take-off:** 155,000 lb (70305 kg)
**Maximum overload:** 175,000 lb (79380 kg)

#### Fuel and load

**Maximum internal fuel capacity:** 6,820 US gal (5,679 Imp gal; 25816 litres)
**Underwing tank capacity (combined):** 2,800 US gal (2,332 Imp gal; 10600 litres)
**Maximum payload (C-130H):** 49,818 lb (22597 kg)

#### Performance

**Maximum cruising speed:** 315 kt (362 mph; 583 km/h)
**Economical cruising speed:** 300 kt (345 mph; 556 km/h)
**Maximum rate of climb:** 1,800 ft (548 m) per minute
**Time to 20,000 ft (6100 m):** 22 minutes
**Service ceiling:** 18,000 ft (5485 m)
**Take-off run:** 4,000 ft (1220 m)
**Landing run:** 1,500 ft (457 m)

#### Range

2,238 miles (3600 km) with 40,000-lb (18144-kg) payload

#### Armament

One single-round loaded M102 105-mm Howitzer and one clip-fed Bofors L-60 40-mm cannon (AC-130H/U); two belt-fed 20-mm M61 Vulcan cannon (AC-130H) or one belt-fed 25-mm GAU-12 rotary cannon (AC-130U)

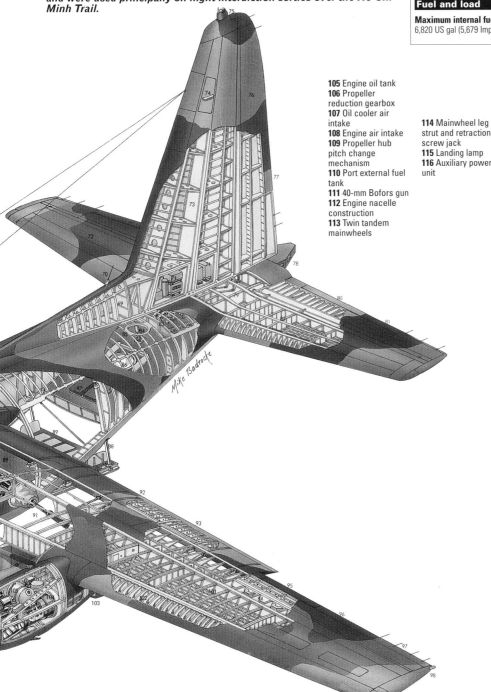

**105** Engine oil tank
**106** Propeller reduction gearbox
**107** Oil cooler air intake
**108** Engine air intake
**109** Propeller hub pitch change mechanism
**110** Port external fuel tank
**111** 40-mm Bofors gun
**112** Engine nacelle construction
**113** Twin tandem mainwheels
**114** Mainwheel leg strut and retraction screw jack
**115** Landing lamp
**116** Auxiliary power unit

# Lockheed F-117 Nighthawk

*An extraordinary shape, revolutionary radar-defeating features and a top secret, yet highly glamorous development have combined with a star combat appearance in Desert Storm to make the Lockheed F-117 Nighthawk the best-known warplane in the world. Able to penetrate hostile airspace without being seen by radars or infra-red sensors, the F-117 can use its sophisticated target acquisition and designation system to score strikes against vital targets with pinpoint accuracy.*

## F-117A Nighthawk

### Cutaway key

1 Air data sensors
2 Nose avionics equipment
3 Air data computer
4 Starboard side downward-looking infra-red (DLIR)
5 Screened sensor aperture
6 Forward-looking infra-red (FLIR), to be replaced by Texas Instruments IRADS sensors in third phase update
7 Cockpit front pressure bulkhead
8 Nosewheel bay
9 Forward-retracting nosewheel
10 Canopy emergency release
11 Position light
12 Cockpit pressure enclosure
13 McDonnell-Douglas ACES II 'zero-zero' ejection seat
14 Instrument panel shroud, central infra-red video monitor and dual head-down multi-function CRT displays
15 Head-up display
16 Windscreen panels, gold film coated
17 Upward-hinging one-piece cockpit canopy

18 Apex-mounted refuelling floodlight
19 Starboard air intake
20 Flush HF aerials
21 Rotating flight-refuelling receptacle
22 Avionics equipment bay
23 Retractable ILS antenna
24 Retractable VHF COMM antenna
25 Port engine air intake
26 Intake screening
27 Intake lip spring-loaded secondary (cooling) air intake
28 Weapons bay doors, open
29 Retractable spoilers
30 Port weapons bay
31 Intake suction relief door aperture
32 Airframe-mounted accessory equipment gearbox
33 Engine bay bulkhead

34 Compressor intake
35 Engine fuel system equipment
36 Mainwheel hydraulic retraction jack
37 Mainwheel bay
38 Removable radar reflector
39 General Electric F404-GE-F1D2 non-augmented turbofan engine
40 Engine bay vent
41 Removable anti-collision beacon
42 Hydraulically actuated weapons loading trapeze mechanism

43 Dorsal fuel tank
44 Retractable communications antenna
45 Starboard wing integral fuel tank
46 RAM-coated skin panels

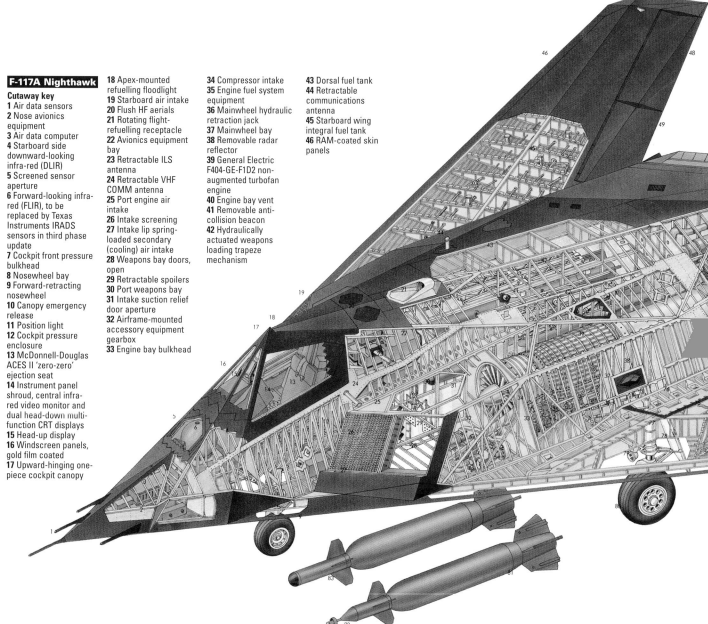

*Above: Nighthawk pilots form an elite within an elite. They have come from a variety of backgrounds, mainly from the USAF's fighter and attack fast jet communities, but have also included former SAC bomber pilots. Undergoing a selection procedure which is almost as rigorous as that for SR-71 aircrew, F-117 pilots are chosen as much for their flying skills as for such intangible qualities as stability of temperament.*

## SPECIFICATION

### F-117A Nighthawk

#### Dimensions

**Length overall:** 65 ft 11 in (20.08 m)
**Wing span:** 43 ft 4 in (13.20 m)
**Wing aspect ratio:** 1.65
**Wing area (estimated):** 1,140 sq ft (105.9 m²)
**Wing sweepback angle:** 67° 30'
**Ruddervator sweep angle:** about 65°
**Overall height:** 12 ft 5 in (3.78 m)
**Wheel track (estimated):** 13 ft 5½ in (4.10 m)
**Wheel base (estimated):** 18 ft 7 in (5.66 m)
**Maximum wing loading:** 46.0 lb/sq ft (225 kg/m²)
**Frontal radar cross section (estimated):** 0.1 sq ft (0.009 m²)

#### Powerplant

Two General Electric F404-GE-F1D2 non-afterburning turbofans each rated at 10,800 lb (48.04 kN) maximum thrust

#### Weights

**Empty operating:** 29,000 lb (13154 kg)
**Normal maximum take-off:** 52,000 lb (23814 kg)
**Maximum overload take-off:** 54,000 lb (24494 kg)

#### Fuel and load

**Total fuel load:** 18,000 lb (8165 kg) of JP-4 fuel
**Total fuel capacity:** 2,769 US gal, (10483 litres)

#### Performance

**(Applies to ISA conditions unless otherwise stated)**
**Maximum level speed:** 561 kt (646 mph; 1040 km/h)
**Normal maximum operating speed:** Mach 0.9 at optimum altitude
**Normal cruising speed:** Mach 0.81, 488 kts (562 mph; 904 km/h) at 30,000 ft (9144 m)
**Undercarriage limiting speed:** 300 kts (345 mph; 556 km/h)
**Service ceiling:** 38,600 ft (11765 m)
**Rotation speed:** 152-195 kts (175-225 mph; 282-361 km/h) at 38,000-54,000 lb (17237-24494 kg) all-up weight (AUW)
**Lift-off speed:** 173-208 kts (199-240 mph; 321-385 km/h) at 38,000-54,000 lb (17237-24494 kg) AUW

**Minimum take-off distance:** 2,500-2,800 ft (762-853 m)
**Minimum take-off distance at maximum take-off weight:** 5,400-6,200 ft (1645-1890 m)
**Approach speeds:** 143-185 kts (165-213 mph; 265-343 km/h) at 30,000-50,000 lb (13608-22680 kg) landing weight
**Approach angle of attack** 9.5°
**Minimum landing distance (from 50-ft/15-m) with brake parachute:** 4,850 ft (1478 m)
**Minimum landing roll with brake parachute:** 2,790 ft (850 m)

#### Range

**Unrefuelled combat radius with 4,000-lb (1814-kg) weapons load, normal diversion fuel and reserves:** 465 nm (535 miles; 862 km) at 30,000 ft (9144 m)

#### g limit

**Maximum:** +7.0

#### Armament

**Maximum weapons load:** 5,000 lb (2268 kg)
**Weapon stations:** internal weapons bay with two stations each stressed for a 2,000-lb (907-kg) weapon
**Internal weapons bay length:** 15 ft 5 in (4.70 m)
**Internal weapons bay width:** 5 ft 9 in (1.75 m)
**Operational weapons (primary):** up to two laser-guided bombs (LGBs) comprising 496-lb (225-kg) GBU-12, 1,984-lb (900-kg) (approximate weight) GBU-10 or 2,169-lb (984-kg) GBU-27A/B; latter two LGBs fitted with either Mk 84 Paveway II or BLU-109B (Lockheed designation I-2000) Paveway III penetration warheads; other stores may include AGM-88 HARM anti-radar missiles
**Probable nuclear strike weapon:** B61 free-fall nuclear bomb weighing 719-765 lb (326-347 kg); F-117A has known nuclear capability and nuclear strike role
**Training/utility stores:** 500-lb (227-kg) Mk 82 free-fall general-purpose bombs dropped during early development; SUU-20 practice bomb and rocket dispenser with six BDU-33 bomb training shapes (no rockets carried)

---

**47** Starboard flush-mounted navigation light, above and below
**48** Outboard elevon
**49** Inboard elevon
**50** Starboard 'platypus' exhaust nozzle
**51** Fixed lower portion of fin
**52** Ruddervator torque shaft

**53** Starboard ruddervator, thermoplastic graphite composite construction replacing earlier all-metal structure
**54** Port ruddervator
**55** Port engine 'platypus' exhaust nozzle

**56** Exhaust nozzle lip heat shielding tiles
**57** Hydraulic ruddervator actuator
**58** Brake parachute housing
**59** Rear equipment bay
**60** Ventral emergency arrester hook
**61** Auxiliary power unit (APU)
**62** Venting air grille
**63** Nickel alloy honeycomb exhaust duct with internal support posts
**64** Inboard elevon hydraulic actuator
**65** Elevon rib construction
**66** Port inboard elevon
**67** Composite trailing-edge structure
**68** Port outboard elevon
**69** Port flush-mounted navigation light, above and below
**70** Outboard elevon hydraulic actuator, GEC Astronics quadruplex fly-by-wire flight control system

**71** Port wing integral fuel tank
**72** Composite leading-edge construction
**73** Three-spar wing torsion box structure
**74** Fuel system piping and contents capacitors
**75** Wingroot rib
**76** Multi-bolt wingroot attachment joints
**77** Main undercarriage leg strut
**78** Torque scissor links
**79** Landing lamp
**80** Forward-retracting mainwheel
**81** GBU-10 2,000-lb (907-kg) laser-guided bomb
**82** Paveway II laser seeker head
**83** GBU-27A/B 2,000-lb (907-kg) laser-guided bomb with BLU-109 Paveway III penetrator warhead

# McDonnell Douglas/BAe Harrier II

The *AV-8B Harrier II Plus* has provided the US Marine Corps and the Italian and Spanish navies with a formidable, radar-equipped fighter and ground-attack aircraft of unparalleled capability.

## AV-8B Harrier II

### Cutaway key

1 Glass-fibre radome
2 Planar radar scanner
3 Scanner tracking mechanism
4 Radar mounting bulkhead
5 Forward-Looking Infra-Red (FLIR)
6 APG-65 radar equipment module
7 Forward pitch control reaction air nozzle
8 Pitot head, port and starboard
9 Cockpit front pressure bulkhead
10 Pitch feel unit and trim actuator
11 Yaw vane
12 Single-piece wrap-round windscreen
13 Instrument panel shroud
14 Rudder pedals
15 Underfloor avionics bay, air data computer and inertial navigation equipment
16 Electro-luminescent and covert night vision goggle (NVG) formation lighting strips
17 Control column
18 Engine throttle and nozzle angle control levers
19 Instrument panel with full-colour multi-function CRT displays
20 Pilot's head-up display (HUD)
21 Sliding cockpit canopy with miniature detonating cord (MDC) emergency breaker

22 UPC/Stencel I lightweight ejection seat
23 Cockpit section framing, all-composite forward fuselage structure
24 Sloping seat mounting rear pressure bulkhead
25 Intake boundary layer separator
26 Port air intake
27 Landing/taxiing light
28 Levered suspension nosewheel, shortens on retraction
29 Intake suction relief doors, free-floating
30 Hydraulic nosewheel retraction jack
31 Hydraulic system accumulator
32 Demountable flight-refuelling probe
33 Cockpit air-conditioning pack
34 Intake boundary layer air spill duct
35 Heat exchanger ram air intakes
36 Rolls-Royce F402-RR-408A Pegasus 11-61 turbofan engine
37 Full-authority digital engine control (FADEC) unit

38 Upper formation lighting strips
39 Accessory equipment gearbox
40 Alternator
41 Engine oil tank
42 Forward fuselage fuel tank
43 Hydraulic system ground connectors and engine monitoring and recording equipment
44 Fuselage lift-improvement device (LID), lateral strake
45 Forward zero-scarf (fan air) swivelling exhaust nozzle
46 Centre fuselage fuel tank
47 Nozzle bearing
48 Gas turbine starter/auxiliary power unit
49 Leading-edge root extension (LERX)
50 Engine bay venting air intake
51 Wing centre-section integral fuel tank
52 Starboard wing integral tank
53 Fuel feed and vent piping

54 Starboard weapons pylons
55 RWR antenna
56 Starboard navigation light
57 Roll control reaction air valve, upper and lower surface vents
58 Wingtip formation lights
59 Fuel jettison
60 Starboard aileron
61 Outrigger wheel fairing
62 Starboard outrigger wheel, retracted position
63 Slotted flap
64 Articulated flap vane
65 VHF/UHF antenna
66 Anti-collision beacon
67 De-mineralised water tank

68 Engine fire suppression bottle
69 Water filler
70 Rear fuselage fuel tank
71 Electrical system distribution panels, port and starboard
72 Chaff/flare launchers

73 Heat exchanger ram air intake
74 Rudder hydraulic actuator
75 Starboard all-moving tailplane

76 Formation lighting strip
77 Fin conventional light alloy structure
78 MAD compensator
79 Temperature probe
80 Broad-band communications antenna

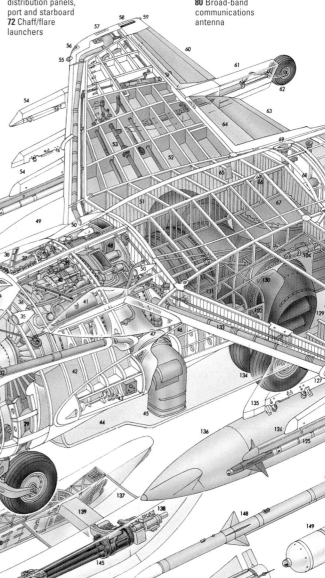

*The APG-65 radar added a 1,000-lb (454-kg) weight penalty to the basic AV-8B, but since all Harrier II Pluses were powered by the more powerful F402-RR-408A engine, this was of little consequence. Other changes to the II Plus included the adoption of the RAF-type wing, with a 100 per cent LERX and, most significantly, four pylons per side, including the dedicated AAM pylons on the undercarriage outriggers.*

## SPECIFICATION

### AV-8B Harrier II Plus

**Dimensions**

**Length:** 47 ft 9 in (14.55 m)
**Wingspan:** 30 ft 4 in (9.25 m)
**Wing aspect ratio:** 4.0
**Tailplane span:** 13 ft 11 in (4.24 m)
**Wing area:** 243.40 sq ft (22.61 m²) including two 6.70-sq ft (0.62-m²) LERXes
**Height:** 11 ft 7¾ in (3.55 m)
**Outrigger wheel track:** 17 ft (5.18 m)

**Powerplant**

One Rolls-Royce F402-RR-408A (Pegasus 11-61) vectored thrust turbofan engine rated at 23,800 lb st (106 kN)

**Weights**

**Empty operating:** 14,860 lb (6740 kg)
**Normal take-off:** 22,950 lb (10410 kg) for 7-*g* operation
**Maximum take-off for 1,427-ft (435-m) STO under standard conditions:** 31,000 lb (14061 kg)
**Maximum take-off for VTO:** 18,950 lb (8596 kg)

**Fuel and load**

**Internal fuel:** 7,759 lb (3519 kg)
**External fuel:** up to 8,070 lb (3661 kg) in four 300-US gal (1136-litre) drop tanks
**Maximum ordnance:** 13,235 lb (6003 kg)

**Performance**

**Maximum level speed 'clean' at sea level:** 575 kt (662 mph; 1065 km/h)
**Maximum rate of climb at sea level:** 14,715 ft (4485 m) per minute
**Service ceiling:** more than 50,000 ft (15240 m)
**STO run at maximum take-off**

**weight at 90°F (32°C):** 1,700 ft (518 m)
**Landing run at up to 19,937 lb (9043 kg):** 0 ft (0 m)
**Anti-ship combat radius with two AGM-84, two AIM-9 and two 300-US gal (1136-litre) drop tanks after a 450-ft (137-m) take-off run with a 6.5° ski-jump:** 609 nm (701 miles; 1128 km)
**Time on station for a CAP (including 2-minute combat) with four AIM-120 and two 300-US gal (1136-litre) drop tanks after a 450-ft (137-m) take-off run with a 6.5° ski-jump:** 2 hours 42 minutes at 100-nm (115-mile, 185-km) radius or 2 hours 6 minutes at 200-nm (230-mile, 370-km) radius
**Sea surveillance combat radius (including 50-nm (57-mile; 92-km) dash at sea level) with two AIM-9 and two 300-US gal (1136-litre) drop tanks after a 450-ft (137-m) take-off run with a 6.5° ski-jump:** 608 nm (700 miles; 1127 km)

**g limits**

-3 to +8

**Armament**

AV-8B Harrier II Plus has four pylons under each wing for the carriage of AIM-9 Sidewinders, AIM-120 AMRAAM, Mk 7 cluster bomb dispensers, Mk 82/83 bombs, LAU-10/68/69 rocket pods, AGM-65 Maverick, AGM-84 Harpoon, CBU-55/72 fuel-air explosive, Mk 77 fire bombs and GBU-12/16 LGBs, the latter requiring designation from another source. The centreline hardpoint is used for an ALQ-167 ECM pod. Two fuselage packs contain a five-barrelled 25-mm GAU-12 cannon (port) and ammunition tank for 300 rounds (starboard)

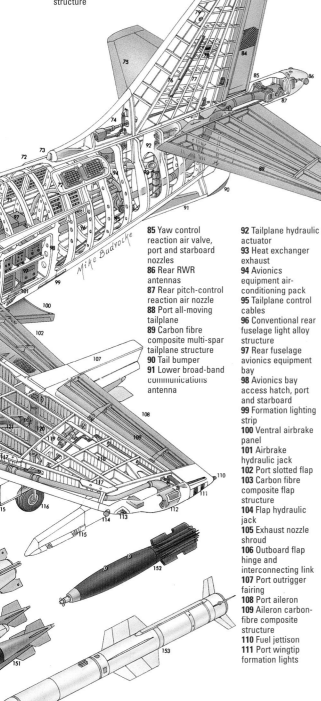

81 Glass fibre fintip antenna fairing
82 Radar beacon antenna
83 Rudder
84 Honeycomb composite rudder structure

85 Yaw control reaction air valve, port and starboard nozzles
86 Rear RWR antennas
87 Rear pitch-control reaction air nozzle
88 Port all-moving tailplane
89 Carbon fibre composite multi-spar tailplane structure
90 Tail bumper
91 Lower broad-band communications antenna

92 Tailplane hydraulic actuator
93 Heat exchanger exhaust
94 Avionics equipment air-conditioning pack
95 Tailplane control cables
96 Conventional rear fuselage light alloy structure
97 Rear fuselage avionics equipment bay
98 Avionics bay access hatch, port and starboard
99 Formation lighting strip
100 Ventral airbrake panel
101 Airbrake hydraulic jack
102 Port slotted flap
103 Carbon fibre composite flap structure
104 Flap hydraulic jack
105 Exhaust nozzle shroud
106 Outboard flap hinge and interconnecting link
107 Port outrigger fairing
108 Port aileron
109 Aileron carbon-fibre composite structure
110 Fuel jettison
111 Port wingtip formation lights

112 Roll control reaction air valve, upper and lower surface vents
113 Port navigation light
114 RWR antenna
115 Port wing stores pylons
116 Port outrigger wheel
117 Pylon attachment hardpoints
118 Outer wing panel dry bay
119 Aileron hydraulic actuator
120 Outrigger wheel strut
121 Hydraulic retraction jack
122 Port wing integral fuel tank
123 Aileron control rod
124 Intermediate missile pylon
125 AIM-9L/M Sidewinder air-to-air missile
126 Missile launch rail
127 Wing leading-edge fence
128 Carbon fibre composite 'sine wave' multi-spar structure
129 Rear, hot steam, swivelling exhaust nozzle
130 Rear nozzle bleed-air cooled bearing housing

131 Hydraulic reservoir, dual system, port and starboard
132 Pressure refuelling connection and control panel
133 Reaction-control air ducting
134 Aft retracting twin-wheel main undercarriage
135 Inboard 'wet' stores pylon
136 External fuel tank
137 Ventral gun pack, replaces fuselage LID strakes
138 Gun pneumatic drive unit
139 Ammunition cross-feed and link return chute
140 Ammunition magazine, 300 rounds
141 Retractable LID cross dam and hydraulic jack
142 Cannon muzzle aperture
143 Gun gas vent
144 Forward recoil mounting
145 GAU-12/U 25-mm five-barrelled rotary cannon
146 Gun pack LID strake
147 AGM-65A Maverick, laser-guided air-to-surface missile

148 AIM-120 AMRAAM, air-to-air missile
149 CBU-89B Gator, submunition dispenser
150 Triple ejector rack
151 Mk 82 LDGP 500-lb (227-kg) bomb
152 Mk 82SE Snakeye, retarded bomb
153 AGM-84A-D Harpoon, air-to-surface anti ship missile

# McDonnell Douglas/BAe Harrier

## Harrier GR.Mk 5

**Cutaway key**
1 Glazed nose aperture
2 Hughes Angle Rate Bombing Set (ARBS)
3 Nose ballast in place of MIRLS
4 IFF aerial
5 Nose avionics equipment
6 ARBS heat exchanger
7 Pitch control reaction air valve
8 Pitot head
9 Pitch feel and trim actuators
10 ARBS signal data converter
11 Yaw vane
12 Rudder pedals
13 Air data computer and inertial navigation system equipment
14 Formation lighting strips
15 Control column and linkages
16 Engine throttle and nozzle control levers
17 Instrument panel shroud
18 Pilot's head-up display
19 Single piece 'wrap-around' windscreen
20 Rearward sliding cockpit canopy cover
21 Miniature detonating cord canopy breaker
22 Martin-Baker Mk 12 ejection seat

23 Nose undercarriage wheel bay
24 Engine air intake
25 Boundary layer bleed duct
26 Hydraulic accumulator
27 Nosewheel hydraulic jack
28 Cockpit air conditioning system
29 Flight refuelling probe stowage
30 Probe hydraulic jack
31 Intake suction relief doors
32 Forward fuselage flank fuel tank
33 Lift augmentation retractable cross-dam
34 Fuselage strakes, port and starboard
35 Engine bay venting air intake
36 Hydraulic system ground connectors and engine monitoring equipment
37 Zero scarf forward (fan air) swivelling nozzle

38 Engine oil tank
39 Rolls-Royce Pegasus Mk 105 engine
40 Alternator
41 Formation lighting strips
42 Leading-edge root extension (LERX)
43 Engine-driven accessory equipment gearbox
44 Gas turbine starter/auxiliary power unit
45 Nozzle bearing cooling air duct
46 Wing centre-section integral fuel tank
47 Water-methanol tank
48 Anti-collision light

49 VHF/UHF aerial
50 Starboard wing integral fuel tank
51 Starboard wing pylons
52 Radar-warning antenna

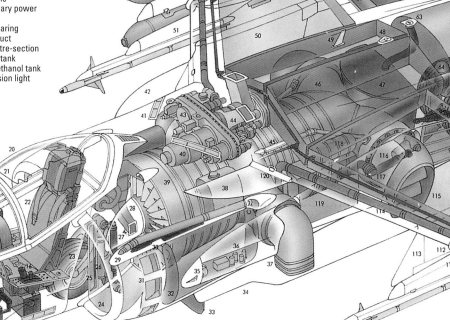

*Above and left: The first-generation Hawker Siddeley Harriers entered service with the RAF in 1969 and brought new capabilities to RAF close support operations with their VTOL performance. However, they were hampered by short range, poor payload-carrying abilities and basic day-attack avionics. These shortcomings have been addressed by the second-generation Harriers which have overcome early teething troubles, to mature into some of the most effective attack aircraft in service today.*

53 Starboard navigation light
54 Starboard/forward missile-warning antenna
55 Roll control reaction air valve
56 Wingtip formation light
57 Fuel jettison
58 Starboard aileron
59 Outrigger wheel fairing
60 Starboard slotted flap
61 Drooping flap vane
62 Wing root fairing
63 Water/methanol tank filler
64 Engine fire suppression bottle

65 Rear fuselage fuel tank
66 Aft avionics equipment bay
67 Electrical distribution panels
68 Heat exchanger ram air intake

69 Rudder hydraulic actuator
70 Starboard all-moving tailplane
71 Formation lighting strip
72 MAD compensator

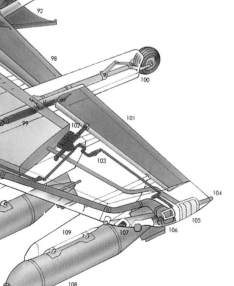

Mike Badrocke

73 Temperature probe
74 Upper broad band communications antenna
75 Fin tip aerial fairing
76 Radar beacon antenna
77 Rudder
78 ECM equipment module
79 Pitch control reaction air valve
80 Yaw control reaction air valves
81 Port all-moving tailplane
82 Rear missile-warning antenna
83 Radar-warning antenna
84 Tail bumper
85 Lower broad band communications antenna
86 Reaction control air ducting
87 Tailplane hydraulic actuator
88 Avionics air conditioning equipment
89 Formation lighting strip

90 Avionics equipment bay access door, port and starboard
91 Airbrake hydraulic jack
92 Ventral airbrake panel
93 Hydraulic system nitrogen pressurisation bottle
94 Main undercarriage wheel bay
95 Flap hydraulic jack
96 Fuselage heat shield
97 Port wing integral fuel tank
98 Port flap
99 Outrigger wheel hydraulic jack
100 Port outrigger wheel
101 Port aileron
102 Aileron hydraulic actuator
103 Aileron/air valve interconnection
104 Fuel jettison
105 Wingtip formation light
106 Port roll control reaction air valve

107 Port navigation light
108 BL755 cluster bombs
109 Outboard weapons pylons
110 AIM-9L/M Sidewinder air-to-air missile
111 Intermediate missile pylon
112 Wing fence
113 Inboard weapon/fuel tank pylon
114 Reaction control air ducting
115 Rear (hot-stream) swivelling exhaust nozzle
116 Main undercarriage hydraulic jack
117 Pressure refuelling connection
118 Hydraulic reservoir
119 Centre fuselage flank fuel tank
120 Engine bay venting air intake

## SPECIFICATION

### Harrier GR.Mk 7

#### Dimensions

**Length overall (flying attitude):** 47 ft 8 in (14.53 m)
**Wing span:** 30 ft 4 in (9.25 m)
**Wing aspect ratio:** 4.0
**Tailplane span:** 13 ft 11 in (4.24 m)
**Wing area (gross, excl. LERX):** 230.0 sq ft (21.37 m²)
**Total LERX area ('100%' LERX):** 15.00 sq ft (1.39 m²)
**Total trailing-edge flaps area:** 31.00 sq ft (2.88 m²)
**Total ailerons area:** 12.40 sq ft (1.15 m²)
**Total ventral fixed strakes area:** 5.50 sq ft (0.51 m²)
**Total retractable fence (LIDs) area:** 2.60 sq ft (0.24 m²)
**Total fin area:** 26.60 sq ft (2.47 m²)
**Total rudder area (excl. tab):** 5.30 sq ft (0.49 m²)
**Tailplane area:** 48.50 sq ft (4.51 m²)
**Overall height:** 11 ft 7¾ in (3.55 m)
**Outrigger wheel track:** 17 ft 0 in (5.18 m)
**Maximum wing loading:** 134.78 lb/sq ft (658.1 kg/m²)

#### Powerplant

**GR Mk.7:** one Rolls-Royce Pegasus Mk 105 vectored-thrust turbofan rated at 21,500 lb st (95.6 kN)

#### Weights

**Empty operating (including pilot and unused fuel):** 15,542 lb (7050 kg)
**Basic flight design gross weight for 7-g operation:** 22,950 lb (10410 kg)
**Maximum take-off (after 1,430-ft (435-m) short take-off):** 31,000 lb (14061 kg); (sea level vertical take-off, ISA conditions) 19,180 lb (8700 kg); (sea level vertical take-off, 32°C) 17,950 lb (8143 kg)
**Design maximum landing weight:** 25,000 lb (11340 kg)
**Maximum vertical landing weight:** 19,937 lb (9043 kg)

#### Fuel and load

**Total fuel capacity:** 1948 Imp gal (8858 litres)
**Total usable internal fuel:** 950 Imp gal (4318 litres)/7,759 lb (3519 kg), comprising integral wing fuel tanks with usable total 604 Imp gal (2746 litres), plus four fuselage tanks; front and rear 134 Imp gal (609 litres) each, plus two centre tanks 39 Imp gal (177 litres) each
**Total usable internal fuel (Harrier T.Mk 10):** 913 Imp gal (4150 litres)
**Water injection tank capacity:** 495 lb (225 kg)
**External fuel:** up to four 250-Imp gal (1135-litre) auxiliary fuel tanks on four inner underwing stations; single-point refuelling plus optional retractable bolt-on flight refuelling probe above port air intake
**Maximum useful load:** (including fuel, water injection for engine, stores, guns and ammunition) approx. 6,750 lb (3062 kg) with vertical take-off and 17,000 lb (7,710 kg) with short take-off

#### Performance

**Maximum level speed at altitude:** 645 mph (1041 km/h)
**Maximum level speed at low level:** 661 mph (1065 km/h)
**Limiting Mach numbers:** 0.98 at altitude; 0.87 at sea level
**Maximum rate of climb at sea level:** 14,715 ft (4485 m) per minute
**Service ceiling above:** 50,000 ft (15240 m)
**STOL take-off run:** (maximum weight, ISA conditions) 1,430 ft (435 m); (maximum weight, 32°C) 1,700 ft (518 m)

#### Range

**Operational radius:** (after short take-off with 12 500-lb (227-kg) bombs, internal fuel and 1-hr loiter) 103 miles (167 km); (hi-lo-hi profile after short take-off with seven 500-lb (227-kg) bombs, two external fuel tanks, no loiter) 684 miles (1101 km)
**Ferry range:** (unrefuelled with four underwing tanks, tanks retained) 1886 miles (3035 km)
**Combat air patrol endurance:** (at 115 miles (185 km) from base) three hours

#### g limits

**Maximum/minimum:** +8/-3, reduced manoeuvring limits apply when auxiliary fuel tanks carried

#### Armament

**Fixed:** two underfuselage pods each housing a single 25-mm Aden 25 cannon with 100 rounds
**Weapon stations:** centreline station stressed for 1,000 lb (454 kg), four stations under each wing stressed for loads up to 2,000 lb (907 kg) inboard, 1,000 lb (454 kg) intermediate and 630 lb (286 kg) outboard, additional weapon station ahead of outrigger wheel fairing for air-to-air missile
**Current weapons:** 540-lb (245-kg) and 1,000-lb (454-kg) general-purpose free-fall bombs, BL755 and CBU-87 cluster bombs, GBU-16, CPU-123/B, GBU-24/B 1,000-lb (454-kg) laser-guided bombs, Matra 155 rocket pods (each with 18 68-mm SNEB rockets) or CRV-7 rocket pods, AIM-9L/M Sidewinder air-to-air missiles for self-defence
**Proposed stores and weapons :** Brimstone anti-armour missiles, AI ARM anti-radiation missile, CASOM, TIALD laser designator pod

# North American F-86 Sabre

In recent years the Sabre has become extremely popular with the warbird fraternity, with about 50 potentially airworthy aircraft in the US and more under restoration. The fliers include single examples of the A, D, E, H and L, and 11 Fs. The remainder are CL-13s. This restored F-86F wears the markings of Maj. John Glenn, USMC who flew with the 25th Fighter Interceptor Squadron during the Korean War. Glenn was on Temporary Deployment (TDY) to the USAF and, during this period, he scored three kills over North Korean MiGs. Later in his career, Glenn was to gain greater fame as America's first man in space and, more recently, as the world's oldest astronaut.

## F-86E Sabre

**Cutaway key**
1 Radome
2 Radar antenna
3 Engine air intake
4 Gun camera
5 Nosewheel leg doors
6 Nose undercarriage leg strut
7 Nosewheel
8 Torque scissor links
9 Steering control valve
10 Nose undercarriage pivot fixing
11 Sight amplifier
12 Radio and electronics equipment bay
13 Electronics bay access panel
14 Battery
15 Gun muzzle blast troughs
16 Oxygen bottles
17 Nosewheel bay doors
18 Oxygen servicing point
19 Canopy switches
20 Machine-gun barrel mountings
21 Hydraulic system test connections
22 Radio transmitter
23 Cockpit armoured bulkhead
24 Windscreen panels
25 A-1CM radar gunsight
26 Instrument panel shroud
27 Instrument panel
28 Control column
29 Kick-in boarding step
30 Used cartridge case collector box
31 Ammunition boxes (267 rounds per gun)
32 Ammunition feed chutes
33 0.5-in (12.7-mm) Colt Browning machine-guns
34 Engine throttle
35 Starboard side console panel
36 North American ejection seat
37 Rear view mirror
38 Sliding cockpit canopy cover
39 Ejection seat headrest
40 ADF sense aerials
41 Pilot's back armour
42 Ejection seat guide rails
43 Canopy handle
44 Cockpit pressure valves

45 Armoured side panels
46 Tailplane trim actuator
47 Fuselage/front spar main frame
48 Forward fuselage fuel tank (total internal fuel capacity 435 US gal/ 1646 litres)
49 Fuselage lower longeron
50 Intake trunking
51 Rear radio and electronics bay
52 Canopy emergency release handle
53 ADF loop aerial
54 Cockpit pressure relief valve
55 Starboard wing fuel tank
56 Leading-edge slat guide rails
57 Starboard automatic leading-edge slat, open
58 Cable drive to aileron actuator
59 Pitot tube

60 Starboard navigation light
61 Wingtip fairing
62 Starboard aileron
63 Aileron hydraulic control unit

64 Aileron balance
65 Starboard slotted flap, down position
66 Flap guide rail
67 Upward identification light
68 Air conditioning plant
69 Intake fairing starter/generator
70 Fuselage/rear spar main frame
71 Hydraulic system reservoirs
72 Longeron/main frame joint
73 Fuel filter de-icing fluid tank
74 Cooling air outlet
75 Engine equipment access panel
76 Heat exchanger exhaust duct

77 Engine suspension links
78 Fuselage skin plating
79 Engine withdrawal rail
80 Starboard side oil tank
81 General Electric J47-GE-27 turbojet
82 Bleed air system

primary heat exchanger
83 Ground power connections

84 Fuel filler cap
85 Fuselage break point sloping frame (engine removal)
86 Upper longeron joint
87 Engine bay air cooling duct
88 Cooling air outlet
89 Engine firewall bulkhead
90 Engine flame cans
91 Rear fuselage framing
92 Fuel jettison pipe

## SPECIFICATION

### F-86E Sabre

#### Dimensions

**Length:** 37 ft (11.27 m)
**Height:** 14 ft (4.26 m)
**Wingspan:** 37 ft (11.27 m)
**Wing area:** 288 sq ft (26.75 m²)

#### Powerplant

One General Electric J47-GE-13 turbojet rated at 5,450 lb (24.24 kN) static thrust

#### Weights

**Empty:** 10,555 lb (4788 kg)
**Normal loaded:** 16,346 lb (7414 kg)
**Maximum take-off:** 17,806 lb (8077 kg)

#### Fuel

**Normal internal fuel:** 435 US gal (1646 litres)
**Maximum internal fuel:** 675 US gal (2555 litres)

#### Performance

**Maximum level speed clean at 35,000 ft (10688 m):** 601 mph (967 km/h)
**Maximum level speed clean at low level:** 679 mph (1093 km/h)
**Cruising speed:** 537 mph (864 km/h)
**Stalling speed:** 123 mph (198 km/h)
**Climb to 30,000 ft (9144 m):** 6 minutes 18 seconds
**Service ceiling:** 47,200 ft (14387 m)
**Range:** 848 miles (1365 km)
**Maximum range:** 1,022 miles (1645 km)

#### Armament

Primary armament consisted of six 0.5-in (12.7-mm) Colt Browning machine-guns mounted in the forward fuselage with a total of 1,800 rounds; provision for either two 1,000-lb (454-kg) bombs or 16 0.5-in (12.7-mm) rocket projectiles mounted on underwing racks, in place of two 120-US gal (454-litre) drop tanks, a variety of other ordnance loads could also be carried

*On 14 December 1953 NAA flew its TF-86F prototype 52-5016, which had been developed in response to a USAF requirement for a high-performance trainer. This aircraft was lost after a few flights, but was replaced by a second aircraft 52-1228 (illustrated), which differed in being fitted with a '6-3' wing. Although no orders were forthcoming, the second TF-86F had a long and productive career as a trainer and test/chase platform.*

**93** Fuselage top longeron
**94** Fin/tailplane root fillet fairing
**95** Control cable duct
**96** Fin spar attachment joint
**97** Tailplane/rudder control cables
**98** All-moving tailplane hydraulic jack
**99** Tailfin construction
**100** Flush HF aerial panel
**101** Starboard tailplane
**102** Fintip dielectric aerial fairing
**103** ADF aerial
**104** Rudder construction
**105** Rudder trim tab

**106** Tail navigation light
**107** Port elevator/tailplane flap
**108** All-moving tailplane construction
**109** Engine exhaust nozzle
**110** Fuel jettison pipe
**111** Heat-shrouded jet pipe
**112** Power control compensator
**113** Emergency hydraulic valves
**114** Airbrake housing
**115** Airbrake hydraulic jack
**116** Port airbrake (open)
**117** Hydraulic system emergency pump
**118** Cooling air intake
**119** Lower longeron joint
**120** Trailing-edge root fillet

**121** Aft main fuel tank
**122** Main undercarriage wheel bay
**123** Hydraulic retraction jack
**124** Main undercarriage pivot fixing
**125** Hydraulic flap jack
**126** Flap shroud ribs
**127** Port slotted flaps
**128** Port aileron construction
**129** Aileron hydraulic power control unit
**130** Gyro compass remote transmitter
**131** Wingtip fairing
**132** Port navigation light
**133** Port automatic leading-edge slat, open position
**134** Leading-edge slat rib construction

**135** Front spar
**136** Wing rib and stringer construction
**137** Wing skin/leading-edge piano hinge attachment joint
**138** 120-US gal (454-litre) drop tank
**139** Drop tank pylon
**140** Port main wheel
**141** Fuel filler cap
**142** Main undercarriage leg strut
**143** Fuel tank bay corrugated double skin
**144** Port wing fuel tank
**145** Tank interconnectors
**146** Skin panel attachment joint strap
**147** Slat guide rails
**148** Fuel feeders
**149** Aileron cable drive

# Panavia Tornado ADV

*Demonstrating the adaptability of Panavia's original Tornado/MRCA design, the ADV has a stretched fuselage, different radar and avionics, plus provision for eight air-to-air missiles. As one of the fastest aircraft at low level, it is ideal for 'running down' bombers attacking down low.*

## Tornado F.Mk 3

**Cutaway key**
1 Starboard taileron construction
2 Honeycomb trailing-edge panels
3 Compound sweep taileron leading edge
4 Taileron pivot fixing
5 Afterburner ducting, extended 14 in (36 cm)
6 Thrust-reverser bucket door actuator
7 Afterburner nozzle jack
8 Starboard fully-variable engine exhaust nozzle
9 Thrust-reverser bucket doors, open
10 Dorsal spine and fairing
11 Rudder hydraulic actuator
12 Honeycomb rudder construction
13 Rudder
14 Fuel jettison pipes
15 Tail navigation light
16 Aft passive ECM housing/radar warning antenna
17 Dielectric fin tip antenna housing
18 VHF aerial
19 Fuel jettison and vent valve
20 ILS aerial, port and starboard
21 Underside view showing semi-recessed missile positions
22 Extended fuselage section
23 Extended radar equipment bay
24 Radome
25 Secondary heat exchanger intake
26 Wing pylon-mounted missile rails
27 External fuel tanks
28 Port taileron
29 Fin leading edge
30 Fin integral fuel tank
31 Tailfin construction
32 Vortex generators
33 Heat shroud
34 Fin spar root attachment joints
35 Engine bay central firewall
36 Starboard airbrake, open
37 Airbrake hydraulic jack
38 Taileron actuator, fly-by-wire control system
39 Turbo-Union RB.199-34R Mk 104 three-spool afterburning turbofan
40 Hydraulic reservoir
41 Hydraulic system filters
42 Engine bay bulkhead
43 Bleed air duct
44 Heat exchanger exhaust duct
45 Primary heat exchanger
46 Ram air intake
47 HF aerial fairing
48 Engine compressor faces
49 Rear fuselage bag-type fuel tank
50 Intake trunking
51 Wing root pneumatic seal
52 KHD/Microtecnica/Lucas T312 APU
53 Engine-driven auxiliary gearbox
54 APU exhaust
55 Flap drive shaft
56 Starboard full-span double-slotted flaps, extended
57 Spoiler housings
58 Starboard wing fully-swept position
59 Flap guide rails
60 Flap screw jacks
61 Wingtip fairing
62 Starboard navigation light
63 Structural provision for outboard pylon attachment
64 Full-span leading-edge slats, extended
65 Starboard external fuel tank, capacity 495 Imp gal (2250 litres)
66 Fuel tank-stabilising fins
67 Swivelling wing stores pylon
68 Missile launching rail
69 AIM-9L Sidewinder air-to-air missiles
70 Leading-edge slat screw jacks
71 Slat guide rails
72 Wing rib construction
73 Two-spar wing torsion box construction
74 Swivelling pylon mounting
75 Starboard wing integral fuel tank
76 Main undercarriage leg strut
77 Starboard mainwheel
78 Mainwheel door
79 Undercarriage breaker strut
80 Wing pivot sealing fairing
81 Telescopic control linkages
82 Pylon swivelling link
83 Main undercarriage hydraulic retraction jack
84 Wing sweep actuator attachment joint
85 Starboard wing pivot bearing
86 Flexible wing seals
87 Wing pivot carry-through (Electron beam welded titanium box construction)
88 Wing pivot box integral fuel tank
89 Pitch and roll control non-linear gearing mechanism
90 Air-conditioning supply ducting (Normalair Garrett system)
91 Dorsal spine fairing
92 Anti-collision light
93 UHF aerials
94 Port wing pivot bearing
95 Flexible trailing-edge seals
96 Spoiler actuators
97 Port spoilers, open

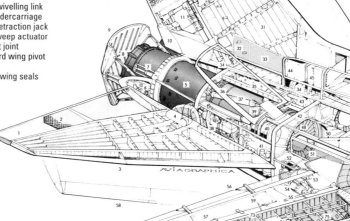

*RAF Tornado F.Mk 3s are occasional visitors to the Red Flag exercises in the USA. These give participating aircrews the opportunity to fly missions in the vast desert ranges of southern Nevada against simulated enemy aggressor units. F.Mk 3s operate with Blue Force (friendly force) and are usually tasked with strike support, as part of the offensive counter-air force.*

## SPECIFICATION

### Tornado F.Mk 3

**Maximum take-off:** 61,700 lb (27986 kg)

### Dimensions

**Length:** 61 ft 3½ in (18.68 m)
**Height:** 19 ft 6¼ in (5.95 m)
**Wingspan spread:** 45 ft 7½ in (13.91 m)
**Wingspan swept:** 28 ft 2½ in (8.60 m)
**Aspect ratio spread:** 7.73
**Aspect ratio swept:** 2.96
**Wing area:** 286.33 sq ft (26.60 m²)
**Tailplane span:** 22 ft 3½ in (6.80 m)
**Wheel track:** 10 ft 2 in (3.10 m)

### Powerplant

Two Turbo-Union RB.199-34R Mk 104 turbofans each rated at 9,100 lb st (40.48 kN) dry and 16,520 lb st (73.48 kN) with afterburning

### Fuel and load

**Internal fuel:** 12,544 lb (5690 kg)
**External fuel:** up to 12,800 lb (5806 kg) in two 495-Imp gal (2250-litre) and two 396-Imp gal (1500-litre) or four 330-Imp gal (1500-litre) drop tanks
**Maximum ordnance:** 18,740 lb (8500 kg)

### Weights

**Empty operating:** 31,970 lb (14502 kg)

### Performance

**Maximum level speed 'clean' at 36,000 ft (10975 m):** 1,262 kt (1,453 mph; 2238 km/h)
**Operational ceiling:** 70,000 ft (21335 m)
**Combat radius:** more than 300 nm (345 miles; 556 km) supersonic or more than 1000 nm (1,151 miles; 1852 km) subsonic

### Armament

One 27-mm IWKA Mauser cannon fitted to the starboard side. Main armament is four BAe SkyFlash semi-active radar-homing or four AIM-120 AMRAAM active radar AAMs with a range of 31 miles (50 km), carried semi-recessed under the fuselage. Four AIM-9L Sidewinders or four ASRAAMS are also carried for short-range combat. Self-defence is provided by a Bofors Phimat chaff dispenser carried on starboard outer Sidewinder pylon or Celsius Tech BOL integral chaff/flare dispenser in Sidewinder rail. Vicon 78 chaff/flare dispensers under rear fuselage. GEC-Marconi Ariel towed-radar decoy can be carried on outboard wing pylon

98 Port wing fully swept back position
99 Full-span double-slotted flaps, extended
100 Port wing fully forward position
101 Wing tip fairing
102 Port navigation light
103 Full-span leading-edge slats, extended
104 Port wing integral fuel tank
105 Swivelling pylon mounting
106 Pylon angle control link
107 Port wing sweep actuator
108 Wing flap and leading-edge slat drive motors
109 Starboard wing sweep actuator
110 Hydraulic drive motor and gearbox
111 Extended wingroot glove fairing
112 Forward radar-warning receiver, port and starboard
113 Supplementary 'blow-in' intake doors
114 Landing lamp, port and starboard
115 Starboard fully-variable engine air intake
116 Navigation light
117 Variable-intake ramp
118 Ramp control linkage
119 Ramp hydraulic jack
120 Bleed air exit louvres
121 Boundary layer spill duct
122 Enlarged forward fuselage bag-type fuel tank
123 Cockpit canopy pivot mounting
124 Air and fuel system ducting
125 Port intake bleed air outlet fairing
126 AIM-9L Sidewinder air-to-air missiles
127 Missile launching rail
128 Port external fuel tank
129 Intake lip
130 Navigator's cockpit enclosure
131 Navigator's ejection seat (Martin-Baker Mk 10A 'zero-zero' seat)
132 Canopy jack strut
133 Cockpit rear pressure bulkhead
134 Engine air intake curved inboard sidewall
135 Starboard avionics equipment and flight control system equipment bay
136 BAe SkyFlash air-to-air missile
137 Ventral semi-recessed missile housing
138 Cartridge case and link collector box
139 Navigator's side console

*The RAF's acquisition of the Sentry AEW.Mk 1, which entered service in 1991, finally allowed the Tornado force to exploit and expand a modern integrated air defence AEW&C system. The belated addition of improved datalink systems and BVR missiles for the F.Mk 3 in the form of JTIDS and AMRAAM has enhanced the Tornado's defence capability still further.*

140 Canopy centre arch
141 Navigator's instrument console
142 One-piece cockpit canopy cover
143 Ejection seat headrest
144 Pilot's ejection seat
145 Side console panel
146 Ammunition feed chute
147 Mauser 27-mm cannon, starboard only
148 Instrument pressure sensor
149 Cannon barrel
150 Radome, open position
151 Nosewheel leg strut
152 Twin nosewheels
153 Torque scissor links
154 Taxiing lamp
155 Nosewheel doors
156 Cannon muzzle blast tube
157 Electrical system equipment and ground test panels
158 Cockpit pressure floor
159 Rudder pedals
160 Control column
161 Instrument panel shroud
162 Pilot's head-up-display
163 Windscreen panels
164 Windscreen rain dispersal duct
165 Cockpit front pressure bulkhead
166 Avionics equipment, communications and navigation systems
167 Angle of attack transmitter
168 Blade antenna
169 In-flight refuelling probe, extended
170 Marconi-Elliot 'Foxhunter' airborne interception radar
171 Scanner tracking mechanism
172 Cassegrain radar antenna
173 Radar unit hinged to starboard for replacement of line replaceable units (LRUs)
174 Extended radome
175 Pitot tube

# Republic F-84F Thunderstreak

### F-84F Thunderstreak

**Cutaway key**
1 Engine air intake
2 Gun tracking radar antenna
3 Machine gun muzzles
4 Pitot tube
5 Nose undercarriage hydraulic retraction jack
6 Leg compression link
7 Nosewheel leg strut
8 Nosewheel
9 Mudguard
10 Steering jack
11 Taxiing lamp
12 Nose undercarriage leg rear strut
13 Nosewheel doors
14 Intake duct framing
15 Nose compartment 0.5-in (12.7-mm) 50 Colt-Browning M3 machine-guns (four)
16 Radar electronics equipment
17 Ammunition tanks, total of 1,800 rounds
18 Forward avionics bay including LABS bombing computer
19 Static ports
20 Battery
21 Intake ducting
22 Cockpit front pressure bulkhead
23 Rudder pedals
24 Instrument panel shroud
25 Windscreen panels
26 A-4 radar gunsight
27 Standby compass
28 Instrument panel
29 Ejection seat footrests
30 Aileron hydraulic booster
31 Intake suction relief door
32 Duct screen clearance access panel
33 Wingroot machine-gun muzzle

34 Intake duct screen
35 Port side console panel
36 Engine throttle
37 External canopy release handle
38 Pilot's ejection seat
39 Safety harness
40 Headrest
41 Ejection seat guide rails
42 Cockpit canopy cover
43 Starboard automatic leading edge slat, open
44 Slat guide rails
45 Starboard navigation light
46 Wingtip fairing
47 Starboard aileron
48 Aileron control rods
49 Starboard wing integral fuel tank; normal maximum fuel capacity 1,475 US gal (5583 litres)
50 Aileron fixed tab
51 Starboard flap
52 Spoiler
53 Starboard main undercarriage leg (retracted position)

54 Canopy rear hinge arm
55 Cockpit aft glazing
56 Ammunition feed chute
57 Cockpit rear pressure bulkhead
58 Wingroot 0.50-in (12.7-mm) Colt Browning M3 machine-gun
59 Engine electric starter/generator
60 Intake compressor face
61 Wing/fuselage spar lug attachment bolts (total four)
62 Fuselage main fuel tanks
63 Engine oil tank
64 Oxygen bottle
65 Air-conditioning and pressurisation pack
66 Fuselage fuel tank filler cap

67 Tail section attachment bolts (four)
68 Fuselage double main frames
69 Fuselage break point
70 Main engine mounting
71 Engine bay cooling intake
72 Wright J65-W-3 turbojet engine
73 Radio-compass antenna
74 Flush aerial fairing
75 Aft radio equipment bay
76 Engine firewall
77 Engine turbine section
78 Fuselage frame and stringer construction

79 Dorsal spine fairing
80 Anti-collision light
81 VHF aerial
82 Tailpipe cooling intake
83 Rear fuselage framing
84 Jet pipe
85 Rudder control rod, elevator on starboard side
86 Finroot fillet

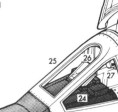

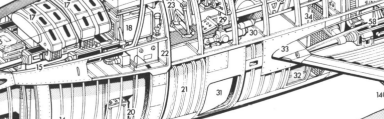

*In 1949, Republic flew the first of its two XF-91 Thunderceptors. Similar to its F-84 forebears only in terms of its fuselage, the XF-91 had butterfly-like wings which were of inverse taper, becoming ever-broader towards the tips, and were mounted on pivots so as to have variable incidence. At the back were not only an afterburning J47 engine (the next engine after the J35), but also a battery of four rocket motors which, on 14 December, thrust the XF-91 beyond the speed of sound (the first time that this had been achieved by a non-Russian fighter). Many other features were also tested on the XF-91s, including a butterfly (V-type) tail, but there was no question of production.*

*Left: Over a 18-year period, F-84Fs served with 24 Air National Guard units in the interceptor (limited use only), special delivery (nuclear) and tactical fighter roles. The last ANG F-84Fs were phased out by Illinois's 170th TDFS and Ohio's 164th TFS (illustrated) in the last quarter of 1972.*

AViAGRAPHiCA

87 Aerial tuning units
88 All-moving tailplane control jack
89 Tailplane pivot fixing
90 Fin/tailplane sealing plates
91 Starboard all-moving tailplane
92 Fin leading edge
93 Tailfin construction
94 Rudder mass balance weight
95 Fintip aerial fairing
96 Tail navigation lights
97 Rudder construction
98 Rudder fixed tab
99 Parallel chord all-moving tailplane construction
100 Jet pipe exhaust nozzle
101 Rudder hinge control
102 Tailfin attachment frames
103 Brake parachute fairing doors
104 Parachute stowage
105 Parachute release link
106 Airbrake hydraulic jack
107 Port perforated airbrake
108 Trailing-edge wingroot fillet
109 Port plain flap construction
110 Port spoiler
111 Drop tank stabilising fins
112 Aileron fixed tab
113 Port aileron construction

114 Aileron control rods
115 Rear spar
116 Port wing integral fuel tank
117 Wingtip fairing
118 Port navigation light
119 Retractable landing lamp
120 5-in (12.7-cm) HVAR ground attack rockets
121 Wing stringers
122 Wing rib construction
123 Port outer wing pylon
124 Undercarriage leg torque scissors
125 Mainwheel doors
126 Port mainwheel
127 Main undercarriage leg strut
128 Undercarriage leg pivot fixing
129 Hydraulic retraction jack
130 Main undercarriage mounting beam
131 Port automatic leading-edge slat (closed position)
132 Mainwheel well
133 Inner wheel door
134 Flying boom in-flight refuelling adaptor (open)
135 Wing tank fuel filler cap
136 Ventral engine access doors
137 Front spar
138 Pylon fixing
139 Fixed leading-edge construction
140 Inboard pylon
141 375-US gal (1420-litre) ferry tank
142 191.5-US gal (725-litre) drop tank
143 Mk 84 1,000-lb (454-kg) HE bomb
144 2,000-lb (907-kg) free fall nuclear weapon

# SEPECAT Jaguar

## Jaguar

### Cutaway key

1 Nose profile (Maritime Strike Variant)
2 Thomson-CSF Agave dual-role (air-air, air-ground) radar
3 Ferranti Type 105 Laser Ranger
4 Pitot tube
5 'Wedge-profile' optical sighting windows
6 Ferranti Laser Ranging and Marked Target Seeker
7 Total pressure probe (both sides)
8 Electronics cooling air duct
9 Air-data computer
10 Radio altimeter
11 Power amplifier
12 Avionics access doors
13 Waveform generator
14 Cooling air intake
15 Marconi Avionics nav/attack system equipment
16 Landing/taxiing lamps
17 Nosewheel leg door
18 Towing lug
19 Nosewheel forks
20 Nosewheel
21 Steering jacks
22 Nose undercarriage leg strut
23 Artificial feel control units
24 Rudder pedals
25 Instrument panel shroud
26 Retractable, in-flight refuelling probe
27 Windscreen panels
28 Smiths electronics head-up-display
29 Instrument panel
30 Smiths FS68 head-down navigational display
31 Control column
32 Engine throttles
33 Pilot's side console panel
34 Martin-Baker Mk 9 'zero-zero' ejection seat
35 Seat and parachute combined safety harness
36 Honeycomb cockpit side panel
37 Plexiglass cockpit canopy cover (upward-opening)
38 Ejection seat headrest
39 Canopy struts
40 Cockpit pressurisation valve
41 Rear pressure bulkhead
42 Gun muzzle blast trough
43 Battery and electrical equipment bay
44 Port engine intake
45 Gun gas vents
46 Spring-loaded secondary air intake doors
47 Boundary layer bleed duct
48 Forward fuselage fuel tank (total system capacity 924 Imp gal; 1200 litres)
49 Air conditioning unit
50 Secondary heat exchanger
51 Starboard engine air intake
52 VHF homing aerials
53 Heat exchanger intake/exhaust duct
54 Cable and hydraulic pipe ducting
55 Intake/fuselage attachment joint
56 Duct frames
57 Integrally-stiffened machined fuselage frames
58 Ammunition tank
59 30-mm ADEN cannon
60 Ground power supply socket
61 Mainwheel stowed position
62 Main undercarriage hydraulic lock strut
63 Leading-edge slat drive motors and gearboxes
64 Fuel system piping
65 Wing panel centreline joint
66 Anti-collision light
67 IFF aerial
68 Wing/fuselage forward attachment joint
69 Starboard wing integral fuel tank
70 Fuel piping provision for pylon-mounted tank
71 Overwing missile pylon
72 Missile launch rail
73 Matra 550 Magic air-to-air missile
74 Starboard leading-edge slat
75 Slat guide rails
76 Starboard navigation light
77 Tacan aerial
78 Flap guide rails and underwing fairings
79 Outboard double-slotted flap
80 Starboard spoilers
81 Inboard double slotted flap
82 Flap honeycomb construction
83 Flap drive shaft and screwjacks
84 Spoiler control links
85 Wing/fuselage aft attachment joint
86 Heat exchanger air scoop

*French SEPECAT Jaguar two-seaters line up on the ramp awaiting another training hop. Although the Jaguar is being increasingly replaced by the Mirage 2000, three squadrons still operate this venerable aircraft.*

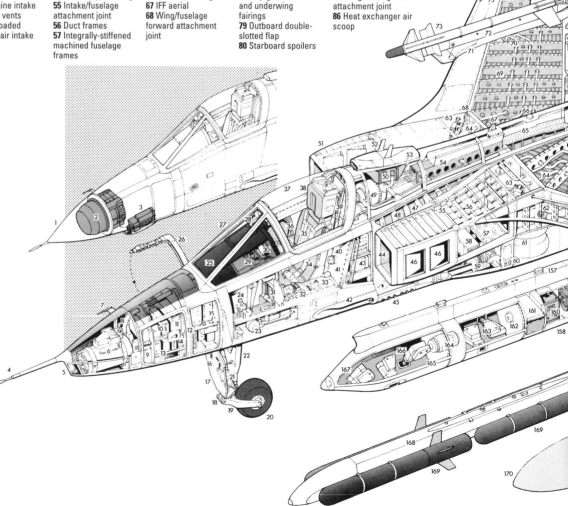

*The **RAF** used this picture as part of its recruitment campaign in the 1970s. Although such a close formation would be tantamount to suicide, this picture displays the power and agility of the **SEPECAT** Jaguar as the formation thunders over a Scottish loch.*

87 Control runs
88 Air conditioning supply ducting
89 Fuselage fuel tank access panels
90 Honeycomb intake duct construction
91 Engine intake frame
92 Hydraulic accumulator
93 Flap hydraulic motor and drive shaft
94 No. 2 system hydraulic reservoir
95 Primary heat exchanger
96 No. 1 system hydraulic reservoir
97 Heat exchanger exhaust ducts
98 Rear fuselage integral fuel tank
99 Inward/outward fuel vent valve
100 Dorsal spine fairing

## SPECIFICATION

**Jaguar GR.Mk 1A
(unless otherwise noted)**

### Dimensions

**Length overall:** 55 ft 2½ in (16.83 m)
**T.Mk 2A:** 57 ft 6¼ in (17.53 m)
**Wingspan:** 28 ft 6 in (8.69 m)
**Wing area:** 260.27 sq ft (24.18 m²)
**Wing aspect ratio:** 3.12
**Wing chord at root:** 11 ft 9 in (3.58 m)
**Wing chord at tip:** 3 ft 8½ in (1.13 m)
**Height overall:** 16 ft ½ in (4.89 m)
**Tailplan span:** 14 ft 10¼ in (4.53 m)
**Wheel track:** 7 ft 11 in (2.41 m)
**T.Mk 2A:** 7 ft 10½ in (2.40 m)
**Wheelbase:** 18 ft 8 in (5.69 m)
**T.Mk 2A:** 18 ft 7¼ in (5.67 m)

### Powerplant

Two Rolls Royce/Turboméca Adour Mk 104 turbofans, each rated at 5,270 lb st (23.4 kN) dry and 7,900 lb st (35.1 kN) with afterburning

### Weights

**Typical empty:** 15,342 lb (7000 kg)
**Normal take-off:** 24,149 lb (10964 kg)
**Maximum take-off:** 34,612 lb (15700 kg)
**Maximum wing loading:** 133 lb/sq ft (649.3 kg/m²)

### Fuel and load

**Internal fuel:** 7,357 lb (3337 kg)
**External fuel:** up to 6,270 lb (2844 kg) in three 264-Imp gal (1200-litre) drop tanks
**Maximum ordnance:** 10,000 lb (4536 kg)

### Performance

**Maximum level speed 'clean' at 36,000 ft (10975 m):** Mach 1.6 or 917 kt (1,056 mph; 1699 km/h)
**Maximum level speed 'clean' at**
**sea level:** Mach 1.1 or 729 kt (840 mph; 1350 km/h)
**Landing speed:** 115 kt (132 mph; 213 km/h)
**Time to 30,000 ft (9145 m):** 1 minute 30 seconds
**Service ceiling:** 45,930 ft (14000 m)
**Take-off run (clean):** 1,854 ft (565 m)
**Take-off run (four 1,000-lb/454-kg bombs):** 4,101 ft (1250 m)
**Landing distance from 50 ft (15 m):** 2,575 ft (785 m)

### Range

**Ferry range with drop tanks:** 1,902 nm (2,190 miles; 3524 km)
**Combat radius on hi-lo-hi attack mission:** 460 nm (530 miles; 852 km)
**Combat radius on lo-lo-lo attack mission:** 290 nm (334 miles; 537 km)

### g-limits

+8.6 at typical weight or +12 ultimate

### Armament

**Fixed:** Two 30-mm ADEN cannon in lower fuselage aft of cockpit with 150 rounds each
**Weapon stations:** One stores attachment on fuselage centreline and two under each wing. Centreline and inboard wing points can each carry up to 2,500 lb (1134 kg) of weapons, and the outboard underwing points up to 1,250 lb (567 kg)
**Weapons carried:** 1,000-lb (454-kg) bombs, various combinations of free-fall and retarded bombs, BL755 or CBU-87 cluster bombs, CPU-123/B Paveway II LGBs and CRV-7 rockets carried in 19-round LAU 5003 launchers. AIM-9L Sidewinder missiles can be carried for self-defence on overwing pylons. The Jaguar has relinquished its nuclear strike role, but could carry the AN 52 tactical nuclear weapon.

---

101 Fin spar attachment joint
102 Tailfin construction
103 Starboard tailplane
104 Fin tip ECM fairing
105 VHF/UHF antenna fairing
106 Recognition light
107 Tail navigation light
108 VOR aerial
109 Rudder honeycomb construction
110 Fuel jettison pipe
111 Tailcone
112 Brake parachute housing
113 Rudder hydraulic jack
114 Tailplane trailing-edge discontinuity
115 Honeycomb panel construction
116 Tailplane rib construction
117 Tailplane spar pivot joint
118 Differential all-moving tailplane hydraulic jack
119 Tailplane mounting frames

120 Fire extinguisher bottle
121 Arrester hook (extended)
122 Variable-area shrouded exhaust nozzle
123 Afterburner duct
124 Port ventral fin
125 Firewall
126 Engine rear suspension joint
127 Rolls-Royce/Turboméca Adour 804 (-26) turbofan
128 Port inboard double-slotted flap
129 Engine accessories
130 Hydraulic system ground servicing connectors
131 Airbrake hydraulic jack
132 Port airbrake (extended)
133 Wing fence (in place of missile pylon)
134 Spoiler hydraulic jack
135 Fixed portion of trailing edge
136 Port spoilers
137 Port outer double-slotted flap

138 Flap honeycomb construction
139 Wingtip fairing
140 Port navigation light
141 Matra Type 155 rocket launcher (18 SNEB rockets)
142 Outboard stores pylon
143 Port leading-edge slat
144 Slat screw jacks
145 Port wing integral fuel tank
146 Machined wing skin/stringer panel
147 Pylon fixing
148 Inboard stores pylon
149 Twin mainwheels
150 Pivoted axle beam
151 Shock absorber strut
152 Main undercarriage leg strut
153 Undercarriage pivot mounting
154 Fuselage sidewall construction
155 Main undercarriage leg door
156 Mainwheel doors

157 Fuselage centreline pylon
158 Reconnaissance pod
159 Infra-red linescan
160 Data converter
161 Air conditioning pack
162 Rear rotating camera drum (role interchangeable)
163 Twin Vinten F95 Mk 10 high oblique cameras
164 Drum rotating electric motor and gearbox
165 Forward-rotating camera drum
166 Twin Vinten F95 Mk 10 low oblique cameras
167 Forward-looking Vinten F95 Mk 7 reconnaissance camera
168 Multiple bomb carrier 430 lb (195 kg)
169 Four Matra Durandal penetration bombs
170 264 Imp-gal (1200-litre) auxiliary fuel tank

# Sukhoi Su-24 'Fencer'

In addition to its standard nuclear strike (now no longer undertaken) and conventional attack roles, the Su-24M is a potent SEAD platform, highlighting the type's versatility. A number of anti-radiation missiles are available, including the Kh-58 (AS-11 'Kilter') seen here under test. Three pylons are available for the carriage of heavy missiles and pods, with another six available in total.

## Su-24M 'Fencer-D'

### Cutaway key

1 Pitot head
2 RSBN ILS antenna
3 Radome, hinged to port
4 Orion-A nav/attack radar
5 'Relyef' terrain-avoidance radar
6 Ventral DISS-7 Doppler antenna
7 Incidence vane, yaw vane in ventral position
8 Radar equipment modules
9 SRZ IFF antenna
10 Retractable flight-refuelling probe
11 Dynamic pressure probes, port and starboard
12 Windscreen rain dispersal air ducts
13 Cockpit front pressure bulkhead
14 Nose undercarriage pivot mounting
15 Hydraulic steering jacks
16 Levered suspension nosewheel strut
17 Twin nosewheels with fixed mudguards, aft-retracting
18 Flight control system equipment
19 Cockpit pressure floor
20 Rudder pedals
21 Control column
22 Engine throttle levers
23 Instrument panel shroud
24 Pilot's HUD
25 Folding glare shield
26 WSO's radar display
27 Individual upward-hinging cockpit canopies
28 WSO's K-36DM ejection seat
29 Pilot's ejection seat
30 Cockpit sloping rear pressure bulkhead
31 Canopy hinge point and actuator
32 Starboard engine air intake
33 APK-15M VHF antenna
34 Dorsal equipment bays
35 Control rod linkages
36 Avionics equipment compartment, port and starboard
37 Intake boundary-layer splitter plate with bleed-air perforations
38 Ground test equipment and connectors
39 Intake FOD protection system high-pressure air blowing duct
40 Kayra-24M laser designator/sighting unit in ventral fairing
41 GSh-6-23 rotary cannon housed in starboard ventral fairing
42 Port fixed-geometry engine air intake
43 Television camera in port ventral fairing
44 Main undercarriage wheel bay forward door/airbrake panel
45 Ammunition magazine, 500 rounds, with transverse feed, link collector box on starboard side
46 SPO-10 radar warning receiver antenna
47 Intake spring-loaded suction relief door
48 Forward fuselage fuel tank, total internal capacity 2,609 Imp gal (11860 litres) in three tanks
49 SPO-15C Beryoza radar warning receiver
50 Boundary layer spill duct
51 ARK-19 ADF antenna
52 Mak L-082 infra-red warning receiver
53 Intake ducting
54 Retractable landing light, port and starboard
55 Fuel feed from glove pylon
56 Main undercarriage hydraulic retraction jack
57 Port wing glove pylon
58 Trailing axle main undercarriage leg strut and shock absorber
59 Port position light
60 Wing sweep hydraulic actuator
61 Port wing pivot bearing
62 Sweep actuator hydraulic power supply, interconnected port and starboard
63 Flap and slat telescopic drive shaft from central actuating motor

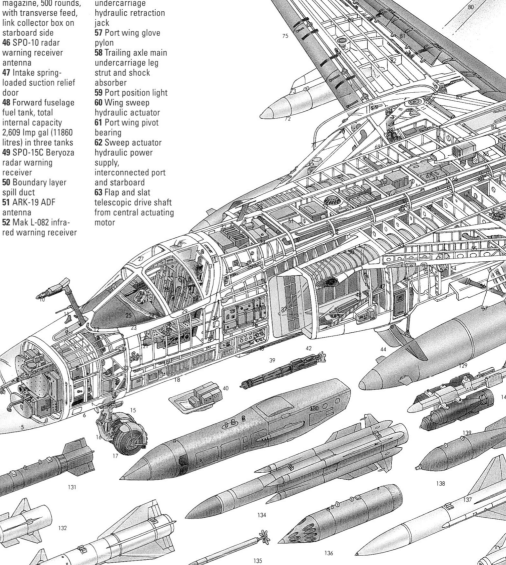

*Inflight refuelling is an important secondary task for the Su-24, for which it employs the UPAZ-1A Sakhalin pod (as also used by the Il-78 'Midas') on the centreline pylon. PTB-3000 tanks are normally carried to increase offloadable fuel. Tanking is usually performed to extend the range of other Su-24s, or to allow them to take off with a small fuel load but a heavy weaponload. The 'Fencer' has also tanked many other aircraft types. Here, the receiver is an Su-30 from the 'Test Pilots' display team, demonstrating the system at an air show.*

## SPECIFICATION

### Su-24M 'Fencer-D'

#### Dimensions

**Length:** 74 ft 1½ in (22.59 m)
**Height:** 20 ft 4 in (6.19 m)
**Maximum wingspan:** 57 ft 10½ in (17.64 m)
**Minimum wingspan:** 34 ft (10.37 m)
**Maximum wing area:** 594.00 sq ft (55.166 m²)
**Minimum wing area:** 549.00 sq ft (51.024 m²)
**Wheel base:** 27 ft 11 in (8.51 m)
**Wheel track:** 10 ft 10 in (3.31 m)

#### Powerplant

Two Lyul'ka AL-21F-3 turbojets rated at 17,230 lb st (76.67) in dry thrust and 24,800 lb st (110.29 kN) with full afterburner activated

#### Weights

**Empty:** 49,162 lb (22300 kg)
**Normal take-off:** 79,365 lb (36000 kg)
**Maximum take-off:** 87,522 lb (39700 kg)
**Maximum landing:** 54,012 lb (24500 kg)

#### Fuel and load

**Maximum internal fuel load:** 21,715 lb (9850 kg)
**Maximum external fuel load:** 14,528 lb (6590 kg)
**Maximum external weaponload:** 19,841 lb (9000 kg)

#### Performance

**Maximum speed at sea level:** 870 mph (1400 km/h)
**Maximum speed at sea level with external tanks:** 823 mph (1325 km/h)
**Maximum speed at 13000 m (theoretical):** 1,317 mph (2120 km/h)
**Minimum speed:** 193 mph (310 km/h)
**Service ceiling:** 55,775 ft (17000 m)
**Take-off run:** 4,265 ft (1300 m)

#### Range

**Maximum range:** 1,770 miles (2850 km)
**Operating radius at sea level:** 348 miles (560 km)
**Operating radius at sea level with external tanks:** 777 miles (1250 km)
**Landing run with parabrake:** 3,120 ft (950 m)
**Landing run without parabrake:** 4,265 ft (1300 m)

#### Armament

'Fencers' can carry an immense array of weaponry. Conventional attacks can be carried out with air-to-surface missiles, unguided rockets, unguided bombs, cluster bombs and gun pods. For SAM hunting Kh-31T and Kh-58U missiles are used. Tactical nuclear bombs (now officially removed from the Russian inventory) carried include the 6U-57, 8U-49, 8U-63, RN-28, 244N and the 10-KT RN-24. Air defence is made possible by two R-60 IR missiles and a GsH-6-23 cannon is carried internally

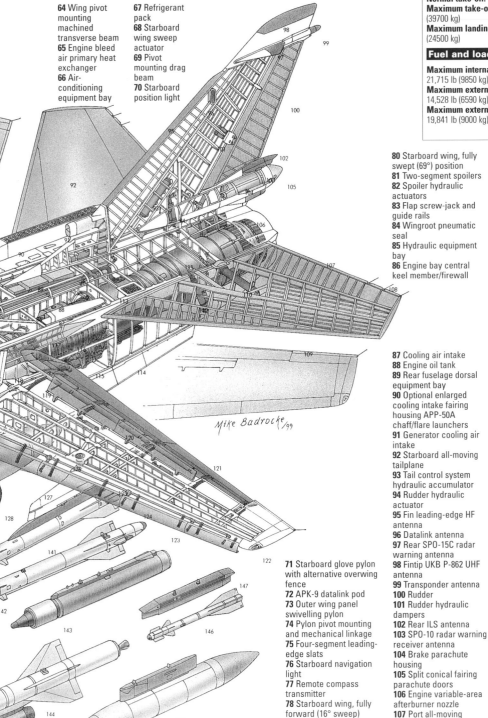

64 Wing pivot mounting machined transverse beam
65 Engine bleed air primary heat exchanger
66 Air-conditioning equipment bay
67 Refrigerant pack
68 Starboard wing sweep actuator
69 Pivot mounting drag beam
70 Starboard position light
71 Starboard glove pylon with alternative overwing fence
72 APK-9 datalink pod
73 Outer wing panel swivelling pylon
74 Pylon pivot mounting and mechanical linkage
75 Four-segment leading-edge slats
76 Starboard navigation light
77 Remote compass transmitter
78 Starboard wing, fully forward (16° sweep) position
79 Two-segment double-slotted trailing-edge flap
80 Starboard wing, fully swept (69°) position
81 Two-segment spoilers
82 Spoiler hydraulic actuators
83 Flap screw-jack and guide rails
84 Wingroot pneumatic seal
85 Hydraulic equipment bay
86 Engine bay central keel member/firewall
87 Cooling air intake
88 Engine oil tank
89 Rear fuselage dorsal equipment bay
90 Optional enlarged cooling intake fairing housing APP-50A chaff/flare launchers
91 Generator cooling air intake
92 Starboard all-moving tailplane
93 Tail control system hydraulic accumulator
94 Rudder hydraulic actuator
95 Fin leading-edge HF antenna
96 Datalink antenna
97 Rear SPO-15C radar warning antenna
98 Fintip UKB P-862 UHF antenna
99 Transponder antenna
100 Rudder
101 Rudder hydraulic dampers
102 Rear ILS antenna
103 SPO-10 radar warning receiver antenna
104 Brake parachute housing
105 Split conical fairing parachute doors
106 Engine variable-area afterburner nozzle
107 Port all-moving tailplane
108 Static dischargers
109 Port wing, fully-swept position
110 Tailplane pivot mounting
111 Afterburner duct
112 Tailplane hydraulic actuator
113 APP-50 12-round flare launcher
114 Ventral fin, port and starboard
115 Engine accessory equipment gearbox
116 Saturn (Lyul'ka) AL-21F-3 afterburning engine
117 Port wingroot pneumatic seal
118 Rear fuselage integral fuel tank
119 Inboard flap guide rail
120 Port two-segment spoiler panels
121 Two-segment double-slotted trailing-edge flap
122 Port navigation light
123 Port four-segment leading-edge slat
124 Slat guide rails
125 Slat drive shaft and screw jack actuators
126 Outer wing pylon pivot mounting
127 Port outer wing swivelling pylon
128 Twin mainwheels with pneumatic brakes, forward retracting
129 PTB-3000 external fuel tank (3000-litre/660-Imp gal) capacity
130 UPAZ-1A Sakhalin 'buddy' refuelling pack
131 KAB-500KR (500-kg/1,102-lb) television-guided bomb
132 Kh-29T television-guided missile nose section
133 Kh-29L (AS-14 'Kedge') laser-guided air-to-surface missile
134 Kh-31P (AS-17 'Krypton') radar-guided air-to-surface anti-shipping missile
135 S-8, 80-mm (3.15-in) FFAR
136 B-8M 20-round rocket pack
137 Kh-58 (AS-11 'Kilter') air-to-surface missile
138 FAB-500M-62 500-kg (1,102-lb) HE bomb
139 FAB-100 100-kg (220-lb) HE bomb
140 Multiple ejector rack
141 Kh-25ML (AS-10 'Karen') laser-guided air-to-surface missile
142 Kh-25MP radar-guided variant
143 S-25-OF, 250-mm (9.84-in) unguided rocket in launcher tube
144 Kh-59M (AS-18 'Kazoo') television-guided air-to-surface missile
145 'Fantasmagoria' passive radar pod
146 R-60 (AA-8 'Aphid') air-to-air 'self-defence' missile
147 R-60 twin missile launch rail, carried on outer wing pylon

Mike Badrocke/99

# Sukhoi Su-25 'Frogfoot'

*With its wingtip airbrakes deployed, this Su-25TM from the Akhtubinsk Scientific and Technical Institute (NII) Flying Centre represents the latest combat variant of the 'Frogfoot' series. Based on the airframe of the two-seat Su-25UB, the Su-25TM introduces a large dorsal hump containing extra fuel and avionics, and a TV sensor in the newly-widened nose.*

## Su-25 'Frogfoot-A'

### Cutaway key

1 Instrument boom
2 Fire-control system transducers
3 Pitot head
4 Glazed nose compartment
5 Laser ranger and marked target seeker
6 Strike camera
7 Localiser aerial port and starboard
8 'Odd-Rods' IFF antennas
9 Nose avionics equipment bays
10 Ventral Doppler aerial (starboard side)
11 30-mm six-barrelled cannon (port side)
12 Gun gas venting ducts
13 Cockpit floor level
14 Rudder pedals
15 Front pressure bulkhead
16 Control column
17 Instrument panel shroud
18 Armoured windscreen panels
19 Pilot's head-up display
20 Canopy open position
21 Rearview mirrors
22 Ejection seat headrest
23 Pilot's ejector seat
24 Canopy latch
25 Seat pan firing handles
26 Engine throttle levers
27 Side console panel
28 Nose undercarriage pivot fixing
29 Levered suspension nosewheel forks
30 Steerable nosewheel (forward-retracting)
31 Mudguard

32 Nosewheel leg door
33 Retractable boarding ladder
34 Fold-out step
35 Armoured cockpit enclosure
36 Rear pressure bulkhead
37 Ejection seat blast screen (retracted)
38 Grab handles
39 Forward fuselage equipment compartment
40 Port air intake
41 Ground power (intercom and telemetry sockets)
42 Intake ducting
43 Mainwheel retracted position
44 Forward fuselage fuel tanks
45 Wing spar centre section carry-through
46 Wing panel root attachment bolted joint
47 Centre-section fuel tank
48 VHF aerial
49 Starboard wingroot attachment joint
50 Inboard leading-edge slat segments (down position)
51 Starboard wing stores pylons
52 Leading-edge dogtooth
53 Starboard missile pylons
54 AA-8 'Aphid' self-defence air-to-air missile

55 Outboard leading-edge slat segments (down position)
56 Retractable landing/taxiing lamp

57 Dielectric ECM aerial fairing
58 Starboard navigation light
59 Wingtip pod fairing
60 Split trailing-edge airbrakes (open)
61 Static dischargers
62 Starboard aileron
63 Aileron tabs
64 Aileron hydraulic actuator
65 Starboard double-slotted tracked flaps (down position)
66 Flap guide rails
67 Flap jacks
68 Engine bay venting air intake
69 Starboard engine installation
70 Dorsal access panels (controls and systems ducting)
71 Rear fuselage fuel tanks
72 Fuel system venting air intake
73 Environmental system ram air intake
74 Tailfin
75 Starboard trimming tailplane
76 Starboard elevator
77 Fintip UHF aerial fairing
78 Tail navigation and position lights
79 Upper rudder segment

80 Rudder tabs
81 Lower rudder segment
82 Rudder hydraulic actuator

83 Radar warning antennas
84 Brake parachute housing
85 Ventral chaff/flare dispenser
86 Elevator tab
87 Port elevator
88 Static discharger
89 Port trimming tailplane

*Developed partly as a result of VVS 'Frogfoot' experience in Chechnya, when bad weather grounded the Su-25 fleet, the Su-25T is an all-weather capable, ground-attack aircraft. Incorporated in the redesigned tail fairing is accommodation for enhanced countermeasures while the UV-26 dispenser is capable of carrying a mixture of PPI-26 infra-red decoys and PPR-26 chaff cartridges. 'Blue 09' carries a weaponload of R-60 (AA-8 'Aphid') AAMs outboard, with a B-13L 122-mm five-round rocket pod inboard.*

**90** Tailplane pivot fixing
**91** Tailplane incidence control
**92** Ventral 'Odd Rods' IFF antennas
**93** Rear fuselage communications and ECM equipment
**94** Ventral towel rail HF aerial
**95** Environmental control system equipment
**96** Engine exhaust nozzle
**97** Soyuz/Gavrilov R-95Sh non-afterburning turbojet
**98** Engine bay venting air intake
**99** Accessory equipment gearbox
**100** Flap guide rails
**101** Flap control jacks
**102** Two-segment, double-slotted flaps
**103** Aileron tabs
**104** Aileron hydraulic actuator
**105** Port aileron
**106** Split trailing-edge airbrake (open)
**107** Static dischargers
**108** Airbrake hydraulic jack
**109** Port navigation light
**110** Retractable landing/taxiing lamp
**111** Dielectric ECM aerial fairing
**112** Leading-edge slat segments
**113** AA-8 'Aphid' self-defence air to-air missile
**114** Missile launch rail
**115** Outboard missile pylon
**116** FAB-500 1,102-lb (500-kg) HE bomb
**117** UV-16-57 rocket pack (16 x 57-mm rockets)
**118** 57-mm high velocity aircraft rocket (HVAR)
**119** Leading-edge dog tooth
**120** Port wing stores pylons
**121** Wingrib construction (dry-bay, no fuel in wings)
**122** Inboard leading-edge slat segments
**123** Port mainwheel
**124** Levered-suspension axle beam
**125** Shock absorber strut
**126** Main undercarriage leg pivot fixing
**127** Hydraulic retraction jack
**128** Leg rotating link
**129** Mainwheel doors
**130** 132-Imp gal (600-litre) external fuel tank
**131** AS-7 'Kerry' air-to-surface missile
**132** BETA B-250 551-lb (250-kg) retarded bomb

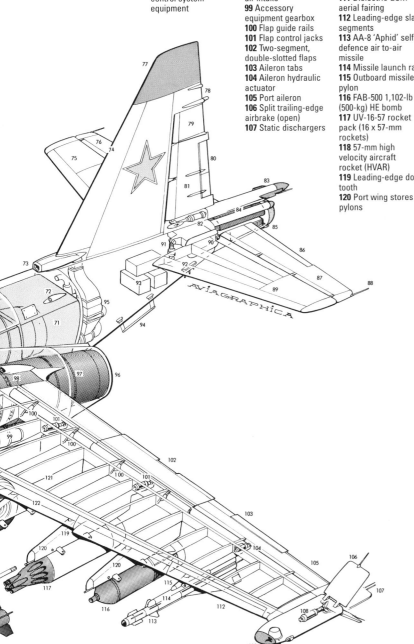

## SPECIFICATION

**Sukhoi Su-25 'Frogfoot-A'**

### Dimensions

**Overall length including probe:** 50 ft 11½ in (15.53 m)
**Fuselage length excluding probe:** 47 ft 10½ in (14.59 m)
**Wingspan:** 47 ft 1 in (14.36 m)
**Wing area:** 324 sq ft (30.1 m²)
**Tailplane span:** 15 ft 3 in (4.65 m)
**Tailplane area:** 69.7 sq ft (6.47 m²)
**Overall height:** 15 ft 9 in (4.8 m)
**Wheel track:** 8 ft 2 in (2.5 m)
**Wheelbase:** 11 ft 9 in (3.58 m)

### Powerplant

Two Soyuz/Gavrilov R-95Sh turbojets each rated at 9,039-lb st (40.21-kN) thrust

### Weights

**Empty operating:** 20,250 lb (9185 kg)
**Normal take-off (early):** 31,415 lb (14250 kg)
**Normal take-off (late):** 32,025 lb (14530 kg)
**Maximum take-off (early):** 38,250 lb (17350 kg)
**Maximum take-off (late):** 38,645 lb (17530 kg)
**Normal landing:** 23,810 lb (10800 kg)
**Maximum landing:** 29,320 lb (13300 kg)

### Fuel load

**Internal fuel:** 6,615 lb (3000 kg)

### Performance

**Maximum level speed clean:** 620 mph (1000 km/h)
**Limiting Mach number (early):** 0.71
**Limiting Mach number (late):** 0.82
**Service ceiling:** 22,950 ft (7000 m)
**Take-off run:** 1,640-2,953 ft (500-900 m)
**Landing roll:** 1,969-2,625 ft (600-800 m)
**Take-off speed:** 149-155 mph (240-270 km/h)
**Landing speed:** 140-162 mph (225-260 km/h)
**g limits:** +6.5 to -3 at basic gross weight

### Range

**With underwing tanks (early):** 1,150 miles (1850 km)
**With underwing tanks (late):** 1,212 miles (1950 km)
**With 6,615 lb (3000 kg) of fuel:** 310 miles (500 km)

### Armament

One GSh-30-2 twin-barrelled 30-mm cannon with 250 rounds; 10 wing pylons to carry a normal weaponload of 2,954 lb (1340 kg), or a maximum weaponload of 9,568 lb (4340 kg)

*As a result of the GSh-30-2 twin-barrelled 30-mm cannon mounted in the starboard side of the front fuselage, the Su-25 features an offset nose gear undercarriage. A mudguard is incorporated to reduce the risk of debris ingestion during operations from unprepared airstrips.*

# Bombers

# Avro Vulcan B Mk.2

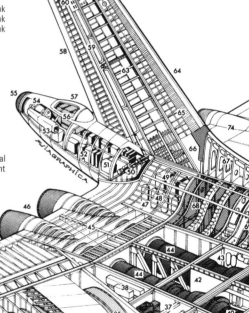

*Between September 1963 and December 1970 the Vulcan B.Mk 2As of the Scampton Wing were equipped with the Avro Blue Steel missile. This used a Bristol Siddeley Stentor rocket motor (consisting of a high-thrust booster and less powerful sustainer) and had a Red Snow thermonuclear warhead. When launched from high altitude in standard mode the Blue Steel had a range of about 115 miles (185 km). In the terminal phase the weapon dived from around 70,000 ft (21336 m) at more than Mach 1.5. After modification for low-level launch, which employed both rocket motors together, range fell dramatically, restricting its use to peripheral targets.*

## Vulcan B.Mk 2

**Cutaway key**
1 Wingtip antennas
2 Starboard navigation light
3 Starboard wingtip construction
4 Outboard aileron
5 Inboard aileron
6 Rear spar
7 Outboard wing panel ribs
8 Front spar
9 Leading-edge ribs
10 Cranked leading edge
11 Corrugated leading-edge inner skin
12 Retractable landing and taxiing lamp
13 Fuel tank fire extinguisher bottles
14 Outer wing panel joint rib
15 Honeycomb skin panel
16 Outboard elevator
17 Inboard elevator
18 Elevator hydraulic jacks
19 No. 7 starboard fuel tank
20 No. 5 starboard fuel tank
21 Diagonal rib
22 Leading-edge de-icing air duct

25 No. 6 starboard fuel tank
26 No. 4 starboard fuel tank
27 No. 3 starboard fuel tank
28 Main undercarriage leg
29 Eight-wheel bogie
30 Mainwheel well door
31 Fuel tank fire extinguishers
32 Inboard leading-edge construction
33 De-icing air supply pipe
34 Fuel collectors and pumps
35 Main undercarriage wheel bay
36 Retracting mechanism
37 Airborne auxiliary power plant (AAPP)
38 Electrical equipment bay
39 Starboard engine bays
40 Rolls-Royce (Bristol Siddeley Olympus 301)
41 Air system piping
42 Engine bay dividing rib
43 Fire extinguishers
44 Jetpipes
45 Fixed trailing-edge construction

49 Batteries
50 Rudder power control unit
51 Rear electronics bay
52 Electronic countermeasures system equipment
53 Cooling air intake
54 Tail warning radar scanner
55 Tail radome
56 Twin brake parachute housing
57 Brake parachute door
58 Rudder construction
59 Rudder balance weights and seals
60 Fin de-icing air outlet
61 Dielectric fin-tip fairing
62 Passive electronic countermeasures (ECM) antennas
63 Fin construction
64 Fin leading edge
65 Corrugated inner skin
66 Communications aerial
67 Fin de-icing air supply
68 Bomb bay rear bulkhead

71 Communications aerial
72 Port Olympus 301 engines
73 Engine bay top panel construction
74 Port jet pipe fairing
75 Electrical equipment bay
76 Chaff dispenser
77 'Green Satin' navigational radar bay
78 Elevator balance weights and seals
79 Elevator hydraulic jacks
80 Inboard elevator
81 Outboard elevator
82 Inboard aileron
83 Aileron balance weights
84 Control rods
85 Aileron power control jacks
86 Jack fairings
87 Outboard aileron
88 Port wingtip antennas
89 Retractable landing and taxiing lamp

92 Cambered leading-edge profile
93 No. 7 port fuel tank
94 No. 5 port fuel tank
95 Leading-edge de-icing air duct
96 No. 6 port fuel tank
97 No. 4 port fuel tank
98 No. 3 port fuel tank
99 Port main undercarriage bay
100 Wing stringer construction
101 Port airbrakes
102 Airbrake drive mechanism
103 Intake ducts
104 Front wing spar attachment joints
105 Centre-section front spar frame
106 Suppressed aerial
107 Anti-collision light
108 Bomb bay longerons
109 Forward limit of bomb bay

23 Wing stringer construction
24 Parallel chord wing skin panels

46 Jetpipe nozzles
47 Rear equipment bay
48 Oxygen bottles

69 Bomb bay roof arch construction
70 Flush air intake

90 Cranked leading edge
91 Fuel tank fire extinguishers

110 Starboard airbrake housings
111 Boundary layer bleed air duct

112 Starboard intake ducts
113 No. 2 fuselage fuel tanks
114 Communications aerials

115 Port engine intake
116 No. 1 fuselage fuel tanks
117 Fuselage frame and stringer construction

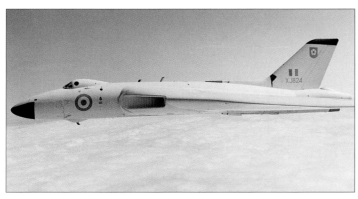

**Vulcan B.Mk 2**

### Dimensions

**Wingspan:** 111 ft (33.83 m)
**Length:** 100 ft 1 in (30.50 m)
**Height:** 27 ft 2 in (8.29 m)
**Wing area:** 3,964 sq ft (368.3 m²)

### Powerplant

Four Rolls-Royce (Bristol) B.O.16 Olympus Mk 201 turbojets, each rated at 17,000-lb (75.66-kN) thrust, or B.O.121 Olympus Mk 301 turbojets, each rated at 20,000-lb (89-kN) thrust

### Weights

**Maximum take-off:** about 250,000 lb (113400 kg)

### Performance

**Maximum speed:** 645 mph (1038 km/h)
**Normal cruise:** Mach 0.84
**Service ceiling:** 65,000 ft (19812 m)
**Take-off run:** 3,500 ft (1067 m) fully loaded with Mk 301 engines
**Time to 40,000 ft (12192 m):** 9 minutes

**Range:** 3,450 miles (5550 km) at low level; 4,600 miles (7400 km) at high altitude with bombload

### Armament

**Conventional** – capability in all variants for 21 1,000-lb (454-kg) bombs carried internally in three clips of seven
**B.Mk 1/1A nuclear** – initially one 11,000-lb (4990-kg) Blue Danube strategic freefall weapon, followed by 9,000-lb (4082-kg) Violet Club. These were replaced by 6,000-lb (2722-kg) US-owned Mk 5 (Waddington Wing aircraft only 1958-62), 7,000-lb (3175-kg) Yellow Sun Mk 1 (1960-63) and by 7,250-lb (3289-kg) Yellow Sun Mk 2 (1962-66);. 2,000-lb (907-kg) Red Beard tactical nuclear bomb also available
**B.Mk 2 nuclear** – initially one Yellow Sun Mk 1/2, but from 1962-1970 aircraft so-modified (B.Mk 2A) could carry one Avro W.105 Blue Steel stand-off missile. From 1966 to 1982 multiple carriage of the 950-lb (431-kg) WE 177B strategic laydown weapon was the principal armament

*The 'schoolhouse' for the Vulcan fleet was No. 230 Operational Conversion Unit, which became the first service operator of both the B.Mk 1 and B.Mk 2 (Illustrated). Initially based at Waddington, the OCU moved to Finningley in 1961, its aircraft acquiring the white rose of Yorkshire on the fin to signify their new base. In 1969 the OCU relocated to Scampton, from where it flew until August 1981. In addition to its Vulcans, between 1974 and 1977 the OCU also parented '1066 Flight', which was equipped with Hastings T.Mk 5 transports, modified with H₂S Mk 9 radar, to train Vulcan navigators.*

118 Intake lip construction
119 Corrugated inner skin
120 Intake divider
121 Starboard intake
122 Boundary layer splitter plate
123 Nose section joint frame
124 Rear pressure bulkhead
125 Nosewheel doors
126 Nosewheel leg
127 Steering jack
128 Twin nosewheels
129 Radio and electronics equipment bay
130 Rearward facing crew members' stations: tactical navigator, radar operator and air electronics operator
131 Cabin side window
132 Chart table
133 Assisted exit seats
134 Jettisonable cockpit canopy
135 Pilot's ejection seat
136 Windscreen panels
142 Ladder
143 Pitot tube
144 Ventral bomb aiming blister fairing (not used on B.Mk 2 aircraft)
145 Destructor
146 Refuelling supply pipe
147 Cockpit pressure dome
148 Radar mounting
149 H₂S radar unit
150 Rotating radar scanner, 80-in (2.03-m) diameter

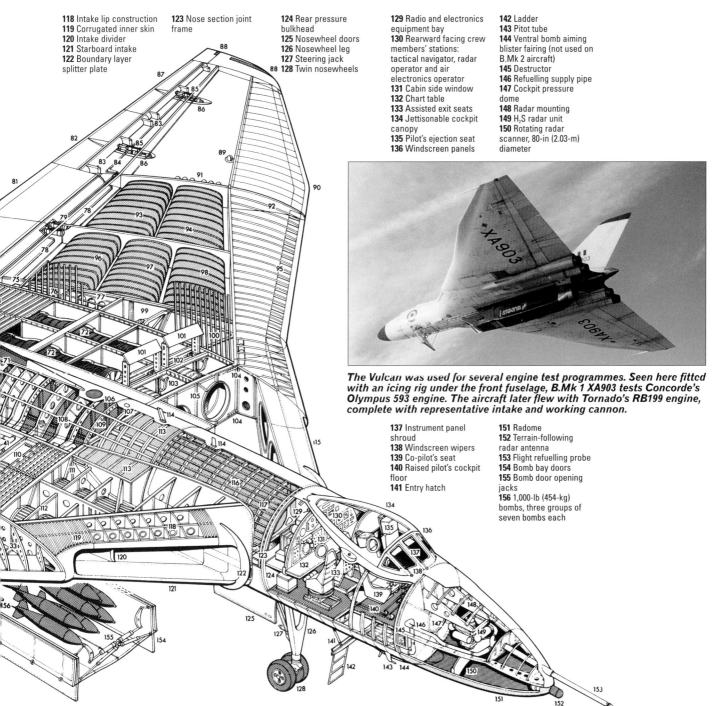

*The Vulcan was used for several engine test programmes. Seen here fitted with an icing rig under the front fuselage, B.Mk 1 XA903 tests Concorde's Olympus 593 engine. The aircraft later flew with Tornado's RB199 engine, complete with representative intake and working cannon.*

137 Instrument panel shroud
138 Windscreen wipers
139 Co-pilot's seat
140 Raised pilot's cockpit floor
141 Entry hatch
151 Radome
152 Terrain-following radar antenna
153 Flight refuelling probe
154 Bomb bay doors
155 Bomb door opening jacks
156 1,000-lb (454-kg) bombs, three groups of seven bombs each

# Blackburn Buccaneer

Front-line service for the Buccaneer ended on 31 March 199_ when Tornados took over the anti-ship role. Many 'Buc_ veterans lamented the aircraft's passing, considering it to b_ a better tool in this role than its replacement. Shortly befor_ withdrawal, a new camouflage scheme was devised for th_ Buccaneer, comprising an overall light/medium- grey pain_ together with pink/light- blue national insignia and whi_ serials. It is widely believed that this scheme had more to d_ with the ongoing 'fashion' for grey paint schemes than wit_ any real operational valu_

## Buccaneer S.Mk 2B

### Cutaway drawing

1 Inflight-refuelling probe
2 Radar scanner
3 Multi-mode search and fire control radar
4 Weapon recorder
5 Radome (folded)
6 Radome hinge
7 Weapon-release computer
8 Windscreen rain dispersal duct
9 Windscreen wiper
10 Birdproof windscreen
11 Pilot's head-up display
12 Instrument panel shroud
13 Rudder pedals
14 Nosewheel leg hinge point
15 Landing and taxi lamp
16 Shock absorber strut
17 Nosewheel forks
18 Aft-retracting nosewheel
19 Avionics equipment
20 Engine throttles
21 Canopy side rail
22 Pilot's ejection seat
23 Seat firing handle
24 Aft-sliding canopy
25 Navigator's blast shield

26 Navigator's instrument display
27 Starboard engine air intake
28 Navigator's ejection seat
29 Cockpit floor structure
30 Head-up display symbol generator
31 Port engine air intake
32 Anti-icing air line
33 Air intake duct
34 Cockpit aft pressure bulkhead
35 Forward main fuselage fuel tank
36 Canopy motor
37 Canopy top rail
38 Rolls-Royce RB.168-1A Spey Mk 101 turbofan
39 Bleed air ducting
40 Detachable bottom cowling
41 Engine front mounting
42 Firewall frame
43 Engine aft mounting
44 Forward fuselage structure
45 Bleed air crossover duct
46 Canopy hand-winding shuttle
47 Detachable engine top cowling
48 Starboard slipper tank

49 Datalink acquisition pod
50 Datalink inboard pylon
51 Martel air-to-surface missile
52 Wing-fold hinge line
53 Leading-edge blowing air duct
54 UHF antenna
55 Dorsal spine structure
56 Anti-collision light
57 Wing-fold actuator
58 Wing-fold operating link
59 Starboard outer pylon
60 ARI 18218 aerial housing
61 Blown leading edge
62 Starboard navigation light
63 Formation light
64 Starboard blown aileron
65 Aileron actuator
66 Starboard wingtip (folded)
67 Aileron and flap blowing ducts
68 Starboard blown flap

69 Port wingtip (folded)
70 Centre fuselage fuel tank
71 Machined spar ring frames
72 Ring frame bolted attachment
73 Aft fuselage fuel tank
74 Electrical cable ducting in dorsal spine
75 Avionics equipment bay
76 Air data computer
77 HF notch aerial
78 Equipment bay cooling air intake
79 Fin spar attachment

80 Fin structure
81 Tailplane actuator
82 Tailplane operating rod
83 Tailplane blowing air duct
84 Bullet fairing
85 Forward passive warning system antenna
86 Blown tailplane leading edge
87 All-moving tailplane structure
88 Tailplane flap
89 Tailplane flap actuator
90 Hinge attachment point

91 Top fairing
92 Rear navigation light
93 Formation light
94 Aft passive warning system antenna
95 Port tailplane flap
96 Rudder structure
97 Rudder operating link

98 Rudder actuator
99 Airbrake jack
100 Drag-link hinge attachment
101 Airbrake operating slide
102 Split tailcone airbrake

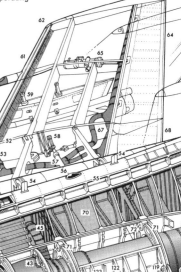

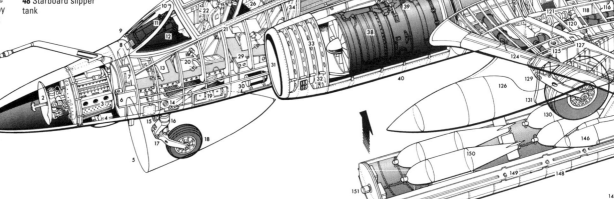

## SPECIFICATION

### Buccaneer S.Mk 2

#### Dimensions

**Length:** 63 ft 5 in (19.33 m)
**Height:** 16 ft 3 in (4.95 m)
**Wingspan:** 44 ft (13.41 m)
**Wing area:** 514.7 sq ft (47.82 m²)

#### Powerplant

Two Rolls-Royce RB.168-1A Spey Mk 101 turbofans each rated at 11,030-lb (49.08-kN) thrust plus (S.Mk 50 only) two Bristol-Siddeley/Rolls-Royce BS.605 rocket engines each rated at 8,000-lb (36-kN) thrust for 30 seconds

#### Weights

**Typical landing:** 35,000 lb (15876 kg)
**Normal take-off:** 46,000-56,000 lb (20866-25402 kg)
**Maximum take-off:** 62,000 lb (28132 lb)

#### Performance

**Maximum speed at sea level:** 691 mph (1112 km/h) or Mach 0.91
**Attack speed at sea level:** 621 mph (1000 km/h)
**Maximum strike range with external fuel load and normal weapons load:** 2,300 miles (3701 km)
**Combat radius with full warload, hi-lo-hi:** 600 miles (966 km)
**Take-off distance at maximum take-off weight:** 3,400 ft (1036 m)
**Landing run:** 3,150 ft (960 m)

#### Armament

(Buccaneer S.Mk 2B for maritime strike) four Martel ASMs (later Sea Eagle ASMs) or up to 16 1,000-lb (454-kg) bombs or (Buccaneer S.Mk 50) four AS30 ASMs or four 68-mm rocket pods, plus internal ordnance

*One of No. 801 Squadron's Buccaneers is seen on the flight deck of HMS Ark Royal during the type's first carrier cruise. This was the work-up prior to the squadron embarking in HMS Victorious. No. 801 Squadron, formed from a nucleus of crews from No. 700Z Sqn, formally commissioned on the Buccaneer in July 1962. Clearly illustrated are the aircraft's folding wings and open speed brake which allowed it to utilise the smaller deck lifts of the British aircraft-carriers.*

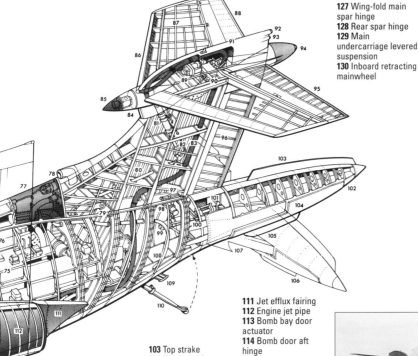

127 Wing-fold main spar hinge
128 Rear spar hinge
129 Main undercarriage levered suspension
130 Inboard retracting mainwheel

131 Mainwheel door
132 Outboard pylon fitting
133 Aileron operating rod
134 Port aileron actuator
135 Outer wing structure
136 Machined skin panels
137 Port wingtip
138 Formation light
139 Crash trip switches
140 Wing lifting lug

141 Port navigation light
142 Blown outboard leading edge
143 Pitot head
144 Port ARI 18218 aerial housing
145 Outboard pylon
146 Port Martel air-to-surface missile
147 36-tube rocket pod
148 Rotary bomb-bay door
149 Bomb door locks
150 1,000-lb (454-kg) bomb

151 Forward hinge point
152 425-Imp gal (1932-litre) bomb door auxiliary tank

103 Top strake
104 Honeycomb reinforcing panel
105 Bottom strake
106 Airbrake (open)
107 Hinge arm
108 Aft fuselage structure
109 Vent pipe
110 Arrester hook

111 Jet efflux fairing
112 Engine jet pipe
113 Bomb bay door actuator
114 Bomb door aft hinge
115 Port blown flap structure
116 Flap actuator
117 Port blown aileron
118 Blowing air duct
119 Wing spar bolted attachment
120 Wing-fold actuator
121 Top of main undercarriage leg
122 Mainwheel well
123 Main undercarriage jack
124 Inboard-blown leading edge
125 Inboard pylon fitting
126 430-Imp gal (1956-litre) slipper tank

*Although most of the 193 British and 16 South African Buccaneers have now been scrapped, finding their way to yards at Elgin, Macclesfield and elsewhere, a few have been kept for display purposes. The first such Buccaneer (an S.Mk 1) went to the FAA Museum at RNAS Yeovilton, where it joined an NA.39. Having formerly flown with both Nos 801 and 809 NAS, it is displayed here in an early gloss finish of Extra Dark Sea Grey and white.*

# Boeing B-47 Stratojet

The 171st example of the B-47E to be manufactured by Lockheed under the Brickbat scheme, No. 23363 features the standard Stratojet finish, being predominantly natural metal with white anti-flash areas on the undersides. Rather unusually, no tail gun armament is carried by this aircraft.

### B-47E-II Stratojet

**Cutaway key**
1 Inflight-refuelling receptacle, open
2 Bomb sight periscope aperture
3 Navigator's instrument panel
4 Bomb sight periscope
5 K-bombing system radar equipment
6 Nose compartment floor level
7 Ventral ejection hatch
8 Navigator/bombardier's downward ejection seat
9 Nose compartment ditching hatch
10 Drift indicator
11 Radio and electronics equipment racks
12 Radar scanner
13 Ventral radome
14 K4A navigation and bombing radar equipment
15 Pressurised crew compartment inner skin
16 Internal walkway
17 Flight deck floor level
18 Rudder pedals
19 Control column
20 Instrument panel shroud
21 Windscreen wiper
22 Windscreen panels
23 Jettisonable cockpit canopy cover
24 Cockpit sunblinds
25 Starboard side console panels
26 Pilot's ejection seat
27 Co-pilot's instrument panel
28 Sextant aperture
29 Aerial mast
30 Co-pilot's ejection seat
31 Tail gunsight and firing controls
32 Oxygen bottles
33 Swivelling seat mounting
34 Pressurised section internal entry door
35 Forward auxiliary fuel tank

36 Maintenance access hatch
37 Crew entry hatch
38 Retractable boarding ladder
39 Cockpit air-conditioning plant
40 Forward main undercarriage hydraulic retraction jack
41 Nose compartment rear bulkhead
42 Forward mainwheel doors
43 Steerable twin wheel forward landing gear
44 Multi-plate disc brakes
45 Steering control unit
46 Main undercarriage leg pivot fixing
47 Bomb bay anti-buffet deflector door, open
48 Bomb door hydraulic jack
49 Hydraulic reservoir
50 Hydraulic equipment bay
51 Forward main fuel cell; total internal capacity 14,610 US gal (55305 litres)
52 Wing spar attachment bulkhead
53 Spar/fuselage attachment joint
54 Wing panel root attachment bolted joint
55 Centre-section fuel tank
56 Wing centre-section carry through
57 Dorsal control and cable ducting
58 Starboard wing panel root joint

59 Starboard fuel injection water/alcohol tanks, total capacity 600 US gal (2271 litres)
60 Fuel and air system piping
61 Starboard outrigger wheel

62 Inboard twin-engine nacelle
63 Detachable engine cowlings
64 Nacelle pylon
65 Inboard engine oil tanks, capacity 9.4 US gal (35.6 litres) each
66 Oil filler caps
67 Fuel piping to external tank
68 Starboard external fuel tank, capacity 1,780 US gal (6738 litres)

69 Fuel tank pylon
70 Outboard engine fuel and air system ducting
71 Vortex generators
72 Outboard engine nacelle
73 Outboard engine oil tank, capacity 9.4 US gal (35.6 litres)
74 Starboard navigation light
75 Wingtip fairing
76 Outboard aileron segment
77 Aileron hydraulic actuators
78 Nacelle tail fairing
79 Inboard aileron segment
80 Aileron tab
81 Outboard Fowler-type flap segment, down position
82 Inboard Fowler-type flap segment, down position

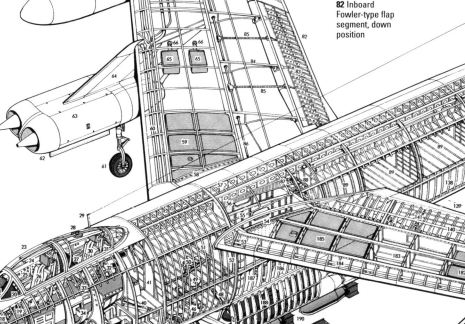

### B-47E-II Stratojet

**Dimensions**

**Length:** 109 ft 10 in (33.48 m)
**Wingspan:** 116 ft (35.36 m)
**Height:** 27 ft 11 in (8.51 m)
**Wing area:** 1,428 sq ft (132.66 m²)
**Aspect ratio:** 11

**Powerplant**

Six General Electric J47-GE-25 or 25A turbojets, each developing 7,200 lb (32 kN) of thrust with water injection

**Weights**

**Empty:** 80,756 lb (36630 kg)
**Maximum take-off with RATO pods:** 198,180 lb (89893 kg)

**Performance**

**Maximum speed at 16,300 ft (4970 m):** 606 mph (975 km/h)
**Cruising speed:** 557 mph (896 km/h)
**Service ceiling:** 40,500 ft (12345 m)
**Range:** 4,000 miles (6437 km)
**Climb:** 2,430 ft (740 m) per minute with normal power, 4,660 ft (1420 m) per minute with water injection

**Armament**

Two 20-mm cannon (though the B model carried twin 0.50-in/12.7-mm guns) with 350 rounds in a remotely-controlled tail turret, plus up to 20,000 lb (9072 kg) of conventional or nuclear bombs such as the Mk 5, 6, 15, 18, 28, 36, 42, 53 and B 43 carried internally

*One of the most radically modified B-47s was aircraft 53-4296, an RB-47H which was given an extended lease of life when it was used for F-111 radar tests and fitted with an F-111 nose. The B-47 had a close association with the F-111, most notably when the Royal Australian Air Force was offered the loan of two squadrons of B/RB-47s, pending the delivery of its Aardvarks.*

83 Flap rib construction
84 Flap guide rails
85 Screw jacks
86 Screw jack drive shaft
87 Central flap drive hydraulic motor
88 Aileron control linkages
89 Centre main fuel tanks
90 Close-pitched fuselage frame construction
95 Equipment air-conditioning plant
96 Finroot fillet
97 Air intake to de-icer heater
98 Tailplane de-icing air ducting
99 Fin/tailplane attachment mainframe
100 Tailplane spar root joint
101 Starboard tailplane
102 HF aerial cable

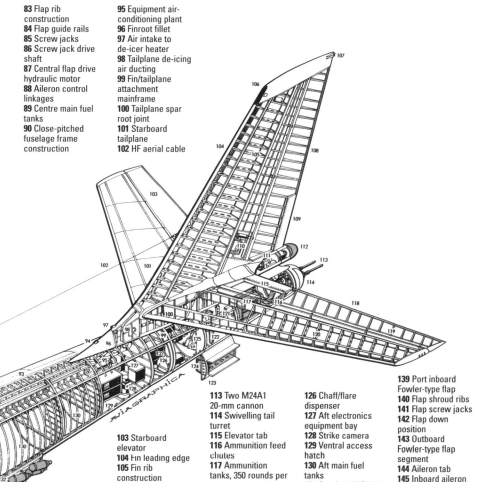

91 Fuel and air system pipe ducting
92 Dorsal maintenance walkway
93 Maintenance access hatches
94 Electronics cooling air intake
103 Starboard elevator
104 Fin leading edge
105 Fin rib construction
106 Fintip aerial fairing
107 Tail navigation and position lights
108 Rudder rib construction
109 Rudder tab
110 Rudder hydraulic actuator
111 Tailgun radar equipment
112 Gun direction radome
113 Two M24A1 20-mm cannon
114 Swivelling tail turret
115 Elevator tab
116 Ammunition feed chutes
117 Ammunition tanks, 350 rounds per gun
118 Port elevator
119 Elevator rib construction
120 Port tailplane construction
121 Elevator control linkage
122 Approach/drogue parachute stowage
123 Ammunition loading door, open
124 Brake parachute housing
125 Rudder control linkages
126 Chaff/flare dispenser
127 Aft electronics equipment bay
128 Strike camera
129 Ventral access hatch
130 Aft main fuel tanks
131 Aerojet 14AS1000 assisted take-off (ATO) bottles (33)
132 ATO bottle jettisonable mounting cradle
133 Aft main undercarriage leg pivot fixing
134 Twin wheel truck
135 Hydraulic retraction jack
136 Wheel bay
137 Aft mainwheel doors
138 Bomb bay fuel tank
139 Port inboard Fowler-type flap
140 Flap shroud ribs
141 Flap screw jacks
142 Flap down position
143 Outboard Fowler-type flap segment
144 Aileron tab
145 Inboard aileron segment
146 Outboard engine nacelle tail fairing
147 Aileron hydraulic actuators
148 Outboard aileron segment
149 Aileron rib construction
150 Wingtip fairing
151 Port navigation light
152 Outboard engine oil tank
153 Outboard engine nacelle
154 Intake centre-body/ starter generator housing
155 General Electric J47-GE-25A turbojet engine
156 Engine flame cans
157 Nacelle pylon
158 Outerwing panel rib construction
159 Rear spar
160 Lower wing skin/ stringer panel
161 Front spar
162 External fuel tank side brace
163 Port external fuel tank
164 Fuel tank rib construction
165 Tank pylon
166 Leading-edge hot air de-icing
167 Leading-edge nose ribs
168 Fuel system piping
169 Inner/outer wing skin panel joint rib
170 Nacelle tail fairing
171 Engine exhaust ducting
172 Outrigger wheel leg strut
173 Torque scissor links
174 Port outrigger wheel
175 Outrigger wheel doors
176 Engine nacelle construction
177 Ventral landing/ taxiing lamp
178 Engine air intakes
179 Inboard General Electric J47 engine
180 Nacelle pylon construction
181 Pylon attachment joint
182 Inboard engine oil tanks
183 Inner wing panel rib construction
184 Leading-edge fuel and air system piping
185 Port wing water/ alcohol injection tanks
186 Internal bomb bay
187 Bomb mounting racks
188 Bomb-door rib construction
189 Bomb-door, open
190 1,000-lb (464-kg) HE bombs; maximum bombload 20,000 lb (9072 kg)
191 2,000-lb (907-kg) HE bomb
192 4,000-lb (1814-kg) HE bomb
193 Mk 28 (B-28IN) free-fall 20-megaton nuclear weapon

# Boeing B-52 Stratofortress

*A heavily-laden Boeing B-52G Stratofortress lifts off from RAF Fairford in England, on its way to contribute to the round-the-clock punishment being inflicted on Iraq's Republican Guard during the Gulf War. B-52s flew 1,624 missions, dropping 25,700 tons of bombs (29 per cent of the total tonnage delivered during the war).*

## B-52G Stratofortress

**Cutaway key**
1 Nose radome
2 ALT28 ECM antenna
3 Electronic countermeasures (ECM)
4 Front pressure bulkhead
5 Electronic cooling air intake
6 Bombing radar
7 Low-light television scanner turret (EVS system), infra-red on starboard side
8 Television camera unit
9 ALQ-117 radar warning antenna
10 Underfloor control runs
11 Control column
12 Rudder pedals
13 Windscreen wipers
14 Instrument panel shroud
15 Windscreen panels
16 Cockpit eyebrow windows
17 Cockpit roof escape/ ejection hatches
18 Co-pilot's ejection seat
19 Drogue chute container
20 Pilot's ejection seat
21 Flight deck floor level
22 Navigator's instrument console
23 Ventral escape/ejection hatch, port and starboard
24 Radar navigator's downward ejection seat, navigator to starboard

25 Access ladder and hatch to flight deck
26 EWO instructor's folding seat
27 Electronics equipment rack
28 In-flight refuelling receptacle, open
29 Refuelling delivery line
30 Electronic warfare officer's (EWO) ejection seat
31 Rear crew members' escape/ejection hatches
32 EWO's instrument panel
33 Gunner's remote control
34 Gunner's ejection seat
35 Navigation instructor's folding seat
36 Radio and electronics racks
37 Ventral entry hatch and ladder
38 Lower deck rear pressure bulkhead
39 ECM aerials
40 ECM equipment bay
41 Cooling air ducting
42 Upper deck rear pressure bulkhead
43 Water injection tank capacity 1,200 US gal (4542 litres)
44 Fuselage upper longeron

45 Astro-navigation antenna
46 Tank access hatches
47 Leading edge 'strakelets' fitted to identify cruise missile carriers
48 Forward fuselage fuel tank
49 Air-conditioning plant
50 Forward starboard main undercarriage bogie

51 Landing lamp
52 Forward port main undercarriage bogie
53 Torque scissor links
54 Steering jacks

55 Main undercarriage door
56 Main undercarriage leg strut

57 Wing front spar/fuselage/main undercarriage attachment frame
58 Main undercarriage wheel bay
59 Doppler aerial
60 Central electronic equipment bay
61 Air-conditioning intake duct
62 Front spar attachment joint
63 Wingroot rib
64 Wing panel bolted attachment joint

65 Centre-section fuel tank bay
66 Wing centre-section carry through
67 Starboard wing attachment joint
68 Vortex generators
69 Starboard wing integral fuel tank bays, total fuel system capacity (includes external tanks) 48,030 US gal (181813 litres)
70 Engine ignition control unit
71 Bleed air ducting

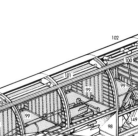

## SPECIFICATION

**B-52H Stratofortress**

### Dimensions

**Length overall:** 160 ft 10⅞ in (49.05 m)
**Wingspan:** 185 ft 9 in (56.39 m)
**Wing area:** 4,000.00 sq ft (371.60 m²)
**Height:** 40 ft 8 in (12.40 m)
**Tailplane span:** 52 ft (15.85 m)
**Tailplane area:** 900 sq ft (83.61 m²)
**Wheel track:** 8 ft 3 in (2.51 m)
**Wheelbase:** 50 ft 3 in (15.48 m)

### Powerplant

Eight Pratt & Whitney TF33-P-3 (JT3D-2) low-bypass turbofans each rated at 17,000 lb st (75.62 kN)

### Weights

**Operating empty:** 138,385 lb (62771 kg)
**Maximum payload:** 51,615 lb (23413 kg)
**Maximum take-off:** 327,000 lb (148325 kg)
**Maximum ramp weight:** 328,000 lb (148780 kg)

### Fuel and load

**Fuel:** 299,434 lb (135821 kg) plus provision for 9,114 lb (4134 kg) in two 700-US gal (2650-litre) non-jettisonable underwing tanks
**Maximum ordnance:** about 50,000 lb (22680 kg)

### Performance

**Maximum speed at high altitude:** 595 mph (957 km/h)
**Cruising speed at high altitude:** 509 mph (819 km/h)
**Penetration speed at low altitude:** between 405 and 420 mph (652 and 676 km/h)
**Range:** more than 10,000 miles (16093 km)
**Service ceiling:** 55,000 ft (16765 m)
**Take-off run:** 9,500 ft (2896 m) at maximum take-off weight

### Armament

In the nuclear role, the B-52H can carry 20 cruise missiles (eight internally on a rotary launcher and six under each wing). These can either be AGM-86B ALCMs or AGM-129 Advanced Cruise Missiles. Free-fall nuclear weapons such as B61 or B83, remain an option, but this capability is at present entrusted mainly to the B-2A Spirit fleet. Conventional weapons include AGM-86C cruise missiles, the AGM-142 Have Nap and AGM-84 Harpoon. Free-fall bombs can be carried on HSABs (heavy stores adaptor beams) or Hound Dog pylons, to a maximum of 51 750-lb (340-kg) class weapons. Alternatives to general-purpose bombs include cluster munitions and mines. The M61A1 Vulcan 20-mm cannon in the tail turret is no longer used

*First delivered to Strategic Air Command (SAC) in June 1955 – to the 93rd Bombardment Wing (Heavy) at Castle AFB, California – B-52s ushered in a new phase in the Cold War. SAC boss General Curtis E. LeMay adopted the procedure of operating the aircraft under wartime conditions in a peacetime era. Across the US, B-52 crews were held on a 15-minute alert, ready to attack the Soviet Union and its allies. Here, the crew of a B-52B serving with the 22nd Bombardment Wing at March AFB, California runs to its aircraft during a simulated alert.*

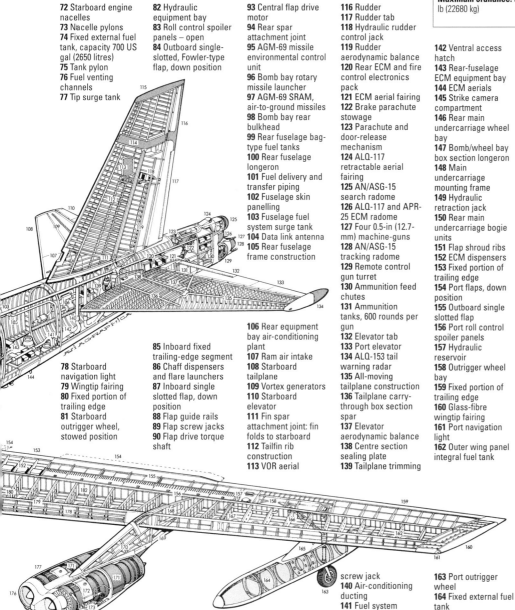

72 Starboard engine nacelles
73 Nacelle pylons
74 Fixed external fuel tank, capacity 700 US gal (2650 litres)
75 Tank pylon
76 Fuel venting channels
77 Tip surge tank
78 Starboard navigation light
79 Wingtip fairing
80 Fixed portion of trailing edge
81 Starboard outrigger wheel, stowed position
82 Hydraulic equipment bay
83 Roll control spoiler panels – open
84 Outboard single-slotted, Fowler-type flap, down position
85 Inboard fixed trailing-edge segment
86 Chaff dispensers and flare launchers
87 Inboard single slotted flap, down position
88 Flap guide rails
89 Flap screw jacks
90 Flap drive torque shaft
91 Life raft stowage
92 Wing centre section/ longeron ties
93 Central flap drive motor
94 Rear spar attachment joint
95 AGM-69 missile environmental control unit
96 Bomb bay rotary missile launcher
97 AGM-69 SRAM, air-to-ground missiles
98 Bomb bay rear bulkhead
99 Rear fuselage bag-type fuel tanks
100 Rear fuselage longeron
101 Fuel delivery and transfer piping
102 Fuselage skin panelling
103 Fuselage fuel system surge tank
104 Data link antenna
105 Rear fuselage frame construction
106 Rear equipment bay air-conditioning plant
107 Ram air intake
108 Starboard tailplane
109 Vortex generators
110 Starboard elevator
111 Fin spar attachment joint: fin folds to starboard
112 Tailfin rib construction
113 VOR aerial
114 Lightning isolator
115 Fintip aerial fairing
116 Rudder
117 Rudder tab
118 Hydraulic rudder control jack
119 Rudder aerodynamic balance
120 Rear ECM and fire control electronics pack
121 ECM aerial fairing
122 Brake parachute stowage
123 Parachute and door-release mechanism
124 ALQ-117 retractable aerial fairing
125 AN/ASG-15 search radome
126 ALQ-117 and APR-25 ECM radome
127 Four 0.5-in (12.7-mm) machine-guns
128 AN/ASG-15 tracking radome
129 Remote control gun turret
130 Ammunition feed chutes
131 Ammunition tanks, 600 rounds per gun
132 Elevator tab
133 Port elevator
134 ALQ-153 tail warning radar
135 All-moving tailplane construction
136 Tailplane carry-through box section spar
137 Elevator aerodynamic balance
138 Centre section sealing plate
139 Tailplane trimming screw jack
140 Air-conditioning ducting
141 Fuel system venting pipes
142 Ventral access hatch
143 Rear-fuselage ECM equipment bay
144 ECM aerials
145 Strike camera compartment
146 Rear main undercarriage wheel bay
147 Bomb/wheel bay box section longeron
148 Main undercarriage mounting frame
149 Hydraulic retraction jack
150 Rear main undercarriage bogie units
151 Flap shroud ribs
152 ECM dispensers
153 Fixed portion of trailing edge
154 Port flaps, down position
155 Outboard single slotted flap
156 Port roll control spoiler panels
157 Hydraulic reservoir
158 Outrigger wheel bay
159 Fixed portion of trailing edge
160 Glass-fibre wingtip fairing
161 Port navigation light
162 Outer wing panel integral fuel tank
163 Port outrigger wheel
164 Fixed external fuel tank
165 Fuel tank pylon
166 Outrigger wheel retraction strut
167 Outer wing panel attachment joint
168 Engine pylon mounting rib
169 Pylon rear attachment strut
170 Engine pylon construction
171 Pratt & Whitney J57-P-43WB turbojet engine
172 Engine oil tank, capacity 8.5 US gal (32 litres)
173 Accessory equipment gearbox
174 Generator cooling air duct
175 Oil cooler ram air Intakes
176 Engine air intakes
177 Detachable cowling panels
178 Leading-edge rib construction
179 Front spar
180 Wingrib construction
181 Rear spar
182 Port wing integral fuel tank bays
183 Inboard pylon mounting rib
184 Leading-edge bleed air and engine control runs
185 Weapons bay doors, open (loading) position
186 Bomb doors, open
187 Wing-mounted cruise missile pylon
188 Boeing AGM-86B Air-Launched Cruise Missiles (ALCMs), six per wing pylon, stowed configuration
189 AGM-86B missile in flight configuration
190 Retractable engine air intake
191 Folding wings
192 AGM-69 SRAM, alternative load
193 Missile adaptors
194 Nacelle pylon
195 Port inboard engine nacelles
196 Central engine mounting bulkhead/ firewall
197 Bleed air ducting
198 Generator cooling air ducting
199 Fuselage bomb-mounting cradle
200 Free-fall 25-megaton nuclear weapons (four)

# Convair B-36 Peacemaker

*In its B-36A form (illustrated), the Peacemaker was far from being an operational bomber, since it lacked a full armament fit and many other key systems were either not installed or were non-operational. BM-004 was the first production B-36A and, like many early B-36s, carried the large 'buzz number' on its forward fuselage to aid civilians when calling the USAF to complain about low flying.*

## B-36J

**Cutaway key**
1 Twin 20-mm nose cannon
2 ILS glideslope aerial
3 Nose-sighting station, hemispherical sight
4 Nose compartment glazing
5 Optically-flat sighting panel
6 Navigator's station
7 Nose turret mounting platform
8 Turret-actuating mechanism
9 Ammunition tanks, 400 rounds per gun
10 Windscreen panels
11 Instrument console
12 Rudder pedals
13 Entry hatch from wheel bay
14 Radar bombardier's station
15 K-system radar bombing equipment
16 ECM aerials
17 Radio compass housing
18 Retractable boarding ladder
19 Observer/radar technician's seat
20 Nosewheel doors
21 Marker beacon aerial
22 Pitot head
23 Electrical power distribution panels
24 Flight deck floor level
25 Pilot's seat
26 Centre instrument console
27 Co-pilot's seat
28 Overhead jet engine control panel
29 Cockpit canopy cover
30 Astrodome observation hatch
31 Flight engineer's seats (2)

32 Engineer's control panels
33 Canopy window panels
34 Lower deck radio operator's station
35 Forward cabin escape hatch
36 Nose undercarriage pivot mounting
37 Forward-retracting twin nosewheels
38 K-system radar antenna housing
39 Food locker
40 Access hatch to communications tunnel
41 Forward cabin pressure bulkhead
42 Port sighting station
43 Cabin pressurisation valve
44 Electrical system equipment
45 Starboard sighting station
46 VHF aerial
47 Life raft stowage
48 Retractable, remotely-controlled dorsal gun turrets, two 20-mm cannon
49 Ammunition feed chutes
50 Cannon bay sliding door, open
51 Ammunition magazines, 600 rounds per gun
52 Fire control equipment
53 Communicating tunnel, forward to rear pressurised crew compartments
54 ECM aerials
55 Bomb bay door frame construction
56 Forward bomb bay doors, open
57 Fuselage lower longitudinal beam

58 Communications tunnel railed personnel cart
59 Bomb bay girder frame construction
60 Oxygen bottles
61 Fuselage upper longitudinal beam
62 Interchangeable bomb racks
63 Frame-stiffened fuselage skin panels
64 No. 1 forward bomb bay
65 Fuselage maintenance walkway
66 No. 2 forward bomb bay
67 Starboard side crawlway
68 Transformer rectifier units
69 Fuselage girder frame/wing spar attachment joint
70 Wing panel centre line joint

71 Inboard integral fuel tank, capacity 4,212 US gal (15944 litres)
72 Fuel system piping

73 Centre integral fuel tank
74 Engine oil tanks, capacity 200 US gal (757 litres) each
75 Engine air intake ducting
76 Leading-edge pitot intakes
77 Outboard integral fuel tank, 2,262 US gal (8563 litres)
78 Leading-edge de-icing air supply ducting

79 Outer wing panel joint strap
80 Wing stringers
81 Wing skin panelling
82 Starboard jet engine nacelle

83 Nacelle pylon
84 Leading-edge thermal de-icing
85 Outer wing panel integral jet fuel tank, capacity 1432 US gal (5421 litres)
86 Wingtip fairing
87 Starboard navigation light
88 Starboard aileron
89 Blue formation lights

90 Aileron geared tab
91 Tab operating linkage
92 Aileron aerodynamic seal and balance
93 Aileron control linkage
94 Hydraulic lock
95 Outboard reciprocating engine nacelle
96 Curtiss-Wright three-bladed variable-pitch propellers, 19-ft (5.79-m) diameter
97 Propeller spinners
98 Outboard single-slotted flap segment, lowered

## SPECIFICATION

### B-36J Peacemaker

#### Dimensions

**Length:** 162 ft 1 in (49.40 m)
**Wingspan:** 230 ft (70.10 m)
**Wing area:** 4,772 sq ft (443.32 m²)
**Height:** 46 ft 8 in (14.22 m)

#### Powerplant

Six 3,800-hp (2834-kW) Pratt & Whitney R-4360-53 radial piston engines and four 5,200-lb st (23.12-kN) General Electric J47-GE-19 turbojet engines
**B-36B:** Six 3,500-hp (2610-kW) Pratt & Whitney R-4360-41 radial piston engines
**B-36D:** Six 3,500-hp (2610-kW) Pratt & Whitney R-4360-41 radial piston engines and four 5,200 lb st (23.12-kN) General Electric J47-GE-19 turbojet engines

#### Weights

**Empty:** 171,035 lb (77580 kg)
**Maximum take-off:** 410,000 lb (185973 kg)
**Empty, B-36B:** 140,640 lb (63794 kg)
**Maximum take-off, B-36B:** 328,000 lb (148780 kg)
**Empty, B-36D:** 158,843 lb (72051 kg)
**Maximum take-off, B-36D:** 357,500 lb (162162 kg)

#### Load

**Maximum ordnance:** 86,000 lb (39010 kg) with weight restrictions or normally up to 72,000 lb (32659 kg)

#### Performance

**Maximum speed at 36,400 ft (11095 m):** 411 mph (661 km/h)
**Cruising speed:** 391 mph (629 km/h)
**Maximum rate of climb:** 1,920 ft (585 m) per minute
**Service ceiling:** 39,900 ft (12160 m)
**Maximum speed at 34,500 ft (10516 m), B-36B:** 381 mph (613 km/h)
**Cruising speed, B-36B:** 202 mph (325 km/h)
**Maximum rate of climb, B-36B:** 1,510 ft (460 m) per minute
**Service ceiling, B-36B:** 42,500 ft (12954 m)
**Maximum speed at 32,120 ft (9790 m), B-36D:** 439 mph (706 km/h)
**Cruising speed, B-36D:** 225 mph (362 km/h)
**Maximum rate of climb, B-36D:** 1,740 ft (530 m) per minute
**Service ceiling, B-36D:** 45,200 ft (13777 m)

#### Range

**With 10,000-lb (4536-kg) bombload:** 6,800 miles (4536 km)
**B-36B:** 8,175 miles (13156 km)
**B-36D:** 7,500 miles (12070 km)

#### Armament

Six retractable and remotely-controlled fuselage turrets, each with twin 20-mm M24A1 cannon and similar weapons in nose and tail turrets. Maximum ammunition load 9,200 rounds. A wide range of conventional and primarily nuclear bombs could be carried

*At the end of World War II, the USAAF closed seven gunnery schools and discharged almost all of its gunners. The few that remained were mostly B-29 crew, but there were insufficient numbers of them to man the guns of the few B-29s involved in the Korean War. Inevitably, when the B-36, with its demand for six gunners per aircraft, entered service this deficit was even more keenly felt and several months had passed before every B-36 could fly with a fully-competent gunnery crew.*

**99** Flap screw jacks
**100** Centre engine nacelle
**101** Flap drive motor and torque shaft
**102** Centre single-slotted flap segment, lowered
**103** Inboard engine nacelle
**104** Detachable engine cowling panels
**105** Induction air ducting
**106** Intercooler, two per engine
**107** Intercooler exhaust
**108** Exhaust primary heat exchanger, heating and pressurising air supply
**109** Exhaust driven turbochargers, two per engine
**110** Ventral oil cooler
**111** Turbocharger and oil cooler combined ventral intake
**112** Cabin heating and pressurising air supply duct
**113** Inboard single-slotted flap
**114** Starboard main undercarriage wheel bay
**115** Electrical power distribution panel
**116** Two bomb bay long-range fuel tanks (rear tank only shown), capacity 3,000 US gal (11356 litres) each
**117** Fuselage formation lights (blue)
**118** No. 3 aft bomb bay
**119** Electrical system equipment
**120** Upper navigation light (white)
**121** Interchangeable bomb racks
**122** Rear fuselage walkway
**123** No. 4 aft bomb bay
**124** Oxygen bottles
**125** Life raft stowage
**126** Cannon fire control equipment
**127** Ammunition tanks, 600 rounds per gun
**128** Retractable, remotely-controlled, dorsal gun turrets, two 20-mm cannon
**129** Hinged turret swivel mounting
**130** Turret retraction strut
**131** Aft crew compartment pressure bulkhead
**132** Crew rest bunks
**133** D/F loop aerial
**134** Galley units
**135** Tailplane de-icing air supply duct
**136** Port dorsal sighting station
**137** Starboard dorsal sighting station
**138** Fin root fillet construction
**139** ADF sense aerial
**140** Starboard tailplane
**141** Starboard elevator
**142** Elevator tabs
**143** HF aerial cables
**144** Fin leading-edge thermal de-icing
**145** Tail fin rib construction
**146** VOR aerial
**147** Sternpost
**148** Fintip VHF aerial
**149** Rudder tip LORAN aerial
**150** Rudder construction
**151** Upper trim tab
**152** Lower geared tab
**153** Tail gun radar scanner
**154** Remotely controlled tail gun turret, two 20-mm cannon
**155** Ammunition tanks, 600 rounds per gun
**156** Rudder hinge control
**157** Tail radar modular unit
**158** Elevator hinge control
**159** Tail navigation lights
**160** Elevator geared tab
**161** Tab control torque shaft
**162** Elevator rib construction
**163** Outboard trim tab
**164** Tailplane tip fairing construction
**165** Leading-edge thermal de-icing
**166** Tailplane rib construction
**167** Fin/tailplane attachment main frames
**168** Tailcone frame and stringer construction
**169** Fin leading-edge attachment main frame
**170** Rear pressure bulkhead
**171** Water tank
**172** Upper gunner's sighting platform
**173** Toilet
**174** Ventral entry hatch
**175** Boarding ladder, stowed
**176** Lateral/ventral sighting station, port and starboard
**177** Lateral gunner's seat
**178** Ventral strike camera
**179** Communications tunnel aft section
**180** Two ventral retractable gun turrets, two 20-mm cannon
**181** Rear bomb bay doors, open
**182** Inboard single-slotted flap segment
**183** Flap rib construction
**184** Port main undercarriage wheel bay
**185** Inboard reciprocating engine nacelle
**186** Engine-driven alternator
**187** Engine accessory equipment gearbox
**188** Pratt & Whitney R-4360-53 28-cylinder, four-row radial engine
**189** Exhaust cooling air outlet ducts
**190** Propeller spinner
**191** Curtiss-Wright three-bladed propellers
**192** Centre single-slotted flap segment
**193** Trailing-edge rib construction
**194** Centre engine nacelle
**195** Induction air ducting
**196** Water tank
**197** Centre Pratt & Whitney R-4360-53 engine
**198** Propeller hub pitch change mechanism
**199** Outboard single-slotted flap segment
**200** Flap shroud ribs
**201** Outboard engine nacelle
**202** Engine-driven cooling air fan
**203** Engine bearer struts
**204** Fireproof bulkhead
**205** Engine bay cooling air variable outlet plug
**206** Port aileron
**207** Aileron geared tab
**208** Aileron rib construction
**209** Wingtip fairing construction
**210** Port navigation light
**211** Port jet engine integral fuel tank
**212** Leading-edge double skin panelling
**213** Leading-edge nose ribs
**214** Nacelle pylon construction
**215** Exhaust tail fairing
**216** General Electric J47-GE-19 engines
**217** Intake fairing
**218** Detachable engine cowling panels
**219** Leading-edge de-icing air ducting
**220** Outer wing panel rib construction
**221** Rear spar
**222** Aileron shroud ribs
**223** Outer wing panel joint strap
**224** Reciprocating engine air ducting
**225** Engine cooling and induction air upper pitot intake
**226** Oil cooler and turbocharger lower pitot intake
**227** Port wing integral fuel tank bays
**228** Engine oil tank bays
**229** Front spar
**230** Inward-retracting four-wheel main undercarriage bogie
**231** Main undercarriage leg
**232** Mainwheel leg pivot mounting
**233** Hydraulic retraction jack
**234** Inboard fuel tank bay
**235** Inboard wing panel rib construction
**236** Leading-edge ribs
**237** Central hydraulic equipment bay
**238** Internal bombload, normal 72,000 lb (32660 kg); maximum 86,000 lb (39000 kg) at restricted gross weight
**239** 4,000-lb (1814-kg) HE bombs
**240** 500-lb (227-kg) bombs
**241** Aerial mine
**242** Mine parachute housing
**243** 43,000-lb (19505-kg) 'special' bomb
**244** Large bomb adaptor racks
**245** 22,000-lb (9980-kg) bombs

# Convair B-58 Hustler

### B-58A Hustler

**Cutaway key**
1 Pitot tube
2 Nose probe
3 AN/ARC-10 long-range communications system antenna
4 Radome
5 Antenna coupler
6 Search radar scanner
7 Radar tracking mechanism
8 Air refuelling ramp door, open
9 Air refuelling receptacle
10 Angle of attack transmitter
11 Radar and nosewheel mounting bulkhead
12 Taxiing lamp
13 Landing lamp
14 Nose undercarriage leg strut
15 ILS glideslope aerial
16 Twin nosewheels
17 Torque scissor links
18 Steering jacks
19 Nose undercarriage hinge links
20 Nosewheel doors
21 Temperature probe
22 Hydraulic retraction jack
23 Secondary pitot tube
24 Search radar modulator unit
25 Liquid oxygen bottles
26 Cockpit front pressure bulkhead
27 Windscreen panels
28 Instrument panel shroud
29 Rudder pedals
30 Cockpit air-conditioning ducting
31 Cockpit pressure floor
32 Engine throttle levers

33 Side console panel
34 Pilot's ejection seat/escape capsule
35 Angle of attack indexer
36 Overhead windows
37 Pilot's escape capsule, deployed configuration
38 Integral control column
39 Folding blast shield
40 Canopy cover/entry hatch
41 Entry hatch, open position
42 Canopy actuator
43 Escape capsule, stowed
44 Ejection seat launch rails
45 Sloping cockpit bulkhead
46 Air data computer
47 Radio and electronics equipment racks
48 Modular navigation instrumentation unit
49 UHF command antenna
50 Navigation unit access/removal hatch
51 Starboard inner engine nacelle
52 Navigator's entry/escape hatch
53 Air-conditioning ducting
54 Hatch actuator

55 Navigator's ejection seat/escape capsule
56 Window panel
57 Side console panel
58 Defence equipment control module, DECM
59 TACAN aerial
60 Defensive systems operator's entry hatch
61 Side window panel
62 Defensive systems operator's ejection seat/escape capsule

63 Cockpit rear pressure bulkhead
64 Ventral air-conditioning pack
65 Fuel vent
66 Forward fuselage fuel tank/reservoir tank; total internal fuel capacity 10,924 US gal (41352 litres)
67 Main fuselage longeron
68 Air system water separators
69 Fuel tank bulkhead
70 Stabilisation amplifier
71 Astrotracker unit
72 Chaff dispenser pneumatic air bottle
73 Starboard main undercarriage, stowed position
74 Hydraulic retraction jack

75 Hydraulic reservoir
76 Fuel feed piping
77 Starboard wing forward main fuel tank
78 Inboard nacelle pylon
79 Main undercarriage wheel well fairing
80 Bleed air system ducting
81 Air/water heat exchanger
82 Water tank
83 Pneumatic starter air ducting to outboard engine
84 Port outboard engine nacelle
85 Engine air intake
86 BLU-2/B-2 fuel pod
87 Fuel and electrical disconnect to upper component pod

*The original Hustler, XB-58 55-660, first flew on 11 November 1956 and accumulated 150 flights (lasting 257 hours and 30 minutes). It was the first B-58 to reach Mach 1 and Mach 2. Nicknamed Old Grandpappy, this aircraft was used for ALBM tests before being scrapped.*

88 Upper component pod housing
89 Pod separation thruster
90 Pod release unit
91 Fuel pod frame construction
92 BLU-2/B-3 combined fuel and weapons pod
93 Forward fuel tank
94 Pod forward latch
95 Electrical disconnect

96 Integral munitions bay
97 Munitions bay access panel
98 Pylon mounting
99 Rear fuel tank
100 Pylon aft latches
101 Pod stabilising fins

102 Outboard nacelle pylon fairing
103 Starboard wing aft main fuel tanks
104 Fuel feed pipe to outer engine

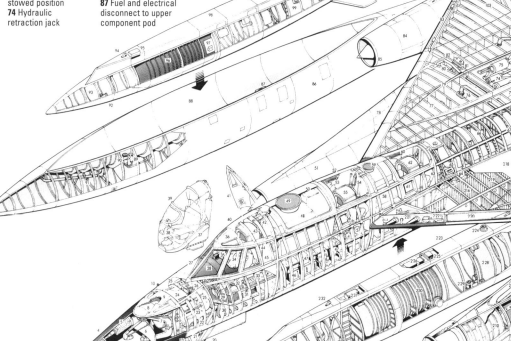

*While the pilot of the B-58 had good visibility, the navigator and defensive systems operator just had two small windows for daylight, making conditions somewhat cramped and claustrophobic.*

## SPECIFICATION

### B-58A Hustler

#### Dimensions

**Overall length:** 96 ft 9 in (29.5 m)
**Wingspan:** 56 ft 9 in (17.3 m)
**Wing aspect ratio:** 2.096
**Wing area:** 1,542 sq ft (143.25 m²)
**Height:** 29 ft 11 in (8.87 m)
**Vertical fin area:** 160 sq ft (48.7 m²)
**Vertical fin height:** 14 ft 6in (4.45 m)

#### Powerplant

Four General Electric J79-GE-5A turbojets, each rated at 15,600 lb (69.3 kN) thrust

#### Weights

**Empty (without pod):** 55,560 lb (25201 kg)
**Basic (without pod):** 57,916 lb (26270 kg)
**Empty (with MB-1C pod):** 64,115 lb (29081 kg)
**Basic (with MB-1C pod):** 66,471 lb (30150 kg)
**Maximum gross weight (in flight):** 176,890 lb (80235 kg)

#### Fuel

**Total internal fuel:** 10,924 US gal (41352 litres)
**Total external fuel (in TCP pod):** 657 US gal (2487 litres)

#### Performance

**Maximum speed below 25,000 ft (7620 m):** Mach 0.91
**Maximum speed at 40,000 ft (12192 m):** Mach 2.1

**Cruise speed:** 531 kt (611.4 mph; 983 km/h)
**Initial climb rate:** 17,400 ft (5310 m) per minute
**Normal cruise altitude:** 38,450 ft (11719 m)
**Service ceiling:** 63,400 ft (19324 m)
**Time to 30,000 ft (9144 m):** 11.2 min

#### Range

**Range with internal fuel:** 1,738 nm (2,000 miles; 3219 km)
**Ferry range:** 4,100 nm (4,718 miles; 7592 km)

#### Armament

**Maximum weaponload:** 19,450 lb (8823 kg)
One 20-mm T-171 rotary barrel cannon was situated in the tail to defend against aircraft attacking from the rear.
A number of weapon pod configurations were designed for the B-58, although few actually reached the production stage.
The MA-1C, with its warhead, was a rocket-propelled version of the MB-1, giving the B-58 stand-off capability. The MB-1C was a standard free-falling weapon. The TCP 'two-component pod' was similar to the MB-1, but was capable of retaining the warhead while ejecting the fuel cell when empty. B-58s were also tested with chemical and conventional weapons.

---

105 Starboard navigation light
106 Cambered leading edge
107 Wingtip fairing
108 Static dischargers
109 Fixed portion of trailing edge
110 Outer engine variable area afterburner nozzle
111 Outboard elevon
112 Linked inboard elevons
113 Elevon hydraulic jacks
114 Fuel pumps
115 Chaff stowage boxes
116 Chaff dispenser doors
117 Radar altimeter
118 Fuselage aft main fuel tank
119 Wing panel centreline joint
120 Fuel system piping
121 Fuel tank bulkhead
122 Power control unit linkage assembly

123 Radar track breaker (T-4) package
124 Aft fuselage fuel tank/balance tank
125 Rudder control linkage
126 Fin root fillet
127 Antenna fairing
128 Position indicating beacon transmitter
129 Rendezvous beacon transmitter
130 IFF transmitter
131 Fin leading edge
132 Remote compass transmitter
133 J-4 compass unit
134 Multi-spar tailfin construction
135 Anti collision light
136 AN/APX-47 IFF aerial
137 Fin tip radome
138 Rudder upper hydraulic jacks
139 AN/APN-135 rendezvous beacon antenna
140 Aft AN/ALQ-16 (T-4) transmitting antenna
141 Position indicating beacon antenna, AN/APN-136
142 AN/ALR-12 radar warning antenna
143 Tail navigation lights

144 VOR localiser aerial
145 Rudder
146 Static discharge wicks
147 Rudder honeycomb construction
148 Position indicator transmitter beacon
149 Tail radome
150 Fire control radar
151 Radar modulator package
152 Rudder lower hydraulic jacks
153 Rudder control linkage
154 Lower anti-collision light
155 Cannon barrels
156 Tailcone/cannon access
157 M61 Vulcan, 6-barrel rotary cannon
158 Cannon gimbal mounting
159 Ammunition feed chute
160 Fire control system tracking control unit
161 Ammunition tank – 1,120 rounds (maximum capacity 1,200 rounds)
162 Bomb damage assessment camera
163 Fuel jettison
164 IFF transponder
165 Doppler receiver aerials
166 Doppler electronics unit
167 Doppler radar transmitter aerials
168 Wing root fillet construction
169 AN/ALQ-16 radar warning receiver aerial
170 Port elevon construction
171 Elevon hinge rib
172 Elevon hydraulic jacks
173 Honeycomb trailing-edge panels

174 Static dischargers
175 Honeycomb wingtip fairing
176 Port navigation light
177 Honeycomb leading-edge panel
178 Engine afterburner duct
179 Variable area exhaust nozzle control jacks
180 Engine cowlings/access panels
181 Accessory equipment compartment
182 Pneumatic starter unit
183 Hydraulic fluid cooler
184 Engine variable air intake
185 Intake conical centre-body
186 Centre-body screw jack
187 Alternator
188 Constant speed drive unit
189 Inlet guide vanes
190 General Electric J79-GE-5B afterburning turbojet engine
191 Outboard nacelle pylon fairing
192 Leading-edge pneumatic air ducting
193 Port wing aft main fuel tanks
194 Diagonal multi-spar aft panel construction
195 Chaff stowage boxes
196 Chaff dispenser doors
197 Port main undercarriage wheel bay
198 Mainwheel doors
199 Hydraulic reservoir

200 Wheel brake hydraulic accumulator
201 Main undercarriage retraction jack
202 Undercarriage leg hinge links
203 Main undercarriage leg strut
204 Honeycomb wing skin panels
205 Fuel pod tail fins
206 Air system heat exchanger
207 Heat exchanger air ducting
208 Eight-wheel main undercarriage bogie
209 Inboard engine nacelle construction
210 Intake ducting
211 Moveable intake conical centre-body
212 Fresh air intake ducting
213 Pneumatic system piping
214 Inboard engine pylon construction
215 Pylon attachment joint
216 Port wing forward main fuel tanks
217 Wheel bay fairing
218 Honeycomb skin panel
219 Forward wing panel multi-spar construction
220 Front spar
221 Forward AN/ALQ-16 radar warning aerials
222 Aerial modulator unit
223 Fuselage centreline pylon
224 Aircraft system fuel connector
225 Ready/safe switch disconnect
226 Control unit disconnect.

227 MB-1C combined fuel and weapons pod
228 Pod integral fuel tank, total capacity 4856 US gal (15732 litres)
229 Integral munitions bay
230 Electrical system disconnect
231 Forward pylon latch
232 Fuel tank bulkhead
233 Retractable pitot tube
234 Camera electronic control units
235 KA-56 reconnaissance camera
236 Camera aperture
237 LA-331A reconnaissance pod, nose section
238 Wing root pylon
239 Ejector release unit
240 B43 free-fall nuclear weapon (four)
241 Ready/safe ground arming switch

# Douglas A3D/A-3 Skywarrior

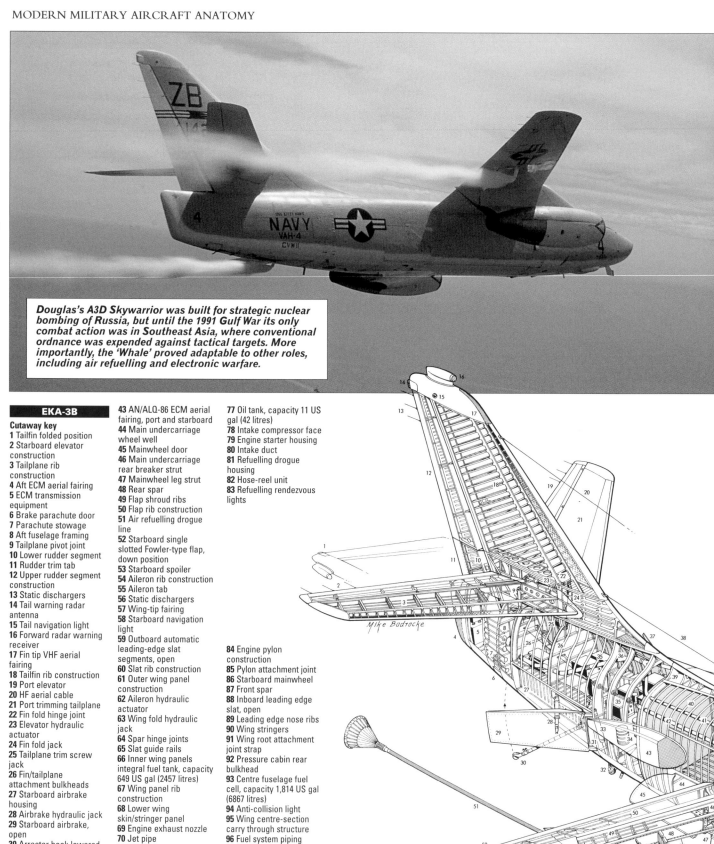

*Douglas's A3D Skywarrior was built for strategic nuclear bombing of Russia, but until the 1991 Gulf War its only combat action was in Southeast Asia, where conventional ordnance was expended against tactical targets. More importantly, the 'Whale' proved adaptable to other roles, including air refuelling and electronic warfare.*

## EKA-3B

**Cutaway key**

1 Tailfin folded position
2 Starboard elevator construction
3 Tailplane rib construction
4 Aft ECM aerial fairing
5 ECM transmission equipment
6 Brake parachute door
7 Parachute stowage
8 Aft fuselage framing
9 Tailplane pivot joint
10 Lower rudder segment
11 Rudder trim tab
12 Upper rudder segment construction
13 Static dischargers
14 Tail warning radar antenna
15 Tail navigation light
16 Forward radar warning receiver
17 Fin tip VHF aerial fairing
18 Tailfin rib construction
19 Port elevator
20 HF aerial cable
21 Port trimming tailplane
22 Fin fold hinge joint
23 Elevator hydraulic actuator
24 Fin fold jack
25 Tailplane trim screw jack
26 Fin/tailplane attachment bulkheads
27 Starboard airbrake housing
28 Airbrake hydraulic jack
29 Starboard airbrake, open
30 Arrester hook lowered
31 Airbrake hinge joint
32 Retractable tail bumper
33 Tail bumper hydraulic jack
34 Hydraulic reservoirs (two)
35 Avionics equipment racks
36 Fuel jettison pipe
37 Port airbrake, open
38 HF aerial cable
39 Fin root fillet construction
40 Rear fuselage fuel cell capacity 1,300 US gal (4921 litres)
41 Fuel vent piping
42 Control cable duct

43 AN/ALQ-86 ECM aerial fairing, port and starboard
44 Main undercarriage wheel well
45 Mainwheel door
46 Main undercarriage rear breaker strut
47 Mainwheel leg strut
48 Rear spar
49 Flap shroud ribs
50 Flap rib construction
51 Air refuelling drogue line
52 Starboard single slotted Fowler-type flap, down position
53 Starboard spoiler
54 Aileron rib construction
55 Aileron tab
56 Static dischargers
57 Wing-tip fairing
58 Starboard navigation light
59 Outboard automatic leading-edge slat segments, open
60 Slat rib construction
61 Outer wing panel construction
62 Aileron hydraulic actuator
63 Wing fold hydraulic jack
64 Spar hinge joints
65 Slat guide rails
66 Inner wing panels integral fuel tank, capacity 649 US gal (2457 litres)
67 Wing panel rib construction
68 Lower wing skin/stringer panel
69 Engine exhaust nozzle
70 Jet pipe
71 Detachable cowling panels
72 Fireproof bulkhead
73 Engine bleed air ducting

74 Bleed air blow-off valve
75 Pratt & Whitney J57-P-10 non after burning turbojet engine
76 Engine accessory equipment

77 Oil tank, capacity 11 US gal (42 litres)
78 Intake compressor face
79 Engine starter housing
80 Intake duct
81 Refuelling drogue housing
82 Hose-reel unit
83 Refuelling rendezvous lights

84 Engine pylon construction
85 Pylon attachment joint
86 Starboard mainwheel
87 Front spar
88 Inboard leading edge slat, open
89 Leading edge nose ribs
90 Wing stringers
91 Wing root attachment joint strap
92 Pressure cabin rear bulkhead
93 Centre fuselage fuel cell, capacity 1,814 US gal (6867 litres)
94 Anti-collision light
95 Wing centre-section carry through structure
96 Fuel system piping
97 Port wing integral fuel tank, capacity 649 US gal (2457 litres)
98 Flap external hinge

99 Port single-slotted Fowler type flap, down position
100 Nacelle tail fairing
101 Flap hydraulic jack

102 Port wing folded position
103 Port spoiler
104 Spoiler hydraulic actuator
105 Fuel pumps

106 Wing fold spar hinge joints
107 Wing fold hydraulic jack
108 Aileron hydraulic actuator

109 Port aileron
110 Aileron tab
111 Mass balance weights
112 Wing tip fairing
113 Port navigation light
114 Outboard leading edge slat segments, open
115 Nacelle pylon

*Flight deck crewmen push an EA-3B belonging to VQ-1 into position aboard the USS Nimitz. The 'Whale' spent 35 years in service with the Navy, and the last ERA-3Bs of VAQ-33 and EA-3Bs of VQ-2 retired as recently as 1991. The longevity of the Skywarrior is of particular note since it was produced only in limited numbers (the last of 283 aircraft being accepted in January 1961). What is more, the aircraft have had busy lives, spending much of their time at sea and flying combat sorties throughout the Vietnam War and Operation Desert Storm.*

**116** Port engine nacelle
**117** Inboard leading edge slat segment, open
**118** Pressure cabin section on roof framing
**119** Cabin roof escape hatch
**120** Electronics equipment racks
**121** ECM operators display panels
**122** ECM operators swivelling seats (four)
**123** Forward fuselage frame and stringer construction
**124** Retractable catapult strop hook
**125** ALQ-100 sideways-looking radar (SLAR) fairing
**126** Ventral access panel
**127** ECM operators cabin

floor level
**128** Forward AN/ALQ-86 ECM aerial fairing, port and starboard
**129** Forward radio and electronics equipment
**130** Circuit breaker panels
**131** Canopy aft glazing
**132** Dinghy stowage
**133** Rear window sunblinds
**134** Signal pistol aperture
**135** Cockpit roof ditching hatch
**136** Rearward-facing navigator 's seat
**137** Co-pilot/Air Refuelling Officer's seat
**138** Side console panel
**139** Heat exchanger air exhaust
**140** Emergency ram air turbine
**141** Ventral entry/escape hatch open
**142** UHF aerial
**143** Nose undercarriage leg strut
**144** Forward retracting nosewheel
**145** Torque scissor links
**146** Cabin air conditioning plant

**147** Cockpit floor level
**148** Instrument panel
**149** Control column handwheel
**150** Pilot's seat
**151** Instrument panel shroud
**152** Windscreen panels
**153** Windscreen wiper
**154** Fresh air NACA intake
**155** Front pressure bulkhead
**156** Nosewheel door mounted landing/taxiing lamp
**157** ALQ -126 ECM aerial
**158** ASB radar scanner

**159** Scanner tracking mechanism
**160** Radar scanner mounting frame
**161** Pitot tube
**162** Radome
**163** ILS aerial
**164** Fixed inflight-refuelling probe

## SPECIFICATION

### A-3B Skywarrior

#### Dimensions

**Length with probe:** 78 ft (23.77 m)
**Length without probe:** 74.5 ft (22.71 m)
**Wing span:** 72.5 ft (22.10 m)
**Span with wings folded:** 49.4 ft (15.06 m)
**Height:** 22.8 ft (6.95 m)
**Height with fin folded:** 15.9 ft (4.85 m)
**Wing area:** 812 sq ft (75.44 m²)

#### Powerplant

Two Pratt & Whitney J57-P-10 non-afterburning turbojets with maximum rating of 10,500 lb st (46.7 kN) and normal rating of 9,000 lb st (40 kN)

#### Weights

**Empty:** 39,620 lb (17971 kg)
**Design:** 55,942 lb (25375 kg)
**Combat:** 62,089 lb (28163 kg)
**Maximum carrier take-off:** 73,000 lb (33112 kg)
**Maximum field take-off:** 78,000 lb (35380 kg)
**Overload field ops:** 83,259 lb (37765 kg)
**Maximum carrier landing:** 49,000 lb (22226 kg)
**Maximum field landing:** 56,000 lb (25401 kg)

#### Fuel and load

**Standard internal fuel:** 4338 US gal (16421 litres) though provisions were made for carrying a 748-US gal (2831-litre) auxiliary tank in the upper bomb bay.
**Tanker operations:** one 1,224-US gal (4633-litre) tank fitted to the lower bomb bay brought maximum fuel up to 40,514 lb (18367 kg)
**Maximum load:** 12,800 lb (5806 kg)

#### Performance

**Maximum speed at sea level:** 556 kt (640 mph; 1030 km/h)
**Maximum speed at 35,000 ft (10670 m):** 508 kt (585 mph; 941 km/h)
**Cruising speed at 35,000 ft (10670m):** 436 kt (501 mph; 807 km/h)
**Maximum climb rate:** 6,510 ft/min (33 m/sec)
**Service ceiling:** 41,000 ft (12495 m)
**Combat ceiling:** 39,900 to 42,300 ft (12160 to 12895 m) depending on weight
**Unrefuelled combat radius with three Mk 27 nuclear bombs and upper bomb bay auxiliary tank:** 1410 nm (1622 miles; 2610 km)
**Tanker radius while transferring 19,200 lb (8710 kg) of fuel on a hi-hi-hi sortie:** 900 nm (1019 miles; 1640 km)

#### Armament

After the Aero-21B turret fitted to the initial production aircraft was removed, the A-3B was left without defensive armament. Although a maximum of 12,800 lb (5806 kg) could be carried internally, load was normally limited to 6,300 lb (2858 kg). Typical load included conventional bombs (either 12 x 500-lb/227-kg GPs, 6 x 1,000-lb/454-kg GPs, 8 x 1,600-lb/726-kg APs or 4 x 2,000-lb/908-kg GPs), mines (two Mk 10s or XA-4As, four Mk 25s, six Mk 36s or Mk 52s, or 12 Mk 50s or Mk 53s), or special stores (such as the Mk 27 thermonuclear free-fall bomb with a yield of a few megatons and the Mk 28 thermonuclear bomb with a yield of 350-1100 kT

# Handley Page Victor

The Victor could carry a theoretical maximum of 48 1,000-lb (454-kg) bombs in its capacious bays, although the normal maximum load was 35 – 14 more than the Vulcan. This remarkable picture captures a full load being dropped by a No. 57 Squadron B.Mk 1, showing the bombs falling as they were stowed: in five clips of seven.

Above right: XA922 was the sixth production B.Mk 1 and the second aircraft to be finished in anti-flash white, instead of the aluminium (silver) scheme adopted by the first four. Later, the serials and national insignia were made much paler.

### Victor K.Mk 2

**Cutaway key**
1 Nose probe
2 Control feel system pressure intake
3 Nose compartment windows
4 Nose construction
5 Inflight-refuelling probe
6 Windscreen
7 Refuelling searchlights
8 Jettisonable roof hatch
9 Co-pilot's Martin Baker ejection seat
10 Pilot's roof hatch windows
11 Pilot's Martin Baker ejection seat
12 Control column
13 Instrument panel
14 Rudder pedals
15 Air intake to air-conditioning system
16 Radome
17 Throttles
18 Pilot's side console
19 Cockpit floor
20 External door handle
21 $H_2S$ radar scanner
22 Radar mounting and equipment
23 Rearward facing crew members' seats
24 Cockpit door
25 Entry steps
26 Front fuselage construction
27 Rear view periscope
28 Rearward facing crew members' work table
29 Cabin side window
30 Air conditioning system
31 Nose freight compartment
32 Instrument panels
33 Radio and electronics racks
34 Pressure bulkhead
35 Air conditioning intake
36 Starboard emergency life-raft hatch
37 Port life-raft pack
38 Forward fuselage connecting construction
39 Wing spar bulkhead
40 Wing centre-section fuel tank
41 Overwing fuel tank
42 Starboard engine intake
43 Intake ducts
44 De-icing air system
45 Underwing fuel tank
46 Starboard wing fuel tanks
47 Fuel flow proportioner
48 De-icing connector to outer wing
49 Vortex generators
50 Starboard Flight Refuelling FR.20B refuelling pod
51 Power turbine propeller
52 Pylon mounting
53 Pitot head
54 Starboard wingtip
55 Starboard aileron
56 Trim tab
57 Refuelling hose
58 Trailing-edge fairing
59 Starboard flap
60 Flap track fairing
61 Flap mechanism
62 Starboard main undercarriage
63 Starboard engine bays
64 Exhaust pipe fairing
65 Bomb bay roof forward fuel tank
66 Forward refuelling bomb bay tank
67 Tank mountings
68 Fuel flow proportioner
69 Fuselage double frames
70 Fuselage stringer construction
71 Bomb-bay roof aft fuel tanks
72 Aft refuelling bomb-bay tank
73 Bomb-bay roof structure
74 Flight Refuelling FR.17B hose reel unit
75 Hose reel jack
76 Reel drive motor
77 Air system piping
78 Bomb-bay aft bulkhead
79 Retractable ram air turbine intakes
80 Rear fuselage fuel tank
81 Air system intake
82 Heat exchanger
83 Fin root fairing
84 Ram air turbine
85 Air exhaust louvres
86 Turbine intake jack
87 Tailplane de-icing air system
88 Fin root fixing
89 Fin leading edge
90 Corrugated inner skin
91 Fin construction
92 Rudder control unit
93 Tailplane fairing
94 Starboard refuelling drogue
95 Starboard tailplane construction
96 Elevator power control unit
97 Elevator construction

## SPECIFICATION

### Victor B.Mk 1

**Range:** 6,000 miles (9656 km)

#### Dimensions

**Length:** 114 ft 11 in (35.02 m)
**Height:** 26 ft 9 in (8.15 m)
**Wingspan:** 110 ft (33.53 m)
**Wing area:** 2,406 sq ft (223.52 m²)

#### Powerplant

Four Armstrong Siddeley Sapphire 202 or 207 turbojets, each rated at 11,050 lb (49.17 kN) thrust

#### Weights

**Empty:** 79,000 lb (35834 kg)
**Maximum take-off:** 205,000 lb (92988 kg)
**Maximum bombload:** 35,000 lb (15876 kg)

#### Performance

**Maximum speed at 40,000 ft (12192 m):** 627 mph (1009 km/h)
**Service ceiling:** 56,000 ft (17069 m)

### Victor B.Mk 2R
### (as for B.Mk 1, except:)

#### Dimensions

**Wingspan:** 120 ft (36.58 m) (113 ft/34.44 m in K.Mk 2)
**Wing area:** 2,597 sq ft (241.26 m²)

#### Powerplant

Four Rolls-Royce RCo.17 Conway 201 turbofans, each rated at 20,600 lb (91.67 kN) thrust

#### Weights

**Empty:** 114,240 lb (51819 kg)
**Maximum take-off:** 223,000 lb (101153 kg)

#### Performance

**Maximum speed at 40,000 ft (12192 m):** 647 mph (1041 km/h)
**Service ceiling:** 60,000 ft (18288 m)

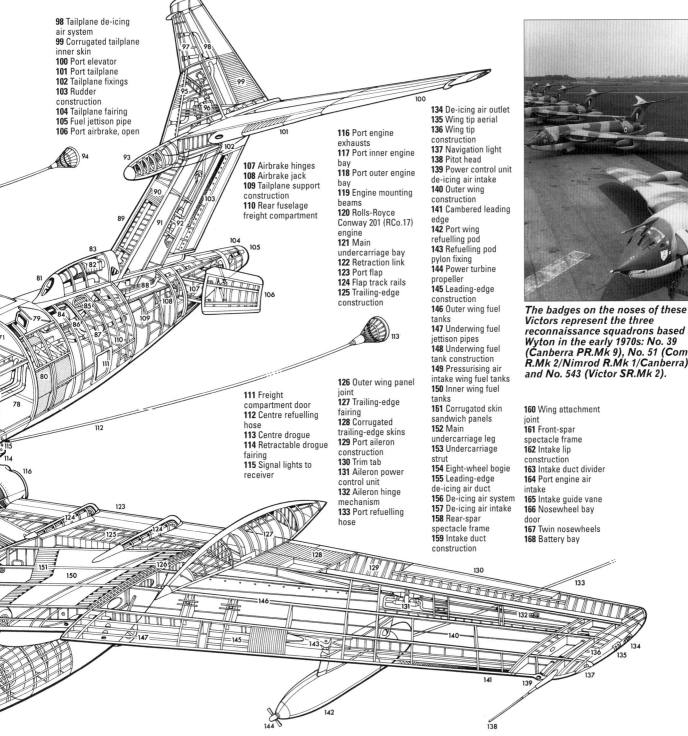

98 Tailplane de-icing air system
99 Corrugated tailplane inner skin
100 Port elevator
101 Port tailplane
102 Tailplane fixings
103 Rudder construction
104 Tailplane fairing
105 Fuel jettison pipe
106 Port airbrake, open

107 Airbrake hinges
108 Airbrake jack
109 Tailplane support construction
110 Rear fuselage freight compartment

111 Freight compartment door
112 Centre refuelling hose
113 Centre drogue
114 Retractable drogue fairing
115 Signal lights to receiver

116 Port engine exhausts
117 Port inner engine bay
118 Port outer engine bay
119 Engine mounting beams
120 Rolls-Royce Conway 201 (RCo.17) engine
121 Main undercarriage bay
122 Retraction link
123 Port flap
124 Flap track rails
125 Trailing-edge construction

126 Outer wing panel joint
127 Trailing-edge fairing
128 Corrugated trailing-edge skins
129 Port aileron construction
130 Trim tab
131 Aileron power control unit
132 Aileron hinge mechanism
133 Port refuelling hose

134 De-icing air outlet
135 Wing tip aerial
136 Wing tip construction
137 Navigation light
138 Pitot head
139 Power control unit de-icing air intake
140 Outer wing construction
141 Cambered leading edge
142 Port wing refuelling pod
143 Refuelling pod pylon fixing
144 Power turbine propeller
145 Leading-edge construction
146 Outer wing fuel tanks
147 Underwing fuel jettison pipes
148 Underwing fuel tank construction
149 Pressurising air intake wing fuel tanks
150 Inner wing fuel tanks
151 Corrugated skin sandwich panels
152 Main undercarriage leg
153 Undercarriage strut
154 Eight-wheel bogie
155 Leading-edge de-icing air duct
156 De-icing air system
157 De-icing air intake
158 Rear-spar spectacle frame
159 Intake duct construction

160 Wing attachment joint
161 Front-spar spectacle frame
162 Intake lip construction
163 Intake duct divider
164 Port engine air intake
165 Intake guide vane
166 Nosewheel bay door
167 Twin nosewheels
168 Battery bay

*The badges on the noses of these Victors represent the three reconnaissance squadrons based at Wyton in the early 1970s: No. 39 (Canberra PR.Mk 9), No. 51 (Comet R.Mk 2/Nimrod R.Mk 1/Canberra) and No. 543 (Victor SR.Mk 2).*

# Ilyushin Il-28 'Beagle'

*Romania's H-5s, exemplified here by an HJ-5 trainer, remain among the 494 H-5 aircraft remaining in service early in 2001. All examples of the original Il-28 have passed out of service, but China, North Korea and Romania all still fly H-5s.*

## Il-28 'Beagle'

### Cutaway key

1 Nose compartment glazing
2 Optically flat sighting panel
3 OPB-5 bombsight
4 Folding chart table
5 Nose undercarriage pivot fixing
6 Cannon muzzle
7 Nosewheel leg door
8 Twin nosewheels, aft retracting
9 Nosewheel steering unit
10 Retraction strut
11 Fixed NR-23 23-mm cannon, port and starboard
12 Ammunition tank, 100 rounds
13 Navigation equipment racks
14 Navigator's instrument panels
15 Nose compartment entry/escape hatch, offset to starboard
16 Navigator/ bombardie's ejection seat
17 Cockpit dividing bulkhead
18 Rudder pedals
19 Pilot's instrument panel
20 Engine throttle levers
21 Control column handwheel
22 Direct vision opening side window panel
23 Instrument panel shroud
24 Windscreen panels
25 Cockpit canopy cover, hinged to starboard
26 Ejection seat headrest
27 Safety harness
28 Canopy latch
29 Pilot's ejection seat
30 Side console panel
31 Underfloor control runs
32 Nosewheel leg doors

33 Oxygen bottles, air conditioning equipment on starboard side
34 Cockpit rear pressure bulkhead

35 Radar transmitter and receiver
36 Navigation and bombing radar scanner
37 Ventral radome
38 Forward fuselage fuel tanks, total internal capacity 9,921 lb (4500 kg)
39 Control duct access panel
40 Fuselage upper longeron
41 Cockpit aft fairing
42 Aerial mast
43 DF aerial fairing
44 Fuselage skin panelling

45 Fuel filler caps
46 Internal bomb bay; maximum load 6,614 lb (3000 kg)

47 Ventral strike/ reconnaissance camera
48 Bomb bay doors
49 5,511-lb (2500-kg) aerial mine
50 Fuselage control and cable ducting
51 Forward fuselage frame and stringer construction
52 Dorsal fuel tank
53 Wing spar attachment fuselage main frame

54 Wing centre-section carry through
55 Bolted wing root attachment joint
56 Wing stringers
57 Inboard leading-edge nose ribs
58 Starboard engine nacelle
59 Starboard mainwheel, stored position
60 Engine bay heat shield above wheel bay
61 Engine bearer struts
62 Starboard engine bay

63 Intake centre body fairing
64 Detachable nose cowling
65 Starboard engine intake
66 Il-28U 'Mascot' trainer variant, nose section profile
67 Leading edge hot air de-icing
68 Starboard outerwing panel
69 Fuel filler cap
70 Detachable long range wing tip tank; overload fuel capacity 14,550 lb (6600 kg)
71 Starboard aileron
72 Aileron hinge control

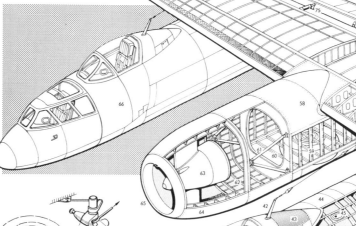

*Above: Groundcrew at work on a Polish Il-28R. The recce 'Beagle' typically carried four vertical or oblique cameras in its modified bomb bay.*

## SPECIFICATION

### Il-28 'Beagle'

### Dimensions

**Fuselage length (excluding cannon):** 57 ft 11 in (17.65 m)
**Height:** 21 ft 11¾ in (6.70 m)
**Wingspan (without tip tanks):** 70 ft 4½ in (21.45 m) without tip tanks
**Wing area:** 654.47 sq ft (60.80 m²)

### Powerplant

two Klimov VK-1A turbojet engines each rated at 5,952 lb st (26.48 kN)

### Weights

**Empty:** 28,417 lb (11890 kg)
**Normal take-off with 8,377 lb (3800 kg) of fuel, and a 2,200-lb (1000-kg) bomb load:** 40,564 lb (1840 kg)
**Maximum take-off:** 46,738 lb (21200 kg)

### Performance

**Maximum speed at 14,765 ft (4500 m):** 560 mph (902 km/h)
**Climb to 32,810 ft (10000 m):** 18 minutes
**Maximum range at 32,810 ft (10000 m):** 1,491 miles
**Service ceiling:** 40,350 ft (12300 m)

### Armament

two 23-mm Nudel'man-Rikhter NR-23 fixed forward-firing cannon in the lower nose and two 23-mm Nudel'man-Rikhter NR-23 trainable rearward-firing cannon in the tail turret, plus up to 6,614 lb (3000 kg) of disposable stores carried in a lower-fuselage weapons bay, and generally comprising one 6,614-lb (3000-kg) FAB-3000 free-fall bomb, or four 1,102-lb (500-kg) FAB-500 free-fall bombs or eight 551-lb (250-kg) FAB-250 free-fall bombs

*.Below right: This photograph of the first Il-28 prototype shows the aircraft after some degree of modification. However, it still retains the ventral strakes and rear-mounted radar location of its original form.*

83 Fin root fillet
84 Fin spar attachment joint
85 HF aerial cable
86 Starboard tailplane
87 Starboard elevator
88 Leading edge hot air de-icing
89 Tailfin construction
90 Flush aerial
91 Fin tip de-icing air outlet louvres
92 Navigation aerial
93 Static discharger
94 Rudder
95 Rudder tab
96 Rear gunner/radio operator's compartment
97 Flexible mounted NR-23 23-mm cannon (two), 225 rounds per gun
98 Tail gun turret
99 Elevator tab
100 Elevator mass balance
101 Port elevator
102 Tailplane tip de-icing air outlet louvres
103 Port tailplane construction
104 Tail gun ranging antenna
105 Tail gunner/radio operator's seat
106 Rudder and elevator hinge controls
107 Tailplane centre-section bolted joint
108 Tail crew compartment pressure bulkhead
109 Door hydraulic jack
110 Ventral entry door/escape hatch
111 Radio and electronics equipment bay
112 Ventral aerials
113 Rear fuselage frame construction
114 Inboard plain flap segment
115 Flap shroud ribs
116 Rear spar
117 Bolted wing root attachment joint
118 Jettisonable rocket assisted take-off bottle (RATO)
119 Engine nacelle attachment main ribs
120 Tailpipe fairing
121 Port exhaust nozzle
122 Outboard plain flap segment
123 Flap rib construction
124 Aileron tab
125 Port aileron rib construction
126 Detachable wing-tip tank
127 Port navigation light
128 Fuel filler cap
129 Wing upper and lower panel half-rib construction
130 Leading-edge hot air de-icing (inoperable with tip tanks fitted)
131 Leading-edge nose ribs
132 Front spar
133 Lower wing skin/ stringer panel
134 Jet pipe cooling air scoop
135 Main undercarriage hydraulic retraction jack
136 Leg swivelling link
137 Mainwheel leg pivot fixing
138 Port mainwheel, forward retracting
139 Mainwheel doors
140 Heat shrouded jet pipe
141 Engine mounting bulkhead
142 Engine bearer struts
143 Klimov VK-1 centrifugal flow turbojet engine
144 Engine flame cans
145 Retractable landing/ taxiing lamp
146 Compressor intake filter screens
147 Gearbox mounting ring frame
148 Engine accessory equipment gearbox
149 Generator
150 Intake plenum chamber
151 Detachable front cowling
152 Intake centre fairing support struts
153 Port engine intake

73 Aileron tab
74 Outboard plain flap segment
75 Flap hydraulic jack
76 Nacelle tail fairing
77 Engine exhaust nozzle
78 Inboard plain flap segment
79 Inboard flap hydraulic jack
80 Rear spar attachment fuselage main frame
81 Fuel filler caps
82 Rear fuselage fuel tanks

# Martin B-57 Canberra

*Conspicuous due to its Dayglo orange and silver colour scheme, the B-57E was configured for target-towing duties. Combat equipment was replaced by four 1,500-ft (457-m) tow reels mounted in the bomb-bay door, though normally only two were carried, with operating equipment fitted in the rear cockpit.*

## RB/WB-57F Canberra

### Cutaway key

1 Starboard navigation light
2 Leading edge anti-erosion sheathing
3 Glassfibre wingtip fairing
4 Outboard fuel tank
5 Spoiler hydraulic actuator
6 Starboard roll control spoiler, open
7 Outboard fixed portion of trailing edge
8 Static dischargers
9 Fuel boost pumps
10 Air sampling pod
11 Fuel system piping
12 Aileron/tab hinge control
13 Starboard aileron
14 Aileron geared tab
15 Fixed tab
16 Inboard fixed trailing-edge segment
17 Ventral fuel jettison pipe
18 Inboard three-bay main fuel tank
19 Fuel filler caps
20 Fuel tank or boost engine-mounting pylon
21 Starboard demountable auxiliary boost engine pod
22 Main engine fan section, detachable cowling panels
23 Fan air intake
24 Intake centre-body
25 Ventral oil cooler
26 Cockpit canopy sun blinds
27 Navigational sextant
28 Cockpit canopy, upward-hinged
29 Pitot head
30 Instrument panel shroud
31 Windscreen panels
32 Windscreen de-icing air duct
33 Alternative nose section (gust response measurement experiments)
34 Nose compartment hinged for access
35 Radome
36 Gas-sampling probes
37 ILS glideslope aerial
38 Temperature probe
39 Radar scanner
40 Scanner tracking mechanism
41 Ventral periscope housing
42 Alternative nose section (X-band sideways-looking radar)
43 Equipment cooling air scoop
44 Forward special mission equipment bay
45 Cockpit front pressure bulkhead
46 Rudder pedals
47 Control column
48 Cockpit floor level
49 Underfloor control linkages
50 Lower UHF aerial
51 Side console panel
52 Engine throttle levers
53 Pilot's McDonnell Escapac IC-6 ejection seat
54 Canopy hydraulic actuator
55 Folding chart board
56 Cockpit section framing
57 Nose wheel leg pivot fixing
58 Twin nose wheels
59 Nose wheel doors
60 Hydraulic retraction jack
61 Special Equipment Operator's (SEO) Escapac IC-6 ejection seat
62 SEO's instrument panel
63 Liquid oxygen converter
64 Cockpit rear pressure bulkhead
65 Radio and electronics equipment bay
66 Battery compartment
67 Ventral equipment pallet
68 Upper pressurised special equipment compartment
69 Avionics and experimental equipment racks
70 Front spar attachment double frame
71 Fuselage keel member
72 Wing main spar attachment bulkhead
73 Upper anti-collision light
74 Starboard main undercarriage wheel bay
75 Starboard mainwheel
76 Landing/taxing lamp
77 Leading-edge honeycomb skin panel
78 Hydraulic reservoir
79 Starboard main engine bay
80 Engine bay cooling air outlet duct
81 Turbine section venting air intakes
82 Main wing spar ring frames
83 Main undercarriage leg pivot fixing
84 Hydraulic retraction jack and side strut
85 Wingroot section construction
86 Fuselage skin panelling
87 VHF/communications aerial
88 Centre fuselage frame and stringer construction
89 Aileron and spoiler differential linkage
90 Wing rear spar attachment bulkhead
91 Aft equipment bay
92 Ground locks and tail stand stowage
93 Radio compass sense aerial
94 Upper UHF/communications aerial
95 Fin leading edge
96 Starboard tailplane
97 HF aerial cable
98 Starboard elevator
99 Two-spar fin construction
100 Fin and rudder honeycomb skin panelling
101 VHF/nav aerial
102 Rudder horn balance
103 Static dischargers
104 Rudder
105 Rudder tab control
106 Rudder trim tab
107 Tailcone
108 Aft air data sensors
109 Tail navigation light
110 Elevator geared tab
111 Port elevator rib construction
112 Elevator horn balance
113 Tailplane rib construction
114 Vortex generators, above and below
115 Tab/elevator control linkage
116 Trimming tailplane incidence control screw jack
117 Tailplane rear-bracing strut
118 Fin-tailplane attachment mainframe
119 Tailplane spar attachment joint
120 Tailbumper
121 Rudder hydraulic actuator
122 Tailplane push-pull control rods
123 Rear fuselage frame and stringer construction
124 Starter kit stowage
125 Lower anti-collision light
126 Fixed trailing-edge panel
127 Jet pipe
128 Engine exhaust nozzle
129 'Eyeshade' exhaust nozzle fairing
130 Fixed trailing-edge honeycomb skin panels
131 Static dischargers
132 Fuel jettison pipe
133 Port aileron
134 Fixed tab
135 Aileron geared tab

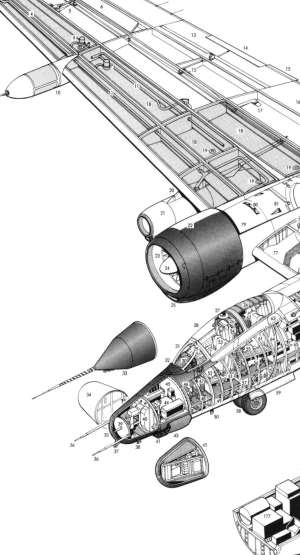

## RB-57E Canberra

### Dimensions

**Wingspan:** 64 ft (19.51 m)
**Length:** 65 ft 6 in (19.96 m)
**Height:** 15 ft 7 in (4.75 m)
**Wing area:** 960.0 sq ft (89.19 m²)

### Powerplant

Two Wright J65-W-1 or W-5 (Sapphire) turbojets each rated at 7,200 lb (32.4 kN) thrust

### Weights

**Empty:** 27,000 lb (12247 kg)
**Normal take-off:** 45,000 lb (20412 kg)
**Maximum take-off:** 55,000 lb (24948 kg)

### Performance

**Maximum speed without tiptanks up to 5,000 ft (1524 m):** 575 mph (925 km/h)
**Maximum speed without tiptanks between 5,000 ft (1524 m) and 20,000 ft (6096 m):** Mach 0.82
**Maximum speed without tiptanks above 20,000 ft (6096 m):** Mach 0.83 to 0.85
**Service ceiling:** 53,000 ft (16154 m)
**Range with reserve fuel tanks:** 2,300 miles (3701 km)

### Armament

The bomber version of the B-57 could house four 750-lb (340-kg), nine 500-lb (227-kg), or 21 260-lb (118-kg) bombs, or two Mk 9 special weapons; four wing pylons could carry four 750-lb (340-kg) bombs, eight 5-in (127-mm) HVAR or 28 2.75-in (70-mm) FFAR rockets (double if eight pylons were used); eight M3 0.5-in (12.7-mm) machine-guns with 300 rounds, or four M39 20-mm cannon with 200 rounds

*Natural metal finish was characteristic of the early production examples of the B-57A, as on this aircraft photographed on a test flight near the company's Middle River production plant. Externally similar to the Canberra B.Mk 2, the B-57A was powered by Wright-built Sapphire turbojets.*

136 Aileron honeycomb core construction
137 Outboard fixed trailing-edge section
138 Static dischargers
139 Glassfibre/honeycomb wingtip fairing construction
140 Port navigation light
141 Leading-edge anti erosion sheathing
142 Honeycomb sandwich wing skin panelling

143 Port spoiler
144 Spoiler hydraulic actuator
145 Spoiler/aileron interconnecting cables
146 Aileron tab hinge control
147 Lower wing skin access panels
148 Port wing outboard fuel tank bays

149 Fuel filler cap
150 Air sampling pod
151 Leading-edge nose ribs
152 Multi-spar outer wing panel construction

153 Tank bay dividing wing ribs
154 Port auxiliary boost engine pod

162 Inboard wing fuel tank bays
163 Fuel filler caps
164 Main sparring frames
165 Pratt & Whitney TF33-P11A turbofan engine
166 Engine bay fire wall
167 Port mainwheel, retracted position
168 Air-conditioning plant
169 Leading-edge heat exchanger air intake

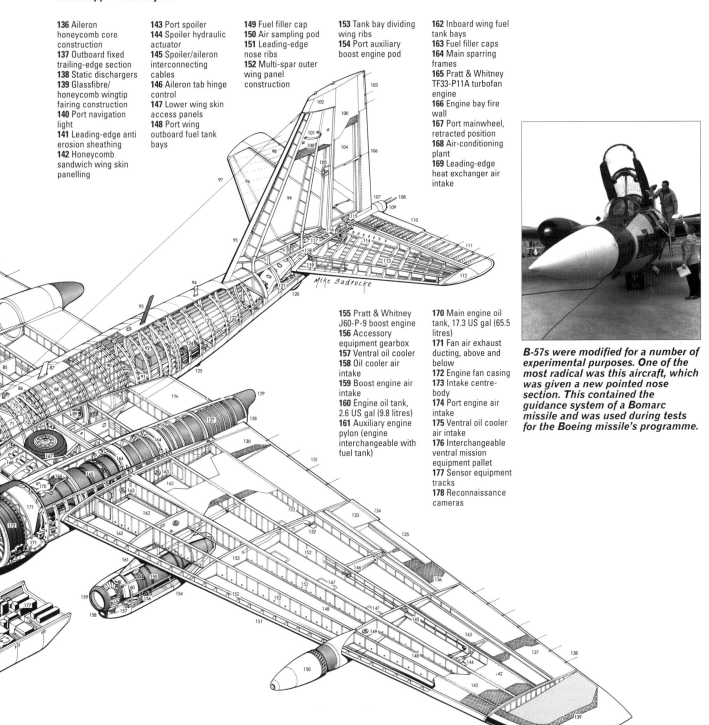

155 Pratt & Whitney J60-P-9 boost engine
156 Accessory equipment gearbox
157 Ventral oil cooler
158 Oil cooler air intake
159 Boost engine air intake
160 Engine oil tank, 2.6 US gal (9.8 litres)
161 Auxiliary engine pylon (engine interchangeable with fuel tank)

170 Main engine oil tank, 17.3 US gal (65.5 litres)
171 Fan air exhaust ducting, above and below
172 Engine fan casing
173 Intake centre-body
174 Port engine air intake
175 Ventral oil cooler air intake
176 Interchangeable ventral mission equipment pallet
177 Sensor equipment tracks
178 Reconnaissance cameras

Mike Badrocke

*B-57s were modified for a number of experimental purposes. One of the most radical was this aircraft, which was given a new pointed nose section. This contained the guidance system of a Bomarc missile and was used during tests for the Boeing missile's programme.*

# Northrop Grumman B-2A Spirit

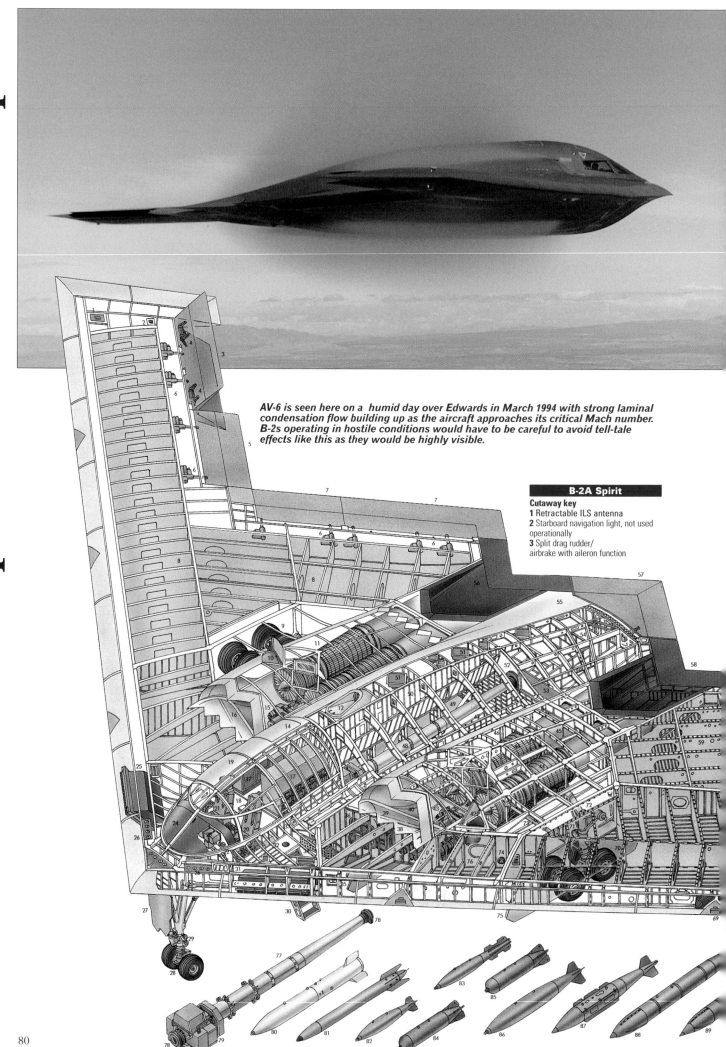

*AV-6 is seen here on a humid day over Edwards in March 1994 with strong laminal condensation flow building up as the aircraft approaches its critical Mach number. B-2s operating in hostile conditions would have to be careful to avoid tell-tale effects like this as they would be highly visible.*

## B-2A Spirit

**Cutaway key**
1 Retractable ILS antenna
2 Starboard navigation light, not used operationally
3 Split drag rudder/
airbrake with aileron function

## SPECIFICATION

### B-2A Spirit

#### Dimensions

**Length:** 69 ft (21.03 m)
**Height:** 17 ft (5.18 m)
**Wingspan:** 172 ft (52.43 m)
**Wing aspect ratio:** 5.92
**Wing area:** 5000 sq ft (464.5 m²) plus
**Wheel track:** 40 ft (12.2 m)

#### Powerplant

Four General Electric F118-GE-100 non-afterburning turbofans each rated at 19,000 lb (84.5 kN)

#### Weights

**Empty:** 153,700 lb (69717 kg)
**Normal take-off:** 336,500 lb (152635 kg)
**Maximum take-off:** 378,000 lb (170550 kg)
**Maximum wing loading:** 75.20 lb/sq ft (367.2 kg/m²)
**Maximum power loading:** 5.43 lb/lb st (554 kg/kN)

#### Fuel and load

**Internal fuel capacity:** 180,000 lb (81635 kg)
**Maximum weapon load:** 40,000 lb (22700 kg)

#### Performance

**Cruising speed at high altitude:** Mach 0.85 or 416 kt (475 mph; 900 km/h)
**Cruising speed at low altitude:** Mach 0.8 or 530 kt (610 mph; 980 km/h)
**Approach speed:** 140 kt (161 mph, 259 km/h)
**Service ceiling:** 50,000 ft plus (15240 m)
**Range with one flight refuelling:** 10,000 nm (11,515 miles; 18532 km)
**Range unrefuelled with 8 SRAM and 8 B83:** 4,410 nm (5075 miles; 8167 km)

#### Armament

Two side-by-side weapons bays in the lower centrebody house Boeing rotary launcher assemblies (RLA) which are detachable and each house eight large stores. Total capacity is 16 AGM-129 ACMs or 16 AGM-69 SRAM IIs. Designed with a nuclear mission in mind, the B-2 can carry 16 B83 or 16 B61 freefall nuclear bombs. For conventional missions, 80 Mk 82 500-lb (227-kg), 16 Mk 84 2,000-lb (908-kg) bombs, 36 CBU-87, -89, -97 and -98 cluster bombs, 80 Mk 36 560-lb (254-kg) or Mk 62 sea mines, 36 M117 750-lb (340-kg) fire bombs, 8 GAM-11 deep penetration bombs, 16 GAM-84s, or 16 JDAMs, can be carried

*AV-1 and AV-2 prepare for an early morning launch at Edwards South Base. Testing for the B-2 was centred at South Base where a secure and purpose-built home for the aircraft was set up. It is now named the Birk Flight Test facility in honour of Colonel Frank Birk, the former B-2 director who was killed in an air crash.*

**4** Drag rudder rotary actuators
**5** Outboard elevon
**6** Elevon hydraulic actuators
**7** Inboard elevons
**8** Starboard integral fuel tankage, total capacity approximately 130,000 lb (58967 kg)
**9** Starboard main undercarriage, stowed position
**10** Intake suction relief doors
**11** Starboard engine bays
**12** Rotating inflight-refuelling receptacle
**13** Cockpit rear pressure bulkhead
**14** Structural cut-out, provision for third crew member ejection seat
**15** Engine-driven auxiliary equipment gearbox
**16** Starboard engine combined air intake
**17** Avionics equipment racks
**18** Two-crew flight deck
**19** Cockpit roof escape hatches, port and starboard
**20** Pilot's Aces II ejection seat
**21** Mission commander's ejection seat
**22** Conventional stick and rudder flight controls, quadruplex digital flight control system
**23** Instrument panel with multi-function full-colour CRT displays
**24** Instrument panel shroud
**25** Starboard AN/APQ-181 Low Probability of Intercept (LPI) electronically scanned multi-function J-band radar unit
**26** Airflow data sensors, above and below
**27** Nosewheel leg door
**28** Twin-wheel nose undercarriage, aft retracting
**29** Taxiing lights
**30** Crew door-mounted boarding ladder
**31** Port AN/APQ-181 radar unit
**32** Astro navigation sensor port
**33** Cockpit hatch emergency release
**34** Weapons bay retractable spoiler panels
**35** Port weapons bay outer door
**36** Environmental control system equipment bay, port and starboard
**37** Hydraulic equipment bay
**38** Boundary layer splitter
**39** Boundary layer secondary intake duct to air systems and APU
**40** Intake S-duct, common to both engines, bypass air to engine bay and exhaust cooling
**41** Allied Signal auxiliary power unit (APU)
**42** APU exhaust
**43** Airframe-mounted auxiliary gearbox
**44** Port General Electric F118-GE-100 non-afterburning turbofan engines
**45** Jet pipes flattened towards aft exhausts
**46** Engine/weapons bay fireproof structural bulkhead
**47** Port weapons bay
**48** Weapons bay rotary launcher
**49** Starboard weapons bay
**50** Centre fuselage keel structure
**51** Flush antenna panels
**52** Weapons bay rear bulkhead
**53** Aft equipment bay
**54** Rear fuselage frame structure
**55** All-composite skin panelling
**56** Exhaust duct thermal protection lining
**57** Gust Load Alleviation System (GLAS) tail surface
**58** Port engine exhaust duct
**59** Rear integral fuel tank bay
**60** Elevon hydraulic actuators
**61** Port inboard elevons
**62** Outboard elevon
**63** Port split drag rudder/airbrake
**64** Port navigation light, not used operationally
**65** Port retractable ILS antenna
**66** Outer wing panel rib structure
**67** Port outboard integral fuel tankage
**68** All-composite leading-edge structure
**69** Leading-edge flush EW antennas
**70** Four-wheel main undercarriage bogie
**71** Landing lights
**72** Main undercarriage leg strut
**73** Retraction breaker strut
**74** Port mainwheel bay pressure refuelling connection
**75** Single-piece mainwheel door
**76** Inboard integral fuel tankage
**77** Weapons bay advanced rotary launcher (ARL)
**78** Launcher mounting adaptors
**79** Launcher drive unit and sequenced release mechanism
**80** B83 nuclear weapon
**81** B61 nuclear weapon
**82** Mk 82 500-lb bomb
**83** Mk 62 mine
**84** CBU-87 CEM sub-munition dispenser
**85** GBU-89 Gator sub-munition dispenser
**86** Mk 84 2,000-lb (907-kg) bomb
**87** GBU-31 2,000-lb (907-kg) Joint Direct Attack Munition (JDAM)
**88** GQM-113
**89** GAM-84
**90** Joint Stand-Off Weapon (JSOW), sub-munitions or 500-lb (227-kg) HE unitary warhead
**91** B61-11 penetrating nuclear weapon

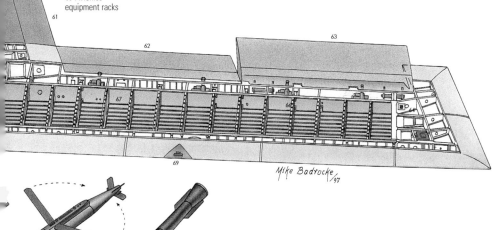

Mike Badrocke /97

# Panavia Tornado GR.Mk 1/4

*The end of the Cold War led to a reduction in the number of Tornados committed to the overland strike role, with two four-squadron wings in RAF Germany being reduced to a single four-squadron wing. Three squadrons (Nos. XV, 16 and 20) were simply disbanded, while a fourth (No. II) returned to the UK. Some of the surplus aircraft were used to re-equip the two remaining maritime strike Buccaneer squadrons, being allocated the designation GR.Mk 1B. This Sea Eagle armed example is from No. 617 Sqn and carries two of the anti-ship missiles on dedicated launchers under the fuselage.*

### Tornado GR.Mk 4

1 Air data probe
2 Radome
3 Lightning conductor strip
4 Terrain following radar antenna
5 Ground mapping radar antenna
6 Radar equipment bay hinged position
7 Radome hinged position
8 IFF aerial
9 Radar antenna tracking mechanism
10 Radar equipment bay
11 UHF/TACAN aerial
12 Laser Rangefinder and Marked Target Seeker (LRMTS), starboard side
13 FLIR housing
14 Ventral Doppler aerial
15 Angle of attack transmitter
16 Canopy emergency release
17 Avionics equipment bay
18 Front pressure bulkhead
19 Windscreen rain dispersal airducts
20 Windscreen (Lucas-Rotax)
21 Retractable, telescopic, inflight refuelling probe
22 Probe retraction link
23 Windscreen open position, instrument access
24 Wide angle HUD
25 Instrument panel
26 Radar 'head down' display

27 Instrument panel shroud
28 Control column
29 Rudder pedals
30 Battery
31 Cannon barrel housing, cannon deleted from port side
32 Nosewheel doors
33 Landing/taxiing lamp
34 Nose undercarriage leg strut (DowtyRotol)

35 Torque scissor links
36 Twin forward-retracting nosewheels (Dunlop)
37 Nosewheel steering unit
38 Nosewheel leg door
39 Electrical equipment bay
40 Ejection seat rocket pack
41 Engine throttle levers
42 Wing sweep control lever
43 Radar hand controller
44 Side console panel
45 Pilot's Martin-Baker Mk 10 ejection seat
46 Safety harness
47 Ejection seat head rest
48 Cockpit canopy cover (Kopperschmidt)
49 Canopy centre arch
50 Navigator's radar displays
51 Navigator's instrument panel and weapons control panels
52 Foot rests
53 Canopy external latch
54 Pitot head
55 Mauser 27-mm cannon, starboard side only

56 Ammunition feed chute
57 Cold air unit ram air intake
58 Ammunition tank
59 Liquid oxygen converter
60 Cabin cold air unit
61 Stores management system computer
62 Port engine air intake
63 Intake lip
64 Cockpit framing

65 Navigator's Martin-Baker Mk 10 ejection seat
66 Starboard engine air intake
67 Intake spill duct
68 Canopy jack
69 Canopy hinge point
70 Rear pressure bulkhead
71 Intake ramp actuator linkage
72 Navigation light
73 Two dimensional variable area intake ramp doors
74 Intake suction relief doors
75 Wing glove Krüger flap
76 Intake bypass air spill ducts
77 Intake ramp hydraulic actuator
78 Forward fuselage fuel tank
79 Wing-sweep control screw jack (Microtecnica)

80 Flap and slat control drive shafts
81 Wing-sweep, flap and slat central control unit and motor (Microtecnica)
82 Wing pivot box integral fuel tank
83 Air system ducting
84 Anti collision light
85 UHF aerials

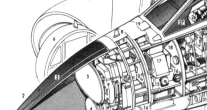

*Saudi Arabia is the only export customer for the Tornado, equipping four squadrons with various IDS versions. The RSAF has adopted the RAF's equipment and weapons, including JP233, ALARM and the GR.Mk 1A reconnaissance system.*

## SPECIFICATION

### Tornado GR.Mk 1

**Dimensions:**

**Fuselage length:** 54 ft 10¼ in (16.72 m)
**Wing span:** 45 ft 7½ in (13.91 m) minimum sweep (25°) and 28 ft 2½ in (8.60 m) maximum sweep (67°)
**Wing aspect ratio:** 7.73
**Tailplane span:** 22 ft 3½ in (6.80 m)
**Tail height:** 19 ft 6¼ in (5.95 m)
**Wing area:** 286.33 sq ft (26.60 m²)
**Wheel track:** 10 ft 2 in (3.10 m)
**Wheel base:** 20 ft 4 in (6.20 m)

**Powerplant**

Two Turbo-Union R.B.199-34R Mk 101 turbofans each rated at 8,475 lb st (37.70 kN) dry and 14,840 lb st (66.01 kN) with afterburning or, in later aircraft, Turbo-Union R.B.199-34R Mk 103 turbofans each rated at 8,650 lb st (38.48 kN) dry and 16,075 lb st (71.50 kN) with afterburning.

**Weights**

**Empty operating:** 31,065 lb (14091 kg)
**Normal take-off:** 45,000 lb (20411 kg)
**Maximum take-off:** 61,620 lb (27951 kg)

**Fuel and load**

**Internal fuel:** 11,221 lb (5090 kg)

**External fuel:** up to 13,200 lb (5988 kg) in two 495-Imp gal (2250-litre) and two 330-Imp gal (1500-litre), or four 330 Imp gal (1500-litre) drop tanks.
**Maximum theoretical weapon load:** more than 19,841 lb (9000 kg)

**g limits**

+7.5 at basic design gross weight

**Performance**

**Maximum level speed 'clean' at altitude:** 1,262 kt (1,453 mph; 2338 km/h)
**Limiting Mach No:** 1.4 with LRMTS
**Service ceiling:** 50,000 ft (15240 m)
**Take-off run:** less than 2,953 ft (900 m)
**Landing run:** 1,214 ft (370 m)

**Range**

**Ferry range:** 2,100 nm (2,420 miles; 3890 km) with four drop tanks
**Combat radius:** 750 nm (863 miles; 1390 km) on a typical hi-lo-hi attack mission with a heavy warload.

**Armament**

**Maximum ordnance:** 19,841 lb (9000 kg) carried on four underwing and three underfuselage hardpoints.

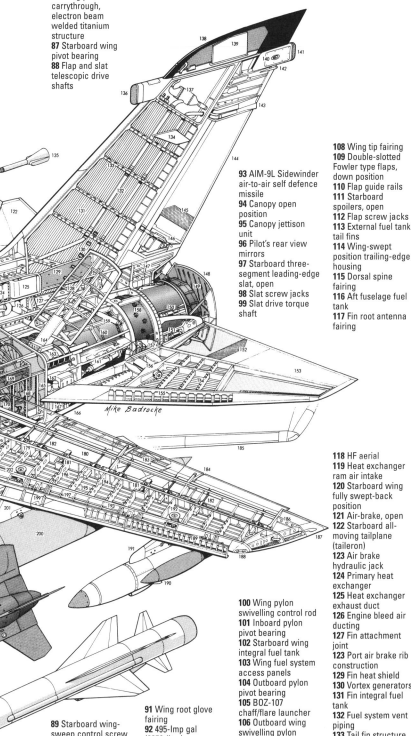

**86** Wing pivot box carrythrough, electron beam welded titanium structure
**87** Starboard wing pivot bearing
**88** Flap and slat telescopic drive shafts
**89** Starboard wing-sweep control screw jack
**90** Leading edge sealing fairing
**91** Wing root glove fairing
**92** 495-Imp gal (2250-litre) 'Hindenburger' fuel tank
**93** AIM-9L Sidewinder air-to-air self defence missile
**94** Canopy open position
**95** Canopy jettison unit
**96** Pilot's rear view mirrors
**97** Starboard three-segment leading-edge slat, open
**98** Slat screw jacks
**99** Slat drive torque shaft
**100** Wing pylon swivelling control rod
**101** Inboard pylon pivot bearing
**102** Starboard wing integral fuel tank
**103** Wing fuel system access panels
**104** Outboard pylon pivot bearing
**105** BOZ-107 chaff/flare launcher
**106** Outboard wing swivelling pylon
**107** Starboard navigation and strobe lights
**108** Wing tip fairing
**109** Double-slotted Fowler type flaps, down position
**110** Flap guide rails
**111** Starboard spoilers, open
**112** Flap screw jacks
**113** External fuel tank tail fins
**114** Wing-swept position trailing-edge housing
**115** Dorsal spine fairing
**116** Aft fuselage fuel tank
**117** Fin root antenna fairing
**118** HF aerial
**119** Heat exchanger ram air intake
**120** Starboard wing fully swept-back position
**121** Air-brake, open
**122** Starboard all-moving tailplane (taileron)
**123** Air brake hydraulic jack
**124** Primary heat exchanger
**125** Heat exchanger exhaust duct
**126** Engine bleed air ducting
**127** Fin attachment joint
**123** Port air brake rib construction
**129** Fin heat shield
**130** Vortex generators
**131** Fin integral fuel tank
**132** Fuel system vent piping
**133** Tail fin structure
**134** ILS aerial
**135** GEC-Marconi Ariel towed radar decoy (TRD)
**136** Forward passive ECM
**138** Fin tip antenna fairing
**139** VHF aerial
**140** Tail navigation light
**141** Aft passive ECM housing
**142** Obstruction light
**143** Fuel jettison
**144** Rudder
**145** Rudder honeycomb construction
**146** Rudder hydraulic actuator (Fairey Hydraulics)
**147** Dorsal spine tail fairing
**148** Thrust reverser bucket doors, open
**149** Variable area afterburner nozzle
**150** Nozzle control jacks (four)
**151** Thrust reverser door actuator
**152** Honeycomb trailing edge construction
**153** Port all-moving tailplane (taileron)
**154** Tailplane rib construction
**155** Leading-edge nose ribs
**156** Tailplane pivot bearing
**157** Tailplane bearing sealing plates
**158** Afterburner duct
**159** Airbrake hydraulic jack
**160** Turbo-Union R.B.199-34R Mk 103 afterburning turbofan engine
**161** Tailplane hydraulic actuator
**162** Hydraulic system filters
**163** Hydraulic reservoir (Dowty)
**164** Air brake hinge point
**165** Intake frame/ production joint
**166** Engine bay ventral access panels
**167** Engine oil tank
**168** Rear fuselage fuel tank
**169** Wing root pneumatic seal
**170** Engine driven accessory gear boxes, port and starboard (KHD), airframe mounted
**171** Integrated drive generator (two)
**172** Hydraulic pump (two)
**173** Gearbox interconnecting shaft
**174** Starboard side Auxiliary Power Unit (KHD)
**175** Telescopic fuel pipes
**176** Port wing pivot bearing
**177** Flexible wing sealing plates
**178** Wing skin panelling
**179** Rear spar
**180** Port spoiler housings
**181** Spoiler hydraulic actuators
**182** Flap screw jacks
**183** Flap rib construction
**184** Port Fowler-type double slotted flaps, down position
**185** Port wing fully swept-back position
**186** Wing tip construction
**187** Fuel vent
**188** Port navigation and strobe lights
**189** Leading-edge slat rib construction
**190** Marconi Sky Shadow ECM pod
**191** Outboard swivelling pylon
**192** Pylon pivot bearing
**193** Front spar
**194** Port wing integral fuel tank
**195** Machined wing skin/ stringer panel
**196** Wing rib construction
**197** Swivelling pylon control rod
**198** Port leading-edge slat segments, open
**199** Slat guide rails
**200** Port 'Hindenburger' external fuel tank
**201** Inboard swivelling pylon
**202** Inboard pylon pivot bearing
**203** Missile launch rail
**204** AIM-9L Sidewinder air-to-air self defence missile
**205** Port mainwheel (Dunlop), forward-retracting
**206** Main undercarriage leg strut (DowtyRotol)
**207** Undercarriage leg pivot bearing
**208** Hydraulic retraction jack
**209** Leg swivelling control link
**210** Telescopic flap and slat drive torque shafts
**211** Leading-edge sealing fairing
**212** Krüger flap hydraulic jack
**213** Main undercarriage leg breaker strut
**214** Main wheel door
**215** Landing lamp
**216** Port fuselage pylon
**217** Triple launch unit
**218** GEC-Marconi Dynamics Brimstone anti-armour missile
**219** ALARM launch rail
**220** Matra-BAe Dynamics ALARM anti-radar missile
**221** 1000-lb (454-kg) HE bomb
**222** Matra-BAe Dynamics Storm Shadow stand-off weapons dispenser
**223** GBU-24/B 2000-lb (908-kg) Laser Guided Bomb
**224** BAe Dynamics Sea Eagle air-to-surface anti-ship missile

Mike Badrocke

# Rockwell B-1B

*The history of the B-1B has been a long and convoluted process, with it emerging as the B-1A, only to be cancelled, and then resurfacing as the B-1B. Having overcome a series of teething troubles, the 'Bone' is now the key element of the USA's strategic bomber force (despite still regularly receiving adverse publicity), being greater in number than the B-2 and more survivable than the B-52.*

## B-1B Lancer

**Cutaway key**
1 Radome
2 Multi-mode phased array radar antenna
3 Low observable shrouded scanner mounting and tracking mechanism
4 AN/APQ-146 offensive radar system equipment bays
5 Pitot heads
6 Foreplane hydraulic actuator
7 Structural mode control system (SMCS) foreplane
8 Nose undercarriage stowed position
9 Control column
10 Rudder pedals
11 Air refuelling receptacle
12 Windscreen panels
13 Fully-shrouded instrument panel
14 Cockpit roof escape hatches
15 Co-pilot's station
16 Weber ACES II zero-zero ejection seats, all positions
17 Pilot's station
18 Crew toilet
19 Conditioned air supply ducting
20 Ventral boarding ladder
21 Defensive Systems Operator's (DSO) station
22 Systems operator's display and control consoles
23 Observer's folding seat
24 Offensive systems operator's station (OSO)
25 Cockpit roof ejection hatches
26 Glideslope antenna
27 SATCOM antenna
28 Avionics racks, port and starboard, flight control and communications equipment

29 Avionics cooling air ground connection
30 Electrical equipment bay
31 Defensive avionics systems transmitting antennas
32 Forward fuselage integral fuel tanks, total system capacity 202,254 lb (91742 kg)
33 Weapons bay movable bulkhead
34 Weapons bay fuel tank, typical, various sizes up to 2,903 US gal (10989 litres)
35 Chaff/flare launchers
36 RFS antenna, port and starboard
37 Starboard leading-edge RFS/ECMS equipment bay
38 UHF/IFF antenna
39 Upper fuselage cable and systems ducting
40 Weapons bay door actuating mechanism
41 Retractable spoiler panel
42 Port leading-edge antenna panel
43 RFS/ECMS transmitting antennas
44 Defensive avionics system equipment
45 Weapons bay doors
46 Rotary weapons carrier/launcher
47 Wing pivot box integral fuel tank
48 Electron beam-welded titanium wing pivot box carry-through structure
49 Blended sidebody integral fuel tank

50 Wing sweep actuator hydraulic drive unit
51 Wing sweep control screw jack
52 Starboard wing integral fuel tank
53 Fuel system vent and feed piping
54 Seven-segment leading-edge slats
55 Starboard navigation and strobe lights
56 Fuel jettison vent
57 Spoiler panels/lift dumpers
58 Starboard single-slotted flap
59 Wing fully-swept position
60 Wing shroud panels
61 Main undercarriage wheel bay
62 Flight control system avionics equipment
63 Undercarriage bay roof fuel tank
64 Air supply ducting
65 Rear weapons bay rotary launcher
66 Weapons bay surround integral fuel tank
67 Starboard engine exhausts
68 Tailplane automatic flight control system equipment

69 Fin/tailplane support structure
70 All-moving tailplane hydraulic actuators
71 Starboard tailplane panel
72 Fin leading-edge HF antenna

73 Fin-tip ECMS and rendezvous beacon antennas
74 Tail navigation and strobe lights
75 Rudder
76 Rudder rotary actuators
77 Rudder SCAS unit

78 RFS/ECMS antenna
79 Port all-moving tailplane
80 Static dischargers
81 Tail radome
82 RFS/ECMS transmitting antennas
83 Defensive system avionics equipment racks

84 Rear fuselage fuel tank
85 Fuel tank pressurant nitrogen bottle
86 Rear weapons bay
87 Main engine mounting beam

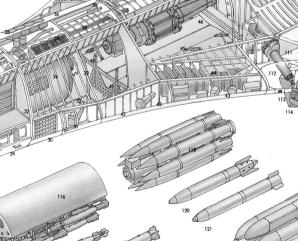

The Reluctant DRAGON

B-1B nose art, as with that of all US aircraft types, has moved away from the traditional glamourous female image following a recent ruling that all such art should be non-gender specific. Hence, decoration is now more carefully chosen, as was with case with **The Reluctant Dragon's** *(86-0103)* nose art, which originally appeared on a 96th Bomb Group B-17G and was applied when this particular 'Bone' took part in a B-1B publicity programme. *UK* visits were made to RAF Alconbury and Fairford in 1993 and 1996, with 86-0103 acting as the main display machine.

## SPECIFICATION

### B-1B Lancer

### Dimensions

**Fuselage length:** 143 ft 3½ in (43.68 m)
**Height:** 34 ft (10.3 m)
**Wingspan (maximum sweep):** 78 ft 2½ in (23.84 m)
**Wingspan (minimum sweep):** 136 ft 8½ in (41.67 m)
**Area:** 1,950 sq ft (181.16 m²)
**Aspect ratio (fully-spread):** 9.58
**Aspect ratio (fully-swept):** 3.14
**Tailplane span:** 44 ft 10 in (13.67 m)
**Wheel track:** 14 ft 6 in (4.42 m)
**Wheelbase:** 57 ft 6 in (17.53 m)

### Powerplant

Four General Electric F101-GE-102 turbofans each rated at 14,600 lb st (64.94 kN) dry and 30,780 lb st (136.92 kN) with afterburning

### Weights

**Basic empty:** 182,360 lb (82840 kg)
**Empty equipped:** 192,000 lb (87091 kg)
**Maximum take-off weight:** 477,000 lb (216365 kg)
**Low-altitude operating weight:** 422,000 lb (191419 kg)
**Nominal payload:** 294,500 lb (133585 kg)

### Fuel and load

**Internal fuel:** 193,405 lb (87728 kg)
**Internal fuel with SIS/SEF FCS software:** 206,160 lb (93514 kg)
**Maximum internal ordnance:** 75,000 lb (34019 kg)
**Maximum external ordnance:** 59,000 lb (26762 kg)

### Performance

**Maximum level speed 'clean' at high altitude:** Mach 1.25 or 715 kt (823 mph; 1324 km/h)
**Penetration speed at approximately 200 ft (61 m):** Mach 0.92 or 521 kt (600 mph; 965 km/h)
**Range with typical weaponload:** 3000 nm (3,444 miles; 5542 km)
**Service ceiling:** 50,000 ft (15240 m)

### Armament

The B-1B is fitted with three internal weapon bays though external stores are also used. In the nuclear role, up to 12 B28 or 14 B23 or 24 B61 or 24 B83 free-fall bombs or 24 AGM-69 SRAM or eight AGM-86B ALCMs can be carried. Conventional weapons may total 84 Mk 82 or 24 Mk 84 GP bombs or 8 AGM-86C ALCMs internally or 44 Mk 82 or 14 Mk 84 or 14 AGM-86C ALCMs externally

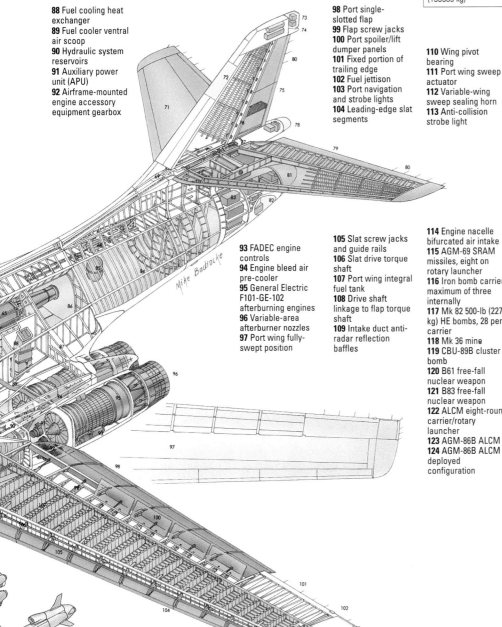

**88** Fuel cooling heat exchanger
**89** Fuel cooler ventral air scoop
**90** Hydraulic system reservoirs
**91** Auxiliary power unit (APU)
**92** Airframe-mounted engine accessory equipment gearbox

**93** FADEC engine controls
**94** Engine bleed air pre-cooler
**95** General Electric F101-GE-102 afterburning engines
**96** Variable-area afterburner nozzles
**97** Port wing fully-swept position

**98** Port single-slotted flap
**99** Flap screw jacks
**100** Port spoiler/lift dumper panels
**101** Fixed portion of trailing edge
**102** Fuel jettison
**103** Port navigation and strobe lights
**104** Leading-edge slat segments

**105** Slat screw jacks and guide rails
**106** Slat drive torque shaft
**107** Port wing integral fuel tank
**108** Drive shaft linkage to flap torque shaft
**109** Intake duct anti-radar reflection baffles

**110** Wing pivot bearing
**111** Port wing sweep actuator
**112** Variable-wing sweep sealing horn
**113** Anti-collision strobe light

**114** Engine nacelle bifurcated air intake
**115** AGM-69 SRAM missiles, eight on rotary launcher
**116** Iron bomb carrier, maximum of three internally
**117** Mk 82 500-lb (227-kg) HE bombs, 28 per carrier
**118** Mk 36 mine
**119** CBU-89B cluster bomb
**120** B61 free-fall nuclear weapon
**121** B83 free-fall nuclear weapon
**122** ALCM eight-round carrier/rotary launcher
**123** AGM-86B ALCM
**124** AGM-86B ALCM deployed configuration

# Tupolev Tu-16 'Badger'

Some redundant 'Badger-C' missile carriers were converted to become Tu-16Ye maritime reconnaissance platforms, known to NATO as 'Badger-D', which could double as electronic intelligence gatherers and provide mid-course guidance for long-range anti-ship missiles. The 'D' looked very like the 'Badger-C', but it had a larger undernose radome and three extra Elint radomes under the fuselage.

## Tu-16 'Badger'

**Cutaway key**
1 Radome, 'Badger-C' & 'D'
2 Weapons ranging and search radar scanner
3 Radar navigator/ bombardier's seat
4 Windscreen wipers
5 Pitot head
6 Windscreen panels
7 Cockpit eyebrow windows
8 Instrument panel shroud
9 Navigation radome
10 Pilot's seat
11 Co-pilot's seat
12 Cockpit roof escape hatches
13 Glazed nose section, all variants except 'C' & 'D'
14 Optically flat sighting window
15 Fixed forward firing NR-23, 23-mm cannon on starboard side only
16 Navigator/ bombardier's seat
17 Navigation radome
18 'Towel-rail' aerial
19 Astrodome observation hatch
20 Forward gunner's swivelling seat
21 Cabin side window panels
22 Ventral entry/exit hatch
23 Extending boarding ladder
24 Retractable landing/ taxiing lamps, port and starboard
25 Nose landing gear leg strut
26 Twin nosewheels, aft retracting
27 Nosewheel doors
28 Nose landing gear hydraulic jack
29 Electronics equipment racks, port and starboard
30 HF blade antenna
31 Remotely controlled dorsal gun turret
32 Twin NR-23, 23-mm cannon
33 Communications aerials, port and starboard
34 Port engine air intake
35 Radar altimeter aerial
36 Intake duct divided around front spar

37 Forward fuselage fuel cells, maximum capacity approximately 10,009 Imp gal (45500 litres)
38 Starboard engine air intake
39 Aerial mast
40 Starboard inboard wing panel
41 Outer wing panel joint
42 Starboard missile pylon
43 AS-6 'Kingfish' air-to-surface missile, 'Badger-G' 'modified'
44 Starboard wing integral fuel tanks
45 Inboard wing fence
46 Outboard wing fence
47 Outer wing panel
48 Starboard navigation light
49 Wing tip faring
50 Fuel jettison pipe
51 Starboard aileron
52 Aileron tab
53 Flap guide rails
54 Flap screw jacks
55 Starboard single-slotted track-mounted flap, down position

56 Starboard main landing gear fairing
57 Inboard flap segment
58 Starboard engine bay
59 Centre section internal weapons bay, capacity 19,842 lb (9000 kg)

60 Rear fuselage fuel cells
61 Blade antenna
62 'Badger-D' electronic reconnaissance variant, ventral view
63 Ventral radomes
64 'Badger-C' maritime strike variant
65 Semi-recessed missile housing, AS-2 'Kipper' air-to-surface missile
66 'Badger-A' bomber, ventral view
67 Weapons bay doors, open
68 Starboard trimming tailplane
69 Starboard elevator
70 HF aerial cable
71 Tailfin
72 Fin tip aerial fairing
73 Rudder

74 Rudder tab
75 Gun ranging radar antenna
76 Rear gunner's station
77 Twin NR-23, 23-mm cannon
78 Elevator tab
79 Port elevator

80 Port tailplane construction
81 Rear pressurised compartment ventral entry/exit hatches
82 Observation blister, port and starboard
83 Radio operator/ observer's station
84 Retractable tail bumper
85 'Odd-Rods' IFF aerials

86 Ventral remotely controlled gun turret, two NR-23, 23mm cannon
87 Exhaust fairing
88 Engine exhaust nozzle
89 Ventral strike camera
90 Outboard canted jet pipe

91 Engine bay access doors, above and below
92 Mikulin RD-3M (AM-3M) single shaft
93 Engine accessory equipment compartment
94 Port inboard flap
95 Port main landing gear housing
96 Main landing gear, stowed position
97 Flap cut-out for missile tail fin
98 Port single-slotted flap

turbojet engine

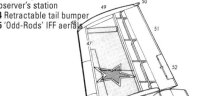

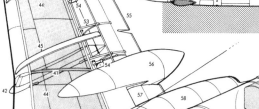

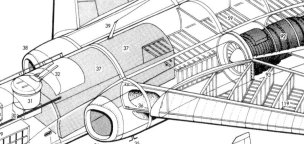

The 'Badger K' is an electronic reconnaissance variant of the Tu-16 first identified in the late 1980s. Probably based on the original anti-shipping 'Badger-B', it is identifiable by the two underfuselage radomes at each end of the weapons bay – much closer together than on the 'Badger-F'. According to some analysts, the 'Badger-K' was probably designed with highly automated systems for the precision collection of Elint in a dense signal environment.

## SPECIFICATION

**Tu-16K-11-16 'Badger-G'**

### Dimensions:

**Wingspan:** 108 ft ½ in (32.93 m)
**Wing area:** 1,772 sq ft (164.65 m²)
**Length:** 118 ft 11¼ in (36.25 m)
**Height:** 45 ft 11¼ in (14.00 m)
**Wheel track:** 32 ft ¾ in (9.77 m)
**Wheel base:** 34 ft 8 in (10.57 m)

### Powerplant:

Two Mikulin KB Type RD-3M (AM-3M-500) single-shaft turbojets, each delivering 20,944-lb (93.16 kN) static thrust

### Weights:

**Empty equipped:** 82,012 lb (37200 kg)
**Max take-off:** 167,110 lb (75800 kg)
**Max landing:** 110,250 lb (50000 kg)
**Max landing (rough field):** 105,840 lb (48000 kg)

### Fuel and load

**Internal fuel:** 75,750 lb (34360 kg)

**Maximum ordnance:** 19,845 lb (9000 kg); normal bomb load 6,600 lb (3000 kg); naval variants carry one or two winged ASMs under wing (AS-5 'Kelt' 6,614 lb/3000 kg each; AS-6 'Kingfish' 11,023 lb/5000 kg each)

### Performance

**Maximum level speed at 19,700 ft (6000 m):** 566 kt (654 mph; 1050 km/h)
**Maximum level speed with combat load:** 495 kt (571 mph; 918 km/h)
**Maximum cruising speed with combat load:** 445 kt (514 mph; 825 km/h)
**Range:** 3,885 nm (4,474 miles; 7200 km)
**Range with 3000 kg warload:** 3,130 nm (3,604 miles; 5800 km)
**Range with 2 missiles underwing:** 2,618 nm (3,013 miles; 4850 km)
**Service ceiling:** 49,215 ft (15000 m)
**Take-off run:** 4,620 ft (1250 m)
**Landing speed:** 120 kt (139 mph; 223 km/h)

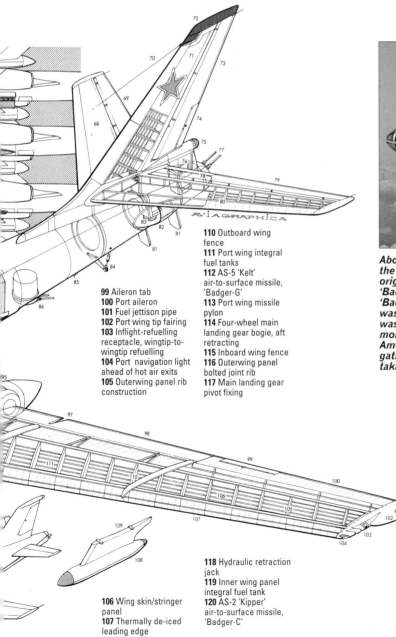

99 Aileron tab
100 Port aileron
101 Fuel jettison pipe
102 Port wing tip fairing
103 Inflight-refuelling receptacle, wingtip-to-wingtip refuelling
104 Port navigation light ahead of hot air exits
105 Outerwing panel rib construction

110 Outboard wing fence
111 Port wing integral fuel tanks
112 AS-5 'Kelt' air-to-surface missile, 'Badger-G'
113 Port wing missile pylon
114 Four-wheel main landing gear bogie, aft retracting
115 Inboard wing fence
116 Outerwing panel bolted joint rib
117 Main landing gear pivot fixing

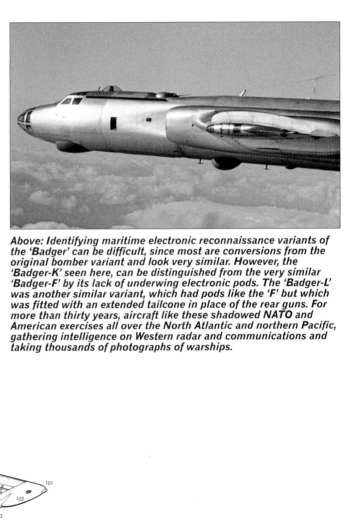

Above: Identifying maritime electronic reconnaissance variants of the 'Badger' can be difficult, since most are conversions from the original bomber variant and look very similar. However, the 'Badger-K' seen here, can be distinguished from the very similar 'Badger-F' by its lack of underwing electronic pods. The 'Badger-L' was another similar variant, which had pods like the 'F' but which was fitted with an extended tailcone in place of the rear guns. For more than thirty years, aircraft like these shadowed NATO and American exercises all over the North Atlantic and northern Pacific, gathering intelligence on Western radar and communications and taking thousands of photographs of warships.

106 Wing skin/stringer panel
107 Thermally de-iced leading edge
108 Electronic intelligence gathering pod, 'Badger-F'
109 Electronic pod pylon

118 Hydraulic retraction jack
119 Inner wing panel integral fuel tank
120 AS-2 'Kipper' air-to-surface missile, 'Badger-C'

# Tupolev Tu-22M 'Backfire'

*The 'Backfire' would probably qualify as the greatest of the West's Cold War bugbears. Few aircraft have been as feared or as mocked, as overestimated or as dismissed.* **Soviet Military Power,** *the* **US** *chronicle of the* **USSR** *in the 1980s, considered the Tu-22M to be a long-range strategic aircraft. However, both it and the 'Blinder' have only ever been used in the medium-range theatre role.*

## Tu-22M2

### Cutaway key

1 Detachable in-flight refuelling probe
2 Radome
3 'Down-Beat' bombing and navigation radar scanner
4 Radar equipment bay
5 Cockpit front pressure bulkhead
6 Pitot head (port and starboard)
7 Forward ECM aerial (port and starboard)
8 Rudder pedals
9 Control column
10 Instrument panel shroud
11 Windscreen panels
12 Cockpit roof escape hatches
13 Co-pilot's ejector seat
14 Pilot's ejector seat
15 Instrument consoles
16 Blade aerial
17 Navigator/ bombardier's and electronic systems officer's seats
18 Rear cockpit side window panel
19 Cockpit floor level
20 Ventral observation and visual bomb-aiming cupola
21 Blade aerial
22 Nose landing gear leg strut
23 Twin nosewheels
24 Nosewheel doors
25 Nose landing gear retraction mechanism
26 Cockpit rear pressure bulkhead
27 Avionics equipment racks
28 Equipment cooling air spill duct
29 'Backfire-C' nose profile
30 Wedge-type engine air intakes

31 Starboard engine air inlet
32 Forward fuselage fuel tank
33 Boundary layer bleed air spill duct
34 Boundary layer splitter plate
35 Variable-area inlet ramp doors
36 Port engine air inlet
37 Inlet ducting
38 Retractable landing/taxiing lamp (port and starboard)
39 Multiple weapons racks (port and starboard)
40 Air system equipment
41 Wing pivot box centre section carry-through
42 Centre fuselage fuel tank
43 Auxiliary air intakes (open)
44 Wing pivot bearing
45 Glove section leading-edge slat (open)
46 Wing fence
47 Starboard wing integral fuel tank
48 Leading-edge slat segments (open)
49 Starboard wing, fully forward (20° sweep) position
50 Starboard navigation lights

51 Wingtip fairing
52 Fixed portion of trailing edge
53 Starboard slotted flap-down position
54 Two-segment spoilers/lift dumpers (open)
55 Wing glove sealing plate
56 Starboard wing, fully-swept (65°) position
57 Flush aerial fairing
58 Centre fuselage weapons bay
59 Extended fin root fillet
60 Flush aerial
61 Fin root fuel tank
62 Starboard all-moving tailplane (taileron)

63 Tailfin
64 Navigational aerials
65 Fin tip fairing
66 ATC transponders and Sirena 3 radar warning receiver
67 Tail navigation light
68 Rudder
69 ECM aerial
70 'Bar-Tail' tail gun control radar
71 Rear ECM aerial (port and starboard )
72 Ammunition magazines
73 Remotely-controlled gun
74 Two twin-barrelled 23-mm cannon
75 Afterburner duct cooling air scoop

76 Variable-area afterburner nozzle
77 Afterburner nozzle control jacks
78 Tailplane/fuselage fillet fairing
79 Port all-moving tailplane (taileron)
80 Tailplane pivot fixing
81 Tailplane hydraulic actuator
82 Afterburner ducting
83 Kuznetsov afterburning turbofan engine
84 Engine accessory equipment gearbox
85 Rear fuselage integral fuel tank

86 Ventral weapons bay doors
87 Main landing gear wheel bay
88 Hydraulic retraction mechanism
89 Mainwheel leg pivot fixing

90 Wing glove section slotted trailing-edge flap
91 Flap hydraulic actuator
92 Ventral landing gear leg pivot fairing

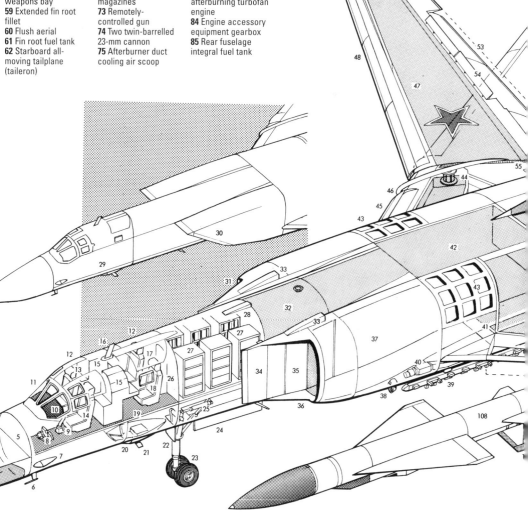

*The dragon badge of the 341st TBAP (Heavy Bomber Regiment) was first worn in Afghanistan, but was retained on its Tu-22Ps in later years. As the Soviet Union dissolved, most of the 'Blinders' were stationed in Belarus. However, the Belarussians allowed the Russians to withdraw the regiments and return them to Engels air base for disbandment. As of 1997, 92 such aircraft were waiting for 'demilitarisation'.*

## SPECIFICATION

### Tu-22M3 'Backfire-C'

### Dimensions

**Length:** 139 ft 4 in (42.46 m)
**Height:** 36 ft 3 in (11.05 m)
**Wingspan (fully-spread):** 112 ft 7 in (34.30 m)
**Wingspan (fully-swept):** 76 ft 11 in (23.40 m)
**Weapons bay length:** 22 ft 11 in (7.00 m)
**Weapons bay width:** 5 ft 10 in (1.80 m)

### Powerplant

Two side-by-side Kuznetsov/KKBM NK-25 turbofans in rear fuselage, each rated at 55,115 lb st (245.2 kN) with afterburning

### Weights and loads

**Maximum weaponload:** 52,910 lb (24000 kg)
**Maximum take-off weight:** 273,370 lb (124000 kg)
**Maximum landing weight:** 194,000 lb (88000 kg)
**Fuel load:** 110,230 lb (50000 kg)

### Performance

**Maximum level speed at high altitude:** Mach 1.88 (1,080 kt; 1,242 mph; 2000 km/h)
**Maximum level speed at low altitude:** Mach 0.86 (567 kt; 652 mph; 1050 km/h)
**Normal cruising speed at height:** 485 kt (560 mph; 900 km/h)
**Take-off speed:** 200 kt (230 mph; 370 km/h)
**Take-off run:** 6,560-6,890 ft (2000-2100 m)
**Normal landing run:** 3,940-4,265 ft (1200-1300 m)

### Armament

Maximum offensive load is three Kh-22 air-to-surface missiles or 52,910 lb (24000 kg) of conventional bombs and mines, half carried internally and half on racks under the wings. Internal bombs can be replaced by rotary launcher for six Kh-15P short-range missiles. Loads can include Kh-31 or Kh-35 missiles and FAB-3000, FAB-1500, FAB-500 or FAB-250 bombs.

93 Wing glove sealing plate
94 Port three-segment slotted flap
95 Two-segment spoilers
96 Port wing fully-swept position
97 Fixed portion of trailing edge
98 Port wing, fully forward position
99 Port navigation lights
100 Leading-edge slat segments
101 Port wing integral fuel tank
102 Wing pivot bearing

103 Wing fence
104 Six-wheel main landing gear bogie
105 Glove section additional stores pylon
106 Wing pivot box integral fuel tank
107 Fixed-wing glove section leading-edge slat
108 AS-4 'Kitchen' air-to-surface missile
109 Folding ventral fin

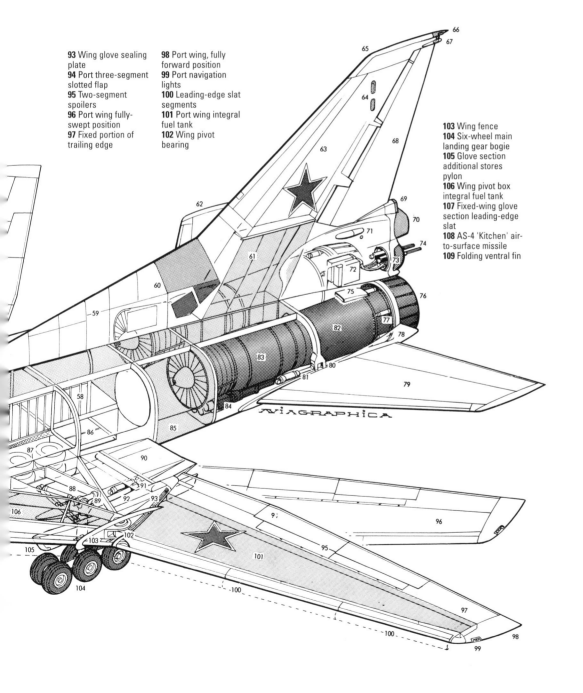

# Vickers Valiant

*A Valiant tanker of No. 214 Squadron is towed past a Bloodhound SAM battery at RAF Marham, Norfolk. This location became the main Valiant operating base in the final years of the type's career, housing two tanker units (Nos 90 and 214 Sqns) and three NATO-assigned bomber units (Nos 49, 148 and 207 Sqns).*

## Valiant B.Mk 1

### Cutaway key

1 Flight refuelling probe, detachable
2 Refuelling probe blanking adaptor
3 De-icing fluid tank
4 Refuelling floodlight
5 $H_2S$ amplifier
6 Gyro unit
7 Radar scanner mounting frame
8 Radome
9 $H_2S$ radar scanner
10 Oxygen and nitrogen bottles
11 Sloping front pressure bulkhead
12 Instrument panel
13 Side mounted control column
14 Rudder pedals
15 Pilot's floor level
16 Bomb sight
17 Ventral bomb aimers windows
18 Bombardier's prone position couch
19 IFF aerial
20 Crew entry door
21 Main crew compartment
22 Air Electronics Officer's seat
23 Door opening bail-out blast shield
24 Dual Navigator's seats to starboard
25 Refuelling line fairing (outside pressurised compartment)
26 Direct vision opening side window panel
27 Curved windscreen panels
28 Jettisonable cockpit roof hatch
29 Second Pilot's Martin-Baker Mk.3A ejection seat
30 Cockpit eyebrow window
31 First Pilot's ejection seat
32 Sextant dome, jettisonable
33 Sextant
34 Cabin roof ditching hatch
35 UHF aerials
36 Radio equipment racks
37 Rear pressure bulkhead
38 Lower crew compartment window, escape hatch on starboard side
39 Nosewheel leg pivot mounting
40 Twin nosewheels, aft retracting
41 Position of HF aerial rail on starboard nosewheel door
42 Mudguard
43 Nosewheel bay
44 Air conditioning equipment
45 Flood-flow cooling air intake
46 Heat exchanger
47 Radar equipment racks
48 Oxygen bottles
49 Dinghy stowage
50 Dinghy inflation bottles
51 ADF aerial
52 Electrical and electronics equipment bay
53 Fuel tank bay bulkhead
54 Fire extinguisher bottles
55 Port engine air intakes
56 Battery compartment
57 Radar altimeter aerials
58 Ground power connection
59 Retractable bomb bay deflectors
60 Intake Spraymat de-icing
61 Inward and upward opening bomb doors
62 Bomb door rack-and-pinion drive mechanism
63 Bomb bay roof
64 Front spar/fuselage frame attachment
65 Reserve tank
66 No 1 fuel tank, total fuel capacity including wing external tanks, 9,972 Imp gal (45,332 litre)
67 Wing front spar, joined on aircraft centreline
68 No 2 fuel tank
69 Fuel recupurators
70 Fuel system piping
71 Upper fuselage central keel member
72 Starboard engine bays
73 Intake ducts
74 Engine bay firewalls
75 De-icing air heat exchanger intake
76 Starboard main undercarriage, stowed position
77 Leading edge de-icing air duct
78 External fuel tank
79 Tank pylon
80 Starboard wing fuel tanks
81 Wing fence
82 Wing stringers
83 Vortex generators
84 Wing skin panelling
85 Pitot head
86 Starboard navigation light
87 ILS glideslope aerial
88 Fuel vent
89 Starboard two-

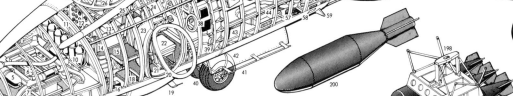

## SPECIFICATION

**Valiant B(K).Mk 1**

### Dimensions
**Length:** 114 ft 4 in (34.85 m)
**Height:** 32 ft 2 in (9.80 m)
**Wing area:** 2,362 sq ft (219.43 m²)

### Powerplant
Four Rolls-Royce Avon RA.28 (200 series), each rated at 10,000 lb (44.48 kN) thrust

### Weights
**Empty:** 75,881 lb (34419 kg)
**Maximum all-up:** 140,000 lb (63503 kg)

### Performance
**Maximum speed at 30,000 ft (9144 m):** 567 mph (912 km/h)
**Service ceiling:** 54,000 ft (16459 m)
**Range:** 4,500 miles (7242 km) with underwing tanks

### Bomb load
No gun armament. Bomb load comprised either one 10,000-lb (4536-kg) nuclear weapon (Blue Danube) or 21 1,000-lb (454-kg) iron bombs. In the tanking role a pair of 1,615-Imp gal (7342-litre) fuel tanks could be carried in the bomb bay.

*Throughout the Valiant's career crew training was performed at Gaydon by 232 Operational Conversion Unit. From 1957 the unit also trained Victor crews, the Valiant element becoming 'B' Squadron. Although formation flying had no operational relevance to the V-force, it was occasionally practised.*

*Only one Valiant was saved from the scrapper's torch, though fortunately it was an airframe with an important and interesting history. XD818 was one of the eight Grapple aircraft and dropped Britain's first thermonuclear weapon on 15 May 1957. After several years at the mercy of the elements, on the gate at RAF Marham, this unique machine was saved by the RAF Museum and resides in the Bomber Command Hall.*

segment aileron
**90** Geared tab
**91** Aileron hinge control
**92** Aileron trim tab
**93** Flap guide rails and screw jacks
**94** Starboard double-slotted flaps, down position
**95** Starboard ventral airbrake
**96** Exhaust nozzles
**97** Jet pipe fairings
**98** No 3 fuel tank
**99** Central aileron power control unit
**100** Water-methanol tanks
**101** Fuel system pressure relief valves
**102** Transfer tanks
**103** De-icing air ducting
**104** Elevator artificial feel unit
**105** Rudder artificial feel unit
**106** Rear fuselage frame and stringer construction
**107** Rudder and elevator power control units
**108** De-icing air manifold
**109** Fin root fillet
**110** De-icing air intake
**111** Artificial feel system pressurisation intake
**112** Fin lower segment
**113** Leading edge de-icing air ducts
**114** Fixed portion of horizontal tailplane
**115** Tailplane hinge joint
**116** Starboard all-moving trimming tailplane
**117** Starboard elevator
**118** Elevator tab
**119** Fin leading edge integral de-icing air duct
**120** Fin rib construction
**121** VHF aerial
**122** De-icing air outlet duct
**123** Fin tip aerial fairing
**124** Gee aerial
**125** Rudder trim tab
**126** Rudder rib construction
**127** Rudder seals
**128** Elevator hinge control
**129** Elevator mass-balance
**130** Trimming tailplane screwjack
**131** Port elevator rib construction
**132** Tail radome
**133** Elevator trim tab
**134** Elevator horn balance
**135** Tailplane rib construction
**136** Rudder control torque shaft
**137** Tailplane trim motor
**138** Sloping fin spar attachment bulkheads
**139** Rear fuselage ventral access hatch
**140** Doppler transceivers
**141** VHF equipment
**142** Refuelling drogue, Valiant B.(K)1
**143** Signal lights
**144** Bomb bay mounted hose drum unit
**145** Fuel pumps
**146** Ventral Doppler antenna
**147** Rear fuselage catwalk
**148** Aileron artificial feel unit
**149** Upward hinged rear bomb bay deflector
**150** Port engine exhaust nozzles
**151** Inboard flap segment beneath jet pipes
**152** Port jet pipes
**153** Rearspar
**154** Engine bay dividing firewall
**155** Bleed air ducting
**156** Rolls-Royce Avon R.A.28 Mk.204 engines
**157** De-icing air manifold
**158** Fire extinguisher bottles
**159** Main undercarriage pivot mounting
**160** Electric main and emergency undercarriage leg actuators
**161** Flap drive shaft and screw jacks
**162** Port ventral airbrake
**163** Flap shroud ribs
**164** Flap rib construction
**165** Flap track fairings
**166** Port double-slotted flaps
**167** Aileron trim tab
**168** Geared tab
**169** Aileron rib construction
**170** Port two-segment aileron
**171** Aileron seals
**172** Fuel vent
**173** VOR localiser aerial
**174** Port navigation light
**175** Pitot head
**176** Leading edge nose ribs
**177** Retractable landing lamp
**178** Fuel vent valve
**179** Wing outboard fuel tanks
**180** External fuel tank
**181** Fuel pump
**182** Nitrogen pressurising bottles
**183** Ground nitrogen and air charging points
**184** Tank rib construction
**185** Tank pylon construction
**186** Port wing fence
**187** Wing inboard fuel tanks
**188** Mainwheel door electric actuator
**189** Leading edge de-icing air duct
**190** Mainwheel door
**191** Twin tandem mainwheels
**192** Disc brakes and anti-skid units
**193** Horizontal telescopic torque link
**194** Shock absorber leg struts
**195** Side stay and breaker strut
**196** Balance strut
**197** Bifurcated de-icing air duct
**198** Bomb bay weapons carrier
**199** 1,000-lb (454-kg) HE bombs, maximum load 21 in groups of 5 and 3
**200** 10,000-lb (4536-kg) free-fall nuclear weapon

# Fighters

# Convair F-102 Delta Dagger

509th FIS F-102As pass over defoliated and bomb-blasted terrain in South Vietnam. With little air threat, the F-102 was used as an escort for the B-52, and in a limited ground attack capacity (for which it was credited with the destruction of 106 buildings, 16 sampans and a bridge during 199 sorties). Vietnam involvement began in March 1962 for the F-102, when four examples were deployed to Tan Son Nhut. Further examples were sent out by President Johnson following the Gulf of Tonkin incident in August 1964 under the codename Water Glass. By the end of 1968, six aircraft were on alert at Bien Hoa, six at Da Nang, and a further 10 were in Thailand.

## F-102A

**Cutaway key**

1 Pitot head
2 Radome
3 Radar scanner
4 Scanner tracking mechanism
5 ILS glideslope aerial
6 Radar mounting bulkhead
7 Radar pulse generator and modulator units
8 Nose compartment access doors
9 Static port
10 Lower IFF aerial
11 Angle of attack transmitter
12 TACAN aerial
13 MG-10 fire control system electronics
14 Nose compartment longeron
15 Infra-red detector
16 Electronics cooling air duct
17 Windscreen panels
18 Central vision splitter
19 Instrument panel shroud
20 Rudder pedals and linkages
21 Cockpit front pressure bulkhead
22 Air-conditioning system ram air intake
23 Boundary layer splitter plate
24 Electrical system equipment
25 Port air intake
26 Nosewheel door
27 Taxiing lamp
28 Nosewheel, forward-retracting
29 Nose undercarriage leg strut
30 Torque scissor links
31 Intake duct framing
32 Nose undercarriage pivot mounting
33 Cockpit pressure floor
34 Port side console panel

35 Engine throttle lever
36 Two-handed control grip, radar and flight controls
37 Pilot's ejection seat
38 Canopy handle
39 Starboard side console panel
40 Radar display
41 Optical sight
42 Cockpit canopy cover, upward-hinging
43 Ejection seat headrest
44 Boundary layer spill duct
45 Sloping cockpit rear pressure bulkhead
46 Air-conditioning plant
47 Canopy external release
48 Canopy jack
49 Air exit louvres
50 Equipment bay access hatches, port and starboard
51 Canopy hinge
52 Radio and electronics equipment bay
53 Forward position light
54 Intake trunking
55 Missile bay cooling air duct
56 Missile bay door pneumatic jacks
57 Canopy emergency release
58 Liquid oxygen converter
59 Electrical system equipment bay
60 Fuselage upper longeron
61 Upper IFF aerial
62 Wing front spar attachment bulkhead

63 Pneumatic system air bottles
64 Bifurcated intake duct
65 Close-pitched fuselage frame construction
66 Engine bleed air duct
67 Anti-collision light
68 Starboard wing forward main fuel tank, total internal capacity 1,085 US gal (4107 litres)
69 Inboard wing fence
70 Fuel system piping
71 Centre-section wing dry bay
72 Wing pylon mountings and connectors
73 Starboard main undercarriage pivot mounting
74 Dorsal spine fairing
75 Intake duct mixing chamber
76 Engine intake centre-body fairing
77 Wing main spar attachment bulkheads
78 Intake compressor face
79 Forward engine mounting
80 Pratt & Whitney J57-P-23A afterburning turbojet engine
81 Engine oil tank, capacity 5.5 US gal (21 litres)
82 Oil filler cap

83 Starboard wing aft main fuel tanks
84 Fuel feed and vent piping
85 Ventral actuator fairing
86 Outboard wing fence
87 Cambered leading edge
88 Wing tip camber wash-out
89 Starboard navigation light
90 Fixed portion of trailing edge
91 Starboard outer elevon
92 Elevon hydraulic actuator
93 Trailing-edge dry bay
94 Fin leading-edge rib construction
95 Aerial tuning units
96 Fin attachment joints
97 Tailfin construction
98 Artificial feel system pitot intakes
99 Sloping front spar
100 Upper fin multi-spar construction
101 Fintip aerial fairing

102 UHF aerials
103 VOR localiser aerial
104 Rudder
105 Honeycomb core rudder construction
106 Split airbrake panels
107 Airbrake pneumatic jacks
108 Airbrake, open position
109 Variable-area afterburner exhaust nozzle
110 Aft fuselage aerodynamic (area-rule) fairing
111 Exhaust nozzle control jacks (eight)
112 Tailcone attachment joint frame (engine removal)
113 Rear position lights
114 Afterburner duct
115 Engine bay internal heat shield

116 Brake parachute housing
117 Rudder hydraulic actuator
118 Rudder trim and feel force control units
119 Afterburner fuel manifold
120 Rear engine mounting
121 Inboard elevon hydraulic actuator
122 Engine turbine section
123 Bleed air connections
124 Bleed air blow-off valve
125 Engine accessory equipment gearbox
126 Wing spar/fuselage frame pin joints
127 Wingroot rib
128 Port wing aft integral fuel tanks

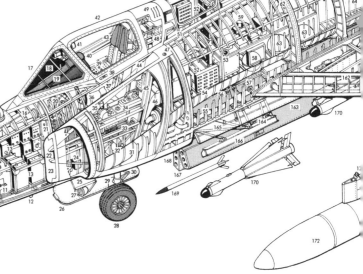

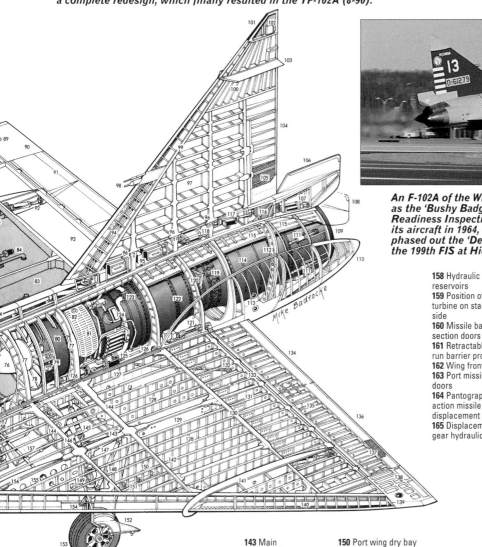

## SPECIFICATION

### F-102A Delta Dagger

**Dimensions**

**Length:** 68 ft 4½ in (20.82 m)
**Wingspan:** 38 ft 1½ in (11.60 m)
**Height:** 21 ft 2½ in (6.45 m)
**Wing area:** 695 sq ft (64.56 m²)

**Powerplant**

One Pratt & Whitney J57-P-23 turbojet developing 11,700 lb (53 kN) of thrust dry and 17,200 lb (77 kN) thrust with afterburning

**Weights**

**Empty:** 19,350 lb (8777 kg)
**Normal loaded, 'clean':** 27,700 lb (12565 kg)
**Normal loaded, point interception:** 28,150 lb (12789 kg)
**Maximum take-off:** 31,500 lb (14288 kg)

**Fuel**

**Internal:** 1,085 US gal (4107 litre)
**Maximum, with two 215-US gal**
**(814-litre) drop tanks:** 1,515 US gal (5735 litre)

**Performance**

**Maximum speed 'clean' at 40,000 ft (12190 m):** 825 mph (1328 km/h)
**Normal cruising speed at 35,000 ft (10670 m):** 540 mph (869 km/h)
**Stalling speed:** 154 mph (248 km/h)
**Service ceiling:** 54,000 ft (16460 m)
**Tactical radius with two 215-US gal (814-litre) drop tanks and full armament:** 500 miles (805 km)
**Maximum range:** 1,350 miles (2173 km)
**Initial climb rate:** 17,400 ft (5304 m) per minute

**Armament**

Three AIM-4C Falcon infra-red homing AAMs and one AIM-26A Nuclear Falcon AAM, or three AIM-4A/E radar-guided and three AIM-4C/F infra-red homing AAMs, or up to 24 unguided 2.75-in (70-mm) folding fin aircraft rockets in early aircraft (this latter facility was later deleted in service)

*The first YF-102 (Model 8-80), 52-7994, is seen on the dry lake at Edwards AFB test facility. After only six flights the aircraft was lost after an engine flame-out during take-off. First flown by test pilot Dick Johnson on 24 October 1953, the YF-102 suffered from severe instability and buffeting in the transonic region, and the second aircraft refused to accelerate past Mach 1. The failure of the initial YF-102 necessitated a complete redesign, which finally resulted in the YF-102A (8-90).*

*An F-102A of the Wisconsin ANG's 176th FIS (sometimes known as the 'Bushy Badgers') takes off during an Operational Readiness Inspection (ORI). The first F-102 squadron gave up its aircraft in 1964, but the bulk of the 23 ANG units so-equipped phased out the 'Deuce' in the 1969-71 period. The final user was the 199th FIS at Hickam AFB, retiring the F-102 in October 1976.*

158 Hydraulic reservoirs
159 Position of ram air turbine on starboard side
160 Missile bay aft section doors
161 Retractable over-run barrier probe
162 Wing front spar
163 Port missile bay doors
164 Pantographic action missile displacement gear
165 Displacement gear hydraulic jack

166 Missile launch rail
167 Missile bay door integral rocket launch tubes
168 Centre missile bay door
169 2.75-in (70-mm) FFAR folding-fin rockets (24)
170 AIM-4D Falcon air-to-air missile (6)
171 Port wing fuel tank pylon
172 215-US gal (814-litre) external fuel tank

129 Fuel tank dividing rib
130 Rear spar
131 Trailing-edge ribs
132 Runway emergency arrester hook, lowered
133 Elevon spar
134 Inboard elevon
135 Elevon rib construction

136 Outboard elevon
137 Trailing-edge honeycomb
138 Wingtip fairing construction
139 Port navigation light
140 Cambered leading-edge rib construction
141 Outboard wing fence
142 Wing rib construction

143 Main undercarriage mounting rib
144 Twin main spars
145 Main undercarriage side strut
146 Hydraulic retraction jack
147 Main undercarriage leg pivot mounting
148 Drag strut and pneumatic brake reservoir
149 Landing lamp

150 Port wing dry bay
151 Wing pylon mountings and connectors
152 Main undercarriage leg door
153 Port mainwheel
154 Torque scissor links
155 Port wing forward integral fuel tank
156 Inboard wing fence
157 Mainwheel door

# Convair F-106 Delta Dart

*'Spittin' Kittens' F-106s originally wore a large tail chevron as seen on this aircraft – the F-106 belonging to the 5th FIS's commanding officer – in May 1974. The more famous lightning bolt and stars appeared several years later.*

## F-106A Delta Dart

**Cutaway key**

1 Pitot head
2 Radome
3 Radar scanner dish
4 Radar tracking mechanism
5 Hughes MA-1 weapons system radar unit
6 Radar mounting bulkhead
7 Pulse generator units
8 TACAN aerial
9 Angle of attack transmitter
10 MA-1 weapons system electronics units
11 Electronics bay access door
12 Infra-red detector fairing
13 Retractable infra-red detector
14 Knife-edged windscreen panels
15 Central vision splitter
16 Instrument panel shroud
17 'Head down' tactical display panel
18 Canopy external release
19 Rudder pedals
20 Cockpit front pressure bulkhead
21 Electrical relay panel
22 Nose undercarriage wheel bay
23 Nosewheel door
24 Taxiing lamp
25 Twin nosewheels
26 Torque scissor links
27 UHF aerial
28 Nose undercarriage leg strut

29 Oxygen filler point and gauge
30 Nosewheel leg pivot fixing
31 Liquid oxygen converter
32 Cockpit air-conditioning ducting
33 Cockpit pressure floor
34 Control column
35 Two-handed control grip, radar and flight controls
36 Engine throttle lever
37 Pilot's ejection seat
38 Radar display
39 Optical sight
40 Cockpit canopy cover
41 Ejection seat headrest
42 Ejection seat launch rails
43 Cockpit rear pressure bulkhead
44 Side console panel
45 Ground power supply connections
46 Doppler navigation unit
47 Aft lower electronics compartment
48 Aft upper electronics equipment bays, port and starboard
49 Electronics bay door
50 Cockpit rear decking
51 Over pressurisation relief valve

52 Canopy pneumatic jack
53 Canopy hinge
54 Air exit louvres
55 Starboard engine air intake
56 Fuel tank access panel
57 Upper longeron
58 Fuselage fuel tank, total internal capacity, 1,514 US gal (5731 litres)
59 Fuselage frame construction
60 Ventral weapons bay
61 Missile pallet hinge arms
62 Bottom longeron
63 Boundary layer splitter plate
64 Port engine air intake
65 Variable area intake ramp
66 Ramp bleed air louvres
67 Air-conditioning system intake duct
68 Intake duct framing
69 Starboard side pressure refuelling connection
70 Forward missile pallet pneumatic jack
71 Air-conditioning plant
72 De-icing fluid reservoir
73 Heat exchanger air exit duct

74 Air refuelling ramp door, open
75 Pneumatic system air bottles
76 Bifurcated intake ducting
77 Aft missile pylon pneumatic jacks
78 AIR-2 Genie air-to-air missile housing
79 Hydraulic accumulators
80 Hydraulic reservoirs, duplex systems
81 Intake trunking
82 Wing spar attachment fuselage main frames
83 Oil cooler air duct
84 Intake centre-body fairing
85 Engine intake compressor face
86 Bleed air ducting
87 Dorsal spine fairing
88 Fuel boost pump
89 Starboard main undercarriage pivot fixing
90 Wing forward fuel tank

91 Dry bay
92 Wing pylon mountings and connectors
93 Fuel system piping
94 Starboard wing main fuel tank
95 Leading-edge slot
96 Cambered leading edge
97 Wingtip fairing
98 Starboard navigation light
99 Outboard elevon
100 Elevon hydraulic jack
101 Elevon jack ventral fairing
102 Inboard elevon
103 Starboard wing aft fuel tank
104 Fuel system vent piping
105 Engine oil tank, 45 US gal (17 litres)
106 Pratt & Whitney J75-P-17 turbojet engine

107 Forward engine mounting
108 Ventral accessory equipment compartment
109 Cooling air ducting
110 Wing and fin spar attachment main frame
111 Inboard elevon hydraulic jack
112 Engine turbine section
113 Exhaust pipe heat shroud
114 Rear engine mounting
115 Aerial tuning units
116 Artificial feel system pitot intakes
117 Fin leading edge
118 Tailfin construction

119 Air-to-air identification (AAI) aerial
120 Fin tip aerial fairing
121 UHF/TACAN aerial
122 Tail navigation light
123 Rudder
124 Rudder honeycomb construction
125 Split air brake panels

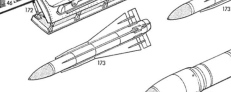

Before the first F-106 even flew, authorisation was given for the construction of a two-seat variant of the Delta Dart. Unlike the TF-102A, with its side-by-side seating and inferior performance to the single-seater, the F-106B was designed to be as close to the F-106A as possible. Due to the fact that it was more than a trainer and carried all the mission equipment of a basic interceptor, it was not given the TF-106A designation. This particular aircraft (57-2540) was, in common with many F-106s, converted into a drone (QF-106) and shot down with an AIM-120 AMRAAM.

## SPECIFICATION

### F-106A Delta Dart

**Dimensions**

**Length (with probe):** 70 ft 8 in (21.55 m)
**Wingspan:** 38 ft 3½ in (11.67 m)
**Wing area:** 697.5 sq ft (64.8 m²)
**Height:** 20 ft 3⅓ in (6.18 m)

**Powerplant**

One Pratt & Whitney J75-P-17 turbojet rated at 17,200 lb (77.4 kN) dry and 24,500 lb (110.25 kN) with full afterburner

**Weights**

**Empty:** 23,814 lb (10800 kg)
**Normal loaded:** 35,500 lb (16012 kg)
**Maximum take-off:** 38,250 lb (17350 kg)

**Performance**

**Maximum speed (without tanks) at 40,000 ft:** Mach 2.25 (1,487 mph/ 2393 km/h)
**Sustained ceiling:** 58,000 ft (17680 m)
**Combat radius (with internal fuel):** 575 miles (925 km)
**Combat radius (with external tanks and aerial refuelling):** 1,950 miles (3138 km)
**Time to 57,000 ft (17374 m):** 4.5 min

**Armament**

Most aircraft had an M61A-1 20-mm cannon. Standard missile armament was four AIM-4E/F and/or AIM-4G Falcon AAMs (Super Falcons) plus one AIR-2A Genie nuclear rocket. The F-106 also tested the XAIM-97A ASAT weapon

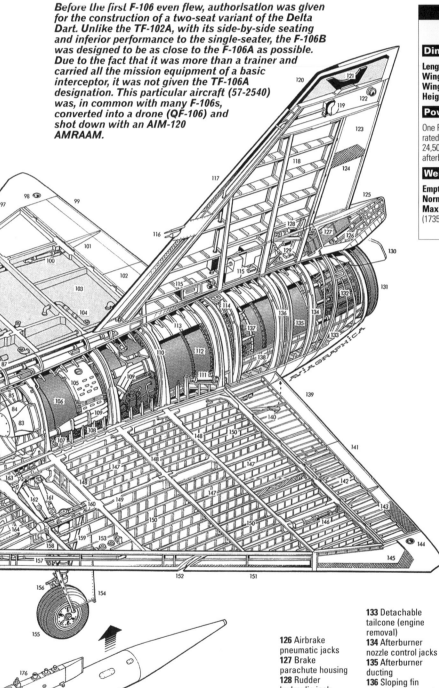

126 Airbrake pneumatic jacks
127 Brake parachute housing
128 Rudder hydraulic jack
129 Rudder trim and feel force control units
130 Air brake, open position
131 Divergent exhaust nozzle
132 Variable-area afterburner exhaust nozzle

133 Detachable tailcone (engine removal)
134 Afterburner nozzle control jacks
135 Afterburner ducting
136 Sloping fin mounting bulkheads
137 Afterburner fuel spray manifold
138 Engine withdrawal rail
139 Port inboard elevon
140 Runway emergency arresting hook, lowered

141 Port outboard elevon
142 Elevon rib construction
143 Honeycomb trailing-edge panels
144 Port navigation light
145 Honeycomb wingtip fairing
146 Outboard elevon hydraulic jack
147 Port wing integral fuel tank
148 Machined wing spars
149 Machined main undercarriage mounting rib
150 Wing rib construction
151 Cambered leading edge
152 Leading-edge slot
153 Port wing pylon connectors
154 Main wheel leg door
155 Port mainwheel
156 Torque scissor links
157 Landing lamp

158 Main undercarriage leg strut
159 Drag brace and pneumatic brake reservoir
160 Main undercarriage leg pivot fixing
161 Breaker strut

162 Hydraulic retraction jack
163 Main undercarriage wheel bay
164 Mainwheel doors
165 Emergency ram air turbine
166 Port wing forward fuel tank bay
167 Fuel system vent pipe
168 Aft single missile pylon, port and starboard, lowered position
169 Weapons bay doors, open
170 Missile launch rail
171 Forward twin missile pallet

172 Weapons bay door pneumatic jack
173 AIM-4F Falcon air-to-air missile (4)
174 Single AIR-2A Genie air-to-air nuclear missile
175 Missile folding fins, deployed position
176 Port wing pylon
177 227-US gal (859-litre) external fuel tank

# Gloster Meteor

As the operational life of the Meteor began to draw to a close, a large number of Meteor F.Mk 8s was modified to become target-towing tugs and advanced trainers. The target tugs were unofficially designated 'F(TT).Mk 8' and the trainers 'T.Mk 8'. Both types received high-visibility markings and a 'T.Mk 8' of No. 85 Sqn, with bright orange Dayglo markings, is seen here accompanying a Lightning of No. 5 Sqn.

## Meteor F.Mk III

**Cutaway key**

1 Starboard detachable wingtip
2 Starboard navigation light
3 Starboard recognition light
4 Starboard aileron
5 Aileron balance tab
6 Aileron mass balance weights
7 Aileron control coupling
8 Aileron torque shaft
9 Chain sprocket
10 Cross-over control runs
11 Front spar
12 Rear spar
13 Aileron (inboard) mass balance
14 Nacelle detachable tail section
15 Jet pipe exhaust
16 Internal stabilising struts
17 Rear spar 'spectacle' frame
18 Fire extinguisher spray ring
19 Main engine mounting frame
20 Engine access panel(s)
21 Nacelle nose structure
22 Intake internal leading-edge shroud
23 Starboard engine intake
24 Windscreen de-icing spray tube
25 Reflector gunsight
26 Cellular glass bulletproof windscreen
27 Aft-sliding cockpit canopy
28 Demolition incendiary (cockpit starboard wall)
29 RPM indicators (left and right of gunsight)
30 Pilot's seat
31 Forward fuselage top deflector skin
32 Gun wobble button
33 Control column grip

34 Main instrument panel
35 Nosewheel armoured bulkhead
36 Nose release catches (10)
37 Nosewheel jack bulkhead
38 Nose ballast weight location
39 Nosewheel mounting frames
40 Radius rod (link and jack omitted)
41 Nosewheel pivot bearings
42 Shimmy-damper/self-centring strut
43 Gun camera
44 Camera access
45 Aperture
46 Nose cone
47 Cabin cold-air intake
48 Nosewheel leg door
49 Picketing rings
50 Tension shock absorber
51 Pivot bracket
52 Mudguard
53 Torque strut
54 Doorhoop
55 Wheel fork
56 Retractable nosewheel
57 Nosewheel doors
58 Port cannon trough fairings
59 Nosewheel cover
60 Intermediate diaphragm
61 Blast tubes
62 Gun front mount rails
63 Pilot's seat pan
64 Emergency crowbar
65 Canopy de-misting silica gel cylinder
66 Bulletproof glass rear view cut-outs
67 Canopy track
68 Sea bulkhead
69 Entry step
70 Link ejection chutes
71 Case ejection chutes
72 20-mm Hispano Mk III cannon
73 Belt feed mechanism

74 Ammunition feed necks
75 Ammunition tanks
76 Aft glazing (magazine bay top door)
77 Leading ramp
78 Front spar bulkhead
79 Oxygen bottles (2)

80 Front spar carry-through
81 Tank bearer frames
82 Rear spar carry-through
83 Self-sealing (twin compartment) main fuel tank, capacity 165 Imp gal (750 litres) in each half
84 Fuel connector pipe
85 Return pipe
86 Drain pipes
87 Fuel filler caps

88 Tank doors (2)
89 T.R.1143 aerial mast
90 Rear spar bulkhead (plywood face)
91 Aerial support frame
92 R.3121 (or B.C.966M IFF installation
93 Tab control cables
94 Amplifier
95 Fire extinguisher bottles (2)
96 Elevator torque shaft
97 T.R.1143 transmitter/ receiver radio installation

98 Pneumatic system filler
99 Pneumatic system (compressed) air cylinders
100 Tab cable fairlead
101 Elevator control cable
102 Top longeron
103 Fuselage frame
104 IFF aerial
105 DR compass master unit
106 Rudder cables
107 Starboard lower longeron
108 Cable access panels (port and starboard)
109 Tail section joint
110 Rudder linkage

111 Tail ballast weight location
112 Fin spar/fuselage frame
113 Rudder tab control
114 Fin structure
115 Torpedo fairing
116 Tailplane spar/upper fin attachment plates
117 Upper fin section
118 Starboard tailplane
119 Elevator horn and mass balance
120 Starboard elevator

## SPECIFICATION

### Meteor F.Mk 8

#### Dimensions

**Length:** 44 ft 7 in (13.59 m)
**Wingspan:** 37 ft 2 in (11.33 m)
**Height:** 13 ft (3.96 m)
**Wing area:** 350 sq ft (32.515 m²)
**Aspect ratio:** 3.9
**Root chord:** 11 ft 9 in (3.6 m)

#### Powerplant

Two 3,500-lb (15.5-kN) thrust Rolls-Royce Derwent 8 turbojets

#### Weights

**Empty:** 10,684 lb (4846 kg)
**Maximum overload:** 15,700 lb (7122 kg)

#### Performance

**Maximum speed at sea level:** 592 mph (953 km/h)
**Maximum speed at 30,000 ft (9144 m):** 550 mph (885 km/h)
**Climb to 30,000 ft (9144 m):** 6 minutes 30 seconds
**Service ceiling:** 44,000 ft (13410 m)
**Range without wing drop tanks:** 690 miles (1111 km)
**Endurance at 40,000 ft (12192 m) with 420 Imp gal (1909 litres) of fuel:** 592 mph (953 km/h)

#### Armament

Four fixed 20-mm British Hispano cannon in the nose with 195 rounds per gun

*EE389 was the first Meteor involved in inflight-refuelling trials, in April 1949. Here it is seen, with its airbrakes deployed and probe clearly evident, about to refuel from a Lancaster Mk III tanker. The neat probe installation in the nose of the aircraft served as the basis of a similar fitting applied to a number of Mk 4s and Mk 8s.*

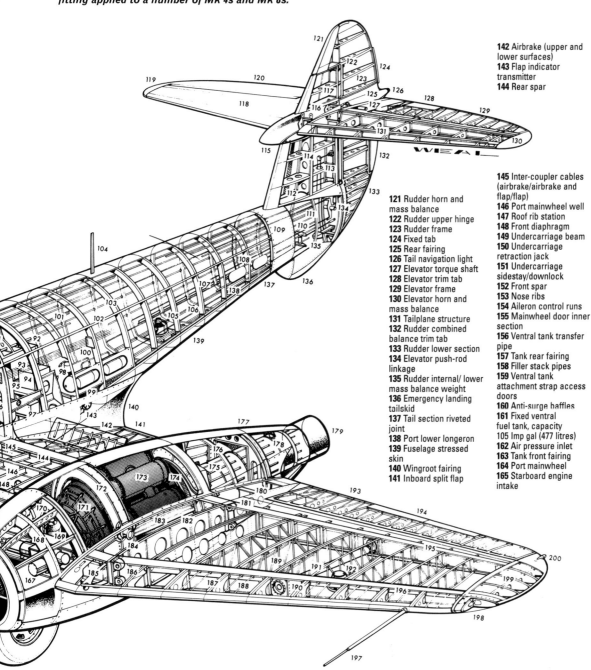

121 Rudder horn and mass balance
122 Rudder upper hinge
123 Rudder frame
124 Fixed tab
125 Rear fairing
126 Tail navigation light
127 Elevator torque shaft
128 Elevator trim tab
129 Elevator frame
130 Elevator horn and mass balance
131 Tailplane structure
132 Rudder combined balance trim tab
133 Rudder lower section
134 Elevator push-rod linkage
135 Rudder internal/ lower mass balance weight
136 Emergency landing tailskid
137 Tail section riveted joint
138 Port lower longeron
139 Fuselage stressed skin
140 Wingroot fairing
141 Inboard split flap

142 Airbrake (upper and lower surfaces)
143 Flap indicator transmitter
144 Rear spar

145 Inter-coupler cables (airbrake/airbrake and flap/flap)
146 Port mainwheel well
147 Roof rib station
148 Front diaphragm
149 Undercarriage beam
150 Undercarriage retraction jack
151 Undercarriage sidestay/downlock
152 Front spar
153 Nose ribs
154 Aileron control runs
155 Mainwheel door inner section
156 Ventral tank transfer pipe
157 Tank rear fairing
158 Filler stack pipes
159 Ventral tank attachment strap access doors
160 Anti-surge baffles
161 Fixed ventral fuel tank, capacity 105 Imp gal (477 litres)
162 Air pressure inlet
163 Tank front fairing
164 Port mainwheel
165 Starboard engine intake

166 Intake internal leading edge shroud
167 Auxiliary gearbox drives (vacuum pump/generator)
168 Nacelle nose structure
169 Starter motor
170 Oil tank
171 Rolls-Royce W.2B/23C Derwent I
172 Main engine mounting frame
173 Combustion chambers
174 Rear spar spectacle frame
175 Jet pipe thermo-coupling
176 Nacelle aft frames
177 Nacelle detachable tail section
178 Jet pipe suspension link
179 Jet pipe exhaust
180 Gap fairing tail section
181 Rear-spar outer wing fixing
182 Outer wing rib No. 1
183 Engine end rib
184 Engine mounting/ removal trunnion
185 Gap fairing nose section
186 Front-spar outer wing fixing
187 Nose ribs
188 Intermediate riblets
189 Wing ribs
190 Aileron drive chain sprocket
191 Aileron torque shaft
192 Retractable landing lamp
193 Port aileron
194 Aileron balance tab
195 Rear spar
196 Front spar
197 Pitot head
198 Port navigation light
199 Outer wing rib No. 10/wingtip attachment
200 Port recognition light

# Lockheed F-94 Starfire

*The 15th production Starfire, 50-970, poses for one of a series of publicity photographs. This aircraft was delivered to the Air Proving Ground Command at Eglin AFB on 3 October 1952 where it was used as a test aircraft in the programme to develop wing rocket pods for the F-94C.*

### F-94C Starfire

**Cutaway key**
1 Radome
2 Radar scanner
3 Radar tracking mechanism
4 Electronics cooling air intake
5 Rocket door hydraulic jack
6 Retractable rocket launching doors
7 Pitot tube
8 Nose compartment rocket launching tubes, 24 x 2.75-in (7-cm) folding fin rockets
9 Battery bay
10 AN/APG-40 radar transmitter
11 AN/APX-6 radar unit
12 Flight data computer
13 AN/ARC-27 radio
14 Nosewheel pivot mounting
15 Landing/taxiing lamps
16 Torque scissors
17 Nosewheel
18 Nose undercarriage leg strut
19 Steering jack and shimmy damper
20 Nosewheel doors
21 Electrical equipment bay
22 Oxygen bottles, port and starboard
23 Nose compartment upper beam construction
24 Front pressure bulkhead
25 Rudder pedals
26 Windscreen de-misting air blower

27 Instrument panel
28 Instrument panel shroud
29 Windscreen framing
30 N-3C standby reflector sight
31 Control column
32 Engine throttle control
33 Pressure refuelling connection
34 Air conditioning plant
35 Port engine air intake

36 Boundary layer bleed air duct
37 Cockpit framing
38 Pilot's ejection seat
39 Cockpit canopy cover
40 Ejection seat headrest
41 AN/ARN-6 radio compass loop antenna
42 Radar operator's AN/APG-40 indicator
43 Accelerometer
44 Intake ducting
45 Side console panel
46 Cockpit pressurisation valve
47 Rear pressure bulkhead
48 Radar operator's blackout hood, folded
49 Radar viewing scope

50 Canopy-mounted ADF sense aerial
51 Radar operator's ejection seat
52 Starboard wing main fuel tanks: total one-wing capacity (with 53 and 66), 129 US gal/ 488 litres)
53 Leading-edge tank
54 Starboard wing rocket pod, 12 x 2.75-in (7-cm) rockets
55 Frangible nose cap
56 Leading-edge de-icing boots
57 Tip tank, 250-US gal (946-litre) capacity
58 Fuel filler cap
59 Tip tank attachment and jettison controls
60 Starboard identification light
61 Aileron spoiler

62 Starboard aileron
63 Aileron hinge control
64 Aileron balance weights
65 Fixed tab
66 Trailing-edge fuel tank

67 Starboard split trailing-edge flap
68 Fuselage fuel tank filler cap
69 Cockpit canopy hinge mechanism

70 Fuselage fuel tank, capacity 65 US gal (246 litres)
71 Fuselage main longeron
72 Centre-section frame construction
73 Hydraulic reservoir

74 Dorsal spine fairing
75 Fuel system vent pipe
76 Engine accessory equipment

77 Engine intake grille
78 Pratt & Whitney J48-P-7A afterburning turbojet
79 Rear fuselage break point

80 Rear fuselage bolted joints (3)
81 Engine flame tubes
82 Firewall
83 Anti-collision light
84 Fin root fairing

85 Fuel jettison valves
86 Tailplane leading-edge de-icing boots
87 Starboard tailplane
88 Fuel jettison pipe
89 Starboard elevator
90 Fin construction
91 Gyrosyn compass transmitter
92 ILS localiser aerial
93 Glideslope antenna
94 AN/ARC-27 radio aerial
95 Rudder construction
96 Fixed rudder tab
97 Rudder and elevator hinge controls
98 Brake parachute housing
99 Tail navigation light

100 Brake parachute doors, open position
101 Elevator trim tab
102 Port elevator construction
103 Elevator mass balance
104 Tailplane tip fuel jettison

*Based at Great Falls (later Malmstrom) AFB, Montana, the 29th FIS was the only USAF squadron to fly the F-94C from the 'Northern Tier' states. These three aircraft were photographed in the mid-1950s, possibly during a gunnery meet: their missing rocket pod nosecones suggest that their FFARs have been fired.*

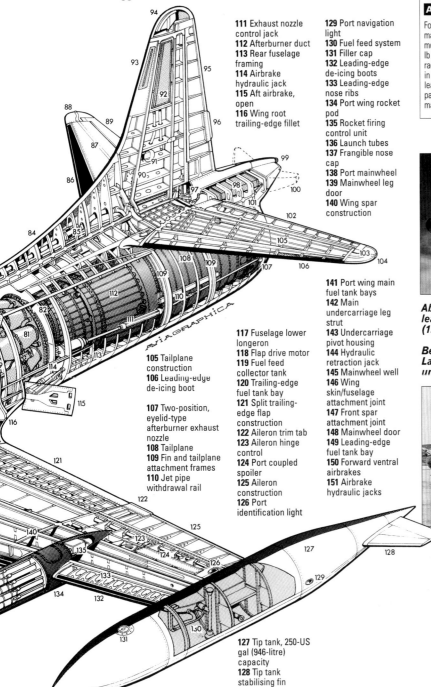

111 Exhaust nozzle control jack
112 Afterburner duct
113 Rear fuselage framing
114 Airbrake hydraulic jack
115 Aft airbrake, open
116 Wing root trailing-edge fillet

105 Tailplane construction
106 Leading-edge de-icing boot
107 Two-position, eyelid-type afterburner exhaust nozzle
108 Tailplane
109 Fin and tailplane attachment frames
110 Jet pipe withdrawal rail

117 Fuselage lower longeron
118 Flap drive motor
119 Fuel feed collector tank
120 Trailing-edge fuel tank bay
121 Split trailing-edge flap construction
122 Aileron trim tab
123 Aileron hinge control
124 Port coupled spoiler
125 Aileron construction
126 Port identification light

129 Port navigation light
130 Fuel feed system
131 Filler cap
132 Leading-edge de-icing boots
133 Leading-edge nose ribs
134 Port wing rocket pod
135 Rocket firing control unit
136 Launch tubes
137 Frangible nose cap
138 Port mainwheel
139 Mainwheel leg door
140 Wing spar construction

141 Port wing main fuel tank bays
142 Main undercarriage leg strut
143 Undercarriage pivot housing
144 Hydraulic retraction jack
145 Mainwheel well
146 Wing skin/fuselage attachment joint
147 Front spar attachment joint
148 Mainwheel door
149 Leading-edge fuel tank bay
150 Forward ventral airbrakes
151 Airbrake hydraulic jacks

127 Tip tank, 250-US gal (946-litre) capacity
128 Tip tank stabilising fin

## SPECIFICATION

| | F-94B | F-94C Starfire |
|---|---|---|
| **Dimensions** | Length: 40 ft 1 in (12.22 m)<br>Height: 12 ft 8 in (3.86 m)<br>Wingspan: 37 ft 6 in (11.43 m)<br>Wingspan (with tip tanks): 38 ft 11 in (11.86 m)<br>Wing area: 234.8 sq ft (21.813 m²) | Length: 44 ft 6 in (13.56 m)<br>Height: 14 ft 11 in (4.55 m)<br>Wingspan: 37 ft 4 in (11.38 m)<br>Wing area: 232.8 sq ft (21.628 m²) |
| **Powerplant** | One Allison J33-A-33 or -33A turbojet, rated at 5,200 lb (23.13 kN) thrust | One Pratt & Whitney J48-P-5, -5A or -7A turbojet, rated at 8,750 lb (38.91 kN) thrust with afterburner |
| **Weights** | Empty: 10,064 lb (4565 kg)<br>Loaded: 13,474 lb (6112 kg)<br>Maximum take-off: 16,844 lb (7640 kg) | Empty: 12,708 lb (5764 kg)<br>Loaded: 18,300 lb (8301 kg)<br>Maximum take-off: 24,184 lb (10970 kg) |
| **Performance** | Maximum speed at sea level: 606 mph (975 km/h)<br>Cruising speed: 452 mph (727 km/h)<br>Initial rate of climb: 6,850 ft/min (2088 m/min)<br>Service ceiling: 48,000 ft (14630 m)<br>Normal range: 665 miles (1070 km)<br>Maximum range: 905 miles (1455 km) | Maximum speed at sea level: 640 mph (1030 km/h)<br>Cruising speed: 493 mph (793 km/h)<br>Initial rate of climb: 7,980 ft/min (2432 m/min)<br>Service ceiling: 51,400 ft (15665 m)<br>Normal range: 805 miles (1295 km)<br>Maximum range: 1275 miles (2050 km) |
| **Armament** | Four Browning M3 0.5-in (12.7-mm) machine-guns, each with 300 rounds, mounted in the nose, plus up to 2,000 lb (907 kg) of bombs on underwing racks. Some aircraft modified to carry, in lieu of bombs, a gun pod on the leading edge of each wing, containing a pair of Browning M3 0.5-in (12.7-mm) machine-guns and 265 rounds per gun. | Twenty-four 2.75-in (6.99-cm) folding-fin aircraft rockets (FFARs) in four clusters of six arranged around the nose, plus (from the 100th aircraft) 12 FFARs in a pod on the leading edge of each wing. |

*Above: This 175th FIS, South Dakota ANG F-94A carries leading-edge gun pods, each with a pair of 0.5-in (12.7-mm) Brownings.*

*Below: Aircrew of the 449th FIS stand by in their F-94As at Ladd AFB, Alaska, ready to scramble and intercept unidentified aircraft reported by AEW radar.*

# Lockheed F-104 Starfighter

*Italy's Starfighters represent the ultimate expression of the F-104 in the interceptor role. Thanks to local upgrades, the aircraft are able to launch the AIM-7 Sparrow AAM or the indigenous Aspide medium-range AAM, as well as the all-aspect AIM-9L Sidewinder.*

## F-104S Starfighter

1 Pitot tube
2 Radome
3 Radar scanner dish
4 R21G/H multi-mode radar equipment
5 Radome withdrawal rails
6 Communications aerial
7 Cockpit front bulkhead
8 Infra-red sight
9 Windscreen panels
10 Reflector gunsight
11 Instrument panel shroud
12 Rudder pedals
13 Control column
14 Nose section frame construction
15 Control cable runs
16 Pilot's side console panel
17 Throttle control
18 Safety harness
19 Martin-Baker IQ-7A ejection seat
20 Face blind seat firing handle
21 Cockpit canopy cover
22 Canopy bracing struts
23 Seat rail support box
24 Angle of attack probe
25 Cockpit rear bulkhead
26 Temperature probe
27 Nosewheel doors
28 Taxiing lamp
29 Nosewheel leg strut
30 Nosewheel
31 Steering linkage
32 AIM-7 Sparrow avionics (replacing M61 gun installation of strike model)

33 Inertial platform
34 Avionics compartment
35 Avionics compartment shroud cover
36 Cockpit aft glazing
37 Ram air turbine
38 Emergency generator
39 Avionics compartment access cover
40 Fuselage frame construction
41 Pressure bulkhead
42 Ammunition compartment auxiliary fuel tank (101.5-Imp gal/462-litre capacity)
43 Fuel feed pipes
44 Flush-fitting UHF aerial panel
45 Anti-collision light
46 Starboard intake
47 Engine bleed air supply to air-conditioning
48 Gravity fuel fillers
49 Fuselage main fuel tanks (total internal capacity 746 Imp gal/3391 litres)
50 Pressure refuelling adaptor
51 Intake shock cone centre body
52 De-iced intake lip
53 Port intake
54 Shock cone boundary layer bleed
55 Boundary layer bleed air duct
56 Auxiliary intake
57 Hinged auxiliary intake door

58 Navigation light
59 Leading-edge flap jack
60 Intake trunking
61 Fuselage main longeron
62 Wingroot attaching members

63 Intake flank fuel tanks
64 Wing-mounting fuselage mainframes
65 Control cable runs
66 Electrical junction box
67 Dorsal spine fairing
68 Starboard inboard pylon
69 Leading-edge flap (lowered)
70 AIM-7 Sparrow AAM
71 Missile launch rail
72 Starboard outer pylon
73 Tip tank vane
74 Tip tank latching unit
75 Starboard wingtip tank
76 Fuel filler caps
77 Starboard aileron
78 Aileron power control jacks
79 Power control servo valves
80 Fuel lines to auxiliary tanks
81 Flap blowing duct
82 Starboard blown flap (lowered)
83 Engine intake compressor face
84 Intake spill flaps
85 Aileron torque shaft
86 Hydraulic reservoir
87 Air-conditioning bleed air supply pipe
88 General Electric J79-GE-19 turbojet
89 Engine withdrawal rail
90 Starboard airbrake (open)
91 Fin root fillet
92 Elevator servo controls

93 Elevator/all-moving tailplane hydraulic jacks
94 Push-pull control rods
95 Tailfin construction
96 Fin tip fairing
97 Tailplane rocking control arm
98 Starboard tailplane
99 One-piece tailplane construction
100 Tailplane spar
101 Tailplane spar central pivot
102 Fin trailing-edge construction

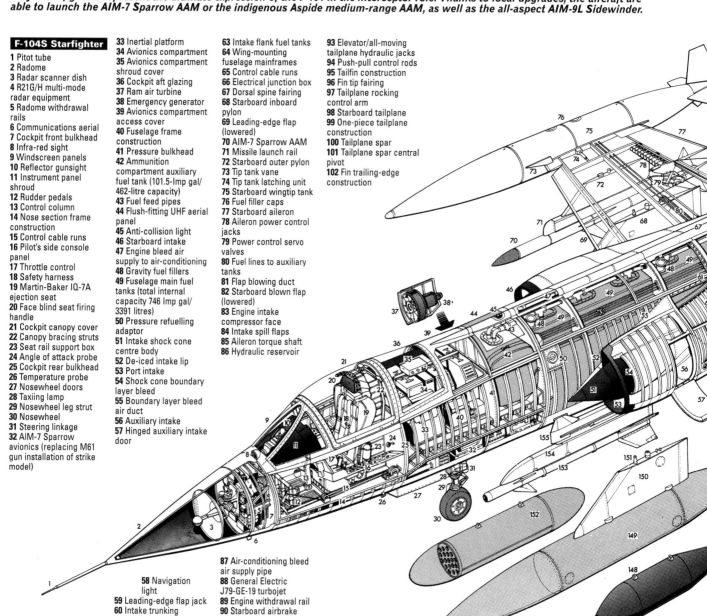

*A willing customer during the original 'sale of the century', the Netherlands was to follow several of its NATO allies in replacing its F-104s with the F-16 Fighting Falcon in the second 'sale of the century'. As it had in the US, the F-104 initially suffered an appallingly high accident rate in European service, the Dutch losing some 35.8 per cent of their Starfighter fleet.*

## SPECIFICATION

### F-104G Starfighter

**Dimensions**

**Length:** 54 ft 9 in (16.69 m)
**Wingspan (without tip-mounted AAMs):** 21 ft 11 in (6.68 m)
**Wing area:** 196.10 sq ft (18.22 m²)
**Wing aspect ratio:** 2.45
**Height** 13 ft 6 in (4.11 m)
**Tailplane span:** 11 ft 11 in (3.63 m)
**Wheel track:** 9 ft (2.74 m)
**Wheelbase:** 15 ft ½ in (4.59 m)

**Powerplant**

One General Electric J79-GE-11A turbojet rated at 10,000 lb st (44.48 kN) dry and 15,800 lb st (70.28 kN) with afterburning

**Weights**

**Empty equipped:** 14,082 lb (6387 kg)
**Normal take-off:** 21,639 lb (9840 kg)
**Maximum take-off:** 28,779 lb (13054 kg)

**Fuel and load**

**Internal fuel:** 896 US gal (3392 litres)
**External fuel:** up to 955 US gal (3615 litres) in one 225-US gal (852-litre) and two 195-US gal (740-litre) drop tanks and two 170-US gal (645-litre) tip tanks
**Maximum ordnance:** 4,310 lb (1955 kg)

**Performance**

**Maximum level speed 'clean' at 36,000 ft (10975 m):** 1,262 kt (1,453 mph; 2338 km/h)
**Cruising speed at 36,000 ft (10975 m):** 530 kt (610 mph; 981 km/h)
**Maximum rate of climb at sea level:** 55,000 ft (16765 m) per minute
**Service ceiling:** 58,000 ft (17680 m)
**Take-off distance to 50 ft (15 m):** 4,600 ft (1402 m)
**Landing distance from 50 ft (15 m):** 3,250 ft (990 m)

**Range**

**Ferry range with four drop tanks:** 1,893 nm (2,180 miles; 3510 km)
**Combat radius:** 648 nm (746 miles; 1200 km)
**Combat radius on hi-lo-hi attack mission with maximum warload:** 261 nm (300 miles; 483 km)

**Armament**

**Fixed:** One General Electric 20-mm M61A-1 Vulcan six-barrelled rotary cannon with 725 rounds
**Weapon stations:** One underfuselage, four underwing and two wingtip hardpoints for AIM-9 AAMs and a variety of bombs, pods and rockets

103 Rudder construction
104 Rudder power control jacks
105 Rudder servo valves
106 Exhaust shroud
107 Fully-variable afterburner exhaust nozzle
108 Fin attachment joints
109 Fin-carrying mainframes
110 Afterburner duct
111 Nozzle control jacks
112 Steel and titanium aft fuselage construction
113 Rear navigation lights
114 Aft fuselage attachment joint
115 Brake parachute housing
116 Port airbrake (open)
117 Airbrake scissor links
118 Fuselage strake (both sides)
119 Emergency runway arrester hook
120 Airbrake jack
121 Air exit louvres
122 Primary heat exchanger
123 Wingroot trailing-edge fillet
124 Flap hydraulic jack
125 Flap blowing slot
126 Port blown flap (lowered)
127 Aileron servo valves
128 Aileron power control jacks
129 Port aileron
130 Tip tank fins
131 Port navigation light
132 Port wingtip fuel tank (283-Imp gal/ 1287-litre) capacity
133 Fuel filler caps
134 Outboard pylon mounting rib
135 Wing multi-spar construction
136 Inboard pylon mounting rib
137 Main undercarriage leg door
138 Shock absorber strut
139 Swivel axle control rods
140 Port mainwheel
141 Leading-edge flap (lowered)
142 Leading-edge flap rib construction
143 Port outboard pylon
144 Missile launch rail
145 Port AIM-7 Sparrow AAM
146 Mk 82 500-lb (227-kg) bomb
147 Mk 83 1,000-lb (454-kg) bomb
148 Bomb mounting shackles
149 Auxiliary fuel tank (163-Imp gal/740-litre) capacity
150 Port inboard wing pylon
151 Pylon attachments
152 LAU-3A 2.75-in (70-mm) FFAR pod (19 rockets)
153 AIM-9 Sidewinder AAM
154 Missile launch rail
155 Fuselage stores pylon adaptor

# Lockheed Martin F-16 Fighting Falcon

*Conceived as a lightweight no-frills air combat fighter, the F-16 has matured into a sophisticated multi-role warplane. This Dutch F-16A is equipped with a centrally mounted Orpheus reconnaissance pod.*

## F-16C Block 50/52

### Cutaway key

1 Pitot head/air data probe
2 Glass-fibre radome
3 Lightning conducting strips
4 Planar radar scanner
5 Radome hinge point, opens to starboard
6 Scanner tracking mechanism
7 ILS glideslope antenna
8 Radar mounting bulkhead
9 Incidence vane, port and starboard
10 IFF antenna
11 GBU-12B laser-guided bomb
12 AN/APG-68 digital pulse-Doppler, multi-mode radar equipment bay
13 Forward oblique radar warning antennas, port and starboard
14 Front pressure bulkhead
15 Static ports
16 Fuselage forebody strake fairing
17 Forward avionics equipment bay
18 Canopy jettison charge
19 Instrument panel shroud
20 Instrument panel, multi-function CRT head-down displays
21 Sidestick controller, fly-by-wire control system
22 Video recorder
23 GEC wide-angle head-up display
24 CBU-52/58/71 submunition dispenser
25 LAU-3A 19-round rocket launcher
26 2.75-in (68-mm) FFAR
27 CBU-87/89 Gator submunition dispenser

28 Starboard intake flank (No. 5R) stores pylon adaptor
29 LANTIRN (FLIR) targeting pod
30 One-piece frameless cockpit canopy
31 Ejection seat headrest
32 McDonnell-Douglas ACES II zero-zero ejection seat
33 Side console panel
34 Canopy frame fairing
35 Canopy external emergency release
36 Engine throttle lever incorporating HOTAS (hands-on throttle-and-stick) radar controls
37 Canopy jettison handle
38 Cockpit section frame structure
39 Boundary layer splitter plate
40 Fixed-geometry engine air intake
41 Nosewheel, aft retracting
42 LANTIRN (FLIR/TFR) navigation pod
43 Port intake flank (No. 5L) stores pylon adaptor

44 Port position light
45 Intake duct framing
46 Intake ducting
47 Gun gas suppression muzzle aperture
48 Aft avionics equipment bay
49 Cockpit rear pressure bulkhead
50 Canopy hinge point
51 Ejection seat launch rails
52 Canopy rotary actuator
53 Conditioned air delivery duct
54 Canopy sealing frame
55 Canopy aft glazing
56 600-US gal (500-Imp gal; 2271-litre) external fuel tank

57 Garrett hydrazine turbine emergency power unit (EPU)
58 Hydrazine fuel tank
59 Fuel tank bay access panel
60 Forward fuselage bag-type fuel tank, total internal capacity 6972 lb (3162 kg)
61 Fuselage upper longeron
62 Conditioned air ducting
63 Cannon barrels
64 Forebody frame construction
65 Air system ground connection
66 Ventral air conditioning system equipment bay

67 Centreline 300-US gal (250-Imp gal; 1136-litre) fuel tank
68 Mainwheel door hydraulic actuator
69 Mainwheel door
70 Hydraulic system ground connectors
71 Gun bay ventral gas vent
72 GE M61A1 Vulcan 20-mm rotary cannon
73 Ammunition feed chute
74 Hydraulic gun drive motor
75 Port hydraulic reservoir

76 Centre fuselage integral fuel tank
77 Leading-edge flap drive hydraulic motor
78 Ammunition drum with 511 rounds
79 Upper position light/refuelling floodlight
80 TACAN antenna
81 Hydraulic accumulator

82 Starboard hydraulic reservoir
83 Leading-edge flap drive shaft
84 Inboard, No. 6 stores station 4,500-lb (2041-kg) capacity
85 Pylon attachment hardpoint

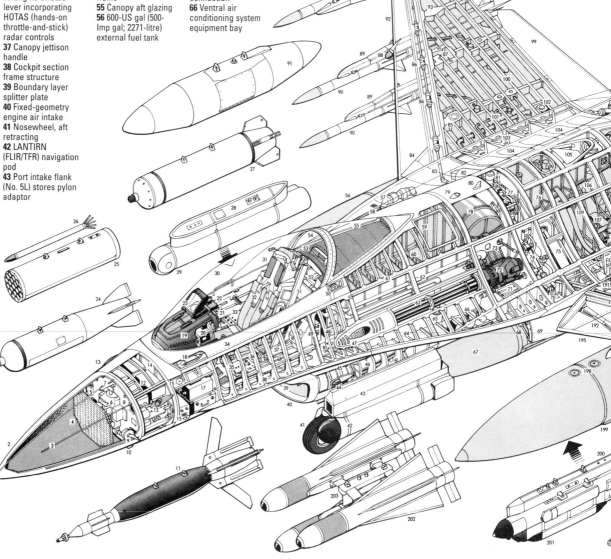

86 Leading-edge flap drive shaft and rotary actuators
87 No. 7 stores hardpoint, capacity 3,500 lb (1588 kg)
88 Starboard forward radar warning antenna
89 Missile launch rails
90 AIM-120 AMRAAM medium-range AAMs
91 MXU-648 baggage pod, carriage of essential ground equipment and personal effects for off-base deployment
92 Starboard leading-edge manoeuvre flap, down position
93 Outboard, No. 8 stores station, capacity 700 lb (318 kg)
94 Wingtip, No. 9 stores station, capacity 425 lb (193 kg)
95 Wingtip AMRAAM
96 Starboard navigation light
97 Fixed portion of trailing edge
98 Static dischargers
99 Starboard flaperon
100 Starboard wing integral fuel tank

101 Fuel system piping
102 Fuel pump
103 Starboard wingroot attachment fishplates
104 Fuel tank access panels
105 Universal air refuelling receptacle (UARSSI), open
106 Engine intake centrebody fairing
107 Airframe mounted accessory equipment gearbox
108 Jet fuel starter
109 Machined wing attachment bulkheads
110 Engine fuel management equipment
111 Pressure refuelling receptacle ventral adaptor
112 Pratt & Whitney F100-PW-229 afterburning turbofan engine
113 VHF/IFF antenna

114 Starboard flaperon hydraulic actuator
115 Fuel tank tail fins
116 Sidebody fairing integral fuel tank
117 Position light
118 Cooling air ram air intake
119 Finroot fairing
120 Forward engine support link
121 Rear fuselage integral fuel tank
122 Thermally insulated tank inner skin
123 Tank access panels
124 Radar warning system power amplifier
125 Finroot attachment fittings
126 Flight control system hydraulic accumulators

The F-16 takes on fuel from tankers via a receptacle in the upper fuselage. Like all USAF tactical combat aircraft, it refuels from 'flying boom'-equipped tankers.

127 Multi-spar fin torsion box structure
128 Starboard all-moving tailplane (tailplane panels interchangeable)
129 General Electric F110-GE-129 alternative powerplant
130 Fin leading-edge honeycomb core
131 Dynamic pressure probe
132 Carbon-fibre fin skin panelling
133 VHF comms antenna (AM/FM)
134 Fintip antenna fairing
135 Anti-collision light
136 Threat warning antennas
137 Static dischargers
138 Rudder honeycomb core structure
139 Rudder hydraulic actuator
140 ECM antenna fairing
141 Tail navigation light
142 Variable-area afterburner nozzle
143 Afterburner nozzle flaps
144 Nozzle sealing fairing
145 Afterburner nozzle fueldraulic actuators (5)

146 Port split trailing-edge airbrake panel, open, upper and lower surfaces
147 Airbrake actuating linkage
148 Port all-moving tailplane
149 Static dischargers
150 Graphite-epoxy tailplane skin panels
151 Leading-edge honeycomb construction
152 Corrugated aluminium sub-structure
153 Tailplane pivot mounting
154 Tailplane hydraulic actuator
155 Fuel jettison chamber, port and starboard
156 Afterburner ducting
157 Rear fuselage machined bulkheads
158 Port navigation light
159 AN/ALE-40(VO-4) chaff/flare launcher, port and starboard
160 Main engine thrust mounting, port and starboard
161 Sidebody fairing frame structure
162 Runway arrester hook
163 Composite ventral fin, port and starboard
164 Port flaperon hydraulic actuator
165 Flaperon hinges
166 Port flaperon, lowered

167 External fuel tank tail fairing
168 Flaperon honeycomb core structure
169 Fixed portion of trailing edge
170 Static dischargers
171 Port navigation light
172 Wingtip, No. 1 stores station, capacity 425 lb (193 kg)
173 Port wingtip AMRAAM
174 AGM-88 HARM (High-speed Anti-Radiation Missile)
175 Mk 84 low-drag 2,000-lb (907-kg) HE bomb
176 Mk 83 Snakeye retarded bomb
177 AIM-9L Sidewinder air-to-air missile
178 Missile launch rails
179 No. 2 stores station, capacity 700 lb (318 Kg)
180 No. 3 stores station, capacity 3,500 lb (1588 Kg)
181 Port forward radar warning antenna
182 Mk 82 500 lb (227 kg) HE bombs
183 Triple ejector rack
184 Intermediate wing pylon
185 Leading-edge manoeuvre flap honeycomb core structure

186 Flap drive shaft and rotary actuators
187 Multi-spar wing torsion box structure
188 Port wing integral fuel tankage
189 No. 4 stores station hardpoint, capacity 4,500 lb (2041 kg)
190 Wing panel root attachment fishplates
191 Undercarriage leg mounted landing light
192 Articulated retraction/drag link
193 Main undercarriage leg strut
194 Shock absorber strut
195 Port leading-edge manoeuvre flap, down position
196 Inboard wing pylon
197 Port mainwheel, forward retracting
198 Fuel filler caps
199 Port 370-US gal (308-Imp gal; 1400-litre) external tank
200 Centreline, No. 5 stores pylon, capacity 2,200 lb (998 kg)
201 AN/ALQ-184(V)-2 (short) ECM pod
202 AGM-65 Maverick air-to-surface missiles
203 LAU-88 triple missile carrier/launcher

Mike Badrocke

## SPECIFICATION

### F-16C Fighting Falcon Block 30

**Dimensions:**

**Fuselage length:** 49 ft 4 in (15.03 m)
**Wing span with tip-mounted AAMs:** 32 ft 9¾ in (10.00 m)
**Wing area:** 300.00 sq ft (27.87 m²)
**Wing aspect ratio:** 3.0
**Tailplane span:** 18 ft 3¾ in (5.58 m)
**Vertical tail surfaces:** 54.75 sq ft (5.09 m²)
**Height:** 16 ft 8½ in (5.09 m)
**Wheel track:** 7 ft 9 in (2.36 m)
**Wheelbase:** 13 ft 1½ in (4.00 m)

**Powerplant:**

One General Electric F110-GE-100 turbofan rated at 28,984 lb st (128.9 kN) with afterburning, or a Pratt & Whitney F100-PW-220 23,770 lb st (105.7 kN) in Blocks 40/42

**Weights:**

**Empty operating:** 19,100 lb (8663 kg)
**Typical combat take-off:** 21,585 lb (9791 kg)
**Maximum take-off for air-to-air mission without drop tanks:**
25,071 lb (11372 kg)
**Maximum take-off, with maximum external load:** 42,300 lb (19187 kg)

### g limits

Max symmetrical design g limit with full internal fuel load ±9

**Performance:**

**Maximum level speed 'clean' at altitude :** 1,146 kt ( 1,320 mph; 2124 km/h)
**Maximum level speed at sea level:**
795 kt (915 mph; 1472 km/h)
**Maximum rate of climb at sea level:** 50,000 ft (15240 m) per minute
**Service ceiling:** more than 50,000 ft (15240 m)
**Combat radius:** 295 nm (340 miles; 547 km) on a hi-lo-hi mission with six 1,000-lb ( 454-kg) bombs

**Armament:**

One internal M61 Vulcan 20-mm cannon; maximum ordnance of 15,200 lb (6894 kg) on one fuselage pylon and six underwing pylons.

# McDonnell Douglas F-4 Phantom II

*The F-4G was the definitive defence suppression Phantom, and the last in front-line USAF service. This pair illustrates the primary weapons employed in this role in later years, the furthest aircraft carrying the AGM-45 Shrike and cluster bombs, while that in the foreground is armed with AGM-65 Maverick and AGM-88 HARM. F-4Gs routinely carried weapons such as Maverick and CBUs to attack missile installations once the anti-radiation missiles had taken out the radars.*

## RF-4C Phantom II

**Cutaway key**

1 Pitot head
2 Radome
3 Radar scanner dish
4 Radar dish tracking mechanism
5 Texas Instruments AN/APQ-99 forward-looking radar unit
6 Nose compartment construction
7 No. 1 camera station
8 KS-87 forward oblique camera
9 Forward radar warning antennas, port and starboard
10 Camera bay access hatches
11 Ventral camera aperture
12 KA-57 low-altitude panoramic camera
13 Lateral camera aperture (alternative KS-87 installation)
14 No. 2 camera station
15 ADF sense aerial
16 Windscreen rain dispersal air duct
17 Camera viewfinder periscope
18 Nose undercarriage emergency air bottles
19 Recording unit
20 No. 3 camera station
21 KA-91 high-altitude panoramic camera
22 Air-conditioning ram air intake
23 Landing/taxiing lamp (2)
24 Lower UHF/VHF aerial
25 Nosewheel leg door
26 Torque scissor links
27 Twin nosewheels, aft retracting
28 Nosewheel steering mechanism
29 AN/AVQ-26 'Pave Tack' laser designator pod
30 Swivelling optical package
31 Fuselage centreline pylon adaptor
32 Sideways-looking radar antenna (SLAR)
33 Electro-luminescent formation lighting strip
34 Canopy emergency release handle
35 Air-conditioning plant, port and starboard
36 Cockpit floor level
37 Front pressure bulkhead
38 Rudder pedals
39 Control column
40 Instrument panel
41 Radar display
42 Instrument panel shroud
43 LA-313A optical viewfinder
44 Windscreen panels
45 Forward cockpit canopy cover
46 Face blind seat firing handle
47 Pilot's Martin-Baker Mk.H7 ejection seat
48 External canopy latches
49 Engine throttle levers
50 Side console panel
51 Intake boundary layer splitter plate
52 APQ-102R/T SLAR equipment
53 AAS-18A infra-red reconnaissance package
54 Intake front ramp
55 Port engine air intake
56 Intake ramp bleed air holes
57 Rear canopy external latches
58 Rear instrument console
59 Canopy centre arch
60 Starboard engine air intake
61 Starboard external fuel tank, capacity 308 Imp gal (1400 litres)
62 Rear view mirrors
63 Rear cockpit canopy cover
64 Navigator/Sensor Operator's Martin-Baker ejection seat
65 Intake ramp bleed air spill louvres
66 Avionics equipment racks
67 Rear pressure bulkhead
68 Liquid oxygen converter
69 Variable intake ramp jack
70 Intake rear ramp door
71 Fuselage centreline external fuel tank, capacity 500 Imp gal (2271 litres)
72 Position of pressure refuelling connection on starboard side
73 ASQ-90B data annotation system equipment
74 Cockpit voice recorder
75 Pneumatic system air bottle
76 Bleed air ducting
77 Fuselage No. 1 fuel cell, capacity 179 Imp gal (814 litres)
78 Intake duct framing
79 Boundary layer spill duct
80 Control cable runs
81 Aft avionics equipment bay
82 IFF aerial
83 Upper fuselage light
84 Fuselage No. 2 fuel cell, capacity 154 Imp gal (700 litres)
85 Centre fuselage frame construction
86 Electro-luminescent formation lighting strip
87 Engine intake centre-body fairing
88 Intake duct rotary spill valve
89 Wing spar attachment fuselage main frames
90 Control cable ducting

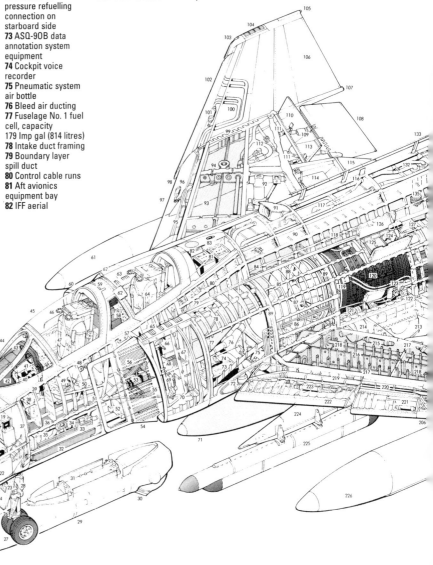

**F-4E Phantom II**

### Dimensions

**Wingspan:** 38 ft 7½ in (11.77 m)
**Wingspan (folded):** 27 ft 7 in (8.41 m)
**Wing aspect ratio:** 2.82
**Wing area:** 530 sq ft (49.2 m²)
**Length:** 63 ft (19.20 m)
**Wheel track:** 17 ft 10½ in (5.45 m)
**Height:** 16 ft 5½ in (5.02 m)

### Powerplant

Two General Electric J79-GE-17A
turbojets, each rated at 17,900 lb
(80 kN) thrust with afterburning

### Weights

**Empty:** 30,328 lb (13757 kg)
**Operating empty:** 31,853 lb (14448 kg)
**Combat take-off:** 41,487 lb (18818 kg)
**Maximum take-off:** 61,795 lb
(28030 kg)

### Fuel and load

**Internal fuel capacity:** 1,855 US gal
(1,545 Imp gal; 7022 litres)
Provision for one 600-US gal
(500-Imp gal; 2271-litre) tank on
centreline and two 370-US gal
(308-Imp gal; 1400-litre) tanks under the
wings
**Maximum weaponload:** 16,000 lb
(7250 kg)

### Performance

**Maximum speed:** approximately
Mach 2.2

**Maximum rate of climb:** 61,400 ft
(18715 m) per minute
**Service ceiling:** 62,250 ft (18975 m)
**Take-off run at maximum take-off
weight:** 4,390 ft (1338 m)
**Landing run at maximum landing
weight:** 3,780 ft (1152 m)

### Range

**Ferry range:** 1,978 miles (3184 km)
**Area intercept combat radius:**
786 miles (1266 km)
**Defensive counter-air combat
radius:** 494 miles (795 km)
**Interdiction combat radius:**
712 miles (1145 km)

### Armament

Fixed internal M61A1 Vulcan 20-mm
six-barrelled cannon; standard intercept
load of four AIM-7 Sparrow missiles in
fuselage recesses and four AIM-9
Sidewinders on wing pylon shoulder
stations; four wing pylons and one
centreline station available for carriage
of wide range of air-to-ground
ordnance, including M117 and Mk 80
series bombs, cluster weapons, laser-
guided bombs, gun pods, napalm, fuel-
air explosives and rocket pods; nuclear
weapon options included B28, B43, B57
and B61; various ECM pods, training
targets and laser designator pods
available; air-to-surface missiles
included AGM-12 Bullpup, AGM-45
Shrike, AGM-65 Maverick and AGM-78
Standard

*USAF Phantoms first went to war in a peacetime grey/white scheme, but soon acquired tactical camouflage. This F-4C carries a mixed load of ground attack weapons, comprising three M117 bombs, four rocket pods and two napalm canisters.*

**91** In-flight refuelling receptacle, open
**92** Starboard main undercarriage leg pivot fixing
**93** Starboard wing integral fuel tank, capacity 262 Imp gal (1192 litres)
**94** Wing pylon mounting
**95** Boundary layer control air duct

**96** Leading-edge flap hydraulic actuator
**97** Inboard leading-edge flap segment, down position
**98** Leading-edge dog-tooth

**99** Outboard wing panel attachment joint
**100** Boundary layer control air ducting
**101** Hydraulic flap actuator
**102** Outboard leading-edge flap
**103** Starboard navigation light

**104** Electro-luminescent formation light
**105** Rearward identification light
**106** Starboard dihedral outboard wing panel
**107** Wing fuel tank vent pipe
**108** Starboard drooping aileron, down position

**109** Aileron flutter damper
**110** Starboard spoilers, open

**111** Spoiler hydraulic actuators
**112** Fuel jettison and vent valves
**113** Aileron hydraulic actuator
**114** Starboard ventral airbrake panel
**115** Starboard blown flap, down position
**116** TACAN aerial

**117** Fuel system piping
**118** No. 3 fuselage fuel cell, capacity 122 Imp gal (566 litres)
**119** Engine intake compressor face
**120** General Electric J79 GE-15 afterburning turbojet engine
**121** Ventral engine accessory equipment gearbox

**122** Wing rear spar attachment joint
**123** Engine and afterburner control equipment
**124** Emergency ram air turbine
**125** Ram air turbine housing
**126** Turbine doors, open
**127** Turbine actuating link
**128** Port engine bay frame construction
**129** No. 4 fuselage fuel cell, capacity 167 Imp gal (759 litres)
**130** Jet pipe heat shroud
**131** No. 5 fuselage fuel cell, capacity 150 Imp gal (681 litres)
**132** Fuel feed and vent system piping
**133** LORAN aerial
**134** Dorsal access panels
**135** Fuel pumps

**136** No. 6 fuselage fuel cell, capacity 177 Imp gal (806 litres)
**137** Photographic flare dispenser, port and starboard
**138** Flare compartment doors, open
**139** Ram air intake, tailcone venting
**140** Tailcone attachment bulkhead
**141** Three-spar fin torsion box construction
**142** Fin rib construction
**143** Electro-luminescent formation lighting strip
**144** HF aerial panel
**145** Anti-collision light
**146** Stabilator feel system pressure head
**147** Fin leading edge
**148** Fin tip aerial fairing
**149** Upper UHF/VHF aerial
**150** Tail navigation light
**151** Rudder horn balance
**152** Rudder
**153** Honeycomb trailing-edge panels

**154** Fuselage fuel cell jettison pipe
**155** Rear radar warning antennas
**156** Tailcone/brake parachute hinged door
**157** Brake parachute housing
**158** Honeycomb trailing-edge panel
**159** Port all-moving tailplane/stabilator
**160** Stabilator mass balance weight
**161** Stabilator multi-spar construction
**162** Pivot sealing plate
**163** All-moving tailplane hinge mounting
**164** Rudder hydraulic actuator
**165** Tailplane hydraulic actuator
**166** Heat-resistant tailcone skinning
**167** Arrester hook, lowered
**168** Arrester hook stowage
**169** Stabilator feel system balance mechanism
**170** Artificial feel system pneumatic bellows
**171** Arrester hook jack and shock absorber
**172** Variable-area afterburner exhaust nozzle
**173** Engine bay cooling exit louvres
**174** Afterburner duct
**175** Exhaust nozzle actuators
**176** Hinged engine cowling panels
**177** Port blown flap, down position
**178** Boundary layer control air-blowing slot
**179** Lateral autopilot servo
**180** Airbrake jack

**181** Flap hydraulic jack
**182** Rear spar
**183** Port spoiler hydraulic jack
**184** Aileron hydraulic actuator
**185** Aileron flutter damper
**186** Port spoiler housing
**187** Aileron rib construction
**188** Port drooping aileron, down position
**189** Wing fuel tank jettison pipe
**190** Honeycomb trailing-edge panels
**191** Port dihedral outer wing panel
**192** Fixed portion of trailing edge
**193** Rearward identification light
**194** Electro-luminescent formation light
**195** Port navigation light
**196** Outboard leading-edge flap, lowered
**197** Boundary layer control air blowing slot
**198** Leading-edge flap actuator
**199** Outer wing panel multi-spar construction
**200** Outer wing panel attachment joint
**201** Leading-edge dog-tooth
**202** Port mainwheel
**203** Mainwheel multi-plate disc brake
**204** Mainwheel leg door
**205** Outboard wing pylon
**206** Inner wing panel outboard leading-edge flap, down position
**207** Leading-edge flap rib construction
**208** Wing pylon mounting

**209** Main undercarriage leg pivot fixing
**210** Hydraulic retraction jack
**211** Undercarriage uplock
**212** Port ventral airbrake panel, open
**213** Main undercarriage wheel bay
**214** Hydraulic reservoir
**215** Hydraulic system accumulator
**216** Port wing integral fuel tank, capacity 262 Imp gal (1192 litres)
**217** Two-spar torsion box fuel tank construction
**218** Wing skin support posts
**219** Leading-edge boundary layer control air duct
**220** Bleed air blowing slot
**221** Outboard flap actuator
**222** Inboard leading-edge flap, lowered
**223** Hydraulic flap actuator
**224** Inboard wing pylon
**225** AN/ALQ-101 ECM pod
**226** Port external fuel tank, capacity 308 Imp gal (1400 litres)

# McDonnell Douglas F-15 Eagle

F-15Es serve with two overseas commands (USAFE and PACAF). Like USAFE's 48th FW, PACAF's 3rd Wing (previously the 21st Composite Wing) operates a mix of F-15Cs and F-15Es, the latter flying with the 90th FS 'Pair o'Dice'. Here the wing commander leads aircraft from the three Eagle squadrons through the Alaskan mountains from the unit's base at Elmendorf AFB.

## F-15E Eagle

**Cutaway key**

1 Glass-fibre radome
2 Hughes AN/APG-70 I-band pulse-Doppler radar scanner
3 Radar mounting bulkhead
4 ADF sense antenna
5 Avionics equipment bay, port and starboard
6 UHF antenna
7 Pitot head
8 AGM-130 TV-guided air-to-surface weapon
9 TACAN antenna
10 Formation lighting strip
11 Incidence probe
12 Rudder pedals
13 Instrument panel shroud
14 Pilot's head-up display
15 Frameless windscreen panel
16 B61 tactical nuclear weapon
17 AIM-7F Sparrow air-to-air missile
18 LANTIRN navigation pod, mounted beneath starboard intake
19 FLIR aperture
20 Terrain-following radar
21 Upward-hinging cockpit canopy
22 Pilot's ACES II ejection seat
23 Side console panel
24 Engine throttle levers
25 Boarding steps
26 Extended boarding ladder
27 Forward-retracting nosewheel
28 Landing/taxiing lights
29 Nosewheel leg shock absorber strut
30 Underfloor control runs
31 Flying controls duplicated in rear cockpit
32 Radar hand controller
33 Weapons Systems Officer's ACES II ejection seat
34 Canopy hinge point
35 Cockpit air-conditioning pack
36 Port variable capture area 'nodding' air intake
37 Boundary layer spill air louvres
38 Nodding intake hydraulic actuator
39 Variable-area intake ramp doors
40 Intake ramp hydraulic actuator
41 Boom-type flight refuelling receptacle, open
42 Air supply duct to conditioning system
43 Ammunition magazine, 512 rounds
44 Forward fuselage fuel tanks
45 Ammunition feed chute
46 Engine intake ducting
47 Centre fuselage fuel tanks3

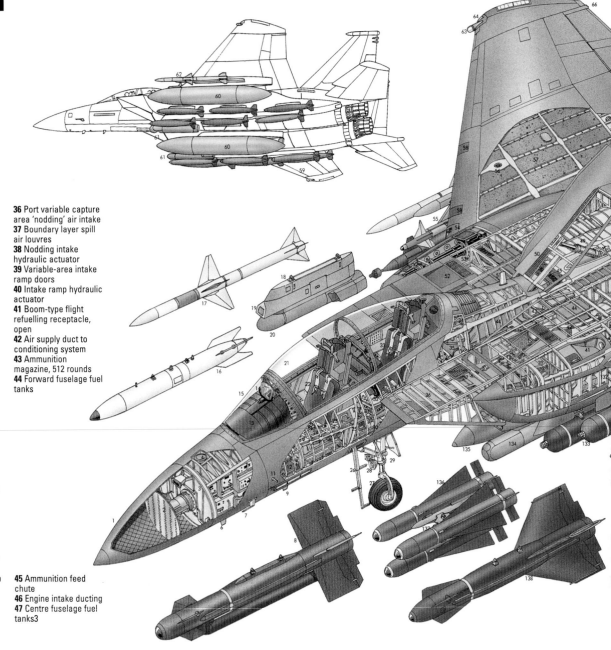

*An F-15A of the now defunct 48th Fighter Interceptor Squadron (FIS) fires an AIM-7. Despite being at the end of its development life, the Sparrow remains an important F-15 weapon even though the AIM-120 is now well established in service. During the Gulf War, most of the kills made by F-15s were achieved with the AIM-7.*

**48** Fuel tank bay access panel
**49** Airbrake hydraulic jack
**50** Dorsal airbrake honeycomb construction
**51** Upper UHF antenna
**52** Starboard intake by-pass air spill duct
**53** M61A-1 Vulcan 20-mm cannon
**54** Anti-collision light
**55** Starboard wing pylon carrying GBU-10, AIM-7M and AIM-120
**56** Pylon mounting hardpoint
**57** Starboard wing integral fuel tank, fire suppressant foam filled
**58** Leading edge flush HF antenna panels
**59** Ventral view showing carriage of 12 Mk 82 500-lb (227-kg) bombs
**60** 610-US gal (2309-litre) external fuel tanks (3)
**61** LANTIRN navigation and targeting pods
**62** Wing pylon mounted AIM-9M and AIM-120 air-to-air missiles
**63** Forward ECM transmitting antenna
**64** Starboard navigation light

## SPECIFICATION

### F-15E

#### Dimensions

**Length:** 63 ft 9 in (19.43 m)
**Height:** 18 ft 5½ in (5.63 m)
**Wingspan:** 42 ft 9 ¾ in (13.05 m)
**Wing aspect ratio:** 3.01
**Tailplane span:** 28 ft 3 in (8.61 m)
**Wheel track:** 9 ft ¼ in (2.75 m)
**Wheelbase:** 17 ft 9 ½ in (5.42 m)

#### Powerplant

Original F-15E had powerplant of F-15C/D, but with option of General Electric F110-GE-129. Aircraft from 135 onwards (90-0233), built from August 1991, have two Pratt and Whitney F100-PW-229s rated at 29,000 lb st (129 kN)

#### Weights

**Empty operating:** 31,700 lb (14379 kg)
**Normal take-off:** 44,823 lb (20331 kg)
**Maximum take-off:** 36,741 lb (81000 kg)

#### Fuel and load

**Internal fuel:** 13,123 lb (5952 kg)
**External fuel:** 21,645 lb (9818 kg)
**Maximum weaponload:** 24,500 lb (11113 kg)

#### Performance

**Maximum level speed:** Mach 2.5
**Maximum combat radius:** 685 nm (790 miles; 1270 km)
**Maximum combat range:** 2,400 nm (2,765 miles; 4445 km)

#### Armament

One 20-mm M61A-1 six-barrel gun, with 512 rounds, in starboard wingroot. Wing pylons for AIM-9 Sidewinder, AIM-120 AMRAAM, and AIM 7 Sparrow. Single or triple rail launchers for AGM-65 Maverick on wing pylons. A wide range of guided and unguided weapons including Mk 20 Rockeye, Mk 82, MK 84, BSU-49 and -50, GBU-10, -12, -15, and -24; CBU-52, -58, -71, -87, -89, -90, -92 and -93; LAU-3A rockets; B57 and B61 nuclear weapons.

**65** Wingtip formation light
**66** Fuel jettison
**67** Starboard aileron
**68** Starboard plain flap
**69** Trailing-edge fuel tank
**70** Engine bay cooling intake bleed air louvres
**71** Compressor intake
**72** Central airframe-mounted engine accessory equipment gearbox
**73** Machined main fuselage/wing spar attachment bulkheads
**74** Pratt & Whitney F100-PW-229 afterburning turbofan engines
**75** Engine bleed air cross-ducting
**76** Forward engine mounting
**77** Main engine mounting 'spectacle' beam
**78** Afterburner ducting
**79** Rear fuselage/engine bay diffusion-bonded all-titanium structure
**80** Tailplane hydraulic actuator
**81** Starboard fin
**82** Fintip ECM antenna
**83** Anti-collision light
**84** Starboard rudder
**85** Starboard all-moving tailplane
**86** Aft ECM transmitting antenna
**87** Variable area afterburner nozzle
**88** Nozzle actuating linkage
**89** Nozzle shroud panels
**90** Fueldraulic afterburner nozzle actuators
**91** Two-spar fin torsion box structure
**92** Boron-fibre fin skin panelling
**93** Radar warning antenna
**94** Port rear ECM antenna
**95** White strobe light
**96** Port rudder honeycomb core construction
**97** Tailplane pivot mounting
**98** Port aft ECM transmitting antenna
**99** Port all-moving tailplane
**100** Boron-fibre tailplane skin panelling
**101** Machined tailplane trunion mounting fitting
**102** Leading edge dog-tooth
**103** Runway emergency arrester hook, lowered
**104** Formation lighting strip
**105** Engine bleed air primary heat exchangers, port and starboard
**106** Port trailing-edge fuel tank bay
**107** Flap hydraulic jack
**108** Port plain flap
**109** Aileron hydraulic actuator
**110** Port aileron honeycomb core construction
**111** Fuel jettison
**112** Port formation light
**113** Port navigation light
**114** Forward ECM transmitting antenna
**115** Engine bleed air primary heat exchanger air intake and exhaust ducts
**116** GBU-28 'Deep-Throat' laser-guided bomb
**117** GBU-12 laser-guided bombs
**118** CFT pylons
**119** Port conformal fuel tank (CFT)
**120** AXQ-14 datalink pod
**121** Mk 84 2,000-lb (907-kg) HE bomb
**122** GBU-24 laser-guided bomb
**123** Outer wing panel dry bay
**124** Port wing integral fuel tankage
**125** Multi-spar wing panel structure
**126** Port pylon hardpoint
**127** Wing stores pylon
**128** Missile launch rails
**129** AIM-120 AMRAAM
**130** AIM-9M Sidewinder air-to-air missile
**131** Leading-edge flush HF antenna
**132** Stores management system equipment
**133** CBU-87 sub-munition dispensers
**134** Port LANTIRN targeting pod
**135** Centreline external tank
**136** AGM-65 Maverick air-to-surface missiles
**137** Triple missile carrier/launch rail
**138** GBU-15 electro-optical guided glide bomb

Mike Badrocke

# McDonnell F-101 Voodoo

Conceived as a long-range fighter to accompany SAC bombers, the F-88 never reached production status, but it did provide the basis for the later F-101 Voodoo. The Voodoo was also initially designed as a strategic fighter, yet it saw service in three other major roles: nuclear bomber, tactical reconnaissance platform and defender of North American airspace. In the latter tasking it served with Canada into the late 1980s

## F-101C

### Cutaway key

1 Radome
2 Scanner dish
3 Radar tracking mechanism
4 Radar mounting bulkhead
5 Refuelling probe doors
6 Radar modulating units
7 Refuelling probe hydraulic jack
8 Flight refuelling probe, extended
9 Forward avionics equipment bay, radar and weapons system equipment
10 Nose compartment access panels
11 Angle of attack transducer
12 Pitot head
13 Nosewheel doors
14 Emergency brake reservoir
15 Cannon muzzles
16 Cockpit pressure floor
17 Cockpit air-conditioning ducting
18 Front pressure bulkhead
19 Rudder pedals
20 Control column
21 Instrument panel
22 Instrument panel shroud
23 K-19 (Mk 7) gunsight
24 Armoured glass windscreen panel

25 MA-7 flight indicator radar scope
26 Canopy cover
27 Canopy mounted flush aerial
28 Headrest
29 Safety harness
30 Canopy external release
31 Pilot's ejection seat
32 Throttle levers
33 Side console panel
34 Cockpit pressurisation valve
35 Cannon barrel seals
36 Nose undercarriage pivot fixing
37 Cannon barrel fairings
38 Nose undercarriage leg strut
39 Landing and taxiing lamps
40 Twin nosewheels
41 Torque scissor links
42 Ventral AW aerial
43 Cannon barrels
44 Control rod runs
45 Anti-'g' valve
46 Rear pressure bulkhead
47 Canopy hydraulic jack

48 Canopy aft fairing
49 Rear avionics equipment bay, navigation and communications systems
50 Canopy hinge
51 Ammunition access door
52 Ammunition magazine, 375 rounds per gun
53 Feed chutes
54 M39 20-mm cannon (single cannon on starboard side, fourth weapon replaced by transponder equipment)
55 Heat exchanger flush air intake
56 Circuit breaker panel
57 Air-conditioning plant
58 Autopilot rate gyros
59 Control linkages
60 Hydraulic accumulators
61 Boundary layer splitter plate

62 Port engine air intake
63 Intake duct framing
64 Port hydraulic system reservoir
65 Boundary layer bleed air spill duct
66 Wing spar attachment main bulkhead
67 Forward fuselage fuel tanks; total system capacity 2,146 US gal (8123 litres)
68 Fuel filler cap, pressure refuelling connector on starboard side
69 Fuel system piping
70 Anti-collision light
71 Starboard wing panel
72 Wing fence
73 Starboard navigation light
74 Fixed portion of trailing edge

75 Starboard aileron
76 Aileron mass-balance weights
77 Aileron hydraulic actuator
78 Main undercarriage pivot fixing
79 Starboard split trailing-edge flap
80 Boom type refuelling receptacle, open
81 Wing spar and engine mounting main bulkheads
82 Centre fuselage fuel tank
83 Fuel vent piping
84 Fuselage upper access panels
85 Fuselage top longeron
86 Aft fuselage fuel tanks
87 Control cable duct
88 Fuel filler cap

89 Finroot fillet
90 Tailcone joint frame
91 Artificial feel system bellows
92 Starboard airbrake, open

93 Tailfin construction
94 Remote compass transmitter
95 Artificial feel system ram air intake
96 VHF aerial

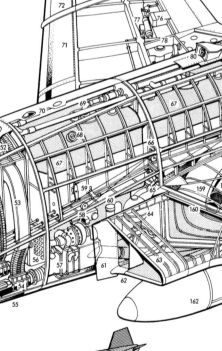

## SPECIFICATION

### RF-101C Voodoo

**Dimensions**

**Length:** 69 ft 3 in (21.1 m)
**Height:** 18 ft (5.49 m)
**Wing span:** 39 ft 8 in (12.09 m)
**Wing area** 368 sq ft (34.19 m²)

**Powerplant**

Two Pratt & Whitney J57-13 turbojets each rated at 14,880 lb (66.2 kN) with maximum afterburner

**Weights**

**Empty:** 25,610 lb (11617 kg)
**Loaded (clean):** 42,550 lb (19300 kg)
**Maximum (with two tanks):** 48,720 lb (22099 kg)

**Wing loading:** 130.8 lb/sq ft (638.6 kg/sq m)
**Power loading:** 1.6 lb/lb st (1.6 kg/kgp)

**Performance**

**Maximum speed (clean, at height):** Mach 1.7 (1,120 mph;1802 km/h)
**Service ceiling:** 52,000 ft (15850 m)
**Range (with internal tanks at high altitude):** 1,890 miles (3040 km)
**Range (with two 375-US gal (1705-litre) drop tanks:** 2,400 miles (3862 km)

**Armament**

No weapons were carried though a single nuclear weapon could be mounted on the centreline hardpoint in the event of nuclear war

*F-101 Voodoo 60236 was the fifth F-101B built and was used for the testing of onboard systems, in this case the MB-1, which would later be named the AIR-2A Genie. The Hughes MG-13 fire-control system on the Voodoo handled both nuclear and non-nuclear air-to-air rocket missiles and projectiles, and it was in 1961 that the Voodoo underwent a modification programme to let it fire the awesome Genie. Designed to scatter incoming Soviet bomb formations, the first 'live' Genie was tested on 19 July 1957 when it was fired from a Northrop F-89 Scorpion over Yucca Flat, Nevada, in a 1.5-kT blast.*

**97** Starboard tailplane construction
**98** Fintip fairing
**99** Tail navigation lights
**100** Rudder mass-balance
**101** Tailplane sealing plate
**102** Tailplane pivot fixing
**103** Port all-moving tailplane
**104** Rudder construction
**105** Tailplane hydraulic actuator
**106** Rudder hydraulic actuator
**107** Fuel jettison, port and starboard
**108** Parachute door

**109** Brake parachute housing
**110** Parachute release mechanism
**111** Tailboom construction
**112** Control system linkages
**113** Tailplane autopilot controller
**114** Port airbrake housing
**115** Airbrake hydraulic jack
**116** Port airbrake, open

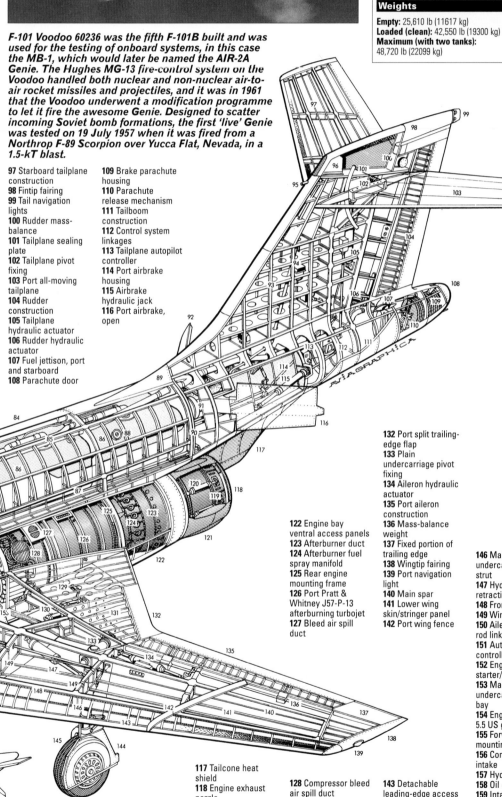

**117** Tailcone heat shield
**118** Engine exhaust nozzle
**119** Variable-area afterburner nozzle
**120** Nozzle control jacks
**121** Nozzle shroud

**122** Engine bay ventral access panels
**123** Afterburner duct
**124** Afterburner fuel spray manifold
**125** Rear engine mounting frame
**126** Port Pratt & Whitney J57-P-13 afterburning turbojet
**127** Bleed air spill duct
**128** Compressor bleed air spill duct
**129** Flap position transmitter
**130** Flap hydraulic jack
**131** Flap shroud ribs

**132** Port split trailing-edge flap
**133** Plain undercarriage pivot fixing
**134** Aileron hydraulic actuator
**135** Port aileron construction
**136** Mass-balance weight
**137** Fixed portion of trailing edge
**138** Wingtip fairing
**139** Port navigation light
**140** Main spar
**141** Lower wing skin/stringer panel
**142** Port wing fence
**143** Detachable leading-edge access panel
**144** Mainwheel doors
**145** Port mainwheel

**146** Main undercarriage leg strut
**147** Hydraulic retraction jack
**148** Front spar
**149** Wing ribs
**150** Aileron control rod linkage
**151** Autopilot controller
**152** Engine starter/generator
**153** Main undercarriage wheel bay
**154** Engine oil tank, 5.5 US gal (21 litres)
**155** Forward engine mounting
**156** Compressor intake
**157** Hydraulic pumps
**158** Oil cooler
**159** Intake conical centre-body
**160** Intake duct main frame
**161** Wing spar attachment joints

**162** Ventral fuel tank 450 US gal (1700 litres)
**163** Mk 84 2,000-lb (907-kg) low-drag HE bomb
**164** Mk 7 1-megaton free-fall nuclear weapon

# Mikoyan-Gurevich MiG-17 'Fresco'

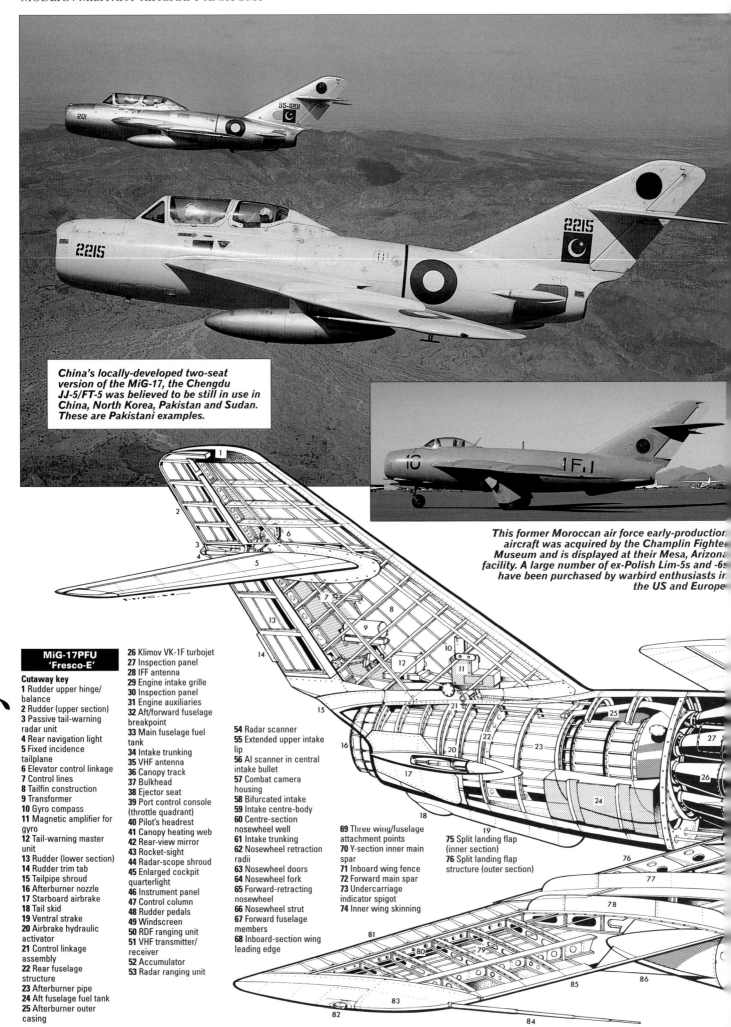

China's locally-developed two-seat version of the MiG-17, the Chengdu JJ-5/FT-5 was believed to be still in use in China, North Korea, Pakistan and Sudan. These are Pakistani examples.

This former Moroccan air force early-production aircraft was acquired by the Champlin Fighter Museum and is displayed at their Mesa, Arizona facility. A large number of ex-Polish Lim-5s and -6s have been purchased by warbird enthusiasts in the US and Europe

## MiG-17PFU 'Fresco-E'

### Cutaway key

1 Rudder upper hinge/balance
2 Rudder (upper section)
3 Passive tail-warning radar unit
4 Rear navigation light
5 Fixed incidence tailplane
6 Elevator control linkage
7 Control lines
8 Tailfin construction
9 Transformer
10 Gyro compass
11 Magnetic amplifier for gyro
12 Tail-warning master unit
13 Rudder (lower section)
14 Rudder trim tab
15 Tailpipe shroud
16 Afterburner nozzle
17 Starboard airbrake
18 Tail skid
19 Ventral strake
20 Airbrake hydraulic activator
21 Control linkage assembly
22 Rear fuselage structure
23 Afterburner pipe
24 Aft fuselage fuel tank
25 Afterburner outer casing

26 Klimov VK-1F turbojet
27 Inspection panel
28 IFF antenna
29 Engine intake grille
30 Inspection panel
31 Engine auxiliaries
32 Aft/forward fuselage breakpoint
33 Main fuselage fuel tank
34 Intake trunking
35 VHF antenna
36 Canopy track
37 Bulkhead
38 Ejector seat
39 Port control console (throttle quadrant)
40 Pilot's headrest
41 Canopy heating web
42 Rear-view mirror
43 Rocket-sight
44 Radar-scope shroud
45 Enlarged cockpit quarterlight
46 Instrument panel
47 Control column
48 Rudder pedals
49 Windscreen
50 RDF ranging unit
51 VHF transmitter/receiver
52 Accumulator
53 Radar ranging unit

54 Radar scanner
55 Extended upper intake lip
56 AI scanner in central intake bullet
57 Combat camera housing
58 Bifurcated intake
59 Intake centre-body
60 Centre-section nosewheel well
61 Intake trunking
62 Nosewheel retraction radii
63 Nosewheel doors
64 Nosewheel fork
65 Forward-retracting nosewheel
66 Nosewheel strut
67 Forward fuselage members
68 Inboard-section wing leading edge

69 Three wing/fuselage attachment points
70 Y-section inner main spar
71 Inboard wing fence
72 Forward main spar
73 Undercarriage indicator spigot
74 Inner wing skinning
75 Split landing flap (inner section)
76 Split landing flap structure (outer section)

## SPECIFICATION

### MiG-17F 'Fresco-C'

**Dimensions:**

**Wingspan:** 31 ft 7 in (9.628 m)
**Wing area:** 243.27 sq ft (22.60 m²)
**Length:** 36 ft 11½ in (11.264 m)
**Height:** 12 ft 5½ in (3.80 m)
**Wheel track:** 12 ft 7½ in (3.849 m)
**Wheel base:** 3.368 m (11 ft ½ in)

**Powerplant:**

one Klimov VK-1F turbojet rated at
5,732 lb st (29.50 kN) dry and
7,451 lb st (33.14 kN) with afterburning

**Weights:**

**Empty equipped:** 8,664 lb (3930 kg)
**Maximum take-off:** 13,380 lb (6069 kg)

**Fuel and load**

**Internal fuel:** 2,579 lb (1170 kg)
**External fuel:** up to 1,444 lb (655 kg)
in two 106- or 63-US gal (400- or
240-litre) drop tanks;
**Maximum ordnance:** 1,102 lb (500 kg)

**Performance**

**Limiting Mach number:** 1.03
**Maximum level speed 'clean' at
9,845 ft (3000 m):** 594 kt (684 mph;
1100 km/h)
**Maximum level speed 'clean' at
32,810 ft (10000 m):** 578 kt (666 mph;
(1071 km/h)
**Speed limit with drop tanks:** 486 kt
(559 mph; 900 km/h)
**Ferry range:** 1,091 nm (1,255 miles;
2020 km) with drop tanks
**Combat radius:** 378 nm (435 miles;
700 km) on a hi-lo-hi attack mission
with two 551-lb (250-kg) bombs and
two drop tanks
**Maximum rate of climb at sea
level:** 12,795 ft (3900 m) per minute;
**Service ceiling:** 49,215 ft (15000 m)
at dry thrust and 54,460 ft (16600 m) at
afterburning thrust
**Take-off run:** 1,936 ft (590 m) at
normal take-off weight
**Landing run:** 2,789 ft (850 m) at
normal landing weight

*Above: This worm's eye view of a
MiG-17PF, with its flaps deployed
for landing, (note the afterburner
nozzle and radar) shows well the
design of the type's wing, with its
virtually untapered planform and
45° sweep angle.*

*Right: After testing in MiG-17
prototype SP-6, a modified radar
set and missile launch boxes were
fitted to all surviving MiG-17PFs,
bringing them up to MiG-17PFU
standard. Known to NATO as
'Fresco-E', this was the first
production fighter in Europe to
feature AAM armament, this
comprising a quartet of K-5
(RS-2US) beam-riding missiles.*

**77** Centre wing fence
**78** Outboard wing fence
**79** Wing construction
**80** Rearspar
**81** Aileron construction
**82** Starboard navigation
light
**83** Wingtip
**84** Starboard pitot head
**85** Outboard-section
wing leading edge
**86** Auxiliary-
tank fin assembly
**87** Triple-strut auxiliary-
tank bracing
**88** Mainwheel leg
**89** Starboard mainwheel
**90** Mainwheel door

**91** Auxiliary tank
(88 Impgal /400 litre
capacity)
**92** Mainwheel
retraction rod
**93** AA-1 'Alkali'-type
beam-riding air-to-air
missiles
**94** Weapon pylons
**95** Altimeter radio
dipole (port outboard/
starboard inboard)

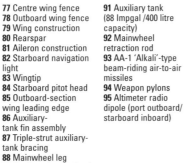

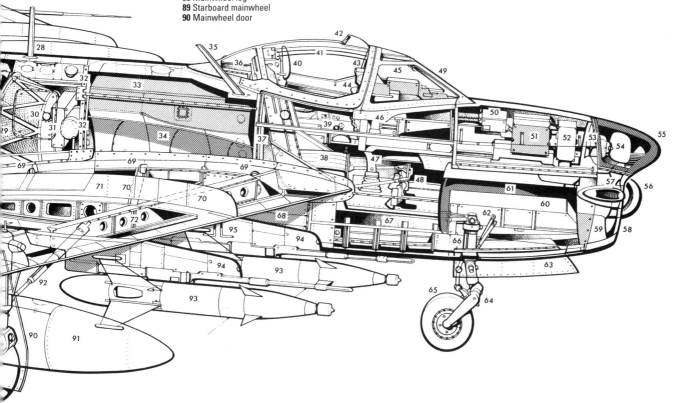

# Mikoyan-Gurevich MiG-21 'Fishbed'

*Finland operated the MiG-21 between 1963 and 1998, when the final aircraft were retired. Along the way, four variants – the MiG-21F-13, U, UM and BIS – were all operated. The picture above shows the very last MiG-21 to fly, MiG-21BIS MG-138 piloted by Captain Yrjö Rantamäki, preparing to at Rissala air base on 7 March 1998. Finland has now replaced its MiG-21s with Boeing F-18s.*

### MiG-21MF 'Fishbed-J'

**Cutaway key**
1 Pitot static boom
2 Pitch vanes
3 Yaw vanes
4 Conical three-position intake centre body
5 'Spin Scan' search-and-track radar antenna
6 Boundary layer slot
7 Engine air intake
8 'Spin Scan' radar
9 Lower boundary layer exit
10 IFF antennas
11 Nosewheel doors
12 Nosewheel leg and shock absorbers
13 Castoring nosewheel
14 Anti-shimmy damper
15 Avionics bay access
16 Attitude sensor
17 Nosewheel well
18 Spill door
19 Nosewheel retraction pivot
20 Bifurcated intake trunking
21 Avionics bay
22 Electronics equipment
23 Intake trunking
24 Upper boundary layer exit

25 Dynamic pressure probe for q-feel
26 Semi-elliptical armour glass windscreen
27 Gunsight mounting
28 Fixed quarterlight
29 Radar scope
30 Control column (with tailplane trim switch and two firing buttons)
31 Rudder pedals
32 Underfloor control runs
33 KM-1 two-position zero-level ejection seat
34 Port instrument console
35 Undercarriage handle
36 Seat harness
37 Canopy release/lock
38 Starboard wall switch pane
39 Rear-view mirror fairing
40 Starboard hinged canopy
41 Ejection seat headrest
42 Avionics bay
43 Control rods
44 Air-conditioning plant
45 Suction relief door
46 Intake trunking
47 Wingroot attachment fairing

48 Wing/fuselage spar-lug attachment points (four)
49 Fuselage ring frames
50 Intermediary frames
51 Main fuselage fuel tank
52 RSIU radio bay
53 Auxiliary intake
54 Leading-edge integral fuel tank
55 Starboard outer weapons pylon
56 Outboard wing construction
57 Starboard navigation light
58 Leading-edge suppressed aerial
59 Wing fence
60 Aileron control jack
61 Starboard aileron
62 Flap actuator fairing
63 Starboard blown flap SPS (*sduva pogranichnovo slova*)
64 Multi-spar wing structure
65 Main integral wing fuel tank

66 Undercarriage mounting/pivot point
67 Starboard mainwheel leg
68 Auxiliaries compartment
69 Fuselage fuel tanks Nos 2 and 3
70 Mainwheel well external fairing
71 Mainwheel (retracted)
72 Trunking contours
73 Control rods in dorsal spine
74 Compressor face
75 Oil tank
76 Avionics pack
77 Engine accessories
78 Tumanskii R-13 turbojet
79 Fuselage break/transport joint
80 Intake
81 Tail surface control linkage
82 Artificial feel unit
83 Tailplane jack
84 Hydraulic accumulator
85 Tailplane trim motor

86 Fin spar attachment plate
87 Rudder jack
88 Rudder control linkage
89 Fin structure
90 Leading-edge panel
91 Radio cable access
92 Magnetic detector
93 Fin mainspar
94 RSIU (*radio-stantsiya istrebitelnaya ultrakorotkykh vol'n* – very short-wave fighter radio) antenna plate
95 VHF/UHF aerials
96 IFF antennas
97 Formation light
98 Tail warning radar
99 Rear navigation light

100 Fuel vent
101 Rudder construction
102 Rudder hinge
103 Braking parachute hinged bullet fairing
104 Braking parachute stowage
105 Tailpipe (variable convergent nozzle)
106 Afterburner installation
107 Afterburner bay cooling intake
108 Tail plane linkage fairing

109 Nozzle actuating cylinders
110 Tailplane torque tube
111 All-moving tailplane
112 Anti flutter weight

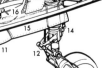

A handful of MiG 21s was delivered to the West during the Cold War by means of defections from Communist countries or by other more covert methods. This example, a Soviet-built MiG-21, is seen flying over the Groom Lake/Area 51 complex and was part of the secret 4477th Test & Evaluation Squadron or 'Red Eagles'. Aircraft like these were flown, in Operation Have Doughnut, against the latest Western types to evaluate their performance, and so enable planners to formulate tactics. The obvious intense secrecy that surrounded these test flights has helped to shape the legend of Area 51 and it is entirely plausible that the supposed 'alien' aircraft are simply foreign aircraft.

## SPECIFICATION

### MiG-21MF 'Fishbed-J'

#### Dimensions

**Length with probe:** 51 ft 8½ in (15.76 m)
**Length excluding probe:** 40 ft 4 in (12.29 m)
**Height:** 13 ft 6 in (4.13 m)
**Span:** 23 ft 6 in (7.15 m)
**Wing area:** 247.5 sq ft (23 m²)
**Wing aspect ratio:** 2.23
**Wheel track:** 9 ft 1¾ in (2.79 m)
**Wheel base:** 15 ft 5½ in (4.71 m)

#### Powerplant

One MNPK 'Soyuz' (Tumanskii/Gavrilov) R-13-300 turbojet rated at 8,972 lb st (39.92 kN) dry and 14,037 lb st (63.66 kN) with afterburning

#### Weights

**Empty:** 11,795 lb (5350 kg)
**Normal take-off with four AAMs and three 129-US gal (490-litre) drop tanks:** 17,967 lb (8150 kg)
**Maximum take-off:** 20,723 lb (9400 kg)

#### Fuel and load

**Internal fuel:** 687 US gal (2600 litres)
**External fuel:** up to 387 US gal (1470 litres) in three drop tanks
**Maximum ordnance:** 4,409 lb (2000 kg)

#### Performance

**Maximum rate of climb at sea level:** 23,622 ft (7200 m) per minute
**Service ceiling:** 59,711 ft (18200 m)
**Take off run:** 2,625 ft (800 m)

#### Range

**Ferry range:** 971 nm (1,118 miles; 1800 km) with three drop tanks
**Combat radius:** 200 nm (230 miles; 370 km) on a hi-lo-hi attack mission with four 551-lb (250-kg) bombs, or 400 nm (460 miles; 740 km) on a hi-lo-hi mission with two 551-lb (250-kg) bombs and drop tanks

#### Armament

Standard gun is the GSh-23L which has a calibre of 23 mm and can fire AP or HE ammunition, with 420 rounds being carried. The only guided missiles normally carried are for air-to-air use. The MF is capable of firing the K-13A (AA-2 'Atoll') and the AA-2-2 Advanced 'Atoll'. As with other MiG-21s, up to eight R-60 (AA-8 'Aphid') infra-red missiles can also be carried. There is provision for various FABs (free-fall general-purpose bombs), up to 1,102 lb (500 kg) in weight. A wide range of fragmentation, chemical, cluster bombs and rocket-boosted penetrators for use against concrete can be carried, as well as 57-mm or 240-mm calibre rockets.

**113** Intake
**114** Afterburner mounting
**115** Fixed tailplane root fairing
**116** Longitudinal lap joint
**117** External duct (nozzle hydraulics)
**118** Ventral fin
**119** Engine guide rail
**120** ATO assembly canted nozzle
**121** ATO assembly thrust plate forks (rear-mounting)
**122** ATO assembly pack

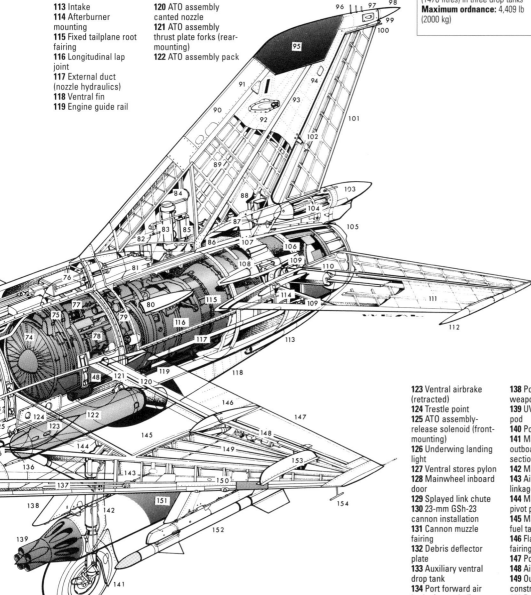

**123** Ventral airbrake (retracted)
**124** Trestle point
**125** ATO assembly-release solenoid (front-mounting)
**126** Underwing landing light
**127** Ventral stores pylon
**128** Mainwheel inboard door
**129** Splayed link chute
**130** 23-mm GSh-23 cannon installation
**131** Cannon muzzle fairing
**132** Debris deflector plate
**133** Auxiliary ventral drop tank
**134** Port forward air brake (extended)
**135** Leading-edge integral fuel tank
**136** Undercarriage retraction strut
**137** Aileron control rods in leading edge
**138** Port inboard weapons pylon
**139** UV-16-57 rocket pod
**140** Port mainwheel
**141** Mainwheel outboard door section
**142** Mainwheel leg
**143** Aileron control linkage
**144** Mainwheel leg pivot point
**145** Main integral wing fuel tank
**146** Flap actuator fairing
**147** Port aileron
**148** Aileron control jack
**149** Outboard wing construction
**150** Port navigation light
**151** Port outboard weapons pylon
**152** 'Advanced Atoll' IR-homing AAM
**153** Wing fence
**154** Radio altimeter antenna

# Mikoyan-Gurevich MiG-25 'Foxbat'

Developed to meet a bomber threat th[at]
never materialised, Mikoyan-Gurevic[h]
MiG-2[5] 'Foxbat' may have lacked t[he]
technology of its NATO adversaries, b[ut]
more than made up for this with [its]
incredible performance. In the MiG-2[5]
the Soviet Union and now, amo[ng]
others, Russia, Azerbaijan, Belar[us]
India, Iraq, Libya and Syria, have [an]
excellent reconnaissance platform a[nd]
bomber destroy[er]

## MiG-25 'Foxbat-A'

**Cutaway key**

1 Ventral airbrake
2 Starboard tailplane (aluminium alloy trailing edge)
3 Steel tailplane spar
4 Titanium leading edge
5 Tail bumper
6 Fully-variable engine exhaust nozzle
7 Exhaust nozzle actuator
8 Starboard rudder
9 Static dischargers
10 Sirena 3 tail warning radar and ECM transmitter
11 Transponder aerial
12 Twin brake parachute housing
13 Port engine exhaust nozzle
14 Port rudder
15 Static dischargers
16 VHF aerial
17 HF leading-edge aerial
18 Port tailfin (steel primary structure)
19 Rudder actuator
20 Titanium rear fuselage skins
21 Dorsal spine fairing
22 Fireproof bulkhead between engine bays
23 Engine afterburner duct
24 Cooling air intake
25 Tailplane hydraulic actuator
26 Starboard ventral fin
27 VHF and ECM aerial housing
28 Aileron actuator
29 Starboard aileron
30 Static discharger
31 All-steel wing construction
32 Wingtip fairing
33 Sirena 3 radar warning receiver and ECM transmitter
34 Continuous-wave target-illuminating radar
35 AA-6 'Acrid' semi-active radar guided-air-to air missile
36 Missile-launching rail
37 Outboard missile pylon
38 Pylon attachments
39 Wing titanium leading edge
40 Inboard pylon
41 Wing fence
42 Engine access panels
43 Engine accessory gearbox
44 Tumanskii R-31 single-shaft afterburning turbojet engine
45 Port flap
46 Aileron hydraulic actuator
47 Port aileron
48 Fixed portion of trailing edge
49 Sirena 3 radar warning receiver and ECM transmitter
50 Continuous-wave target-illuminating radar
51 Titanium leading edge
52 Port wing fences
53 AA-6 'Acrid' semi-active radar-guided air-to-air missile
54 Infra-red-guided AA-6 'Acrid' missile
55 Stainless steel wing skins
56 Intake flank fuel tanks
57 Controls and systems ducting
58 Main fuel tanks (welded steel integral construction), total system capacity 31,575 lb (14322 kg), nitrogen-pressurised
59 Intake bleed air ducts engine bay cooling
60 Engine compressor face
61 Wing spar attachments
62 Main undercarriage leg strut
63 Starboard mainwheel
64 Mainwheel doors
65 Mainwheel stowed position
66 Starboard infra-red guided AA-6 'Acrid' missile
67 Retractable landing/taxiing lamp
68 Intake duct control vanes
69 Steel fuselage primary structure
70 Intake bleed air outlet ducts
71 UHF communications aerials
72 Variable-intake ramp doors
73 Ramp jacks
74 Intake water/methanol injection duct
75 Electric intake tip actuator
76 Variable lower intake lip
77 Nose wheel door/mudguard
78 Twin nose wheels
79 Nose wheel leg doors
80 Starboard navigation light
81 Curved intake inboard sidewall
82 Rear avionics bay, communications and ECM equipment
83 Cockpit canopy cover, hinges to starboard
84 Pilot's ejection seat
85 Cockpit rear pressure bulkhead
86 UHF communications aerial
87 Radar altimeter
88 Pilot's side console panel
89 Control column
90 Instrument panel shroud
91 Stand-by visual sighting system for infra-red missiles
92 Windscreen panels
93 'Odd Rods' IFF aerials
94 Pitot tube
95 Forward avionics compartment, radar and navigation equipment
96 'Fox Fire' fire control radar system
97 Angle-of-attack probe
98 Scanner tracking mechanism
99 Radar scanner dish, 2ft 9½-in (85-cm) diameter
100 Radome
101 'Swift Rod' ILS antenna
102 Pitot tube

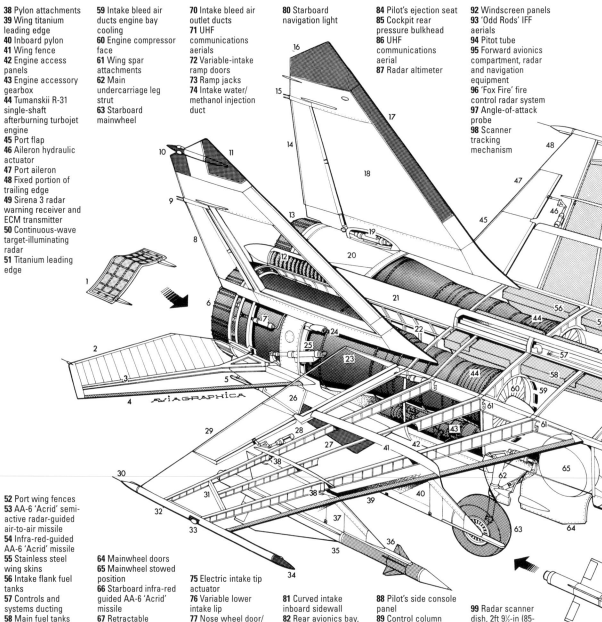

*A refuelling capability was considered an important asset for the MiG-25 and a single MiG-25PD (coded 'Blue 45') was modified as an inflight-refuelling receiver testbed. The aircraft was fitted with an inverted-L-shaped probe immediately in front of the windscreen. Ultimately, the PVO and VVS remained pitifully short of tankers, and priority was given to equipping newer aircraft types with probes, so nothing came of the proposal to retro-fit in-service MiG-25PDs for inflight refuelling.*

## SPECIFICATION

### MiG-25PDS 'Foxbat-E'

#### Dimensions

**Length:** 78 ft 1¾ in (23.82 m)
**Length for aircraft modified with IFR capability:** 78 ft 11½ in (24.07 m)
**Height:** 20 ft ¼ in (6.10 m)
**Wingspan:** 45 ft 11¾ in (14.02 m)
**Wing aspect ratio:** 3.2
**Wing area:** 660.93 sq ft (61.40 m²)
**Wheel track:** 12 ft 7½ in (3.85 m)
**Wheel base:** 16 ft 10¼ in (5.14 m)

#### Powerplant

Two MNPK 'Soyuz' (Tumanskii) R-15BD-300 turbojets each rated at 24,691 lb st (109.83 kN) with afterburning

#### Weights

**Normal take-off weight with four R-40s (AA-6s) and 100 per cent internal fuel:** 80,952 lb (36720 kg)

#### Fuel and loads

**Internal fuel:** 32,121 lb (14570 kg)
**External fuel in an underbelly tank:** 9,634 lb (4370 kg)
**Maximum ordnance:** 8,818 lb (4000 kg)

#### Performance

**Maximum level speed 'clean' at 42,650 ft (13000 m):** Mach 2.8 or 1,619 kt (1,864 mph; 3000 km/h)
**Maximum level speed 'clean' at sea level:** Mach 2.8 or 647 kt (745 mph; 1200 km/h)
**Climb to 65,615 ft (20000 m):** 8 minutes 54 seconds
**Service ceiling:** 67,915 ft (20700 m)
**Take-off run at normal take-off weight:** 4,101 ft (1250 m)
**Landing run at normal landing weight with brake chutes:** 2,624 ft (800 m)
***g* limits:** + 4.5 supersonic

#### Range

**With internal fuel at subsonic speed:** 933 nm (1,075 miles; 1730 km)
**With internal fuel at supersonic speed:** 675 nm (776 miles; 1730 km)
**Endurance:** 2 hours 5 minutes

#### Armament

Standard intercept fit is two or four R-40 (AA-6 'Acrid') missiles. MiG-25PDS aircraft are armed with two R-40s and four R-60 (AA-8 'Aphid') AAMs

**103** MiG-25U 'Foxbat-C' two-seat operational training variant
**104** Student pilot's cockpit enclosure
**105** Instructor's cockpit
**106** MiG-25R 'Foxbat-B' reconnaissance variant
**107** Reconnaissance cameras, one vertical and four oblique
**108** Sideways-looking airborne radar (SLAR) aperture
**109** Ground mapping and Doppler radar antenna
**110** 'Jay-Bird' forward-looking radar

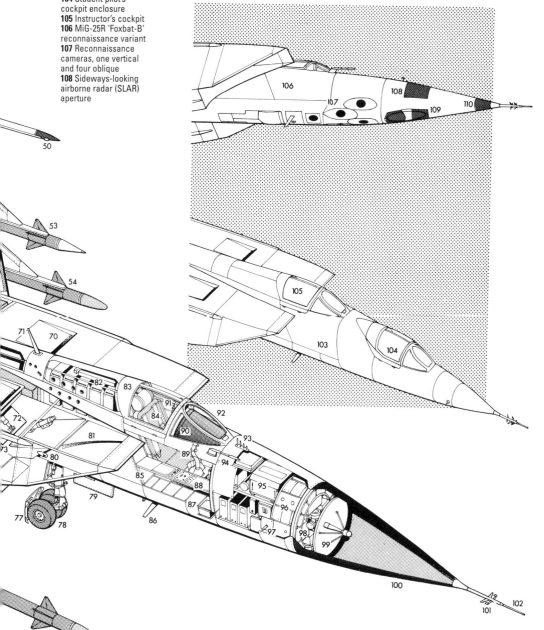

# Mikoyan-Gurevich MiG-29 'Fulcrum'

*The first squadron of Poland's No. 1 PLM (Pulk Lotnictwa Mysliwskiego/Air Fighter Regiment) operates some 19 'Fulcrum-As', nine of which were obtained from the Czech Republic. Four 'Fulcrum UBs' are also used and one of these was also obtained from the Czechs. Poland still hopes to replace its remaining MiG-21Ms with new 'Fulcrums'.*

## MiG-29 'Fulcrum-A'

**Cutaway Key**

1 Pitot head
2 Vortex generating nose strake
3 Glass-fibre radome
4 Pulse-Doppler radar scanner
5 Scanner tracking mechanism
6 N-019 (NATO: 'Slot Back') radar equipment module
7 Angle-of-attack transmitter
8 ILS aerial fairing
9 SRO-2 (NATO: 'Odd Rods') IFF aerial
10 UHF antenna
11 Forward avionics equipment bay
12 Infra-red search and track sensor and laser ranger
13 Dynamic pressure probe
14 Frameless windscreen panel
15 Pilot's head-up-display
16 Instrument panel shroud
17 Rudder pedals and control column
18 Fuselage blended chine fairing
19 Cannon muzzle aperture
20 Cannon barrel
21 Slide mounted engine throttle levers
22 Canopy latch
23 K-36D 'zero-zero' ejection seat
24 Upward-hingeing cockpit canopy cover
25 Electrical distribution centre
26 Cockpit rear pressure bulkhead
27 Cannon bay venting air louvres
28 Nosewheel retraction jack
29 Levered suspension nosewheel leg
30 Twin nosewheels, aft retracting

31 Mudguard
32 ECM aerial panels
33 Cartridge case and link collector box
34 Ammunition magazine
35 Centre avionics equipment bay
36 Canopy hinge point
37 Canopy hydraulic jack
38 HF aerial
39 Mechanical control rods
40 Rear avionics equipment bay
41 Air intake louvres/blow-in doors
42 Variable area intake ramp doors
43 Ramp hydraulic actuator
44 Port engine air intake
45 Weapons interlock access
46 Landing lamp
47 Mainwheel door
48 Forward fuselage integral fuel tank
49 Port main undercarriage wheel bay
50 Flight control system hydraulic equipment module
51 ADF aerial
52 Starboard main undercarriage wheel bay
53 Chaff/flare cartridge housing
54 Starboard wing integral fuel tank
55 Starboard wing missile carriage
56 Leading edge manoeuvre flap
57 Starboard navigation light

58 Radar warning antenna
59 Starboard aileron
60 Plain flap
61 Flap hydraulic jack
62 Centre fuselage integral fuel tank
63 Engine compressor face
64 Cooling air scoop
65 Top-mounted engine accessory equipment gear boxes
66 Central gas turbine starter/APU
67 Engine bay/tailplane attachment machined main frames
68 Airbrake hydraulic jack
69 RD-33D afterburning turbofan engine
70 Fin rib construction
71 Carbon fibre fin skin panelling
72 Fin tip VHF aerial fairing
73 Radar warning antenna
74 'Swift Rod' ILS aerial
75 Starboard rudder
76 Rudder hydraulic actuator

77 Tailplane hydraulic actuator
78 Starboard all-moving tailplane
79 Airbrake, upper and lower split surfaces
80 Brake parachute housing
81 Variable area afterburner nozzle
82 Port tailfin
83 Tail navigation light
84 Sirena-3 ECM aerial fairing
85 Static discharger
86 Port rudder composite construction
87 Port all-moving tailplane
88 Static dischargers
89 Carbon fibre trailing edge skin panelling

90 Tailplane spar box construction
91 Tailplane pivot point
92 Fuselage side-body fairing construction
93 Artificial feel system pitot heads and control valves
94 Port plain flap composite construction
95 Main undercarriage hydraulic retraction jack
96 Port chaff/flare cartridge
97 Main undercarriage leg pivot fixing

98 Pylon attachment hardpoints
99 Flap hydraulic jack
100 Port wing integral fuel tank
101 Aileron hydraulic actuator
102 Port aileron composite construction

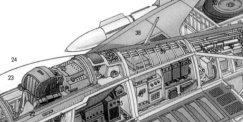

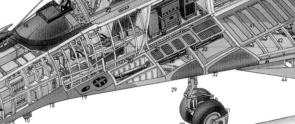

*Despite being conceived in the early 1970s, the MiG-29 remains in service around the world today. The MiG-MAPO design and production facility has also decided that the MiG-29 will remain its basic export product until 2005, by which time a new fighter will have been designed. It is a tribute to the 'Fulcrum' and its designers that it is still in service and, with upgrades, should remain there for many years.*

**103** Carbon fibre skin panelling
**104** Static dischargers
**107** Downward identification light and remote compass housing
**108** Outer wing panel rib construction
**109** Port leading edge manoeuvre flap
**110** Port wing missile pylons
**111** Leading edge flap hydraulic jacks
**112** Port mainwheel
**113** Main undercarriage leg strut
**114** Three-spar wing torsion box construction
**115** Spar root attachment joints
**116** Undercarriage bay pressure refuelling connection
**117** AA-10 'Alamo' long-range air-to-air missile
**118** AA-11 'Archer' intermediate-range air-to-air missile
**119** AA-8 'Aphid' short-range air-to-air missile
**120** 57-mm rocket pack
**121** Cluster bomb
**122** Wing-mounted external fuel tank
**123** Tank pylon
**124** Centre fuselage 'tunnel' fuel tank
**125** Tank pylon attachment

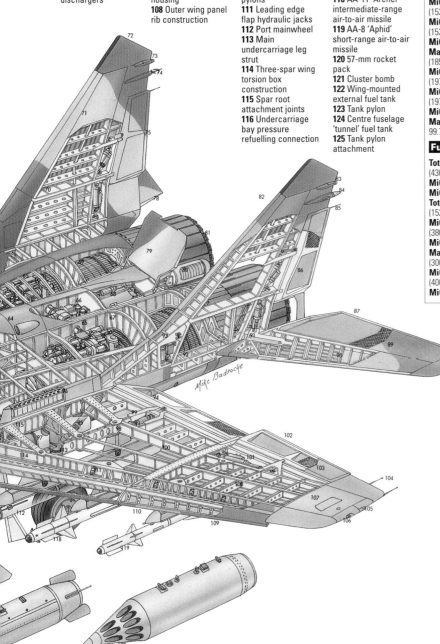

## SPECIFICATION

**MiG-29 'Fulcrum-A'**
**(unless otherwise noted)**

### Dimensions
**Fuselage length (including probe):** 56 ft 10 in (17.32 m)
**Wing span:** span 37 ft 3¼ in (11.36m)
**Wing aspect ratio:** 3.4
**Wing area:** 409.04 sq ft (38 m²)
**Tailplane span:** 25 ft 6¼ in (7.78m)
**Wheel track:** 10 ft 2 in (3.10m)
**Wheel base:** 12 ft 0.5 in (3.67m)
**Height:** 15 ft 6.¼ in (4.73m)

### Powerplant
Two Klimov/Leningrad (Isotov/Sarkisov) RD-33 augmented turbofans each rated at 11,111 lb st (49.42 kN) dry and 18,298 lb st (81.39 kN) with afterburning.
**MiG-29M:** Two Klimov/Leningrad (Isotov/Sarkisov) RD-33K turbofans rated at 12,125 lb st (53.95 kN) dry. 19,400 lb st (86.33 kN) with afterburning, and with an 'emergency regime' rating of 20,725 lb st (92.22 kN)

### Weights
**Empty operating:** 24,030 lb (10900 kg)
**Normal take-off interceptor:** 33,600 lb (15240 kg)
**MiG-29UB 'Fulcrum-B':** 33,730 lb (15300 kg)
**MiG-29 'Fulcrum-C':** 33,730 lb (15300 kg)
**MiG-29K:** 40,705 lb (18480 kg)
**Maximum take-off:** 40,785 lb (18500 kg)
**MiG-29UB 'Fulcrum-B':** 43,430 lb (19700kg)
**MiG-29 'Fulcrum-C':** 42,680 lb (19700 kg)
**MiG-29K:** 49,340 lb (22400 kg)
**Maximum wing loading:** 99.71 lb/sq ft (486.8 kg/m²)

### Fuel and load
**Total internal fuel:** 960 Imp gal (4365 litres)
**MiG-29C:** 998 Imp gal (4540 litres)
**MiG-29M:** 1,375 Imp gal (6250 litres)
**Total external fuel:** 334 Imp gal (1520 litres)
**MiG-29 'Fulcrum-C':** 836 Imp gal (3800 litres)
**MiG-29M:** 1,100 Imp gal (5000 litres)
**Maximum weapon load:** 6,614 lb (3000 kg)
**MiG-29 'Fulcrum-C':** 8,818 lb (4000 kg)
**MiG-29M:** 9,921lb (4500 kg)

### Performance
**Maximum level speed 'clean' at 36,090 ft (11000 m):** 1,320 kt (1,520 mph; 2445 km/h)
**MiG-29K:** 1,242 kt (1,430 mph; 2300 km/h)
**Maximum level speed at low level:** 810 kt (932 mph; 1500 km/h)
**Limiting Mach numbers:** 2.3 at 36,090 ft (11000 m); 1.22 at sea level
**Take-off speed:** 119 kt (137 mph; 220 km/h)
**Take-off run:** 820 ft (250 m)
**Approach speed:** 140 kt (162 mph; 260 km/h)
**Landing speed:** 127 kt (146 mph; 235 km/h)
**Landing run with brake chute:** 1,970-2,300 ft (600-700 m)
**Acceleration at 3,280 ft (1000 m):** 325-595 kt (373-683 mph; 600-1100 km/h) in 13.5 s 595-700 kt (683-805 mph; 1100-1300 km/h) in 8.7 s
**G-Limits:** +9 below Mach 0.85 and +7 above Mach 0.85
**Service ceiling:** 55,780 ft (17000 m)

### Range
**With maximum internal fuel:** 810 nm (932 miles; 1500 km)
**MiG-29M:** 1,080 nm (1,243 miles; 2000 km)
**Ferry range with three external tanks:** 1,134 nm (1,305 miles; 2100 km)
**MiG-29M** 1,728 nm (1,988 miles; 3200 km)

### Armaments
**Maximum weapon load:** 4,410 lb (2000 kg)
**MiG-29 'Fulcrum-C':** 6,614 lb (3000 kg) of ordnance on six underwing hardpoints, with provision for two 253-Imp gal (1150-litre) drop tanks underwing and an optional centreline hardpoint for a 330 Imp gal (1500 litre) fuel tank
**Cannon:** one 30-mm GSh-301 cannon in port wingroot leading edge with 150 rounds
**Air-to-Air missiles:** R-60 (AA-8 'Aphid'), R-27 (AA-10 'Alamo'), R-73 (AA-11 'Archer')
**Ground attack weapons:** FAB-250 and -500 bombs, KMGU-2 submunitions dispenser, ZB-500 napalm tank, 20 round 80-mm rocket pods, 130-mm and 240-mm rockets. One 30-kT RN-40 nuclear bomb on port inboard pylon

# North American F-100 Super Sabre

Although it suffered from more than its fair share of problems, the F-100 represented the absolute cutting-edge of US fast-jet technology when the F-100A entered operational service in 1954. As a combat aircraft the F-100A lacked capability, however, and was soon replaced by the more capable -100C. These F-100Cs demonstrate the original straight-wing trailing edge, which was 'cranked' on the F-100D and F thanks to their increased-area flaps.

## F-100D Super Sabre

**Cutaway key**
1 Pitot tube, folded for ground handling
2 Engine air intake
3 Pitot tube hinge point
4 Radome
5 IFF aerial
6 AN/APR-25(V) gun tracking radar
7 Intake bleed air electronics cooling duct
8 Intake duct framing
9 Cooling air exhaust duct
10 Cannon muzzle port 11 UHF aerial
12 Nose avionics compartment
13 Hinged nose compartment access door
14 Inflight refuelling probe

15 Windscreen panels
16 A-4 radar gunsight
17 Instrument panel shroud
18 Cockpit front pressure bulkhead
19 Rudder pedals
20 Gunsight power supply

21 Armament relay panel
22 Intake ducting
23 Cockpit canopy emergency operating controls
24 Nosewheel leg door
25 Torque scissors
26 Twin nosewheels
27 Nose undercarriage leg strut
28 Pontiac M39 20-mm cannon (four)
29 Kick-in boarding steps
30 Ejection seat footrests
31 Instrument panel
32 Engine throttle
33 Canopy external handle
34 Starboard side console panel

35 Ejection seat
36 Headrest
37 Cockpit canopy cover
38 Ejection seat guide rails
39 Cockpit rear pressure bulkhead
40 Port side console panel

41 Cockpit floor level
42 Control cable runs
43 Gun bay access panel
44 Ammunition feed chutes
45 Ammunition tanks, 200 rpg
46 Power supply amplifier
47 Rear electrical and electronics bay
48 Cockpit pressurisation valve
49 Anti-collision light
50 Air-conditioning plant
51 Radio compass aerial
52 Intake bleed air heat exchanger
53 Heat exchanger exhaust duct

54 Secondary air turbine
55 Air turbine exhaust duct (open)
56 Starboard wing integral fuel tank, capacity 174 Imp gal (791 litres)
57 Starboard automatic leading-edge slat, open
58 Slat guide rails
59 Wing fence

60 Starboard navigation light
61 Wingtip faring
62 Fixed portion of trailing edge
63 Starboard aileron
64 Aileron hydraulic jack
65 Starboard outer plain flap
66 Flap hydraulic jack
67 UHF aerial
68 Engine intake centrebody
69 Wing attachment fuselage main frames
70 Fuselage fuel tanks, total internal capacity 641 Imp gal (2915 litres)
71 Wing spar centre section carry through beams

72 Engine intake compressor face
73 Main engine mounting
74 Pratt & Whitney J57-P-21A afterburning turbojet engine
75 Dorsal spine fairing
76 Fuel vent pipe
77 Engine oil tank
78 Fuselage upper longeron
79 Engine accessory gearbox
80 Compressor bleed air blow off valve
81 Fuselage break point

82 Rear fuselage attachment bolts (four)
83 Finroot filet
84 Engine turbine section
85 Engine rear mounting ring

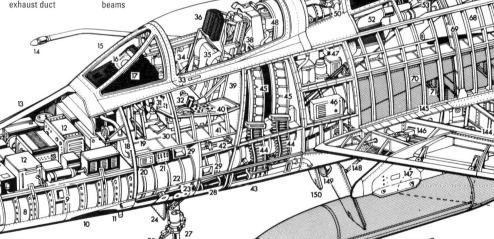

*As the F-100's front-line service career began drawing to a close, airframes became available for conversion as target drones. The first YQF-100 prototype was converted and flown by Sperry Flight Systems in 1979 and was followed by a second YQF-100, three QF-100s for the USAF, three for the US Army and a single QF-100F. A major programme then got underway, with Tracor producing a further 72 QF-100Ds and Tracor/Flight Systems another 209 QF-100D/F drones. A QF-100D is illustrated.*

## SPECIFICATION

### F-100D Super Sabre

#### Dimensions
**Length:** 49 ft 6 in (15.09 m)
**Height:** 16 ft 2⅝ in (4.95 m)
**Wingspan:** 38 ft 9 in (11.81 m)
**Wing area:** 385.20 sq ft (35.79 m²)

#### Powerplant
One Pratt & Whitney J57-P-21A turbojet rated at 11,700 lb st (52.02 kN) dry and 16,950 lb st (75.40 kN) with afterburning

#### Weights
**Empty:** 21,000 lb (9525 kg)
**Loaded:** 29,762 lb (13500 kg)
**Combat:** 30,061 lb (13633 kg)
**Maximum take-off:** 38,048 lb (17256 kg)

#### Fuel and load
**Internal fuel:** 1,189 US gal (4500 litres)
**External fuel:** up to 1,070 US gal (4050 litres)
**Drop tanks:** normally flown with two 450-US gal (1703-litre) tanks, although 200-US gal (757-litre), 275-US gal (1041-litre) and 335-US gal (1268-litre) tanks were also available
**Maximum external load:** 7,500 lb (3402 kg)

#### Performance
**Maximum speed at 35,000 ft (10670 m):** 864 mph (1390 km/h)
**Rate of climb:** 16,000 ft (4875 m) per minute
**Climb to 35,000 ft (10670 m) at combat weight with maximum power:** 3 minutes 30 seconds

#### Range
**Combat:** 1,500 miles (2415 km)
**Ferry:** 1,973 miles (3176 km)

#### Armament
Four 20-mm Pontiac M39E 20-mm cannon with 200 rounds per gun, plus provision for tactical nuclear weapons and a wide range of conventional stores including Mk 80 series and M117 bombs, cluster munitions, practice bomb dispensers, rocket pods, fire bombs and napalm tanks, AGM-12A/B/C ASMs and AIM-9B AAMs

86 Afterburner fuel spray manifold
87 Fin attachment sloping frame
88 Rudder hydraulic jack
89 Fin sub attachment joint
90 Tailfin construction
91 Fin leading edge
92 Fintip aerial fairing
93 Upper UHF aerial
94 Fixed portion of trailing edge
95 AN/APR-26(V) radar warning antenna
96 Tail navigation light
97 Fuel jettison pipe
98 Rudder construction
99 Rudder trim control jack
100 Externally braced trailing-edge section

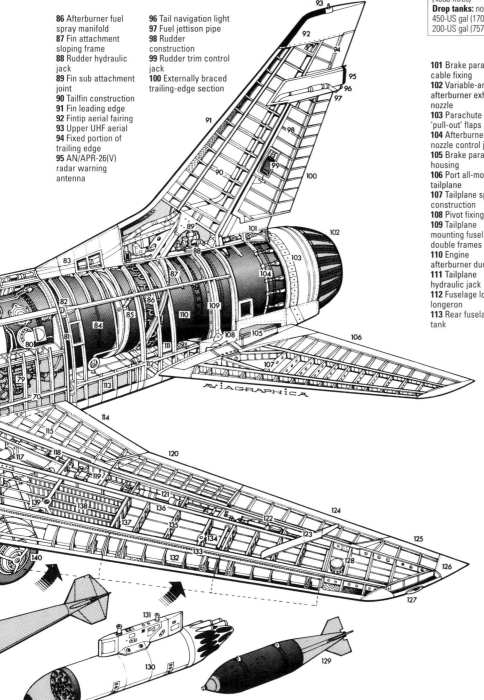

101 Brake parachute cable fixing
102 Variable-area afterburner exhaust nozzle
103 Parachute cable 'pull-out' flaps
104 Afterburner nozzle control jacks
105 Brake parachute housing
106 Port all-moving tailplane
107 Tailplane spar box construction
108 Pivot fixing
109 Tailplane mounting fuselage double frames
110 Engine afterburner duct
111 Tailplane hydraulic jack
112 Fuselage lower longeron
113 Rear fuselage fuel tank
114 Port inner plain flap
115 Flap rib construction
116 Main undercarriage wheel bay
117 Undercarriage leg pivot fixing
118 Flap hydraulic jack
119 Flap interconnecting linkage
120 Port outer flap
121 Flap hydraulic jack
122 Aileron jack
123 Wing fence
124 Port aileron
125 Fixed portion of trailing edge
126 Wingtip fairing
127 Port navigation light
128 Compass master transmitter
129 750-lb (340-kg) M117 HE bomb
130 SUU-7A CBU 19-round rocket pod and bomblet dispenser
131 Outboard wing pylon
132 Leading-edge slat rib construction
133 Hinged leading-edge attachment joint
134 Outboard pylon fixing
135 Wing rib construction
136 Rear spar
137 Port wing integral fuel tank, 174 Imp gal (791 litres)
138 Multi-spar inner wing panel construction
139 Centre pylon fixing
140 Multi-plate disc brake
141 Port mainwheel
142 Main undercarriage leg strut
143 Undercarriage mounting rib
144 Front spar
145 Wing/fuselage attachment skin joint
146 Aileron cable control run
147 Inboard pylon
148 Airbrake hydraulic jacks (two)
149 Retractable landing/taxiing lamps, port and starboard
150 Ventral airbrake
151 166.5-Imp gal (757-litre) napalm container
152 AGM-12C Bullpup B tactical missile
153 Centre wing pylon
154 279-Imp gal (1268-litre) air refuellable supersonic fuel tank
155 Tank side bracing strut

# Northrop F-5

Around 45 Brazilian F-5E/Fs are to undergo an upgrade programme by Elbit Systems. The aircraft are to receive a new multi-mode fire-control radar, HOTAS controls and large-format multi-function LCD displays. Brazil's F-5Es are used mainly for ground-attack and this pre-upgrade F-5E is carrying four unguided bombs on its underwing hardpoints, MAA-1 missiles on the wingtip launchers and an auxiliary fuel tank on the centreline pylon.

## RF-5E 'Tigereye'

**Cutaway key**

1 Pilot head
2 Forward radar-warning antennas
3 KS-87B forward camera, station 1
4 Forward camera compartment
5 Pallet 3, HIAC-1 Long-Range Oblique Photography (LOROP) camera, requires reconfigured window aperture panel
6 LOROP camera rotary drive
7 Main camera compartment
8 Pallet 1 option, KA-95B medium-altitude panoramic camera, station 2
9 KA-56E low-altitude panoramic camera, station 3
10 RS-710 infra-red linescanner, station 4
11 Pallet 2 option, KA-93B high-altitude panoramic camera, stations 2 and 3
12 KA-56E low-altitude panoramic camera, station 4
13 Camera-mounting pallet
14 Optical viewing panel, hinged to starboard
15 Optional vertical KS-87B camera replacing IR linescanner at station 4 of pallet 1
16 Forward-retracting nosewheel
17 Temperature probe
18 Gun gas venting retractable air scoop
19 Ammunition magazine, 280 rounds

20 Ammunition feed chute
21 Single M39A2 20-mm cannon
22 Central avionics equipment compartment
23 Avionics equipment relocated to starboard cannon bay
24 Television sighting camera, located at base of starboard cannon bay
25 Windscreen de-icing fluid tank
26 Gun gas venting air ducts
27 Cartridge case ejector chute
28 Static ports
29 UHF/IFF antenna
30 Rudder pedals
31 Canopy emergency release
32 Position of angle-of attack transmitter on starboard side
33 Control column
34 Instrument panel shroud
35 Frameless windscreen panel
36 AN/ASG-31 lead computing gunsight

37 Upward-hinged canopy
38 Pilot's lightweight rocket-powered ejection seat
39 External canopy handle
40 Engine throttle levers
41 Fold-out boarding steps
42 275-US gal (1041-litre) centreline fuel tank
43 Port engine air intake
44 Liquid oxygen converter
45 Cabin air-conditioning plant
46 Rear avionics equipment bay, port and starboard access
47 Electro-luminescent formation lighting strip
48 Canopy hinge arms and hydraulic actuator
49 Engine bleed air duct to air conditioning heat exchanger

50 Forward fuel cell, bag-type tanks, total internal capacity 677 US gal (2563 litres)
51 Inverted flight reservoir
52 Pressure refuelling connection
53 Port navigation light
54 Ventral retractable landing light
55 Missile control relay boxes
56 Wing leading-edge root extension
57 Leading-edge flap actuator
58 Ventral airbrake panel, port and starboard
59 Airbrake hydraulic jack
60 Intake ducting
61 Centre fuselage fuel cell
62 Gravity fuel fillers

63 Starboard wing tank pylon
64 Leading-edge manoeuvring flap
65 Wingtip missile installation
66 Starboard position light
67 Aileron control linkage
68 Starboard aileron
69 Starboard plain flap
70 Fuel feed pipes
71 Rear fuselage fuel cell

78 UHF antenna
79 Trailing-edge communications antennas
80 Fuel jettison
81 Rudder
82 Rudder and hydraulic actuators
83 Parachute anchorage and release link
84 Brake parachute housing

89 Port all-moving tailplane
90 Tailplane pivot mounting and hydraulic actuator
91 General Electric J85-GE-21 afterburning engine
92 Engine accessory equipment

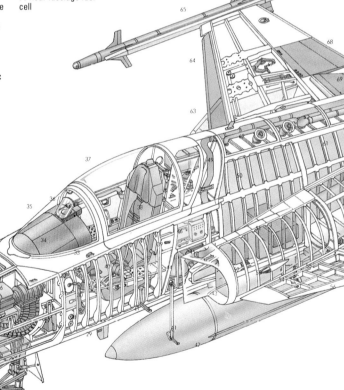

72 Fuel jettison pipe
73 Starboard all-moving tailplane
74 Anti-collision flashing beacon
75 Pressure head
76 Tail position light
77 Fintip antenna fairing

85 Exhaust nozzle shrouds
86 Variable-area afterburner nozzle
87 Rear radar warning antenna, port and starboard
88 Afterburner ducting

93 Runway emergency arrester hook
94 Engine auxiliary air intake doors
95 Hydraulic reservoir, dual systems port and starboard

*Thirty years after their introduction, Norway's F-5s are still soldiering on in service. This F-5A(G) is seen cruising over Norwegian fjords in the 1970s prior to the aircraft receiving a new light-grey colour scheme in the 1980s to help prevent excessive corrosion of the airframe. During the 1980s the F-5s also underwent the associated Service Life Extension Programme (SLEP), and in the 1990s underwent a further upgrade with the Programme for Avionics and Weapon System (PAWS). The F-5s are likely to remain in service until at least 2003.*

## SPECIFICATION

### F-5E Tiger II

#### Dimensions

**Length including probe:** 47 ft 4¾ in (14.45 m)
**Height:** 13 ft 4½ in (4.08 m)
**Wingspan without wingtip AAMs:** 26 ft 8 in (8.13 m)
**Wingspan with wingtip AAMs:** 28 ft (8.53 m)
**Wing area:** 186.00 sq ft (17.28 m²)
**Wing aspect ratio:** 3.82
**Tailplane span:** 14 ft 1½ in (4.31 m)
**Wheel track:** 12 ft 5½ in (3.80 m)
**Wheel base:** 16 ft 11½ in (5.17 m)

#### Powerplant

Two General Electric J85-GE-21B turbojets each rated at 3,500 lb st (15.5 kN) dry and 5,000 lb st (22.2 kN) with afterburning

#### Weights

**Empty:** 9,558 lb (4349 kg)
**Maximum take-off:** 24,664 lb (11187 kg)

#### Fuel and load

**Maximum internal fuel:** 677 US gal (2563 litres)
**Maximum external fuel:** up to three 275-US gal (1040-litre) auxiliary drop tanks
**Maximum ordnance:** 7,000 lb (3175 kg)

#### Performance

**Maximum level speed 'clean' at 36,000 ft (10975 m):** 917 kt (1,056 mph; 1700 km/h)
**Cruising speed at 36,000 ft (10975 m):** 562 kt (647 mph; 1041 km/h)
**Maximum rate of climb at sea level:** 34,300 ft (10455 m) per minute
**Service ceiling:** 51,800 ft (15590 m)
**Take-off run:** 2,000 ft (610 m) at 15,745 lb (7142 kg)
**Take-off distance to 50 ft (15 m):** 2,800 ft (853 m) at 15,745 lb (7142 kg)
**Landing run:** 2,450 ft (747 m) at 11,340 lb (5143 kg) with brake parachute

#### Range

**Ferry range:** 2,010 nm (2,314 miles; 3720 km) with empty auxiliary tanks dropped
**Combat radius:** 760 nm (875 miles; 1405 km) with two AIM-9 Sidewinder air-to-air missiles

#### Armament

Two 20-mm Pontiac (Colt-Browning) M39A2 cannon in fuselage nose with 280 rounds per gun; two AIM-9 Sidewinder air-to-air missiles on wingtip launchers and up to 7,000 lb (3175 kg) of mixed ordnance on one underfuselage and four wing hardpoints, including M129 leaflet bombs, 500-lb (227-kg) Mk 82 and Snakeye bombs, 2000-lb (907-kg) Mk 84 bomb, various air-launched rockets, CBU-24, -49, -52 or -58 cluster bomb units and SUU-20 bomb and rocket packs. Can also be adapted to carry AGM-65 Maverick, a centreline multiple ejector rack and laser guided bombs

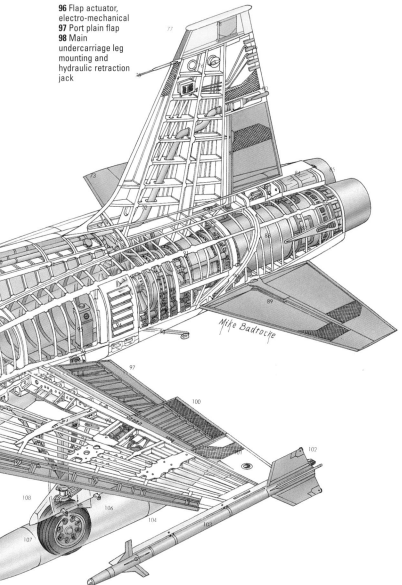

96 Flap actuator, electro-mechanical
97 Port plain flap
98 Main undercarriage leg mounting and hydraulic retraction jack

Mike Badrocke

*The 425th Tactical Fighter Training Squadron (formerly the 4441st CCTS) was formed in 1969 and, during its 20-year existence, operated the F-5A, B, E and F. Its primary role was the training of foreign F-5 pilots, although from 1979 the parent 405th TTW also acted as the replacement training unit for the F-15.*

99 Aileron tandem hydraulic actuators
100 Port aileron
101 Port position light
102 Navigation light repeater
103 AIM-9L Sidewinder air-to-air missile

104 Missile launch rail
105 Outboard pylon hardpoint (unused)
106 150-US gal (568-litre) external fuel tank
107 Port mainwheel

108 External tank pylon
109 Port leading-edge manoeuvring flap

# Republic F-84 Thunderjet

F-84G-26-RE 51-16719 displays the well-known colours of the USAF's Thunderbirds display team. The F-84G was the team's first type upon its formation in 1953. Five aircraft were assigned to the team and the F-84G was employed for two years. In 1955 they were replaced by F-84F Thunderstreaks.

## F-84G Thunderjet

**Cutaway key**

1 Engine air intake
2 Gun laying radar seeker
3 Machine gun muzzles
4 Pitot tube
5 Main undercarriage leg strut
6 Steering control
7 Nosewheel
8 Shimmy damper
9 Taxiing lamp
10 Nosewheel retraction strut
11 Nosewheel doors
12 Bifurcated intake ducting
13 Nosewheel hydraulic retraction jack
14 Machine gun barrels
15 Gyro compass unit
16 Ballast weights
17 Ammunition tanks (300 rounds per gun)
18 M3 0.5-in (12.7-mm) machine guns
19 Spent cartridge case collector chute
20 Nosewheel bay between intake ducts
21 Battery
22 Servicing access panels
23 Gun bay access panel latch
24 Oxygen converter
25 Hydraulic system header tank
26 Gun bay access panel
27 Armoured bulkhead
28 Cockpit front pressure bulkhead
29 Rudder pedals
30 Instrument panel
31 Control column
32 Instrument panel shroud
33 Sperry radar gunsight
34 Bullet-proof windscreen
35 Cockpit canopy cover
36 Canopy framing
37 Starboard side console panel
38 Pilot's ejection seat
39 Engine throttle control
40 Cockpit floor level
41 Intake suction relief door
42 Intake trunking
43 Port side console panel
44 Cockpit rear pressure bulkhead
45 Canopy external latch
46 Ejection seat headrest
47 Pilot's back and head armour
48 Cockpit air system
49 Starboard wing fuel tank bays, total internal fuel system capacity 450 US gal (1709 litre)
50 Fuel tank interconnecting piping
51 Starboard navigation light
52 Fixed tip tank, capacity 230 US gal (870 litre)
53 Tip tank stabilising fin
54 Rear identification light
55 Starboard aileron
56 Aileron aerodynamic seal
57 Fixed tab
58 Aileron hinge control
59 Starboard Fowler flap
60 Hydraulic flap jack
61 Starboard main undercarriage pivot fixing
62 D/F loop aerial
63 Cockpit air system vent
64 Sliding canopy cover electric motor and rail
65 Fuselage top longeron
66 Main fuselage fuel tank
67 Intake centre fairing accessory compartment
68 Fuselage/main spar attachment frame
69 Wing root machine gun ammunition tank (300 rounds)
70 Ammunition feed chute
71 Allison J35-A-29 axial-flow turbojet
72 Fuselage/rear spar attachment main frame
73 Rear fuselage break point (engine removal)
74 Engine flame cans
75 Cooling air vent
76 Radio and electronics equipment bay
77 VHF radio transmitter and receiver
78 Jet pipe cooling air intake
79 Jet pipe heat shroud
80 Control cable runs
81 Fin root fillet
82 Fin/tailplane attachment joints
83 Starboard tailplane

*Large numbers of F-84s were supplied to NATO and other allied air forces under the Mutual Defense Assistance Program, including that of the Netherlands (pictured). The Dutch received 21 F-84Es in 1951-52 (most of which were later converted as photo-reconnaissance aircraft) and 166 F-84Gs. Other Thunderjet operators have included France (below right), Greece, Portugal, Taiwan, Turkey and Yugoslavia.*

## SPECIFICATION

### F-84G Thunderjet

**Dimensions**

**Wingspan:** 36 ft 5 in (11.09 m)
**Length:** 38 ft 1 in (11.60 m)
**Height:** 12 ft 7 in (3.83 m)
**Wing area:** 260.00 sq ft (24.25 m²)

**Powerplant**

one Allison J35-A-29 axial-flow turbojet rated at 5,600 lb st (24.91 kN)

**Weights**

**Empty:** 11,095 lb (5033 kg)
**Normal loaded:** 18,645 lb (8457 kg)
**Maximum loaded:** 23,525 lb (10670 kg)

**Fuel load**

**Internal fuel:** 451 US gal (1709 litres)
**External fuel:** two wingtip fuel tanks and two underwing drop tanks, each of 230-US gal (870-litre) capacity

**Performance**

**Maximum speed at sea level:** 622 mph (1001 km/h)

**Maximum speed at 20,000 ft (6095 m):** 575 mph (925 km/h)
**Maximum speed at 36,000 ft (10970 m):** 540 mph (869 km/h)
**Cruising speed at 35,000 ft (10670 m):** 483 mph (777 km/h)
**Time to 35,000 ft (10670 m):** 7 minutes 54 seconds; 9 minutes 24 seconds with external tanks
**Service ceiling:** 40,500 ft (12345 m)
**Range with internal fuel:** 670 miles (1078 km)
**Range with tiptanks:** 1,330 miles (2140 km)
**Range with maximum external fuel:** 2,000 miles (3217 km)

**Armament**

Six 0.5-in (12.7-mm) Colt-Browning M3 machine-guns, with 300 rounds per gun, and provision for up to 4,000 lb (1184 kg) of external ordnance, including 100-, 500- and 1,000-lb (45-, 227-, 454-kg) GP bombs, napalm and 'Tiny Tim' 12-in (30-cm) and 5-in (12.7-cm) HVARs

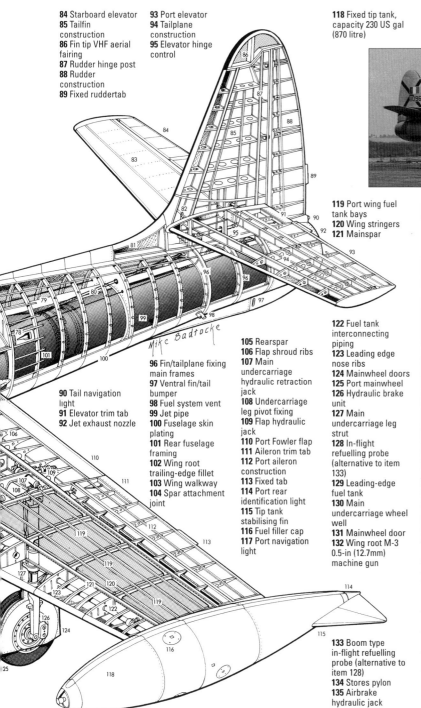

84 Starboard elevator
85 Tailfin construction
86 Fin tip VHF aerial fairing
87 Rudder hinge post
88 Rudder construction
89 Fixed ruddertab

90 Tail navigation light
91 Elevator trim tab
92 Jet exhaust nozzle

93 Port elevator
94 Tailplane construction
95 Elevator hinge control

96 Fin/tailplane fixing main frames
97 Ventral fin/tail bumper
98 Fuel system vent
99 Jet pipe
100 Fuselage skin plating
101 Rear fuselage framing
102 Wing root trailing-edge fillet
103 Wing walkway
104 Spar attachment joint

105 Rearspar
106 Flap shroud ribs
107 Main undercarriage hydraulic retraction jack
108 Undercarriage leg pivot fixing
109 Flap hydraulic jack
110 Port Fowler flap
111 Aileron trim tab
112 Port aileron construction
113 Fixed tab
114 Port rear identification light
115 Tip tank stabilising fin
116 Fuel filler cap
117 Port navigation light

118 Fixed tip tank, capacity 230 US gal (870 litre)

119 Port wing fuel tank bays
120 Wing stringers
121 Mainspar
122 Fuel tank interconnecting piping
123 Leading edge nose ribs
124 Mainwheel doors
125 Port mainwheel
126 Hydraulic brake unit
127 Main undercarriage leg strut
128 In-flight refuelling probe (alternative to item 133)
129 Leading-edge fuel tank
130 Main undercarriage wheel well
131 Mainwheel door
132 Wing root M-3 0.5-in (12.7mm) machine gun

133 Boom type in-flight refuelling probe (alternative to item 128)
134 Stores pylon
135 Airbrake hydraulic jack

136 Perforated ventral airbrake
137 Drop tank, capacity 230 US gal (870 litre)
138 500-lb (227-kg) HE bomb
139 'Tiny Tim' 30-cm air-to-ground rocket
140 Rocket fixing shackles
141 HVAR ground attack rockets

*USAF experiments with the zero-length launcher (ZELL) concept, which culminated in test flights employing F-100s and F-104s, began with this F-84. Equipped with a booster bottle and mounted on a mobile launcher developed by Martin Aircraft of Baltimore, the ZELL system was mooted as the future for air defence aircraft, rendering vulnerable conventional airstrips obsolete. However, the concept did not find sufficient favour in official circles and was ultimately abandoned.*

# Republic F-105 Thunderchief

A flight of F-105D Thunderchiefs of 335th TFS, Tactical Air Command is seen during a practice mission over North Carolina in 1964. In May of that year, the squadron had the distinction of being the first 'Thunderchief' unit to temporarily deploy to Europe to take part in Operation Long Thrust. This exercise saw TAC units operating alongside NATO forces under simulated wartime conditions. The Thunderchief in the foreground (FH-161) was one of the 30 'Thuds' later converted to the T-Stick II configuration.

## F-105D Thunderchief

### Cutaway key

1 Pitot tube
2 Radome
3 Radar scanner dish
4 Radar mounting and tracking mechanism
5 Forward electronic countermeasures (ECM) antenna
6 Aft-facing strike camera
7 Radome hinge
8 ADF sense aerial
9 Fire-control radar transmitter/receiver
10 Cannon muzzle
11 Instrument electronics
12 In-flight refuelling position light
13 Air refuelling receptacle
14 Cannon ammunition drum, 1,028 rounds
15 Liquid oxygen converter
16 Angle of attack transmitter
17 Cannon barrels
18 Nosewheel doors
19 M61, 20-mm, six-barrelled rotary cannon
20 Ammunition feed chute
21 Gun gas venting pipe
22 Air refuelling probe housing

23 Alternator and electrical bay
24 Air-driven turbine
25 Air refuelling probe
26 Windshield rain dispersal duct
27 Bulletproof windscreen panels
28 Radar attack sight
29 Instrument panel shroud
30 Navigation radar display
31 Rudder pedals
32 Cockpit front pressure bulkhead
33 Cannon mounting
34 Nosewheel leg strut
35 ILS system radar reflector
36 Taxiing lamps
37 Nosewheel
38 Torque scissor links
39 Hydraulic steering controls
40 Flight control system hydraulics bay
41 Electronics cooling air outlet
42 IFF aerial
43 UHF aerial
44 Underfloor radio and electronics bay

45 Cockpit pressure floor level
46 Pilot's side console panel

47 Engine throttle
48 Control column
49 Pilot's ejection seat
50 Seat back parachute pack
51 Headrest
52 Cockpit canopy cover
53 3,000-lb (1360-kg) HE bomb (inboard pylon)
54 Starboard air intake
55 Cockpit canopy jack
56 Canopy hinge
57 Air-conditioning pack
58 Cockpit rear pressure bulkhead
59 Secondary electronics bay
60 Air data computer
61 Port air intake
62 Bomb bay fuel tank, 390-US gal (1476-litre)
63 Boundary layer splitter plate

64 Intake duct variable-area sliding ramp

65 Forward group of fuselage fuel tanks; total internal fuel capacity 1,160 US gal (4391 litres)
66 Gyro compass platform
67 Bomb bay fuel tank fuel transfer lines
68 Fuselage/front spar main frame
69 Dorsal spine fairing
70 Starboard mainwheel, stowed position

71 450-US gal (1703-litre) external fuel tank
72 AIM-9 Sidewinder air-to-air missile
73 Missile launcher rail
74 Twin missile carrier (outboard pylon)
75 Starboard leading-edge flap

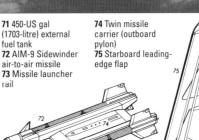

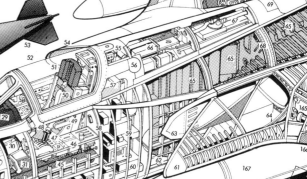

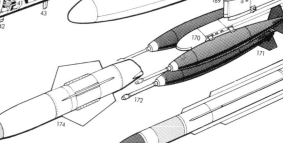

*The USAF's* **Thunderbirds** *flight demonstration team usually flew the 'hottest' aircraft on the inventory, but the Thunderchief seemed to be too much for them. The team adopted the F-105B Thunderchief for the 1964 season. The transition was fairly smooth and the first display was at Norfolk, Virginia in April 1964. Modifications were necessary to convert the Thunderchiefs to the aerobatic team role, with changes in the rudder, flap and fuel systems, for extended inverted flight. The life of the F-105B with the Thunderbirds was short-lived, only six displays being given before a fatal accident, in May 1964, resulted in a decision to revert to the F-100 Super Sabre for the remainder of the season.*

76 Outboard pylon fixing/drop tank filler cap
77 Starboard navigation light
78 Static dischargers
79 Starboard aileron
80 Starboard fowler flap
81 Trim tab, starboard only
82 Flap guide rails
83 Roll control spoilers
84 Anti-collision light
85 Air intake ducting
86 Ground running secondary air intake
87 Wing spar attachment joint
88 Fuselage/rear spar main frame
89 Engine compressor face
90 Forward engine mounting frame

91 Rear fuselage group of fuel tanks
92 Fuel pipe ducting
93 Drop tank tail fins
94 Afterburner duct cooling ram air intake
95 Starboard all-moving tailplane
96 Tailfin construction
97 Fin tip ECM aerials
98 Tail position light
99 Static dischargers
100 Rudder mass balance
101 Rudder
102 Formation light

103 Water injection tank 36-US gal (136-litre) capacity
104 Rudder-power control unit
105 Brake parachute housing
106 Parachute door
107 Petal-type airbrakes, open position

108 Republic convergent/ divergent ram air ejector nozzle flaps
109 Airbrake/nozzle flap jacks
110 Internal variable-area afterburner nozzle

111 Afterburner nozzle actuators
112 Afterburner ducting
113 Tailplane pivot fixing
114 Port all-moving tailplane construction

## SPECIFICATION

### F-105D Thunderchief

**Dimensions**

**Length:** 64 ft 4 in (19.61 m)
**Height:** 19 ft 7 in (5.97 m)
**Wingspan:** 34 ft 9 in (10.59 m)
**Wing area:** 385 sq ft (35.77 m²)

**Powerplant**

One Pratt & Whitney J75-P-19W turbojet rated at 17,200 lb (76.0 kN) thrust dry and 24,500 lb (110.25 kN) thrust with afterburning; water injection permitted 60-second rating of 26,500 lb (117.7 kN) thrust in afterburner mode

**Weights**

**Empty:** 27,500 lb (12474 kg)
**Maximum overload take-off:** 52,838 lb (23967 kg)

**Fuel**

**Normal internal fuel:** 435 US gal (1646 litres)
**Maximum internal fuel:** 675 US gal (2555 litres)

**Performance**

**Maximum level speed clean at 36,000 ft (10970 m):** 1,390 mph (2237 km/h)
**Initial climb rate:** 34,400 ft (10485 m) per minute in clean configuration
**Service ceiling:** 41,200 ft (12560 m)
**Range:** 920 miles (1480 km) with two 450-US gal (1703 litres) drop-tanks underwing, one 650-US gal (2461-litre) drop-tank on centreline and two AGM-12 Bullpup ASMs; ferry range 2,390 miles (3846 km) with maximum external fuel at 584 mph (940 km/h)

**Armament**

Combination of 750-lb (340-kg) M117 bombs, 1,000-lb (454-kg) Mk 83 bombs, 3,000-lb (1361-kg) M118 bombs, AGM-12 Bullpup ASMs, AIM-9 Sidewinder AAMs, 2.75-in (70-mm) rocket pods, napalm containers, Mk 28/43 special weapons, chemical bombs, leaflet bombs, 5-in (127-mm) rocket pods and MLU-10/B mines; also one M61 Vulcan 20-mm cannon with 1,028 rounds of ammunition

*Big Sal, flown by Capt. John Hoffman, is seen on the way back from a bombing mission over North Vietnam. Hoffman's F-105D (61-0086) survived the war to serve with the Virginia Air National Guard until 1979.*

134 Five-section roll control spoilers
135 Flap screw jacks
136 Aileron mass balance
137 Port drop tank tail fins
138 Honeycomb aileron construction
139 Static dischargers
140 Wingtip fairing
141 Port navigation light
142 AGM-45 Strike anti-radar missile
143 ECM pod
144 Outboard stores pylon
145 Pylon fixing/fuel filler cap
146 Aileron hinge control
147 Aileron/spoiler mixer linkage
148 Multi-spar wing construction
149 Aileron power control unit
150 Inboard pylon fixing
151 Inboard stores pylon
152 Mainwheel leg door
153 Port mainwheel
154 450-US gal (1703-litre) drop tank
155 Main undercarriage leg torque scissor links
156 Landing lamp
157 Port leading-edge flap
158 Leading-edge flap rotary actuators

159 Main undercarriage pivot mounting
160 Undercarriage side breaker strut
161 Hydraulic retraction jack
162 Diagonal wing spar
163 Mainwheel housing
164 Inner mainwheel door
165 Leading-edge flap actuator
166 Leading-edge flush aerial
167 650-US gal (2461-litre) centreline fuel tank
168 Fuel tank filler cap
169 Centreline stores pylon
170 Triple ejection rack
171 Six M117, 750-lb (340-kg) HE bombs
172 Anti-personnel extended bomb fuse
173 AGM-78 Standard anti-radar missile
174 AGM-12C Bullpup air-to-ground missile

121 Rear engine mounting
122 Engine turbine section heat shroud
123 Engine bay venting ram air intake
124 Rear fuselage frame and stringer construction
125 Runway arrester hook
126 Ventral fin
127 Accessory cooling air duct
128 Cartridge starter
129 Fuselage top longeron
130 Engine-driven accessory gearbox
131 Oil tank, 4.5-US gal (17-litre) capacity
132 Pratt & Whitney J75-P-19W afterburning turbojet
133 Port Fowler-type flap construction

115 Tailplane titanium box spar
116 Leading-edge nose ribs
117 Ventral fuel vent
118 All-moving tailplane control jack
119 Rear fuselage break point
120 Engine firewall

AVIAGRAPHICA

# Saab J-35 Draken

As the final J 35J Drakens underwent major overhaul in the early 1990s, they were repainted in this highly effective two-tone air superiority grey camouflage. This was the final colour scheme worn by Swedish air force Drakens before the last front-line squadron was eventually retired at the end of 1998.

## Saab J 35F-2 Draken

### Cutaway key

1 Nose probe
2 Glass-fibre nose cone
3 Radar scanner
4 Scanner mounting frame
5 Radar pack
6 Saab S7-collision-course fire control
7 L. M. Ericsson (Hughes licence) infra-red seeker
8 Electronics pack
9 Front pressure bulkhead
10 Data-handling unit
11 Rudder pedal assembly
12 Port instrument console
13 Side panel
14 Instrument panel/radar scope shroud
15 Windscreen frame
16 Weapons sight
17 Windscreen
18 Starboard intake
19 Glassfibre intake lip
20 Aft-hinged cockpit canopy
21 Cockpit sill
22 Control panel
23 Control column
24 Throttle quadrant
25 Pilot's Saab RS 35 ejection seat
26 Canopy hinge mechanism
27 Seat support frame
28 Rear pressure bulkhead
29 Navigation computer
30 Forward avionics equipment bay
31 Gyro unit

32 TACAN transmitter-receiver
33 Auxiliary air intake
34 Starboard intake trunk
35 Starboard fuel tanks
36 Dorsal spine
37 Starboard forward bag-type fuel tank,
38 30-mm ADEN cannon
39 Ammunition magazine (100 rounds)
40 Dorsal antenna
41 Electrical wiring
42 Mid-fuselage production break line
43 Intake trunking
44 Oil-cooler air intake
45 Volvo Flygmotor RM6C (Rolls-Royce Avon 300 series) turbojet
46 Louvres
47 Access panels
48 Fuselage frames
49 Engine firewall
50 Cooling air inlet scoop
51 Finroot fairing
52 Fuel transfer
53 Starboard mainwheel door
54 Door actuating rod
55 Inner/outer wing joint strap
56 Starboard navigation light
57 Wing skinning
58 Starboard outer elevon
59 Hinge point
60 Actuating jack access

61 Control hinge
62 Access panels
63 Starboard aft integral fuel tank
64 Starboard aft bag-type fuel tanks (3)
65 Intake grille
66 Jet pipe
67 Engine aft mounting ring
68 Access
69 Tailfin main spar attachment
70 Control stick angle indicator unit
71 Computer amplifier
72 Synchroniser pack
73 Tailfin structure
74 Pitot tube
75 Rudder mass balance
76 Rudder structure
77 Rudder post
78 Tailfin rear spar
79 Rudder servo mechanism and actuator
80 Attachment point
81 Speed brake
82 Fuselage structure
83 Detachable tail cone (engine removal)
84 Access panel
85 Brake parachute housing
86 Aft fairing
87 Afterburner assembly
88 Exhaust
89 Air intake (afterburner housing)

90 Control surface blunt trailing edge
91 Port inner elevon
92 Hinge points
93 Elevon actuator
94 Rear spar
95 Twin (retractable) tailwheels
96 Port aft
97 Inner/outer wing joint
98 Wing outer structure
99 Rib stations
100 Port outer elevon
101 Elevon actuator
102 Hinge points
103 Port wingtip
104 Anti-buffet underwing fences (6)
105 Stores pylons (maximum 8)
106 Nose ribs
107 Forward spar
108 Wheel door
109 Port navigation

light
110 Port main wheel
111 Door inboard section
112 Port main wheel well
113 Fuel transfer
114 Wing join strap
115 Port aft bag-type fuel tanks (3)
116 Fuel collector
117 Mainwheel retraction mechanism
118 Mainwheel oleo leg mounting
119 Engine accessory gearbox
120 Port cannon ammunition magazine
121 Port 30-mm ADEN cannon (Saab 35F has starboard gun only, earlier intercept and export 35X versions retaining port gun as illustrated)

122 Port forward bag-type fuel tank
123 Port forward integral fuel tanks
124 Cannon port
125 Inner wing/fuselage integral structure
126 Angled frame member
127 Emergency ventral ram-air turbine
128 Trunking formers
129 Gyro amplifiers
130 Intake trunking
131 Nosewheel leg
132 Glassfibre intake lip
133 Forward retracting nosewheel

134 Steering mechanism
135 Possible stores (including jettisonable tanks)
136 Pod containing 19 x 3-in (75-mm) rockets
137 Rb 28 (Sidewinder) IR-homing missile
138 5.3-in (13.5-cm) rocket
139 Rb 27 (Falcon) radar-homing missile
140 1,102-lb (500-kg) bomb

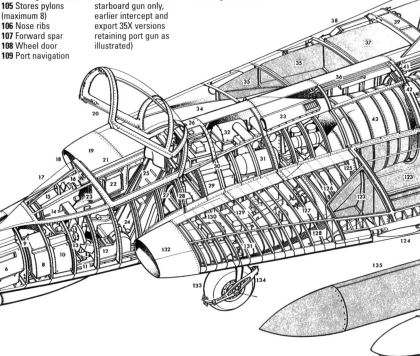

*Above: HavLlv 21 was one of two squadrons to operate the Draken in Finnish air force service. The unit operated the type for 25 years from 1972, before becoming the first operational unit in the Finnish air force to fly the F-18C/D Hornet. The remaining Draken operator, HavLlv 11, will operate the type into the next century.*

*Above right: At its introduction into service, the Draken was one of the best-performing warplanes in the world, thanks in part to its excellent powerplant. The large flame emitted in reheat was courtesy of a locally-produced afterburner added to the licence-built Rolls-Royce Avon engine.*

## SPECIFICATION

### J 35J Draken

### Dimensions

**Length:** 50 ft 4 in (15.35 m)
**Wingspan:** 30 ft 10 in (9.40 m)
**Height:** 12 ft 9 in (3.89 m)
**Wing area:** 529.60 sq ft (49.20 m²)
**Wing aspect ratio:** 1.77
**Wheel track:** 8 ft 10½ in (2.70 m)

### Powerplant

One 12,790-lb st (56.89-kN) dry or 17,650-lb st (78.5-kN) with afterburning Volvo Flygmotor RM6C turbojet (licence-built Rolls-Royce Avon Series 300 turbojet fitted with a Swedish-designed afterburner)

### Weights

**Empty:** 18,188 lb (8250 kg)
**Normal take-off:** 25,132 lb (11400 kg)
**Maximum take-off:** 27,050 lb (12270 kg) for interceptor mission or 33,069 lb (17650 kg) for attack mission

### Fuel

**Internal fuel:** 1,057 US gal (4000 litres)
**External fuel:** provision for up to 1,321 US gal (5000 litres) in external drop tanks

### Performance

**Maximum level speed 'clean' at 36,000 ft (10975 m):** more than 1,147 kt (1,317 mph; 2119 km/h)
**Maximum speed at 300 ft (90 m):** 793 kt (910 mph; 1465 km/h)
**Maximum climb rate at sea level:** 34,450 ft (10500 m) per minute with afterburning
**Service ceiling:** 65,600 ft (19995 m)
**Take-off run:** 2,133 ft (650 m) at normal take-off weight
**Take-off distance to 50 ft (15 m):** 3,150 ft (960 m) at normal take-off weight

### Range

**Ferry range:** 1,533 nm (1,763 miles; 2837 km)
**Combat radius:** 304 nm (350 miles; 564 km) on a hi-lo-hi attack mission with internal fuel only

### Armament

Usual air-to-air armament of 2 x AIM-9J Sidewinder air-to-air missiles on centre-section pylons, 2 x Hughes Falcon air-to-air missiles on wing pylons and one 30-mm ADEN cannon with 90 rounds in starboard wing. Maximum ordnance of 6,393 lb (2900 kg)

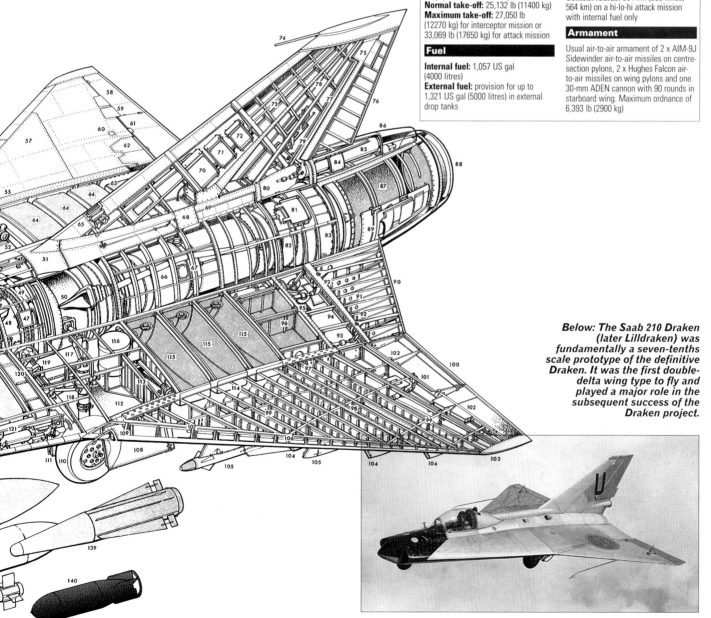

*Below: The Saab 210 Draken (later Lilldraken) was fundamentally a seven-tenths scale prototype of the definitive Draken. It was the first double-delta wing type to fly and played a major role in the subsequent success of the Draken project.*

# Saab Viggen

*Displaying the Viggen's distinctive wing planform, this JA 37 is loaded with inert training BAe Sky Flash and AIM-9 Sidewinder missiles. This load is representative of the Viggen's intercept mission although a fuel tank would normally be carried on the fuselage centreline to help overcome the aircraft's poor range.*

### SH 37 Viggen

**Cutaway key**
1 Pitot head
2 Glass-fibre radome
3 Radar scanner housing
4 LM Ericsson PS-37/A radar equipment module
5 Incidence probe
6 Cockpit pressure bulkhead
7 Forward avionics equipment bay
8 Rudder pedals
9 Instrument panel shroud
10 One piece frameless windscreen panel
11 Pilot's head-up display
12 Upward-hinging cockpit canopy
13 Ejection seat arming lever
14 Saab rocket-powered ejection seat
15 Engine throttle lever
16 Boundary layer splitter plate
17 Port air intake
18 Landing/taxiing lamp
19 Twin nosewheels, forward retracting
20 Hydraulic steering control
21 Red Baron multi-sensor reconnaissance pod
22 Centreline external fuel tank
23 Electro-luminescent formation lighting strip
24 Central avionics equipment bay
25 Intake ducting
26 Boundary layer spill duct

27 Forward fuselage integral fuel tank
28 Dorsal avionics equipment bay
29 Starboard canard foreplane
30 Canard flap
31 SATT AQ31 ECM jamming pod
32 SSR transponder aerial
33 Anti-collision light
34 Air-conditioning equipment bay
35 Heat exchanger air exhaust
36 Intake flank fuel tankage
37 Engine compressor face
38 Accessory equipment gearbox
39 Foreplane spar attachment joint
40 Fuselage flank avionics equipment bays, port and starboard
41 Emergency ram air turbine
42 Port canard foreplane flap honeycomb panel
43 Hydraulic reservoirs
44 Formation lighting strip
45 Centre fuselage integral fuel tankage
46 Main engine mounting
47 Volvo Flygmoto RM8A afterburning turbofan engine
48 Engine bleed air pre-cooler
49 Fuel-cooled engine oil cooler
50 Wing spar attachment fuselage main frame

51 Fuel system recuperators
52 ADF aerial
53 Starboard wing panel
54 Outboard missile pylon
55 ECM antenna fairing
56 Extended-chord outboard leading edge
57 Starboard navigation light
58 Starboard elevon panels
59 Artificial feel system pressure head
60 Fin tip aerial fairing
61 Multi spar fin construction
62 Rudder hydraulic actuator
63 Fin spar attachment joints
64 Hydraulic hand pump for hangaring fin folding
65 Port lateral airbrake
66 Airbrake hydraulic jack
67 Afterburner ducting
68 Variable area afterburner nozzle control jack
69 Exhaust duct ejector seal (closed at speeds above Mach 1)
70 Ejector seal screw jack

71 Thrust reverser door pneumatic actuator
72 Radar warning antennas
73 Engine/afterburner exhaust nozzle
74 Thrust reverser blocker doors
75 Tail navigation light
76 Lower thrust reverser door pneumatic actuator
77 Port inboard elevon
78 Elevon hydraulic actuators
79 Elevon honeycomb construction
80 Port outboard elevon
81 Port navigation lights
82 Outboard elevon hydraulic actuator
83 Saab Bofors Rb 24 (licence-built Sidewinder) air-to-air self-defence missile
84 Missile launch rail
85 ECM antenna fairing
86 Bofors BOZ-9 flare launcher pod

87 Wing stores pylon
88 Honeycomb wing skin panels
89 Multispar wing panel construction
90 Wing panel integral fuel tank
91 Main spar
92 Main undercarriage wheel bay
93 Side breaker strut
94 Hydraulic retraction jack
95 Main undercarriage mounting rib
96 Mainwheel leg strut
97 Torque scissor links
98 Tandem mainwheels

99 Starboard fuselage pylon
100 Long-range camera pod
101 Rb 05A air-to-surface missile
102 Rb 04E air-to-surface anti-ship missile
103 Missile launch adaptor

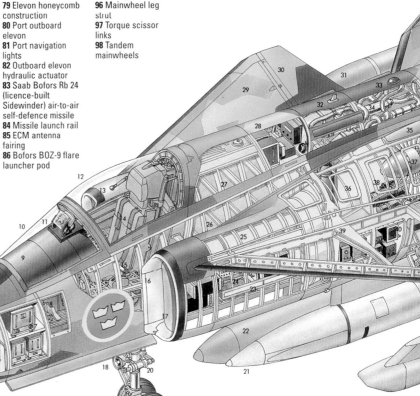

## Viggen reconnaissance pods

There are two Viggen reconnaissance variants: the SH 37 is used for maritime surveillance, while the SF 37 is employed in the overland role. The SH 37 is equipped with an RKA 40 recording camera and can carry a night-photography pod on its port or starboard sides. There is also provision for a single, forward-facing long-range optical pod (LOROP) on the starboard shoulder pylon containing an SKA 24D camera with 600-mm lens (top left).

Mounted on the shoulder pylons of the SF 37 are reconnaissance pods (top right). To the port side is a pod (Mörkerspaningskapsel) which contains three SKA 34 cameras with 75-mm lenses, each having a 120° field of view, and situated at the rear are two flash windows. The starboard pod (Blixtkapsel) contains capacitors which are charged from the aircraft's electrical generators to release power to the flashguns when required for illumination from heights of up to approximately 1,640 ft (500 m).

### SPECIFICATION

#### JA 37 Viggen

**Dimensions**

**Length:** 53 ft 9¾ in (16.40 m)
**Height:** 19 ft 4¼ in (5.90 m)
**Wingspan:** 34 ft 9¼ in (10.60 m)
**Wing area:** 495.16 sq ft (46.00 m²)
**Canard foreplane span:** 17 ft 10½ in (5.45 m)
**Canard foreplane area:** 66.74 sq ft (6.20 m²)
**Wheel base:** 18 ft 8 in (5.69 m)
**Wheel track:** 15 ft 7½ in (4.76 m)

**Powerplant**

One Volvo Flygmotor RM8B turbofan (Pratt & Whitney JT8D-22 with Swedish-designed afterburner and thrust reverse) rated at 16,600 lb st (73.84 kN) maximum military dry and 28,109 lb st (125 kN) with afterburning

**Weights**

**Normal take-off:** 33,069 lb (15000 kg)
**Maximum take-off interceptor:** 37,478 lb (17000 kg)
**Maximum take-off attack:** 45,194 lb (20500 kg)

**Fuel and load**

**Internal fuel:** 1,506 US gal (5700 litres)

**Performance**

**Maximum level speed clean at 36,000 ft (10975 m):** More than 1,147 kt (1,321 mph; 2126 km/h)
**Climb to 32,800 ft (10000 m):** Less than 1 minute 40 seconds from brakes off with afterburning
**Service ceiling:** 60,000 ft (18290 m)
**Take-off run at typical take-off weight:** 1,312 ft (400 m)
**Landing run:** 1,640 ft (500 m) at normal landing weight
**Combat radius on hi-lo-hi mission:** 539 nm (621 miles; 1000 km)
**Combat radius on lo-lo-lo mission:** 270 nm (311 miles; 500 km)

**Armament**

Primary armament consists of six AAMs. The standard BVR weapon is the medium-range, semi-active radar-guided, all-weather BAeD Rb 71 Sky Flash. Rb 74 (AIM-9L) IR-homing Sidewinders are fielded for short-range work. The JA 37 also has an integral 30-mm Oerlikon KCA revolver cannon with 150 rounds. Seven to nine pylons accommodate up to 13,000 lb (5987 kg) of external stores. These include four pods each containing six Bofors 5.3-in (13.5-cm) rockets for air-to-surface use.

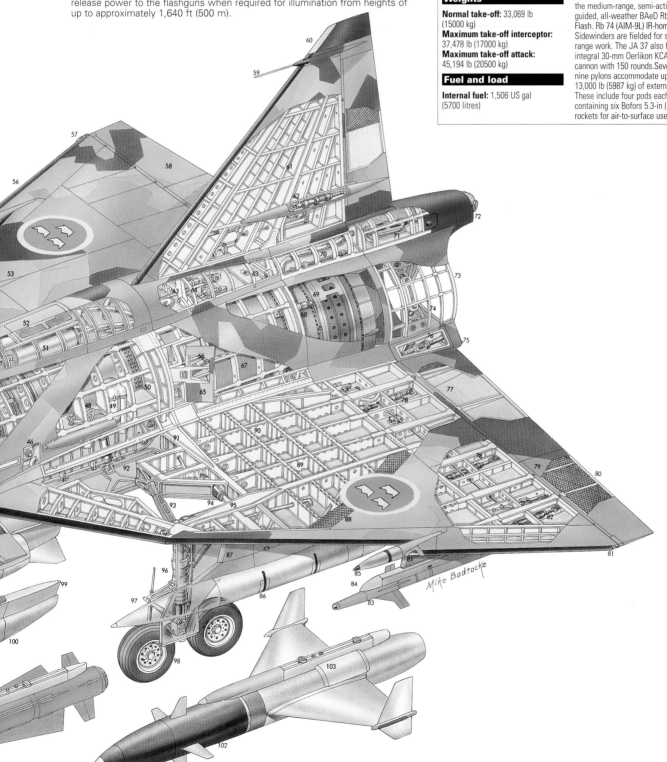

Mike Badrocke

# Sukhoi Su-7 'Fitter'

In Indian Air Force service, the Su-7 gained a reputation as a formidable combat asset during the confrontation with Pakistan in 1971. Approximately 150 Su-7BMs were operational during the war, equipping seven units, five of which were based on the Western Front. 221 Sqn was particularly active: raiding the sole PAF airbase at Tezgaon, outside Dacca and the airfield at Jessore. Some 32 'Fitter-As' were lost.

### Su-7BMK 'Fitter-A'

**Cutaway key**
1 Pitot tube
2 Pitch vanes
3 Yaw vanes
4 Engine air intake
5 Fixed intake centre-body
6 Radome
7 Ranging radar scanner
8 ILS aerial
9 Radar controller
10 Weapon release ballistic computer
11 Retractable taxiing lamp
12 SRO-2M 'Odd-rods' IFF aerials
13 Intake suction relief doors
14 Intake duct divider
15 Instrument access panel
16 Su-7UM 'Moujik' two-seat operational training variant
17 Armoured glass windscreen
18 Reflector sight
19 Instrument panel shroud
20 Control column
21 Rudder pedals
22 Control linkages
23 Nose undercarriage wheel well
24 Nosewheel doors
25 Torque scissor links
26 Steerable nosewheel
27 Low pressure 'rough-field' tyre
28 Hydraulic retraction jack
29 Cockpit pressure floor
30 Engine throttle
31 Pilot's side console panel
32 Ejection seat
33 Canopy release handle

34 Parachute pack headrest
35 Rear view mirror
36 Sliding cockpit canopy cover
37 Instrument venturi
38 Radio and electronics equipment bay
39 Intake ducting
40 Air conditioning plant
41 Electrical and pneumatic systems ground connections
42 Cannon muzzle
43 Skin doubler/blast shield
44 Fuel system components access
45 Main fuel pumps
46 Fuel system accumulator
47 Filler cap
48 External piping ducts

49 Starboard main undercarriage leg pivot fixing
50 Shock absorber pressurisation charging valve
51 Gun camera
52 Starboard wing integral fuel tank
53 Starboard wing fence
54 Outer wing panel dry bay
55 Wing tip fence
56 Static discharger
57 Starboard aileron
58 Flap guide rail
59 Starboard fowler flap
60 Flap jack
61 Fuselage skin plating
62 Fuselage fuel tank
63 Wing/fuselage attachment double frame

64 Engine compressor face
65 Ram air intake
66 Engine oil tank
67 Bleed air system 'blow-off' valve
68 Fuselage break point, engine removal
69 Lyulka AL-71F-1 turbojet
70 Afterburner duct
71 Fin root fillet
72 Autopilot controller
73 Starboard upper airbrake, open
74 Rudder power control unit
75 Artificial feel unit
76 Tailfin construction
77 VHF/UHF aerial fairing
78 RSIU (very short wave fighter radio) aerial
79 Tail navigation light

80 Sirena-3 tail warning radar
81 Rudder
82 Brake parachute release tank
83 Brake parachute housing
84 Parachute doors
85 Engine exhaust nozzle
86 Port all-moving tailplane
87 Static discharger
88 Tailplant anti-flutter weight
89 Tailplane construction
90 Pivot mounting
91 Tailplane limit stops
92 Variable area exhaust nozzle flaps
93 Nozzle control jacks

94 Fin/tailplane attachment fuselage frame
95 Afterburner cooling air intake
96 Rear fuselage frame and stringer construction
97 Insulated tailplane
98 Airbrake housing
99 Hydraulic jack
100 Tailplane power control unit
101 'Odd rods' IFF aerials
102 Port lower airbrake, open
103 Engine accessories
104 Jettisonable RATO bottle
105 Port fowler flap
106 Port wing integral fuel tanks
107 Aileron control rod

108 Port aileron construction
109 Static discharger
110 Wing tip fairing
111 Port navigation light
112 Wing tip fence
113 Pitot tube
114 Wing rib and stringer construction
115 Port outer stores pylon

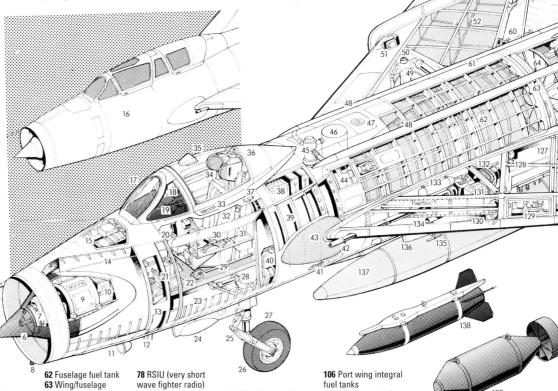

79

## SPECIFICATION

### Su-7BMK 'Fitter-A'

#### Dimensions

**Wingspan:** 29 ft 3½ in (8.93 m)
**Length:** 57 ft (17.37 m) including probe
**Height:** 15 ft (4.57 m)
**Wing area:** 297.09 sq ft (27.60 m²)
**Aspect ratio:** 2.89

#### Powerplant

One NPO Saturn (Lyul'ka) AL-7F-1 turbojet rated at 15,432 lb st (68.65 kN) dry and 22,282 lb st (99.12 kN) with afterburning

#### Weights

**Empty equipped:** 19,004 lb (8620 kg)
**Normal take-off:** 26,455 lb (12000 kg)
**Maximum take-off:** 29,762 lb (13500 kg)

#### Fuel load

**Internal fuel:** 5,181 lb (2350 kg)
**External fuel:** up to two 159-US gal (600-litre) and two 458- or 238-US gal (1800- or 900-litre) drop tanks; maximum ordnance 5,511 lb (2500 kg)

#### Performance

**Maximum level speed 'clean' at 36,090 ft (11000 m):** 1,055 mph (1700 km/h)
**Maximum level speed at sea level:** 840 mph (1350 km/h)
**Maximum rate of climb at sea level:** about 29,920 ft (9120 m) per minute
**Service ceiling:** 49,705 ft (15150 m)
**Take-off run:** 2,887 ft (880 m)
**Ferry range with drop tanks:** 901 miles (1450 km)
**Combat radius on a hi-lo-hi attack mission with a 2,205-lb (1000-kg) warload and two drop tanks:** 214 miles (345 km)

#### Armament

Two 30-mm Nudelmann Richter NR-30 cannon in the wing roots, plus a wide range of bombs, rockets and unguided missiles

*These Polish Su-7BM 'Fitter-As' appear to have been updated to Su-7BMK standard with the enlarged fairing – obscured here by the technicians who appear to be repacking the 'chutes – for the twin brake 'chutes of this variant. All single-seat Su-7s were designated 'Fitter-A' by ASCC/NATO, while the two-seat Su-7UM was known as 'Moujik'. Experimental Su-7s included the 100LDU testbed of 1968, which was derived from a n Su-7UM, and as a remotely-piloted aircraft was used to investigate flight stability for the T-4.*

80
77
78
81
76
75
74
73
72
71
70
69
68
98
99
100
101
102
103
104
105
106
106
107
108
109
110
111
112
113
114
115
116
117
118
119
120
121
122
123
82
83
84
85
86
87
88
89
90
91
92
93
94
95
96
97

AVIAGRAPHICA

**116** UV-16-57 rocket launcher pack
**117** Auxiliary fuel tank, inner pylon
**118** Port mainwheel
**119** Low-pressure 'rough-field' main undercarriage
**120** Inner stores pylon
**121** Port wing fence
**122** Mainwheel doors
**123** Main undercarriage leg strut
**124** Leg shortening link
**125** Hydraulic retraction jack
**126** Wing fuel tank filler cap
**127** Port mainwheel bay
**128** Main undercarriage up-lock
**129** Aileron power control unit

**130** Retractable landing lamp
**131** Ammunition tank (80 rounds per gun)
**132** 30-mm NR-30 cannon
**133** Cannon pressurisation bottle
**134** Ventral gun gas venting intake
**135** Radar altimeter
**136** Fuselage pylon, port and starboard
**137** Twin fuselage mounted auxiliary fuel tanks
**138** 551-lb (250-kg) concrete piercing bomb
**139** 1,102-lb (500-kg) HE bomb

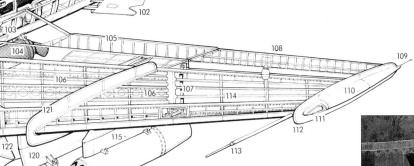

*This pair of specially-marked Su-7s was photographed in a poor condition at an Indian air force base. Both aircraft have UB-16 rockets pods under their outer wings and both are moored to concrete blocks and in a poor state of finish.*

# Sukhoi Su-17/20/22 'Fitter'

Formerly the prime operator of the Su-17 family, the 'Fitter' is now rapidly disappearing from the air forces of the former Soviet Union .The intended replacement for the Su-17M (and MiG-27) in Soviet service was the now aborted MiG-29M, specifically developed to meet the requirements of the Group of Soviet Forces in Germany. The Su-17M-4 (illustrated) has now left the front-line of the Russian inventory in response to post-Cold War CFE guidelines.

### Su-22M-4 'Fitter-K'
**Cutaway key**

1 Instrumentation data probe
2 Yaw and pitch vanes
3 Fire control system computer transducers
4 Pitot head
5 Conical intake centre-body shock cone/ radome
6 Engine air intake
7 'High Fix' 1-band ranging radar
8 Laser marked target designator
9 Radar altimete r
10 Ventral doppier navigation aerial
11 Angle of attack transmitter
12 Radar equipment module
13 Bifurcated intake ducting
14 Spring loaded intake suction relief doors, open
15 Temperature probe
16 Nose avionics equipment compartment, ASP-5ND fire control system
17 Su-17'Fitter G' two-seat tandem trainer variant, nose profile
18 Student pilot's cockpit
19 Retractable forward vision periscope
20 Instructor's cockpit
21 Armoured glass windscreen panels
22 Pilot's head-up display and attack sight

23 Instrument panel shroud
24 Control column
25 Rudder pedals
26 Nose undercarriage wheel bay

27 Retractable landing/ taxiing lamp, port and starboard
28 Nosewheel doors

29 Nosewheel forks
30 Steerable nosewheel forward retracting
31 SRO-21VI 'Odd Rods'IFF aerials
32 Nosewheel leg pivot fixing
33 Hydraulic retraction jack
34 Cockpit floor level
35 Close pitched fuselage frames
36 Port console panel
37 Engine throttle lever
38 Canopy latch
39 Pilot's 'zero-zero' ejection seat
40 Ejection seat headrest
41 Rear view mirror

42 Cockpit canopy cover, upward tingeing
43 Canopy jack
44 Cockpit pressurisation valve
45 Rear pressure bulkhead
46 Air conditioning plant
47 intake duct framing
48 Ground power and intercom sockets
49 Cannon muzzle blast- shield/skin doubler
50 Avionics equipment racks
51 Cockpit aft fairing additional avionics equipment
52 Fuel system access panel

53 Intake trunking
54 Main fuel pumps
55 Inverted fight accumulator

56 Front wing spar attachment main frame

57 Centre fuselage frame and stringer construction
58 Fuselage fuel tanks
59 Fuel system components
60 Dorsal spine fairing
61 ADF aerial
62 Starboard wing fixed root section
63 Strike camera
64 Wing pivot bearing
65 Outboard wing fence
66 Fuselage centreline reconnaissance pod
67 GSh-231-cannon pod
68 Leading edge slats, down position
69 Slat hydraulic actuator
70 Starboard wing integral fuel tank
71 Aileron hydraulic actuator
72 Slat guide rails
73 Starboard navigation light
74 Wing tip fairing
75 Static discharger
76 Starboard aileron
77 Starboard wing fully swept position

78 Outboard single-slotted flap, down postion
79 Wing glove section
80 Spine fairing access panels
81 Fuselage skin panelling
82 Wing main spar attachment double frame
83 Engine compressor intake
84 Engine oil tank
85 Lyulka AL-21 F-3 afterburning engine (Tumanskii R-29B alternative instailation)
86 Rear fuselage break point (engine removal)
87 Engine turbine section
88 Cooling air intakes
89 Forward 'Sirena-3' radar warning and ECIA aerial (repositioned from leading edge of three-pylon wing)

90 Starboard upper airbrake, open
91 Autopilot controller
92 HF aerial
93 Starboard tailplane anti flutterweight
94 Rudder control linkages
95 Rudder hydraulic actuator
96 Tailfin construction
97 PSI U (very short wave fighter control) aerial
98 Fin tip UHF aerial fairing
99 Tail navigation light
100 Rudder
101 Rear'Sirena-3' radar warning and ECM aerial
102 Parachute release link
103 Brake parachute housing
104 Tailcone/parachute door conic fairing

105 Transponder aerial
106 Engine exhaust nozzle
107 Port all-moving tailplane
108 Static discharger
109 Tailplane tip anti-flutter weight
110 Tailplane rib construction
111 Tailplane spar
112 Pivot mounting
113 Tailplane limit stops
114 Variable area afterburner nozzle

115 Nozzle control jacks
116 Fin and tailplane attachment fuselage double frame
117 Afterburner ducting
118 Tailplane hydraulic actuator
119 RO-2M'Odd Rods'IFF aerial
120 Airbrake housing
121 Airbrake hydraulic jack
122 Rear fuselage frame and stringer construction

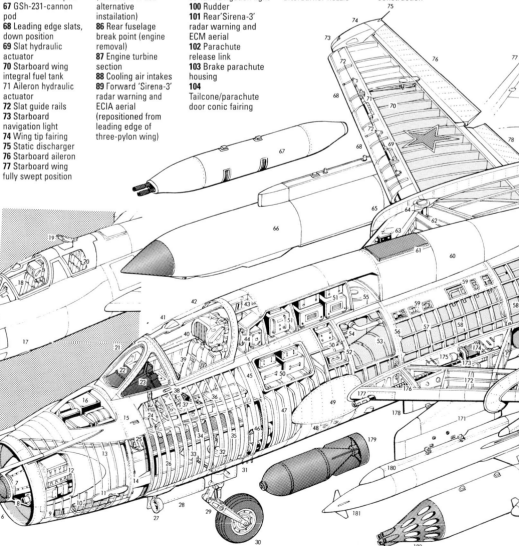

*Above: The definitive two-seat 'Fitter' was exported to allied air forces as the R-29BS-300-engined Su-22UM-3, delivered from 1982. This was quickly superceded by the Su-22UM-3K delivered from 1983, and incorporating the AL-21F-3 powerplant carried as standard by Soviet Su-17Ms. East Germany operated eight examples of the Su-22UM-3K within a total 'Fitter' fleet comprising 53 aircraft. During 1979-80 all Soviet Su-17UM two-seaters were updated to Su-17UM-3 standard.*

## SPECIFICATION

### Su-17M-4 'Fitter-K'

### Dimensions

**Length (including probes):**
61 ft 6¼ in (18.75 m)
**Height:** 16 ft 5 in (5.00 m)
**Span (spread):** 45 ft 3 in (13.80 m)
**Span (swept):** 32 ft 10 in (10.00 m)
**Wing area (spread):** 430.57 sq ft (40.00 m²)
**Wing area (swept):** 398.28 sq ft (37.00 m²)

### Powerplant

One NPO Saturn (Lyul'ka) AL-21F-3 turbojet rated at 17,196 lb st (76.49 kN) dry and 24,802 lb st (110.32 kN) with afterburning, plus provision for two RATO units

### Weights

**Normal take-off:** 36,155 lb (16400 kg)
**Maximum take-off:** 42,989 lb (19500 kg)

### Performance

**Maximum level speed 'clean' at sea level:** 870 mph (1400 km/h)
**Maximum rate of climb at sea level:** 45,276 ft (13800m) per minute
**Service ceiling:** 49,870 ft (15200 m)
**Combat radius:** 621 nm (715 miles; 1150 km) on a hi-lo-hi mission with a 4,409 lb (2000-kg) warload, or 378 nm (435 miles; 700 km) on a lo-lo-lo mission with a 4,409 lb (2000-kg) warload

### Armament

A wide range of freefall bombs and podded and unpodded unguided rocket projectiles ranging in calibre from 57 mm to 330 mm; for precision attacks a variety of air-to-surface missiles, including Kh-25 (AS-10 'Karen' and AS-12 'Kegler') and Kh-29, and the Kh-58E (AS-11 'Kilter') anti-radar missile. To further improve self-defence capability, four 32-round upward-firing ASO chaff/flare dispensers can be scabbed on to either side of the tailfin, augmenting the two six-tube KDS-23 dispensers mounted flush with the dorsal spine.For strafe attacks, the 'Fitter-K's wingroot-mounted NR-30 30-mm cannon (each with 80 rounds) can be augmented by gun pods carried under the wings or fuselage. .The 'Fitter-K' can be used in the tactical reconnaissance role, carrying the same KKR reconnaissance pod as has been applied to the 'Fitter-C' and 'Fitter-H'. This contains three optical cameras, flares and Elint modules, and is usually carried in association with the SPS ECM pod

---

123 Ventral fin
124 Port lowerairbrake, open
125 Engine accessory equipment access panel
126 Accessory equipment gearbox compartment
127 Port inboard single-slotted flap
128 Flap actuator
129 Auxiliary rear spar
130 Wing sweep control hydraulic jack
131 Rear spar guide rails
132 Wing glove section external stiffeners
133 Outboard wing fence
134 Outboard single-slotted flap
135 Flap rib construction

136 Flap actuator
137 Aileron construction
138 Port wing fully swept (63 deg) position
139 Port aileron
140 Aileron hinge control linkage
141 Static discharger
142 Wing tip fairing
143 Port wing fully forward (28 deg) position
144 Port navigation light
145 Three-segment leading edge slats, down position

146 BETA-B 250-kg (551-1b) retarded concrete piercing bomb
147 S-24 240-mm aircraft rocket
148 AA-2 (K-13A)'Atoli' air-to air self-defence missile
149 Missile launch rail

150 Leading edge slat rib construction
151 Aileron hydraulic actuator

152 Portwing integral fuel tank
153 Wing rib construction
154 Leading edge slat hydraulic actuator
155 Outer wing panel main spar
156 Wing pivot bearing
157 Mainwheel doors
158 Port mainwheel
159 Levered suspension axle beam
160 600-litre (1 22-1mp gal) external fuel tank

164 Main undercarriage pivot fixing
165 Hydraulic retraction jack
166 Fixed wing section main spar
167 Main undercarriage wheel bay
168 Inboard wing fence
169 Front spar
170 Centre wing pylon
171 Inboard wing pylon
172 Leading edge nose ribs
173 N R 30-mm cannon, port and starboard

161 Main undercarriage leg strut
162 Leg rotation and shortening link
163 Outboard wing pylon

174 Ammunition feed chute, 70-rounds per gun
175 Cannon pressurisation bottle
176 Recoil mounting
177 Cannon muzzle
178 Fuselage stores pylons, port and starboard, one or two per side
179 FAB 500, 500-kg (1 102-1b) HE bomb
180 Missile launch rail
181 AS-7 'Kerry' air-to-surface missile
182 UV-32-57 rocket pack 32x57-mm rockets

# Sukhoi Su-27 'Flanker'

*The formidable Sukhoi Su-27 'Flanker' family of fighter aircraft is one of the most successful ever to emerge from the former Soviet Union. Supremely manoeuvrable, heavily armed and blessed with exceptional range, it has been compared favourably with the best Western fighters.*

## Su-27K (Su-33)

**Cutaway key**

1 Pitot head
2 Upward-hinging radome
3 Radar scanner
4 Scanner mounting
5 Radome hinge point
6 Infra-red search and tracking scanner
7 Refuelling probe housing
8 Radar equipment module; tilts down for access
9 Lower SRO-2 'Odd-Rods' IFF aerial
10 Incidence transmitter
11 Cockpit front pressure bulkhead
12 Retractable spotlight, port and starboard
13 Cockpit side console panel
14 Slide-mounted throttle levers
15 Flight-refuelling probe, extended
16 Instrument panel shroud
17 Pilot's head-up display
18 Upward-hinging cockpit canopy
19 K-36MD 'zero-zero' ejection seat
20 Canopy hydraulic jack
21 Dynamic pressure probe, port and starboard

22 Cockpit rear pressure bulkhead
23 Temperature probe
24 Nosewheel door
25 Twin nosewheels, forward-retracting
26 ASM-MSS long-range ramjet and rocket-powered anti-shipping missile
27 Missile folding fins
28 Nosewheel hydraulic steering jacks
29 Deck approach 'traffic-lights'
30 Leading-edge flush EW aerial
31 Avionics equipment bay
32 Ammunition magazine, 149 rounds
33 HF aerial
34 Starboard fuselage GSh-30-1 30-mm cannon
35 Canard foreplane
36 Starboard wing missile armament
37 Dorsal airbrake
38 Gravity fuel filler cap
39 Centre fuselage fuel tank
40 Forward lateral fuel tanks
41 ASM-MSS missile carrier on fuselage centreline station
42 Variable-area intake ramp doors
43 Ramp hydraulic jack
44 Foreplane hydraulic actuator

45 Port canard foreplane
46 Engine air intake
47 Boundary layer bleed air louvres
48 Segmented ventral suction relief doors
49 Retractable intake FOD screen
50 Mainwheel door
51 Door hydraulic jack
52 Port mainwheel bay
53 Intake trunking
54 Wing panel attachment joints
55 Engine compressor face
56 Wing centre-section integral fuel tanks
57 ADF antenna
58 Airbrake hydraulic jack
59 Starboard mainwheel, stowed position
60 Fuel tank access panels
61 Wing-fold hydraulic jack
62 Leading-edge flap, down position
63 Starboard outer, folding, wing panel
64 Outboard plain flap, down position
65 Starboard wing, folded position

66 Inboard double-slotted flap segments
67 Engine bleed air pre-cooler air intake
68 Engine accessory equipment gearbox
69 Central auxiliary power unit
70 Chaff/flare launchers
71 Rear fuselage integral fuel tank
72 Engine oil tank
73 Fin structure
74 Leading-edge HF aerial
75 Rudder hydraulic actuator
76 Fintip UHF/VHF aerial
77 ILS aerial
78 Tail navigation light
79 Radar warning antenna
80 Starboard rudder
81 Starboard tailplane folded position

82 AL-31F afterburning turbofan engine
83 Port tailfin
84 ILS aerial
85 ECM antenna
86 Upper SRO-2 'Odd Rods' IFF aerial
87 Tailcone fairing
88 Rear EW antenna fairing
89 Deck arrester hook
90 Variable-area afterburner nozzle
91 Port tailplane
92 Tailplane fold joint rotary actuator
93 Tailplane pivot bearing

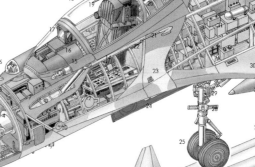

*Above: The sheer size of the 'Flanker' is evident in this view of two Su-27Ks of the 1st Squadron, Severomorsk Regiment, AV-MF (Russian naval aviation). The Su-27K (Su-33) is a naval variant of the 'Flanker-B' interceptor. The large lifting area makes the Su-27 suitable for operations from aircraft-carriers, while its size enables a huge internal fuel load to be carried, conferring excellent long-range performance. Clearly visible are the Su-27K's canards and double-slotted trailing-edge flaps.*

## SPECIFICATION

### Su-27P 'Flanker-B'

### Dimensions

**Fuselage length (including probe):** 72 ft 0 in (21.94 m)
**Wing span over tip missile launch rails:** 48 ft 3 in (14.70 m)
**Wing aspect ratio:** 7.76
**Tailplane span:** 32 ft 5 in (9.88 m)
**Wing area:** 667.8 sq ft (62.04 m²)
**Horizontal tail area:** 131.75 sq ft (12.24 m²)
**Total fin area:** 165.76 sq ft (15.40 m²)
**Distance between fin tips:** 14 ft 1¼ in (4.30 m)
**Overall height:** 19 ft 6 in (5.93 m)
**Wheel track:** 14 ft 3 in (4.34 m)
**Wheelbase:** 19 ft 4 in (5.88 m)
**Maximum wing loading:** 93.4 lb/sq ft (456.2 kg/m²)

### Powerplant

Two Saturn Lyul'ka AL-31F afterburning turbofans each rated at 16,755 lb st (74.53 kN) dry and 27,558 lb st (122.59 kN) with afterburning

### Weights

**Empty operating:** 36,112 lb (16380 kg)
**Normal take-off:** 50,705 lb (23000 kg)
**Maximum take-off:** 62,391 lb (28300 kg)

### Fuel and load

**Internal fuel:** (normal) 11,620 lb (5270 kg), (maximum) 20,723 lb (9400 kg) or 2,640 Imp gal (12000 litres) in three main fuselage tanks, with additional tanks in outer wing panels; the basic Su-27 has no provision for inflight refuelling or for the carriage of external fuel tanks (but see under individual variant briefings for exceptions)
**Maximum theoretical weapon load:** 17,636 lb (8000 kg)

**Normal weapon load:** 8,818 lb (4000 kg)

### g limits

8-9 at basic design gross weight

### Performance

**Maximum level speed at sea level (estimated):** 743 kt (850 mph; 1370 km/h)
**Maximum level speed 'clean' at altitude:** 1,236 kt (1,418 mph; 2280 km/h)
**Limiting Mach No.:** 2.35
**Absolute ceiling:** 60,700 ft (18500 m)
**Practical service ceiling (estimated):** 58,070 ft (17700 m)
**Take-off run:** 1,640 ft (500 m) or 1,476 ft (450 m)
**Landing roll:** 1,968 ft (600 m) or 2,297 ft (700 m)
**Landing speed:** 121-124 kt (140-143 mph; 225-230 km/h)

### Range

**Maximum range:** 1,987 nm (2,285 miles; 3680 km) at altitude, 740 nm (851 miles; 1370 km) at low level
**Radius of action (high-altitude):** 590 nm (677 miles; 1090 km)
**Radius of action (low-altitude):** 227 nm (261 miles; 420 km)

### Armament

Note: This specification should be treated with some caution. Sukhoi has released widely differing performance figures on different occasions (and even releases different dimensions for the same aircraft), while rarely specifying the loads carried for particular range or performance figures.

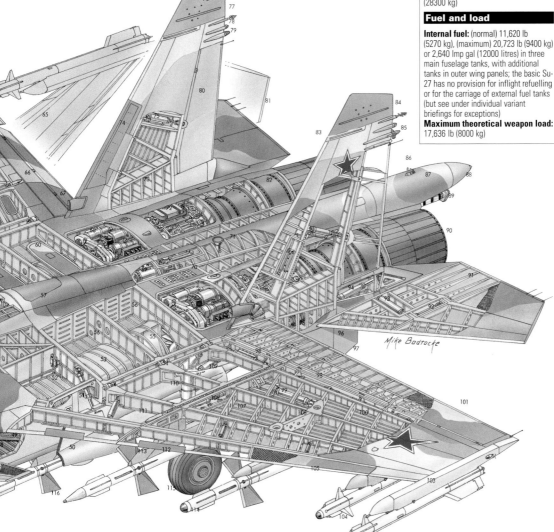

Mike Badrocke

94 Hydraulic actuator
95 Hydraulic accumulator
96 Ventral fin
97 Port inboard double-slotted flap segments
98 Flap hydraulic actuators
99 Wing-fold hydraulic jack
100 Outer wing panel structure
101 Outboard plain flap segment
102 Port navigation light
103 Wingtip missile launch rail
104 Vympel R-73 (AA-11 'Archer') air-to-air missiles
105 Leading-edge flap
106 Pylon attachment hardpoints
107 Port wing integral fuel tank
108 Wing-fold locking mechanism jack
109 Main undercarriage hydraulic retraction jack
110 Mainwheel leg strut
111 Wing-fold hinge joint
112 Leading-edge flush EW aerial panels
113 Missile pylon
114 Vympel R-27 (AA-10 'Alamo-B') IR-homing air-to-air missile
115 Port mainwheel
116 Vympel R-27 (AA-10 'Alamo-C') RHAAM

# Helicopters

# Aérospatiale Alouette III

*Aérospatiale's SA.316B is one of the world's top selling light helicopters – nearly 1,500 examples have been built and the helicopter has been exported to 190 civil and military operators in 7? countries. A further 400 examples have been built by HAL in India (the Chetak) and by ICA-Brasov in Romania (where they were designated the IAR 316B). This example is from the South African Air Force and is being escorted by a Puma*

## SA.316B Alouette III

**Cutaway key**

1 FM homing antennas, port and starboard
2 Pitot head
3 Instrument access panel
4 Cockpit ventilating air intake
5 Antenna mounting
6 Downward-view windows
7 Curved windscreen panels
8 Standby compass
9 Instrument panel shroud
10 Pilot's instrument console
11 Weapons system control panel
12 Centre control pedestal
13 Yaw control rudder pedals
14 Landing lamp
15 Floor beam construction
16 Levered suspension nose landing gear leg strut
17 Non-retracting castoring nosewheel
18 Port navigation light
19 Door jettison linkage
20 Cyclic pitch control column
21 Central power and engine condition levers
22 Collective pitch control lever
23 Control column handgrip
24 Missile hand-controller
25 Safety harness
26 Starboard jettisonable cockpit door
27 Outside air temperature gauge
28 Starboard sliding cabin door
29 Cabin roof glazing
30 APX-Bezu 260 gyro-stabilised sight
31 Retractable sight controller and binocular viewer
32 Pilot's seat
33 Co-pilot/weapons officer's seat
34 Sliding side window panel
35 Port jettisonable cockpit door
36 Collective pitch-control lever
37 Seat mounting rails (three-abreast front seat row)
38 Boarding step
39 Lower fuselage 'raft' section skin panelling
40 Port sliding cabin door
41 Passenger/cargo loading
42 Door hatches/ stretcher handle apertures
43 Door latches
44 Troop-carrying folding seats (four)
45 Fixed backrest
46 Control rod linkages
47 Sliding doortop rail
48 Cabin rear-sloping bulkhead
49 Trim/insulating panelling
50 First-aid kit
51 Anti-collision light
52 VHF aerial
53 Cabin roof skin panelling
54 Rotor head control rods
55 Main transmission gearbox
56 Swash plate mechanism
57 Blade pitch angle control rods
58 Torque scissor links
59 Rotor head hinge fitting
60 Lifting fitting
61 Hydraulic drag hinge dampers
62 Bracing cables

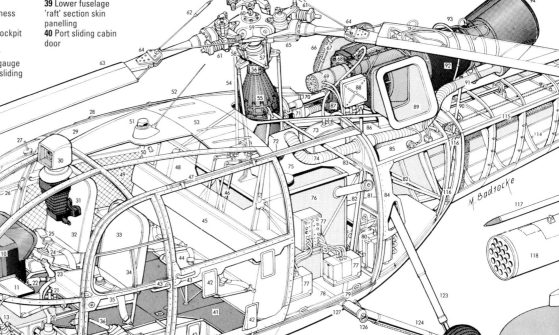

M. Badrocke

*France still retains a significant Alouette capability and the Aéronavale is the major operator. These ageing aircraft remain in service due to the delays over the entry into service of the NH 90. About 70 examples of the Alouette II and the Alouette III are operated by 20, 22 and 23 Escadrille de Servitude, performing in the general utility and training roles.*

## SPECIFICATION

**SA.319 Alouette III Astazou**

### Dimensions

**Fuselage length:** 32 ft 10 ¾ in (10.03 m)
**Length with rotors turning:** 42 ft 1½ in (12.84 m)
**Height:** 9 ft 10 in (3 m)
**Wheeltrack:** 8 ft 6¾ in (2.60 m)
**Main rotor diameter:** 36 ft 1¾ in (11.02 m)
**Tail rotor diameter:** 6 ft 3¼ in (1.90 m)
**Main rotor disk area:** 1,026.68 sq ft (95.38 m²)
**Tail rotor disk area:** 30.84 sq ft (2.87 m²)

### Powerplant

One 870-shp (649 kW) Turboméca Astazou XIV derated to 600 shp (447 kW)

### Weights

**Empty:** 2,513 lb (1140 kg)
**Maximum take-off:** 4,960 lb (2250 kg)

### Fuel and load

**Internal fuel:** 126.5 Imp gal (575 litres)
**External fuel:** None

**Maximum payload:** 1,653 lb (750 kg)

### Performance

**Maximum level speed 'clean' at sea level:** 118 kt (136 mph; 220 km/h)
**Maximum cruising speed at sea level:** 106 kt (136 mph; 220 km/h)
**Maximum rate of climb at sea level:** 885 ft (270 m) per minute
**Hovering ceiling:** 10,170 ft (3100 m)
**Range:** 326 nm (375 miles; 605 km)

### Armament

A wide range of light weaponry can be carried by the Alouette when it is engaged in combat duties. A 0.3-in (7.62-mm) machine-gun can be fired through the port door, while a 20-mm cannon in a fixed axial fairing can be mounted on the port side of the cabin. One or two MATRA 155H rocket pods firing 2⅔ in (68-mm) unguided rockets are useful against soft or dispersed targets. For anti-armour missions, the Euromissile HOT, the AS11 or the FN ETNA TMP-5-twin 0.3-in (7.62-mm) machine gun pod is used. Naval Alouettes carry a pair of Mk 44 torpedoes or a MAD bird and single torpedo or search radar.

**63** Three-bladed main rotor
**64** Blade root attachment joints
**65** Blade pitch angle control horn
**66** Engine inlet filter screen
**67** Starboard engine inlet
**68** Accessory equipment gearbox
**69** Generator
**70** Engine transmission shaft
**71** Rotor brake
**72** Transmission oil cooler
**73** Oil tank
**74** Oil cooler airduct
**75** Gearbox mounting deck

**76** Fuel tank, capacity 126.5 Imp gal (575 litres)
**77** Electrical system equipment
**78** Equipment loading deck
**79** Sliding cabin door bottom rail
**80** Missile system avionics equipment
**81** Position of fuel filter on starboard side
**82** Welded steel tube centre fuselage framework
**83** Gearbox mounting struts
**84** Non-structural skin panelling

**85** Fireproof engine mounting deck
**86** Angled tail rotor transmission shaft
**87** Engine reduction gearbox
**88** Ignition control unit
**89** Port engine bellmouth air inlet
**90** Rear engine mounting strut
**91** Tailpipe negative pressure cooling air duct
**92** Engine combustion section

**93** Turboméca Artouste IIIB turboshaft engine
**94** Engine exhaust duct
**95** Tailboom top decking/access panel
**96** Tail rotor transmission shaft
**97** Transmission shaft bearings
**98** Tail rotor control cables
**99** Starboard fixed tailplane
**100** Endplate tailfin
**101** Three-bladed tail rotor
**102** All-metal tail rotor blades
**103** Blade pitch control mechanism
**104** Right-angle final drive gearbox
**105** Tail navigation light

**106** Steel tube tailskid/ rotor protector
**107** Port fixed tailplane
**108** Port endplate tailfin
**109** Tailplane bracing struts
**110** Main rotor blade balance weights
**111** Aluminium alloy blade spar
**112** Moltoprene foam trailing-edge filler
**113** Bonded aluminium alloy rotor blade skin panels
**114** Tailboom frame and stringer construction
**115** Upper longeron

**116** Tailboom attachment joints
**117** 68-mm folding fin aircraft rocket (FFAR)
**118** MATRA rocket launcher pack
**119** Missile pylon adaptor
**120** Missile launch rail
**121** AS12 wire-guided air-to-surface missiles (two)
**122** Port mainwheel
**123** Shock absorber leg strut
**124** Trailing axle beam
**125** Hydraulic brake pipe
**126** Tie-down point
**127** Axle beam pivot fixing
**128** Weapons pylon mount

**129** Detachable missile pylons
**130** AS11 wire guided air-to-surface missiles (four)

*Still remaining in service with several Alouette III operators, the AS12 air-to-surface missile entered service in 1960. Four of these missiles can be carried by the SA.316B and are generally used in the anti-tank role. The AS12 has three different warhead fits: semi-armour piercing, shaped charge and fragmentation. Detonation of the missile is delayed until the missile has passed through ¾ in (20 mm) of armour; it will then explode 6½ feet (2 m) beyond the entry point. The most famous use of the AS12 was by British Wasp helicopters, which used the weapon to damage the Argentine submarine, Santa Fé. Most Alouette III operators now use the HOT missile rather than the AS12.*

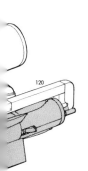

# Aérospatiale SA321 Super Frelon

*One of France's few remaining Super Frelons is seen wearing the new two-tone colour scheme, which has replaced the all-over sea-grey finish of old. Aéronavale SA 321s lost their ASW role to the Westland Lynx and now see limited operational use.*

## SA 321GM Super Frelon

### Cutaway key

1 Nose radome (Exocet armed anti-shipping role)
2 Target designation radar scanner
3 Omera Segid ORB 32 radar equipment
4 Radome mounting fairing
5 FM homing aerials, port and starboard
6 Pitot heads
7 Windscreen wipers
8 Windscreen panels
9 Pilot's instrument console
10 Instrument panel shroud
11 Centre control pedestal
12 Cyclic pitch control column
13 Rudder pedals
14 Downward view window
15 Lower IFF aerial
16 Anti-collision light
17 Fixed steerable twin nosewheels
18 Boat hull chine member
19 Collective pitch control lever
20 Door jettison handle
21 Jettisonable cockpit doors
22 Safety harness
23 Co pilot's seat
24 Observer's folding seat
25 Cockpit doorway
26 Sliding side window panel
27 Pilot's seat
28 Engine power levers
29 Folding sun visors
30 Overhead systems switch panel
31 Circuit breaker panel
32 Starboard side maintenance access ladder
33 Rescue hoist/winch

34 Flight control rod linkages
35 Engine control runs
36 Cabin heater
37 Heater intake grille
38 Starboard side main cabin doorway (sliding door)
39 Cockpit rear bulkhead
40 Avionics and electrical equipment racks, port and starboard
41 Radar altimeter equipment
42 Tie-down ring
43 Boat hull waterproof bulkheads
44 Position of pressure refuelling connection on starboard side
45 Main cabin loading floor

46 Cargo tie down rings
47 Forward group of underfloor, bag type fuel tanks total fuel capacity 874 Imp gal (3975 litres )
48 Honeycomb floorpanels
49 Cabin window panels
50 HF aerial rail
51 Aerial support masts
52 Fuselage frame and stringer construction
53 Cabin wall soundproof lining
54 Engine mounting deck
55 Forward engine air intakes

56 Cooling air intake
57 Starboard engine bay hinged cowling/work platform
58 Main rotor blade hollow D-section aluminium alloy main spar
59 Starboard engine exhaust fairing
60 Engine bay dividing fireproof bulkhead
61 Generator

62 Engine oil tank
63 Ignition control unit
64 Turboméca Turmo 111 C6 turboshaft engine
65 Engine transmission gearbox
66 Bifurcated exhaust ducts
67 Oil cooler fan
68 Forward engine power take-off shafts
69 Combining gearbox
70 Main reduction gearbox

71 Rotor head swash plate mechanism

72 Blade pitch control rods
73 Main rotor hub
74 Hydraulic fluid reservoirs
75 Folding rotor blade hinge joints
76 Six-bladed main rotor
77 Blade root attachment joints
78 Pressurised blade crack detection indicator

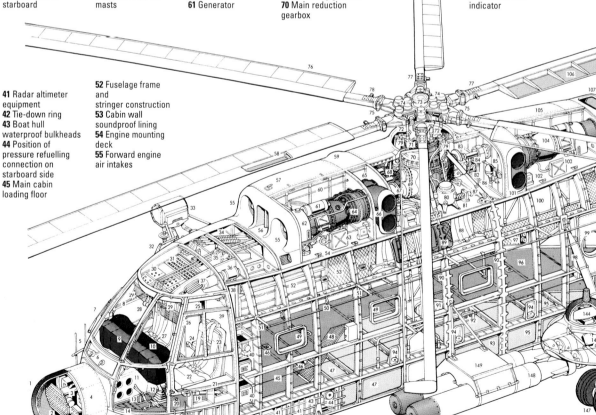

*The SA 321F was the unsuccessful civil version of the SA 321 Super Frelon. It was designed to transport 34-37 passengers and had a soundproofed cabin that was claimed to be 'as comfortable as that of any modern airliner'. It had a cruise speed of 130 kt (150 mph; 241 km/h) and it was designed to be used for feeder and short haul shuttle services over medium distance routes.*

**79** Rotor head hydraulic control actuator (three)
**80** Hydraulic reservoir
**81** Gearbox mounting deck
**82** Tail rotor transmission shaft
**83** Rotor brake
**84** Rear engine power take-off shaft
**85** Fireproof bulkhead
**86** Engine fire extinguisher bottle
**87** Gearbox mounting struts (four)
**88** Troop seats (marine assault role), 27 troops
**89** Stainless steel exhaust heat shield
**90** Gearbox mounting fuselage main frames

**98** Main undercarriage upper energy absorbing strut
**99** Emergency escape hatch, port and starboard
**100** Troop seats folded against cabin wall
**101** Aft engine bifurcated exhaust duct
**102** Fireproof engine bay decking
**103** Ignition control unit

**114** Dorsal spine fairing
**115** Bevel drive gearbox
**116** Tailrotor angled drive shaft
**117** Tailplane bracing strut
**118** Fixed tailplane
**119** Upper IFF aerial
**120** Tailplane rib construction
**121** Tail rotor control linkage

**138** Tailboom access hatch
**139** Ramp hydraulic jacks, port and starboard
**140** Cargo loading ramp (flight openable), down position
**141** Ramp frame and stringer construction

**142** Port stabilising float
**143** Port lateral radome
**144** ASW search radar scanner
**145** Main undercarriage lower mounting struts
**146** Shock absorber leg strut
**147** Fixed twin mainwheels
**148** L5 2,200-lb (1000-kg) homing torpedoes (four)
**149** Twin torpedo carrier/launcher
**150** Dipping sonar (ASW operations)
**151** AM 39 Exocet-air-to surface anti-shipping missile (two)

**91** Central hatch for dipping sonar or cargo hook
**92** Hydraulic system ground connections
**93** Central fuel tank group
**94** Position of gravity fuel fillers on starboard side
**95** Rear underfloor fuel tank group
**96** Rear cabin sloping floor section
**97** Fuel pump

**104** Aft Turboméca Turmo II C6 turboshaft engine
**105** Starboard side fairing panels (aft engine on port side only)
**106** Main rotor blade aluminium alloy trailing-edge pocket construction
**107** Aft engine air intake
**108** Intake plenum
**109** Tail rotor transmssion shaft
**110** Tail rotor control cables
**111** VHF aerial
**112** Venting air grilles
**113** Transmission shaft bearings

**122** Final drive right-angle gearbox
**123** Anti-collision light
**124** Tail navigation light
**125** Blade pitch control mechanism
**126** Five-bladed tail rotor
**127** Aluminium alloy tail rotor blades
**128** Tail rotor pylon construction
**129** Hinged pylon latch mechanism, pylon folds to starboard
**130** Transmission gearbox mounting main frame
**131** Internal bracing strut
**132** VOR aerial
**133** Tailboom frame and stringer construction
**134** Main rotor blade balance weights
**135** Tracking weights
**136** Aluminium alloy blade skin panelling
**137** IFF transceiver

## SPECIFICATION

### SA 321G Super Frelon

#### Dimensions

**Main rotor diameter:** 62 ft (18.90 m)
**Tail rotor diameter:** 13 ft 1½ in (4 m)
**Length overall (rotors turning):** 75 ft 6⅔ in (23.03 m)
**Height overall:** 22 ft 2¼ in (6.76 m)
**Wheel track:** 14 ft 1 in (4.30 m)

#### Powerplant

Three Turboméca Turmo IIIC3 turboshafts each rated at 1,475 hp (1100 kW) or, in later helicopters, three Turboméca Turmo IIIC7 turboshafts each rated at 1,610 hp (1201 kW)

#### Weight

**Empty:** 15,130 lb (6863 kg)
**Maximum take-off in early versions:** 27,557 lb (12500 kg)
**Maximum take-off in late versions:** 28,660 lb (13000 kg)

#### Performance

**Maximum rate of climb at sea level:** 984 ft (300 m) per minute

**Service ceiling:** 10,170 ft (3100 m)
**Hovering ceiling (in ground effect):** 6,400 ft (1950 m)
**Never-exceed speed at sea level:** 149 kt (171 mph; 275 km/h)
**Maximum cruising speed at sea level:** 134 kt (154 mph; 248 km/h)
**Range with a 7,716-lb (3500-kg) payload:** 550 nm (633 miles; 1020 km)
**Endurance:** Up to four hours

#### Fuel and load

**Internal fuel:** 1,050 US gal (3975 litres) plus provision for 262 US gal (1191 litres) of auxiliary fuel in two cabin tanks
**External fuel:** Up to two 132-US gal (600-litre) auxiliary tanks
**Maximum payload:** 11,023 lb (5000 kg )

#### Armament

Two AM39 Exocet missiles or four Mk 46 homing torpedoes

*An SA 321G development aircraft fires an Aérospatiale Exocet anti-shipping missile. The Exocet/Super Frelon combination proved deadly during the Gulf War between Iraq and Iran.*

## Super Frelon at war

First to see combat were the assault transport SA 321Ks of the Israeli Defence Force/Air Force (IDF/AF). The initial few from an order for 12 had only just been delivered when they were involved in the Six-Day War of June 1967. They transported troops for a daring assault on the airfield at Sharm el Sheikh at the southern tip of the Sinai peninsula, and literally carried off an Egyptian missile guidance radar station so that electronics experts could reveal its secrets at their leisure. Over a decade later, in 1978, plans were announced to re-engine Israeli Super Frelons with 1,896-hp (1413-kW) General Electric T58-16 turboshafts to improve hot-and-high performance and to give powerplant commonality with the IDF's other transport helicopter, the Sikorsky CH-53. Eventually, the CH-53, with its greater lifting capacity and power, replaced the Super Frelon, though one heavy lift squadron; 114 Tayeset, has retained the name 'The Super Frelon Squadron'. During Desert Storm, at least one of Iraq's Super Frelons was destroyed by the Allies.

# Puma/Super Puma Puma/Cougar

Due to its relatively large size, the Puma is vulnerable to return fire if employed in the attack role. However, under favourable circumstances, it may be equipped with 72 rocket projectiles with blast, hollow-charge, fragmentation or smoke warheads, as demonstrated by this Aérospatiale-owned SA 330L.

## AS 332 Super Puma

### Cutaway key

1 Radome
2 Weather radar scanner
3 Retractable landing/taxiing lamp
4 Communications and navigation system electronic equipment
5 Pitot tubes
6 Cockpit front bulkhead
7 Fresh air scoop
8 Windscreen wipers
9 Windscreen panels
10 Instrument panel shroud
11 Instrument panel
12 Centre control console
13 Cyclic pitch control column
14 Yaw control rudder pedals
15 Brake pedal connections
16 Nose undercarriage leg strut
17 Downward-vision window
18 Twin nosewheels
19 Nose undercarriage wheel bay
20 Cockpit step
21 Flight-deck floor level
22 Collective pitch control lever
23 Hydraulic system hand pump
24 Cockpit door
25 Co-pilot's seat
26 Safety harness
27 Opening side-window panel
28 Cockpit bulkhead
29 Fire extinguisher bottle
30 Control rod linkages
31 Pilot's seat
32 Starboard side cockpit door
33 Engine power levers and fuel cocks
34 Overhead control panel
35 Cabin air intake
36 Cabin heater unit
37 Intake ice and debris shield
38 Engine air intake
39 Starboard engine cowling panels
40 Engine bay central firewall
41 Accessory equipment
42 Engine oil tank
43 Engine mounting deck

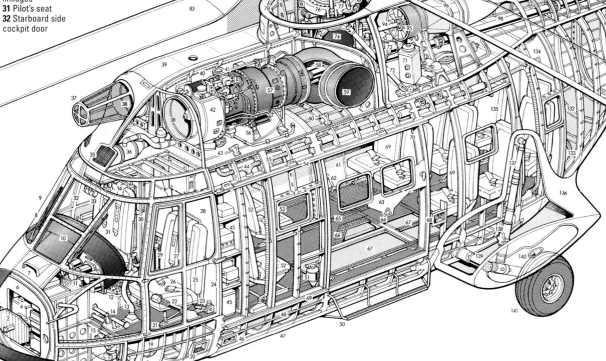

*The French deployed the Puma early in Operation Desert Shield as part of the French Army Light Aviation (ALAT) advanced party. By the outbreak of Desert Storm, a total of 38 French Pumas was in theatre; during the conflict, they were mainly used for army support, carrying 16 troops or 2.5 tonnes of underslung load, such as ammunition.*

## SPECIFICATION

### SA 330L Puma

**Dimensions**

**Length (rotors turning):** 50 ft 6½ in (18.15 m)
**Fuselage length:** 46 ft 1½ in (14.06 m)
**Main rotor diameter:** 49 ft 2½ in (15.00 m)
**Tail rotor diameter:** 9 ft 11½ in (3.04 m)
**Main rotor disc area:** 1,902.20 sq ft (176.71 m²)
**Tail rotor disc area:** 78.13 sq ft (7.26 m²)
**Height overall:** 16 ft 10½ in (5.14 m)
**Height to top of rotor head:** 14 ft 4½ in (4.38 m)
**Wheel base:** 13 ft 3 in (4.05 m)
**Wheel track:** 7 ft 10¾ in (2.38 m)

**Powerplant**

Two Turboméca Turmo IVC turboshafts each rated at 1,575 shp (1175 kW)

**Weights**

**Empty:** 7,970 lb (3615 kg)
**Maximum take-off:** 16,534 lb (7500 kg)

**Fuel and load**

**Internal fuel load:** 408 US gal (1544 litres) plus provision for 502 US gal (1900 litres) of auxiliary fuel in four cabin tanks
**External fuel load:** up to two 93-US gal (350-litre) auxiliary tanks
**Maximum payload:** 7,055 lb (3200 kg)

**Performance**

**Never-exceed speed:** 158 kt (182 mph; 293 km/h)
**Maximum cruising speed 'clean' at optimum altitude:** 146 kt (168 mph; 270 km/h)
**Maximum rate of climb at sea level:** 1,810 ft (552 m) per minute
**Service ceiling:** 19,685 ft (6000 m)
**Hover ceiling (IGE):** 14,435 ft (4400 m)
**Hover ceiling (OGE):** 13,940 ft (4250 m)
**Range:** 308 nm (355 miles; 572 km)

**Armament**

The Puma can carry a wide variety of weaponry for several different roles, including one or two 0.3-in (7.62-mm) general-purpose machine-guns for self-defence, 72 SNEB 2.68-in (68-mm) rocket projectiles for close support, two Aérospatiale AM39 Exocets for the long-range anti-shipping role or six Aérospatiale AS15TT missiles for the medium-range anti-shipping role

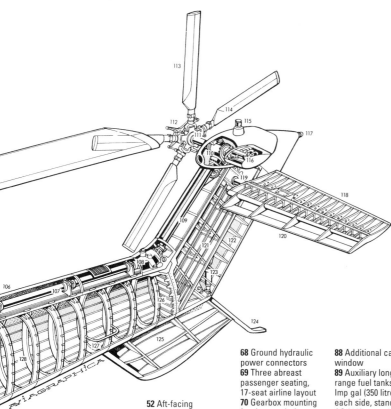

44 Cabin heater air ducting
45 Radio and electronics equipment rack
46 Ground electrical power socket
47 External cable and pipe duct
48 Forward underfloor fuel cell
49 Lower sliding door rail
50 Boarding step
51 Fuel system filter
52 Aft-facing passenger seating
53 Cabin window panels
54 Upper sliding door rail
55 Engine mounting fuselage main frame
56 Main engine mounting
57 Turboméca Makila 1A turboshaft engine
58 Engine drive shaft
59 Exhaust duct
60 Cabin roof framing
61 Cabin wall trim panelling
62 Starboard side refuelling pipe
63 Sliding main cabin door, port and starboard
64 Door emergency release handle
65 Main cabin flooring
66 Honeycomb floor panels
67 Underfloor fuel tanks; total fuel capacity 343 Imp gal (1560 litres)

68 Ground hydraulic power connectors
69 Three abreast passenger seating, 17-seat airline layout
70 Gearbox mounting fuselage main frame
71 Hydraulic system reservoir
72 Gearbox mounting strut
77 Hydraulic pump
74 Main gearbox
75 Rotor head hydraulic control jack (3)
76 Swashplate mechanism
77 Torque scissor links
78 Rotor head fairing
79 Main rotor drive shaft
80 Blade pitch control rods
81 Vibration damper
82 Blade root fixing
83 Composite construction main rotor blades
84 Main rotor hub mechanism
85 Rotor head fairing
86 AS 332L stretched variant
87 AS 332L 2-ft 6-in (0.76-m) fuselage plug

88 Additional cabin window
89 Auxiliary long-range fuel tanks, 77 Imp gal (350 litres) each side, standard AS 332L capacity 453 Imp gal (2060 litres)
90 Flotation bag stowage
91 VHF aerial
92 Anti-collision light
93 Rotor head tail fairing
94 Fan drive shaft
95 Oil cooler fan
96 Gearbox oil cooler
97 Oil cooler exhaust duct
98 Tail rotor transmission shaft
99 Glass-fibre shaft fairing
100 Cooling air grille
101 Rotor blade titanium leading-edge capping strip
102 Glass-fibre roving blade spar
103 Honeycomb blade core
104 Carbon fibre inner skins
105 Glass-fibre outer skin covering
106 Dorsal spine fairing

107 Drive shaft bearings
108 Bevel drive gearbox
109 Tail rotor angled transmission shaft
110 Right-angled final drive gearbox
111 Tail rotor hub fixing
112 Blade pitch control mechanism
113 Five-bladed tail rotor
114 Composite construction tail rotor blades
115 Anti-collision light
116 Tail rotor hydraulic control jack
117 Tail navigation light
118 Fixed tailplane construction
119 Tailplane mounting shaft
120 Fixed leading-edge slat
121 Tail pylon construction
122 Glass-fibre trailing-edge section
123 Skid shock absorber
124 Tail skid

125 Ventral fin construction
126 Gearbox/tail pylon mounting bulkhead
127 VOR aerial
128 Tailboom frame and stringer construction
129 Main rotor blade tip fairing
130 Blade tracking weights
131 Fuselage/tailcone production joint
132 Ventral hatch/emergency exit
133 Downward vision window
134 Cabin rear bulkhead
135 Aft cabin seating
136 Glass-fibre main undercarriage fairing
137 Hydraulic retraction jack
138 Shock absorber leg strut
139 Pivoted suspension main axle beam
140 Port navigation light
141 Port mainwheel

*This atmospheric shot of ALAT Pumas was taken during their deployment to the Gulf after the invasion of Kuwait in 1990. As well as the support role, the Puma carried out communications duties, one example – using a simplified version of the Orchidée system – being used for battlefield surveillance.*

# Bell AH-1 Huey Cobra

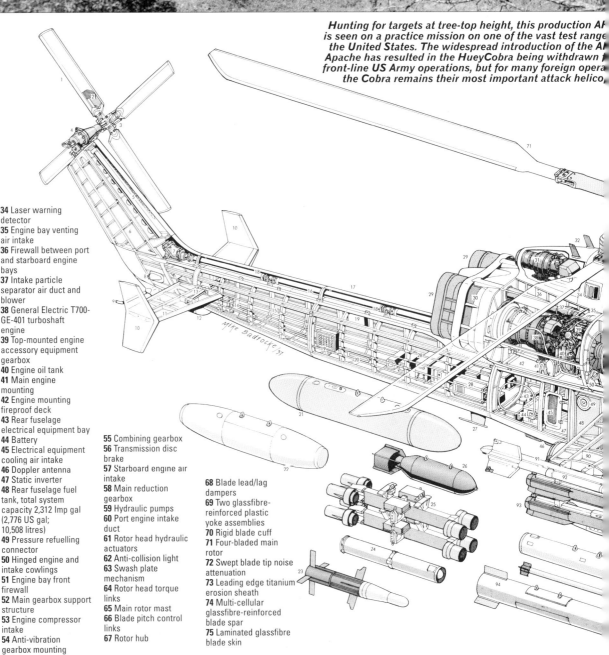

*Hunting for targets at tree-top height, this production AH[...] is seen on a practice mission on one of the vast test range[...] the United States. The widespread introduction of the A[...] Apache has resulted in the HueyCobra being withdrawn [...] front-line US Army operations, but for many foreign opera[...] the Cobra remains their most important attack helico[...]*

## AH-1(4B)W

**Cutaway key**
1 Four-bladed tail rotor
2 All-composite tail rotor blades
3 Pitch control links
4 Final drive right-angle gearbox
5 Angled drive shaft
6 Tail pylon structure
7 Angle-drive intermediate gearbox
8 Rear radar warning antenna
9 Tail protection skid
10 Endplate fins
11 Elevator
12 Ventral fin
13 Elevator hinge mounting
14 Control rod linkages
15 Tail boom frame and stringer structure
16 Tail rotor drive shaft
17 Detachable shaft housing
18 Shaft bearings and couplings
19 Rear chaff/flare launcher, port and starboard
20 Electro-luminescent external lighting strip
21 83.3 Imp gal (100 US gal; 379 litre) external fuel tank
22 83.3 Imp gal (100 US gal; 379 litre) napalm tank
23 BGM-71 TOW air-to-surface anti-armour missile
24 TOW missile container
25 Four-round TOW missile carrier/launcher
26 250-lb (113-kg) fragmentation bomb
27 Lower UHF/IFF antenna
28 Tail boom avionics equipment bay, access on port side
29 Infra-red suppression engine exhaust ducts
30 Exhaust cooling air intake
31 Auxiliary power unit (APU)
32 VHF homing antennae
33 Infra-red jammer

34 Laser warning detector
35 Engine bay venting air intake
36 Firewall between port and starboard engine bays
37 Intake particle separator air duct and blower
38 General Electric T700-GE-401 turboshaft engine
39 Top-mounted engine accessory equipment gearbox
40 Engine oil tank
41 Main engine mounting
42 Engine mounting fireproof deck
43 Rear fuselage electrical equipment bay
44 Battery
45 Electrical equipment cooling air intake
46 Doppler antenna
47 Static inverter
48 Rear fuselage fuel tank, total system capacity 2,312 Imp gal (2,776 US gal; 10,508 litres)
49 Pressure refuelling connector
50 Hinged engine and intake cowlings
51 Engine bay front firewall
52 Main gearbox support structure
53 Engine compressor intake
54 Anti-vibration gearbox mounting

55 Combining gearbox
56 Transmission disc brake
57 Starboard engine air intake
58 Main reduction gearbox
59 Hydraulic pumps
60 Port engine intake duct
61 Rotor head hydraulic actuators
62 Anti-collision light
63 Swash plate mechanism
64 Rotor head torque links
65 Main rotor mast
66 Blade pitch control links
67 Rotor hub

68 Blade lead/lag dampers
69 Two glassfibre-reinforced plastic yoke assemblies
70 Rigid blade cuff
71 Four-bladed main rotor
72 Swept blade tip noise attenuation
73 Leading edge titanium erosion sheath
74 Multi-cellular glassfibre-reinforced blade spar
75 Laminated glassfibre blade skin

*The Bell company endeared itself to the US Army with a succession of highly successful utility/transport helicopters. The AH-1G, seen in the foreground flying with a UH-1B (centre) and a UH-1D (rear), was radically different, yet used many components of the earlier UH-1 models.*

## SPECIFICATION

| | AH-1F HueyCobra | AH-1W SuperCobra |
|---|---|---|
| **Dimensions** | | |

**AH-1F HueyCobra**

**Dimensions**

**Length overall, rotors turning:** 53 ft 1 in (16.18 m)
**Fuselage length:** 44 ft 7 in (13.59 m)
**Main rotor diameter:** 44 ft (13.41 m)
**Tail rotor diameter:** 8 ft 6 in (2.59 m)
**Height to top of rotor head:** 13 ft 5 in (4.09 m)
**Main rotor disc area:** 1,520.23 sq ft (141.26 m²)
**Tail rotor disc area:** 56.75 sq ft (5.27 m²)
**Stabiliser span:** 6 ft 11 in (2.11 m)
**Skid track:** 7 ft (2.13 m)

**Powerplant**

One 1,800-shp (1342-kW) Textron Lycoming T53-L-703 turboshaft, transmission-limited to 1,290 shp (962 kW) for take-off and 1,134 shp (845 kW) for continuous running

**Weights**

**Operating weight:** 6,598 lb (2993 kg)
**Normal take-off:** 9,975 lb (4524 kg)
**Maximum take-off:** 10,000 lb (4536 kg)

**Performance**

**Never exceed speed in TOW configuration:** 195 mph (315 km/h)
**Maximum level speed at optimum altitude in TOW configuration:** 141 mph (227 km/h)
**Service ceiling:** 12,200 ft (3720 m)
**Range:** 315 miles (507 km)

**Armament**

Primary armament is the TOW missile, eight of which can be carried along with 2.75-in (70-mm) FFARs with a variety of warheads. Secondary armament is the M197 triple-barrelled 20-mm cannon in a chin turret

**AH-1W SuperCobra**

**Dimensions**

**Length overall, rotors turning:** 58 ft (17.68 m)
**Fuselage length:** 45 ft 6 in (13.87 m)
**Main rotor diameter:** 48 ft (14.63 m)
**Tail rotor diameter:** 9 ft 9 in (2.97 m)
**Height to top of rotor head:** 13 ft 6 in (4.11 m)
**Main rotor disc area:** 1,809.56 sq ft (168.11 m²)
**Tail rotor disc area:** 74.7 sq ft (6.94 m²)
**Stabiliser span:** 6 ft 11 in (2.11 m)
**Skid track:** 7 ft (2.13 m)

**Powerplant**

Two 1,625-shp (1212-kW) General Electric T700-GE-401 turboshafts, transmission-limited to a total of 2,032 shp (1515 kW) for take-off and 1,725 shp (1286 kW) continuous running

**Weights**

**Empty weight:** 10,200 lb (4627 kg)
**Maximum take-off:** 14,750 lb (6691 kg)

**Performance**

**Never exceed speed:** 219 mph (352 km/h)
**Maximum level speed 'clean' at sea level:** 175 mph (282 km/h)
**Service ceiling:** more than 12,200 ft (3720 m)
**Range:** 395 miles (635 km)

**Armament**

Uniquely qualified to carry both TOW and Hellfire, plus up to four seven-round LAU-69A rocket pods containing 2.75-in (70-mm) Hydra 70 rockets. Self-defence is provided by a single AIM-9L Sidewinder AAM mounted on a hardpoint above each wingtip

---

**76** Honeycomb trailing edge core structure
**77** Kevlar trailing edge spline
**78** Blade root attachment joint with provision for semi-automatic folding
**79** Upper UHF/IFF antenna
**80** Pitot head
**81** Cooling air grille
**82** Upper cable cutter
**83** Hydraulic filters
**84** Avionics equipment bay, access port and starboard
**85** Hydraulic equipment bay, air conditioning on port side

**90** All-composite stub wing structure
**91** Wingtip missile launch rail
**92** AIM-9L Sidewinder or Sidearm air-to-air missile
**93** AGM-114 Hellfire air-to-surface missiles
**94** CBU-55 fuel/air explosive weapon
**95** 2.75-in (70-mm) rocket
**96** LAU-68 seven-round rocket launcher
**97** GPU-2/A 20mm gun pod with 300-rounds
**98** Landing skid
**99** Four-round Hellfire missile carrier/launcher

**86** Cockpit air delivery duct
**87** Gravity fuel filler
**88** Stub wing attachment joints
**89** Stub wing fuel cell

**100** LAU-69 19-round rocket launcher
**101** Forward fuselage fuel tank

**102** Fuel tank bay kevlar composite armoured structure
**103** Forward chaff/flare launcher, port and starboard
**104** Control stability augmentation system actuators
**105** Front skid strut with aerodynamic fairing
**106** Ground handling wheel attachment points
**107** Forward fuselage equipment bay access door, port and starboard
**108** Boarding steps
**109** Flight control linkages
**110** TOW missile system avionics equipment
**111** Lower cable cutter
**112** Forward fuselage lateral equipment bay, port and starboard
**113** Pilot's cockpit armoured floor
**114** Yaw control rudder pedals
**115** Collective pitch control column
**116** Side console panel
**117** Starboard side pilot's entry hatch
**118** Circuit breaker panel
**119** Detachable shoulder armour
**120** Pilot's seat

**121** Armament and weapons display control handgrips; flight controls and weapons system can be operated from either cockpit
**122** Pilot's instrument console, full-colour CRT displays
**123** Cyclic pitch control lever
**124** ADF antenna
**125** Port wingtip missile installation
**126** Helmet-mounted sight provision for possible future integration
**127** Co-pilot/gunner's entry hatch open
**128** Single-piece curved windscreen panel
**129** Windscreen wire deflecting strakes
**130** Low-speed air data sensor
**131** Co-pilot/gunner's armoured seat
**132** Front cockpit instrument console
**133** CRT cockpit displays
**134** Front cockpit sidestick controller
**135** Ammunition feed chute
**136** Cannon ammunition magazine, 750 rounds
**137** Retractable landing light

**138** GE universal gun turret
**139** M197 three-barrel 20-mm rotary cannon
**140** Turret protection cable cutter
**141** Forward radar warning antenna, port and starboard
**142** Windscreen rain dispersal air duct
**143** Forward-looking infra-red (FLIR)
**144** Night targeting system turret
**145** High resolution FLIR dual field-of-view low-light television camera and laser rangefinder designator

# Boeing CH-47 Chinook

*The CH-47JA has radar, AAQ-16 FLIR and long-range tanks to increase greatly the operational capability of the type in JGSDF service. In addition to the Kyoiku Sien Hiko-tai at Akeno, CH-47JAs serve with the JGSDF's Dai 1 Konsei-Dan and Dai 1 Herikoputa-dan. The Seibu Homen Herikoputa-tai (Western Army Helicopter Squadron) has, in 1999, begun to receive this advanced variant to replace the KV-107-II.*

## CH-47D Chinook

**Cutaway key**

1 Pitot tubes
2 Forward lighting
3 Nose compartment access hatch
4 Vibration absorber
5 IFF aerial
6 Windscreen panels
7 Windscreen wipers
8 Instrument panel shroud
9 Rudder pedals
10 Yaw sensing ports
11 Downward vision window
12 Pilot's footboards
13 Collective pitch control
14 Cyclic pitch control column
15 Co-pilot's seat
16 Centre instrument console
17 Pilot's seat
18 Glideslope indicator
19 Forward transmission housing fairing
20 Cockpit overhead window
21 Doorway from main cabin
22 Cockpit emergency exit doors
23 Sliding side window panel
24 Cockpit bulkhead
25 Vibration absorber
26 Cockpit door release handle
27 Radio and electronics racks
28 Sloping bulkhead
29 Stick boost actuators
30 Stability augmentation system actuators
31 Forward transmission mounting structure
32 Windscreen washer bottle
33 Rotor control hydraulic jack
34 Forward transmission gearbox
35 Rotor head fairing
36 Forward rotor head mechanism

37 Pitch change control levers
38 Blade drag dampers
39 Glassfibre rotor blades
40 Titanium leading-edge capping with de-icing provision
41 Rescue hoist/winch
42 Forward transmission aft fairing
43 Hydraulic system modules
44 Control levers
45 Front fuselage frame and stringer construction
46 Emergency exit window, main entry door on starboard side
47 Forward end of cargo floor
48 Fuel tank fuselage side fairing
49 Battery
50 Electrical system equipment bay
51 Aerial cable
52 Stretcher rack (up to 24 stretchers)
53 Cabin window panel
54 Cabin heater duct outlet
55 Troop seats stowed against cabin wall

56 Cabin roof transmission and control run tunnel
57 Formation-keeping lights
58 Rotor blade cross section
59 Static dischargers
60 Blade balance and tracking weights pocket
61 Leading-edge anti-erosion strip
62 Fixed tab
63 Fuselage skin plating
64 Maintenance walkway
65 Transmission tunnel access doors
66 Troop seating, up to 44 troops
67 Cargo hook access hatch

68 VOR aerial
69 Cabin lining panels
70 Control runs
71 Main transmission shaft
72 Shaft couplings
73 Centre fuselage construction
74 Centre aisle seating (optional)
75 Main cargo floor, 1,440-cu ft (40.78-m³) cargo volume
76 Ramp-down 'dam' for waterborne operations
77 Ramp hydraulic jack
78 Engine bevel drive gearbox
79 Transmission combining gearbox
80 Rotor brake
81 Transmission oil tank
82 Oil cooler
83 Engine drive shaft fairing

84 Engine screen
85 Starboard engine nacelle
86 Cooling air grilles
87 Tail rotor pylon construction
88 Hydraulic equipment
89 Access door
90 Maintenance step
91 Tail rotor drive shaft
92 Tail rotor bearing mounting
93 Rotor head fairing

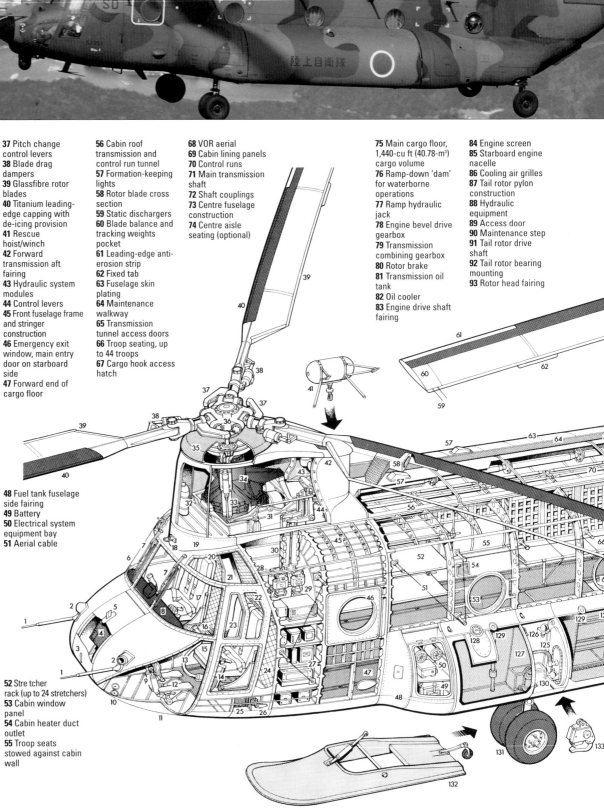

*The ultimate expression of the Special Forces Chinook is the MH-47E, a purpose-built version for the US Army. Dripping with defensive avionics and low-level night penetration aids, the MH-47E also introduced a 'glass' cockpit, and bulged 'saddle' tanks based on those developed for the Model 234LR Commercial Chinook.*

**94** Tail rotor head mechanism
**95** Main rotor blades, glassfibre construction
**96** Rotor control hydraulic jack
**97** Vibration absorber
**98** Pylon aft fairing construction
**99** Rear lighting
**100** Solar T62T-2B auxiliary power unit
**101** APU-driven generators
**102** Maintenance walkways
**103** Engine exhaust duct
**104** Avco Lycoming T55-L-712 turboshaft engine
**105** Detachable engine cowlings
**106** Aft fuselage frame and stringer construction
**107** Rear cargo doorway
**108** Ramp extensions
**109** Cargo ramp, lowered
**110** Ramp ventral strake
**111** Fuselage side fairing aft extension
**112** Ramp control lever
**113** Ramp hydraulic jack
**114** Rear landing gear shock absorber
**115** Landing gear leg strut
**116** Single rear wheels
**117** Rear wheel optional ski fitting
**118** Maintenance steps
**119** Rear fuel tank
**120** Fuel tank interconnections
**121** Ventral strake
**122** Main fuel tank; total system capacity 1,030 US gal (3899 litres)
**123** Floor beam construction
**124** Fuel tank attachment joint
**125** Fuel system piping
**126** Fire extinguishers
**127** Forward fuel tank
**128** Fuel filler caps
**129** Fuel capacity transmitters
**130** Front landing-gear mounting
**131** Twin forward wheels
**132** Forward wheels optional ski-fitting
**133** Triple cargo hook system; forward and rear hooks 20,000-lb (9072-kg) capacity
**134** Main cargo hook, 28,000-lb (12701-kg) capacity

## SPECIFICATION

### CH-47D Chinook

**Dimensions**

**Length overall, rotors turning:** 98 ft 10¾ in (30.14 m)
**Fuselage:** 51 ft (15.54 m)
**Height to top of rear rotor head:** 18 ft 11 in (5.77 m)
**Wheel track:** 10 ft 6 in (3.20 m)
**Wheel base:** 22 ft 6 in (6.86 m)
**Rotor diameter:** 60 ft (18.29 m)
**Rotor disc area:** 5,654.86 sq ft (525.34 m²)

**Powerplant**

Two Textron Lycoming T55-L-712 turboshafts each rated at 3,750 shp (2796 kW) for take-off and 3,000 shp (2237 kW) for continuous running, or two Textron Lycoming T55-L-712 SSB turboshafts each rated at 4,378 shp (3264 kW) for take-off and 3,137 shp (2339 kW) for continuous running, in both cases driving a transmission rated at 7,500 shp (5593 kW) on two engines and 4,600 shp (3430 kW) on one engine

**Weights**

**Empty:** 22,379 lb (10151 kg)
**Normal take-off:** 46,000 lb (20866 kg)

**Maximum take-off:** 50,000 lb (22679 kg)

**Fuel and load**

**Internal fuel:** 1,030 US gal (3899 litres)
**External fuel:** None
**Maximum payload:** 22,798 lb (10341 kg)

**Range**

**Ferry range:** 1,093 nm (1,259 miles; 2026 km)
**Operational radius with maximum internal and maximum external payloads respectively:** Between 100 and 30 nm (115 and 35 miles; 185 and 56 km)

**Performance**

**Maximum level speed at sea level:** 161 kt (185 mph; 298 km/h)
**Maximum cruising speed at optimum altitude:** 138 kt (159 mph; 256 km/h)
**Maximum rate of climb at sea level:** 2,195 ft (669 m) per minute
**Service ceiling:** 22,100 ft (6735 m)
**Hovering ceiling:** 10,550 ft (3215 m)

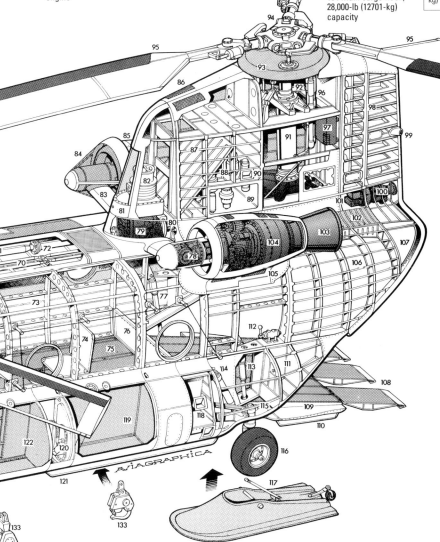

*A Dutch CH-47D repositions a tactical vehicle during manoeuvres. Equipped with EFIS cockpit, nose radar and T55-L-714 engines, the Dutch Chinooks are among the most advanced in service. The first seven were converted from ex-Canadian CH-147s.*

# Kamov Ka-25/Ka-27

*Civil versions of the 'Helix' are designated Ka-32 by Kamov. The models are often simplified military versions lacking any offensive equipment and radar. This particular example is a Ka-32T (wearing Aeroflot airline markings), a variant which has been heavily marketed in the US. Despite its low purchase price of US$3 million however, the Ka-32 series has yet to make a real impact on the civil market.*

### Ka-29TB 'Helix-B'

**Cutaway key**

1 Pitch and yaw vanes
2 Dual pitot heads
3 Air data instrumentation boom
4 Ventral periscope sighting unit and FLIR
5 Retractable landing lamps
6 Instrumentation and autostabilisation equipment racks
7 ECM antenna
8 Gun compartment hinged door, open
9 Flexibly-mounted 7.62-mm four-barrel Gatling gun
10 Rear view mirror, port and starboard
11 Armoured windscreen panels
12 Weapons Systems Officer sighting unit
13 Windscreen wipers
14 Outside temperature gauge
15 Weapons control panel
16 Gunner's periscope sight
17 Remote gun controller
18 Pilot's head-up display
19 Cyclic pitch control column
20 Instrument panel
21 Radar warning antenna
22 Yaw control rudder pedals
23 Radar director unit for AT-6 Spiral missile
24 Cockpit armour panelling
25 Nose undercarriage torque scissor links
26 Nose wheel rebound position
27 Steerable nose wheel
28 Shock absorber leg strut
29 Cockpit floor level
30 Collective pitch control lever and throttle
31 Pilot's seat
32 Sliding cockpit door
33 Centre control pedestal
34 Gunner's folding seat
35 Cockpit bulkhead doorway
36 IFF aerial
37 Overhead switch panel
38 Starboard split cabin door, upper segment, open
39 Engine air intakes, bleed air de-iced
40 Control rod linkages
41 Cockpit door rail
42 Pilot's shoulder armour
43 ECM antenna
44 Avionics equipment racks
45 Battery compartment
46 Step
47 Lower fuselage strake
48 Fuselage chine member
49 Underfloor fuel cells; maximum capacity 8,113 lb (3680 kg)
50 Stub wing pylon assembly support struts
51 Seat mounting rails
52 Cabin window panel
53 Engine bay armoured panel
54 Isotov TV3-117BK turboshaft engine
55 Engine accessory equipment gearbox
56 Generator
57 Engine bay firewall
58 Oil tank access panels
59 Generator cooling air scoop
60 Glass/carbon fibre D-section rotor blade spar
61 Honeycomb core trailing-edge pockets
62 Composite skin panelling
63 Hinged engine cowling/work platform
64 Starboard engine exhaust duct
65 Rotor head hydraulic actuators
66 Lower rotor swashplate mechanism
67 Articulated rotor hub
68 Blade pitch control rods
69 Upper/lower rotor (interconnecting)
70 Upper rotor swash plate mechanism
71 Blade pitch control links and rods
72 Upper rotor articulated hub
73 Blade-folding hinge joints, manual
74 Three-bladed, coaxial, contra-rotating main rotors
75 Electro-thermal leading-edge de-icing
76 Vibration-damping pendulum weights, lower rotor only
77 Blade root attachment fittings
78 Radar warning antenna
79 Maintenance handgrips
80 Cooling air louvres
81 Oil cooler fan
82 Rotor brake
83 Gearbox mounting struts
84 Port engine lateral exhaust
85 Engine/gearbox coupling shaft
86 Central combining and main reduction gearbox
87 Cabin fresh air scoop
88 Gearbox sump fairing
89 Folding troop seats along cabin wall (12)
90 Gearbox mounting fuselage double main frames
91 Cabin floor panelling
92 Main undercarriage leg shock absorber strut
93 Gravity fuel filler
94 Central underfloor internal weapons bay ([torpedoes, depth charges, etc.)
95 Split main cabin door, upper segment
96 Air intake grilles
97 Auxiliary Power Unit (APU)
98 Cabin heater
99 ESM 'Flower Pot' antenna
100 Anti-collision light
101 Rear avionics equipment racks
102 Cabin rear bulkhead
103 Tailcone joint frame
104 'Hot Brick' infra-red jammer
105 Radar warning antenna
106 Tailcone frame and stringer construction
107 Communications aerial
108 Starboard tailplane
109 Radar warning antenna
110 Starboard elevator
111 Rudder control linkage
112 Tailfin fixed leading-edge slat
113 Starboard tailfin
114 Starboard rudder
115 Upper rotor blades [folded position]
116 Blade locking struts
117 Lower rotor blades [folded position]
118 IFF aerial
119 ESM antenna fairing
120 Aft radome
121 Port rudder
122 Rudder composite construction
123 Fin/tailplane joint rib
124 Port navigation light
125 UB-32 rocket pod
126 2¼-in (57-mm) rocket projectiles
127 Port fin leading-edge slat

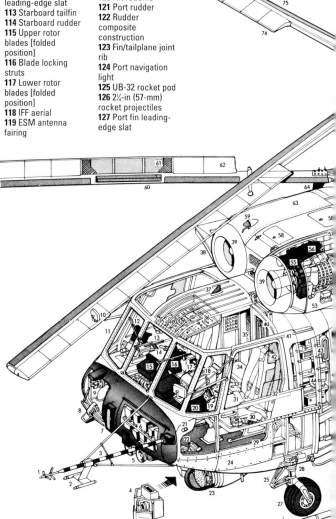

## SPECIFICATION

### Ka-25BSh 'Hormone-A'

**Dimensions**

**Fuselage length:** 32 ft (9.75 m)
**Height overall:** 17 ft 5 in (5.37 m)
**Stabiliser span including endplate surfaces:** 12 ft 4 in (3.76 m)
**Wheel track:** 4 ft 7½ in (1.41 m) for the front unit and 11 ft 6½ in (3.52 m) for the rear unit
**Rotor diameter (each):** 52 ft 7¾ in (15.74 m)
**Rotor disc area:** 4,188.83 sq ft (389.15 m²)

**Powerplant**

Two OMKB Isotov (Glushenkov) GTD-3F turboshafts each rated at 898 shp (671 kW) in early helicopters, or two OMKB Isotov (Glushenkov) GTD-3BM turboshafts each rated at 900 shp (738 kW) in late helicopters

**Performance**

**Maximum speed 'clean' at optimum altitude:** 130 mph (209 km/h)

**Normal cruising speed at optimum altitude:** 120 mph (193 km/h)
**Ferry range with auxiliary fuel:** 404 miles (650 km)
**Range with standard fuel:** 249 miles (400 km)

**Weights**

**Empty:** 10,505 lb (4765 kg)
**Maximum take-off:** 16,534 lb (7500 kg)
**Maximum payload:** 2,866 lb (1300 kg)

**Armament**

Armament is not normally carried although the helicopter can be fitted with a long 'coffin-like' weapons bay which runs along the belly from the radome back to the tailboom, and small bombs or depth charges can be carried on tiny pylons just aft of the nosewheels. The underfuselage weapons bay can carry a variety of weapons, including nuclear depth charges. When wire-guided torpedoes are carried, a wire reel is mounted on the port side of the forward fuselage

*This Ka-25BSh 'Hormone-A' (displaying the flag of the Soviet navy) is bereft of flotation gear, fuel tanks and all the usual ASW equipment. In this configuration, the Ka-25 can carry a useful load of freight or 12 passengers, enabling it to perform an important secondary ship-to-shore transport role. Throughout the Cold War years, 'Hormones' were often seen shadowing NATO warships for intelligence-gathering purposes. For this role, a photographer would hang out of the main cabin door to record images of the warship of interest.*

**128** Tailplane bracing strut
**129** Horizontal tailplane construction
**130** Tailplane mounting bulkhead
**131** Rear navigation avionics equipment bay
**132** Twin gyromagnetic compass unit

**133** Pressure refuelling connection
**134** Ground power socket
**135** Ventral weapons bay loading doors, open

**136** Chaff/flare dispenser housing, port and starboard
**137** Split cabin door lower segment

**138** Integral boarding steps
**139** External fuel tank
**140** Fixed blade tab

**141** Spiral missile launch tubes
**142** Missile pylon adaptor

**143** UPK-23 twin barrel, 23-mm cannon pod
**144** AT-6 'Spiral' command guidance air-to-surface missile
**145** Mainwheel rebound position
**146** Port fixed mainwheel
**147** Mainwheel forks
**148** Main undercarriage leg strut
**149** Upper and lower wishbone links
**150** Pylon stub wing
**151** Fixed stores pylons

**152** UB-20 rocket pods
**153** 3.15-in (80-mm) rocket projectiles

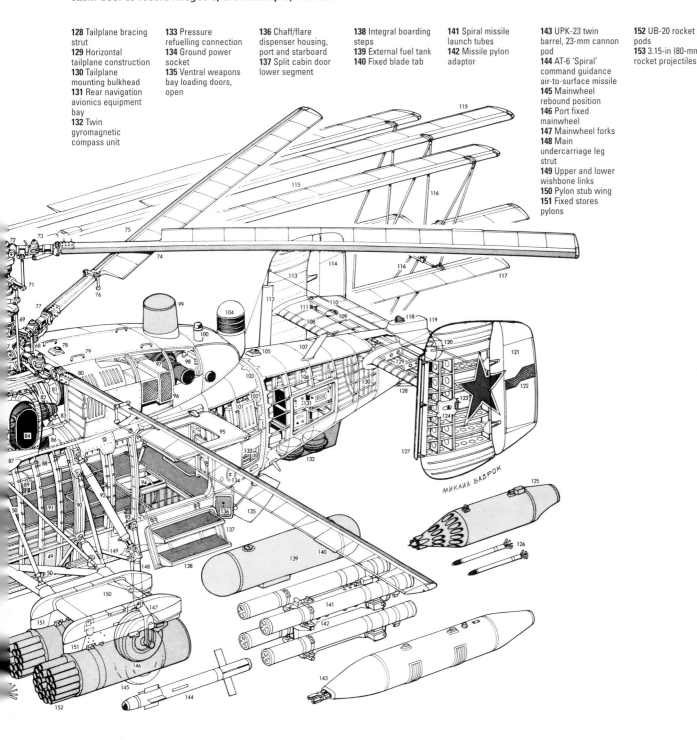

# McDonnell Douglas AH-64 Apache

### AH-64A Apache
**Cutaway key**
1 Night systems sensor scanner
2 Pilot's Night Vision System (PNVS)
3 Electro-optical target designation and night sensor systems turret
4 Target Acquisition and Designation System (TADS) daylight scanner
5 Azimuth motor housing
6 TADS/PNVS swivelling turret
7 Turret drive motor housing
8 Sensor turret mounting
9 Rear-view mirror
10 Nose compartment access hatches
11 Remote terminal unit
12 Signal data converter
13 Co-pilot/gunner's yaw control rudder pedals
14 Forward radar warning antenna
15 M230E1 Chain Gun barrel
16 Fuselage sponson fairing
17 Avionics cooling air ducting
18 Boron armoured cockpit flooring
19 Co-pilot/gunner's 'fold down' control column
20 Weapons control panel
21 Instrument panel shroud
22 Windscreen wiper
23 Co-pilot/gunner's armoured windscreen
24 Head-down sighting system viewfinder
25 Pilot's armoured windscreen panel
26 Windscreen wiper
27 Co-pilot/gunner's Kevlar armoured seat
28 Safety harness
29 Side console panel
30 Engine power levels
31 Avionics equipment bays, port and starboard
32 Avionics bay access door
33 Collective pitch control lever
34 Adjustable crash-resistant seat mouldings
35 Pilot's rudder pedals
36 Cockpit side window panel
37 Pilot's instrument console
38 Inter-cockpit acrylic blast shield
39 Starboard side window entry hatches
40 Rocket launcher pack
41 Starboard wing stores pylon
42 Cockpit roof glazing
43 Instrument panel shroud
44 Pilot's Kevlar armoured seat
45 Collective pitch control lever
46 Side console panel
47 Engine power levers
48 Rear cockpit floor level
49 Main landing gear shock absorber mounting
50 Linkless ammunition feed chute
51 Forward fuel tank: total fuel capacity 312 Imp gal (1419 litres)
52 Control rod linkages
53 Cockpit ventilating air louvres
54 Display adjustment panel
55 Grab handles/ maintenance steps
56 Control system hydraulic actuators (three)
57 Ventilating air intake
58 UHF aerial
59 Starboard stub wing
60 Main rotor blade
61 Laminated blade-root attachment joints
62 Vibration absorbers
63 Blade pitch bearing housing
64 Air data sensor mast
65 Rotor hub unit
66 Offset flapping hinges
67 Elastomeric lead/lag dampers
68 Blade pitch control rod
69 Pitch control swashplate
70 Main rotor mast
71 Airturbine starter/ auxiliary power unit (APU) input shaft
72 Rotor head control mixing linkages
73 Gearbox mounting plate
74 Transmission oil coolers, port and starboard
75 Rotor brake
76 Main gearbox

*This Apache is one of those operated by the US Army's 1st Aviation Training Brigade, located at Ft Rucker, Alabama – the home of US Army aviation. All training helicopters based at Ft Rucker wear large white identification codes. Students who have graduated onto the AH-64 from basic flying training join the 1-14 AVN for the 12 week conversion course. They first learn all about basic aircraft systems before progressing onto advanced flying training and weapons familiarisation. Increasing numbers of foreign air crew are now travelling to Ft Rucker for their Apache training.*

*The Apache's performance during Operation Desert Storm persuaded several nations, such as Greece, the UK and the Netherlands, to finally accelerate their search for a new attack helicopter – while existing customers (such as Saudi Arabia and the UAE) came back for more. Over 200 Apaches have now been exported.*

## SPECIFICATION

### AH-64A Apache
(unless otherwise noted)

#### Dimensions

**Fuselage length including both rotors turning:**
58 ft 3⅛ in (17.76 m)
**Main rotor diameter:** 48 ft (14.63 m)
**Tail rotor diameter:** 9 ft 2 in (2.79 m)
**Height over tail rotor:** 14 ft 1¼ in (4.30 m)
**Total height AH-64D:** 16 ft 3 in (4.95 m)
**Main rotor disc area:** 1,809.5 sq ft (168.11 m²)
**Tail rotor disc area:** 66 sq ft (6.13 m²)
**Wingspan:** 17 ft 2 in (5.23 m)
**Tailplane span:** 11 ft 2 in (3.4 m)
**Wheelbase:** 34 ft 9 in (10.59 m)
**Wheel track:** 6 ft 8 in (2.03 m)
**Main rotor ground clearance (turning):** 11 ft 9¼ in (3.59 m²)

#### Powerplant

Two 1,696-shp (1265-kW) General Electric T700-GE-701 turboshafts, each derated for normal operations or, from 604th helicopter, two General Electric T700-GE-701C turboshafts, each rated at 1,890 shp (1409 kW)
**AH-64D:** two General Electric T700-GE-701C turboshafts, each rated at 1,800 shp (1342 kW)

#### Weights

**Empty:** 11,387 lb (5165 kg)
**AH-64D:** 11,800 lb (5352 kg)
**Normal take-off for primary mission:** 14,445 lb (6552 kg)
**Design mission weight:** 17,650 lb (8006 kg)
**Maximum external stores:** 1,700 lb (772 kg)
**Maximum take-off:** 21,000 lb (9525 kg)

#### Fuel and load

**Internal fuel:** 2,550 lb (1157 kg)
**External fuel (four Brunswick tanks):** 2,712 lb (5980 kg)

#### Performance

**Maximum level and cruising speed:** 158 kt (182 mph; 293 km/h)
**AH-64D:** 141 kt (162 mph; 261 km/h)
**Never-exceed speed:** 197 kt (227 mph; 365 km/h)
**Maximum rate of climb at sea level:** 3,240 ft (990 m) per minute
**AH-64D:** 3,090 ft (942 m) per minute
**Maximum vertical rate of climb at sea level:** 2,500 ft (762 m) per minute
**AH-64D:** 1,555 ft (474 m) per minute
**Service ceiling:** 21,000 ft (6400 m)
**Service ceiling, one engine out:** 10,800 ft (3290 m)
**Hovering ceiling:** 15,000 ft (4570 m)
**AH-64D:** 13,500 ft (4115 m)

#### Range

**Maximum range, internal fuel only:** 260 nm (300 miles; 482 km)
**AH-64D:** 220 nm (253 miles; 407 km)
**Ferry range, max internal and external fuel in still air:** 1,024 nm (1,180 miles; 1899 km)

#### Armament

**Maximum ordnance:** some 1,700 lb (771 kg) of ordnance can be carried by the Apache. One McDonnell Douglas M230 30-mm Chain Gun is located between the mainwheel legs in an underfuselage mounting. Normal rate of fire is 625 rds/min of HE (high-explosive) or HEDP (high-explosive, dual-purpose) ammunition, with a maximum load of 1,200 rounds. There are four underwing hardpoints, upon which can be carried 16 Rockwell AGM-114A Hellfire anti-tank missiles or up to 77 2.75-in (70-mm) FFAR (folding fin aircraft rockets) in their launchers, or a combination of Hellfires and FFAR. Planned modifications include two extra hardpoints for four Stinger, four Mistral or two Sidewinder missiles for an air-defence role. The co-pilot has responsibility for firing the gun and missiles, but the pilot can override his controls in the event of an emergency.

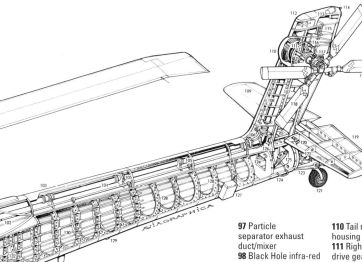

77 Gearbox mounting struts
78 Generator
79 Input shaft from port engine
80 Gearbox mounting deck
81 Tail rotor control rod linkage
82 Ammunition magazine
83 Stub wing attachment joints
84 Engine transmission gearbox
85 Air intake
86 Engine integral oil tank
87 General Electric T-700-GE-701 turboshaft
88 Intake particle separator
89 Engine accessory equipment gearbox
90 Oil cooler plenum
91 Gas turbine starter/auxiliary power unit
92 Starboard engine cowling panels/fold-down maintenance platform
93 Starboard engine exhaust ducts
94 APU exhaust
95 Pneumatic system and environmental control equipment
96 Cooling air exhaust louvres

97 Particle separator exhaust duct/mixer
98 Black Hole infra-red suppressors
99 Hydraulic reservoir
100 Gearbox/engine bay tail fairings
101 Internal maintenance platform
102 Tail rotor control rod
103 Spine shaft housing
104 Tail rotor transmission shaft
105 Shaft bearings and couplings
106 Bevel drive intermediate gearbox
107 Fin/rotor pylon construction
108 Tail rotor drive shafts
109 All-moving tailplane

110 Tail rotor gearbox housing
111 Right-angle final drive gearbox
112 Fin tip aerial fairing
113 Rear radar warning antennas
114 Tail navigation light
115 Cambered trailing-edge section (directional stability)
116 Tail rotor pitch actuator
117 Tail rotor hub mechanism
118 Asymmetric (noise attenuation) tail rotor blades
119 Tailplane construction
120 Tailplane pivot bearing
121 Castoring tailwheel
122 Tailwheel shock absorber
123 Tailwheel yoke attachment

124 Handgrips/maintenance steps
125 Tailplane control hydraulic jack
126 Fin/rotor pylon attachment joint
127 Chaff and flare dispenser
128 Tailboom ring frames
129 Ventral radar warning aerial
130 Tailcone frame and stringer construction
131 UHF aerial
132 ADF loop aerial
133 ADF sense aerial
134 Access hatch
135 Handgrips/maintenance steps
136 Radio and electronics equipment bay
137 Rear fuel tank
138 Reticulated foam fire suppressant tank bay linings
139 VHF aerial
140 Main rotor blade stainless steel spars (five)
141 Glassfibre sparlinings
142 Honeycomb trailing-edge panel
143 Glassfibre blade skins
144 Trailing-edge fixed tab
145 Swept-blade tip fairing
146 Static discharger
147 Stub wing trailing-edge flap

148 Stub wing rib construction
149 Twin spar booms
150 Port navigation and strobe lights
151 Port wing stores pylons
152 Rocket pack: 19 x 2.75-in (70-mm) FFAR rockets
153 Rockwell Hellfire AGM-114 anti-tank missiles
154 Missile launch rails
155 Fuselage sponson aft fairing
156 Boarding step
157 Port mainwheel
158 Main landing gear leg strut
159 Shock absorber strut
160 Boarding steps
161 Main landing gear leg pivot fixing
162 Ammunition feed and cartridge case return chutes
163 Gun swivelling mounting
164 Azimuth control mounting frame
165 Hughes M230E1 Chain Gun 30-mm cannon
166 Blast suppression cannon muzzle

# Mil Mi-8/9/17 'Hip'

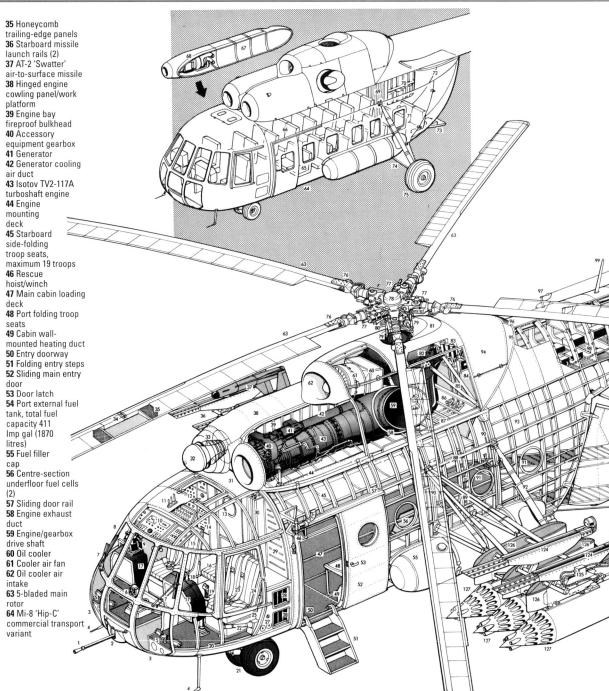

*Fitted with a Doppler navigation box beneath th[e] tailboom, this Mi-8T belongs to the Karinès Oro Pajègo[s] (Lithuanian air force) and was one of three acquire[d] shortly after the air arm was established in 1993. On[e] example was destroyed in an accident and the remainin[g] two examples serve with 13 Squadron at Zoknia[i].*

## Mi-8TB 'Hip-E'

**Cutaway key**

1 0.5-in (12.7-mm) machine-gun barrel
2 Flexible gun mounting
3 Downward vision windows
4 Pitot heads
5 Yaw control rudder pedals
6 Gunsight
7 Windscreen wipers
8 Windscreen panels
9 Weapons Systems Officer's sighting unit
10 Overhead switch panels
11 'Odd-Rods' IFF aerials
12 Cockpit roof escape hatch
13 Main cabin doorway
14 Radio and electrical equipment racks
15 Co-pilot/Weapons Systems Officer's armoured seat
16 Gunner's folding seat
17 Instrument consoles
18 Stand-by compass
19 Cyclic pitch control column
20 Cockpit floor level
21 Twin nosewheels
22 Collective pitch control lever
23 Safety harness
24 Pilot's armoured seat
25 Adjustable seat mounting
26 Sliding cockpit side-window panel
27 Ground power and intercom sockets
28 Batteries (2)
29 Cockpit rear bulkhead
30 Control rod ducting
31 Engine air intake
32 Anti-ingestion intake guard
33 Internal particle separator
34 Main rotor blade hollow steel spar boom
35 Honeycomb trailing-edge panels
36 Starboard missile launch rails (2)
37 AT-2 'Swatter' air-to-surface missile
38 Hinged engine cowling panel/work platform
39 Engine bay fireproof bulkhead
40 Accessory equipment gearbox
41 Generator
42 Generator cooling air duct
43 Isotov TV2-117A turboshaft engine
44 Engine mounting deck
45 Starboard side-folding troop seats, maximum 19 troops
46 Rescue hoist/winch
47 Main cabin loading deck
48 Port folding troop seats
49 Cabin wall-mounted heating duct
50 Entry doorway
51 Folding entry steps
52 Sliding main entry door
53 Door latch
54 Port external fuel tank, total fuel capacity 411 Imp gal (1870 litres)
55 Fuel filler cap
56 Centre-section underfloor fuel cells (2)
57 Sliding door rail
58 Engine exhaust duct
59 Engine/gearbox drive shaft
60 Oil cooler
61 Cooler air fan
62 Oil cooler air intake
63 5-bladed main rotor
64 Mi-8 'Hip-C' commercial transport variant

*Above: The Eesti Piirivalve (Estonian Border Guard) acquired four Mi-8s (three ex-Luftwaffe and one ex-East German civil) in November 1995. This Mi-8T is one of two which have been updated with new radar, IR sensor and hoist to make them more effective in the SAR role; the other two are in storage, awaiting funds for upgrade.*

## SPECIFICATION

### Mi-8T 'Hip-C'

#### Dimensions

**Length (rotors turning):** 82 ft 9¾ in (25.24 m)
**Fuselage length:** 59 ft 7⅓ in (18.17 m)
**Main rotor diameter:** 69 ft 10¼ in (21.29 m)
**Tail rotor diameter:** 12 ft 10 in (3.91 m)
**Main rotor disc area:** 3,832.08 sq ft (356.00 m²)
**Tail rotor disc area:** 129.25 sq ft (12.01 m²)
**Height overall:** 18 ft 6½ in (5.65 m)
**Wheel base:** 13 ft 11¾ in (4.26 m)
**Wheel track:** 14 ft 9 in (4.50 m)

#### Powerplant

Two Klimov (Isotov) TV2-117A turboshafts each rated at 1,481 shp (1104 kW)

#### Weights

**Typical empty:** 15,784 lb (7160 kg)
**Normal take-off:** 24,471 lb (11100 kg)
**Maximum take-off:** 26,455 lb (12000 kg)

#### Fuel load

**Standard fuel load:** 494 US gal (1870 litres)
**External fuel load:** 258 US gal (980 litres)

#### Performance

**Maximum level speed at sea level:** 134 kt (155 mph; 250 km/h)
**Maximum rate-of-climb at sea level:** 14 ft 8¾ in (4.50 m) per second
**Service ceiling:** 14,760 ft (4500 m)
**Hover ceiling (IGE):** 6,235 ft (1900 m)
**Hover ceiling (OGE):** 2,625 ft (800 m)
**Ferry range:** 501 nm (577 miles; 930 km)
**Radius of action:** 188 nm (217 miles; 350 km)

#### Armament

Outriggers carry four pylons each capable of carrying a UV-16-57, a UV-32-57 rocket pod or alternatively each pylon can carry a bomb of up to 551 lb (250 kg)

**65** Cabin window panels
**66** 4-abreast passenger seating (28 passengers)
**67** Starboard external fuel tank
**68** Optional air-conditioning plant
**69** Wardrobe
**70** Baggage stowage
**71** Emergency exit window hatch, port and starboard
**72** Rear entry hatch
**73** Rear airstairs
**74** Main undercarriage hinged axle beam

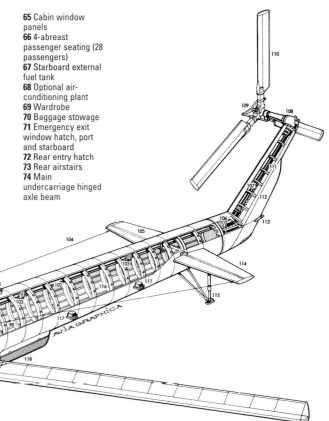

*East Germany, like most Warsaw Pact states, obtained Mi-8s/17s. This Mi-8TB was operated by that nation's Volksmarine and was fitted with three pylons on each side of the fuselage. After German re-unification, the Marineflieger continued to operate the type until the mid-1990s.*

**75** Port mainwheel
**76** Blade root attachment joints
**77** Hydraulic drag dampers
**78** Rotor head hydraulic reservoir
**79** Blade pitch control rods
**80** Swash plate mechanism
**81** Rotor head tail fairing
**82** Main reduction gearbox
**83** Rotor head hydraulic control jacks (3)
**84** Fuel system collector and feed tank
**85** Gearbox mounting struts
**86** Control rod linkages
**87** Gearbox mounting deck

**88** Fuselage upper longeron
**89** External stores pylon mounting struts
**90** Gearbox mounting fuselage main frames
**91** Cabin window panels
**92** Main undercarriage shock absorber leg strut
**93** Fuselage frame and stringer construction
**94** Control system access hatch
**95** Engine/gearbox aft fairing
**96** Cooling air exit louvres
**97** Aerial mast
**98** Radio communications and navigation equipment
**99** HVF aerial

**100** Tailboom attachment joint ring frame
**101** Anti-collision light
**102** Tail rotor transmission shaft
**103** Shaft bearings
**104** HF aerial cable
**105** Starboard variable-incidence tailplane
**106** Bevel drive gearbox
**107** Tail rotor drive shaft
**108** Final drive right-angle gearbox
**109** Tail rotor pitch control mechanism
**110** 3-bladed tail rotor
**111** Tail rotor pylon
**112** Pylon tail fairing
**113** Tail navigation light
**114** Port variable-incidence tailplane

**115** Fixed tail bumper
**116** Tailboom frame and stringer construction
**117** Radio altimeter aerials
**118** Doppler aerial fairing
**119** Aft clamshell doors, open
**120** Door hydraulic jacks
**121** Vehicle loading ramps
**122** Ramp toe-plate
**123** AT-2 'Swatter' air-to-surface missile
**124** Missile launch rails
**125** Missile fire control unit
**126** Port stores pylons (3)
**127** UV-32-57 rocket launcher, 32 x 57-mm folding fin rockets

# Mil Mi-24 'Hind'

*In addition to its normal underwing load of rocket pods and guided-missiles, the 'Hind' is capable of carrying a variety of stores including bombs, napalm tanks and fuel tanks, as illustrated by these Czech 'Hind-Es'.*

## Mi-24RCh & -24K 'Hind-G1 & G-2'

### Cutaway key

1 Remotely-controlled camera (Mi-24K) mounted beneath nose cannon barbette
2 Hinged lens cover
3 Low-speed precision airflow sensors
4 Air data sensor boom
5 IFF antenna
6 Armoured windscreen panel
7 Windscreen wiper
8 Gunsight
9 Pitot heads
10 Turret mechanism access doors
11 Ammunition feed mechanism
12 Four-barrelled 9-A-624 12.7-mm rotary machine-gun with 1,470 rounds
13 Gun turret; ±20° traverse and +20°/-60° elevation/depression
14 Radar warning antenna
15 Retractable landing lamp
16 Boarding step
17 Kick-in steps
18 Oxygen bottle
19 Weapons Systems Officer (WSO) hatch
20 Collective pitch control column, flying controls duplicate in front cockpit
21 WSO's seat
22 Safety harness
23 Side console panel
24 WSO's hatch, open position
25 Cabin-mounted camera pallet (Mi-24K)
26 Hinged lens aperture, replaces starboard cabin door
27 Film magazine
28 Cabin-mounted data-link console (Mi-24RCh)
29 Pilot's entry door, open position
30 Armoured windscreen panel
31 Windscreen wiper
32 Head-up-display
33 Instrument panel shroud
34 Cyclic pitch control column
35 Yaw control rudder pedals
36 Underfloor control linkages
37 Search light
38 Nosewheel leg door and indicator light
39 Levered suspension axle beam
40 Aft-retracting twin nosewheels
41 Conditioned air ducting (ammunition magazine on starboard side)
42 Nosewheel bay (semi-retracted housing)
43 Cockpit section armoured skin panelling
44 Cyclic pitch control lever
45 Fuel cocks
46 Circuit-breaker panel
47 Oxygen bottle
48 Rear view mirror
49 Pilot's seat
50 Engine air intake vortex-type dust/debris extractors
51 Debris ejection chute
52 Intake cowling
53 Generator cooling air intake
54 Starboard engine cowling/hinged work platform

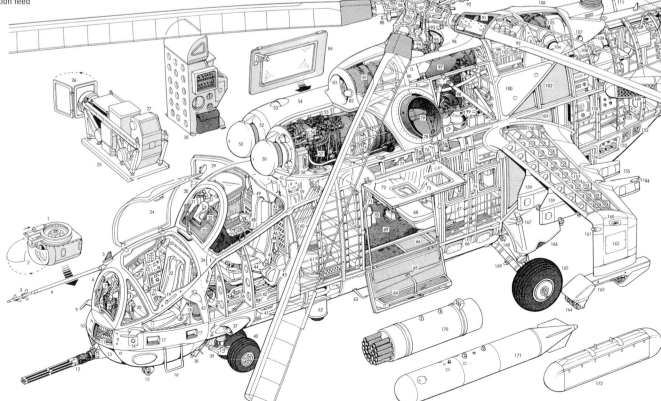

*The Mi-24DU 'Hind-D' trainer saw extensive use in the Soviet Union, for training both Soviet pilots and those of client nations, almost all of whom sent their students to the USSR. These helicopters belonged to the Syzran Air Force Academy.*

## SPECIFICATION

### Mi-24D 'Hind-D'

#### Dimensions

**Length overall, rotors turning:**
64 ft 11 in (19.79 m)
**Fuselage length (excluding rotors and gun):** 57 ft 5½ in (17.51 m)
**Main rotor diameter:** 56 ft 9 in (17.30 m)
**Tail rotor diameter:** 12 ft 10 in (3.91 m)
**Height overall, rotors turning:** 21 ft 4 in (6.50 m)
**Height to top of rotor head:** 14 ft 6¾ in (4.44 m)
**Main rotor disc area:** 2,529.52 sq ft (235 m²)
**Tail rotor disc area:** 129.12 sq ft (11.99 m²)
**Wingspan:** 21 ft 5½ in (6.54 m)
**Tailplane span:** 10 ft 9 in (3.27 m)
**Wheel base:** 14 ft 5 in (4.39 m)
**Wheel track:** 9 ft 11½ in (3.03 m)
**Maximum rotor disc loading:** 10.46 lb/sq ft (51.05 kg/m²)

#### Powerplant

Two 2,200-shp (1640-kW) Klimov (Isotov) TV3-117 Series III turboshafts

#### Weights

**Empty:** 18,519 lb (8400 kg)
**Normal take-off:** 24,250 lb (11000 kg)
**Maximum take-off:** 27,557 lb (12500 kg)

#### Fuel and load

**Internal fuel:** 3,307 lb (1500 kg) or 469 Imp gal (2130 litres) plus provision for 2,205 lb (1000 kg) or 187 Imp gal (850 litres) of auxiliary fuel in an optional cabin tank
**External fuel (with auxiliary internal tank removed):** 2,646 lb (1200 kg) in four 110-Imp gal (500-litre) drop tanks
**Maximum ordnance:** 5,291 lb (2400 kg)

#### Performance

**Maximum level speed 'clean' at optimum altitude:** 168 kt (192 mph; 310 km/h)
**Maximum cruising speed at optimum altitude:** 140 kt (162 mph; 260 km/h)
**Maximum rate of climb at sea level:** 2,461 ft (750 m) per minute
**Service ceiling:** 14,765 ft (4500 m)
**Hovering ceiling (out-of-ground effect):** 7,220 ft (2200 m)

#### Range

**Maximum range, internal fuel only:** 405 nm (466 miles; 750 km)
**Combat radius with maximum military load:** 86 nm (99 miles; 160 km)
**Combat radius with two drop tanks:** 135 nm (155 miles; 250 km)
**Combat radius with four drop tanks:** 155 nm (179 miles; 288 km)

#### Armament

One four-barrelled 12.7-mm (0.5-in) YakB-12.7 Gatling-type machine-gun in remotely-controlled undernose USPU-24 turret, plus four 9M17P Skorpion (AT-2 'Swatter') radio-guided anti-tank missiles, and four UV-32 rocket pods each containing 32 S-5 57-mm (2.24-in) unguided rockets; or four twenty-round B-8V-20 80-mm (3.15-in) S-8 rocket pods; or four five-round B-13L 130-mm (5.12-in) S-13 rocket pods; or four 240-mm (9.45-in) S-24B rockets. Possible underwing stores also include UPK-23-250 gun pods containing one GSh-23L twin-barrelled 23-mm cannon; GUV gun pods containing one four-barrelled 12.7-mm (0.5-in) machine-gun or two four-barrelled 7.62-mm (0.3-in) 9-A-622 machine-guns or one 30-mm AGS-17 Plamia grenade launcher; bombs, mine dispensers and napalm tanks

55 Engine bay dividing firewall
56 Accessory equipment gearbox
57 Klimov TV3-117 turboshaft engine
58 Engine oil tank
59 Starboard side avionics equipment racks
60 Flight control rods
61 Cabin air filtration system equipment
62 Cabin air intake
63 Ventral aerial mast
64 Boarding step
65 Cabin lower door segment
71 Door interconnecting linkage
72 Tactical navigator's seat
73 Upper door segment
74 Cabin rear window panels
75 Cabin equipment racks
76 Winch mounting pads
77 Cabin air distribution ducting
78 Port exhaust duct
79 Engine/gearbox drive shaft
92 Electric leading-edge de-icing
93 Blade pitch control rods
94 Swash plate
112 UHF aerial mast
113 VHF aerial
114 Anti-collision light
115 Tail rotor transmission shaft
116 Transmission shaft bearings
117 HF aerial cable
118 Starboard all-moving tailplane
119 Gearbox cooling air intake
120 Bevel drive gearbox
121 Tail rotor drive shaft

80 Transmission oil cooler
81 Oil cooler fan
82 Ice detector
83 Oil cooler air intake
84 Starboard upper door segment with bulged observation window (Mi-24RCh)
85 Five-bladed main rotor
86 Blade root hinge joints
87 Titanium rotor head
88 Hydraulic drag dampers
89 Hydraulic reservoir
90 Blade root cuffs
91 Blade spar crack indicator (pressurised nitrogen-filled)

66 Underfloor fuel tanks Nos 4 and 5, total internal fuel capacity 427 Imp gal (1940 litres)
67 Cabin equipment consoles
68 Observer's seat
69 Main cabin floor panelling
70 Starboard side data-link console (Mi-24RCh)

mechanism
95 Rotor head actuating linkage
96 Rotor head fairing
97 Main reduction gearbox
98 Gearbox mounting struts
99 Fire extinguisher bottles
100 Fuel system equipment access
101 Main fuselage tank No. 3
102 Collector tanks Nos 1 & 2
103 Rotor head control hydraulic module
104 APU exhaust
105 AI-9V auxiliary power unit
106 Hinged access panels
107 Air system vent
108 Auxiliary equipment gearbox
109 Generator
110 L-166V-11E Ispanka, microwave-pulse infra-red jammer
111 Aerial lead-in

122 Tail pylon construction
123 Final drive right-angle gearbox
124 Pylon tip fairing
125 Three-bladed tail rotor
126 Aluminium alloy tail rotor blades
127 Electric leading-edge de-icing
128 Blade pitch control mechanism
129 Tail navigation light
130 Lower IFF antenna
131 Flight recorder
132 Port all-moving tailplane
133 Tailplane rib construction
134 Tail bumper
135 Aft-facing camera mounting
136 Tailplane spar pivot mounting
137 Tail assembly joint frame
138 Tailcone frame and stringer construction
139 Radar altimeter antennas
140 Signal cartridge firing unit
141 Short-wave aerial cable
142 DISS-15D gyromagnetic compass units
143 Tailcone joint frame
144 Hollow D-section titanium blade spar

145 Honeycomb trailing-edge panels
146 Glass-fibre skin panelling
147 Fixed blade tab
148 Leading-edge anti-erosion sheath
149 Chaff-flare dispensers, port and starboard
150 Rear avionics equipment bay
151 Ventral access hatch
152 Ground power socket
153 Pneumatic system around connectors
154 Battery bay, both sides
155 Wing pylon tail fairings
156 Radar warning antenna
157 Stub wing rib and spar structure
158 Stub wing attachment joints
159 Port stores pylons
160 Port navigation light
161 Radar warning antenna
162 Stub wing endplate pylon fairing
163 'Clutching-hand' ground sample collector
164 Hydraulically-operated scoops, three per side
165 Port mainwheel
166 Mainwheel leg door
167 Mainwheel leg aft pivot mounting

168 Shock absorber strut
169 Undercarriage indicator light
170 UV-32A-24 rocket launcher
171 PTB-450 110-Imp gal (500-litre) auxiliary fuel tank
172 Container store

# Sikorsky H-3/Westland Sea King

*Westland achieved considerable export success with the Sea King, including the supply of three Commando Mk 2As to Qatar (two of which are illustrated). The Commando was originally conceived as a dedicated assault version of the Sea King but, through a number of variants, its roles now include AEW, anti-ship and VIP transport operations.*

## Sea King HAS. Mk 5

**Cutaway key**

1 Fixed-tailplane construction
2 Static dischargers
3 Tail navigation light
4 Anti-collision light
5 Tail rotor gear box
6 Six-bladed tail rotor
7 Blade pitch change mechanism
8 Tail rotor drive shaft
9 Tail pylon construction
10 Glassfibre trailing-edge panel
11 Intermediate shaft gearbox
12 Shaft coupling
13 Folding tail pylon hinges
14 Transponder aerial
15 Rotor blade cross section
16 Blade tracking weight
17 Blade balance weights
18 D-section aluminium spar
19 Tail rotor control gear
20 Tailcone frame and stringer construction
21 Tail rotor transmission shaft
22 Dorsal spine fairing
23 UHF aerial
24 Shaft bearings
25 Tie-down ring
26 Fuselage/tailcone production joint
27 Maintenance walkway
28 Fuel jettison pipe
29 Non-retracting tailwheel
30 Tailwheel levered suspension leg strut
31 Tailwheel castoring leg fixing
32 Mk 46 torpedo
33 Torpedo propellers
34 Parachute launch pack
35 Mk 11 depth charge
36 Weapon pylon shackles

37 Weapon release unit
38 Cabin flooring
39 Smoke marker container
40 Door latch
41 Cabin rear bulkhead
42 Radar scanner support mounting
43 MEL Sea Searcher radar scanner
44 HF aerial cable
45 Cabin wall soundproofing panels
46 Rescue hoist/winch
47 Winch floodlight
48 Transponder transmitter/receiver
49 Radar transmitter/receiver
50 Data-processing station (Marconi LAPADS)
51 Crew emergency exit window
52 Sonobuoy launch tube
53 Swivelling seat mounting
54 Pressure refuelling connection
55 Plessey Type 195 dipping sonar
56 Emergency flotation bag (shown inflated)
57 Flotation bag inflation bottles
58 Bilge pump access covers
59 Underfloor fuel tanks, total fuel capacity 704 Imp gal (3200 litres) in five cells
60 Fuselage main longeron
61 Sonobuoy stowage racks
62 Winch operating control lever
63 Sliding freight door
64 Freight door rail
65 Data display panels
66 Sonar operator's seat

67 Portside radar observer's seat
68 Sonar/radar instrumentation racks
69 Gearbox mounting support structure

70 Hydraulic system connectors
71 Oil cooler
72 Oil cooler air outlet
73 Rotor head tail fairing
74 Engine fire extinguisher bottles
75 Handhold
76 Oil cooler fan
77 Gearbox driven accessory units
78 Rotor head hydraulic control jack (3)
79 Main gearbox
80 Swash plate mechanism
81 Blade pitch control rods
82 Blade attachment joints
83 Master (non-folding) rotor blade
84 Nos 2-5 rotor blades, folded position
85 Rotor head fairing
86 Hydraulic oil reservoir
87 Blade folding hinge joints
88 Rotor head mechanism
89 Cooling air louvres
90 Engine exhaust duct
91 Cabin roof construction
92 Folding step/handhold
93 Tie down ring

94 Main undercarriage strut mounting
95 Kick-in steps
96 Undercarriage energy absorbing side strut
97 Main undercarriage housing sponson
98 Starboard navigation light
99 Main undercarriage leg strut
100 Refraction strut
101 Twin mainwheels
102 Stub wing/walkway
103 Folding step
104 Forward underfloor fuel tanks
105 Cabin air ducting
106 Dipping sonar housing

107 Sonar winch cable drum
108 Winch 'pithead' gear
109 Tape recorder
110 Engine-mounting deck

111 Rolls-Royce Gnome H.1400-1 turboshaft engine
112 Engine bay firewall
113 Port engine nacelle
114 Engine oil tank
115 Port engine air intake

*Since the late 1970s, the Sea King HAR.Mk 3 has been the RAF's standard SAR helicopter. An initial batch of 16 had been delivered by 1979, with a further three delivered in 1985. Six examples of the advanced HAR.Mk 3A are also now in service.*

**116** Engine starter housing
**117** Starboard engine air intake
**118** Engine mounting strut
**119** Intake foreign object deflector
**120** Pitot tube
**121** Control rod linkages
**122** Heating/ventilation system air intake
**123** Fuel control computers
**124** Cabin heater/blower
**125** Boat hull chine longeron
**126** Electrical equipment bay
**127** Cockpit floor level
**128** Fire extinguisher
**129** Sliding side window pane
**130** Pilot's seat
**131** Cockpit bulkhead
**132** Radio rack
**133** Port entry doorway
**134** Rotor brake lever
**135** Overhead switch panels
**136** Engine control cables
**137** Entry door upper segment (open)
**138** Pitot tube
**139** Cockpit eyebrow windows
**140** Windscreen panels
**141** Windscreen wipers
**142** Air temperature probe
**143** Co-pilot's seat
**144** Instrument panel shroud
**145** Centre control console
**146** Cyclic pitch control column
**147** Back of instrument panel
**148** Yaw control rudder pedals
**149** Downward vision window
**150** Radio and electronics equipment
**151** Anti-collision light
**152** Homing aerials
**153** Retractable landing/taxiing lamps
**154** Vertical landing lamps
**155** Bow compartment hinged access door
**156** Battery compartment
**157** Fresh air intakes
**158** VHF aerial

## SPECIFICATION

### Advanced Sea King

#### Dimensions

**Length overall, rotors turning:** 72 ft 8 in (22.15 m)
**Fuselage length:** 55 ft 10 in (17.02 m)
**Length with main rotor blades folded:** 57 ft 2 in (17.42 m)
**Length with main rotor blades and tail pylon folded:** 47 ft 3 in (14.40 m)
**Main rotor diameter:** 62 ft (18.90 m)
**Tail rotor diameter:** 110 ft 4 in (3.16 m)
**Height overall, rotors turning:** 16 ft 10 in (5.13 m)
**Height overall, rotors stationary:** 15 ft 11 in (4.85 m)
**Height to top of rotor head:** 15 ft 6 in (4.72 m)
**Main rotor disc area:** 3,019.07 sq ft (280.47 m²)
**Tail rotor disc area:** 83.86 sq ft (7.79 m²)
**Wheel base:** 23 ft 5 in (7.14 m)
**Wheel track:** 13 ft (3.96 m)

#### Powerplant

Two Rolls-Royce Gnome H.1400-1T turboshafts each rated at 1,660 shp (1238 kW) for take-off and 1,465 shp (1092 kW) for continuous running

#### Weights

**Basic empty with sponsons:** 11,891 lb (5393 kg)
**Basic empty without sponsons:** 11,845 lb (5373 kg)
**Empty equipped (ASW role):** 16,377 lb (7428 kg)
**Empty equipped (ASV role):** 16,689 lb (7570 kg)
**Empty equipped (AEW role):** 17,143 lb (7776 kg)
**Empty equipped (SAR role):** 13,760 lb (6241 kg)
**Empty equipped (troop transport role):** 12,594 lb (5712 kg)
**Empty equipped (freight role):** 12,536 lb (5686 kg)
**Empty equipped (VIP role):** 15,917 lb (7220 kg)
**Maximum take-off:** 21,500 lb (9752 kg)

#### Fuel and load

**Internal fuel capacity:** 817 Imp gal (3714 litres)
**Auxiliary fuel:** 190 Imp gal (863 litres) in an auxiliary fuselage tank
**Maximum ordnance:** 2,500 lb (1134 kg)

#### Performance

**Never-exceed speed at sea level:** 140 mph (226 km/h)
**Maximum cruising speed at sea level:** 126 mph (204 km/h)
**Maximum rate of climb at sea level:** 2,030 ft (619 m) per minute
**Service ceiling (one engine out):** 4,000 ft (1220 m)
**Hovering ceiling (in ground effect):** 6,500 ft (1980 m)
**Hovering ceiling (out of ground effect):** 4,700 ft (1435 m)

#### Range

**Ferry range with auxiliary fuel:** 1,082 miles (1742 km)
**Range with standard fuel:** 921 miles (1482 km)

#### Armament

Up to four Mk 46, A244S or Sting Ray torpedoes can be carried externally, or four Mk 11 depth charges. Sea Eagle or Exocet anti-ship missiles are anti-ship options. Pintle-mounted machine-guns can be fitted to starboard door.

# Sikorsky H-19/Westland Whirlwind

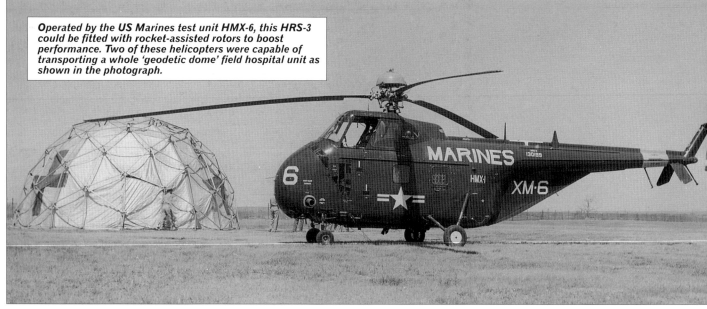

*Operated by the **US** M**arines** test unit **HMX-6**, this **HRS-3** could be fitted with rocket-assisted rotors to boost performance. Two of these helicopters were capable of transporting a whole 'geodetic dome' field hospital unit as shown in the photograph.*

## S-55

**Cutaway key**
1 Two-bladed tail rotor
2 Tail rotor pitch change mechanism
3 Feathering counterweights
4 Right-angle final drive gearbox
5 Tail rotor drive shaft
6 Tail rotor pylon
7 Rear navigation lights
8 Tailcone fairing
9 Tail bumper/rotor guard
10 Bevel drive intermediate gearbox
11 Pylon attachment ring frame
12 Anhedral stabiliser, port and starboard
13 VHF aerial
14 Tailboom
15 Tail rotor transmission shaft
16 Dorsal spine fairing
17 Shaft bearings
18 Tail rotor control cables
19 Tailboom frame and stringer construction
20 Ventral fairing construction
21 Main rotor blade trailing-edge construction

22 Extruded aluminium blade spar
23 Tailcone joint ring frame
24 Bolted tailcone joint
25 Cabin heater intake
26 Combustion heater unit
27 Winch cable hydraulic motor
28 Baggage/equipment stowage space
29 Radio and electronics equipment bay
30 Equipment bay access door
31 Main undercarriage shock absorber strut
32 Starboard mainwheel
33 Float mainwheel
34 Pivoted axle beam
35 Hydraulic brake pipe
36 Sliding cabin door lower rail
37 Rear fuel tank group filler cap
38 3-abreast passenger seating, 8-seat all-passenger layout
39 Cabin window panel
40 Heater air ducting

41 Cabin rear bulkhead
42 Baggage compartment door
43 Sliding door top rail
44 Winch cable emergency cutter
45 Gearbox support deck double frame
46 Rear underfloor fuel tanks, total system capacity 150 Imp gal (180 US gal; 682 litres)
47 Axle beam pivot fixing
48 Floor beam construction
49 Jettisonable window panel
50 Cabin wall trim panelling
51 Folding maintenance platform, open
52 Rescue hoist floodlight
53 Cockpit sliding entry hatch rail
54 Internal maintenance platform
55 Cockpit rearward vision window panels
56 Gearbox mounting deck
57 Gearbox oil cooler
58 Oil cooler air outlet fairing

59 Oil cooler belt drive
60 Gearbox mounting strut
61 Main gearbox
62 Rotor head control jacks (3)
63 Swash plate assembly
64 Blade pitch angle control rods
65 Torque scissor links
66 Pitch control arm
67 Drag damper
68 Blade root attachment joints
69 Main rotor head
70 3-bladed main rotor
71 Cockpit eyebrow windows
72 Co-pilot's seat
73 Control linkages
74 Rotor brake
75 Pilot's seat
76 Sliding side window/entry hatch
77 Rescue hoist/winch
78 Main cabin sliding door
79 Door latch
80 Forward group of underfloor fuel tanks
81 Cabin floor panelling
82 Winch hook

83 External load sling, 2000-lb (907-kg) capacity
84 Forward float mounting strut
85 Grab handle/step
86 Forward fuel tank filler cap
87 Aft-facing seat row
88 Boarding steps
89 Oil tank
90 Oil filler cap
91 Ventilating air grille
92 Cockpit floor level
93 Cockpit heater duct
94 Cyclic pitch control column
95 Collective pitch control lever
96 Centre control console, engine controls
97 Instrument panel shroud
98 Temperature probe
99 Windscreen panels
100 Windscreen de-misting air duct
101 Yaw control rudder pedals
102 Engine cooling air intake grille
103 Sloping engine bay fireproof bulkhead
104 Cooling air fan
105 Engine bay door hinges
106 Engine oil cooler

107 Nose undercarriage leg strut
108 Torque scissor links
109 Starboard castoring nosewheel
110 Cooling air ventral outlet
111 Carburettor intake duct
112 Main engine mounting
113 Carburettor
heater intake duct
114 Exhaust pipe heater muff
115 Exhaust collector ring, exhaust on port side
116 Pratt & Whitney R-1340-40 nine-cylinder radial engine
117 Engine bay clamshell doors
118 Clamshell door latch
119 Engine accessory equipment housing
120 Generator

121 Carburettor
122 Port castoring nosewheel
123 Fixed float, H-19B amphibious rescue variant
124 Bilge pump access panels
125 Mooring attachment
126 Float castoring nosewheels

*Four specially-painted H-19Ds were employed by the US Army as a 'square dance display team' operating at air shows and other demonstrations around the USA. The 'female' H-19 in the foreground is seen wearing a 'skirt' whereas the 'male' H-19 behind is 'smoking a pipe'.*

## SPECIFICATION

### Whirlwind HAR.Mk 2

#### Dimensions

**Length overall:** 62 ft 4 in (19.00 m)
**Nose-to-tail rotor distance:** 44 ft 2 in (13.50 m)
**Main rotor diameter:** 53 ft (16.15 m)
**Height overall:** 15 ft 7½ in (4.76 m)
**Wheel track:** 11 ft 3 in (3.45 m)
**Main rotor disc area:** 2,205 sq ft (204.84 m²)

#### Powerplant

One Pratt & Whitney R-1340-40 nine-cylinder radial air cooled geared and supercharged engine rated at 600 hp (447 kW)

#### Performance

**Maximum level speed:** 99 mph (159 km/h)
**Maximum cruising speed:** 85 mph (137 km/h)
**Rate of climb at sea level:** 600 ft (183 m) per minute
**Service ceiling at normal weight:** 8,600 ft (2621 m)
**Standard range at normal operating weight:** 320 miles (515 km)

#### Weights

**Empty:** 5,327 lb (2416 kg)
**Normal loaded:** 7,200 lb (3266 kg)

#### Armament

Up to four Nord SS.11 ASMs

*In the late 1950s and early 1960s the Royal Canadian Air Force not only operated the Sikorsky H-19 (bottom two), but also the Sikorsky H-34 (second from top, first ordered in 1955) and the Piasecki (later Vertol) H-21 (top). All three types were heavily used during the construction of the Mid-Canada Line for NORAD and were mainly operated by civilian contractors.*

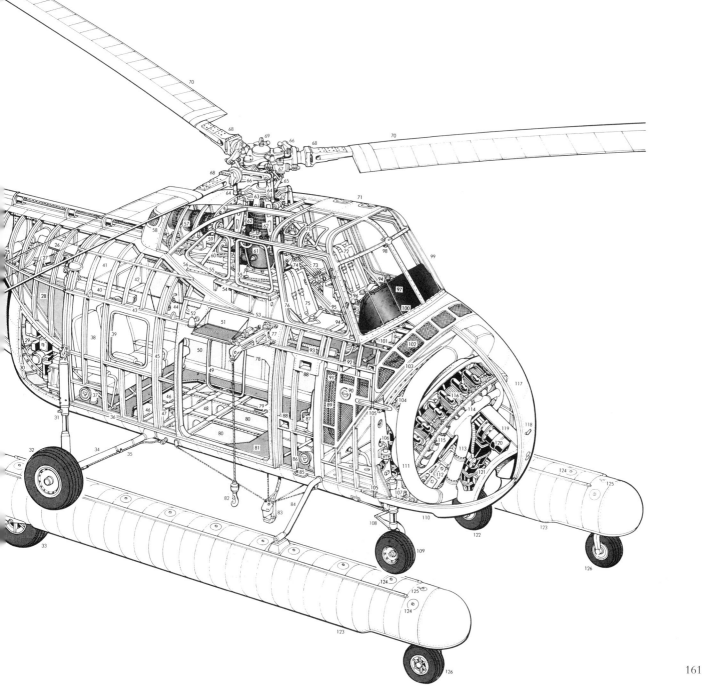

# Sikorsky H-53

**Bulky loads are carried underneath a central cargo hook. This CH-53 is delivering a field gun to troops. Such capability allows rapid mobility around the battlefield for heavy equipment, or early deployment so that artillery is in place soon after the first troops land.**

## CH-53E

**Cutaway key**
1 Retractable-in-flight refuelling boom
2 Refuelling boom fairing
3 Instrument compartment access door
4 Glideslope aerial
5 Fresh air intakes
6 Yaw control rudder pedals
7 Landing lamp
8 Downward vision windows
9 Nose undercarriage leg strut
10 Twin nosewheels
11 Radio and electronics bay, port and starboard
12 Cockpit floor level
13 Collective pitch control lever
14 Cyclic pitch control column
15 Co-pilot's armoured seat
16 Instrument panel shroud
17 Windscreen wipers
18 Windscreen panels
19 Rescue hoist/winch
20 Pitot tube
21 UHF aerial
22 Overhead control panel
23 Pilot's armoured seat
24 Cockpit eyebrow window
25 Flight leader's folding jump seat
26 Cockpit bulkhead
27 Jettisonable side window panel
28 Starboard side crew entry door
29 Fuselage and stringer construction
30 Emergency exit window
31 Engine air intake particle separator
32 Bevel drive gearbox
33 Engine oil cooler
34 Auxiliary power unit (APU)

35 Cabin heater unit
36 Starboard engine intake particle separator

37 Engine cowlings armoured on lower surface
38 Auxiliary gearbox
39 Hydraulic reservoirs
40 Gearbox drive shaft
41 Port engine transmission shaft
42 Folding troop seats maximum 37 troops
43 Cargo loading floor

44 Roller conveyor
45 Cargo hook support links
46 General Electric T64-GE-416 turboshaft engine
47 Gearbox mounting fuselage main frame
48 Engine exhaust duct
49 Centre engine intake
50 Main transmission gearbox

51 Blade pitch control rotating swashplate
52 Rotor head mechanism
53 Blade pitch control links
54 Blade folding hinge points
55 Rotor head fairing

56 Seven-bladed main rotor 79-ft (24.08-m) diameter
57 Centre engine oil cooler

58 Maintenance handrail
59 Engine compartment firewall
60 Centre General Electric T64-GE-416 turboshaft engine
61 Cabin wall soundproofing trim panel

62 Rear troop seats
63 Fuselage/main undercarriage main frame
64 Cargo ramp hydraulic jack
65 Production break double frame
66 Centre engine exhaust duct
67 Oil cooler exhaust
68 Rotor blade cross-section
69 D-section titanium spar

70 Honeycomb trailing edge panel
71 Glass-fibre blade skin
72 Leading edge anti-erosion strip
73 Dorsal spine fairing
74 Tail rotor transmission shaft
75 TACAN aerial

## H-53 in Vietnam

It was the shortcomings of other helicopters in Vietnam that provided the impetus for the construction of the H-53. First entering service in 1967, the CH-53A, and soon after the HH-53B, proved popular for transporting supplies and rescuing downed aircrew all over the region. Two years later, in September 1969, the HH-53C made its combat debut. Outwardly similar but possessing many upgraded capabilities the Super Jolly was equipped with an external cargo hook which enabled it to carry loads of up to 20,000 lb (9072 kg), while for the rescue mission it was fitted with a hoist complete with a 250-ft (76-m) cable to penetrate the tallest jungle canopy. For defence up to three 0.3-in (7.62-mm) Miniguns were carried, and these could suppress enemy forces intent on reaching the downed crews before the rescue helicopter.

### SPECIFICATION

**CH-53E Super Stallion**

#### Dimensions

**Length overall, rotors turning:** 99 ft ½ in (30.19 m)
**Fuselage length:** 73 ft 4 in (22.35 m)
**Length with rotor and tail folded:** 60 ft 6 in (18.44 m)
**Height overall:** 29 ft 5 in (8.97 m)
**Main rotor diameter:** 79 ft (24.08 m)
**Tail rotor diameter:** 20 ft (6.10 m)
**Main rotor disc area:** 4,901.7 sq ft (455.38 m²)
**Tail rotor disc area:** 314.2 sq ft (29.19 m²)

#### Powerplant

Three General Electric T64-GE-416 engines rated at 4,380 shp (3266 kW) for ten minutes, 4,145 shp (3091 kW) for 30 minutes and 3,696 shp (2756 kW) for continuous running

#### Weights

**Empty:** 33,228 lb (15072 kg)
**Maximum take-off with an internal payload:** 69,750 lb (31640 kg)
**Maximum take-off with an external payload:** 73,500 lb (33340 kg)

#### Fuel and load

**Internal fuel:** 1,017 US gal (3849 litres)
**External fuel:** up to two 650 US gal (2461-litre) drop tanks
**Maximum payload internally over 115-mile (185-km) radius:** 36,000 lb (16330 kg)
**Maximum payload externally over 57.5-mile (92.5-km) radius:** 32,000 lb (14515 kg)

#### Performance

**Maximum level speed 'clean' at sea level:** 196 mph (315 km/h)
**Cruising speed at sea level:** 173 mph (278 km/h)
**Maximum rate of climb at sea level with a 25,000-lb (11340-kg) payload:** 2,500 ft (762 m) per minute
**Service ceiling:** 18,500 ft (5640 m)
**Hovering ceiling:** 11,500 ft (3520 m)

#### Range

**Ferry range without aerial refuelling:** 1,290 miles (2075 km)
**Radius with a 20,000-lb (9072-kg) external payload:** 575 miles (925 km)
**Radius with a 32,000-lb (14515-kg) external payload:** 57.5 miles (92.5 km)

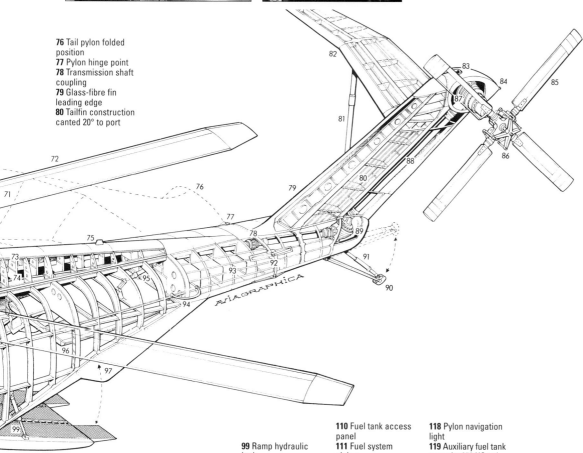

**76** Tail pylon folded position
**77** Pylon hinge point
**78** Transmission shaft coupling
**79** Glass-fibre fin leading edge
**80** Tailfin construction canted 20° to port

**81** Stabiliser bracing strut
**82** Gull-wing horizontal stabiliser
**83** Anti-collision light
**84** Tail navigation light
**85** Four-bladed tail rotor, 20-ft (6.1-m) diameter
**86** Tail rotor pitch control mechanism
**87** Tail rotor gearbox
**88** Final drive shaft
**89** Bevel gear box
**90** Retractable tail bumper

**91** Bumper hydraulic jack
**92** Folding tail pylon latches
**93** Tail boom construction
**94** VOR/localiser aerial
**95** Upper cargo door hydraulic jack
**96** Upper cargo door, open position
**97** Doorway side strakes
**98** Cargo loading ramp down position

**99** Ramp hydraulic jack
**100** Formation keeping light
**101** Fuel jettison pipe
**102** Main undercarriage leg strut
**103** Twin mainwheels
**104** Mainwheel bay
**105** Hydraulic retraction jack
**106** Maintenance platform walkway
**107** Fuselage sponson main frame
**108** Fuel filler cap
**109** Port navigation light

**110** Fuel tank access panel
**111** Fuel system piping
**112** Port main fuel tank; total internal capacity 1,017 US gal (3850 litres)
**113** Secondary fuel tank
**114** Sponson nose fairing
**115** Two-point suspension cargo hooks
**116** Single-point cargo hook; maximum external slung load 32,200 lb (14606 kg)
**117** Auxiliary fuel tank pylon

**118** Pylon navigation light
**119** Auxiliary fuel tank capacity 650 US gal (2461 litres)

# Sikorsky UH-60 Black Hawk

*Black Hawks were designed from the outset to have an offensive capability on their external pylons. Up to 10,000 lb (4536 kg) of armament can be carried, including Hellfire missiles, 20-mm cannon, and 2.75-in (70-mm) FFARs (Folding Fin Aerial Rockets), which can be seen here being fired.*

## UH-60A Black Hawk

### Cutaway key

1 Nose radio and electronics bay
2 Nose glazing
3 Radio compartment access door
4 Air grille
5 Windscreen wipers
6 Windscreen panels
7 Instrument panel shroud
8 Rudder pedals
9 Downward vision window
10 Boarding step
11 Cockpit door
12 Cyclic pitch control lever
13 Sliding side window
14 Co-pilot's seat
15 Control column
16 Centre instrument console
17 Armoured seat backs
18 Pilot's seat
19 Sliding side armour panels
20 Cockpit eyebrow windows
21 Armoured headrests
22 Electrical fuse panels
23 Pitot tubes
24 Control equipment sliding access cover
25 Cooling intake grille
26 Sliding fairing guide rails
27 Control runs
28 Handrail/aerial bar
29 Gunner's sliding side windows, open
30 Cockpit step/main axle fairing
31 Port navigation light

32 Main undercarriage pivoted axle
33 Ground power supply
34 Swivelling gun mounting
35 Gunner's side-facing seat
36 Port M-23D 0.3-in (7.62-mm) machine-gun
37 Undercarriage shock-absorber strut
38 Port mainwheel
39 Cabin floor level
40 Folding maintenance step
41 Undercarriage mounting main frames
42 Hydraulic pump
43 Flight control mixer unit
44 Cabin heater
45 Engine-driven accessory units
46 Rotor blade titanium main spar
47 Bevel gearboxes
48 Starboard engine intake
49 Central main reduction gearbox
50 Rotor control swash plate
51 Rotor mast
52 Main rotor head (elastomeric non-lubricated bearings)
53 Bifilar vibration damper
54 Rotor head fairing
55 Blade root attachments
56 Composite titanium spar/glass-fibre main rotor blades
57 Rotor blade drooped leading edge
58 Fixed trailing-edge tabs
59 Blade pitch control rods

60 Port engine intake
61 Engine drive shaft
62 Aft-sliding cabin door
63 Emergency door release handle
64 Cargo hook, 8,000-lb (3650-kg) maximum capacity
65 Cabin accommodation, 13 troops plus up to two crew chief/gunners or four stretchers or internal cargo
66 Cabin rear bulkhead
67 Troop seats
68 Sliding door rail fairings

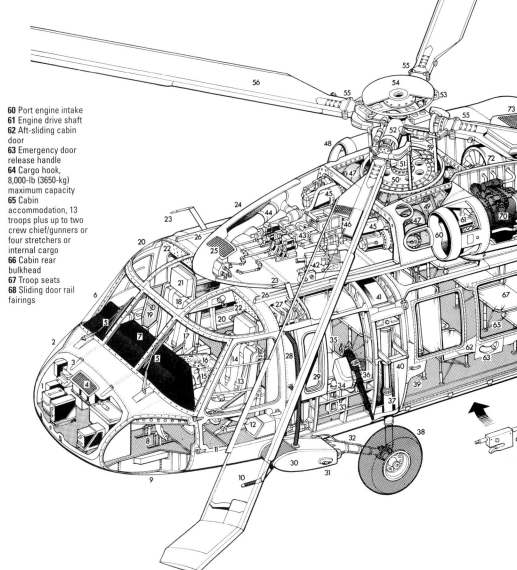

## SPECIFICATION

**UH-60A Black Hawk**

### Dimensions

**Length overall with rotors turning:** 64 ft 10 in (19.76 m)
**Height overall:** 16 ft 10 in (5.13 m)
**Main rotor diameter:** 53 ft 8 in (16.36 m)
**Tail rotor diameter:** 11 ft (3.35 m)
**Wheel track:** 8 ft 10½ in (2.71 m)
**Wheel base:** 28 ft 11¾ in (8.83 m)

### Powerplant

Two General Electric T700-GE-700 turboshafts each rated at 1,560 shp (1151 kW) or in export S-70s, two General Electric T700-GE-701A turboshafts each rated at 1,723 shp (1285 kW)

### Performance

**Maximum level 'clean' speed at sea level:** 160 kt (184 mph; 296 km/h)
**Maximum cruising speed at 4,000 ft (1220 m):** 145 kt (167 mph; 268 km/h)
**Ferry range with four external auxiliary tanks:** 1200 nm (1,382 miles; 2224 km)
**Standard range:** 319 nm (368 miles; 592 km)

### Fuel and load

**Internal fuel:** 360 US gal (1361 litres) plus provision for 370 US gal (1400 litres) of auxiliary fuel in two fuselage tanks
**External fuel:** Up to two 230-US gal (870-litre) and/or two 450-US gal (1703-litre) tanks
**Maximum payload:** 2,640 lb (1197 kg) carried internally or 8,000 lb (3629 kg) carried externally

### Weights

**Empty:** 11,284 lb (5118 kg)
**Normal take-off:** 16,994 lb (7708 kg)
**Maximum take-off:** 20,250 lb

*The UH-60L superseded the A model on the production line. It introduces more powerful engines, uprated transmission and a refined gearbox to give a much improved performance, especially in 'hot-and-high' conditions or with external loads. The Hover Infra-Red Suppressor Subsystem (HIRSS – pronounced 'herz') was fitted as standard on all production UH-60s from 1987. This system, which redirects engine exhaust and mixes cool air into the exhaust stream, is effective in all flight profiles.*

69 Engine cowlings
70 General Electric T700-GE-700 turboshaft engine
71 Exhaust cooling air fan, infra-red suppression
72 Oil cooler fan
73 Infra-red suppression oil cooler exhaust
74 Fire extinguishers
75 Formation light
76 Solar T-62T-40-1 auxiliary power unit
77 Engine exhaust pipe

84 APU exhaust
85 Engine/transmission rear fairing
86 Chaff dispenser
87 Anti-collision light
88 Tailcone frame and stringer construction
89 Dorsal spine fairing
90 Transmission shaft
91 Shaft bearings
92 Tail rotor control cables
93 Communications aerial
94 Tailwheel axle strut and fairing

78 Spring-loaded maintenance steps
79 Fireproof main fuel tanks, port and starboard, capacity 157 US gal (594 litres) each
80 Pressure refuelling connection
81 Fuselage frame and stringer construction
82 Tailcone joint frame
83 Engine exhaust shroud

95 Tailwheel
96 Shock absorber strut
97 Formation light
98 Bevel drive gearbox
99 Folding footrest
100 Tailcone rear fairing
101 Pull-out maintenance steps
102 Tail rotor drive shaft
103 Starboard tailplane
104 Formation light
105 Static discharge wicks
106 Fin leading-edge suppressed aerial
107 Fin construction
108 Tail rotor drive gearbox

109 Canted (20°) tail rotor
110 Lightweight cross beam rotor hub
111 Pitch change spider
112 Graphite epoxy composite rotor blades
113 Anti-collision light
114 Tail navigation light
115 Troop commander's communications aerial
116 Cambered section fin
117 Tailplane hydraulic jack
118 Tailplane pivot fixing
119 Port tailplane construction
120 Formation light
121 Static discharge wicks

# Westland Wessex

## Wessex HAS.Mk 3

### Cutaway key

**1** Tail navigation lights
**2** Anti-collision light
**3** Cooling air grilles
**4** Tail rotor gearbox fairing
**5** Final drive right-angle gearbox
**6** Tail rotor hub mechanism
**7** Blade pitch angle control linkage
**8** Four-bladed tail rotor
**9** Handgrip
**10** Tail rotor drive shaft
**11** Tail pylon construction
**12** Fixed horizontal tailplane construction
**13** Ground handling grips
**14** Cooling air grilles
**15** Bevel drive gearbox
**16** Port tailplane
**17** Folding tail pylon hinge
**18** Tail pylon latching mechanism
**19** Tailwheel shock absorber strut
**20** Castoring tailwheel
**21** Hinged axle beam
**22** Mooring ring
**23** Aerial mast
**24** HF aerial cable
**25** Rotor blade trailing edge rib construction
**26** Tip fairing
**27** Blade tracking weight
**28** Blade balance weights
**29** 'D'-section aluminium blade spar
**30** Transponder aerial
**31** Tailcone frame and stringer construction
**32** Tail rotor control cables
**33** Tail rotor transmission shaft
**34** Upper IFF aerial
**35** UHF aerial

**36** Tailcone/fuselage joint frame
**37** Equipment bay bulkhead
**38** Dorsal radome
**39** Search radar scanner
**40** Radome mounting structure
**41** Port side cabin heater
**42** Electrical system equipment
**43** Fuel delivery piping
**44** Rear fuel tank group filler cap
**45** Pressure refuelling connection
**46** Mk 46 torpedo
**47** External fuel tank. capacity 100 Imp gal (454 litres)
**48** External cable ducting
**49** Aft crashproof fuel cells; total fuel capacity 266 Imp gal (1209 litres)
**50** Cabin window/escape hatch
**51** Cabin rear bulkhead
**52** Curtained aperture to equipment bay
**53** Vent piping
**54** Oil cooler air exit louvres
**55** Rotor head rear aerodynamic fairing
**56** Oil cooler
**57** Rear fairing access panels
**58** Cabin heating ducting
**59** Smoke marker stowage
**60** Marker launch tube cover
**61** Cabin floor panelling
**62** External stores carrier
**63** Stores pylon fixing
**64** Dipping sonar
**65** Floor beam construction
**66** Cabin door
**67** Seat mounting rails

**68** Tactical navigator and sonar operator seats
**69** Instrument consoles
**70** Rescue hoist/winch
**71** Gearbox mounting deck
**72** Gearbox support struts
**73** Rotor brake
**74** Oil cooler fan
**75** Gearbox deck access panels
**76** Rotor head servo control units
**77** Blade pitch control linkage
**78** Torque scissor links
**79** Blade drag damper
**80** Hydraulic oil reservoir
**81** Rotor head mechanism
**82** Four-bladed main rotor
**83** Blade root attachment joints
**84** Cooling air grilles
**85** Cockpit roof glazing
**86** Overhead switch panel
**87** Chart case
**88** Servomotor switching control panel
**89** Cockpit rear bulkhead
**90** Pilot's seat
**91** Sliding side window/ entry hatch
**92** Main undercarriage leg strut attachment
**93** Cabin door jettison lever

**94** Sliding cabin door
**95** Door latch
**96** Shock absorber leg strut
**97** Boarding step
**98** Flotation bag inflation bottle
**99** Starboard mainwheel
**100** Flotation bag stowage
**101** Mooring ring
**102** Pivoted main axle beam
**103** Step
**104** Hydraulic brake pipe
**105** Forward group of fuel cells
**106** Fuel filler cap
**107** Dipping sonar winch mechanism
**108** Cockpit access steps
**109** Bifurcated engine exhaust pipes, port and starboard
**110** Cockpit floor level

**111** External cable ducting
**112** Handgrip
**113** Rudder pedals
**114** Instrument panel
**115** Cyclic pitch control column
**116** Collective pitch lever
**117** Co-pilot's seat
**118** Rotor brake control lever
**119** Temperature gauge

**120** Windscreen panels
**121** Windscreen wipers
**122** Instrument panel shroud
**123** Windscreen de-icing fluid spray nozzle
**124** Sloping cockpit front bulkhead
**125** Engine/gearbox transmission shaft
**126** Electrical equipment bay, radio and electronics bay on port side
**127** Nose equipment bay access hatches
**128** Cooling air scoop

## SPECIFICATION

### Wessex HC.Mk 2

#### Dimensions

**Overall length with rotors turning:** 65 ft 9 in (20.04 m)
**Fuselage length:** 48 ft 4½ in (14.74 m)
**Length with main rotor blades and tail folded:** 38 ft 6 in (11.73 m)
**Height to top of rotor head:** 14 ft 5 in (4.39 m)
**Height overall:** 16 ft 2 in (4.93 m)
**Main rotor diameter:** 56 ft (17.07 m)
**Tail rotor diameter:** 9 ft 6 in (2.90 m)
**Main rotor disc area:** 2,643.01 sq ft (228.81 m²)
**Tail rotor disc area:** 70.88 sq ft (6.58 m²)
**Wheel track:** 12 ft (3.66 m)

#### Powerplant

two Rolls-Royce (Bristol Siddeley) Gnome Mk 110/111 coupled turboshafts each rated at 1,350 shp (1007 kW)

#### Weights

**Empty operating:** 8,304 lb (3767 kg)
**Maximum take-off:** 13,500 lb (6123 kg)

#### Fuel and load

**Internal fuel:** 300 Imp gal (1364 litres)
**Auxiliary fuel:** 200 Imp gal (909 litres)
**Maximum payload:** 4,000 lb (1814 kg)

#### Performance

**Maximum level speed at sea level:** 132 mph (212 km/h)
**Maximum cruising speed at optimum altitude:** 121 mph (195 km/h)
**Ferry range with standard fuel:** 478 miles (769 km)
**Ferry range with auxiliary fuel:** 645 miles (1040 km)
**Maximum rate of climb at sea level:** 1,650 ft (503 m) per minute
**Service ceiling:** 12,000 ft (3658 m)
**Hovering ceiling:** 4,000 ft (1220 m)

*Above: The Wessex HC.Mk 2 saw widespread service with the RAF and as late as 1994, when this photograph was taken, Nos 28, 60, 72 and 84 Sqns were still operational with the type.*

*Left: This Wessex HU.Mk 5 was photographed on operations in Malaysia during 1965 while serving with No. 848 Sqn Fleet Air Arm aboard HMS Albion. No. 848 reformed on the Wessex in May 1964.*

129 Batteries (two)
130 Engine oil tank
131 Engine turbine section
132 Exhaust compartment firewalls
133 Ground power socket
134 Ventilating air intake
135 Starboard navigation light
136 Main axle beam mounting
137 Nose compartment framing
138 Engine bay access door
139 Throttle control linkage
140 Engine withdrawal rail
141 Engine mounting struts
142 Rolls-Royce (Napier) Gazelle 22 turboshaft engine
143 Engine bay ventilating air intake
144 Starter cartridge magazine
145 Hydraulic pump
146 Fire extinguisher bottles
147 Engine air intake
148 Hinged nose cone access panel
149 Engine accessory equipment gearbox
150 Generator
151 Intake plenum
152 Retractable landing lamp
153 Lower IFF aerial

*For hangar stowage aboard ship, the Wessex has a folding main rotor, as demonstrated by this FAA Wessex HAS.Mk 1. Not illustrated in this photograph is the folding tail pylon, which served to reduce the overall length of the aircraft by 27 ft (8.23 m).*

# Sikorsky SH-60 Sea Hawk

## SH-60B Seahawk

**Cutaway key**
1 Graphite epoxy composite tail rotor blades
2 Lightweight cross beam rotor hub
3 Blade pitch change spider
4 Anti-collision light
5 Tail rotor final drive bevel gearbox
6 Rotor hub canted 20°
7 Horizontal tailplane folded position
8 Pull-out maintenance steps
9 Port tailplane
10 Tail rotor drive shaft
11 Fin pylon construction
12 Tailplane hydraulic jack
13 Cambered trailing edge section
14 Tail navigation light
15 Tailplane hinge joint (manual folding)
16 Handgrips
17 Static dischargers
18 Starboard tailplane construction
19 Towed magnetic anomaly-detector (MAD) bird
20 Tail bumper
21 Shock absorber strut
22 Bevel drive gearbox
23 Tail pylon latch joint
24 Tail pylon hinge frame (manual folding)
25 Transmission shaft disconnect
26 Tail rotor transmission shaft
27 Shaft bearings
28 Tail pylon folded position
29 Dorsal spine fairing
30 UHF aerial
31 Tailcone frame and stringer construction
32 Magnetic compass remote transmitters
33 MAD detector housing and reeling unit
34 Tail rotor control cables
35 HF aerial cable
36 MAD unit fixed pylon
37 Ventral data link antenna housing
38 Lower UHF/TACAN aerial
39 Fuel jettison
40 Anti-collision light
41 Tie-down shackle
42 Tailcone joint frame
43 Air system heat exchanger exhaust
44 Engine exhaust shroud
45 Emergency locater aerial
46 Engine fire suppression bottles
47 IFF aerial
48 Port side auxiliary power unit (APU)
49 Oil cooler exhaust grille
50 Starboard side air conditioning plant
51 Engine exhaust pipe
52 HF radio equipment bay
53 Sliding cabin door rail
54 Aft AN/ALQ-142 ESM aerial fairing, port and starboard
55 Tailwheel leg strut
56 Fireproof fuel tanks, port and starboard; total capacity 361 US gal (1368 litres)
57 Starboard stores pylon
58 Castoring twin tail wheels
59 Torpedo parachute housing
60 Mk 46 lightweight torpedo
61 Cabin rear bulkhead
62 Passenger seat
63 Honeycomb cabin floor panelling
64 Sliding cabin door
65 Recovery Assist, Secure and Traverse (RAST) aircraft haul-down fitting
66 Ventral cargo hook, 6,000 lb (2722-kg) capacity
67 Floor beam construction
68 Spring-loaded door segment in way of stores pylon
69 Pull-out emergency exit window panel
70 Pneumatic sonobuoy launch rack (125 sonobuoys)
71 Rescue hoist/winch
72 General Electric T700-GE-401 turboshaft engine
73 Engine accessory equipment gearbox
74 Intake particle separator air duct
75 Engine bay firewall
76 Oil cooler fan
77 Rotor brake unit
78 Engine intake ducts
79 Maintenance step
80 Engine drive shafts
81 Bevel drive gearboxes
82 Central main reduction gearbox
83 Rotor control swash plate
84 Rotormast
85 Blade pitch control rods
86 Bi-filar vibration absorber
87 Rotorhead fairing
88 Main rotor head (elastomeric, non-lubricated, bearings)
89 Blade pitch control horn
90 Lead-lag damper
91 Individual blade folding joints, electrically actuated
92 Blade spar crack detectors
93 Blade root attachment joints
94 Main rotor composite blades
95 Port engine intake
96 Control equipment sliding access cover
97 Engine driven accessory gearboxes
98 Hydraulic pump
99 Flight control servo units
100 Flight control hydro- mechanical mixer unit
101 Cabin roof panelling
102 Radar operator's seat
103 AN/APS-124 radar console
104 Tie-down shackle
105 Gearbox and engine mounting main frames
106 Maintenance steps
107 Main undercarriage leg

*Above: An SH-60F Ocean Hawk departs USS Nimitz. The Ocean Hawk was designed to replace the SH-3H Sea King, two examples of which can be seen in the background. Among the A-6s, A-7s, F-14s and SH-3s on this late-1980's carrier deck, the SH-60F plays an unexpectedly important role in the carrier's survival, performing as it does the close-in ASW mission and therefore acting as the ship's last line of defence against enemy submarines.*

*Left: The Seahawk has never been noted for its bright markings, this HSL-41 SH-60B proving that the red and yellow MAD bird is often the only thing to relieve the type's grey camouflage.*

## SPECIFICATION

### SH-60B Seahawk

#### Dimensions

**Overall length with rotors turning:** 64 ft 10 in (19.76 m)
**Fuselage length:** 50 ft ¼ in (15.26 m)
**Length with main rotor blades and tail folded:** 40 ft 11 in (12.47 m)
**Length with main rotor blades and tail folded (HH-60H):** 41 ft ⅝ in (12.51 m)
**Length with main rotor blades and tail folded (HH-60J):** 43 ft ⅛ in (13.13 m)
**Height to top of rotor head:** 11 ft 11 in (3.63 m)
**Height overall, rotors turning:** 17 ft (5.18 m)
**Height with tail folded:** 13 ft 3¼ in (4 04 m)
Stabiliser span: 14 ft 4½ in (4.38 m)
**Main rotor diameter:** 53 ft 8 in (16.36 m)
**Tail rotor diameter:** 11 ft (3.35 m)
**Main rotor disc area:** 2,262.03 sq ft (210.05 m²)
**Tail rotor disc area:** 95.03 sq ft (8.83 m²)
**Wheel track:** 9 ft 2 in (2.79 m)
**Wheel base:** 15 ft 10 in (4.83 m)

#### Powerplant

Two General Electric T700-GE-401 turboshafts each rated at 1,690 shp (1260 kW) or, in helicopters delivered from 1988, two General Electric T700-GE-401C turboshafts each rated at 1,900 shp (1417 kW)

#### Weights

**Empty (for the ASW mission):** 13,648 lb (6191 kg)

**Empty (HH-60H):** 13,480 lb (6114 kg)
**Empty (HH-60J):** 13,417 lb (6086 kg)
**Mission take-off (for the ASW mission):** 20,244 lb (9182 kg)
**Maximum take-off (HH-60H and SH-60B for the utility mission):** 21,884 lb (9926 kg)
**Maximum take-off (SH-60F and SH-60R):** 23,500 lb (10659 kg)
**Maximum take-off (HH-60J):** 21,246 lb (9637 kg)

#### Fuel and load

**Internal fuel:** 590 US gal (2233 litres)
**External fuel:** up to two 120-US gal (455-litre) drop tanks
**Internal payload (HH-60H):** 4,100 lb (1860 kg)
**Useful load (HH-60J):** 7,829 lb (3551 kg)
**Maximum payload:** 8,000 lb (3629 kg)

#### Performance

**Dash speed at 5,000 ft (1525 m):** 145 mph (234 km/h)
**Cruising speed at sea level (HH-60H):** 169 mph (272 km/h)
**Cruising speed at sea level (HH-60J):** 168 mph (271 km/h)
**Operational radius (for a 3-hour loiter):** 58 miles (93 km)
**Operational radius (for a 1-hour loiter):** 173 miles (278 km)
**Operational radius (HH-60H on a SAR mission):** 288 miles (463 km)
**Operational radius (HH-60H on a SEAL insertion/extraction mission):** 230 miles (370 km)
**Maximum vertical rate of climb at sea level:** 700 ft (213 m) per minute

mounting
**108** Shock absorber leg strut
**109** Starboard mainwheel
**110** Pivoted axle beam
**111** Starboard navigation light
**112** Cockpit step/main axle fairing
**113** Forward cabin access panel
**114** Collective and cyclic pitch control rods
**115** Sliding fairing guide rails
**116** Cooling air grille

**117** Main rotor blade glass-fibre skins
**118** Honeycomb trailing edge panel
**119** Titanium tube blade spar
**120** Rotor blade drooped leading edge
**121** Leading edge anti-erosion sheathing
**122** Fixed trailing edge tab
**123** Cockpit eyebrow window
**124** Rearview mirrors

**125** Overhead engine throttle and fuel cock control levers
**126** Circuit breaker panel
**127** Pilot's seat
**128** Safety harness
**129** Crash resistant seat mounting
**130** Pull-out emergency exit window panel

**131** Flight deck floor level
**132** Cockpit door
**133** Boarding step
**134** AN/APS-124 search radar antenna
**135** Ventral radome
**136** Retractable landing/hovering lamp
**137** Downward vision window
**138** Yaw control

rudder pedals
**139** Cyclic pitch control column
**140** Instrument panel
**141** Centre instrument console
**142** Stand-by compass
**143** ATO/co-pilot's seat
**144** Outside air temperature gauge
**145** Instrument panel shroud
**146** Air data probes
**147** Windscreen panels
**148** Windscreen wipers

**149** Hinged nose compartment access panel
**150** Pitot tubes
**151** Avionics equipment bay
**152** Forward data link antenna
**153** Forward AN/ALQ-142 ESM aerial housings

*Early SH-60Bs used the lower-rated T700-GE-401 engine, which was later replaced in production by the T700-GE-401C of the HH-60H and HH-60J. By 2002, the US Navy expects its SH-60R to begin entering service. The SH-60R sees all the capabilities of the SH-60B combined with the dipping sonar of the SH-60F to produce the so-called LAMPS Block 2 helicopter. Up to 170 SH-60Bs, 77 SH-60Fs and 42 HH-60Hs are likely to be brought up to the new standard, which is optimised for littoral warfare.*

# Westland Lynx

*The Brazilian navy received nine Lynx Mk 21s, based on the Royal Navy's HAS.Mk 2 with some minor changes in avionics equipment. The surviving seven airframes are being upgraded to Super Lynx standard as Mk 21As and are being joined by nine new-build examples from Westland.*

### Lynx AH.Mk 9

**Cutaway key**
1 Nose cone
2 Circuit-breaker panel
3 Forward radar warning antennas, port and starboard
4 Electrical system relays
5 Nose avionics equipment bay
6 Gyro platform
7 UHF aerials
8 Ventilating air intake
9 Flight-control computer
10 Avionics bay access door, port and starboard
11 Battery
12 Cockpit front bulkhead
13 Pitot head
14 Underfloor control linkages
15 Yaw control rudder pedals
16 Cyclic pitch control column
17 Downward-vision window
18 Instrument panel
19 Instrument panel shroud
20 Windscreen wipers
21 Curved windscreen panels
22 Outside air temperature probe
23 Composite rotor blade construction
24 Honeycomb core trailing edge
25 Glassfibre blade skins
26 Leading-edge anti-erosion sheath
27 Rescue hoist/winch, 600-lb (272-kg) capacity
28 Hoist pintle mounting, starboard cabin doorway
29 Cockpit roof glazing
30 Engine power and condition levers
31 Overhead switch panel
32 Safety harness
33 Pilot's seat

34 Centre control pedestal
35 Chart case
36 Boarding step
37 Port navigation light
38 Collective pitch control lever
39 Jettisonable cockpit door
40 Control rod linkages
41 Forward fuselage arch double main frame
42 Direct-vision sliding side window panel
43 Co-pilot/observer's seat
44 TOW missile sight periscope
45 Swivelling turret mounting
46 Hughes (British Aerospace licence-built) TOW sighting unit
47 Optical sighting aperture
48 Miniaturised thermal imaging system scanners
49 Control system ducting
50 Sliding cowling rail
51 Starboard aft-sliding main cabin door
52 Cabin wall trim/soundproofing panelling
53 Glassfibre honeycomb cabin roof construction
54 Lightweight detachable troop seats (nine fully-armed troops)
55 Side window panel
56 Port aft sliding cabin door
57 Sliding door latch
58 Emergency jettison handle
59 Forward underfloor fuel tank, total fuel capacity 1,616 lb (773 kg)
60 Lower sliding door rail
61 Floor beam construction

62 Lower fuselage access panels
63 Fuselage keel web member
64 Fuel collector tanks (two)
65 Forged gearbox mounting main frame
66 Forward gearbox mounting
67 Lateral control auto-stabilised servo-actuator
68 Hydraulic reservoir, dual system
69 Hydraulic equipment module, port and starboard
70 Alternators (two)
71 Alternator cooling air duct

72 Collective pitch servo-actuator
73 Longitudinal pitch control autostabilised servo-actuator
74 Forward-sliding equipment bay cowling
75 Hingeless main rotor hub, titanium
76 Blade pitch control horns

77 Pitch bearings
78 Flexible blade arm
79 Blade root attachment joints
80 Four-bladed main rotor
81 Drag hinge dampers

82 Blade pitch control rods
83 Main rotor mast
84 Main gearbox
85 Gearbox mounting deck
86 Sliding cabin door top rail fairing
87 Main cabin frame and stringer construction
88 Fuel tank access panel

89 Main fuel tanks, port and starboard
90 Fuel filler cap
91 Intake dust/debris ejector
92 Engine air intake filter screen

93 Engine/gearbox transmission shaft
94 Rotor brake
95 Compressor air intake
96 Starter/generator intake/exhaust fairing
97 Starboard engine cowling

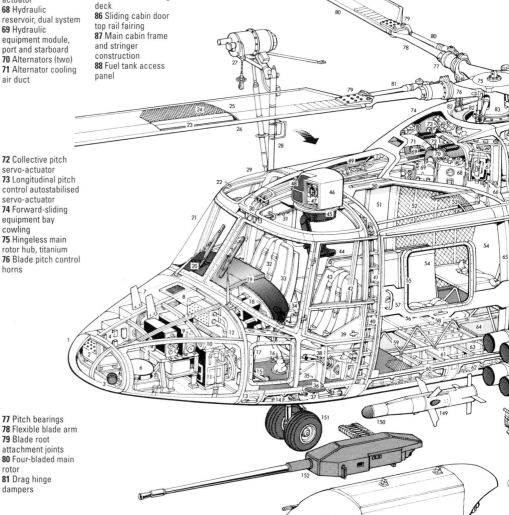

West Germany eventually received a total of 19 Lynx Mk 88s for the ASW role. The aircraft were delivered to a standard similar to that of the FAA's HAS.Mk 2, but with Gem 41-2 turboshafts and a non-folding tail boom.

## SPECIFICATION

### Lynx AH.Mk 7

### Dimensions

**Length overall, rotors turning:** 49 ft 9 in (15.16 m)
**Fuselage length:** 39 ft 7 in (12.06 m)
**Main rotor diameter:** 40 ft (12.80 m)
**Tail rotor diameter:** 7 ft 3 in (2.21 m)
**Height overall, rotors stationary:** 12 ft (3.66 m)
**Main rotor disc area:** 1,385.44 sq ft (128.71 m²)
**Tail rotor disc area:** 41.28 sq ft (3.84 m²)
**Stabiliser span:** 5 ft 10 in (1.78 m)
**Skid track:** 6 ft 8 in (2.03 m)

### Powerplant

Two Rolls-Royce Gem 41-1 turboshafts each rated at 1,120 shp (835 kW), from 1987 the engines were upgraded to Gem 42-1 standard, rated at 1,135 shp (846 kW)

### Weights

**Empty:** 5,683 lb (2578 kg)
**Maximum take-off:** 10,750 lb (4876 kg)

### Performance

**Maximum continuous cruising speed:** 140 kt (161 mph; 259 km/h)
**Economical cruising speed:** 70 kt (81 mph; 130 km/h)
**Hover ceiling out-of-ground effect:** 10,600 ft (3230 m)
**Maximum rate of climb:** 2,480 ft (756 m) per minute at sea level
**Ferry range:** 724 nm (835 miles; 1342 km) with auxiliary fuel
**Standard range:** 340 nm (392 miles; 630 km)
**Typical range on troop-carrying mission:** 292 nm (336 miles; 540 km)
**Endurance:** 3 hours

### Fuel and load

**Internal fuel:** 214 Imp gal (973 litres) plus provision for 47 Imp gal (214 litres) in one fuselage tank or 192 Imp gal (873 litres) in two fuselage ferry tanks
**Maximum ordnance:** about 1,210 lb (549 kg)

### Armament

One or two 20-mm cannon, 0.3-in (7.62-mm) Miniguns or rocket projectile pods; six AS11s, two Stinger or eight HOT, Hellfire, TOW or ATOW air-to-surface missiles

---

98 Engine bay dividing fireproof bulkhead, titanium
99 Starter/generator
100 Engine accessory equipment gearbox
101 Main engine mounting
102 Fireproof engine mounting deck, titanium
103 Rolls-Royce Gem 42-1 turboshaft engines
104 Engine bay rear fireproof bulkhead
105 Multi-lobe exhaust duct
106 Exhaust cooling air intakes
107 Infra-red suppressor fairings
108 Tail rotor transmission shaft
109 Shaft bearings
110 Dorsal spine fairings/access panels
111 Bevel drive intermediate gearbox
112 Tail pylon bracing struts
113 Tail rotor angled drive shaft
114 Gearbox cooling air intake
115 Fixed horizontal stabiliser
116 Stabiliser tubular spar
117 Final drive right-angled gearbox
125 Tail rotor control linkage
126 Tail pylon construction
127 Tailboom ring frame construction
143 Cooling air scoop
144 HF homing aerial rail, port and starboard
157 Rocket-launcher pack (19 FFARS)
158 SURA 3.1-in (80-mm) air-to-surface unguided rockets
159 Ammunition magazine

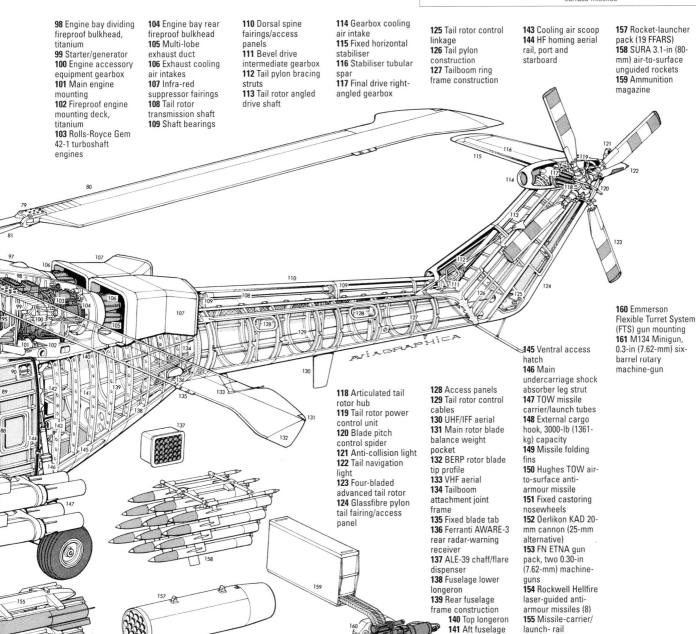

118 Articulated tail rotor hub
119 Tail rotor power control unit
120 Blade pitch control spider
121 Anti-collision light
122 Tail navigation light
123 Four-bladed advanced tail rotor
124 Glassfibre pylon tail fairing/access panel
128 Access panels
129 Tail rotor control cables
130 UHF/IFF aerial
131 Main rotor blade balance weight pocket
132 BERP rotor blade tip profile
133 VHF aerial
134 Tailboom attachment joint frame
135 Fixed blade tab
136 Ferranti AWARE-3 rear radar-warning receiver
137 ALE-39 chaff/flare dispenser
138 Fuselage lower longeron
139 Rear fuselage frame construction
140 Top longeron
141 Aft fuselage equipment bay
142 Electrical system equipment racks
145 Ventral access hatch
146 Main undercarriage shock absorber leg strut
147 TOW missile carrier/launch tubes
148 External cargo hook, 3000-lb (1361-kg) capacity
149 Missile folding fins
150 Hughes TOW air-to-surface anti-armour missile
151 Fixed castoring nosewheels
152 Oerlikon KAD 20-mm cannon (25-mm alternative)
153 FN ETNA gun pack, two 0.30-in (7.62-mm) machine-guns
154 Rockwell Hellfire laser-guided anti-armour missiles (8)
155 Missile-carrier/launch- rail
156 2.75-in (70-mm) folding-fin aircraft rockets (FFAR)
160 Emmerson Flexible Turret System (FTS) gun mounting
161 M134 Minigun, 0.3-in (7.62-mm) six-barrel rotary machine-gun

# Naval Aircraft

# Breguet Atlantic/Dassault Atlantique 2

The most noticeable differences between the Atlantique 2 (seen here) and the Atlantic are the former's wingtip ECM pods, nose-mounted Tango FLIR turret, the prominent cooling intakes below the cockpit and the re-shaped fin top, housing an ECM aerial.

## Atlantique 2

**Cutaway key**

1 Nose compartment glazing
2 Forward-looking infra-red sensor (FLIR)
3 Observer's sight
4 Side window
5 Forward observer's seat
6 Access doorway to flight deck
7 Nose landing gear pivot fixing
8 Nosewheel steering jacks
9 Taxiing lamps
10 Nosewheel leg door
11 Twin nosewheels
12 Nose landing-gear leg strut
13 Hydraulic retraction jack
14 Air-conditioning system ram air intake
15 Heat exchangers
16 Air-conditioning plant, electronics systems cooling air
17 Control rod linkages
18 Rudder pedals
19 Instrument panel
20 Flight deck bulkhead
21 Windscreen-wipers
22 Instrument panel shroud
23 Windscreen panels
24 Overhead switch panel
25 VHF aerial
26 Starboard propeller spinner
27 Four-bladed constant-speed propeller
28 Engine air inlet
29 Detachable engine cowling panels
30 Cockpit roof escape hatch
31 Aircraft commander's seat
32 Flight engineer's swivelling seat
33 Cockpit eyebrow window
34 Control column handwheel
35 Pilot's seat
36 Side console panel
37 Observer's folding seat
38 Main cabin bulkhead
39 Curtained doorway

40 TACAN aerials
41 Periscope sextant mounting
42 Radio navigator's station
43 Moving map display
44 Starboard underfloor APU bay
45 Radome raising and lowering hydraulic motor
46 Fuselage lower lobe frame construction
47 Thomson-CSF Iguane search radar
48 Air-conditioning system exhaust duct
49 Retractable radome
50 Weapons bay forward bulkhead
51 Externally sliding weapons bay doors
52 Door guide rails
53 Bomb door honeycomb construction
54 Fuselage pressurised section honeycomb skin panels
55 Port side radio and electronics racks
56 ESM, ECM and MAD systems operator's seat
57 Radar operator's seat
58 Tactical co-ordinator's seat
59 Display consoles
60 IFF aerial
61 Starboard engine nacelle fairing
62 Outer-wing panel joint
63 Starboard wing integral fuel tank; total system capacity 5,086 Imp gal (23120 litres)
64 Landing/search light
65 Wing stores pylons
66 AM39 Exocet air-to-surface missiles
67 Leading-edge pneumatic de-icing boots
68 Wing access panels
69 UHF aerial
70 Wingtip ECM pod
71 Starboard navigation light
72 Static dischargers

73 Starboard outer aileron
74 Starboard inner aileron
75 Aileron mass balance weights
76 Aileron hydraulic jack
77 Spoiler/airbrake panels, open
78 Spoiler hydraulic jacks
79 Outboard, two-segment double-slotted flaps
80 Flap screw jacks
81 Starboard engine exhaust nozzle
82 Anti-collision light
83 Wing/fuselage attachment main frames
84 Sonobuoy display consoles
85 Teleprinters
86 Sonobuoy operators' seats (two)
87 Electronics racks cooling air ducting
88 Wing centre-section carry through
89 Central flap hydraulic motor
90 Starboard escape hatch
91 DF aerial
92 Life raft stowage
93 Port escape hatch
94 Pressure floor beam construction
95 Bomb-bay door hydraulic motor
96 Crew rest area seating, port and starboard
97 Galley compartment
98 Dining table
99 Toilet compartment
100 Wardrobe
101 Curtained doorway
102 Rear observers' seats, port and starboard
103 Binocular mounting rail
104 Observation bubble window
105 Cabin doorway
106 Rear pressure bulkhead
107 Flare stowage rack
108 Sonobuoy stowage rack, maximum load 72 A or A3 sonobuoys

109 Rear fuselage frame and stringer construction
110 Tailplane mounting bulkhead
111 Finroot fillet
112 Tailplane leading-edge de-icing boots
113 Starboard HF aerial cable
114 Starboard tailplane
115 Starboard elevator
116 Static dischargers
117 Fin leading-edge de-icing boot
118 Fin construction
119 Fin honeycomb skin panels
120 Fintip ECM aerial housing
121 Static dischargers
122 Rudder mass balance weights
123 Rudder construction

124 Rudder hydraulic jack
125 Tail navigation light
126 Tailboom extension
127 MAD boom
128 MAD detector head
129 Port elevator construction
130 Elevator hydraulic jack
131 Tailplane construction
132 Tailplane honeycomb skin panels
133 Leading-edge de-icing boot
134 Port HF aerial cable
135 Rudder and elevator control rods
136 Rear entry hatch
137 Extending boarding ladder

*The five crew positions on the starboard side of the Atlantique 2's cabin are used for monitoring the aircraft's various systems. The two closest positions are sonobuoy display consoles, which are the responsibility of the sonobuoy operators. Next is the tactical co-ordinator's screen which displays correlated information from all of the systems. To the left is the radar operator and, finally, the ESM, ECM and MAD systems operator's position.*

## SPECIFICATION

### Atlantique 2

### Dimensions

**Length:** 103 ft 9 in (31.62 m)
**Height:** 35 ft 8¼ in (10.89 m)
**Wingspan:** 122 ft 9¼ in (37.42 m)
**Wing area:** 1,295.37 sq ft (120.34 m²)
**Wing aspect ratio:** 10.94
**Tailplane span:** 40 ft 4½ in (12.31 m)
**Wheel track:** 29 ft 6¼ in (9.00 m)
**Wheel base:** 30 ft 10 in (9.40 m)

### Powerplant

Two Rolls-Royce Tyne RTy.20 Mk 21 turboprops each rated at 6,100 ehp (4549 ekW)

### Weights

**Empty equipped:** 56,437 lb (25600 kg)
**Normal take-off:** 97,443 lb (44200 kg) for ASW role or 99,206 lb (45000 kg) for combined ASW and ASV roles
**Maximum take-off:** 101,852 lb (46200 kg)

### Fuel and load

**Internal fuel:** 40,785 lb (18500 kg)
**External fuel:** none
**Maximum external ordnance:** 7,716 lb (3500 kg)
**Maximum internal ordnance:** 5,512 lb (2500 kg)

### Performance

**Maximum level speed 'clean':** 349 kt (402 mph; 648 km/h)
**Maximum cruising speed at 23,620 ft (7200 m):** 300 kt (345 mph; 556 km/h)
**Normal patrol speed between sea level and 5,000 ft (1525 m):** 170 kt (196 mph; 315 km/h)
**Maximum rate of climb at sea level:** 2,900 ft (884 m) per minute
**Service ceiling:** 30,000 ft (9145 m)
**Take-off distance to 35 ft (10.50 m) at maximum take-off weight:** 6,037 ft (1840 m)
**Landing distance from 35 ft (10.50 m) at normal landing weight:** 4,921 ft (1500 m)
**Ferry range:** 4,897 nm (5,639 miles; 9075 km)
**Operational radius:** 1,799 nm (2,071 miles; 3333 km) for a 2-hour ASV patrol or 599 nm (690 miles; 1110 km) for an 8-hour ASW patrol at low-level
**Endurance:** 18 hours

### Armament

The weapons bay can accommodate all NATO-standard bombs, depth charges, two ASMs, up to eight Mk 46 torpedoes or seven Murène advanced torpedoes; the four wing pylons can carry additional stores, including future ASMs, AAMs and equipment pods

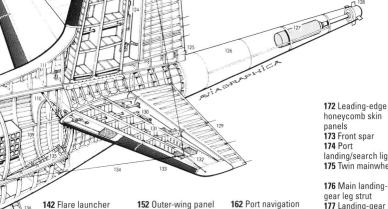

172 Leading-edge honeycomb skin panels
173 Front spar
174 Port landing/search light
175 Twin mainwheels

176 Main landing-gear leg strut
177 Landing-gear leg pivot fixing
178 Mainwheel leg doors
179 Hydraulic retraction jack
180 Mainwheel bay doors, closed
181 Main landing-gear wheel bay
182 Heat shrouded exhaust pipe
183 Port engine nacelle construction
184 Engine cowling doors
185 Fireproof bulkhead

186 Engine bleed air and pre-cooler exhaust louvres
187 Rolls-Royce Tyne RTy.20 Mk 21 turboprop engine
188 Ventral oil cooler duct
189 De-iced engine air inlet
190 Oil cooler ram air intake
191 Propeller hub pitch change mechanism
192 Spinner
193 Four-bladed constant-speed propeller
194 Propeller blade root de-icing cuffs
195 Mk 46 lightweight torpedo
196 Depth charge

138 Tail bumper
139 Tailplane trim feel units
140 Camera
141 Sonobuoy/flare launcher, inflight loadable
142 Flare launcher door
143 AM39 Exocet air-to-surface missile
144 Aft bomb bay door
145 Bomb door actuating mechanism
146 Inboard double-slotted flap
147 Centre wing panel construction
148 Port engine tailpipe
149 Exhaust nozzle
150 Flap guide rails
151 Inner-wing integral fuel tank bay
152 Outer-wing panel bolted skin joint
153 Rear spar
154 Port airbrake/spoiler panels
155 Outboard two-segment double-slotted flaps
156 Flap rib construction
157 Aileron rib construction
158 Port inboard aileron
159 Port outboard aileron
160 Static dischargers
161 Wingtip ECM pod
162 Port navigation light
163 Wing rib construction
164 UHF aerial
165 Pitot tube
166 Port wing stores pylons
167 AM39 Exocet air-to-surface missiles
168 Leading-edge de-icing boots
169 Aluminium honeycomb wing skin panels
170 Wing centre spar
171 Outer wing panel integral fuel tank bay

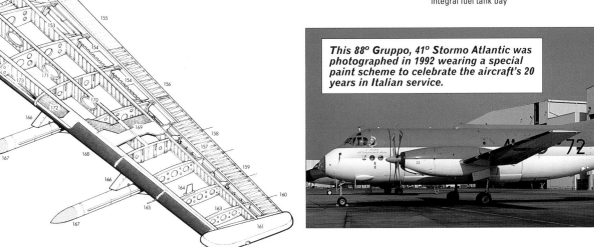

*This 88° Gruppo, 41° Stormo Atlantic was photographed in 1992 wearing a special paint scheme to celebrate the aircraft's 20 years in Italian service.*

# British Aerospace Sea Harrier

Following the success of the Sea Harrier/AIM-9L Sidewinder combination during the Falklands conflict, the Royal Navy's aircraft were modified to carry twin launcher rails under each wing, thus doubling their potential AAM capacity. The two aircraft illustrated wear the 'winged fist' insignia of No. 899 NAS, a squadron which formed at Yeovilton in April 1980 from the existing No. 700A Squadron. A No. 899 Squadron pilot scored the first Argentine fighter kill (a Mirage III) in the Falklands.

## Sea Harrier FRS.Mk 1

**Cutaway key**
1 Pitot head
2 Radome
3 Ferranti Blue Fox radar scanner
4 Radar equipment module
5 Radome hinge
6 Nose pitch reaction control valve
7 Pitch feel and trim control mechanism
8 Rudder pedals
9 Starboard side oblique camera
10 Inertial platform
11 IFF aerial
12 Cockpit ram air intake
13 Yaw vane
14 Pressurisation spill valve
15 Windscreen wiper
16 Head-up display
17 Instrument panel shroud
18 Control column and linkages
19 Doppler antenna
20 TACAN aerial
21 UHF aerial
22 Nose undercarriage wheel bay
23 Radar hand controller
24 Throttle and nozzle angle control levers
25 Martin-Baker Mk 10H zero-zero ejection seat
26 Miniature detonating cord (MDC) canopy breaker
27 Boundary layer spill duct
28 Cockpit air-conditioning pack
29 Nose undercarriage hydraulic retraction jack
30 Hydraulic accumulator
31 Boundary layer bleed duct
32 Engine air intake
33 Intake suction relief doors (spring-loaded)
34 Forward fuselage flank fuel tank
35 Hydraulic system ground connectors
36 Engine monitoring and recording equipment
37 Engine oil tank
38 Rolls-Royce Pegasus Mk 104 turbofan engine
39 UHF homing aerials
40 Alternator
41 Accessory equipment gearbox
42 Gas turbine starter/auxiliary power unit (GTS/APU)
43 Starboard external fuel tank
44 Starboard wing integral fuel tank
45 Twin missile pylon
46 Starboard navigation light
47 Roll control reaction air valve
48 Outrigger wheel fairing
49 Starboard outrigger wheel
50 Starboard aileron
51 Aileron hydraulic actuator
52 Fuel jettison valve
53 Starboard plain flap
54 Anti-collision light
55 Water methanol tank
56 Engine-fire suppression bottle
57 Flap hydraulic actuator
58 Water-methanol filler cap
59 Rear fuselage fuel tank
60 Emergency ram air turbine extended
61 Ram air turbine actuator
62 Heat exchanger air intake
63 HF tuner
64 HF notch aerial
65 Rudder control linkage
66 Starboard all-moving tailplane
67 Temperature probe
68 Forward radar-warning antenna
69 VHF aerial
70 Rudder
71 Rudder trim tab
72 Rear rudder-warning antenna
73 Tail pitch control reaction air valve
74 Yaw control reaction air valves
75 Port all-moving tailplane
76 IFF notch aerial
77 Tail bumper
78 Radar altimeter aerials
79 Reaction control air duct
80 Tailplane hydraulic actuator
81 Rear equipment bay air conditioning pack
82 Chaff/flare dispensers
83 Avionics equipment bay
84 Airbrake hydraulic jack
85 Ventral airbrake
86 Liquid oxygen converter
87 Hydraulic system nitrogen pressurising bottle
88 Main undercarriage stowage

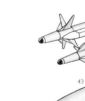

*The new-generation Sea Harrier (initially known as the FRS.Mk 2) features a stretched fuselage (with a plug inserted behind the wing) and a refined wing, with new wingtips and a revised, kinked leading edge. A further advance was the introduction of the Ferranti Blue Vixen radar, providing a new multiple target-tracking and all-weather look-down/shoot-down capability.*

## SPECIFICATION

### Sea Harrier FRS.Mk 1

#### Dimensions

**Overall length:** 47 ft 7 in (14.50 m)
**Length with nose folded:** 41 ft 9 in (12.73 m )
**Wingspan:** 25 ft 3 in (7.70 m)
**Wingspan with ferry tips:** 29 ft 8 in (9.04 m)
**Wing area:** 202.10 sq ft (18.68 m²)
**Wing aspect ratio:** 3.175

#### Powerplant

One Rolls-Royce Pegasus Mk 104 vectored thrust turbofan rated at 21,500 lb st (95.6 kN)

#### Weights

**Basic empty:** 13,000 lb (5897 kg)
**Operating empty:** 14,502 lb (6374 kg)
**Maximum take-off weight:** 26,200 lb (11884 kg)

#### Fuel load

**Maximum internal fuel:** 5,060 lb (2295 kg)
**Maximum external fuel:** 5,300 lb (2404 kg) in two 100-Imp gal (455-litre) drop tanks or two 330- or 190-Imp gal (1500- or 864-litre) ferry tanks; maximum ordnance 8,000 lb (3629 kg)

#### Performance

**Maximum speed at high altitude:** 825 mph (1328 km/h)
**Maximum speed 'clean' at sea level:** more than 736 mph (1185 km/h)

**Cruising speed at 36,000 ft (10975 m):** 528 mph (850 km/h)
**Maximum rate of climb at sea level:** 50,000 ft (15240 m) per minute
**Service ceiling:** 51,000 ft (15545 m)
**Take-off run:** 1,000 ft (305 m) at maximum take-off weight without 'ski jump'; landing run 0 ft (0 m) at normal landing weight

#### Range

**Combat radius:** 460 miles (750 km) on a hi-hi-hi interception mission with four AAMs, or 288 miles (463 km) on a hi-lo-hi attack mission.
**g limit:** +7.8/-4.2

#### Armament

Underfuselage mounts for two 30-mm ADEN cannon, and four underwing hardpoints stressed for up to 8,000 lb (3629 kg). Standard carrying capabilities as follows: underfuselage and inboard wing hardpoints 2,000 lb (907 kg) each; outboard wing pylons 650 lb (295 kg) each. Cleared for carriage of standard British 1,000-lb (454-kg) free-fall and retarded HE bombs, BAe Sea Eagle ASM, AGM-84 Harpoon ASM, WE177 tactical nuclear free-fall bomb, Lepus flare units, CBLS 100 practice bomb dispenser and most NATO-standard bombs, rockets and flares. Air-to-air armament can comprise four AIM-9L Sidewinders on twin-rail launchers, or MATRA Magic missiles on Indian aircraft

---

89 Nozzle blast shield
90 Port wing integral fuel tank
91 Port plain flap
92 Fuel jettison
93 Port aileron
94 Outrigger wheel hydraulic retraction jack
95 Port outrigger wheel
96 Roll control reaction air valve
97 Port navigation light
98 AIM-9L Sidewinder air-to-air missiles
99 Twin missile carrier/launcher
100 Outboard stores pylon

101 Reaction control air duct
102 Port aileron hydraulic actuator
103 External fuel tank
104 Inboard wing pylon
105 Rear (hot-stream) swivelling exhaust nozzle
106 Main undercarriage hydraulic retraction jack
107 Pressure refuelling connection

108 Nozzle bearing cooling air duct
109 Hydraulic system reservoir, port and starboard
110 Centre fuselage flank fuel tank
111 Fan air (cold-stream) swivelling nozzle

112 Ammunition magazine
113 ADEN 30-mm cannon
114 Ventral gun pack, port and starboard

Mike Badrocke

*India acquired four two-seat Harrier T.Mk 60s to complement its squadron of FRS.Mk 51s. Indian Sea Harriers operate alongside Sea King helicopters on the nation's remaining carrier, INS Viraat (ex-HMS Hermes).*

*As the first Sea Harriers entered Royal Navy service, high-visibility unit markings, inherited from their operator's Phantoms, were de rigeur. The colourful fin flashes and gloss white bellies of these No. 800 Squadron aircraft were removed during the Falklands War.*

# De Havilland D.H.110 Sea Vixen

*In 1961 two Sea Vixen FAW.Mk 1s fresh off the Christchurch production line – XN684 and XN685 – were flown to Hatfield and converted to an interim FAW.Mk 2 standard. Once procedures for the conversion programme were established both aircraft were employed in development work concerning the Red Top AAM. XN684 carries four in this view and has a special test camera fitted under its nose.*

## Sea Vixen FAW.Mk 1/2

**Cutaway key**

1 Glass-fibre radome
2 GEC A1 radar scanner
3 Scanner gimballing mechanism
4 Radome hinge point, opens to starboard
5 Wave form generator
6 Power pulse unit
7 Radar modulator
8 Radome latch
9 Radar transmitter/receiver
10 Lower IFF aerial
11 UHF aerial
12 2-in folding fin rocket
13 Landing taxiing and carrier approach lights
14 Nosewheel leg door
15 Levered suspension nosewheel forks
16 Nosewheel, aft-retracting
17 Microcell 14-round rocket launcher, extended
18 Rocket launcher hydraulic jack
19 Nose undercarriage pivot mounting
20 Front pressure bulkhead
21 Rudder pedals
22 Control column
23 Nosewheel housing
24 Cockpit rain dispersal air duct fairing
25 Instrument panel shroud

26 Ferranti gun sight
27 Upper IFF aerial
28 Knife-edged windscreen panels
29 Observer's instrument panel
30 Sliding cockpit canopy cover
31 Canopy framing, FAW.Mk 1 (clear canopy on FAW.Mk 2)
32 Observer's instrument console
33 Pilot's Martin-Baker Mk 4 ejection seat
34 Engine throttle levers
35 Fuel cocks
36 Rudder Q-feel dashpot
37 Airbrake hinge point
38 Ventral airbrake, open
39 Airbrake strake
40 Airbrake hydraulic jack
41 Boundary layer splitter plate
42 Electronics equipment racks
43 Port engine air intake
44 Ventral air-conditioning system ram air intake
45 Boundary layer spill duct
46 Canopy release strut
47 Canopy de-misting air duct
48 Observer's ejection seat
49 Bulged hatch fairing (on modified FAW.Mk 2 aircraft)
50 Observer's entry hatch

51 Starboard engine air intake
52 Rear pressure bulkhead
53 Electrical and Low-Altitude Bombing System (LABS) equipment bays, port and starboard
54 Boundary layer spill air louvres
55 Centre section fuel tank
56 Fuel filler, port and starboard
57 Intake de-icing air duct
58 Engine intake ducting
59 Central air-conditioning equipment bay
60 Intake flank fuel tank
61 Ventral catapult strop hook
62 Mainwheel door actuator
63 Engine fire suppression bottle

64 Port main undercarriage wheel bay
65 Engine bleed air ducting
66 Rolls-Royce Avon 208 engine
67 Starter housing intake fairing
68 Bleed air spill duct
69 Air-conditioning controllers
70 VHF aerials
71 Starboard mainwheel, stowed position
72 Starboard intake flank fuel tank
73 Tailboom fuel tank
74 Extended tailboom fairing (FAW.Mk 2 only)
75 Outer wing panel integral fuel tank
76 Wing fence
77 Aileron trim actuator
78 Autopilot actuator

79 Extended chord outboard leading edge
80 Pitot head
81 Starboard navigation light
82 Aileron horn balance
83 Starboard aileron
84 Aileron hydraulic actuator
85 Chain and sprocket flap drive
86 Outboard Fowler-type flap
87 Extended tailboom aft fairing
88 Flap drive shafts
89 Wing fold hydraulic deck

90 Hydraulic reservoir, leader tank and accumulator
91 Inboard flap segment guide rails

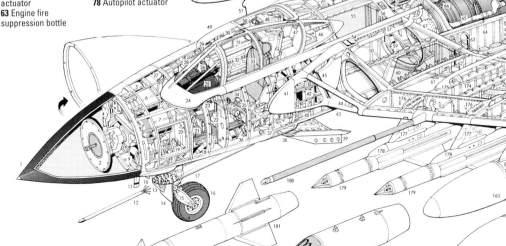

## SPECIFICATION

**Sea Vixen FAW.Mk 1**

### Dimensions

**Length:** 55 ft 7 in (16.94 m)
**Length (nose folded):** 50 ft 2½ in (15.3 m)
**Height:** 10 ft 9 in (3.28 m)
**Wingspan:** 50 ft (15.24 m)
**Wing area:** 648 sq ft (60.20 m²)

### Powerplant

Two Rolls-Royce Avon 208 turbojet engines each rated at 11,230 lb st (49.95 kN)

### Weights

**Empty:** 27,952 lb (12679 kg)
**All-up:** 35,000 lb (15876 kg)
**Maximum take-off:** 41,575 lb (18858 kg)

### Fuel and load

**External fuel:** Provision for two 150-Imp gal (682-litre) drop tanks
**Maximum ordnance:** up to 2,000 lb

(907 kg) of ordnance on underwing pylons

### Performance

**Maximum speed at sea level:** 690 mph (1110 km/h)
**Maximum speed at 10,000 ft (3048 m):** 645 mph (1038 km/h)
**Time to 10,000 ft (3048 m):** 1½ minutes
**Time to 40,000 ft (12192 m):** approximately 6½ minutes
**Service ceiling:** 48,000 ft (14630 m)

### Armament

Up to four de Havilland Firestreak IR-homing air-to-air missiles on underwing pylons; two retractable Microcell rocket packs under the forward fuselage, each holding 14 2-in (5.08-cm) rockets; a 500-lb (227-kg) or 1,000-lb (454-kg) GP bomb, napalm tank, rocket pod (carrying either 2-in/5.08-cm or 3-in/7.62-cm rockets) or Martin Bullpup A air-to-surface missile on each of the inner pair of AAM pylons

*A concession in the DH.110's design, made to improve the aircraft's suitability for deck operations, was the offset cockpit. This allowed the Sea Vixen's pilot to see forward over the large radome, forward visibility being an important consideration when landing an aircraft on a carrier deck. This aircraft, seen being catapulted from the deck of a carrier, has the 'V' tailcode of HMS Victorious.*

**92** Engine bay venting air intakes
**93** Starboard engine bay
**94** Fuselage centre keel member
**95** Detachable firewall upper segment (for engine removal)
**96** Flap drive cable drum
**97** Flap hydraulic actuator
**98** Arrester hook jack and damper
**99** Engine jet pipe
**100** Arrester hook stowage
**101** Exhaust nozzle fairing
**102** Emergency ram air turbine, extended
**103** Static inverters
**104** Tailboom electrical equipment bay
**105** Hydraulic accumulators
**106** Tail bumper
**107** Starboard rudder
**108** Tailplane rib and stringer construction
**109** Wing panels, folded position
**110** Rudder hydraulic actuator
**111** All-moving horizontal tailplane
**112** Tailplane rib construction
**113** Fin/tailplane fairing
**114** Tail navigation lights
**116** Tab balance weights
**117** Tailplane tip fairing
**118** Tab control linkage
**119** Tailplane pivot mounting
**120** Tailplane hydraulic actuator
**121** Rudder mass balance weight
**122** Port rudder hydraulic actuator
**123** Rudder rib construction
**124** Tie-down point
**125** Tail bumper
**126** Bumper strut
**127** Tailboom/fin joint frame
**128** Tailboom frame construction
**129** Telebriefing socket
**130** Tailplane control cables
**131** Port electrical equipment bay
**132** Inverter cooling air intake
**133** Tailboom joint ring frame
**134** Air bottles
**135** Port inboard flap segment
**136** Autopilot control unit
**137** Flap drive shafts and gearboxes
**138** Wing fold hydraulic jack
**139** Wing fold hinge fittings
**140** Outboard flap segment guide rails
**141** Flap rail fairings
**142** Flap shroud ribs
**143** Rear spar
**144** Aileron hydraulic actuator
**145** Port aileron rib construction
**146** Refuelling drogue, extended
**147** Port aileron horn balance
**148** Tip fairing construction
**149** Outer wing panel rib construction
**150** Port navigation light
**151** Leading-edge nose ribs
**152** Red Top air-to-air missile (arming FAW.Mk 2 only)
**153** Pitot head
**154** Aileron control rod linkage
**155** Leading-edge dog-tooth
**156** Wing fence honeycomb construction
**157** Fuel tank end rib
**158** Semi-span centre spar
**159** Port outer wing panel integral fuel tank
**160** Front spar
**161** Mainwheel leg door
**162** 'Buddy' refuelling pack
**163** 150-Imp gal (682-litre) external fuel tank
**164** Fuel filler
**165** Fuel tank pylon
**166** Port mainwheel
**167** Torque scissor links
**168** Pylon hard point
**169** Main undercarriage leg strut
**170** Side breaker strut
**171** Undercarriage leg pivot mounting
**172** Hydraulic retraction jack
**173** Wing fold hinge rib
**174** Wing inboard segment integral fuel tank
**175** Tailboom forward fairing (FAW.Mk 1)
**176** Light stores pylon fittings
**177** Missile pylons
**178** Missile launch rails
**179** Firestreak air-to-air missiles (arming FAW.Mk 1)
**180** Flight refuelling boom
**181** Bullpup A air-to-surface missile
**182** 36 x 2-in (50-mm) rocket pack

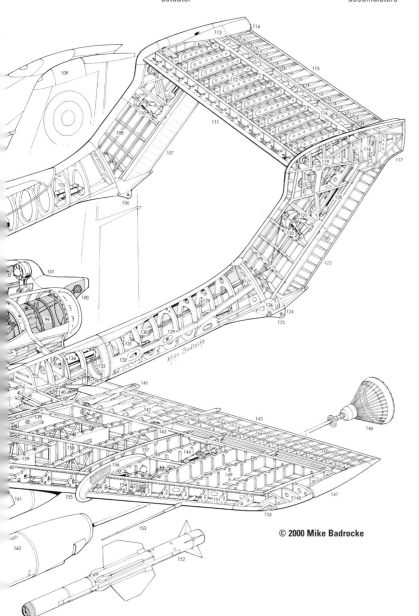

© 2000 Mike Badrocke

# Douglas AD/A-1 SkyRaider

With its distinctive exhaust staining around the engine cowling, this early unmarked Skyraider is seen on a test flight. It wears the second colour scheme introduced on the Skyraider family, consisting of gull-grey upper surfaces and white undersides

## A-1H Skyraider
### Cutaway key

1 Aeroproducts four-bladed, variable-pitch propeller, 13 ft 6-in (4.1-m) diameter
2 Propeller hub pitch change mechanism
3 Gearbox cowling
4 Retractable cooling air baffles
5 Starboard underwing fuel tank
6 Cowling nose ring
7 Propeller reduction gearbox
8 Wright R-3350-26WA 18-cylinder, two-row radial engine
9 Detachable cowling panels
10 Starboard mainwheel
11 Mainwheel disc brake
12 Centre line auxiliary fuel tank, capacity 300 US gal (1136 litres)
13 Oil cooler intake
14 Exhaust stubs
15 Oil cooler
16 Engine bearer lower segment
17 Oil tank, capacity 38.5 US gal (146 litres)
18 Engine mounting ring
19 Engine accessory equipment
20 Port magneto
21 Carburettor
22 Carburettor intake
23 Cockpit air-ducting
24 Armoured front bulkhead
25 Engine bearer upper segment
26 Cowling air exit flaps
27 Exhaust shields
28 Rudder pedals
29 Cockpit floor level
30 Hydraulic reservoir
31 Oxygen bottle
32 Electrical system distribution box
33 Autopilot controller
34 Boarding step
35 Control linkages
36 Port side console panel

37 Engine throttle and propeller control levers
38 Control column
39 Circuit-breaker panel
40 Instrument panel
41 Windscreen de-misting air duct
42 Instrument panel shroud
43 Reflector gun sight
44 Armoured glass windscreen
45 Starboard mainwheel, retracted position
46 Ammunition tank, 200 rounds
47 Main undercarriage retraction jack
48 Gun camera
49 Starboard inboard pylon
50 Approach light
51 BLU-11B, 500-lb (227-kg) napalm tanks
52 Cannon barrels
53 M3 20-mm cannon
54 Front spar hinge joint
55 Ammunition feed drums
56 Outboard ammunition tank, 200 rounds
57 Starboard outer underwing pylons (six)
58 Ventral pitot tube
59 Radar warning antennae
60 Starboard navigation light
61 Wingtip fairing
62 Static dischargers
63 Starboard aileron
64 Starboard wing, folded position
65 Cannon bay access panels
66 Rear spar hinge joint
67 Wing fold hydraulic jack
68 Starboard Fowler-type flap
69 Sliding cockpit canopy cover

70 Armoured headrest
71 Pilot's seat
72 Canopy external handle
73 Safety harness
74 Adjustable seat mountings
75 Armoured cockpit rear bulkhead
76 Main fuel tank; internal fuel capacity 378 US gal (1431 litres)

77 Hand grip
78 Fuselage top longeron
79 Fuel vent pipe
80 Sliding canopy rail

81 Port wing, folded position

82 VHF aerial
83 Dorsal section frame and stringer construction
84 IFF aerial
85 ADF antenna
86 Fuselage dorsal skin panelling

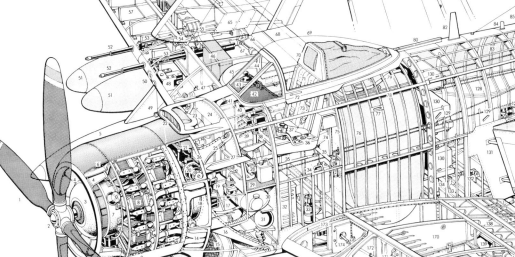

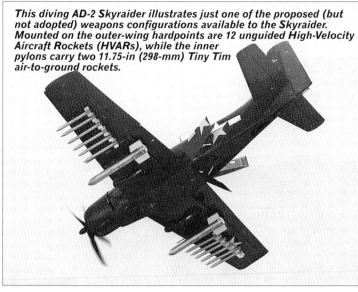

*This diving AD-2 Skyraider illustrates just one of the proposed (but not adopted) weapons configurations available to the Skyraider. Mounted on the outer-wing hardpoints are 12 unguided High-Velocity Aircraft Rockets (HVARs), while the inner pylons carry two 11.75-in (298-mm) Tiny Tim air-to-ground rockets.*

## SPECIFICATION

### A-1H Skyraider

**Dimensions**

**Length:** 38 ft 10 in (11.84 m)
**Wingspan:** 50 ft ¼ in (15.25 m)
**Wing area:** 400 sq ft (37.19 m²)
**Height:** 15 ft 8¼ in (4.78 m)

**Powerplant**

One 2,700-hp (2013-kW) Wright R-3350-26WA 18-cylinder, two-row radial piston engine driving a four-bladed constant-speed propeller.

**Weights**

**Empty:** 11,968 lb (5429 kg)
**Normal take-off:** 18,106 lb (8213 kg)
**Maximum take-off:** 25,000 lb (11340 kg)

**Fuel and load**

**Total main internal fuel:** 314.5 Imp gal (1431 litres)

**Maximum bombload:** 8,000 lb (3629 kg)

**Performance**

**Maximum speed:** 322 mph (518 km/h) at 18,000 ft (5485 m)
**Cruising speed:** 198 mph (319 km/h)
**Initial climb rate:** 2,850 ft (869 m) per minute
**Service ceiling:** 28,500 ft (8685 m)
**Take-off run (to 50 ft/15 m):** 4,649 ft (1417 m)
**Landing run (from 50 ft/15 m):** 3,002 ft (915 m)

**Range**

**Operational range :** 1,315 miles (2116 km)

**Armament**

Four wing-mounted 20-mm cannon, each with 200 rounds of ammunition plus up to 8,000 lb (3629 kg) of external stores

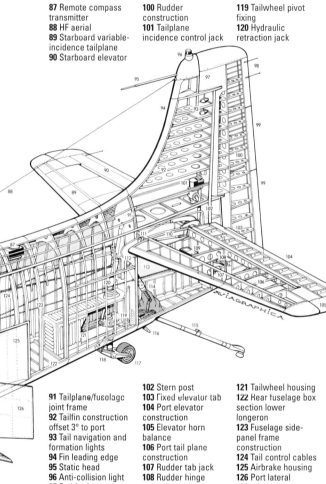

87 Remote compass transmitter
88 HF aerial
89 Starboard variable-incidence tailplane
90 Starboard elevator
91 Tailplane/fuselage joint frame
92 Tailfin construction offset 3° to port
93 Tail navigation and formation lights
94 Fin leading edge
95 Static head
96 Anti-collision light
97 Rudder horn balance
98 Static dischargers
99 Rudder tabs
100 Rudder construction
101 Tailplane incidence control jack
102 Stern post
103 Fixed elevator tab
104 Port elevator construction
105 Elevator horn balance
106 Port tail plane construction
107 Rudder tab jack
108 Rudder hinge control
109 Radar altimeter transmitter/receiver
110 Elevator control rod
111 Variable-incidence tailplane pivot fixing
112 Tailplane sealing plate
113 Starboard side access panel
114 Arrester hook jack damper
115 Deck arresting hook, down
116 Catapult hold-back link
117 Tailwheel solid tyre
118 Castoring tailwheel forks
119 Tailwheel pivot fixing
120 Hydraulic retraction jack
121 Tailwheel housing
122 Rear fuselage box section lower longeron
123 Fuselage side-panel frame construction
124 Tail control cables
125 Airbrake housing
126 Port lateral airbrake, open
127 Airbrake hydraulic actuators
128 Starboard lateral airbrake housing
129 Handgrips
130 Radio and electronics equipment racks
131 Airbrake-reinforced hinge panel
132 Central flap hydraulic jack
133 Flap torque shaft
134 Battery
135 Boarding step
136 Ventral airbrake, open
137 Port Fowler-type flap construction
138 Flap shroud ribs
139 Flap external hinge
140 Wing fold hydraulic jack
141 Rear spar hinge joint
142 Trailing-edge fence
143 Aileron tab
144 Auxiliary fuel tank tail fins
145 Port aileron construction
146 Aileron balance weights
147 Static dischargers
148 Wingtip fairing
149 Port navigation light
150 5-in (127-mm) HVAR air-to-ground rocket
151 Rocket pack, 19 x 2.75-in (70-mm) folding fin rockets
152 Radar warning antenna
153 Main spar
154 Port wing rib construction
155 Inter-rib stiffeners
156 Outboard ammunition tank, 200 rounds
157 Leading-edge rib construction
158 Port outboard wing pylons
159 Auxiliary fuel tank. capacity 300 US gal (1136 litres)
160 Inboard pylon
161 Cannon barrels
162 Approach light
163 Recoil spring
164 Front spar hinge joint
165 Ammunition feed drums
166 Aileron control rod
167 M3 20-mm cannon
168 Cartridge case ejector chute
169 Inboard ammunition tank, 200 rounds
170 Main undercarriage wheel bay
171 Hydraulic retraction jack
172 Main undercarriage mounting diagonal ribs
173 Wing spar/fuselage attachment joint
174 Aileron push/pull control rod
175 Catapult strop attachment link
176 Main undercarriage pivot fixing
177 Retraction linkage
178 Folding rear struts
179 Main undercarriage leg strut
180 Leg strut fairing
181 Wheel rotation push rod, wheel rotated 90° to lie flat in wing bay
182 Port mainwheel
183 AN-M66A2 2,000-lb (907-kg) HE bomb
184 Mk 82 500-lb (227-kg) bomb
185 Mk 81 250-lb (113-kg) low-drag bomb
186 SUU-11A rocket launcher, 4 x 5-in (12.7-cm) folding fin rockets
187 5-in (12.7-cm) folding fin air-to-ground rocket

## Douglas Skyraider variants

**XBT2D:** first version with 2,300-hp (1716-kW) R-3350-24W, included prototypes of five other versions; total 25
**AD-1:** redesignation of BT2D-1, with 2,500-hp (1865-kW) R-3350-24W engine and strengthened structure; total 242
**AD-1Q:** ECM platform with jammer pod on left wing and ECM operator in fuselage cabin; total 35
**AD-2:** further strengthening, more fuel, 2,700-hp (2014-kW) R-3350-26W engine, mainwheel doors added; total 156
**AD-2D:** conversion to drone (RPV) directors
**AD-2Q:** ECM version; total 22
**AD-2Q(U):** further rebuild to tow Mk 22 target
**AD-3:** further strengthening, long-stroke main gears; Aeroproducts propeller and new canopy; total 124
**AD-3E:** conversion for ASW search
**AD-3N:** night-attack version; total 15
**AD-3Q:** ECM version; total 23
**AD-3S:** anti-submarine attack, partner to AD-3E; all conversions
**AD-3W:** AEW version with improved APS-20 surveillance radar and two operators in fuselage cabin, plus auxiliary fins; total 31
**AD-4:** refined structure, cleared for great increase in gross weight from 18,500 lb (8392 kg) to 24,000 lb (10886 kg); P-1 autopilot, modified windscreen, improved radar (APS-19A) option; total 344
**AD-4B:** four cannon, provision for nuclear bombs; total 194
**AD-4L:** conversion for winter (Arctic)
**AD-4N:** night-attack version with APS-19A; total 248
**AD-4NA:** night version stripped for day attack; total 23 plus conversions; redesignated (A-1D) from 1962
**AD-4NL:** winterised night version; total 36
**AD-4Q:** ECM version; total 39
**AD-4W:** RN designation AEW.Mk 1; total 168
**AD-5 (A-1E):** redesigned multi-role model with wide forward and longer overall fuselage, side-by-side cockpit, taller fin, side dive brakes removed (leaving ventral brake), four guns standard, provision for quick role conversions; cleared to 25,000 lb (11340 kg); total 212
**AD-5N (A-1G):** night-attack version; total 239
**AD-5Q (EA-1F):** ECM conversions of 54 aircraft
**AD-5S:** (no 1962 designation) anti-submarine conversion
**AD-5U (UA-1E):** conversions as target tow/transport for 12 seats or 3,000 lb (1361 kg) of freight
**AD-5W (EA-1E):** AEW version; total 156
**AD-6 (A-1H):** new standard close-support single-seater, LABS toss-bombing avionics and reinforced wing as AD-4B; total 713
**AD-7 (A-1J):** further reinforced wing and main gear, 3,050-hp (2275-kW) R-3350-26WB engine; total 72

# Douglas A-4 Skyhawk

Two-seat Skyhawks provided carrier-capab... training facilities for USN/USMC aircrew from 19(... until 1999, when the last training examples we... replaced by T-45A Goshawks. Pictured is a TA-4J... VT-7, which finally retired the type from the USN... training establishment in September 1999, leavin... Puerto Rico-based target facilities squadron VC... as the only Navy unit with Skyhawks in 200...

## A-4M Skyhawk

### Cutaway key

1 Fixed inflight refuelling probe
2 Nose ECM recording and suppression aerials
3 Angle-Rate Bombing System (ARBS) laser seeker head
4 Hinged nose compartment access door
5 Laser seeker system electronics
6 Electronics cooling air inlet
7 Pitot tube
8 Avionics access panel
9 APN-153(V) navigation radar
10 Lower TACAN aerial
11 Communications electronics
12 Cockpit front pressure bulkhead
13 Pressurisation valve
14 Windshield rain dispersal air duct
15 Rudder pedals
16 Angle-of-attack sensor
17 Air conditioning refrigeration plant
18 Nosewheel door
19 Control system access
20 Cockpit floor level
21 Pilot's side console panel
22 Engine throttle
23 Control column
24 Instrument panel shroud
25 Head-up display (HUD)
26 Windscreen panels
27 AIM-9L Sidewinder air-to-air missile
28 Missile launch rail
29 D-704 flight refuelling pack containing 300 US gal (1135 litres)
30 Cockpit canopy cover
31 Face blind firing handle

32 Ejection seat headrest
33 Safety harness
34 McDonnell Douglas ESCAPAC IG-3 'zero-zero' ejection seat
35 Anti-*g* valve
36 Cockpit insulation and fragmentation blanket
37 Rear pressure bulkhead
38 Emergency canopy release handle
39 Nose undercarriage leg strut
40 Steering linkage
41 Nosewheel
42 Leg shortening link
43 Hydraulic retraction strut

44 Emergency wind-driven generator
45 Port cannon muzzle
46 Intake gun gas shield
47 Port air intake
48 Boundary layer splitter plate
49 Self-sealing fuselage fuel cell, capacity 240 US gal (908 litres)
50 Fuel system piping
51 Canopy hinge cover
52 Starboard air intake duct
53 Fuel system gravity filler cap
54 UHF aerial

55 Electronics cooling air inlet
56 Engine-driven generator
57 Constant-speed drive
58 Bifurcated intake duct
59 Reel-type ammunition magazine (200 rounds per gun)
60 Intake compressor face
61 Electrical system power amplifier
62 Engine accessory drive gearbox

63 Wing spar attachment fuselage double frame
64 Engine mounting trunnion
65 Engine fuel system access panel
66 Pratt & Whitney J52-P-408 turbojet
67 Dorsal avionics bays
68 Compressor bleed air exhaust duct
69 Upper TACAN aerial

70 Starboard wing integral fuel tank (total wing capacity 560 US gal/2120 litres)
71 Wing tank access panels
72 Slat guide rails
73 Starboard automatic leading-edge slat (open)
74 Wing fences
75 Vortex generators
76 Starboard navigation light
77 Wing tip communications aerial

78 Aileron horn balance
79 Starboard aileron
80 Split trailing-edge spoiler (open position)
81 Starboard split trailing-edge flap (down position)
82 Anti-collision light
83 Cooling air exit louvres

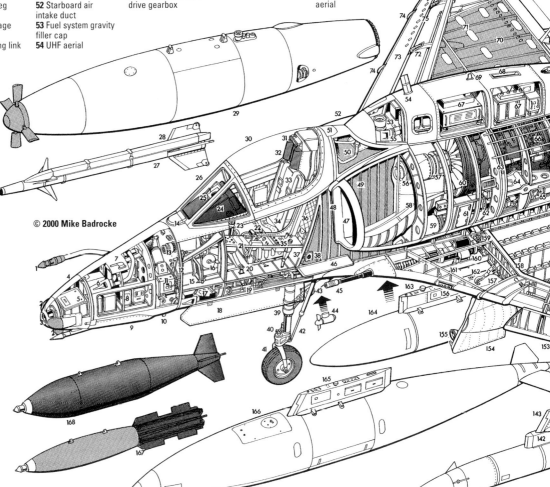

© 2000 Mike Badrocke

*BuNo. 160264 was the 2,960th and last Skyhawk constructed, after a production run that had lasted no less than 27 years and finally ended in 1979. An A-4M for the USMC, the aircraft incorporated all the improvements introduced during the 'Mike's 10-year production life, including a redesigned cockpit, Elliott HUD, laser spot tracker, ECM equipment and a new GE generator. An angle-rate bombing system (ARBS) had been added in 1977. With so many changes to the A-4M consideration was given to redesignating these late-production aircraft as A-4Ys, but this was not proceeded with as most early A-4Ms were eventually upgraded.*

## SPECIFICATION

| A4D-2N Skyhawk | A-4M Skyhawk |
| --- | --- |
| **Dimensions** | **Dimensions** |
| **Fuselage length:** 39 ft 4¾ in (12.01 m)<br>**Height:** 15 ft (4.57 m)<br>**Wingspan:** 27 ft 6 in (8.38 m)<br>**Wing area:** 260.00 sq ft (24.15 m²) | **Fuselage length:** 40 ft 3½ in (12.29 m)<br>**Height:** 15 ft (4.57 m)<br>**Wingspan:** 27 ft 6 in (8.38 m)<br>**Wing area:** 260.00 sq ft (24.15 m²) |
| **Powerplant** | **Powerplant** |
| One Wright J65-W-16A turbojet rated at 7,700 lb st (34.25 kN) | One Pratt & Whitney J52-P-408A turbojet rated at 11,200 lb st (49.80 kN) |
| **Weights** | **Weights** |
| **Empty:** 9,559 lb (4336 kg)<br>**Normal loaded:** 17,295 lb (7845 kg) | **Empty:** 10,465 lb (4747 kg)<br>**Maximum take-off:** 24,500 lb (11113 kg) |
| **Fuel and load** | **Fuel and load** |
| **Internal fuel capacity:** 770 US gal (2910 litres)<br>**External fuel capacity:** 500 US gal (1893 litres) | **Internal fuel capacity:** 800 US gal (3028 litres)<br>**External fuel capacity:** up to 1,000 US gal (3786 litres) |
| **Performance** | **Performance** |
| **Maximum speed at sea level:** 680 mph (1094 km/h) | **Maximum speed at sea level:** 685 mph (1102 km/h)<br>**Maximum rate of climb at sea level:** 10,300 ft (3140 m) per minute<br>**Service ceiling:** 38,700 ft (11795 m)<br>**Combat radius:** 345 miles (547 km) with a 4,000-lb (1814-kg) warload |
| **Armament** | **Armament** |
| Two Colt Mk 12 20-mm cannon, each with 200 rounds of ammunition, plus up to 5,000 lb (2268 kg) of weapons on three external hardpoints | Two Colt Mk 12 20-mm cannon, each with 200 rounds of ammunition, plus up to 9,155 lb (4153 kg) of weapons on five external hardpoints |

**84** Rear fuselage double frame break point
**85** Engine firewall
**86** Cooling air intake
**87** VHF aerial
**88** Upper fuselage stringers
**89** Fin root dorsal fairing
**90** Remote compass flux valve
**91** Rear electronics bay cooling air inlet
**92** Fin rib construction
**93** Fin spar attachment joint
**94** Rudder hydraulic jack
**95** Artificial feel spring unit
**96** Pitot tube
**97** Fin tip ECM antenna housing
**98** Externally-braced rudder construction

**99** Fixed rudder tab
**100** Tail navigation light
**101** ECM antennas
**102** Tailplane trim jack
**103** Tailplane seal plate
**104** Elevator hydraulic jack
**105** Tailpipe fairing
**106** Port elevator
**107** All-moving tailplane construction
**108** Elevator horn balance
**109** Jet pipe exhaust nozzle
**110** Brake parachute housing for 16-ft (4.88-m) diameter, ribbon type 'chute
**111** Brake parachute release linkage
**112** Insulated jet pipe
**113** Electronics bay heat shield
**114** Rear electronics bay, automatic flight control system (AFCS)
**115** Port airbrake (open)
**116** JATO bottle attachment hardpoints
**117** Airbrake hydraulic jack
**118** 2.65-US gal (10-litre) liquid oxygen (LOX) converter
**119** Arrester hook (down position)
**120** Arrester hook hydraulic jack
**121** Control cable runs
**122** Inertial platform
**123** Ventral pressure refuelling connection
**124** Central hydraulic flap drive linkage
**125** Port upper surface spoiler
**126** Spoiler hydraulic jack
**127** Ventral anti-collision light
**128** Wing rib construction
**129** Stringer construction

**130** Port wing integral fuel tank (single tank tip-to-tip)
**131** Rear spar
**132** Port split trailing-edge flap
**133** Port aileron construction
**134** Aileron trim tab
**135** Tip fairing
**136** Aileron horn balance
**137** Wing tip antenna fairing
**138** Port navigation light
**139** LAU-10A Zuni rocket launcher
**140** 5-in (12.7-cm) folding fin rocket
**141** AGM-12 Bullpup air-to-ground missile
**142** Missile launcher rail
**143** Outboard wing pylon (1,000-lb/454-kg capacity)
**144** Port automatic leading-edge slat (open)
**145** Wing fences
**146** Vortex generators
**147** Aileron control rod linkage
**148** Leading-edge ribs
**149** Wing centre spar
**150** Main undercarriage hydraulic retraction jack
**151** Undercarriage leg pivot mounting
**152** Slat guide rail fuel sealing can
**153** Port mainwheel
**154** Mainwheel door
**155** Position of landing lamp on starboard mainwheel door
**156** Approach lights
**157** Retractable catapult hook
**158** Cranked wing front spar
**159** Aileron servo control

**160** Colt Mk 12 20-mm cannon
**161** Spent cartridge case and link ejector chutes
**162** Mainwheel well
**163** Centreline pylon (3,575-lb/1622-kg capacity)
**164** 150-US gal (568-litre) fuel tank
**165** Inboard wing pylon (2,240-lb/1016-kg capacity)
**166** 400-US gal (1514-litre) long-range fuel tank
**167** Snakeye 500-lb (227-kg) retarded bomb
**168** Mk 83 1,000-lb (454-kg) HE bomb

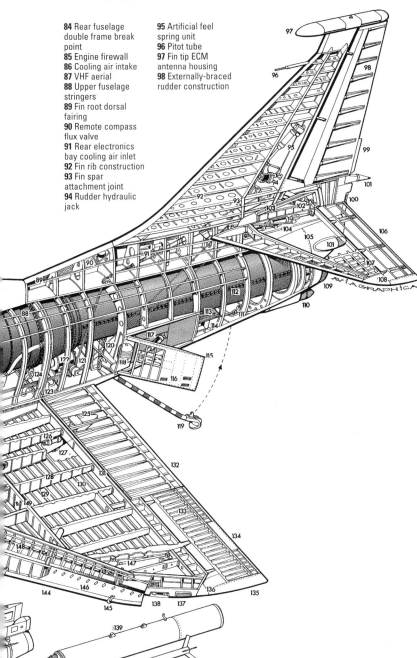

# Grumman A-6E Intruder

An A-6E from VA-34, carrying one ATM-84E Stand-off Land Attack Missile, receives fuel from a Kansas Air National Guard KC-135E during the SLAM-O-RAMA exercise over the Naval Air Weapons Station, Patuxent River, MD. During Desert Storm, an A-6E from the USS Kennedy made the first-ever combat launch of a SLAM.

## A-6E (TRAM) Intruder

### Cutaway key

1 Radome
2 Radome open position
3 Norden AN/APQ-148 multi-mode radar scanner
4 Scanner-tracking mechanism
5 Intermediate frequency unit
6 ILS aerials
7 TRAM rotating turret mounting
8 Target Recognition and Attack Multisensor turret (TRAM)
9 Taxiing lamp
10 Deck approach lights
11 Nosewheel leg door
12 Hydraulic nosewheel steering unit
13 Catapult launch strap
14 Twin nosewheels (aft-retracting)
15 Retraction/breaker strut
16 Shock-absorber leg strut
17 Torque scissor links
18 Radome latch
19 Hinged avionics equipment pallet (port and starboard)
20 Radar scanner mounting
21 Radome hydraulic jack
22 Flight-refuelling probe
23 ALQ-165 ECM system forward spiral antenna
24 Refuelling probe spotlight
25 Windscreen rain-repellent air duct
26 Front-pressure bulkhead
27 Nosewheel bay-mounted pressure refuelling connection
28 Boundary layer splitter plate

29 Port engine air intake
30 Nosewheel bay electronic equipment racks
31 VHF aerial
32 UHF aerial
33 Intake duct framing
34 Temperature probe
35 Canopy emergency release handle
36 TACAN aerial
37 Folding boarding ladder
38 Integral boarding steps
39 Angle-of-attack transmitter
40 Boundary layer spill duct
41 Cockpit floor level
42 Rudder pedals
43 Engine throttle levers
44 Control column
45 Instrument panel shroud
46 Pilot's optical sighting unit/head-up display
47 Windscreen panels
48 Aft-sliding cockpit canopy cover
49 Forward-Looking Infra-Red (FLIR) viewing scope
50 Navigator/ Bombardier's Martin Baker GRU-7 ejection seat
51 Ejection seat headrests
52 Seat-reclining mechanism
53 Centre console
54 Pilot's GRU-7 ejection seat
55 Safety/parachute harness
56 Port side console panel
57 Electrical system equipment
58 Destruct initiator
59 Leading-edge stall warning buffet strip
60 Engine intake compressor face
61 Engine bay venting air scoop
62 Accessory equipment gearbox

63 Pratt & Whitney J52-P-8B non-afterburning turbofan
64 Mainwheel door
65 Leading-edge antenna fairing (port and starboard)
66 ILQ-165 high-, mid- and low-band ECM aerials
67 Mainwheel well
68 Hydraulic system reservoir
69 Cockpit rear-pressure bulkhead
70 Cooling air spill louvres
71 Electrical equipment bay
72 Electronics and avionics equipment bay
73 Forward fuselage bag-type fuel tank

74 Weapons-monitoring module
75 Sliding canopy rail
76 Canopy hydraulic jack

77 Canopy aft fairing
78 Starboard wing inboard integral fuel tank; total fuel capacity 1,951 Imp gal (2344 US gal/8870 litres)

79 Fuel system piping
80 Inboard wing fence
81 Leading-edge slat drive shaft
82 Slat guide rails
83 Slat screw jacks
84 AGM-65 Maverick air-to-surface missiles
85 Triple missile carrier/launcher
86 Starboard wing stores pylons

87 AIM-9P Sidewinder 'self-defence' air-to-air missile
88 Wing fold twin hydraulic jacks
89 Spar hydraulic latch pins
90 Wing fold hinge joint

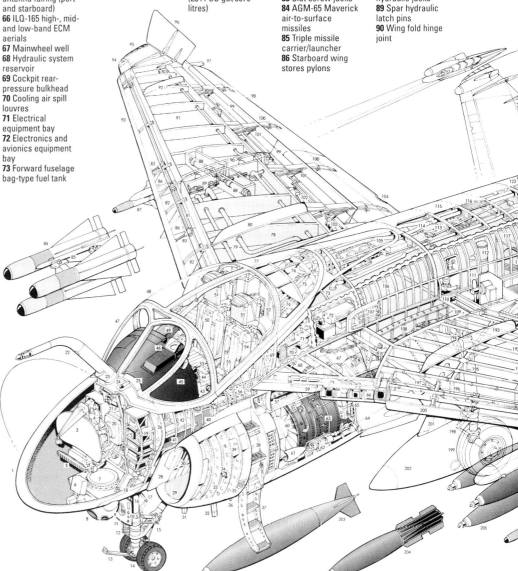

*EA-6B Prowlers performed sterling service throughout the Gulf War, providing stand-off (nicknamed 'white snow') jamming on every strike. Desert Storm also gave the Prowler the chance to demonstrate its ability as a HARM-shooter on strike escort missions.*

## SPECIFICATION

### A-6E Intruder

**Dimensions**
Length: 54 ft 9 in (16.69 m)
Height: 16 ft 2 in (4.93 m)
Wingspan: 53 ft (16.15 m)
Width, folded: 25 ft 4 in (7.72 m)
Wing area: 528.90 sq ft (49.13 m²)
Wing aspect ratio: 5.31
Wheel track: 10 ft 10½ in (3.32 m)

**Powerplant**
Two Pratt & Whitney J52-P-8B turbojets, each rated at 9,300 lb st (41.4 kN) dry

**Weights**
Empty: 27,613 lb (12525 kg)
Maximum take-off for catapult launch: 58,600 lb (26580 kg)
Maximum take-off for field launch: 60,400 lb (27397 kg)

**Fuel and load**
Internal fuel: 15,939 lb (7230 kg)
External fuel: up to 10,050 lb (4558 kg) in five 400-US gal (1514-litre) drop tanks
Maximum ordnance: 18,000 lb (8165 kg)

**Performance**
Never-exceed speed: 700 kt (806 mph; 1297 km/h)
Maximum level speed 'clean' at sea level: 560 kt (644 mph; 1037 km/h)
Cruising speed at optimum altitude: 412 kt (474 mph; 763 km/h)
Service ceiling: 42,400 ft (12925 m)

**Range**
Ferry range: 2,818 nm (3,245 miles; 5222 km) with empty tanks dropped
Ferry range: 2,380 nm (2,740 miles; 4410 km) with empty tanks retained
Range with maximum military load: 878 nm (1,011 miles; 1627 km)

**Armament**
The A-6 carried its stores on one centreline and four wing pylons. Virtually all the US Navy/Marine Corps inventory of stores could be carried. Stand-off weapons included the AGM-62 Walleye, AGM-84 Harpoon, AGM-84E SLAM, AGM-88 HARM and AGM-123 Skipper. Mk 82 and 83 general-purpose bombs, B57 and B61 nuclear bombs, ADM-141 decoy drones and AIM-9s were also compatible.

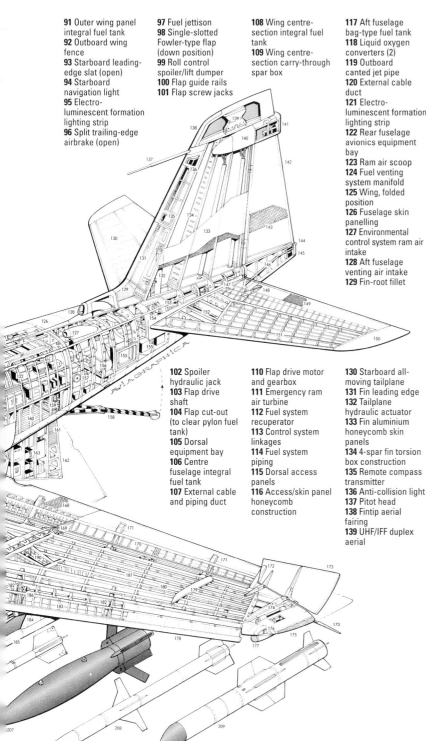

91 Outer wing panel integral fuel tank
92 Outboard wing fence
93 Starboard leading-edge slat (open)
94 Starboard navigation light
95 Electro-luminescent formation lighting strip
96 Split trailing-edge airbrake (open)
97 Fuel jettison
98 Single-slotted Fowler-type flap (down position)
99 Roll control spoiler/lift dumper
100 Flap guide rails
101 Flap screw jacks
102 Spoiler hydraulic jack
103 Flap drive shaft
104 Flap cut-out (to clear pylon fuel tank)
105 Dorsal equipment bay
106 Centre fuselage integral fuel tank
107 External cable and piping duct
108 Wing centre-section integral fuel tank
109 Wing centre-section carry-through spar box
110 Flap drive motor and gearbox
111 Emergency ram air turbine
112 Fuel system recuperator
113 Control system linkages
114 Fuel system piping
115 Dorsal access panels
116 Access/skin panel honeycomb construction
117 Aft fuselage bag-type fuel tank
118 Liquid oxygen converters (2)
119 Outboard canted jet pipe
120 External cable duct
121 Electro-luminescent formation lighting strip
122 Rear fuselage avionics equipment bay
123 Ram air scoop
124 Fuel venting system manifold
125 Wing, folded position
126 Fuselage skin panelling
127 Environmental control system ram air intake
128 Aft fuselage venting air intake
129 Fin-root fillet
130 Starboard all-moving tailplane
131 Fin leading edge
132 Tailplane hydraulic actuator
133 Fin aluminium honeycomb skin panels
134 4-spar fin torsion box construction
135 Remote compass transmitter
136 Anti-collision light
137 Pitot head
138 Fintip aerial fairing
139 UHF/IFF duplex aerial
140 ECM aerial fairing
141 ALQ-165 high-, mid-and low-band ECM transmitting aerials
142 Rudder
143 Rudder honeycomb construction
144 Tail navigation light
145 ALQ-165 ECM receiving aerials
146 Tailcone rudder segment
147 Rudder hydraulic actuator
148 Fuel jettison
149 Tailplane honeycomb trailing-edge section
150 Tailplane tip fairing
151 Multi-spar tailplane construction
152 All-moving tailplane pivot fixing
153 Tailplane hinge control arm
154 Tailplane sealing plate
155 ECM transmitting and receiving equipment
156 Avionics equipment environmental control system
157 Static discharge port
158 Deck arrester hook (lowered)
159 Arrester hook hydraulic jack and damper
160 Structural provision for fuselage air brake (deleted)
161 ALE 45 chaff and flare dispensers
162 Avionics bay ventral access door, open
163 'Birdcage' avionics equipment rack (lowered)
164 Telescopic access ladder
165 Port engine exhaust nozzle
166 Flap rib construction
167 Spoiler hydraulic actuator
168 Flap honeycomb trailing-edge segment
169 Wing fold control linkage breakers
170 Port spoiler rib construction
171 Flap track fairings
172 Fuel jettison
173 Port split trailing-edge airbrake (open)
174 Airbrake hydraulic jack
175 Wingtip electro-luminescent formation lighting strip
176 Port navigation light
177 ALR 45 radar warning receiver
178 Port leading-edge slat (open)
179 Outboard wing fence
180 Multi-spar outer wing panel construction
181 Port wing integral fuel tank
182 Slat guide rails
183 Slat rib construction
184 Additional outer wing missile pylon
185 Missile launch rail
186 Slat screw jack
187 Multiple ejector rack
188 Port outer stores pylon
189 Wing fold hinge joint
190 Wing fold hydraulic jacks
191 Inboard integral fuel tank
192 Inner wing panel multi-spar construction
193 Inboard wing fence
194 Main undercarriage leg pivot fixing
195 Main undercarriage leg strut
196 Leading-edge slat drive shaft
197 Undercarriage leg retraction/breaker strut
198 Torque scissor links
199 Port mainwheel
200 Inboard leading-edge slat segment
201 Inboard stores pylon
202 External fuel tank, capacity 250 or 330 Imp gal (300 or 400 US gal/1135 or 1514 litres)
203 2000-lb (907-kg) low-drag HE bomb
204 Snakeye Mk 92 retarded bomb
205 Mk 83 500-lb (227-kg) HE bombs (6 per rack)
206 AIM-9P Sidewinder 'self-defence' air-to-air missile
207 GBU-10 Paveway (2000-lb/907-kg) laser-guided bomb
208 AGM-88 Harm air-to-surface anti-radar missile
209 AGM-84A Harpoon air-to-surface anti-shipping missile

# Grumman EA-6B Prowler

This EA-6B Prowler is an ICAP (Improved Capability) II Block 82 aircraft with just two dorsal antennas and none under the nose. ICAP II Prowlers were retrospectively dubbed 'Block 82' after the introduction of the so-called 'Block 86' avionics upgrade in 1986.

## EA-6B Prowler

1 Inflight-refuelling probe
2 Radome, upward-hinging
3 APQ-92 radar antenna
4 Pitot head, port and starboard
5 TACAN aerial
6 IFF L-band antenna
7 Forward avionics equipment bay
8 Rudder pedals
9 Pilot's head-down radar display
10 Control column
11 Instrument panel shroud
12 Refuelling probe spotlight
13 Windscreen rain dispersal air duct
14 Upward-hinging cockpit canopy
15 Electronic countermeasures officer No. 1 ejection seat (ECMO-1)
16 Pilot's Martin-Baker GRUEA-7 ejection seat
17 Engine throttle levers
18 Fold-down boarding step
19 Boundary layer splitter plate
20 Nosewheel leg door-mounted landing and approach lights

21 Port engine air intake
22 Temperature probe
23 Canopy emergency release
24 Hinged boarding ladder
25 Nose undercarriage, stowed position
26 Hydraulic retraction jack
27 ECMO display and control consoles
28 Forward canopy actuator
29 Tactical jamming system pod
30 Rear upward-hinging canopy
31 ECMO-2 ejection seat
32 Rear canopy actuator
33 ECMO-3 ejection seat
34 Leading-edge stall-warning buffet strip
35 Stand-by hydraulic pump and selector valves
36 Generator cooling air intake
37 Engine accessory equipment gearbox

38 Pratt & Whitney J52-P-408 turbojet engine
39 Leading-edge radome panel
40 Forward ECM transmitting antennas
41 Main undercarriage stowed position
42 Hydraulic reservoir
43 Central electrical and avionics equipment bay
44 Anti-collision light
45 Starboard wing inboard integral fuel tank
46 Inboard wing fence
47 Wing-fold hydraulic jacks
48 Wing-fold hinge joint
49 Leading-edge slat
50 Outboard integral fuel tank
51 Outboard wing fence
52 Radar warning antenna
53 Starboard navigation light

54 Formation light
55 Split trailing-edge airbrake
56 Fuel jettison
57 Port single-slotted Fowler-type flap
58 Port spoiler/lift dumper
59 UHF/TACAN aerial
60 Fuselage fuel tanks
61 Fuel recuperator
62 ADF aerial

63 Flight control system mechanical linkages
64 Avionics cooling air intakes
65 Cooling system air cycle machine
66 Downward-hinging avionics equipment pallet
67 HF antenna
68 Starboard all-moving tailplane
69 Tailplane hydraulic actuator
70 Band 1 and 2 transmitting antennas
71 Fintip radome

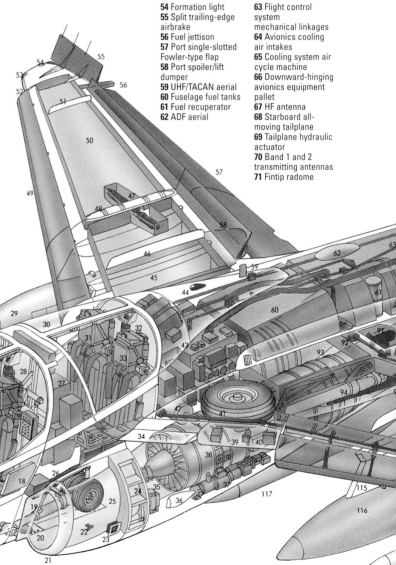

*The key to the EA-6B's success as a jamming system – and one of the reasons it survived and the EF-111A did not – is its four-man crew. Having three dedicated ECMOs, plus a pilot, allows a far greater division of duties between the crew than in comparable aircraft. Here, the ground crew prepare a VAQ-137 aircraft before a mission from USS America.*

## SPECIFICATION

### EA-6B Prowler

#### Dimensions

**Length:** 59 ft 10 in (18.24 m)
**Wingspan:** 53 ft (16.15 m)
**Wingspan, folded:** 25 ft 10 in (7.87 m)
**Wing aspect ratio:** 5.31
**Wing area:** 528.90 sq ft (49.13 m²)
**Height:** 16 ft 3 in (4.95 m)
**Tailplane span:** 20 ft 4½ in (6.21 m)
**Wheel track:** 10 ft 10½ in (3.32 m)
**Wheel base:** 17 ft 2 in (5.23 m)

#### Powerplant

Two Pratt & Whitney J52-P-408 turbojets each rated at 11,200 lb st (49.80 kN) dry

#### Weights

**Empty:** 31,572 lb (14321 kg)
**Normal take-off (equipped):** 54,461 lb (24703 kg)
**Normal take-off (equipped) with maximum fuel:** 60,610 lb (27493 kg)
**Maximum take-off:** 65,000 lb (29484 kg )

#### Fuel

**Internal fuel:** 15,422 lb (6995 kg)
**External fuel:** up to 10,025 lb (4547 kg) in five 400-US gal (1514-litre) drop tanks

#### Performance

**Never-exceed speed:** 710 kt (817 mph; 1315 km/h)
**Maximum level speed 'clean' at sea level:** 566 kt (651 mph; 1048 km/h)
**Maximum level speed carrying five jammer pods at sea level:** 530 kt (610 mph; 982 km/h)
**Cruising speed at optimum altitude:** 418 kt (481 mph; 774 km/h)
**Maximum rate of climb 'clean' at sea level:** 12,900 ft (3932 m) per minute
**Maximum rate of climb with five jammer pods at sea level:** 10,030 ft (3057 m) per minute
**Service ceiling 'clean':** 41,200 ft (12550 m)
**Service ceiling with five jammer pods:** 38,000 ft (11580 m)
**Take-off run with five jammer pods:** 2,670 ft (814 m)
**Take-off distance to 50 ft (15 m) with five jammer pods:** 3,495 ft (1065 m)
**Landing distance from 50 ft (15 m) at maximum landing weight:** 2,700 ft (823 m)
**Landing run with five jammer pods:** 2,150 ft (655 m)
**Ferry range:** 2,085 nm (2,399 miles; 3861 km) with empty tanks dropped
**Range:** 955 nm (1,099 miles; 1769 km) with maximum external load

*Air-to-air refuelling with drogue-equipped USAF aircraft, such as this KC-135R, has become routine for Prowler crews. However, they must now adapt to a new era of completely integrated operations.*

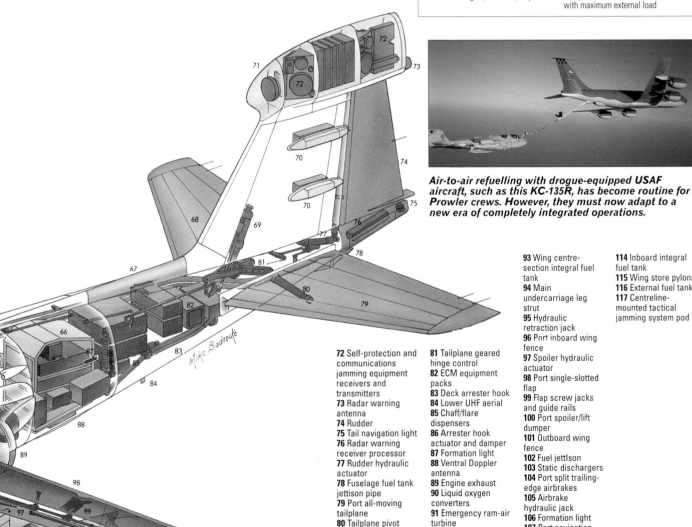

72 Self-protection and communications jamming equipment receivers and transmitters
73 Radar warning antenna
74 Rudder
75 Tail navigation light
76 Radar warning receiver processor
77 Rudder hydraulic actuator
78 Fuselage fuel tank jettison pipe
79 Port all-moving tailplane
80 Tailplane pivot bearing
81 Tailplane geared hinge control
82 ECM equipment packs
83 Deck arrester hook
84 Lower UHF aerial
85 Chaff/flare dispensers
86 Arrester hook actuator and damper
87 Formation light
88 Ventral Doppler antenna
89 Engine exhaust
90 Liquid oxygen converters
91 Emergency ram-air turbine
92 Central flap drive motor and gearbox
93 Wing centre-section integral fuel tank
94 Main undercarriage leg strut
95 Hydraulic retraction jack
96 Port inboard wing fence
97 Spoiler hydraulic actuator
98 Port single-slotted flap
99 Flap screw jacks and guide rails
100 Port spoiler/lift dumper
101 Outboard wing fence
102 Fuel jettison
103 Static dischargers
104 Port split trailing-edge airbrakes
105 Airbrake hydraulic jack
106 Formation light
107 Port navigation light
108 Radar warning antenna
109 Wing outboard integral fuel tank
110 Slat screw jacks and guide
111 Port leading-edge slat
112 AGM-88A HARM anti-radar missile
113 Wing-fold hydraulic jack
114 Inboard integral fuel tank
115 Wing store pylons
116 External fuel tank
117 Centreline-mounted tactical jamming system pod

Mike Badrocke

# Grumman F-14 Tomcat

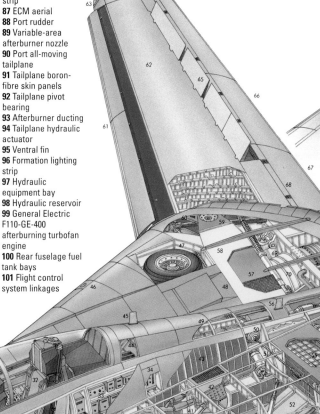

*Symbolising the might of the US Navy's carrierborne air power, the Grumman F-14 Tomcat has been the world's premier long-range interceptor for over 20 years. This F-14A Tomcat of VF-2 'Bounty Hunters' climbs with afterburners blazing at full power.*

## F-14D Tomcat

**Cutaway key**

1 Pitot head
2 Glass-fibre radome
3 IFF aerial array
4 AN/APG-71 flat plate radar scanner
5 Scanner tracking mechanism
6 Infra-red search and track sensor (IRST) and television camera housing
7 Cannon port
8 Weapons system avionics equipment bay
9 Angle of attack transmitter
10 ADF aerial
11 Flight refuelling probe
12 Pilot's head-up display
13 Instrument panel shroud
14 Temperature probe
15 Rudder pedals
16 Control column
17 Electro-luminescent formation lighting strip
18 Nosewheel doors
19 Catapult strop link
20 Twin nosewheels, forward-retracting
21 Boarding ladder, extended
22 M61A1 Vulcan cannon
23 Ammunition drum
24 Pull-out steps
25 Pitot static head
26 Engine throttle levers
27 Pilot's Martin-Baker Mk 14 Navy Aircrew Common Ejection Seat (NACES)

28 Upward-hinged cockpit canopy cover
29 Naval flight officer's instrument console
30 Kick-in step
31 Tactical information display hand controller
32 NFO's ejection seat
33 Rear avionics equipment bay
34 Air data computer
35 Electrical system relays
36 Fuselage missile pallet
37 AIM-54A Phoenix air-to-air missile
38 Port engine air intake
39 Port navigation light
40 Variable-area intake control ramps
41 Intake ramp hydraulic actuators
42 Air conditioning pack
43 Forward fuselage fuel tanks
44 Canopy hinge point
45 UHF/TACAN aerial
46 Starboard navigation light
47 Mainwheel stowed position
48 Starboard intake duct spill door

49 Dorsal control and cable duct
50 Central flap and slat drive hydraulic motor
51 Emergency hydraulic generator
52 Intake by-pass door
53 Electron-beam welded titanium wing pivot box
54 Port wing pivot bearing
55 Pivot box beam integral fuel tank
56 UHF datalink/IFF aerial
57 Honeycomb skin panels
58 Wing glove stiffeners
59 Starboard wing pivot bearing
60 Flap and slat drive shaft and gearbox
61 Starboard leading-edge slat
62 Wing panel fully forward position
63 Navigation light

64 Wingtip formation light
65 Roll control spoilers
66 Outboard manoeuvre flaps
67 Inboard high-lift flap
68 Flap sealing vane
69 Mainwheel leg hinge fitting
70 Variable wing-sweep screw jack
71 Wing glove sealing plates
72 Wing glove pneumatic seal
73 Starboard wing fully swept position
74 Starboard all-moving tailplane
75 Fin-tip aerial fairing
76 Tail navigation light
77 Starboard rudder
78 Rudder hydraulic actuator
79 Variable-area afterburner nozzle control jack
80 Dorsal airbrake (split ventral surfaces)
81 Chaff/flare dispensers
82 Fuel jettison
83 ECM antenna
84 Aluminium honeycomb fin skin panels

85 Anti-collision light
86 Formation lighting strip
87 ECM aerial
88 Port rudder
89 Variable-area afterburner nozzle
90 Port all-moving tailplane
91 Tailplane boron-fibre skin panels
92 Tailplane pivot bearing
93 Afterburner ducting
94 Tailplane hydraulic actuator
95 Ventral fin
96 Formation lighting strip
97 Hydraulic equipment bay
98 Hydraulic reservoir
99 General Electric F110-GE-400 afterburning turbofan engine
100 Rear fuselage fuel tank bays
101 Flight control system linkages

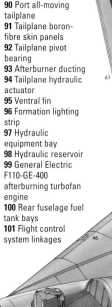

*Left: Exploitation of the Tomcat's air-to-ground capability has turned it into a true multi-role combat aircraft, able to provide a formidable self-escort capability. An F-14A of VF-51 'Screaming Eagles' banks to show a heavy ordnance load of four 2,000-lb (907-kg) 'slick' Mk 84 free-fall bombs.*

**102** Engine bleed air ducting
**103** Port wing-sweep crew jack
**104** Inboard high-lift flap hydraulic jack
**105** Flap hinge links
**106** Flap honeycomb construction
**107** Port wing fully swept position
**108** Port manoeuvre flaps
**109** Wingtip formation light

**110** Navigation light
**111** Port leading-edge slat
**112** Slat guide rails
**113** Wing integral fuel tank
**114** Machined wing rib construction
**115** Main undercarriage leg strut

**116** Port mainwheel, forward-retracting
**117** Wing glove mounted AIM-54A Phoenix air-to-air missile
**118** AIM-9L Sidewinder air-to-air missile
**119** Wing glove pylon
**120** Mainwheel door
**121** External fuel tank
**122** GBU-12D/B Paveway II, 500-lb (227-kg) laser-guided bomb

**123** Mk 82 Snakeye, 500-lb (227-kg) retarded bomb
**124** Phoenix pallet weapons adapter
**125** GBU-24A/B Paveway III, 2,000-lb (907-kg) laser-guided bomb
**126** AN/AAQ-14 LANTIRN navigation and targeting pod, carried on starboard glove pylon
**127** GBU-16 Paveway II, 1,000-lb (454-kg) laser-guided bomb

**128** Mk 83 AIR, 1,000-lb (454-kg) retarded bomb
**129** Mk 83 AIR inflated ballute
**130** Mk 7 submunition dispenser
**131** LAU-97, 4-round rocket launcher

**132** 5-in (127-mm) Zuni FFAR (Folding-Fin Air Rocket)
**133** TARPS reconnaissance pod, carried in centreline tunnel
**134** ALQ-167 countermeasures pod, carried on forward fuselage Phoenix pallet station

## SPECIFICATION

**F-14A Tomcat (unless otherwise noted)**

### Dimensions

**Fuselage length (including probe):** 62 ft 8 in (19.10 m)
**Wing span:** (unswept) 64 ft 1½ in (19.54 m); (swept) 38 ft 2½ in (11.65 m); (overswept) 33 ft 3½ in (10.15 m)
**Wing aspect ratio:** 7.28
**Tailplane span:** 32 ft 8½ in (9.97 m)
**Wing area:** 565 sq ft (52.49 m²)
**Total slat area:** 46.2 sq ft (4.29 m²)
**Total flap area:** 106.3 sq ft (9.87 m²)
**Total spoiler area:** 21.2 sq ft (1.97 m²)
**Horizontal tail area:** 140 sq ft (13.01 m²)
**Total fin area:** 85 sq ft (7.90 m²)
**Total rudder area:** 33 sq ft (3.06 m²)
**Tailplane area:** 140 sq ft (13.01 m²)
**Distance between fin-tips:** 10 ft 8 in (3.25 m)
**Overall height:** 16 ft (4.88 m)
**Wheel track:** 16 ft 5 in (5.00 m)
**Wheelbase:** 23 ft 0½ in (7.02 m)
**Wing loading:** 90 lb/sq ft (439 kg/m²)
**Wing/fuselage loading:** 55 lb/sq ft (269 kg/m²)

### Powerplant

**F-14A:** two Pratt & Whitney TF30-P-412A/414A turbofans each rated at 20,900 lb st (92.97 kN) with afterburning
**F-14B & F-14D:** two General Electric F110-GE-400 turbofans each rated at 14,000 lb st (62.27 kN) dry and 27,600 lb st (122.8 kN) with afterburning

### Weights

**Empty operating:** (F-14A) 40,104 lb (18191 kg); (F-14B) 41,780 lb (18951 kg); (F-14D) 43,735 lb (19838 kg)
**Normal take-off, four Sparrow:** 59,714 lb (27086 kg)
**Normal take-off, six Phoenix:** 70,764 lb (32098 kg)
**Maximum take-off (all versions, service limit):** 72,000 lb (32659 kg)
**Maximum take-off (manufacturer's limit):** 74,349 lb (33725 kg)
**Design landing weight:** 51,830 lb (23510 kg)

### Fuel load

**Total internal fuel:** 2385 US gal (9030 litres) [approx 16,200 lb/ 7348 kg] in six main tanks, comprising: forward fuselage tank 691 US gal (2616 litres); rear fuselage tank 648 US gal (2453 litres); combined left and right feed tanks 456 US gal (1727 litres); wing tanks 295 US gal (1117 litres) each
**External fuel:** two 267-US gal (1011-litre) under-intake fuel tanks; single-point pressure refuelling via port on starboard lower fuselage, below inflight refuelling probe
**Normal weapon load:** (air-to-ground and tactical reconnaissance) up to 14,500 lb (6577 kg) of stores

### Performance

**Maximum level speed at altitude:** 1,342 kt (1,544 mph; 2485 km/h)
**Maximum level speed at low level:** 792 kt (912 mph; 1468 km/h)
**Limiting Mach numbers:** 2.38 at altitude; 2.4 attained, but initially limited to 2.25 in service; 1.2 at low level
**Maximum cruising speed:** 550 kt (633 mph; 1019 km/h)
**Maximum rate of climb at sea level:** 30,000 ft (9140 m) per minute
**Absolute ceiling:** 56,000 ft (17069 m)
**Service ceiling:** 50,000 ft (15240 m) (F-14A); 53,000 ft (16154 m) (F-14B/D)
**Normal carrier approach speed:** 134 kt (154 mph; 248 km/h)
**Stalling speed, landing configuration:** 115 kt (132 mph; 213 km/h)
**Take-off run:** (with full fuel, and four AIM-7s) 1,400 ft (427 m)
**Landing run:** 2,900 ft (884 m)

### Range

**Combat air patrol endurance:** (with four AIM-54s, two AIM-7, two AIM-9s and external fuel) 90 min at 150 nm (173 miles; 278 km); one hour at 253 nm (292 miles; 470 km)
**Radius:** (deck-launched intercept with four AIM-54s, two AIM-7s, two AIM-9s and external fuel) 171 nm (197 miles; 317 km) at Mach 1.3; 134 nm (154 miles; 248 km) at Mach 1.5
**Ferry range:** (F-14A with two tanks) 1,730 nm (2,000 miles; 3200 km); (F-14B with two tanks) 2,050 nm (2,369 miles; 3799 km)

# Grumman F-14A+/B/D Tomcat

*Applying the superb F110 engine to the Tomcat made it the aircraft it had always promised to be. As a dogfighter, the F-14 now possessed carefree engine handling, while as a long-range air defence machine it could fly further or stay on station longer. In addition, it could carry a hefty weight of air-to-ground ordnance, while burning less fuel for greater performance and, on top of all this, it offered safer carrier operations.*

## F-14D Tomcat

**Cutaway key**
1 Pitot head
2 Radar target horn
3 Upward-hinging glass-fibre radome
4 Radome hinge point
5 AN/APG-71 radar scanner
6 Articulated scanner mounting
7 Undernose IRST/TCS sensor pod
8 Infra-Red Search and Track (IRST)
9 Television camera set (TCS)
10 Anti-collision light
11 Cannon barrel aperture
12 Incidence transmitter
13 Weapons system avionics equipment
14 ADF antenna
15 Retractable inflight-refuelling probe
16 Windscreen panels
17 Pilot's head-up display
18 Instrument panel shroud
19 Temperature probe
20 Rudder pedals
21 Avionics cooling air exhaust
22 Electro-luminescent formation lighting strips
23 Gun gas purging intake
24 Nosewheel doors
25 Canopy emergency release
26 Dynamic pressure probe
27 Engine throttle levers
28 Control column
29 Pilot's instrument panel with dual multi-function displays
30 Cockpit canopy, open position
31 Rear-view mirrors
32 Ejection seat headrest with canopy breakers
33 Martin-Baker Mk 14 NACES ejection seat
34 Boarding step
35 M61 Vulcan six-barrelled rotary cannon
36 Catapult strop link
37 Fold-out boarding ladder
38 Steerable twin nosewheels, forward retracting
39 Nosewheel undercarriage leg strut
40 Hydraulic retraction jack
41 Ammunition magazine, 675 rounds
42 Ammunition feed and cartridge case return chutes
43 Tactical information display hand controller
44 Radar Intercept Officer's display console
45 RIO's ejection seat
46 Canopy hydraulic jack
47 Electrical system controller
48 Electrical relays
49 Engine intake lip
50 Ventral missile pallet
51 EW antenna
52 Port engine air intake
53 Intake sidewall honeycomb core structure
54 Port navigation light
55 Conditioned air ducting
56 Rear avionics equipment bay
57 Canopy hinge point
58 UHF/TACAN antenna
59 Starboard wing glove fairing
60 Starboard navigation light
61 Dorsal control and cable ducting
62 Forward fuselage fuel tank bays, total internal fuel capacity 1,986 Imp gal (9029 litres)
63 Air-conditioning system heat exchanger, port and starboard dual system for crew and avionics
64 Variable-area intake ramp doors
65 Intake ramp hydraulic actuators
66 Main undercarriage wheel bay
67 Mainwheel door
68 Rear intake ramp
69 Wing glove sealing horn fairing
70 Telescopic flap/slat drive shaft
71 Port wing pivot bearing
72 Electron beam welded titanium wing pivot box
73 Intake bypass air spill duct
74 Emergency hydraulic generator
75 Central flap/slat drive motor
76 UHF datalink/IFF antenna
77 Fuselage upper longeron/pivot box attachment links
78 Wing pivot box integral fuel tank
79 Telescopic fuel feed pipes
80 Variable wing sweep control screw jacks
81 Centre-section fuel tankage
82 Intake ducting
83 Honeycomb skin panels
84 Starboard mainwheel, stowed position
85 Starboard wing

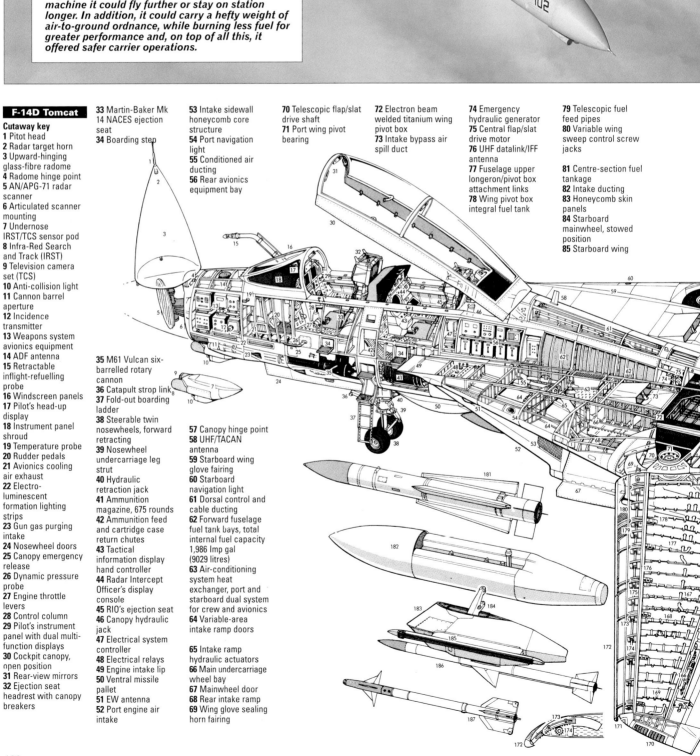

*VF-74 was just completing its transition to the F-14A+ when it left for the Red Sea on 7 August 1990 aboard USS Saratoga. The squadron returned on 28 March 1991, making a further cruise on Saratoga in 1992. A subsequent stint aboard Constellation was followed by a rearrangement of units, which left VF-74 without a front-line role. It then flew in the adversary role from NAS Oceana, using specially painted aircraft such as this F-14B, until disbanded on 28 April 1994.*

## SPECIFICATION

### F-14D Tomcat

**Dimensions**

As F-14A, see File 133 Sheet 02

**Powerplant**

Two General Electric F110-GE-400 turbofans each rated at 14,000 lb st (62.27 kN) dry and 23,100 lb st (102.75 kN) with afterburning

**Weights**

**Empty:** 41,780 lb (18951 kg)
**Normal take-off, fighter/escort mission:** 64,093 lb (29072 kg)
**Normal take-off, fleet air defence mission:** 73,098 lb (33157 kg)
**Maximum take-off:** 74,349 lb (33724 kg)

**Fuel**

**Internal fuel:** 16,200 lb (7348 kg)
**External fuel:** up to 3,800 lb (1724 kg) in two 267-US gal (1011-litre) drop tanks

**Performance**

**Maximum level speed 'clean' at high altitude:** 1,078 kt (1,241 mph; 1997 km/h)
**Cruising speed at optimum altitude:** 413 kt (475 mph; 764 km/h)
**Maximum climb rate at sea level:** more than 30,000 ft (9145 m) per minute
**Service ceiling:** more than 53,000 ft (16150 m)
**Take-off run, on land:** 2,500 ft (762 m) at maximum take-off weight
**Landing run, on land:** 2,400 ft (732 m)

**Range**

**Maximum range with internal and external fuel:** about 1,600 nm (1,842 miles; 2965 km)

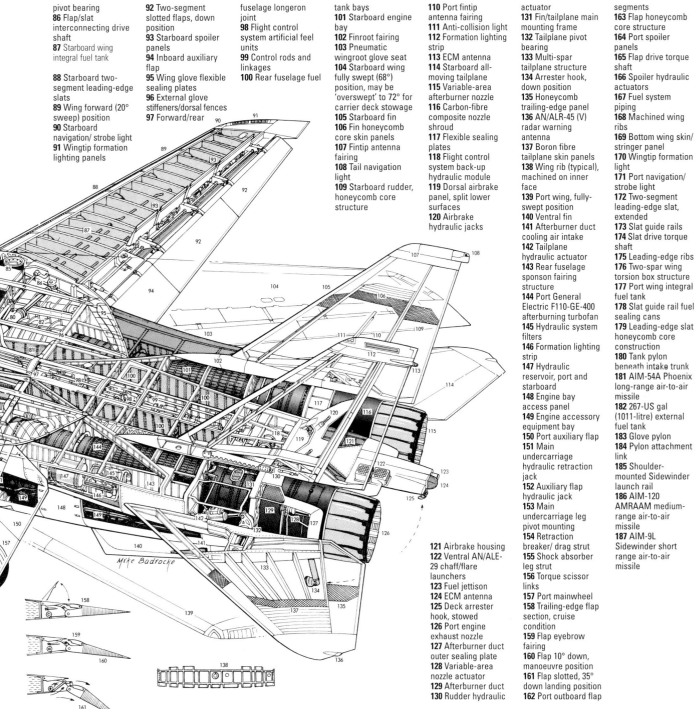

pivot bearing
**86** Flap/slat interconnecting drive shaft
**87** Starboard wing integral fuel tank
**88** Starboard two-segment leading-edge slats
**89** Wing forward (20° sweep) position
**90** Starboard navigation/ strobe light
**91** Wingtip formation lighting panels

**92** Two-segment slotted flaps, down position
**93** Starboard spoiler panels
**94** Inboard auxiliary flap
**95** Wing glove flexible sealing plates
**96** External glove stiffeners/dorsal fences
**97** Forward/rear

fuselage longeron joint
**98** Flight control system artificial feel units
**99** Control rods and linkages
**100** Rear fuselage fuel

tank bays
**101** Starboard engine bay
**102** Finroot fairing
**103** Pneumatic wingroot glove seat
**104** Starboard wing fully swept (68°) position, may be 'overswept' to 72° for carrier deck stowage
**105** Starboard fin
**106** Fin honeycomb core skin panels
**107** Fintip antenna fairing
**108** Tail navigation light
**109** Starboard rudder, honeycomb core structure

**110** Port fintip antenna fairing
**111** Anti-collision light
**112** Formation lighting strip
**113** ECM antenna
**114** Starboard all-moving tailplane
**115** Variable-area afterburner nozzle
**116** Carbon-fibre composite nozzle shroud
**117** Flexible sealing plates
**118** Flight control system back-up hydraulic module
**119** Dorsal airbrake panel, split lower surfaces
**120** Airbrake hydraulic jacks
**121** Airbrake housing
**122** Ventral AN/ALE-29 chaff/flare launchers
**123** Fuel jettison
**124** ECM antenna
**125** Deck arrester hook, stowed
**126** Port engine exhaust nozzle
**127** Afterburner duct outer sealing plate
**128** Variable-area nozzle actuator
**129** Afterburner duct
**130** Rudder hydraulic

actuator
**131** Fin/tailplane main mounting frame
**132** Tailplane pivot bearing
**133** Multi-spar tailplane structure
**134** Arrester hook, down position
**135** Honeycomb trailing-edge panel
**136** AN/ALR-45 (V) radar warning antenna
**137** Boron fibre tailplane skin panels
**138** Wing rib (typical), machined on inner face
**139** Port wing, fully-swept position
**140** Ventral fin
**141** Afterburner duct cooling air intake
**142** Tailplane hydraulic actuator
**143** Rear fuselage sponson fairing structure
**144** Port General Electric F110-GE-400 afterburning turbofan
**145** Hydraulic system filters
**146** Formation lighting strip
**147** Hydraulic reservoir, port and starboard
**148** Engine bay access panel
**149** Engine accessory equipment bay
**150** Port auxiliary flap
**151** Main undercarriage hydraulic retraction jack
**152** Auxiliary flap hydraulic jack
**153** Main undercarriage leg pivot mounting
**154** Retraction breaker/ drag strut
**155** Shock absorber leg strut
**156** Torque scissor links
**157** Port mainwheel
**158** Trailing-edge flap section, cruise condition
**159** Flap eyebrow fairing
**160** Flap 10° down, manoeuvre position
**161** Flap slotted, 35° down landing position
**162** Port outboard flap

segments
**163** Flap honeycomb core structure
**164** Port spoiler panels
**165** Flap drive torque shaft
**166** Spoiler hydraulic actuators
**167** Fuel system piping
**168** Machined wing ribs
**169** Bottom wing skin/ stringer panel
**170** Wingtip formation light
**171** Port navigation/ strobe light
**172** Two-segment leading-edge slat, extended
**173** Slat guide rails
**174** Slat drive torque shaft
**175** Leading-edge ribs
**176** Two-spar wing torsion box structure
**177** Port wing integral fuel tank
**178** Slat guide rail fuel sealing cans
**179** Leading-edge slat honeycomb core construction
**180** Tank pylon beneath intake trunk
**181** AIM-54A Phoenix long-range air-to-air missile
**182** 267-US gal (1011-litre) external fuel tank
**183** Glove pylon
**184** Pylon attachment link
**185** Shoulder-mounted Sidewinder launch rail
**186** AIM-120 AMRAAM medium-range air-to-air missile
**187** AIM-9L Sidewinder short range air-to-air missile

Mike Badrocke

# Grumman F9F Panther/Cougar

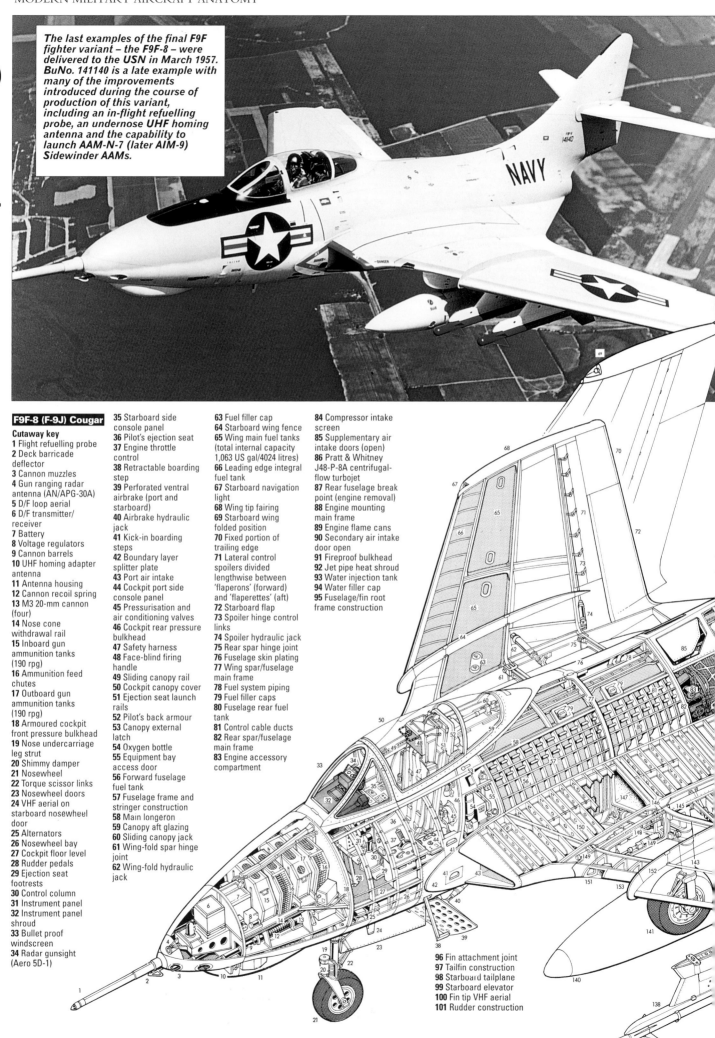

*The last examples of the final F9F fighter variant – the F9F-8 – were delivered to the USN in March 1957. BuNo. 141140 is a late example with many of the improvements introduced during the course of production of this variant, including an in-flight refuelling probe, an undernose UHF homing antenna and the capability to launch AAM-N-7 (later AIM-9) Sidewinder AAMs.*

## F9F-8 (F-9J) Cougar

### Cutaway key

1 Flight refuelling probe
2 Deck barricade deflector
3 Cannon muzzles
4 Gun ranging radar antenna (AN/APG-30A)
5 D/F loop aerial
6 D/F transmitter/ receiver
7 Battery
8 Voltage regulators
9 Cannon barrels
10 UHF homing adapter antenna
11 Antenna housing
12 Cannon recoil spring
13 M3 20-mm cannon (four)
14 Nose cone withdrawal rail
15 Inboard gun ammunition tanks (190 rpg)
16 Ammunition feed chutes
17 Outboard gun ammunition tanks (190 rpg)
18 Armoured cockpit front pressure bulkhead
19 Nose undercarriage leg strut
20 Shimmy damper
21 Nosewheel
22 Torque scissor links
23 Nosewheel doors
24 VHF aerial on starboard nosewheel door
25 Alternators
26 Nosewheel bay
27 Cockpit floor level
28 Rudder pedals
29 Ejection seat footrests
30 Control column
31 Instrument panel
32 Instrument panel shroud
33 Bullet proof windscreen
34 Radar gunsight (Aero 5D-1)

35 Starboard side console panel
36 Pilot's ejection seat
37 Engine throttle control
38 Retractable boarding step
39 Perforated ventral airbrake (port and starboard)
40 Airbrake hydraulic jack
41 Kick-in boarding steps
42 Boundary layer splitter plate
43 Port air intake
44 Cockpit port side console panel
45 Pressurisation and air conditioning valves
46 Cockpit rear pressure bulkhead
47 Safety harness
48 Face-blind firing handle
49 Sliding canopy rail
50 Cockpit canopy cover
51 Ejection seat launch rails
52 Pilot's back armour
53 Canopy external latch
54 Oxygen bottle
55 Equipment bay access door
56 Forward fuselage fuel tank
57 Fuselage frame and stringer construction
58 Main longeron
59 Canopy aft glazing
60 Sliding canopy jack
61 Wing-fold spar hinge joint
62 Wing-fold hydraulic jack

63 Fuel filler cap
64 Starboard wing fence
65 Wing main fuel tanks (total internal capacity 1,063 US gal/4024 litres)
66 Leading edge integral fuel tank
67 Starboard navigation light
68 Wing tip fairing
69 Starboard wing folded position
70 Fixed portion of trailing edge
71 Lateral control spoilers divided lengthwise between 'flaperons' (forward) and 'flaperettes' (aft)
72 Starboard flap
73 Spoiler hinge control links
74 Spoiler hydraulic jack
75 Rear spar hinge joint
76 Fuselage skin plating
77 Wing spar/fuselage main frame
78 Fuel system piping
79 Fuel filler caps
80 Fuselage rear fuel tank
81 Control cable ducts
82 Rear spar/fuselage main frame
83 Engine accessory compartment

84 Compressor intake screen
85 Supplementary air intake doors (open)
86 Pratt & Whitney J48-P-8A centrifugal-flow turbojet
87 Rear fuselage break point (engine removal)
88 Engine mounting main frame
89 Engine flame cans
90 Secondary air intake door open
91 Fireproof bulkhead
92 Jet pipe heat shroud
93 Water injection tank
94 Water filler cap
95 Fuselage/fin root frame construction

96 Fin attachment joint
97 Tailfin construction
98 Starboard tailplane
99 Starboard elevator
100 Fin tip VHF aerial
101 Rudder construction

## Blue Angels

The first F9F-2s to enter US Navy service were those assigned to the *Blue Angels* demonstration team on 20 August 1949 (top). The team's first jet aircraft, the jet-age Panthers replaced F8F Bearcats and were employed until July 1950, when the team was stood-down to form the nucleus of VF-191 in anticipation of the war in Korea. After a 14-month stand-down and a 1952 season spent with the F7U-1 Cutlass, the *Angels* were reunited with members of the F9F family the following year. It had been intended that F9F-6 Cougars be issued to the team at this point, but the grounding of the type in 1953 forced the team to use overhauled F9F-5 Panthers instead. These remained in use until 1955, when the Cougar was finally made available. The first F9F-8s (above) were debuted on the air show circuit in 1955 and stayed with the team until 1957, when the first F11F-1 Tigers were introduced. This was not the last word however; the team acquired an F9F-8T when it transitioned to the F11F (replacing a Lockheed TV-2) and this was retained until 1969, when the team received McDonnell Phantom IIs.

### SPECIFICATION

| | F9F-2 Panther | F9F-8 Cougar |
|---|---|---|

**Dimensions**

| F9F-2 Panther | F9F-8 Cougar |
|---|---|
| **Length:** 37 ft 5¾ in (11.41 m) | **Length:** 42 ft 2 in (12.85 m) |
| **Height:** 11 ft 4 in (3.45 m) | **Height:** 12 ft 3 in (3.73 m) |
| **Span:** 38 ft (11.58 m) | **Span:** 34 ft 6 in (10.52 m) |
| **Span (folded):** 23 ft 5 in (7.14 m) | **Span (folded):** 14 ft 2 in (4.32 m) |
| **Wing area:** 250 sq ft (23.23 m²) | **Wing area:** 337 sq ft (31.31 m²) |

**Powerplant**

| F9F-2 Panther | F9F-8 Cougar |
|---|---|
| One Pratt & Whitney J42-P-4, P-6 or P-8 turbojet rated at 5,000 lb (22.24 kN) thrust dry, or 5,750 lb (25.58 kN) thrust with water injection | One Pratt & Whitney J48-P-8A or P-8C turbojet rated at 6,250 lb (27.80 kN) thrust dry, or 7,250 lb (32.25 kN) thrust with water injection |

**Weights**

| F9F-2 Panther | F9F-8 Cougar |
|---|---|
| **Empty:** 9,303 lb (4220 kg) | **Empty:** 11,866 lb (5382 kg) |
| **Loaded:** 16,450 lb (7462 kg) | **Loaded:** 20,098 lb (9116 kg) |
| **Maximum take-off:** 19,494 lb (8842 kg) | **Maximum take-off:** 24,763 lb (11232 kg) |

**Performance**

| F9F-2 Panther | F9F-8 Cougar |
|---|---|
| **Maximum speed:** 575 mph (925 km/h) at sea level | **Maximum speed:** 647 mph (1041 km/h) at 2,000 ft (607 m) |
| **Cruising speed:** 487 mph (784 km/h) | **Cruising speed:** 516 mph (830 km/h) |
| **Climb rate:** 6,000 ft (1829 m) per minute | **Climb rate:** 5,750 ft (1753 m) per minute |
| **Service ceiling:** 44,600 ft (13594 m) | **Service ceiling:** 42,000 ft (12802 m) |
| **Normal range:** 1,353 miles (2177 km) | **Normal range:** 1,208 miles (1944 km) |
| | **Maximum range:** 1,312 miles (2111 km) |

**Armament**

| F9F-2 Panther | F9F-8 Cougar |
|---|---|
| Four 20-mm cannon, each with 190 rounds per gun. Most F9F-2s were later modified with four racks under each wing; the inner pair was stressed to carry a 1,000-lb (454-kg) bomb or 150-US gal (568-litre) drop tank, while the outer racks could each carry a 250-lb (114-kg) bomb or a 5-in (127-mm) HVAR. Total external load was 3,000 lb (1361-kg) | Four 20-mm cannon, plus two bomb racks each able to carry one 1,000-lb (454-kg) bomb or 150-US gal (568-litre) drop tank. Late production aircraft were equipped with four additional pylons, each wired to carry an AAM-N-7 Sidewinder air-to-air missile |

*The only other nation to operate F9Fs took delivery of examples of both the Panther and Cougar. Argentina's Servicio de Aviación Naval received 24 refurbished F9F-2s (below) in 1958. Issued to 1ª Escadrilla Aeronavale de Ataque, 2ª Escuadra Aeronavale at BAN Comandante Espora the aircraft were confined to operations from land bases as the catapults aboard the carrier ARA Independencia were not sufficiently powerful to launch a jet aircraft of this type at normal operating weights. In April 1963 four of the Panthers were destroyed on the ground and a fifth collided with a Corsair during a three-day coup in which navy personnel fought with those of the army and air force. Two years later, by which time the 1ª Escadrilla Aeronavale de Ataque, had been transferred to the 3ª Escuadra Aeronavale, the Panthers were again in action, flying border patrols during a dispute with neighbouring Chile. Surviving aircraft were grounded in 1969 by a lack of spare parts. Meanwhile, in 1962 a pair of F9F-8Ts had been acquired for use by the 1ª Escadrilla Aeronavale de Ataque. Both had been withdrawn by 1971.*

**109** Port tailplane construction
**110** Trimming tailplane hinge joint
**111** Tailplane trim jack
**112** Exhaust nozzle shroud
**113** Jet exhaust nozzle
**114** Sting-type deck arrester hook
**115** Retractable tail bumper
**116** Wing root trailing edge fillet
**117** Arrester hook damper and retraction jack
**110** Rear fuselage framing
**119** Jet pipe
**120** Intake duct aft fairing
**121** Port Fowler flap
**122** Spoiler hydraulic jack
**123** Rear spar

**126** Trim tab electric actuator
**127** Electrically-operated trim tab (port only)
**128** Fuel jettison vent
**129** Port wing tip fairing
**130** Fuel vent valve
**131** Port navigation light
**132** Fuel venting ram air intake
**133** Port wing main fuel tanks
**134** Main spar
**135** Cambered leading-edge ribs

**102** Rudder mass balance
**103** Fin/tailplane fairing
**104** Tail navigation lights

**105** Lower rudder segment trim tab
**106** Elevator trim tab
**107** Port elevator
**108** Elevator horn balance

**124** Wing rib construction
**125** Lateral control spoilers 'flaperons' (forward) and 'flaperettes' (aft)

**136** Leading edge integral fuel tank
**137** Wing ordnance pylon (four)
**138** Missile launch rail
**139** AIM-9B Sidewinder air-to-air missile

**140** 150 US gal (568 litre) auxiliary fuel tank
**141** Port mainwheel
**142** Fuel tank bay corrugated double skin
**143** Main undercarriage leg strut
**144** Wing fold hydraulic jack
**145** Main undercarriage pivot housing

**146** Main spar hinge joint
**147** Intake duct
**148** Undercarriage hydraulic retraction jack
**149** Wing-fold locking cylinders
**150** Intake duct framing
**151** Landing/taxiing lamp
**152** Port wing fence
**153** Leading-edge dog-tooth

# Grumman S2F/S-2 Tracker

When it first appeared, Grumman's stubby Tracker (commonly known as the 'Stoof' due to its S2F designation) was the first aircraft to combine submarine hunter/killer operations in one carrierborne airframe. A stalwart of US Navy operations, it was widely exported and spawned several vastly differing variants

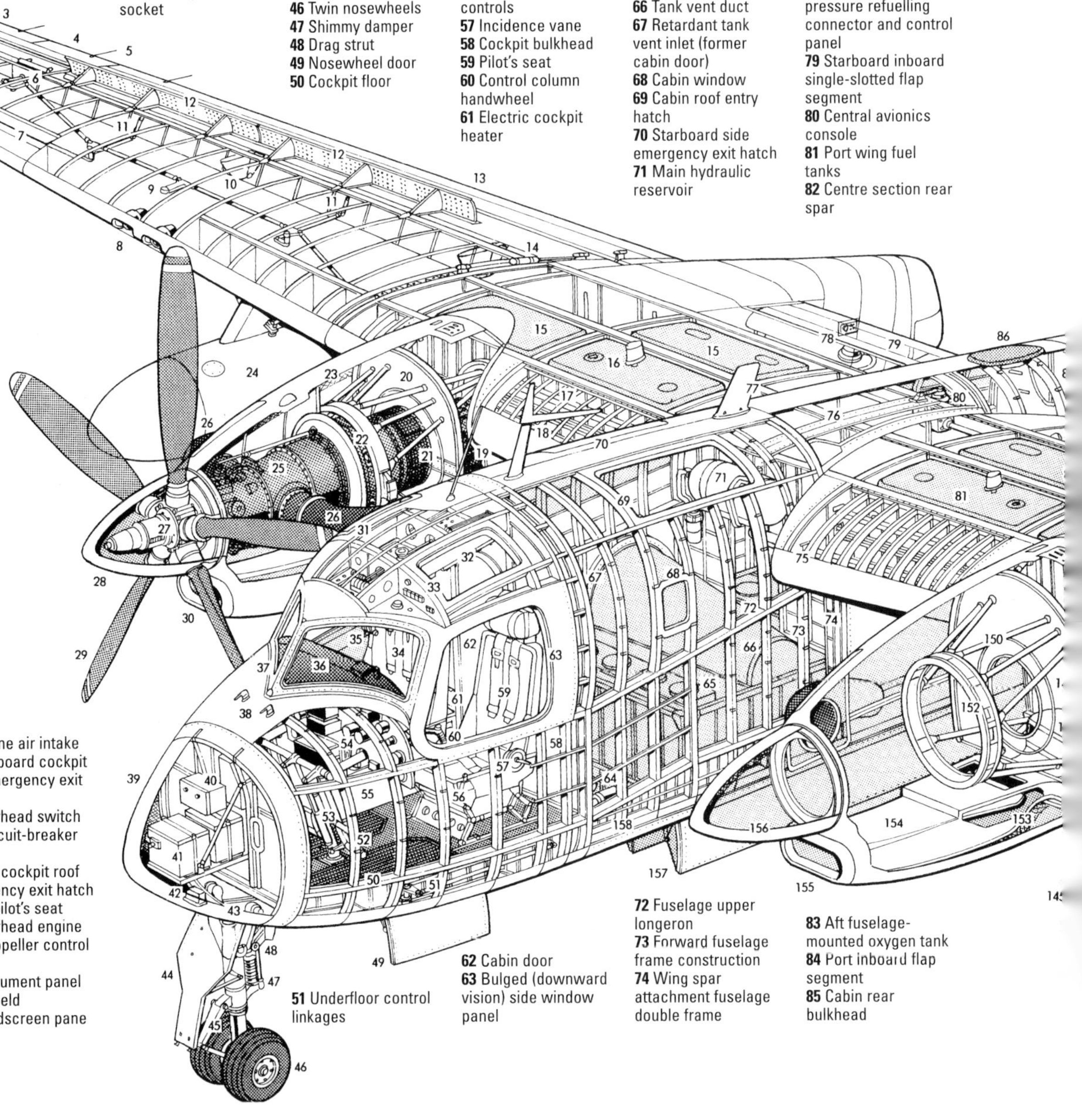

**Conair Turbo Firecat**

**Cutaway key**
1 Starboard navigation light
2 Wingtip fairing
3 Starboard aileron
4 Aileron spring tab
5 Static dischargers
6 Aileron hinge control
7 Fixed leading-edge slot
8 Landing and taxiing lamps
9 Aileron and spoiler control rods
10 External flap hinges
11 Spoiler actuating links
12 Starboard spoiler panels, extended
13 Single-slotted Fowler-type outboard flap segment
14 Starboard wing fold joint (operable with ground hydraulic power supply only)
15 Starboard wing fuel tanks
16 Fuel vent
17 Leading-edge control and cable runs
18 FM antenna
19 Engine accessory equipment compartment
20 Aft firewall
21 Engine intake filter screen
22 Anti-vibration engine mountings (4)
23 Composite engine cowling panels
24 Starboard external fuel tank, 105-Imp gal (126-US gal/477-litre) capacity
25 Pratt & Whitney Canada PT6A-67AF engine

26 Exhaust stubs
27 Propeller hub pitch change mechanism
28 Spinner
29 Hartzell five-bladed constant-speed propeller
30 Engine air intake
31 Starboard cockpit roof emergency exit hatch
32 Overhead switch and circuit-breaker panel
33 Port cockpit roof emergency exit hatch
34 Co-pilot's seat
35 Overhead engine and propeller control levers
36 Instrument panel flareshield
37 Windscreen pane

38 Dual pitot heads
39 Composite nosecone
40 Radio junction box
41 Twin NiCd battery installation
42 Ground power socket
43 Nose undercarriage trunion fittings
44 Nosewheel leg door
45 Torque scissor links
46 Twin nosewheels
47 Shimmy damper
48 Drag strut
49 Nosewheel door
50 Cockpit floor
51 Underfloor control linkages

52 Rudder pedals
53 Brake master cylinders
54 Instrument panel
55 Central avionics console
56 Adjustable seat controls
57 Incidence vane
58 Cockpit bulkhead
59 Pilot's seat
60 Control column handwheel
61 Electric cockpit heater
62 Cabin door
63 Bulged (downward vision) side window panel

64 Retardant tank dump door rotary actuators (4)
65 Retardant tank, capacity 735 Imp gal (882 US gal/3341 litres)
66 Tank vent duct
67 Retardant tank vent inlet (former cabin door)
68 Cabin window
69 Cabin roof entry hatch
70 Starboard side emergency exit hatch
71 Main hydraulic reservoir
72 Fuselage upper longeron
73 Forward fuselage frame construction
74 Wing spar attachment fuselage double frame

75 Hinged inboard leading-edge segment (control access)
76 Wing panel centreline joint
77 No. 1 VHF aerial
78 Starboard nacelle pressure refuelling connector and control panel
79 Starboard inboard single-slotted flap segment
80 Central avionics console
81 Port wing fuel tanks
82 Centre section rear spar
83 Aft fuselage-mounted oxygen tank
84 Port inboard flap segment
85 Cabin rear bulkhead

## SPECIFICATION

### S-2E Tracker

#### Dimensions

**Length:** 43 ft 6 in (13.26 m)
**Height:** 16 ft 7 in (5.06 m)
**Wingspan:** 72 ft 7 in (22.13 m)
**Width, wings folded:** 27 ft 4 in (8.33 m)
**Wing area:** 496.00 sq ft (46.08 m²)
**Aspect ratio:** 10.63
**Wheel track** 18 ft 6 in (5.64 m)

#### Powerplant

Two Wright R-1820-82 WA Cyclones each rated at 1,525 hp (1137 kW)

#### Weight

**Empty:** 18,750 lb (8505 kg)
**Normal take-off:** 24,413 lb (11074 kg)
**Maximum take-off:** 29,150 lb (13222 kg)

#### Fuel and load

**Internal fuel:** 4,368 lb (1981 kg)
**Maximum ordnance:** 4,810 lb (2182 kg)

#### Performance

**Maximum level speed 'clean' at sea level:** 230 kt (265 mph; 426 km/h)
**Cruising speed at optimum altitude:** 180 kt (207 mph; 333 km/h)
**Patrol speed at 1,500 ft (457 m):** 130 kt (150 mph; 241 km/h)
**Ferry range:** 1,130 nm (1,301 miles; 2094 km)
**Range:** 1,000 nm (1,152 miles; 1853 km)
**Endurance:** 9 hours
**Maximum rate of climb at sea level:** 1,390 ft (425 m) per minute
**Service ceiling:** 21,000 ft (6400 m)
**Take-off run at maximum take-off weight:** 1,300 ft (396 m)

#### Armament

Early Trackers could carry either one Mk 34 or one Mk 41 or two Mk 43 torpedoes or one Mk 24 mine in the ventral bomb bay and either four Mk 19 mines or four Mk 43 torpedoes or four Mk 54 depth charges or six HVAR rockets beneath the wings. The S-2F-2 version had an enlarged bomb bay which enabled carriage of the Mk 90 nuclear depth charge; this weapon was later replaced by the smaller Mk 101 'Lulu'. Later models could also carry rocket pods, Mk 44 or Mk 46 torpedoes or the Mk 57 nuclear weapon. The varying export operators have each added weapons packages of their own, such as gun pods or ASMs to meet individual needs

*Utilising the fuselage of a TF-1 Trader, replacing the original vertical tail with twin fins and rudders and adding a 17-ft 6-in (5.33-m) diameter radome, Grumman created the E-1B Tracer. A total of 88 aircraft was built and the first operational example was delivered on 20 January 1969. Typical sorties for this AEW machine saw Tracers operating some 150 nm (172 miles; 278 km) from carriers on missions lasting up to seven hours. In the anti-submarine warfare support role, Tracers were used to control S-2s and to ensure that they were flying precise search patterns.*

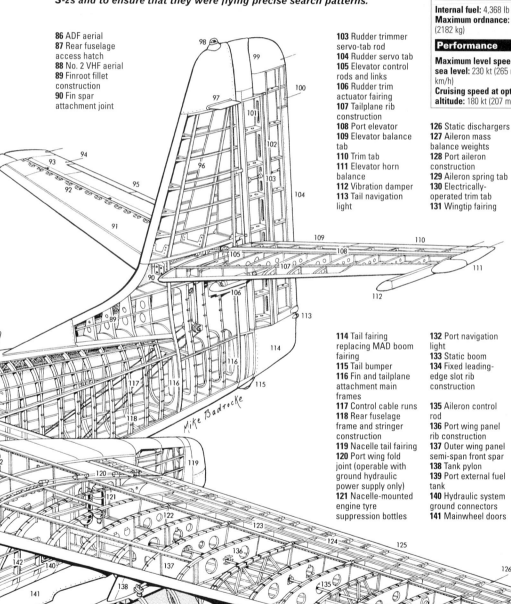

**86** ADF aerial
**87** Rear fuselage access hatch
**88** No. 2 VHF aerial
**89** Finroot fillet construction
**90** Fin spar attachment joint

**103** Rudder trimmer servo-tab rod
**104** Rudder servo tab
**105** Elevator control rods and links
**106** Rudder trim actuator fairing
**107** Tailplane rib construction
**108** Port elevator
**109** Elevator balance tab
**110** Trim tab
**111** Elevator horn balance
**112** Vibration damper
**113** Tail navigation light

**126** Static dischargers
**127** Aileron mass balance weights
**128** Port aileron construction
**129** Aileron spring tab
**130** Electrically-operated trim tab
**131** Wingtip fairing

**142** Port nacelle frame construction
**143** Main undercarriage mounting sub-frame
**144** Port mainwheel with low-pressure tyre
**145** Torque scissor links
**146** Hydraulic retraction jack
**147** Oil cooler exhaust, ram air intake on starboard side
**148** Engine bay firewall
**149** Nacelle fireseal
**150** Engine mounting truss frame
**151** Oil cooler
**152** Engine mounting ring frame
**153** Intake particle separator
**154** Intake ducting
**155** Port engine air intake
**156** Port spinner
**157** Retardant dump doors (4), open
**158** Fuselage door aperture longeron

**114** Tail fairing replacing MAD boom fairing
**115** Tail bumper
**116** Fin and tailplane attachment main frames
**117** Control cable runs
**118** Rear fuselage frame and stringer construction
**119** Nacelle tail fairing
**120** Port wing fold joint (operable with ground hydraulic power supply only)
**121** Nacelle-mounted engine tyre suppression bottles

**132** Port navigation light
**133** Static boom
**134** Fixed leading-edge slot rib construction
**135** Aileron control rod
**136** Port wing panel rib construction
**137** Outer wing panel semi-span front spar
**138** Tank pylon
**139** Port external fuel tank
**140** Hydraulic system ground connectors
**141** Mainwheel doors

*Mike Badrocke*

**91** Starboard tailplane
**92** Vortex generators
**93** Starboard elevator
**94** Static dischargers

**95** Elevator tabs
**96** Fin spar and rib construction
**97** VOR localiser/glidescope aerial
**98** Anti-collision light
**99** Rudder horn balance

**100** Static discharger
**101** Trimming rudder, electric trim, hydraulic rudder assist
**102** Rudder rib construction

**122** Outer wing panel rear spar
**123** Port spoiler housing
**124** Flap rib construction
**125** Port outboard single-slotted flap

# Hawker Sea Fury

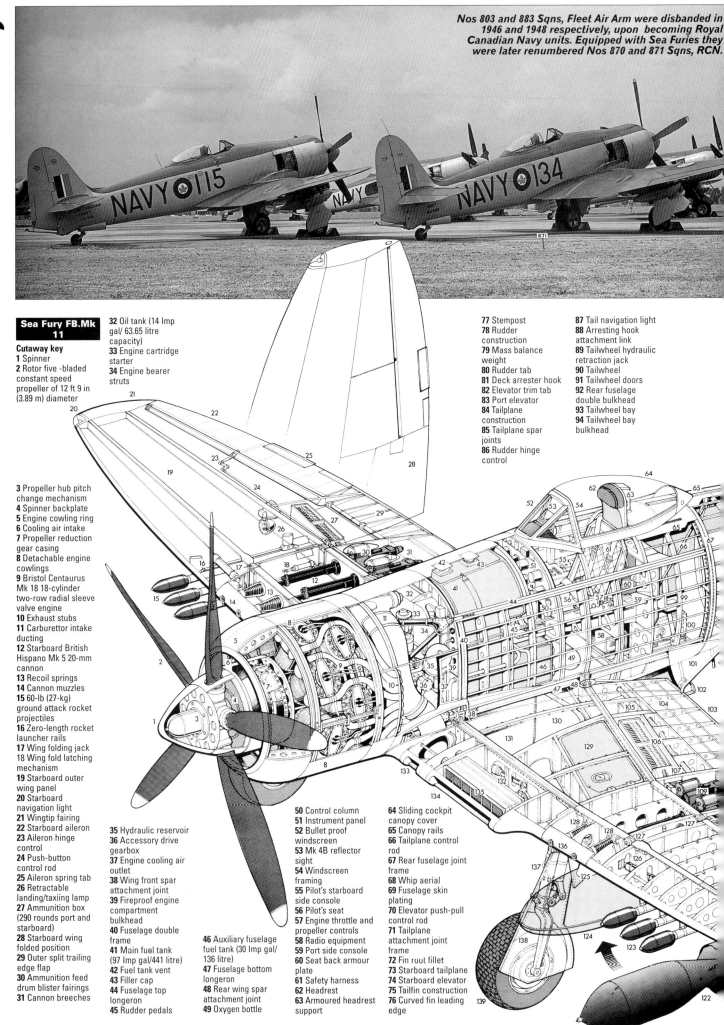

Nos 803 and 883 Sqns, Fleet Air Arm were disbanded in 1946 and 1948 respectively, upon becoming Royal Canadian Navy units. Equipped with Sea Furies they were later renumbered Nos 870 and 871 Sqns, RCN.

**Sea Fury FB.Mk 11**

**Cutaway key**
1 Spinner
2 Rotor five -bladed constant speed propeller of 12 ft 9 in (3.89 m) diameter
3 Propeller hub pitch change mechanism
4 Spinner backplate
5 Engine cowling ring
6 Cooling air intake
7 Propeller reduction gear casing
8 Detachable engine cowlings
9 Bristol Centaurus Mk 18 18-cylinder two-row radial sleeve valve engine
10 Exhaust stubs
11 Carburettor intake ducting
12 Starboard British Hispano Mk 5 20-mm cannon
13 Recoil springs
14 Cannon muzzles
15 60-lb (27-kg) ground attack rocket projectiles
16 Zero-length rocket launcher rails
17 Wing folding jack
18 Wing fold latching mechanism
19 Starboard outer wing panel
20 Starboard navigation light
21 Wingtip fairing
22 Starboard aileron
23 Aileron hinge control
24 Push-button control rod
25 Aileron spring tab
26 Retractable landing/taxiing lamp
27 Ammunition box (290 rounds port and starboard)
28 Starboard wing folded position
29 Outer split trailing edge flap
30 Ammunition feed drum blister fairings
31 Cannon breeches

32 Oil tank (14 Imp gal/ 63.65 litre capacity)
33 Engine cartridge starter
34 Engine bearer struts
35 Hydraulic reservoir
36 Accessory drive gearbox
37 Engine cooling air outlet
38 Wing front spar attachment joint
39 Fireproof engine compartment bulkhead
40 Fuselage double frame
41 Main fuel tank (97 Imp gal/441 litre)
42 Fuel tank vent
43 Filler cap
44 Fuselage top longeron
45 Rudder pedals

46 Auxiliary fuselage fuel tank (30 Imp gal/ 136 litre)
47 Fuselage bottom longeron
48 Rear wing spar attachment joint
49 Oxygen bottle
50 Control column
51 Instrument panel
52 Bullet proof windscreen
53 Mk 4B reflector sight
54 Windscreen framing
55 Pilot's starboard side console
56 Pilot's seat
57 Engine throttle and propeller controls
58 Radio equipment
59 Port side console
60 Seat back armour plate
61 Safety harness
62 Headrest
63 Armoured headrest support

64 Sliding cockpit canopy cover
65 Canopy rails
66 Tailplane control rod
67 Rear fuselage joint frame
68 Whip aerial
69 Fuselage skin plating
70 Elevator push-pull control rod
71 Tailplane attachment joint frame
72 Fin root fillet
73 Starboard tailplane
74 Starboard elevator
75 Tailfin construction
76 Curved fin leading edge

77 Stempost
78 Rudder construction
79 Mass balance weight
80 Rudder tab
81 Deck arrester hook
82 Elevator trim tab
83 Port elevator
84 Tailplane construction
85 Tailplane spar joints
86 Rudder hinge control

87 Tail navigation light
88 Arresting hook attachment link
89 Tailwheel hydraulic retraction jack
90 Tailwheel
91 Tailwheel doors
92 Rear fuselage double bulkhead
93 Tailwheel bay
94 Tailwheel bay bulkhead

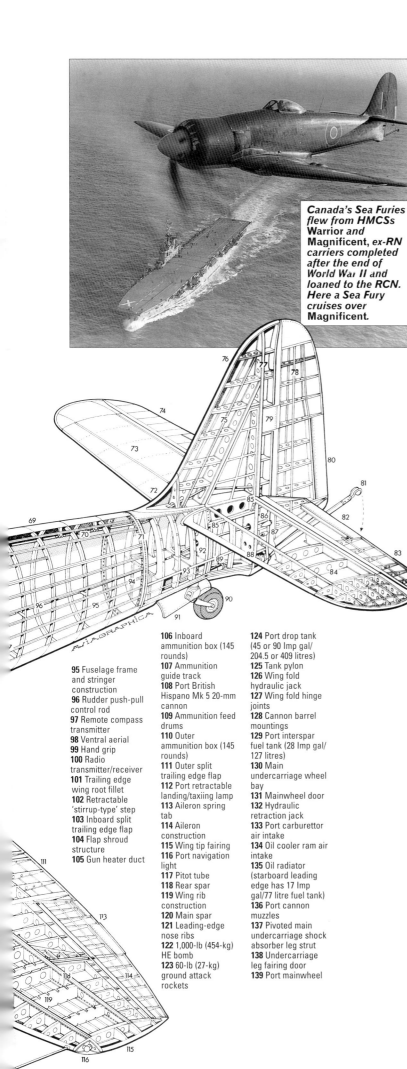

*Canada's Sea Furies flew from HMCSs* Warrior *and* Magnificent, *ex-RN carriers completed after the end of World War II and loaned to the RCN. Here a Sea Fury cruises over* Magnificent.

## SPECIFICATION

| | Sea Fury F.Mk X | Sea Fury FB.Mk 11 |
|---|---|---|
| **Dimensions** | **Length:** 34 ft 3 in (10.44 m)<br>**Wingspan:** 38 ft 4½ in (11.70 m)<br>**Wingspan (folded):** 16 ft 1 in (4.90 m)<br>**Wing area:** 280 sq ft (26.01 m²) | **Length:** 34 ft 3 in (10.44 m)<br>**Wingspan:** 38 ft 4½ in (11.70 m)<br>**Wingspan (folded):** 18 ft 2 in (5.54 m)<br>**Wing area:** 280 sq ft (26.01 m²) |
| **Powerplant** | One Bristol Centaurus Mk 18 18-cylinder, air-cooled radial rated at 2,480 hp (1849 kW) and driving a Rotol four-bladed propeller | One Bristol Centaurus Mk 18 18-cylinder, air-cooled radial rated at 2,480 hp (1849 kW) and driving a Rotol five-bladed propeller |
| **Weights** | **Empty:** 9,070 lb (4114 kg)<br>**Loaded:** 10,660 lb (4835 kg) | **Empty:** 9,240 lb (4191 kg)<br>**Loaded:** 12,300 lb (5579 kg) |
| **Performance** | **Maximum speed at 18,000 ft (5486 m):** 465 mph (748 km/h)<br>**Climb to 30,000 ft (9144 m):** 9 minutes 48 seconds<br>**Range (clean):** 710 miles (1142 km)<br>**Service ceiling:** 36,180 ft (11028 m) | **Maximum speed at 18,000 ft (5486 m):** 450 mph (724 km/h)<br>**Climb to 30,000 ft (9144 m):** 10 minutes 48 seconds<br>**Range (clean):** 810 miles (1304 km)<br>**Service ceiling:** 37,800 ft (11521 m) |
| **Armament** | Four 20-mm Hispano Mk 5 cannon | Four 20-mm Hispano Mk 5 cannon, plus an underwing stores load comprising a pair of 500-lb or 1,000-lb (227-kg or 454-kg) bombs (or equivalent weights in napalm or sea mines), or up to 12 25-lb (11-kg) rocket projectiles |

*With Sea Furies of No. 802 Sqn and Fireflies of No. 825 Sqn ranged on her deck, HMS* Ocean *steams from Japan to the waters off Korea, July 1952.* Ocean *made two deployments to the region, in 1952 and 1953, including the last by a Royal Navy carrier during the Korean conflict.*

**95** Fuselage frame and stringer construction
**96** Rudder push-pull control rod
**97** Remote compass transmitter
**98** Ventral aerial
**99** Hand grip
**100** Radio transmitter/receiver
**101** Trailing edge wing root fillet
**102** Retractable 'stirrup-type' step
**103** Inboard split trailing edge flap
**104** Flap shroud structure
**105** Gun heater duct

**106** Inboard ammunition box (145 rounds)
**107** Ammunition guide track
**108** Port British Hispano Mk 5 20-mm cannon
**109** Ammunition feed drums
**110** Outer ammunition box (145 rounds)
**111** Outer split trailing edge flap
**112** Port retractable landing/taxiing lamp
**113** Aileron spring tab
**114** Aileron construction
**115** Wing tip fairing
**116** Port navigation light
**117** Pitot tube
**118** Rear spar
**119** Wing rib construction
**120** Main spar
**121** Leading-edge nose ribs
**122** 1,000-lb (454-kg) HE bomb
**123** 60-lb (27-kg) ground attack rockets

**124** Port drop tank (45 or 90 Imp gal/ 204.5 or 409 litres)
**125** Tank pylon
**126** Wing fold hydraulic jack
**127** Wing fold hinge joints
**128** Cannon barrel mountings
**129** Port interspar fuel tank (28 Imp gal/ 127 litres)
**130** Main undercarriage wheel bay
**131** Mainwheel door
**132** Hydraulic retraction jack
**133** Port carburettor air intake
**134** Oil cooler ram air intake
**135** Oil radiator (starboard leading edge has 17 Imp gal/77 litre fuel tank)
**136** Port cannon muzzles
**137** Pivoted main undercarriage shock absorber leg strut
**138** Undercarriage leg fairing door
**139** Port mainwheel

# Vought A-7 Corsair II

*Pictured are A-7Ds of the 57th Fighter Weapons Wing of the Tactical Fighter Weapons Center (TFWC), Nellis AFB, Nevada, a unit which more recently flew the A-10A, F-15C/D and F-16A/B/C/D. The TFWC was established in 1966 and the 57th FWW (formerly 57th FIW) became part of the unit in 1969. The TFWC has established small detachments at other USAF bases, assisting the service entry of new types; for the A-7D, this included an establishment at Luke AFB, Arizona.*

## A-7D

**Cutaway key**

1 Radome
2 Radar scanner dish
3 AN/APQ-126 radar equipment module
4 Scanner tracking mechanism
5 Radar-mounting bulkhead
6 Pitot tubes
7 Windscreen rain dispersal air ducts
8 Cooling air louvres
9 Radar transmitter/receiver equipment
10 Engine air intake
11 ILS aerial
12 Forward radar warning antenna
13 Pave Penny laser ranger and marked target seeker
14 Pave Penny avionics pack
15 Intake duct framing
16 Cockpit floor level
17 Boron carbide (HCF) cockpit armour panelling
18 Cockpit pressurisation valve
19 Armoured front pressure bulkhead
20 Rudder pedals
21 Control column
22 Instrument panel
23 Head-down projected map display
24 Instrument panel shroud
25 Armoured windscreen panels
26 AN/AVQ-7(V) head-up display (HUD)
27 Pilot's rear view mirrors
28 Cockpit canopy cover, upward-hinged
29 Ejection seat headrest
30 Seat arming/safety lever
31 Safety harness

32 McDonnell Douglas Escapac 1-C2 rocket-powered 'zero-zero' ejection seat
33 Starboard side console panel
34 External canopy latch
35 Engine throttle lever
36 Port side console panel
37 Static ports
38 Boarding steps
39 Cannon muzzle
40 Retractable boarding ladder
41 Taxiing lamp
42 Nose undercarriage leg strut
43 Levered suspension axle beam
44 Twin nosewheels, aft retracting
45 Nosewheel doors
46 Cannon barrels
47 Intake trunking
48 Cockpit rear-pressure bulkhead
49 Angle-of-attack transmitter
50 Electrical system equipment bay
51 Ejection seat launch rails
52 Canopy aft framing
53 Hydraulic canopy jack
54 Canopy hinge point
55 TACAN antenna
56 Ammunition feed drive mechanism
57 Canopy emergency release
58 Ammunition feed and link return chutes
59 M61A1 Vulcan, 20-mm rotary cannon
60 Gun gas spill duct
61 Rotary cannon/ammunition drive, flexible interconnection
62 Cannon bay, air-conditioning plant on starboard side

63 Liquid oxygen converter
64 Emergency hydraulic accumulator
65 Electronics systems built-in test equipment panel (BITE)
66 Ground power socket
67 Ventral Doppler navigation aerial
68 Port avionics equipment bay
69 Cooling air extractor fan
70 Forward fuselage fuel cell; total internal fuel capacity 1,249 US gal (4728 litres)
71 Fuselage stores pylon, capacity 500 lb (227 kg)
72 Wing front spar/fuselage attachment joint
73 Control rod runs
74 Ammunition drum, 1,000 rounds
75 Universal air refuelling receptacle, open
76 Centre-section integral fuel tank
77 Wing panel centre-section carry-through structure
78 Wing skin panel centreline joint strap
79 Upper anti-collision light
80 Starboard wing integral fuel tank
81 Fuel system piping
82 Pylon attachment hardpoints
83 Inboard leading-edge flap
84 Flap hydraulic actuators
85 Centre wing pylon, capacity 3,500 lb (1558 kg)

86 AIM-9 Sidewinder air-to-air missile
87 Missile launch rail
88 Fuselage missile pylon
89 Mk 82 HE bombs, 500 lb (227 kg)
90 Multiple ejector rack
91 Outboard wing pylon, 3,500-lb (1558-kg) capacity
92 Leading-edge dog-tooth
93 Wing fold hydraulic jack
94 Outer wing panel hinge joint
95 Leading-edge flap hydraulic actuators
96 Snakeye, retarded bomb, 500 lb (227 kg)
97 Outboard leading-edge flap segment
98 Starboard navigation light
99 Wingtip fairing
100 Formation light
101 Outer wing panel, folded position

102 Starboard aileron
103 Aileron hydraulic actuator
104 Fuel jettison pipe
105 Starboard single-slotted trailing-edge flap (down)
106 Flap hydraulic jack
107 Starboard spoiler
108 Spoiler hydraulic actuator
109 Dorsal spine fairing

110 Control rod linkages
111 Rear spar/fuselage attachment joint
112 Gravity fuel filler cap
113 Rear fuselage fuel cell

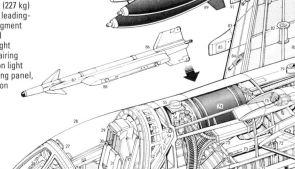

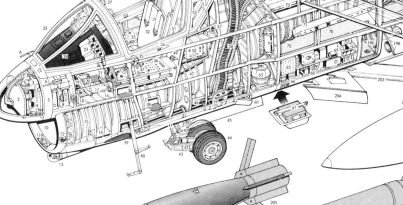

*The first two-seat TA-7C made its maiden flight in mid-1975. Used for pilot familiarisation by the USN, the TA-7C was initially delivered with the TF30 engine, and from March 1983 six aircraft were redesignated EA-7L and assigned to VAQ-34 for electronic warfare training and simulation. The USN began taking delivery of re-engined (TF41) and upgraded TA-7Cs in January 1985. The TA-7Cs pictured served with VA-174 'Hell Razors' of the east coast Replacement Air Group (RAG), based at NAS Cecil Field, Florida.*

## SPECIFICATION

### A-7D

#### Dimensions

**Wingspan:** 38 ft 9 in (11.81 m)
**Length:** 46 ft 1½ in (14.06 m)
**Height:** 16 ft ¾ in (4.90 m)
**Wing area:** 375 sq ft (34.84 m²)

#### Powerplant

One 14,500-lb (64.5-kN) Allison TF41-A-1 (licence-built Rolls-Royce Spey) turbojet, without afterburning

#### Weights

**Empty:** 19,781 lb (8973 kg)
**Maximum take-off:** 42,000 lb (19051 kg)

#### Fuel and load

Internal fuel 9,263 lb (4202 kg); external fuel up to four 300-US gal (1136-litre) drop tanks; maximum ordnance 20,000 lb (9072 kg) theoretical, 15,000 lb (6804 kg) practical with reduced internal fuel and 9,500 lb (4309 kg) with maximum internal fuel

#### Performance

**Maximum speed (clean):** 662 mph (1065 km/h) at 2,000 ft (610 m)
**Maximum speed with 6,000-lb (2722-kg) of stores:** 647 mph (1041 km/h) at 5,000 ft (1525 m)
**Radius of action:** ferry range 2,485 nm (2,861 miles; 4604 km) with maximum internal and external fuel or 1,981 nm (2,281 miles; 3671 km) with internal fuel; combat radius 620 nm (714 miles; 1149 km) on a hi-lo-hi mission
**Ferry range:** 2,870 miles (4619 km) with four 250-Imp gal (1137-litre) tanks

#### Armament

One internal 20-mm M61 Vulcan cannon with up to 1,000 rounds, plus up to 15,000 lb (6804 kg) of ordnance on six underwing pylons, and two fuselage hardpoints

---

**114** Control rod spring damper
**115** Engine compressor intake
**116** Intake centre-body fairing
**117** Fuselage upper longeron
**118** Engine bleed air ducting
**119** Rear fuselage main frames
**120** Hydraulic system reservoir
**121** Vertical tail control rod
**122** Finroot fillet
**123** Vertical tail trim feel unit
**124** Vertical tail autopilot controller
**125** Rudder feel control unit
**126** Tailfin construction
**127** Flush VHF aerial
**128** Starboard all-moving tailplane
**129** Fin leading-edge ribs
**130** Dielectric fintip aerial fairing
**131** UHF/IFF aerial
**132** VOR aerial
**133** Tail navigation light
**134** Tail radar warning antenna (electronic countermeasures, ECM)
**135** Rudder
**136** Rudder rib construction
**137** Rudder hydraulic actuator
**138** Fin attachment post
**139** Detachable tail cone
**140** Jet pipe
**141** Engine exhaust nozzle
**142** Port all-moving tailplane
**143** Tailplane rib construction
**144** Tailplane spar box
**145** Leading-edge nose ribs
**146** Tailplane pivot fixing
**147** Tailplane control lever arm
**148** Hydraulic actuator
**149** Back-up tailplane control interconnecting yoke
**150** Rear engine mounting
**151** Allison TF41-A-1 turbofan
**152** Fuselage lower longeron
**153** Ventral chaff dispenser
**154** Engine bay access panels
**155** Boron carbide (HCF) engine bay armour
**156** Emergency runway arrester hook
**157** Hook hydraulic actuator/damper
**158** Engine accessory equipment gearbox
**159** Main engine mounting trunion
**160** Hydraulic accumulators
**161** Position of strike camera on starboard side
**162** Fuel vent mast
**163** Port spoiler
**164** Flap hinge arms
**165** Flap hydraulic jack
**166** Flap rib construction
**167** Port single-slotted trailing-edge flap
**168** Fuel jettison pipe
**169** External fuel tank tail fins
**170** Aileron hydraulic actuator
**171** Port aileron
**172** Fixed portion of trailing edge
**173** Port formation light
**174** Wingtip fairing
**175** Port navigation light
**176** Outboard leading-edge flap
**177** Leading-edge flap (down)
**178** Leading-edge flap rib construction
**179** Flap hydraulic jacks
**180** Outer wing panel multi-spar construction
**181** Wing hinge rib
**182** Wing fold hydraulic actuator
**183** Port outer stores pylon
**184** Leading-edge dog-tooth
**185** Port mainwheel
**186** Inner wing panel multi-spar construction
**187** Port wing integral fuel tank
**188** Centre pylon attachment hardpoint
**189** Main undercarriage leg strut
**190** Hydraulic retraction jack
**191** Shock/absorber strut
**192** Main undercarriage leg pivot fixing
**193** Aileron feel trim control unit
**194** Centre fuselage fuel cell
**195** Inner wing pylon hardpoint, capacity 2,500 lb (1134 kg)
**196** Hydraulic reservoir
**197** Undercarriage bay pressure refuelling connection
**198** Position of landing lamp in starboard wheel bay
**199** Fuel sump cell
**200** Main wheel doors
**201** Port centre wing pylon
**202** 250-Imp gal (1137-litre) external fuel tank
**203** Ventral airbrake
**204** Airbrake retractable side flap
**205** GBU-10 Paveway II laser-guided bomb (2,000-lb/907-kg Mk 84)
**206** Rockeye cluster bomb
**207** AGM-65A Maverick TV or laser-guided air-to-ground missile
**208** LAU-37 air-to-ground rocket launcher

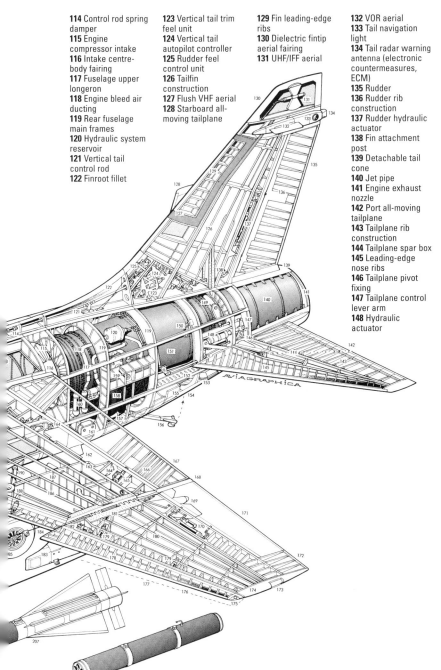

# Vought F-8 Crusader

*Fighter Squadron One Hundred and Three (VF-103) transitioned to the F8U in 1957, then to the F-8E in 1963. Known as the 'Sluggers', the squadron was aboard USS Forestal in the eastern Mediterranean at the time of the Lebanon crisis (1958), during which US Marines undertook an amphibious landing in an effort to restore peace to the area.*

## F-8E Crusader

### Cutaway key

1 Fintip VHF aerial fairing
2 Tail warning radar
3 Tail navigation light
4 Rudder construction
5 Rudder hydraulic jack
6 Engine exhaust nozzle
7 Variable-area nozzle flaps
8 Afterburner cooling air duct
9 Nozzle control jacks
10 Starboard all-moving tailplane construction
11 Tailplane spar box
12 Leading-edge ribs
13 Tailplane pivot fixing
14 Tailplane hydraulic control jack
15 Tailpipe cooling air vents
16 Fin attachment main frame
17 Afterburner duct
18 Rudder control linkages
19 Fin leading-edge construction
20 Port all-moving tailplane
21 Fin-root fillet construction
22 Rear engine mounting
23 Fuselage break point double frame (engine removal)
24 Afterburner fuel spray manifold
25 Tailplane autopilot control system
26 Deck arrester hook
27 Starboard ventral fin
28 Rear fuselage fuel tank
29 Pratt & Whitney J57-P-20A afterburning turbojet
30 Engine bay cooling air louvres
31 Wingroot trailing-edge fillet

32 Bleed air system piping
33 Engine oil tank (85 US gal/322 litres)
34 Wing spar pivot fixing
35 Hydraulic flap jack
36 Starboard flap
37 Control rod linkages
38 Rear spar
39 Engine accessory gearbox compartment
40 Inboard wing panel multi-spar construction
41 Starboard wing integral fuel tank, total fuel system capacity 1,348 US gal (5103 litres)
42 Aileron power control unit
43 Starboard drooping aileron construction
44 Hydraulic wing fold jack
45 Trailing-edge ribs
46 Fixed portion of trailing edge
47 Wingtip fairing
48 Starboard navigation light
49 Leading-edge flap, lowered position
50 Leading-edge flap rib construction
51 Outer wing panel spar construction
52 Leading-edge flap hydraulic jack
53 Wingfold hinge
54 Front spar
55 Leading-edge flap inboard section
56 Leading-edge dog-tooth
57 Wing pylon
58 AGM-12B Bullpup A air-to ground missile
59 Starboard mainwheel
60 Main undercarriage leg strut
61 Shock absorber strut
62 Hydraulic retraction jack
63 Landing lamp

64 Wheel bay doors
65 Main undercarriage pivot fixing
66 Wing spar/front engine mounting main bulkhead
67 Engine compressor intake
68 Wingroot rib
69 Centre-section fuel tank
70 Wing spar carry-through structure
71 Dorsal fairing
72 Port flap jack
73 Port plain flap, lowered position
74 Port drooped aileron, lowered position
75 Aileron power control unit
76 Fuel system piping
77 Wing-fold hydraulic jack

78 Fixed portion of trailing edge
79 Port wing folded position
80 Wingtip fairing
81 Port navigation light
82 Port outboard leading-edge flap, lowered
83 Outboard flap hydraulic jack
84 Leading-edge dog-tooth
85 Wing-fold hinge

86 Inboard leading-edge flap hydraulic jacks
87 Port wing integral fuel tank
88 Anti-collision light
89 Missile system avionics
90 Two-position variable-incidence wing, raised position
91 Intake trunking
92 Wing incidence hydraulic jack

93 Fuselage upper longeron
94 Air system exhaust heat shield
95 Main fuselage fuel tank
96 Airbrake hydraulic jack
97 Airbrake housing

98 Ventral airbrake, lowered
99 Rocket launch tubes
100 Rocket launcher pylon adaptor
101 Zuni folding-fin ground attack rockets (8)
102 Emergency air-driven generator
103 Liquid oxygen bottle (LOX)
104 Fuselage stores pylon

## SPECIFICATION

### F-8E Crusader

**Dimensions**

**Length:** 54 ft 6 in (16.61 m)
**Height:** 15 ft 9 in (4.80 m)
**Wingspan:** 35 ft 2 in (10.72 m)
**Wing area:** 350 sq ft (35.52 m²)

**Powerplant**

One Pratt & Whitney J57-P-20A turbojet rated at 10,700 lb (48.15 kN) static thrust or 18,000 lb st (81 kN) with afterburner

**Weights**

**Empty:** 17,541 lb (7957 kg)
**Gross weight:** 28,765 lb (13048 kg)
**Combat weight:** 25,098 lb (11304 kg)
**Maximum take-off:** 34,000 lb (15422 kg)

**Performance**

**Maximum level speed at sea level:** 764 mph (1230 km/h)

**Maximum level speed at 40,000 ft (12192 m):** 1,120 mph (1802 km/h)
**Cruising speed:** 570 mph (917 km/h)
**Stalling speed:** 162 mph (261 km/h)
**Rate of climb in one minute:** 31,950 ft (9738 m)
**Service ceiling:** 58,000 ft (17678 m)
**Combat ceiling:** 53,400 ft (16276 m)

**Range**

**Range:** 453 miles (729 km)
**Maximum range:** 1,737 miles (2795 km)

**Armament**

Four Colt-Browning (20-mm) Mk 12 cannon with 144 rounds per gun; plus up to four AIM-9 Sidewinder AAMs; or 12 250-lb (113-kg) bombs; or eight 500-lb (227-kg) bombs; or eight Zuni rockets; or two AGM-12A or AGM-12B Bullpup A AGMs

*The exceptional speed of the Crusader meant that the aircraft was used to accomplish a number of high-profile speed records. By far the best-known was the record coast-to coast flight of 16 July 1957, known as 'Project Bullet'. This was carried out in an F8U-1P flown by Major John Glenn (illustrated) and an F8U-1 flown by LCdr Charles Demmler. Taking off from Los Angeles, the pair flew supersonically to the first refuelling, where Demmler's probe was damaged, forcing him to retire. Glenn carried on, landing at New York 3 hours and 23 minutes after take-off, having photographed the entire strip of land beneath his aircraft during the run.*

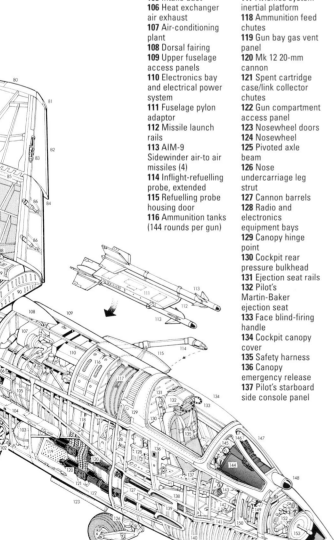

105 Intake duct
106 Heat exchanger air exhaust
107 Air-conditioning plant
108 Dorsal fairing
109 Upper fuselage access panels
110 Electronics bay and electrical power system
111 Fuselage pylon adaptor
112 Missile launch rails
113 AIM-9 Sidewinder air-to air missiles (4)
114 Inflight-refuelling probe, extended
115 Refuelling probe housing door
116 Ammunition tanks (144 rounds per gun)

117 Avionics system inertial platform
118 Ammunition feed chutes
119 Gun bay gas vent panel
120 Mk 12 20-mm cannon
121 Spent cartridge case/link collector chutes
122 Gun compartment access panel
123 Nosewheel doors
124 Nosewheel
125 Pivoted axle beam
126 Nose undercarriage leg strut
127 Cannon barrels
128 Radio and electronics equipment bays
129 Canopy hinge point
130 Cockpit rear pressure bulkhead
131 Ejection seat rails
132 Pilot's Martin-Baker ejection seat
133 Face blind-firing handle
134 Cockpit canopy cover
135 Safety harness
136 Canopy emergency release
137 Pilot's starboard side console panel

138 Cockpit floor level
139 Cannon muzzle blast troughs
140 Intake duct framing
141 Radar cooling air piping
142 Rudder pedals
143 Control column
144 Instrument panel shroud
145 Engine throttle control
146 Radar gunsight
147 Bullet-proof windshield
148 Infra-red seeker head
149 Radar electronics package
150 Cockpit front pressure bulkhead
151 Engine air intake
152 Radar scanner tracking mechanism
153 Radar antenna
154 Glass-fibre radome
155 Pitot tube

*Vought modified the 74th F-8A into a dual (tandem)-seat aircraft, designated F8U-1T (later TF-8A). As a one-of-a-kind prototype, the lone TF-8A performed extremely well. After serving with the US Navy (illustrated), the 'Two-sader' served with NASA/Vought at Edwards AFB, where one of its roles was as a chase-plane. The TF-8A was lost on 28 July 1978 while on a training mission.*

# Reconnaissance
# Aircraft

# Boeing E-3 Sentry

*The size of the AN/APY-1 radar held within t...
rotodome is clearly evident in this view o...
USAF E-3B. The radar's sophistication allows...
to operate in several modes, providi...
comprehensive surveillance tailored to t...
E-3B's tactical needs over a wide rang...*

## Boeing E-3C/D Sentry (AWACS)

**Cutaway key**
1 Fixed flight-refuelling probe, British and French aircraft only
2 Refuelling lights
3 Refuelling receptacle, open
4 Flight deck, two pilots, navigator and flight engineer
5 Forward 'Quick-Look' ESM system antennas, retrofitted to USAF and NATO aircraft
6 Forward entry door
7 Forward toilet
8 Safety equipment locker
9 Communications console with Joint Tactical Information Distribution System (JTIDS)
10 Communications equipment racks
11 Lateral 'Quick-Look' antennas, port and starboard

12 Underfloor flight-essential avionics racks
13 Bale-out chute
14 Computer racks
15 Communications technician's console
16 Data display controller
17 Underfloor power distribution centre
18 Operator consoles (14)
19 GPS antenna
20 Escape hatch with automatic life raft

21 Standard overwing escape hatches, port and starboard
22 CFM56-2A-3 engines, British, French and Saudi aircraft, USAF and NATO aircraft have Pratt & Whitney TF33-P-100/-100A
23 Wingtip Loral 10171 ('Yellow Gate') ESM pod, British aircraft only
24 HF antenna

25 Rotodome, rotates at 6 rpm operationally
26 IFF antenna
27 TADIL-C array
28 Radar-cooling air duct
29 Antenna ancillary equipment
30 Westinghouse APY-2 phased-array antenna
31 Radar maintenance station
32 Radar receiving and signal processing racks

33 Supernumerary and relief crew seats
34 JTIDS terminal
35 Underfloor radar equipment bay, regulators, filters and pulser/Klystron equipment
36 Radar-cooling system ram air intake to heat exchanger
37 Auxiliary power unit (APU) bay
38 ESM equipment rack
39 Relief crew seating

40 Bunks, port and starboard
41 Starboard-side service door
42 Galley
43 Rear entry door
44 Toilet compartments, port and starboard
45 Rear 'Quick-Look' ESM antenna

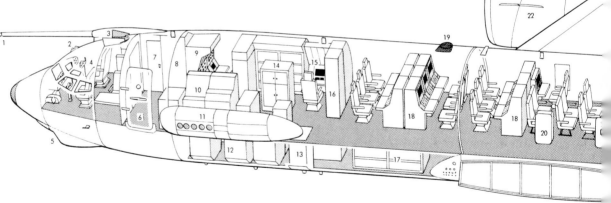

## Boeing E-767

In December 1991 Boeing announced the project for an AWACS version of the Boeing 767-200ER airliner, fitted with the Northrop Grumman AN/APY-2 radar. Japan expressed an immediate interest and in November 1993 two examples were ordered for the JASDF. Two further examples were ordered the following year and in March 1998 the first two examples were delivered. The aircraft has a flight crew of two and up to 19 mission crew, although this number can vary depending on the mission profile. Substantial structural modifications were needed, including two additional bulkheads and reinforced floor beams as well as the rotodome to hold the rotating radar. The aircraft offers twice the floor space and three times the internal volume of the Boeing E-3. When operational, the four aircraft will be based at Hamamatsu Air Base.

*Left: To mark the 50th anniversary of NATO in 1999, NE-3A Sentry LX-N-90442 was repainted in this spectacular colour scheme. The flags of all 19 member states of NATO are depicted on the side of the aircraft.*

*Below left: During the 1990s, NATO's E-3 fleet underwent a major upgrade. This included the installation of an AN/AYR-1 ESM system, identified by the additional bulges beneath the nose and on the side of the front fuselage, and an upgraded computer system.*

## SPECIFICATION

**Sentry AEW.Mk 1 (E-3D)**

### Dimensions

**Length:** 152 ft 11 in (46.61 m)
**Wingspan:** 147 ft 7 in (44.98 m)
**Wingspan (E-3A/B/C):** 145 ft 9 in (44.42 m)
**Wing area:** 3,050 sq ft (283.35 m²)
**Height:** 41 ft 9 in (12.73 m)

### Powerplant

Four CFM56-2A-3 turbofan engines each rated at 24,000 lb st (106.8 kN) for take-off or 23,405 lb st (104.1 kN) maximum continuous power
**E-3A/B/C:** Four Pratt & Whitney TF33-P-100/-100A turbofan engines each rated at 21,000 lb st (93.41 kN)

### Weights

**Normal take-off:** 325,000 lb (147417 kg)
**Maximum take-off:** 332,500 lb (150820 kg)

**Maximum ramp:** 335,000 lb (151953 kg)

### Fuel load

**Total fuel weight (JP4):** 155,448 lb (70,510 kg)

### Performance

**Maximum level speed at operating altitude:** 460 kt (530 mph; 853 km/h)
**Service ceiling:** more than 35,000 ft (10670 m)
**Maximum unrefuelled range:** more than 5,000 nm (5,758 miles; 9266 km)
**Operational radius:** 870 nm (1,000 miles; 1610 km) with six hours on allocated station
**Maximum unrefuelled endurance:** more than 11 hours

### Accommodation

**Flight crew:** 4
**Mission crew and operators:** 17

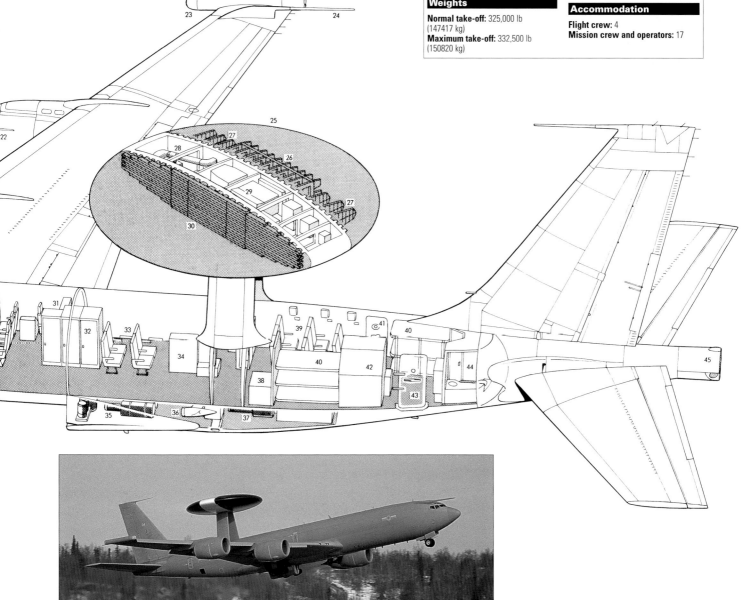

*As the UK component of the NATO Airborne Early Warning Force (AEWF), the RAF's E-3Ds are equipped with a refuelling probe to allow air-to-air refuelling from the RAF's VC10 and TriStar tanker assets. Each of the seven aircraft is named after characters in the story, Snow White and the Seven Dwarfs.*

# Boeing RC-135

*Despite the collapse of the Soviet threat, the disbandment of Strategic Air Command in 1992 and the introduction of modern spy satellites and J-STARS, the RC-135 remains an important type in the USAF's reconnaissance inventory. During Operation Allied Force in 1999, elements of the RC-135V/W Rivet Joint fleet operated from Mildenhall as a vital component of the electronic warfare/surveillance effort over the former Yugoslavia.*

## RC-135W

**Cutaway key**
1 Radome
2 Forward radar antenna
3 Front pressure bulkhead
4 Ventral antennas
5 Extended nose radome fairing
6 Nose compartment framing
7 Cockpit floor level
8 Pilot's side console panel
9 Rudder pedals
10 Control column
11 Instrument panel
12 Windscreen wipers
13 Windscreen panels
14 Cockpit eyebrow windows
15 Overhead systems switch panels
16 Co-pilot's seat
17 Direct vision opening side window panel
18 Pilot's seat
19 Safety equipment stowage
20 Chart-plotting table
21 Navigator's instrument console
22 Boom type inflight refuelling receptacle, open
23 Dual navigators' seats
24 Retractable escape spoiler, stowed position
25 Entry hatch floor grille
26 Nose landing gearwheel bay
27 Crew entry hatch, open
28 Retractable boarding ladder
29 Twin nosewheels, forward retracting
30 Nose landing gear pivot fixing

31 Underfloor avionics equipment racks
32 Electrical equipment racking
33 Super numerary crew seal
34 Star tracking windows, celestial navigation system
35 Cockpit doorway
36 Circuit breaker panels
37 Overhead air distribution ducting
38 No. 1 UHF/VHF aerial
39 Starboard side avionics equipment racks
40 Toilet compartment
41 Water heater
42 Wash basin
43 Water storage tanks
44 Toilet
45 Side-Looking Airborne Radar (SLAR) antenna panels
46 SLAR equipment fairing
47 Cargo doorway, electronic equipment loading
48 Main cabin flooring
49 Modular equipment package
50 Cargo door hydraulic jacks and hinges
51 Cargo door, open
52 ADF aerials
53 Electronics equipment racks
54 Air conditioning ducting
55 Aerial lead-in
56 Front spar attachment fuselage main frame
57 Centre section fuel tanks, 27656 litres (7,306 US gal) capacity

58 Overwing emergency exit hatch, port only
59 Floor beam construction
60 AN/ASD-1 avionics equipment racks
61 Tacan aerial
62 No. 1 satellite navigation system aerial
63 Inboard wing fuel tank, 8612 litres (2,275 US gal) capacity
64 Fuel filler cap
65 Detachable engine cowling panels
66 No. 3 starboard inboard engine nacelle
67 Intake cowling
68 Nacelle pylon
69 Pylon strut access panels
70 Wing centre main fuel tank, 7805 litres (2,062 US gal) capacity
71 Fuel venting channels
72 Leading edge flap hydraulic jacks
73 Krueger-type leading edge flap, down position
74 No. 4 starboard outboard engine nacelle
75 Outboard nacelle pylon
76 Outer wing panel joint rib
77 Wing outboard fuel tank, 1643 litres (434 US gal) capacity
78 HF antenna tuner
79 Lightning arrester panel
80 HF aerial mast

81 Pitot static boom
82 Starboard navigation light
83 Static dischargers
84 Outboard, low speed, aileron
85 Aileron internal balance panels
86 Spoiler interconnection linkage
87 Aileron hinge control mechanism
88 Aileron tab
89 Outboard double-slotted Fowler-type flap, down position
90 Outboard spoilers, open
91 Spoiler hydraulic jacks
92 Flap guide rails
93 Flap screw jacks
94 Aileron control and trim tab
95 Inboard, high speed, aileron
96 Gust damper
97 Aileron hinge control linkage
98 Inboard spoilers, open
99 Spoiler hydraulic jacks
100 Inboard double-slotted Fowler-type flap, down position
101 Rear spar attachment fuselage main frame

102 Pressure floor above wheel bay
103 ECM operator's seats
104 AN/ASD-1 Elint system control console
105 No. 2 UHF/VHF aerial
106 Cabin divider
107 Production break fuselage mainframe
108 Main cabin floor beams
109 Rear underfloor fuel cells, not used on Sigint aircraft
110 Signals Intelligence (Sigint) operator's seats
111 Sigint instrument and control consoles
112 No. 2 satellite navigation system aerial
113 QRC-259 superheterodyne receiver system console
114 Rear cabin emergency exit and service hatch, starboard only
115 QRC-259 operator's seat
116 Avionics equipment racks

117 Equipment modules
118 Table
119 Crew rest area seating

120 Hatches to underfloor radar equipment bay
121 Recorder unit
122 Rear fuselage close pitched frame construction

123 Galley unit
124 Aft toilet compartment

© 2001 Mike Badrocke/Aviagraphica

## SPECIFICATION

### RC-135V Rivet Joint

**Dimensions:**

**Wingspan:** 130 ft 10 in (39.88 m)
**Wing area (less ailerons):**
2,313.4 sq ft (214.9 m²)
**Wing area (flaps extended):**
2,754.4 sq ft (255.9 m²)
**Length:** 135 ft 1 in (41.17 m)
**Height:** 41 ft 9 in (12.73 m)

**Powerplant:**

Four Pratt & Whitney TF33-P-9

turbofans, each rated at 18,000 lb st (80.07 kN) dry; re-engined aircraft powered by four CFM International F108-CF-100 turbofans, each rated at 22,000 lb st (97.86 kN)

**Weights:**

**Maximum gross (taxi):** 301,600 lb (136803 kg)

**Performance**

Generally similar to KC-135E Stratotanker

*The basic flight crew of the RC-135 comprises two pilots and two navigators, with the rear part of the cabin containing seven operator stations for Sigint missions. Today's Rivet Joint crew includes members of several 55th Wing squadrons. Pilots, navigators and maintainers are assigned to the 38th Reconnaissance Sqn, EWOs ('Ravens') and maintainers are drawn from the 343rd RS while the remaining crew are provided by the 97th Intelligence Sqn.*

125 Equipment stowage racks
126 Relief crew bunks
127 Rear pressure bulkhead
128 Fin root fillet
129 Tail fin attachment joints
130 Artificial feel system pressure head
131 Fin rib construction
132 VOR aerial
133 HF notch aerial
134 Starboard tailplane
135 HF aerial cable
136 Fin leading edge
137 Fin tip aerial fairing
138 HF aerial mast
139 Lightning arrester panel
140 HF tuner
141 Loran aerial
142 Rudder fixed trailing edge, segment
143 Rudder rib construction
144 Internal balance panels
145 Rudder operating control rod

146 Rudder control tab
147 Anti-balance tab
148 Tailcone
149 Crash locator beacon
150 Tail navigation light
151 Elevator tab
152 Port elevator
153 Elevator internal balance panels
154 Tailplane tip fairing
155 Tailplane rib construction
156 All-moving trimming tailplane hinge mountings
157 Centre section carry through
158 Tailplane sealing plate
159 Trimming tailplane operating arm
160 Screw jack
161 Fuel jettison pipe
162 Fin attachment main frames

165 Fuselage skin panelling
166 Ventral aerial array

167 Fuselage lower lobe frame and stringer construction
168 Wing root trailing edge fairing

182 Flap rib construction
183 Outboard double-slotted flap
184 Aileron hinge control mechanism
185 Aileron tab
186 Outboard, low speed, aileron
187 Static dischargers
188 Fixed portion of trailing edge
189 Wing tip fairing
190 Port navigation light
191 Fuel system vent tank
192 Ventral NACA-type venting air intake
193 Pitot static boom

201 Aft translating exhaust cowling, open
202 Thrust reverser cascades
203 Engine cowling panels
204 Fan air reverser, open
205 Spring loaded intake pressure relief doors
206 No. 1 outboard engine cowling
207 Port leading edge Krueger flap, down position
208 Leading edge nose ribs
209 Front spar
210 Wing rib construction

215 Engine hot stream exhaust nozzle
216 Tailpipe

217 Pratt & Whitney TF33-9 turbofan engine
218 Engine accessory equipment gearbox
219 Main engine mounting
220 Fan air, cold stream, exhaust duct
221 Engine oil tank
222 Compressor intake face
223 Inboard nacelle pylon
224 Bleed air ducting
225 Four-wheel main landing gear bogie
226 Wing skin panelling
227 Inboard integral fuel tanks
228 Ventral air conditioning pack, port and starboard
229 Leading edge rib construction
230 Landing taxiing lamps
231 Sigint antennae

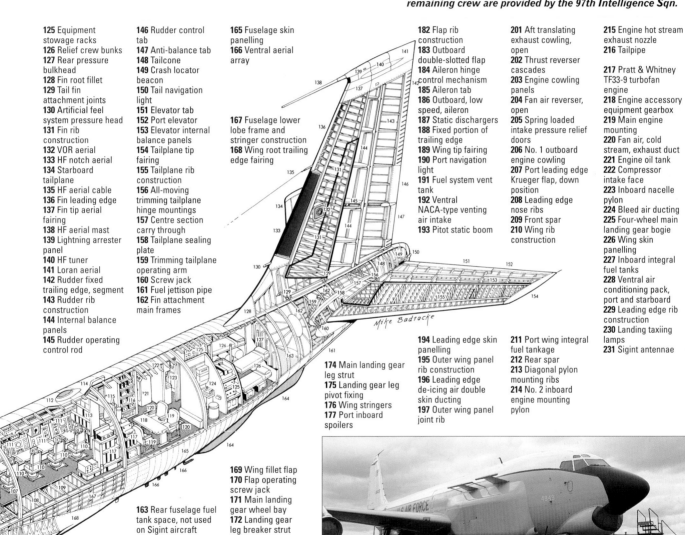

Mike Badrocke

174 Main landing gear leg strut
175 Landing gear leg pivot fixing
176 Wing stringers
177 Port inboard spoilers

169 Wing fillet flap
170 Flap operating screw jack
171 Main landing gear wheel bay
172 Landing gear leg breaker strut
173 Hydraulic retraction jack

163 Rear fuselage fuel tank space, not used on Sigint aircraft
164 Ventral radomes

194 Leading edge skin panelling
195 Outer wing panel rib construction
196 Leading edge de-icing air double skin ducting
197 Outer wing panel joint rib

211 Port wing integral fuel tankage
212 Rear spar
213 Diagonal pylon mounting ribs
214 No. 2 inboard engine mounting pylon

178 Inboard double-slotted flap
179 Inboard, high-speed, aileron
180 Aileron tab
181 Outboard spoilers

198 Pylon rear support strut
199 Nacelle pylon attachment joint
200 Pylon construction

*RC-135U Bark like a Dawg operated out of Mildenhall during the late 1980s. Initially a minor modification program, Combat Sent later added a chin radome, a second radome below the forward fuselage, two 'rabbit's ear' fairings above the cheek fairings, and an angular fairing over the boom position, to produce the most radically-altered sub-type in service.*

# British Aerospace Nimrod

A number of Nimrods was modified for the carriage of **BOZ** chaff/flare pods during the Gulf War. These aircraft also received an underwing **FLIR** turret to starboard and a fin-mounted **TRD** (Towed Radar Decoy).

## Nimrod MR.Mk 2

**Cutaway key**
1 Radome
2 Taxiing lamp
3 EMI Searchwater radar scanner
4 Windscreen panels and wipers
5 Flight refuelling probe
6 Two-pilot flight deck
7 Pitot head
8 Interrogator unit
9 Doppler antenna
10 Forward radio crate
11 Flight engineer's station

12 Escape hatch (inoperable with refuelling boom fitted)
13 Starboard electrical equipment crate
14 Scarbe aerials
15 Upper IFF aerial
16 Periscope sextant aperture
17 Starboard side forward entry door
18 Systems equipment crate
19 Toilet compartment
20 Nose undercarriage wheel bay

21 Weapons bay door ground control panel
22 AGM-86A Harpoon air-to-surface anti-shipping missile
23 Weapons bay doors
24 Underfloor weapons bay
25 Armament distribution panel
26 Black-out curtain
27 Domed observation window, port and starboard
28 Port beam observer's station

29 Starboard beam observer's station
30 Dual sonic homers
31 ADF loop aerial
32 Navigation console
33 Route navigator's station
34 Tactical navigator's station
35 Observation window, starboard only
36 AEO's seat
37 Communications officer's seat
38 Searchwater radar equipment crates

39 Sonics operators' stations (2)
40 UHF/VHF aerials
41 Loran aerial
42 Avionics equipment cooling air ducts
43 ASV operator's seat
44 AC electrical equipment crate, port and starboard
45 Emergency exit window hatches, port and starboard

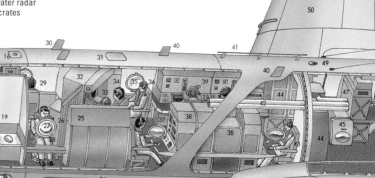

46 Document stowage
47 ESM/MAD console
48 ESM/MAD operator's station
49 Anti-collision light
50 Starboard wing panel
51 Steerable searchlight, 70-million candlepower
52 External fuel tank
53 Wingtip ECM pod

54 Starboard aileron
55 Airbrake panel, upper and lower surfaces
56 Starboard plain flaps
57 Galley compartment
58 Crew rest area
59 Curtained bulkheads

60 Acoustic equipment crates (2)
61 Sonobuoy stowage racks, two-port, six-starboard
62 Stores loader's station
63 Pressurised launcher
64 Rotary launchers (2)

*For onboard crew training in the ASW role, the Nimrod can utilise the Airborne Crew Trainer Mk 1 (ACT-1). This consists of a single exercise control unit driven by a reel of magnetic tape containing a software programme which simulates submarine threats on the AQS-901 acoustic detection and display system. This allows the crew to train in authentic conditions, without expending sonobuoys.*

## SPECIFICATION

### Nimrod MR.Mk 2

#### Dimensions

**Length:** 126 ft 9 in (38.63 m)
**Height:** 29 ft 8½ in (8.60 m)
**Wing span:** 114 ft 10 in (35.00 m)
**Wing area:** 2,121 sq ft (197.04 m²)
**Tailplane span:** 47 ft 7¼ in (14.51 m)
**Wheel track:** 28 ft 2½ in (8.60 m)
**Wheel base:** 46 ft 8½ in (14.24 m)

#### Powerplant

Four Rolls-Royce RB.168-20 Spey Mk 250 turbofans each rated at 12,140 lb st (54.00 kN)

#### Weights

**Typical empty:** 86,000 lb (39010 kg)
**Maximum normal take-off:** 177,500 lb (80514 kg)
**Maximum overload take-off:** 192,000 lb (87091 kg)

#### Fuel and load

**Internal fuel:** 85,840 lb (38937 kg) plus provision for 15,100 lb (6849 kg) of auxiliary fuel in six weapon-bay tanks
**Maximum ordnance:** 13,500 lb (6124 kg)

#### Performance

**Maximum speed at optimum altitude:** 500 kt (575 mph; 926 km/h)

**Maximum cruising speed at optimum altitude:** 475 kt (547 mph; 880 km/h)
**Economical cruising speed at optimum altitude:** 425 kt (490 mph; 787 km/h)
**Typical patrol speed at low level:** 200 kt (230 mph; 370 km/h) on two engines
**Service ceiling:** 42,000 ft (12800 m)
**Take-off run at normal maximum take-off weight:** 4,800 ft (1463 m)
**Landing run at normal landing weight:** 5,300 ft (1615 m)
**Ferry range:** 5,000 nm (5,758 miles; 9266 km)
**Endurance:** 12 hours typical, 15 hours maximum and 19 hours with one refuelling

#### Armament

Weapons bay can hold up to six lateral rows of ASW weapons including up to nine torpedoes as well as bombs or depth charges. Bay in rear fuselage for storing and launching active and passive sonobuoys and marine markers through two rotary and two single-barrel launchers. Hardpoints beneath each wing can carry two AIM-9 Sidewinder AAMs, a Harpoon air-surface missile, rockets, cannon pods, torpedoes or ECM equipment

65 Starboard side emergency door
66 UHF aerial
67 Intercom panel
68 Retro-launcher
69 Spare camera magazines
70 Hat rack
71 ECM pre-amplifier
72 Conditioning air intake, port only
73 Extended finroot fillet

74 HF aerial cables
75 Starboard tailplane
76 Fintip ECM aerial fairing
77 Rudder
78 MAD sensor boom
79 Elevator trim tab
80 Port elevator
81 Auxiliary fins, above and below
82 Port tailplane
83 Ventral fin
84 Tail bumper

85 Lower sonics aerial
86 Systems equipment air-conditioning pack
87 Auxiliary Power Unit (APU)
88 Internal walkway and tailcone access
89 Rear pressure dome
90 Cooling air blowers

96 Wingroot fillet
97 Dinghy stowage compartment
98 Engine exhaust nozzles
99 Thrust reverser cascades, outboard engines only
100 Port two-segment plain flaps
101 Fuel vent pipe
102 Dual fuel jettison pipes
103 Port airbrake panel

111 Aileron actuator linkage
112 Wing bumper
113 Port external fuel tank

128 Heat exchanger air intake
129 Taxiing lamp

91 Crew baggage stowage
92 Safe
93 Liquid oxygen converter
94 External cooling air duct
95 Rear entry door

104 Aileron trim tab
105 Port aileron
106 Aft high- and low-band ESM aerials
107 Port wingtip ESM pod
108 Port navigation light
109 Forward high- and low-band ESM aerials
110 Vortex generators

114 Wing tank fairing
115 Fixed slot
116 AIM-9 Sidewinder air-to-air 'self-defence' missiles
117 Wing stores pylon
118 Port wing rib construction
119 Wing panel integral fuel tankage
120 Flap hydraulic jack
121 Four-wheel main undercarriage bogie
122 Main undercarriage bay
123 Rolls-Royce Spey 250 turbofan engines
124 Engine bay dividing firewall
125 Landing lamp
126 Engine air intakes
127 Cabin air-conditioning bay

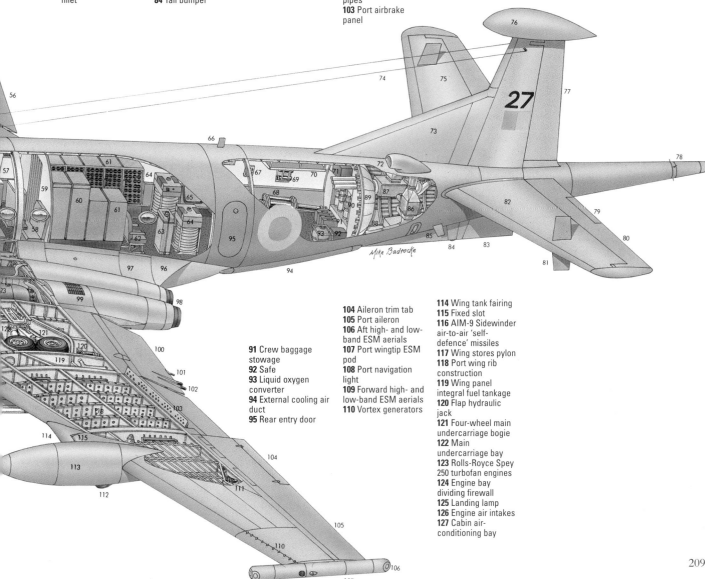

# Grumman E-2 Hawkeye

*A VAW-116 E-2 serenely cruises over the Pacific. All five Hawkeye squadrons of the Pacific Fleet are equipped with the Group II version, as was VAW-114 'Hormel Hawgs' before its disbandment in March 1995*

## E-2C Hawkeye

**Cutaway key**

1 Two-section rudder panels
2 Starboard outboard fin
3 Glassfibre fin construction
4 Passive detection system (PDS) antenna
5 Rudder construction
6 Static discharger
7 Fin construction
8 Leading-edge de-icing
9 Wing-fold jury strut lock
10 Wing folded position
11 Rudder jack
12 PDS receivers
13 Starboard inboard rudder sections
14 Starboard inboard glassfibre fin
15 Port elevator construction
16 Port inboard fixed fin
17 Port outboard rudder sections
18 Rudder controls
19 Tailplane construction
20 Fuel jettison pipes
21 Rearward PDS antenna
22 Tailplane fixing
23 Rear fuselage construction
24 Tailskid jack

25 Arrester hook
26 Tailskid
27 Arrester hook jack
28 Lower PDS receiver and antenna

29 Rear pressure dome
30 Toilet
31 Rotodome rear mounting struts
32 Rotating radar scanner housing (Rotodome)
33 Rotodome edge de-icing
34 UHF aerial array, AN/APS-125 set

35 Pivot bearing housing
36 IFF aerial array
37 Rotodome motor
38 Hydraulic lifting jack

39 Front mounting support frame
40 Radar transmission line
41 Fuselage frame construction
42 Toilet compartment doorway
43 Antenna coupler
44 Rear cabin window

45 Air controller's seat
46 Radar and instrument panels

47 Combat information officer's seat
48 Combat information radar panel
49 Radar operator
50 Radar panel and instruments

51 Swivelling seat mountings
52 Wing rear fixing
53 Wing-fold break-point
54 Spar locking mechanism
55 Wing-fold hinge jack
56 Wing-folding hydraulic jack
57 Starboard outboard flap
58 Flap construction

59 Flap guide rails
60 Flap drive motors and shaft
61 Starboard drooping aileron
62 Flap to drooping aileron connection
63 Aileron jack
64 Aileron construction
65 Aileron hinges
66 Starboard wingtip
67 Navigation light

68 Jury strut locking mechanism
69 Outer wing construction
70 Leading-edge construction

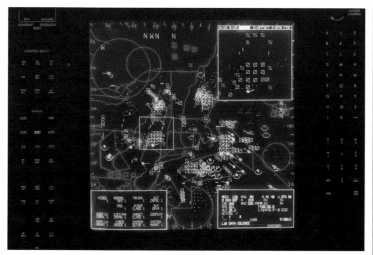

## SPECIFICATION

### E-2C Hawkeye

#### Dimensions

**Length:** 57 ft 6¾ in (17.54 m)
**Height:** 18 ft 3¾ in (5.58 m)
**Wingspan:** 80 ft 7 in (24.56 m)
**Wing, folded width:** 29 ft 4 in (8.94 m)
**Wing, aspect ratio:** 9.3
**Wing area:** 700.00 sq ft (65.03 m²)
**Tailplane span:** 26 ft 2½ in (7.99 m)
**Wheel track:** 19 ft 5¾ in (5.93 m)
**Wheel base:** 23 ft 2 in (7.06 m)

#### Powerplant

Two Allison T56-A-425 turboprop engines, each rated at 4,910 ehp (3661 kW)

**Empty:** 38,063 lb (17265 kg)
**Maximum take-off:** 51,933 lb (23556 kg)

**Internal fuel:** 12,400 lb (5624 kg)

#### Performance

**Maximum level speed:** 323 kt (372 mph; 598 km/h)
**Maximum cruising speed at optimum altitude:** 311 kt (358 mph; 576 km/h)
**Ferry cruising speed at optimum altitude:** 268 kt (308 mph; 496 km/h)
**Ferry range:** 1,394 nm (1,605 miles; 2583 km)
**Operational radius:** 175 nm (200 miles; 320 km) for a patrol of 3 to 4 hours
**Endurance with maximum fuel:** 6 hours 6 minutes
**Maximum rate of climb at sea level:** 2,515 ft (767 m) per minute
**Service ceiling:** 30,800 ft (9390 m)
**Minimum take-off run:** 2,000 ft (610 m)

*Hawkeye WSOs view tactical displays like the one above. The 11-in (27.94-cm) screen displays a background map, with colour-coded symbols detailing the origin, status, vector and intentions of the objects causing the radar returns.*

**71** Leading-edge de-icing
**72** Lattice rib construction
**73** Engine exhaust pipe fairing
**74** Front spar locking mechanism
**75** Main undercarriage leg

**81** Allison T56-A-425 engine
**82** Oil cooler
**83** Oil cooler intake
**84** Engine intake
**85** Hamilton Standard four-bladed propeller
**86** Gearbox drive shaft
**87** Propeller mechanism

**91** Bleed air supply duct
**92** Vapour cycle air-conditioning plant
**93** Wing front fixing
**94** Computer bank
**95** Wing centre rib joint

**96** Inboard wing section fuel tank, capacity 912 US gal (3452 litres) each wing
**97** Lattice rib construction
**98** Port inboard flap
**99** Wing-fold hinge
**100** Wing-fold joint line

**101** Sloping hinge rib
**102** Port outboard flap
**103** Aileron jack
**104** Port aileron
**105** Port outer wing panel
**106** Port wingtip
**107** Navigation light
**108** Leading-edge de-icing
**109** Aileron control

**121** Radar processor
**122** IFF processor
**123** Radar transmission line
**124** Range finder amplifier
**125** Port side entry doorway
**126** Equipment cooling air duct
**127** Port side equipment rack
**128** Starboard side radio and electronics racks
**129** Radar duplexer
**130** Electronics boxes
**131** Forward fuselage frame construction
**132** Lower electronics racks
**133** Scrambler boxes
**134** Navigation equipment
**135** Cockpit air-conditioning duct
**136** Cockpit doorway
**137** Electrical system junction box
**138** Air-conditioning diffuser
**139** Signal equipment
**140** Cockpit floor level
**141** Co-pilot's seat
**142** Parachute stowage
**143** Pilot's seat
**144** Headrest
**145** Cockpit roof window
**146** Cockpit roof construction
**147** Instrument panel shroud
**148** Windscreen wiper
**149** Bulged cockpit side window
**150** Instrument panel
**151** Control column
**152** Nose undercarriage strut
**153** Nose undercarriage door
**154** Rudder pedals
**155** Nose construction

**158** Navigation code box
**159** Nose electrical junction box
**160** Rudder pedal linking mechanism
**161** Windscreen heater unit
**162** Nose undercarriage leg
**163** Steering mechanism
**164** Twin nosewheels
**165** Catapult strop attachment arm
**166** Nosewheel leg door
**167** Nosewheel emergency air bottle

**168** Nose PDS receivers
**169** Oxygen tank
**170** Landing lamp
**171** Landing and taxi light window
**172** Nose PDS antenna array
**173** Nose aerial fairing

cable mechanism
**110** Engine mounting strut attachment
**111** Engine-to-propeller gearbox
**112** Propeller spinner fairing
**113** Hamilton Standard four-bladed propeller
**114** Engine intake
**115** Gearbox drive shaft
**116** Port engine
**117** Fuel system piping
**118** Cooling air intake
**119** Vapour cycle system radiator
**120** Cooling air outlet duct

**76** Undercarriage leg door
**77** Single mainwheel
**78** Mainwheel door
**79** Engine pylon construction
**80** Engine mounting strut

**88** Cooling air intake
**89** Engine-to-propeller gearbox
**90** Oil tank, usable capacity 9.25 US gal (35 litres) each nacelle

**156** Pilot head
**157** Sloping front bulkhead

# Grumman OV-1/RV-1 Mohawk

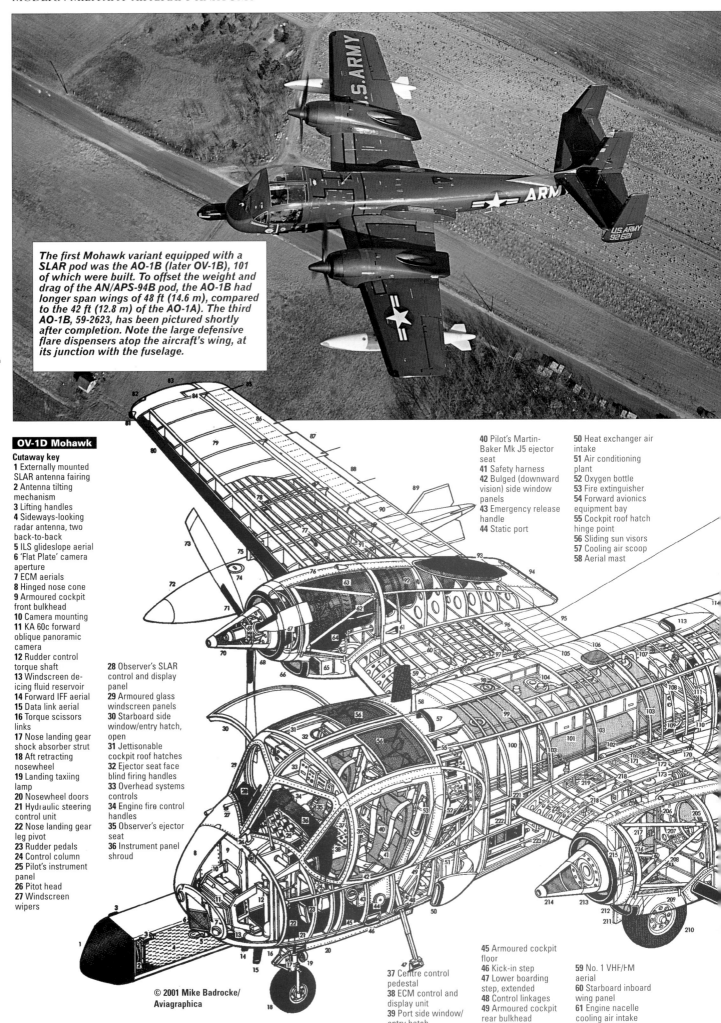

*The first Mohawk variant equipped with a SLAR pod was the AO-1B (later OV-1B), 101 of which were built. To offset the weight and drag of the AN/APS-94B pod, the AO-1B had longer span wings of 48 ft (14.6 m), compared to the 42 ft (12.8 m) of the AO-1A. The third AO-1B, 59-2623, has been pictured shortly after completion. Note the large defensive flare dispensers atop the aircraft's wing, at its junction with the fuselage.*

## OV-1D Mohawk
### Cutaway key
1 Externally mounted SLAR antenna fairing
2 Antenna tilting mechanism
3 Lifting handles
4 Sideways-looking radar antenna, two back-to-back
5 ILS glideslope aerial
6 'Flat Plate' camera aperture
7 ECM aerials
8 Hinged nose cone
9 Armoured cockpit front bulkhead
10 Camera mounting
11 KA 60c forward oblique panoramic camera
12 Rudder control torque shaft
13 Windscreen de-icing fluid reservoir
14 Forward IFF aerial
15 Data link aerial
16 Torque scissors links
17 Nose landing gear shock absorber strut
18 Aft retracting nosewheel
19 Landing taxiing lamp
20 Nosewheel doors
21 Hydraulic steering control unit
22 Nose landing gear leg pivot
23 Rudder pedals
24 Control column
25 Pilot's instrument panel
26 Pitot head
27 Windscreen wipers

28 Observer's SLAR control and display panel
29 Armoured glass windscreen panels
30 Starboard side window/entry hatch, open
31 Jettisonable cockpit roof hatches
32 Ejector seat face blind firing handles
33 Overhead systems controls
34 Engine fire control handles
35 Observer's ejector seat
36 Instrument panel shroud
37 Centre control pedestal
38 ECM control and display unit
39 Port side window/entry hatch

40 Pilot's Martin-Baker Mk J5 ejector seat
41 Safety harness
42 Bulged (downward vision) side window panels
43 Emergency release handle
44 Static port
45 Armoured cockpit floor
46 Kick-in step
47 Lower boarding step, extended
48 Control linkages
49 Armoured cockpit rear bulkhead

50 Heat exchanger air intake
51 Air conditioning plant
52 Oxygen bottle
53 Fire extinguisher
54 Forward avionics equipment bay
55 Cockpit roof hatch hinge point
56 Sliding sun visors
57 Cooling air scoop
58 Aerial mast
59 No. 1 VHF/FM aerial
60 Starboard inboard wing panel
61 Engine nacelle cooling air intake

© 2001 Mike Badrocke/Aviagraphica

| SPECIFICATION | |
|---|---|
| **OV-1D Mohawk** | **Power loading\*:** 5.6 lb/shp (2.6 kg/shp) |
| **Dimensions** | **Performance** |
| **Wingspan:** 48 ft (14.63 m) **Wing area:** 360 sq ft (33.45 m²) **Length (including SLAR pod):** 44 ft 11 in (13.69 m) **Height:** 13 ft (3.96 m) | **Maximum speed:** 305 mph (491 km/h) at 5,000 ft (1525 m) **Cruising speed:** 207 mph (333 km/h) **Climb rate:** 3,618 ft/min (18 m/sec) **Service ceiling:** 25,000 ft (7620 m) **Maximum range:** 1,010 miles (1625 km) |
| **Powerplant** | |
| Two Lycoming T53-L-701 turboprops each rated at 1,400 hp (1044 kW) | |
| **Weights** | \*Wing and power loadings are calculated at normal loaded weight and maximum take-off power |
| **Empty:** 11,757 lb (5333 kg) **Loaded:** 15,741 lb (7140 kg) **Maximum:** 10,109 lb (8214 kg) **Wing loading\*:** 43.7 lb/sq ft (213.5 kg/m²) | |

*In order to evaluate the suitability of the Mohawk in the armed reconnaissance/ ground support role, two OV-1As were modified as JOV-1As, equipped with an extra 500-lb (227-kg) stores station on each wing. A cockpit gunsight, gun firing and stores release equipment and armour plating were also added. Stores cleared for carriage by the aircraft included 0.50-in (12.7-mm) machine gun pods, 2.75-in (7-cm) and 5-in (12.7-cm) FFARs, 5-in (12.7-cm) HVARs, 250-, 500- and 1,000-lb (114-, 227 and 454-kg) low-drag bombs, fire bombs and Sidewinder air-to-air missiles.*

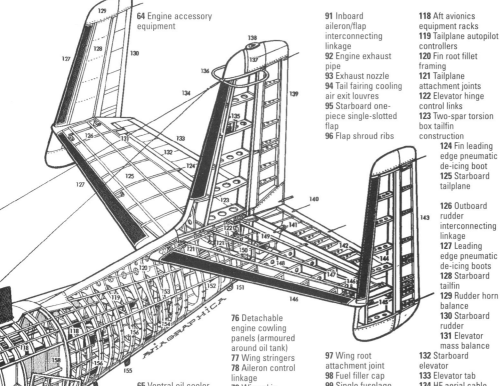

64 Engine accessory equipment

62 Engine bearer struts
63 Avco Lycoming T53-L-701A turboprop engine
65 Ventral oil cooler
66 Oil cooler air intake
67 Engine compressor inlet
68 Inlet lip de-icing
69 Propeller hub pitch change mechanism
70 Spinner
71 Propeller blade root de-icing
72 Starboard 150-US gal (567-litre) external fuel tank
73 Hamilton Standard three-bladed fully feathering and reversible constant-speed propeller
74 Fuel filler cap
75 Starboard tank pylon
76 Detachable engine cowling panels (armoured around oil tank)
77 Wing stringers
78 Aileron control linkage
79 Wing skin panelling
80 Leading edge pneumatic de-icing boot
81 Radar warning antenna
82 Starboard navigation light
83 Wingtip fairing
84 Aileron mass balance
85 Static dischargers
86 Starboard aileron
87 Aileron trim tab
88 Spring tab
89 External fuel tank tail fins
90 Inboard (low-speed) drooping aileron

91 Inboard aileron/flap interconnecting linkage
92 Engine exhaust pipe
93 Exhaust nozzle
94 Tail fairing cooling air exit louvres
95 Starboard one-piece single-slotted flap
96 Flap shroud ribs
97 Wing root attachment joint
98 Fuel filler cap
99 Single fuselage fuel tank, capacity 297 US gal (1125 litres)
100 Lateral cable and control ducting, port and starboard
101 Self-sealing main fuel tank
102 Flap hydraulic jack
103 Wing spar/fuselage attachment main frames
104 Fuel tank access panel
105 Fuselage skin panelling
106 ADF loop aerial
107 Fuel jettison pipe
108 Camera control unit
109 KA 76a vertical camera
110 KA 60c aft oblique panoramic camera
111 Control linkages
112 Avionics equipment racks
113 Cooling air scoop
114 TACAN aerial
115 Starboard airbrake, open
116 Aerial cable lead-in
117 No. 2 VHF/FM aerial

118 Aft avionics equipment racks
119 Tailplane autopilot controllers
120 Fin root fillet framing
121 Tailplane attachment joints
122 Elevator hinge control links
123 Two-spar torsion box tailfin construction
124 Fin leading edge pneumatic de-icing boot
125 Starboard tailplane
126 Outboard rudder interconnecting linkage
127 Leading edge pneumatic de-icing boots
128 Starboard tailfin
129 Rudder horn balance
130 Starboard rudder
131 Elevator mass balance
132 Starboard elevator
133 Elevator tab
134 HF aerial cable
135 Compass flux valve
136 VOR aerial
137 Centre rudder horn balance
138 Anti-collision light
139 Rudder rib construction
140 Static dischargers
141 Tail navigation light
142 Port elevator rib construction
143 Port rudder
144 Outboard tailplane rib construction
145 Fin/tailplane attachment joints
146 Leading edge pneumatic de-icing boots
147 Tailplane rib construction
148 Three-spar tailplane torsion box construction
149 Rear IFF aerial
150 Rudder torque shaft
151 Ventral tail bumper/ tie-down point
152 Tailplane attachment main frames

153 Rear fuselage frame and stringer construction
154 Fuselage lower longeron
155 Lower TACAN aerial
156 Radar altimeter aerials
157 FM homing aerial
158 Port airbrake housing
159 Hydraulic jack
160 Port airbrake construction
161 ADF sense aerial
162 Airbrake hinge point
163 Equipment bay access door, port and starboard
164 Electrical system equipment
165 Ground power socket
166 Battery
167 Ventral VHF/UHF aerial
168 Camera equipment light sensor
169 Marker beacon antenna
170 Port flap operating rod
171 Stub wing construction
172 Rear spar bolted joint
173 Main landing gear leg pivot fixing
174 Port single slotted flap
175 Port engine exhaust nozzle
176 Nacelle tail fairing
177 Flap rib construction
178 Outboard flap operating rod
179 Flap/drooping aileron interconnection
180 Swinging link flap/aileron hinge
181 Port low-speed drooping aileron
182 Aileron geared tab
183 Rear spar
184 Aileron rib construction
185 External tank tail fins
186 Port aileron
187 Static dischargers
188 Aileron mass balance
189 Wingtip fairing
190 Port navigation light
191 Radar warning antenna
192 Leading edge de-icing boot

193 Port 150-US gal (567-litre) external fuel tank
194 Fuel filler cap
195 Port fuel tank pylon
196 Wing rib construction
197 Aileron control linkage
198 Front spar
199 Aileron interconnecting link
200 Auxiliary centre spar
201 Main landing gear wheel bay
202 Engine nacelle framing
203 Port engine exhaust duct
204 Nacelle venting air intake
205 Rear engine mounting mainframe
206 Main landing gear hydraulic retraction jack
207 Side breaker strut
208 Engine bearer struts
209 Lower hinged engine cowling panels
210 Port main wheel
211 Main wheel doors
212 Oil cooler air intake
213 Engine air inlet
214 Port spinner
215 Cowling nose ring
216 Forward engine mounting ring frame
217 Engine oil tank, capacity 2½ US gal (9.50 litres)
218 Forward and centre spar bolted joints
219 Aileron autopilot controller
220 Leading edge engine control runs
221 SLAR signal receiver (interchangeable with IR receiver)
222 SLAR signal processor (interchangeable with IR recorder)
223 Ventral equipment bay access doors

# Lockheed S-3 Viking

In all 187 of 199 planned Vikings were built, about 119 of these eventually being reworked to S-3B standard. Eight of the original aircraft were pre-production prototypes and test airframes. Production ended in 1978.

## S-3B Viking

**Cutaway key**

1 Upward-hinging glass-fibre radome
2 Scanner protective housing
3 AN/APS(V)1 radar scanner
4 Rotating scanner mounting
5 Retractable flight refuelling probe
6 Windscreen wipers
7 Windscreen de-icing fluid reservoir
8 Forward identification light
9 Cockpit front pressure bulkhead
10 Nose undercarriage leg pivot mounting
11 Catapult strop link
12 Trailing link nosewheel suspension
13 Cabin conditioning and pressurisation outflow valves
14 Pitot head
15 Canopy external release
16 Rudder pedals
17 Instrument panel
18 Instrument panel shroud
19 Electrically heated windscreen panels
20 Overhead switch panels
21 Second pilot's seat
22 Tactical co-ordinator's (TACCO's) console
23 Pilot's Escapac 1-E ejection seat
24 Seat mounting/ejection rails
25 Jettisonable side window hatch
26 Electro-luminescent formation lighting strip
27 Engine throttle levers
28 OR-89AA infra-red equipment bay, radar equipment to starboard

29 Retractable Forward-Looking Infra-Red (FLIR) turret
30 FLIR turret doors
31 Auxiliary Power Unit (APU) bay, crew entry hatch on starboard side
32 APU exhaust duct
33 Port weapons bay door
34 Cabin conditioning air ducting
35 Sloping seat mounting bulkhead
36 Side window with rotating Polaroid blind
37 Sensor operator's (SENSO's) seat
38 SENSO's instrument console
39 TACCO's seat
40 Circuit breaker panels
41 Rear crew compartment ejection/escape hatch
42 UHF L-band UHF/IFF antenna
43 VHF antenna
44 Fixed inboard wing panel integral fuel tank, total internal capacity 1900 US gal (7192 litres)
45 Engine fire suppression bottles
46 Starboard engine pylon
47 CNU-264 cargo pod
48 De-icing air ducting
49 Starboard wing-fold hinge joint and rotary actuator
50 Leading-edge torque shaft and actuating links
51 Starboard drooped leading edge
52 Forward and forward oblique ECM antennas
53 Starboard navigation light
54 Wing-tip ECM equipment pod
55 Aft and aft oblique ECM antennas
56 Starboard aileron
57 Aileron hinge link

58 Starboard single-slotted flap
59 Outboard spoiler panels
60 Ventral airbrake/spoiler panel
61 Inboard spoiler panel
62 Flap guide rails
63 ADF antenna
64 Avionics equipment racks, port and starboard
65 Starboard weapons bay
66 Equipment bay centre aisle
67 Port weapons bay
68 BRU-14A bomb racks
69 Univac main computer
70 'Cold-plate' avionics cooling air ducts
71 Control surface actuators, ailerons and spoilers, on rear face of rear spar
72 Central flap drive unit

73 Magnetic Anomaly Detector (MAD) boom housing
74 Air conditioning pack
75 UHF L-band comm/TACAN antenna
76 Starboard wing asymmetrically folded position

77 Port wing asymmetrically folded position
78 Underwing sonobuoy reference antenna

79 Air system heat exchanger ram air intake
80 HF tuner
81 HF flush antenna

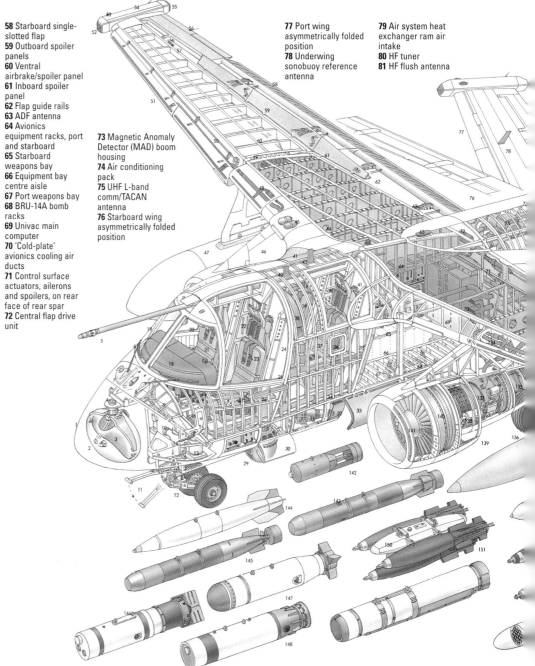

*Sharing ramp space at Palmdale with the first, third, and seventh prototype and first production aircraft, the fifth S-3A prototype (BuNo. 157996) is run-up prior to another test flight.*

## SPECIFICATION

### S-3A Viking

**Dimensions**

**Wingspan:** 68 ft 8 in (20.93 m)
**Wingspan (folded):** 29 ft 6 in (8.99 m)
**Wing area:** 598.00 sq ft (55.56 m²)
**Length overall:** 53 ft 4 in (16.26 m)
**Length (tail folded):** 49 ft 5 in (15.06 m)
**Height overall:** 22 ft 9 in (6.93 m)
**Height (tail folded):** 15 ft 3 in (4.65 m)

**Powerplant**

Two General Electric TF34-GE-2 turbofans each rated at 9,275 lb st (41.26 kN) dry

**Weights**

**Empty:** 26,650 lb (12088 kg)
**Normal take-off:** 42,500 lb (19277 kg)
**Maximum take-off:** 52,540 lb (23832 kg)

**Fuel and load**

**Internal fuel:** 12,863 lb (5753 kg)
**External fuel:** up to two 300-US gal (1136-litre) drop tanks
**Maximum ordnance:** 7,000 lb (3175 kg) including 4,000 lb (1814 kg) carried internally

**Performance**

**Maximum level speed 'clean' at sea level:** 439 kt (506 mph; 814 km/h)
**Maximum cruising speed at optimum altitude:** more than 350 kt (403 mph; 649 km/h)
**Patrol speed at optimum altitude:** 160 kt (184 mph; 296 km/h)
**Ferry range:** more than 3,000 nm (3,454 miles; 5558 km)
**Operational radius:** more than 945 nm (1,088 miles; 1751 km)
**Endurance:** 7 hours 30 minutes
**Maximum rate of climb at sea level:** more than 4,200 ft (1280 m) per minute
**Service ceiling:** more than 35,000 ft (10670 m)

**Armament (S-3B)**

The S-3B has two internal weapon bays on the 'corners' of its fuselage, able to carry four Mk 46 or 50 torpedoes, four Mk 36, 62 or 82 bomb/destructors, or two B57 nuclear depth charges (no longer carried on US carriers). A wing pylon outboard of each nacelle is able to carry two Mk 52, 55, 56 or 60 mines, six Mk 36, 62 or 82 destructor/bombs, six Mk 7 cluster dispensers, six ADM-141 decoys, six rocket pods, six flare dispensers or two AGM-84 Harpoons or AGM-84E SLAM. In refuelling role the D-704 pod is carried under the port wing, with a 300-US gal (1135-litre) fuel tank to starboard

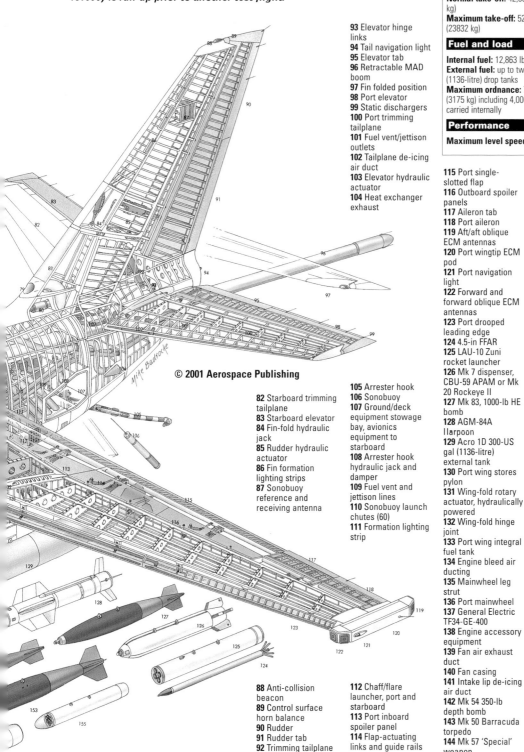

© 2001 Aerospace Publishing

Mike Badrocke

93 Elevator hinge links
94 Tail navigation light
95 Elevator tab
96 Retractable MAD boom
97 Fin folded position
98 Port elevator
99 Static dischargers
100 Port trimming tailplane
101 Fuel vent/jettison outlets
102 Tailplane de-icing air duct
103 Elevator hydraulic actuator
104 Heat exchanger exhaust

82 Starboard trimming tailplane
83 Starboard elevator
84 Fin-fold hydraulic jack
85 Rudder hydraulic actuator
86 Fin formation lighting strips
87 Sonobuoy reference and receiving antenna

105 Arrester hook
106 Sonobuoy
107 Ground/deck equipment stowage bay, avionics equipment to starboard
108 Arrester hook hydraulic jack and damper
109 Fuel vent and jettison lines
110 Sonobuoy launch chutes (60)
111 Formation lighting strip

88 Anti-collision beacon
89 Control surface horn balance
90 Rudder
91 Rudder tab
92 Trimming tailplane hydraulic actuator

112 Chaff/flare launcher, port and starboard
113 Port inboard spoiler panel
114 Flap-actuating links and guide rails

115 Port single-slotted flap
116 Outboard spoiler panels
117 Aileron tab
118 Port aileron
119 Aft/aft oblique ECM antennas
120 Port wingtip ECM pod
121 Port navigation light
122 Forward and forward oblique ECM antennas
123 Port drooped leading edge
124 4.5-in FFAR
125 LAU-10 Zuni rocket launcher
126 Mk 7 dispenser, CBU-59 APAM or Mk 20 Rockeye II
127 Mk 83, 1000-lb HE bomb
128 AGM-84A Harpoon
129 Aero 1D 300-US gal (1136-litre) external tank
130 Port wing stores pylon
131 Wing-fold rotary actuator, hydraulically powered
132 Wing-fold hinge joint
133 Port wing integral fuel tank
134 Engine bleed air ducting
135 Mainwheel leg strut
136 Port mainwheel
137 General Electric TF34-GE-400
138 Engine accessory equipment
139 Fan air exhaust duct
140 Fan casing
141 Intake lip de-icing air duct
142 Mk 54 350-lb depth bomb
143 Mk 50 Barracuda torpedo
144 Mk 57 'Special' weapon

145 Mk 46 torpedo
146 Mk 52 mine
147 Mk 55 moored mine
148 Mk 56 mine
149 Mk 60 Captor mine
150 Triple ejector rack (TER)
151 Mk 36 destructor mines
152 Mk 82 500-lb HE bomb
153 Mk 84 2000-lb HE bomb
154 LAU-69, 19-round 2.75-in rocket launcher
155 LAU-68, 7-round 2.75-in rocket launcher

*In 2002 the Viking is very much in the twilight of its career, relegated to anti-surface and land attack offensive taskings and an increasingly important tanking role. Some aircraft will be converted to a permanent IFR role, possible redesignated as KS-3Bs.*

# Lockheed SR-71 Blackbird

*Undoubtedly the most impressive military jet ever built, Lockheed's SR-71 is still officially the world's fastest air-breathing aircraft twelve years after its premature retirement from service in 1990. Tasked with performing highly classified reconnaissance missions, the aircraft's sensor systems collected material that helped to formulate US foreign policy for more than 20 years.*

## SR-71 Blackbird

**Cutaway key**
1 Pitot tube
2 Air data probe
3 Radar warning antennas
4 Nose mission equipment bay
5 Panoramic camera aperture
6 Detachable nosecone joint frame
7 Cockpit front pressure bulkhead
8 Rudder pedals
9 Control column
10 Instrument panel
11 Instrument panel shroud
12 Knife-edged windscreen panels
13 Upward-hinged cockpit canopy covers
14 Ejection seat headrest
15 Canopy actuator
16 Pilot's Lockheed F-1 'zero-zero' ejection seat
17 Engine throttle levers
18 Side console panel
19 Fuselage chine close-pitched frame construction
20 Liquid oxygen converters (2)
21 Side console panel
22 Reconnaissance Systems Officer's (RSO) instrument display
23 Cockpit rear pressure bulkhead
24 RSO's Lockheed F-1 'zero-zero' ejection seat
25 Canopy hinge point
26 SR-71B dual-control trainer variant, nose profile

27 Raised instructor's rear cockpit
28 Astro-inertial navigation star tracker
29 Navigation and communications systems electronic equipment
30 Nosewheel bay
31 Nose undercarriage pivot fixing
32 Landing and taxiing lamps
33 Twin nosewheels, forward-retracting

34 Hydraulic retraction jack
35 Cockpit environmental system equipment bay
36 Air refuelling receptacle, open
37 Fuselage upper longeron
38 Forward fuselage frame construction
39 Forward fuselage integral fuel tanks
40 Palletised, interchangeable reconnaissance equipment packs

41 Fuselage chine member
42 Forward/centre fuselage joint ring frame
43 Centre fuselage integral fuel tanks; total system capacity 12,219 US gal (46254 litres)
44 Beta B.120 titanium alloy skin panelling
45 Corrugated wing skin panelling

*The inability of surveillance satellites to provide the specific, targetted reconnaissance required by US military commanders saw the brief resurrection of the SR-71, although the type has now once more been retired by the USAF.*

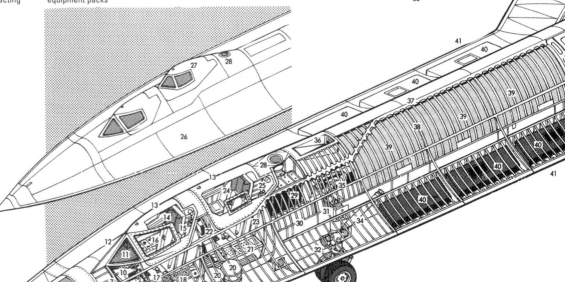

46 Starboard main undercarriage, stowed position
47 Intake centre-body bleed air louvres
48 Bypass duct suction relief louvres
49 Starboard engine air intake
50 Moveable intake conical centre-body
51 Centre-body retracted (high-speed position)
52 Boundary layer bleed air holes
53 Automatic intake control system air data probe
54 Diffuser chamber
55 Variable inlet guide vanes
56 Hinged engine cowling/outer wing panel

57 Pratt & Whitney JT11D-20B (J58) single-spool bleed-bypass engine
58 Engine accessory equipment
59 Bypass duct suction relief doors
60 Compressor bleed air bypass doors
61 Afterburner fuel manifold
62 Tailfin fixed root section
63 Starboard outer wing panel
64 Under-cambered leading edge
65 Outboard roll control elevon
66 All-moving starboard fin
67 Continuously-operating afterburner duct

68 Afterburner nozzle
69 Engine bay tertiary air flaps
70 Exhaust nozzle ejector flaps
71 Variable-area exhaust nozzle
72 Starboard wing integral fuel tank bays
73 Brake parachute doors, open
74 Ribbon parachute stowage
75 Aft fuselage integral fuel tanks
76 Skin doubler
77 Aft fuselage frame construction
78 Elevon mixer unit
79 Inboard elevon torque control unit
80 Tailcone
81 Fuel vent
82 Port all-moving fin
83 Fin rib construction

## SPECIFICATION

### SR-71A Blackbird

#### Dimensions

**Length overall:** 103 ft 10 in (31.65 m)
**Length overall (including probe):** 107 ft 5 in (32.74 m)
**Wing span:** 55 ft 7 in (16.94 m)
**Wing area:** 1,605 sq ft (149.10 m²)
**Moving vertical tail area:** 70.2 sq ft (6.52 m²)
**Height:** 18 ft 6 in (5.64 m)
**Wheel track:** 16 ft 8 in (5.08 m)
**Wheel base:** 37 ft 10 in (11.53 m)

#### Powerplant

Two Pratt & Whitney J58 afterburning bleed turbojets, each rated at 32,500 lb (144.57 kN) of thrust with afterburning

#### Weights

**Empty:** 67,500 lb (30617 kg)
**Maximum take-off:** 172,000 lb (78017 kg)

#### Fuel and load

**Total fuel capacity:** 12,219 US gal (46254 litres)
**Internal sensor payload (approximate):** 2,770 lb (1256 kg)

#### Performance

**Design maximum speed:** Mach 3.2 - 3.5 at 80,000 ft (24385 m) (limited by structural integrity of windscreen)
**Maximum speed:** Mach 3.35 at 80,000 ft (24385 m)
**Maximum cruising speed:** Mach 3.35 at 80,000 ft (24385 m)
**Maximum sustained cruising speed:** Mach 3.2 or approximately 2,100 mph (3380 km/h) at 80,000 ft (24385 m)
**Maximum altitude (approximate):** 100,000 ft (30480 m)
**Operational ceiling:** 85,000 ft (25908 m)
**Take-off run at 140,000-lb (63503-kg) gross weight:** 5,400 ft (1646 m)
**Landing run at maximum landing weight:** 3,600 ft (1097 m)

#### Range

**Maximum unrefuelled range at Mach 3.0:** 3,250 miles (5230 km)
**Operational radius (typical):** 1,200 miles (1931 km)
**Maximum unrefuelled endurance at Mach 3.0:** 1 hour 30 minutes

84 Torque shaft hinge mounting
85 Fin hydraulic actuator
86 Port engine exhaust nozzle
87 Ejector flaps
88 Port outboard elevon
89 Elevon titanium alloy rib construction
90 Under-cambered leading edge
91 Leading-edge diagonal rib construction
92 Outer wing panel titanium alloy construction
93 Outboard elevon hydraulic actuator
94 Engine bay tertiary air flaps

95 Engine nacelle/outer wing panel integral construction
96 Engine cowling/wing panel hinge axis
97 Port nacelle ring frame construction
98 Inboard wing panel integral fuel tank bays
99 Multi-spar titanium alloy wing construction
100 Main undercarriage wheel bay
101 Wheel bay heat shield
102 Hydraulic retraction jack
103 Main undercarriage pivot fixing
104 Mainwheel leg strut
105 Intake duct framing

106 Outer wing panel/nacelle chine
107 Three-wheel main undercarriage bogie, inward retracting
108 Port engine air intake
109 Moveable conical intake centre-body
110 Centre-body frame construction
111 Inboard leading-edge diagonal rib construction
112 Inner wing panel integral fuel tank
113 Wingroot/fuselage attachment root rib
114 Close-pitched fuselage titanium alloy frames

115 Wing/fuselage chine blended fairing panels

# Lockheed U-2

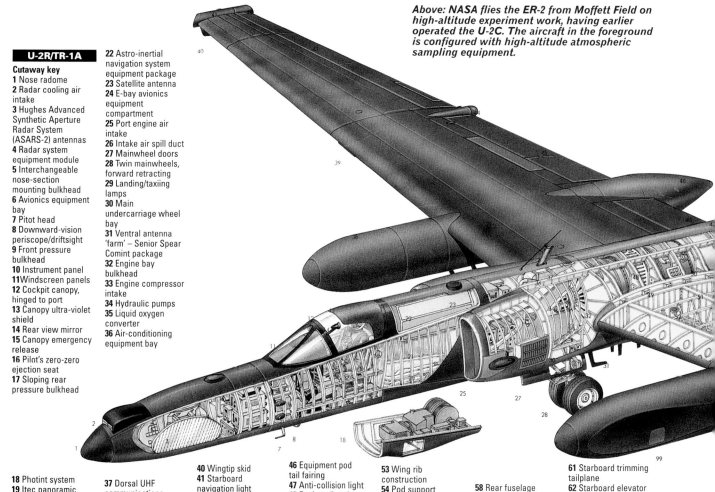

*Above: NASA flies the ER-2 from Moffett Field on high-altitude experiment work, having earlier operated the U-2C. The aircraft in the foreground is configured with high-altitude atmospheric sampling equipment.*

## U-2R/TR-1A

### Cutaway key
1 Nose radome
2 Radar cooling air intake
3 Hughes Advanced Synthetic Aperture Radar System (ASARS-2) antennas
4 Radar system equipment module
5 Interchangeable nose-section mounting bulkhead
6 Avionics equipment bay
7 Pitot head
8 Downward-vision periscope/driftsight
9 Front pressure bulkhead
10 Instrument panel
11 Windscreen panels
12 Cockpit canopy, hinged to port
13 Canopy ultra-violet shield
14 Rear view mirror
15 Canopy emergency release
16 Pilot's zero-zero ejection seat
17 Sloping rear pressure bulkhead

18 Photint system
19 Itec panoramic (horizon-to-horizon) optical bar camera
20 Equipment conditioning airducts
21 Q-bay mission equipment compartment

22 Astro-inertial navigation system equipment package
23 Satellite antenna
24 E-bay avionics equipment compartment
25 Port engine air intake
26 Intake air spill duct
27 Mainwheel doors
28 Twin mainwheels, forward retracting
29 Landing/taxiing lamps
30 Main undercarriage wheel bay
31 Ventral antenna 'farm' – Senior Spear Comint package
32 Engine bay bulkhead
33 Engine compressor intake
34 Hydraulic pumps
35 Liquid oxygen converter
36 Air-conditioning equipment bay

37 Dorsal UHF communications aerial
38 Starboard interchangeable mission equipment superpod
39 Leading-edge stall strip

40 Wingtip skid
41 Starboard navigation light
42 Wingtip threat warning receiver pod
43 Starboard aileron
44 IRCM dummy pod
45 Starboard plain flap, inboard and outboard segments

46 Equipment pod tail fairing
47 Anti-collision light
48 Engine oil tank
49 Wing panel attachment joints
50 Machined wing support mainframes
51 Port wing integral fuel tank
52 Fuel filler cap

53 Wing rib construction
54 Pod support machined ribs
55 Flap shroud ribs
56 Inboard plain flap segment
57 Pratt & Whitney J75-P-13B non-afterburning turbojet

58 Rear fuselage break point, engine removal
59 Extended fin root fillet fairing
60 Communications equipment compartment

61 Starboard trimming tailplane
62 Starboard elevator
63 Fin leading-edge HF-aerial
64 Tail navigation light
65 Fuel vent
66 ECM antenna
67 Rudder
68 Fixed rudder tab

*When the USAF retired its final Convair F-106 Delta Dart, the U-2R became the last type in the inventory powered by the Pratt & Whitney J75. Moreover, just as with the U-2A in the 1950s, the U-2R was becoming airframe-limited. Re-engining with the General Electric F118 (similar to the B-2's engine) was the answer, a test aircraft flying for the first time on 23 May 1989. Despite highly encouraging test results, it was not until 1994 that the first production U-2S took to the air. The F118 engine is mounted centrally in the airframe, exhausting through a long duct to the jet pipe. The engine produces much less thrust at its operating altitude, where the U-2 coasts along at a cruise speed not far from its stall speed.*

69 Rear threat warning radar receiver
70 Trimming tailplane incidence control jack
71 Elevator tab
72 Port elevator
73 Tailplane leading-edge skin stiffeners
74 Convergent-divergent thrust augmentor nozzle
75 Trimming tailplane pivot point
76 Heat-shrouded jet pipe
77 Ventral mission equipment bay
78 Datalink antenna
79 Tailwheel doors
80 Solid-tyre twin tailwheels
81 Port airbrake
82 Airbrake hydraulic jack
83 Port superpod tail fairing
84 Spoiler/lift dump panels
85 Outboard plain flap segment
86 Fuel jettison
87 Port aileron
88 Wingtip threat warning receiver pod
89 Port navigation light
90 Abradable wingtip skid
91 Manually-folding wingtip hinge joint
92 Port jettisonable outrigger wheel
93 Wing panel outboard integral fuel tank
94 Fuel filler cap

95 Leading-edge stall strip
96 Three-spar wing torsion box construction
97 Leading-edge integral fuel tank
98 Ventral 'canoe' antenna – electronic intelligence receiver
99 Outward-facing Elint antenna

## SPECIFICATION

### U-2R

**Dimensions**

**Length:** 62 ft 9 in (19.13 m)
**Height:** 16 ft (4.88 m)
**Wingspan:** 103 ft (31.39 m)
**Wing aspect ratio:** 10.6
**Wing area:** about 1,000 sq ft (92.90 m²)

**Powerplant**

One Pratt & Whitney J75-P-13B turbojet rated at 17,000 lb st (75.62 kN)

**Weights and loads**

**Basic empty weight without powerplant and equipment pods:** 10,000 lb (4536 kg)
**Operating empty:** about 15,500 lb (7031 kg)
**Maximum take-off:** 41,300 lb (18733 kg)

**Fuel load:** 7,649 lb (3469 kg)
**Sensor payload:** 3,000 lb (1361 kg)

**Performance**

**Never-exceed speed:** Mach 0.8
**Maximum cruising speed at 70,000 ft (21335 m):** more than 430 mph (692 km/h)
**Maximum rate of climb at sea level:** about 5,000 ft (1525 m) per minute
**Time to climb:** climb to 65,000 ft (19812 m) in 35 minutes
**Operational ceiling:** 80,000 ft (24385 m)
**Take-off run:** about 650 ft (198 m) at maximum take-off weight
**Landing run:** about 2,500 ft (762 m) at maximum landing weight

**Range**

**Maximum range:** about 6,250 miles (10060 km)
**Maximum endurance:** 12 hours

# North American RA-5C Vigilante

The large size of the Vigilante made it an unpopular aircraft with commanders and a dangerous one for inexperienced pilots. However, upon its conversion to a tactical reconnaissance platform, it proved peerless in its abilities and still today, 20 years after its retirement, a comparable successor has yet to be found.

## RA-5C Vigilante

**Cutaway key**
1 Pitot static boom
2 Hinged radome
3 Search radar antenna
4 Hinged radar and AN/ASB-12 forward package (servicing position)
5 TV optical scanner
6 Inflight-refuelling line
7 Inflight-refuelling probe (stowed)
8 AN/ASB-12 bomb directing set
9 Radome actuator
10 Radome (folded)
11 LOX converter
12 Instrument panel shroud
13 One-piece acrylic windscreen
14 Radar-flight projected display indicator
15 Control column
16 Rudder controls
17 TACAN antenna
18 ADF antenna
19 AN/APR-27 antenna
20 Viewfinder
21 Pilot's ejection seat
22 Underseat high-pressure emergency oxygen bottle
23 Cockpit air supply
24 Canopy emergency air bottle
25 Headrest
26 Pilot's canopy
27 Emergency escape system ballistic charges
28 Pilot's canopy actuator
29 Indicating power supply
30 Bombing computer
31 UHF antenna
32 Radar altimeter
33 AN/ALQ-100 antenna
34 Navigator's side console
35 Underseat high-pressure emergency oxygen bottle
36 Navigator's ejection seat
37 Canopy emergency air bottle
38 Navigator's window
39 Headrest
40 Navigator's canopy actuator
41 LOX storage converters (2)
42 Master flight reference gyro
43 Nosewheel well
44 Pre-closing nose-wheel doors
45 Nosewheel gear steering unit
46 Taxiing light
47 Forward-retracting nosewheel
48 Nosewheel centring unit
49 Nosewheel gear actuator
50 Flight control main electronics bay
51 Flight control relays
52 IFF antenna
53 Bulkhead
54 Forward fuselage fuel cell (455 US gal/ 1722 litres)
55 Inlet sidewall structure
56 Forward variable ramp
57 Nacelle inlet assembly
58 Port intake
59 Nacelle structure
60 Aft variable ramp
61 Ramp actuator
62 Intake duct
63 (Ventral) launch catapult hooks (2)
64 Main wing/fuselage frame forging
65 Wing forward attachment pick-up point
66 BLC ducting
67 Fuselage sump fuel cell (490 US gal/ 1855 litres)
68 Starboard wingroot fillet
69 Starboard auxiliary drop-tanks (400 US gal/ 1514 litres each)
70 AN/ALQ-41 and -100 forward transmit antennas
71 AN/APR-25 and AN/ALQ-41 and -100 forward receive antennas
72 Leading-edge wing-droop (inner section)
73 Droop actuator and torque rod
74 Conduit to wing fold (hydraulic and electrical)
75 Wing structure
76 Starboard wing integral fuel (715 US gal/2707 litres)
77 Span-wise corrugated stiffeners
78 Wing-fold line
79 Leading-edge wing-droop (outer section)
80 Starboard navigation lights
81 Starboard formation light
82 Wing outer section (folded)
83 Outboard spoiler deflector (downward airflow)
84 AN/ALQ-4 and-100 aft receiver antennas
85 Central (closed) and inboard spoiler deflectors (upward airflow)
86 Starboard flaps
87 BLC flap-blowing duct
88 Wing aft attachment pick-up point
89 Dorsal fairing
90 Overwing saddle tank (210 US gal/ 795 litres)
91 Wing centreline splice assembly
92 Starboard intake ducting
93 Bomb-bay forward fuel cell
94 Hydraulic reservoir air storage tank
95 Port intake ducting
96 Port mainwheel well
97 Retraction jack
98 Universal pivot
99 Mainwheel leg down-lock
100 Wing aft attachment pick-up point
101 Steel mainframe and firewall (canted)
102 General Electric J79-GE-10 turbojet
103 BLC cross-over ducting
104 Bomb-bay central fuel cell
105 No. 1 hydraulic system reservoir
106 No. 2 hydraulic system reservoir
107 Aft fuselage saddle tank (130 US gal/ 492 litres)
108 Anti-collision beacon
109 Starboard engine oil tank (6.10 US gal/ 23 litres)
110 Fuselage aft structure
111 Horizontal stabiliser
112 Horizontal stabiliser attachment frame
113 Horizontal stabiliser actuator
114 Vertical stabiliser actuator
115 Bomb-bay aft fuel cell (total internal capacity: 885 US gal/ 3350 litres)
116 Fuselage aft frame
117 Vertical stabiliser pivot
118 Vertical stabiliser lower section structure
119 Conduits (front to rear: electrical, hydraulic, tail-fold cable)
120 Leading-edge dielectric panel
121 Tail-fold hinge line
122 Tail-fold actuator
123 Vertical stabiliser upper-section structure
124 Front spar
125 Duplex UHF comm/ALQ-55 antenna
126 Electrical conduit
127 Vertical stabiliser (folded)
128 Rear formation light
129 DECM antenna, AN/APR-18, AN/APR-25(v) or AN/ALR-45(v)
130 Buddy tanker lights
131 Fuel vent
132 AN/APR-18 antenna, if fitted
133 Fuel vent line
134 Electrical conduits
135 Honeycomb structure

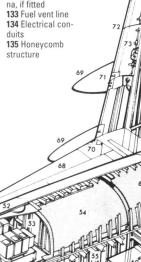

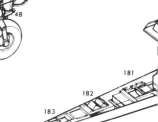

### RA-5C Vigilante

**Dimensions**

**Length:** 76 ft 6 in (23.35 m)
**Length (with vertical fin and radome folded):** 65 ft 4⅞ in (19.92 m)
**Wingspan:** 53 ft (16.17 m)
**Wingspan (folded):** 42 ft (12.8 m)
**Wing area:** 753.7 sq ft (70.02 m²)
**Height:** 19 ft 4¾ in (5.91 m)
**Height (with vertical tail folded):** 15 ft 6 in (4.72 m)

**Powerplant**

Two General Electric J79-GE-10 turbo-jets each rated at 17,900 lb (79.63 kN) thrust with maximum afterburner

**Weights**

**Empty:** 37,498 lb (17024 kg)
**Basic:** 38,219 lb (17336 kg)
**Combat:** 55,617 lb (25227 kg)
**Maximum landing (field):** 65,988 lb (29931 kg)
**Maximum landing (arrested):** 47,000 lb (21319 kg)

**Performance**

**Maximum speed at sea level:** 806 mph (1297 km/h)
**Maximum speed at 40,000 ft (12192 m):** 1,320 mph (2124 km/h)
**Initial climb rate:** 6,600 ft (2012 m) per minute at sea level
**Service ceiling:** 49,000 ft (14935 m)
**Combat radius (attack):** 1,284 miles (2066 km)
**Combat radius:** 1,508 miles (2427 km)
**Ferry range:** 2,050 miles (3299 km)

**Armament**

None normally carried, though two pylons could be fitted under each wing and a full weapons delivery capability was retained

*It was not unknown for Vigilantes to lose their linear bay fuel tanks during a 'cat shot', all three fuel cells landing unceremoniously on the flight deck. An explosion and fire on the deck would usually result although, more often than not, damage to the ship was minor and experienced pilots were able to continue their take-offs normally, as in this example, where Cdr John H. Huber of RVAH-12 lost his fuel cells, and the 885 US gal (3350 litres) of fuel they contained, aboard USS Independence on 4 September 1969. Others were not so lucky, including the crew of BuNo. 156609 from the same unit which, during spring 1973, lost one fuel tank and caught fire during a 'cat shot'. The crew ejected as the aircraft rolled out of control; both survived.*

**136** Tailcone
**137** DECM boom antenna, AN/ALQ-100
**138** As item 137, AN/ALQ-41
**139** Exhaust nozzle fairing
**140** Variable-area convergent-divergent expansion nozzle
**141** Honeycomb structure
**142** Horizontal sta-biliser structure

**147** Exhaust nozzle cable pulley feedback system
**148** Arresting hook
**149** Launch catapult holdback yoke
**150** Central and inboard spoiler deflectors
**151** Wing spoiler actuators
**152** Port flaps

**158** Port formation light
**159** Port navigation lights
**160** Outer section leading-edge droop
**161** Droop actuator and torque rod
**162** Wing-fold actua-tor

**180** Interchangeable camera module (two side oblique serial frame cameras, two panoramic cameras. or two vertical serial frame cameras)
**181** PECM antennas, AN/ALQ-61
**182** Vertical serial frame camera (KA-50 or -51)
**183** Forward oblique serial frame camera (KA-51A)

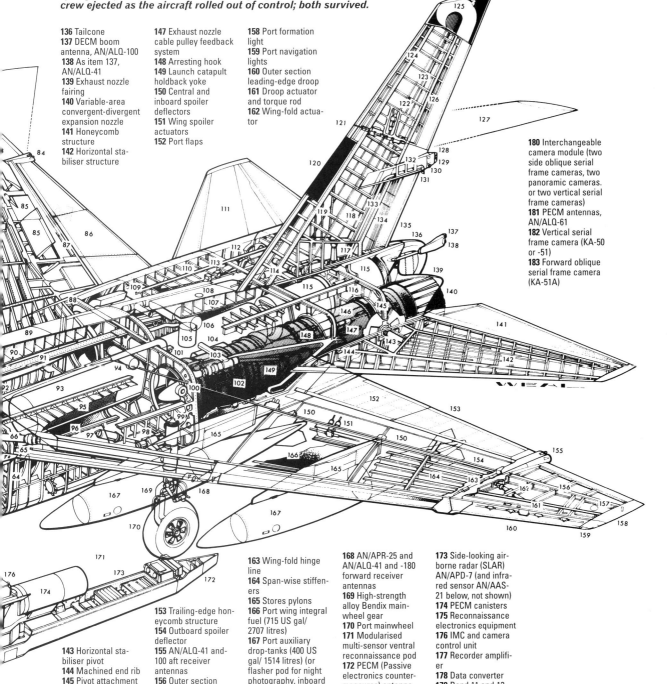

**143** Horizontal sta-biliser pivot
**144** Machined end rib
**145** Pivot attachment frame
**146** Afterburner

**153** Trailing-edge hon-eycomb structure
**154** Outboard spoiler deflector
**155** AN/ALQ-41 and -100 aft receiver antennas
**156** Outer section wing structure
**157** Compass

**163** Wing-fold hinge line
**164** Span-wise stiffen-ers
**165** Stores pylons
**166** Port wing integral fuel (715 US gal/ 2707 litres)
**167** Port auxiliary drop-tanks (400 US gal/ 1514 litres) (or flasher pod for night photography, inboard pylons only)

**168** AN/APR-25 and AN/ALQ-41 and -180 forward receiver antennas
**169** High-strength alloy Bendix main-wheel gear
**170** Port mainwheel
**171** Modularised multi-sensor ventral reconnaissance pod
**172** PECM (Passive electronics counter-measures) antenna

**173** Side-looking air-borne radar (SLAR) AN/APD-7 (and infra-red sensor AN/AAS-21 below, not shown)
**174** PECM canisters
**175** Reconnaissance electronics equipment
**176** IMC and camera control unit
**177** Recorder amplifi-er
**178** Data converter
**179** Band 11 and 12 receivers

# Trainers

# Aermacchi MB326/MB339

Although not as glamorous as the front-line fast jets to which their pilots graduate, Aermacchi's MB-326 and MB-339 have proved to be highly capable in both the training and attack roles. This photograph shows an MB-339CB of the Royal New Zealand Air Force. RNZAF aircraft are equipped to deliver AGM-65 Maverick air-to-ground missiles and AIM-9 Sidewinder IR-homing air-to-air missiles. In addition to gem pods, un-guided weapons include the Matra 155 rocket pod (illustrated), containing 18 Brandt 68mm spin-stabilised SNEB rocket projectiles. These may be fitted with different types of warhead according to the type of target to be attacked.

## MB-339A

**Cutaway key**

1 Starboard fixed wingtip tank (69.5-Imp gal/316-litre capacity)
2 Fuel filler point
3 Starboard servo-powered aileron
4 Aileron balance tab
5 Aileron balance weights
6 Wingtip tank fuel line
7 Starboard outer pylon (507-lb/230-kg capacity)
8 Missile launcher rail
9 Matra R550 Magic IR-guided air-to-air missile
10 Starboard centre pylon (750-lb/340-kg capacity)
11 Jettisonable auxiliary fuel tank (71-Imp gal/ 325-litre capacity)
12 Starboard wing fence
13 Aileron hinge mechanism
14 Aileron servo
15 Starboard single-slotted flap
16 Flap control linkage
17 Pod attachment spigot
18 Macchi 0.5-in (12.7-mm) AN/M-3 machine-gun pod
19 Ammunition feed chute
20 Ammunition box (350 rounds)
21 Cartridge case ejection chute
22 Starboard-hinged canopy
23 Rear Martin-Baker Mk 1T-10F zero-zero ejection seat
24 Headrest parachute container
25 Seat safety harness
26 Rear Aeritalia fixed reflector sight
27 Rear instrument panel shroud

28 Front Martin-Baker Mk 1T-10F zero-zero ejection seat
29 Headrest parachute container
30 Starboard instrument console
31 Front Aeritalia fixed reflector sight (Aeritalia Saab RGS2 computer gyroscopic sight or Thomson/CSF RD 21 simple gyroscopic sight optional)
32 Fully automatic OMERA-SEGID 110-3 gun camera
33 Front instrument panel shroud
34 Curved one-piece windshield
35 Pitot tubes
36 Antenna
37 Nosewheel retraction jack
38 Nosewheel well
39 Nosewheel bay front bulkhead
40 Nose cone
41 Landing/taxi light
42 Nosewheel shock absorber
43 Chined steerable nosewheel
44 Nose wheel doors
45 Front radio and electronics bay
46 Cockpit forward bulkhead
47 Rudder pedals
48 Control column
49 Underfloor control linkage
50 Throttle
51 C-section forward fuselage frames
52 Niche-type step
53 Ventral antenna
54 Control runs
55 Rear flight controls
56 Canopy emergency release handle
57 Access panel
58 Rear cockpit niche-type steps
59 Rear throttle
60 Port instrument side console
61 Ventral air brake
62 Air brake jack

63 Port engine air intake
64 Aft-sloping rear cockpit bulkhead
65 Intake trunk cut-out
66 Fuselage/main spar attachment
67 Main spar carry-through
68 Forward fuselage frame-and-stringer construction
69 Fuselage double frame
70 Top longeron
71 Rear radio and electronics bay

72 Antenna
73 Access panel
74 Engine air intake trunking
75 Cooling air louvres
76 Fuel filler
77 Fuel system piping
78 Batteries (2 x 24V)
79 Access panel
80 Engine intake
81 Hydraulic system reservoirs

82 Side access panel
83 Engine electrical accessories
84 Piaggio-built Rolls-Royce Viper 632-43 engine
85 Engine bay air louvres
86 Dorsal navigation light
87 Dorsal spine construction

88 Engine mounting frame
89 Fuselage break point
90 Firewall
91 Fuel jettison pipe
92 Jet pipe flush cooling air intakes
93 Jet pipe
94 Fuselage/fin spar attachment
95 Elevator linkage
96 Fin construction
97 Starboard tailplane
98 Starboard elevator
99 Fin leading edge
100 Dielectric fin tip
101 Anti-collision light

102 UHF antenna
103 Fin VOR antenna
104 Rudder balance
105 Rudder construction
106 Fixed tab
107 Trim tab jack
108 Rudder trim tab
109 Rudder control linkage
110 Tailplane centre section
111 Elevator hinge control
112 Tailcone
113 Jet pipe nozzle shroud
114 Tail navigation light
115 Elevator trim tab
116 Port elevator
117 Balance weight

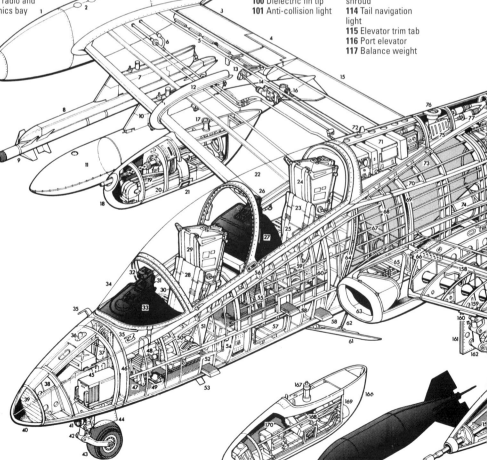

*Left: For many years the MB-326 was the backbone of the AMI's jet training force. For this role, the aircraft wore a highly conspicuous orange colour scheme. The docile handling characteristics of the machine soon came to be appreciated by novice jet pilots, resulting in an accident rate of only 0.8 per 10,000 flying hours. Today, the type has given way to the MB-339, but a few examples still soldier on in the communications role and as squadron 'hacks'.*

## SPECIFICATION

### MB-339A

**Dimensions**

**Length:** 36 ft (10.97 m)
**Height:** 13 ft 1¼ in (3.99 m)
**Wingspan:** 35 ft 7½ in (10.86 m) over tip tanks
**Wing area:** 207.74 sq ft (19.30 m²)
**Wing aspect ratio:** 6.1
**Wheel track:** 8 ft 1¾ in (2.48 m)
**Wheel base:** 14 ft 4 in (4.37 m)

**Powerplant**

One Piaggio-built Rolls-Royce (Bristol Siddeley) Viper Mk 632-43 rated at 4,000 lb st (17.79 kN) dry

**Weights**

**Empty equipped:** 6,889 lb (3125 kg)
**Operating empty:** 6,913 lb (3136 kg)
**Normal take-off:** 9,700 lb (4400 kg)
**Maximum take-off:** 12,996 lb (5895 kg)

**Fuel and load**

**Internal fuel:** 2,425 lb (1100 kg)
**External fuel:** up to two 71-Imp gal (325-litre) drop tanks
**Maximum ordnance:** 4,497 lb (2040 kg)

**Performance**

**Never-exceed speed:** 575 mph (926 km/h)
**Maximum level speed 'clean' at 30,000 ft (9145 m):** 508 mph (817 km/h)
**Maximum speed at sea level:** 558 mph (898 km/h)

**Stalling speed:** 93 mph (149 km/h)
**Maximum rate of climb at sea level:** 6,595 ft (2010 m) per minute
**Climb to 30,000 ft (9145 m):** in 7 minutes 6 seconds
**Service ceiling:** 48,000 ft (14630 m)

**Range/Armamente 1**

**Ferry range:** 1,311 miles (2110 km) with drop tanks; range 1,094 miles (1760 km); combat radius 369 miles (593 km) on a hi-lo-hi attack mission with four Mk 82 bombs and two drop tanks, or 244 miles (393 km) on a hi-lo-hi attack mission with six Mk 82 bombs, or 317 miles (510 km) on a hi-lo-hi attack mission with two 30-mm cannon pods, two rocket launchers and two drop tanks, or 351 miles (565 km) on a hi-lo-hi attack mission with four rocket launchers and two drop tanks, or 190 miles (306 km) on a hi-lo-hi attack mission with six rocket launchers, or 230 miles (371 km) on a lo-lo-lo attack mission with four Mk 82 bombs and two drop tanks, or 168 miles (271 km) on lo-lo-lo attack mission with six Mk 82 bombs, or 219 miles (352 km) on a lo-lo-lo attack mission with two 30-mm cannon pods, two rocket launchers and two drop tanks, or 222 miles (358 km) on a lo-lo-lo attack mission with four rocket launchers and two drop tanks, or 142 miles (228 km) on a lo-lo-lo attack mission with six rocket launchers; endurance 3 hours 45 minutes with drop tanks or 2 hours 50 minutes on internal fuel

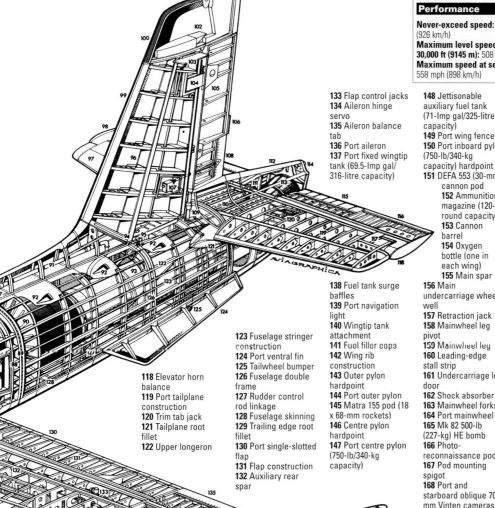

**133** Flap control jacks
**134** Aileron hinge servo
**135** Aileron balance tab
**136** Port aileron
**137** Port fixed wingtip tank (69.5-Imp gal/316-litre capacity)

**118** Elevator horn balance
**119** Port tailplane construction
**120** Trim tab jack
**121** Tailplane root fillet
**122** Upper longeron
**123** Fuselage stringer construction
**124** Port ventral fin
**125** Tailwheel bumper
**126** Fuselage double frame
**127** Rudder control rod linkage
**128** Fuselage skinning
**129** Trailing edge root fillet
**130** Port single-slotted flap
**131** Flap construction
**132** Auxiliary rear spar

**138** Fuel tank surge baffles
**139** Port navigation light
**140** Wingtip tank attachment
**141** Fuel filler caps
**142** Wing rib construction
**143** Outer pylon hardpoint
**144** Port outer pylon
**145** Matra 155 pod (18 x 68-mm rockets)
**146** Centre pylon hardpoint
**147** Port centre pylon (750-lb/340-kg capacity)

**148** Jettisonable auxiliary fuel tank (71-Imp gal/325-litre capacity)
**149** Port wing fence
**150** Port inboard pylon (750-lb/340-kg capacity) hardpoint
**151** DEFA 553 (30-mm) cannon pod
**152** Ammunition magazine (120-round capacity)
**153** Cannon barrel
**154** Oxygen bottle (one in each wing)
**155** Main spar
**156** Main undercarriage wheel well
**157** Retraction jack
**158** Mainwheel leg pivot
**159** Mainwheel leg
**160** Leading-edge stall strip
**161** Undercarriage leg door
**162** Shock absorber
**163** Mainwheel forks
**164** Port mainwheel
**165** Mk 82 500-lb (227-kg) HE bomb
**166** Photo-reconnaissance pod
**167** Pod mounting spigot
**168** Port and starboard oblique 70-mm Vinten cameras
**169** Heater and blower unit
**170** Vertical 70-mm Vinten camera
**171** Forward 70-mm Vinten camera

# Aero L-39 Albatros

The L-39 has scored heavily in the 'real' export market (as opposed to Warsaw Pact nations), notably in the Middle East, from where Egypt, Iraq, Libya and Syria placed large orders for 'first-generation' aircraft. Egypt followed up by buying the L-59E, this example being illustrated in the four-tank ferry fit used to deliver the jets.

## L-139 Albatros

**Cutaway key**
1 Glass-fibre nosecone
2 ILS antenna
3 Ground intercom socket
4 Navigational antenna
5 Nosewheel door, closed after cycling of undercarriage
6 Avionics equipment compartment
7 Nosewheel housing
8 Pitot head
9 Hinged access doors, port and starboard
10 On-Board Oxygen Generator System (OBOGS)
11 Front pressure bulkhead
12 Nosewheel pivot mounting
13 Nosewheel leg strut
14 Levered suspension shock absorber
15 Forward-retracting nose wheel
16 Shimmy damper
17 Ventral cannon pack
18 Rudder pedals
19 Incidence transmitter
20 Control column, fully duplicated controls
21 Instrument console
22 Undercarriage position visual indicator
23 Hot air de-iced one-piece windscreen
24 Front cockpit instrument panel with Electronic Flight Information System (EFIS) displays
25 Rear cockpit instrument panel with EFIS displays
26 Pilot's head-up display (HUD)
27 Stand-by horizon
28 Rear cockpit monitor screen
29 Stand-by compass
30 Individual cockpit canopies, hinged to starboard
31 Student pilot's VS-2R rocket-assisted ejection seat
32 Seat harness
33 Engine throttle lever
34 Side console panel
35 Front cockpit floor level
36 Boarding steps
37 Underfloor equipment bays
38 Rear cockpit floor level
39 Canopy external release
40 Canopy lifting handle
41 Rear instrument console
42 Canopy centre arch
43 Instructor's VS-2R ejection seat
44 Rear side console panel
45 Kick-in steps
46 Rear pressure bulkhead
47 Fuselage centre bag-type fuel tanks, total internal capacity (excluding tip tanks) 232 Imp gal (1055 litres)
48 Boundary layer splitter plate
49 Port air intake
50 Fuselage tank gravity filler
51 Tailplane control rods
52 Starboard air intake
53 Flap actuating linkage
54 Starboard outer wing pylon
55 Starboard wing panel
56 Pitot head
57 Landing/taxiing light
58 Starboard navigation light
59 22-Imp gal (100-litre) fixed wingtip fuel tank
60 Starboard aileron
61 Servo tab
62 Aileron operating linkage
63 Flap track fairing
64 Starboard double-slotted flap
65 Anti-collision

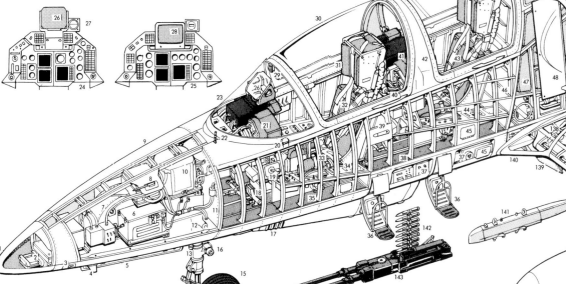

*Flying from Korat with No. 1 Wing, Thailand's two L-39ZA/ART squadrons provide fighter lead-in training and a light attack capability. The black/yellow chequerboard markings on the tail denotes No. 101 Squadron.*

## SPECIFICATION

### L-39ZO Albatros

**Dimensions**

**Length:** 39 ft 9½ in (12.13 m)
**Height:** 15 ft 7¾ in (4.77 m)
**Wingspan:** 31 ft ½ in (9.46 m)
**Aspect ratio:** 4.4 or 5.2 including tip tanks
**Wing area:** 202.37 sq ft (18.80 m²)
**Tailplane span:** 14 ft 5 in (4.40 m)
**Wheel track:** 8 ft (2.44 m)
**Wheel base:** 14 ft 4¾ in (4.39 m)

**Powerplant**

One ZMDB Progress (Ivchenko) AI-25TL turbofan engine rated at 3,792 lb (16.87 kN) dry

**Weights**

**Empty equipped:** 7,804 lb (3540 kg)
**Normal take-off:** 9,976 lb (4525 kg)
**Maximum take-off:** 10,362 lb (4700 kg)

**Fuel and load**

**Internal fuel:** 1,816 lb (824 kg) plus provision for 344 lb (156 kg) in two 48-US gal (180-litre) non-jettisonable tip tanks
**External fuel:** up to 1,199 lb (544 kg) in two 110-US gal (420-litre) drop tanks
**Maximum ordnance:** 2,200 lb (1000 kg)

**Performance**

**Never-exceed speed at 36,090 ft (11000 m):** 459 kt (528 mph; 850 km/h)

**Maximum level speed 'clean' at 16,405 ft (5000 m):** 407 kt (466 mph; 755 km/h)
**Maximum speed at sea level:** 388 kt (447 mph; 720 km/h)
**Ferry range:** 944 nm (1,087 miles; 1750 km) with drop tanks
**Standard range:** 593 nm (683 miles; 1100 km) with internal fuel
**Endurance at 22,975 m (7000 m):** 3 hours 50 minutes with drop tanks or 2 hours 30 minutes with internal fuel
**Maximum rate of climb at sea level:** 4,134 ft (1260 m) per minute
**Climb to 16,405 ft (5000 m):** 5 minutes
**Service ceiling:** 36,090 ft (11000 m)
**Take-off run:** 1,740 ft (530 m) at normal take-off weight
**Landing run:** 2,135 ft (650 m) at normal landing weight
**g limits:** -4 to +8 at operational weights or up to +12 at 9,259 lb (4200 kg)

**Armament**

Four underwing hardpoints, inboard pair each stressed for loads of up to 1,102 lb (500 kg) and the outer pair for loads of up to 551 lb (250 kg) each. Typical underwing stores can include various combinations of bombs (two 1,102-lb/500-kg, four 551-lb/250-kg or six 220-lb/100-kg) or four UB-16-57 M pods containing 16 S-5 2½ (57-mm) air-to-surface rockets or infra-red air-to-air missiles (outer pylons only) or a five-camera day reconnaissance pod (port inboard pylon only)

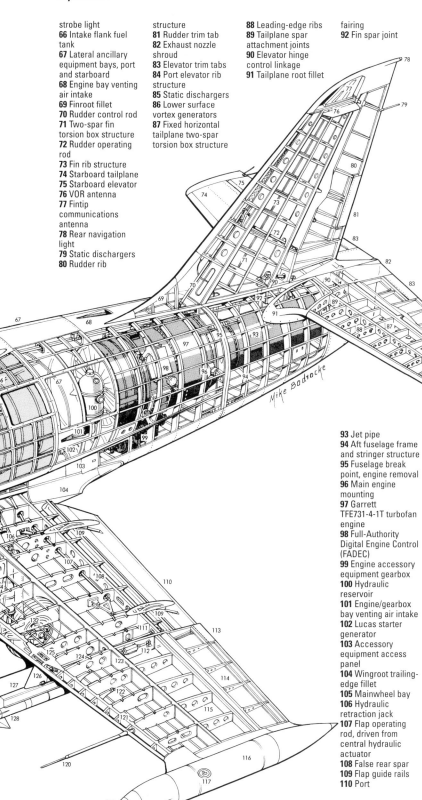

65 strobe light
66 Intake flank fuel tank
67 Lateral ancillary equipment bays, port and starboard
68 Engine bay venting air intake
69 Finroot fillet
70 Rudder control rod
71 Two-spar fin torsion box structure
72 Rudder operating rod
73 Fin rib structure
74 Starboard tailplane
75 Starboard elevator
76 VOR antenna
77 Fintip communications antenna
78 Rear navigation light
79 Static dischargers
80 Rudder rib

structure
81 Rudder trim tab
82 Exhaust nozzle shroud
83 Elevator trim tabs
84 Port elevator rib structure
85 Static dischargers
86 Lower surface vortex generators
87 Fixed horizontal tailplane two-spar torsion box structure

88 Leading-edge ribs
89 Tailplane spar attachment joints
90 Elevator hinge control linkage
91 Tailplane root fillet

fairing
92 Fin spar joint

double-slotted flap
111 Aileron operating link
112 Tab actuator
113 Port servo/trim tab
114 Port aileron rib structure
115 Trailing-edge ribs
116 Port wingtip fixed fuel tank

93 Jet pipe
94 Aft fuselage frame and stringer structure
95 Fuselage break point, engine removal
96 Main engine mounting
97 Garrett TFE731-4-1T turbofan engine
98 Full-Authority Digital Engine Control (FADEC)
99 Engine accessory equipment gearbox
100 Hydraulic reservoir
101 Engine/gearbox bay venting air intake
102 Lucas starter generator
103 Accessory equipment access panel
104 Wingroot trailing-edge fillet
105 Mainwheel bay
106 Hydraulic retraction jack
107 Flap operating rod, driven from central hydraulic actuator
108 False rear spar
109 Flap guide rails
110 Port

117 Tip tank filler cap
118 Port navigation fight
119 Landing/taxiing light
120 Pitot head
121 Front spar
122 Lower wing skin/stringer panel
123 Main spar
124 Wing panel rib structure
125 Pylon mounting hardpoint
126 Outboard stores pylon
127 Missile launch rail
128 R-35 (AA-2 Atoll) air-to-air missile
129 77-Imp gal (350-litre) external fuel tank
130 Inboard stores pylon
131 Inboard pylon hardpoint
132 Port mainwheel
133 Levered suspension shock absorber
134 Mainwheel leg strut
135 Undercarriage leg pintle mounting
136 Main spar attachment joint

137 Fuselage lower main longeron
138 Airbrake hydraulic jack
139 Ventral airbrake panels (2)
140 Extended chord wingroot fairing
141 Light stores dispenser
142 Ammunition feed, 150 rounds housed beneath rear cockpit floor
143 GSh-23 twin-barrel 23-mm cannon
144 250-lb (113-kg) HE bomb
145 UV-16-57, 16-round rocket launcher
146 57-mm (2½-in) rocket

Mike Badrocke

# British Aerospace Hawk

*Originally intending to buy licence-built Aermacchi MB.326s, the Indonesian air force abandoned its plans in favour of becoming the third Hawk export customer in 1978 with an initial order for eight T.Mk 53s. Another 12 examples were subsequently ordered and the aircraft are used for both advanced training (in a red and white scheme) and for tactical weapons training, as is the case with this example, in two-tone camouflage.*

## Hawk 60 series

**Cutaway key**

1 Starboard all-moving tailplane
2 Tailplane multi-spar construction
3 Engine exhaust nozzle
4 Tail navigation light
5 Optional brake parachute housing
6 Tailplane pivot fixing
7 Tailplane sealing plate
8 Hydraulic tailplane actuator
9 Port all-moving tailplane
10 Rudder trim tab
11 Trim tab rotary actuator
12 Rudder hinge control
13 Mass balance weights
14 Rudder honeycomb construction
15 Rudder
16 Fintip aerial fairing
17 VHF aerial
18 Fin leading edge
19 Tailfin construction
20 Rudder control rod linkage
21 Fin spar attachment joints
22 Aft fuselage frame construction
23 Heat-shrouded exhaust pipe
24 Tail bumper
25 Lower IFF aerial
26 Ventral fin, port and starboard
27 Airbrake hydraulic jack
28 Ventral airbrake, lowered
29 Engine bay access panel
30 Fireproof bulkhead
31 Hydraulic reservoir, port and starboard
32 Finroot fillet
33 Ram air turbine actuator
34 Emergency ram air turbine, extended
35 Ram air turbine doors

36 Equipment bay decking
37 Engine combustion and turbine section
38 Rolls-Royce/ Turboméca Adour 861 turbofan engine
39 Engine oil tank
40 Wing trailing-edge root fillet
41 Engine accessory equipment gearbox
42 Engine bay framing
43 Bleed air ducting
44 Gas turbine starter
45 Starter exhaust
46 Starter turbine intake grille, port and starboard
47 Wing rear spar attachment frame
48 Engine compressor face
49 Rear spar attachment joint
50 Trailing-edge hinged access panels
51 Flap rib construction
52 Starboard double-slotted flap

53 Flap operating link
54 Rear spar
55 Reduced span flap vane
56 Aileron hydraulic actuator
57 Aileron honeycomb construction

58 Starboard aileron
59 Localiser aerial
60 Brandt 100-4 rocket launcher, 3.9-in (100-mm) rockets (four)

61 Starboard navigation light
62 Outer wing panel dry bay
63 Matra 155 18-tube rocket-launcher

64 2.75-in (70-mm) HVAR folding-fin rockets
65 Outboard stores pylon
66 Wing tank end rib
67 Wing fence
68 Stall strip
69 Leading-edge rib construction
70 Auxiliary wing fences
71 Inboard stores pylon
72 Two 550-lb (250-kg) low-drag bombs

73 Twin stores carrier
74 250-lb (113-kg) low-drag bomb
75 Starboard mainwheel
76 Mainwheel leg doors
77 Levered suspension axle beam
78 Mainwheel shock absorber leg strut
79 Auxiliary front spar
80 Main spar
81 Wingrib construction
82 Machined wing skin/ stringer panel
83 Starboard wing integral fuel tank; total internal fuel capacity 375 Imp gal (1705 litres)

84 Main undercarriage leg pivot fixing
85 Hydraulic retraction jack
86 Main spar attachment joint
87 Fuel system access panels
88 Fuselage bag-type tank
89 Bleed air control valve
90 Rudder control rod (elevator control on port side)

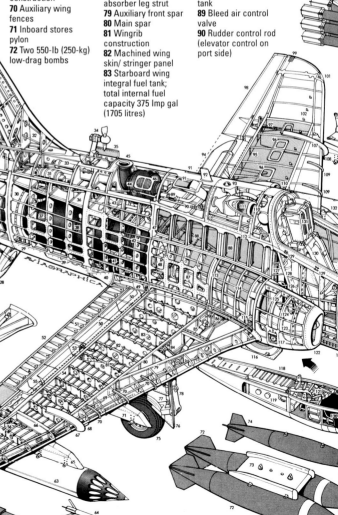

## SPECIFICATION

### Hawk T.Mk 1A

#### Dimensions

**Wingspan:** 30 ft 10 in (9.39 m)
**Overall length:** 38 ft 11 in (11.85 m)
**Height:** 13 ft 1 in (4.00 m)
**Wing area:** 180 sq ft (16.90 m²)
**Wheel track:** 11 ft 5 in (3.47 m)
**Wheel base:** 14 ft 9 in (4.50 m)

#### Powerplant

One Rolls-Royce/Turboméca Adour Mk 151-01 turbofan rated at 5,200 lb st (23.13 kN), also quoted as 5,340 lb st (23.67 kN)

#### Weights

**Empty equipped:** 8,013 lb (3635 kg)
**Maximum take-off:** 18,390 lb (8340 kg)
**Maximum landing:** 17,000 lb (7650 kg)

#### Performance

**Maximum level speed:** 560 kt (646 mph; 1040 km/h), Mach 0.88 at sea level
**Maximum speed (shallow dive):** 572 kt (658 mph; 1060 km/h), Mach 1.2 at 3,000 ft (914 m)
**Demonstrated Mach No.:** 1.2 IMN
**Service ceiling:** 50,000 ft (15240 m)
**Maximum rate of climb:** 9,300 ft (2835 m) per minute
**Time to 30,000 ft (9144 m):** 6 minutes
**Take-off run:** 1,600 ft (488 m)
**Maximum endurance:** 5 hours 30 minutes

**Ferry range:** 1,300 nm (1,491 miles; 2400 km) with internal fuel; 1,700 nm (1,957 miles; 3150 km) with external fuel
**Combat radius:** 500 nm (578 miles; 930 km) hi-lo-hi with gun, four 1,000-lb (454-kg) bombs and two fuel tanks
**g limit:** -4 to +7.5 g (service limit, cleared to 9 g); sustained turn 4.7 g at 1,600 ft (487 m)

#### Fuel and load

**Internal fuel:** 2,970 lb (1347 kg), 375 Imp gal (1705 litres)
**Maximum external fuel:** two 190-Imp gal (864-litre) fuel tanks
**Maximum external load:** tested up to 6,500 lb (2948 kg), weaponload up to 6,800 lb (3100 kg) on export versions

#### Armament

All Hawks can be fitted with a centre-line gun pod, containing a single 30-mm ADEN Mk 4 cannon and 120 rounds of ammunition. Two underwing pylons are fitted as standard, but most Hawk series can be fitted with four underwing pylons. RAF Hawk T.Mk 1As have provision for underwing AIM-9L Sidewinder missiles. In service, they are usually limited to external loads of 1,500 lb (680 kg), carrying carrier, bomb. light store (CBLS) practice bomb carriers or SNEB rocket pods. The Hawk 60 and Hawk 100 can carry up to 6,614 lb (3000 kg), including a wide range of weapons plus wingtip AAM launch rails

*After rigorous evaluation in competition with the Aero L-39 Albatross, Aermacchi MB.339, Dassault/Dornier Alpha Jet and the Saab 105A, the Hawk gained its first export order, from the Finnish air force. Used for advanced training, Finnish Hawks originally wore this attractive three-tone camouflage, which has now been replaced by a flat grey scheme. The success of the aircraft in service led to follow-up orders and, to date, Finland has received 57 Hawk Mk 51/51As.*

**91** Heat exchanger exhaust ducts
**92** Upper UHF aerial
**93** Anti-collision light
**94** Port double-slotted flap, down position
**95** Port wing integral fuel tank
**96** Fuel tank access panels
**97** Aileron hydraulic actuator
**98** Port aileron
**99** Localiser aerial
**100** Thomson Brandt BAT 120 runway-cratering retarded bombs (nine)
**101** Port navigation light
**102** Vortex generators

**103** AIM-9L Sidewinder air-to-air missiles
**104** Missile launch rails
**105** Twin missile carrier
**106** Outboard stores pylon
**107** Port wing fence
**108** Leading-edge stall strip
**109** Auxiliary wing fences
**110** Air-conditioning system heat exchanger intakes
**111** Heat exchangers (two)
**112** Fuselage upper longeron

**113** Mainspar attachment double frame
**114** Intake duct framing
**115** Auxiliary front spar attachment joint
**116** Mainwheel door
**117** Position of pressure refuelling connection on port side
**118** Ventral gun pack
**119** Ammunition magazine
**120** 30-mm ADEN cannon
**121** Ammunition feed and link return chutes
**122** Starboard air inlet

**123** Bifurcated inlet ducting
**124** Fire extinguisher bottle
**125** Nitrogen bottle, port and starboard (emergency pressurisation of hydraulic system)
**126** Boundary layer spill duct
**127** Oxygen bottle (two)
**128** Cockpit rear pressure bulkhead
**129** Canopy hinge joints
**130** Instructor's Martin-Baker 'zero-zero' ejection seat
**131** Ejection seat headrest
**132** Port inboard stores pylon
**133** Canopy, hinged to starboard
**134** Rear cockpit internal windshield
**135** Ferranti F.195 weapons sight
**136** Rear instrument panel shroud
**137** Side console panels
**138** Rear control column
**139** Rudder pedals
**140** Rear cockpit pressurised floor panels
**141** External fuse panel, port and starboard
**142** Position of retractable boarding step on port side
**143** Underfloor electrical equipment bay
**144** Lower UHF aerial
**145** Ventral gun pack attachment link
**146** Cannon barrel

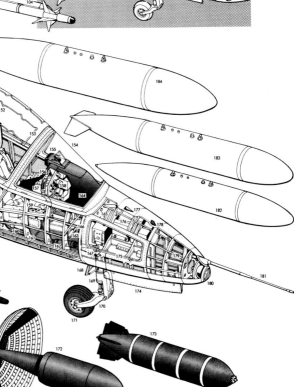

**147** Cannon muzzle fairing
**148** Electrical cable ducting, port and starboard
**149** Fuselage lower longeron
**150** Position of fold-out step handhold on port side
**151** Student pilot's Martin Baker 'zero-zero' ejection seat
**152** Canopy miniature detonating cord (MDC)
**153** Canopy arch frame
**154** Curved frameless windscreen panel
**155** Student pilot's F.195 weapon sight and recording camera
**156** Engine throttle lever
**157** Front control column
**158** Instrument panel
**159** Starboard side console panel
**160** Ejection seat rocket pack
**161** Forward cockpit pressurised floor panels
**162** Nose-landing gear hydraulic retraction jack
**163** Rudder pedals
**164** Instrument panel shroud

**165** Avionics equipment bay
**166** Cockpit front pressure bulkhead
**167** Nose-landing gear pivot fixing
**168** Nosewheel leg door
**169** Shock absorber nosewheel leg strut
**170** Levered suspension nosewheel forks
**171** Nosewheel, forward-retracting
**172** 1,000-lb (454-kg) retarded bomb, deployed configuration
**173** BL755 600-lb (272 kg) cluster bomb
**174** Nosewheel doors
**175** Avionics bay doors, port and starboard
**176** Avionics equipment racks
**177** Fresh air intake
**178** Upper IFF aerial
**179** Nosewheel bay construction
**180** Landing/taxiing lamp
**181** Pitot head
**182** 100-Imp gal (455-litre) auxiliary fuel tank
**183** 130-Imp gal (591-litre) auxiliary fuel tank
**184** 190-Imp gal (864-litre) auxiliary fuel tank
**185** Hawk 200 single-seat conflguration
**186** Built-in cannon (two) 25-mm, 27-mm or 30-mm

**187** Ammunition magazine
**188** Pilot's seat
**189** Radar head-down display
**190** Head-up display
**191** Avionics equipment and radar processing equipment bay
**192** Radar transmitter/receiver
**193** Radar scanner
**194** Radome
**195** Alternative nose configuration with Laser Ranger and Marked Target Seeker (LRMTS)
**196** Alternative nose configuration with Laser Ranger and Infra-Red detector
**197** Boeing/British Aerospace T-45A Goshawk, nose configuration
**198** Catapult towbar
**199** Twin-wheel nose landing gear
**200** Lowered fuselage nose profile
**201** Liquid oxygen converter
**202** Advanced Cathode-Ray Tube (CRT) cockpit displays
**203** T-45A Goshawk long-stroke main landing gear leg, carrier-compatible
**204** T-45A main landing gear leg pivot, moved outboard
**205** T-45A Goshawk rear fuselage configuration
**206** Ventral fin and tail bumper
**207** Deck arrester hook, lowered
**208** Repositioned lateral airbrakes, port and starboard

# Casa C.101 Aviojet

*The C.101 has fulfilled the basic jet training role for the Spanish air force since 1980 and has proved to be safe and economical in this role. Sales of the aircraft never reached the 300 mark, which CASA had proposed in 1978, but this was due more to overenthusiastic predictions than to any shortcomings in the aircraft.*

## C.101CC

**Cutaway key**
1 Glassfibre nosecone
2 ILS glideslope antenna
3 Nosewheel doors
4 Nose undercarriage wheel bay
5 Oxygen bottles
6 Pitot head
7 TACAN antenna
8 Temperature probe
9 Cockpit fresh air intake
10 Avionics equipment bay
11 Nosewheel leg pivot mounting
12 Hydraulic retraction jack
13 Avionics bay access doors, port and starboard
14 Nosewheel leg strut
15 Forward-retracting nosewheel
16 Electro-luminescent formation lighting strip
17 Cockpit front pressure bulkhead
18 Static ports
19 Rudder pedals
20 Control column
21 Front instrument console
22 Avimo gunsight
23 Frameless windscreen panel
24 Canopy open position, individual canopy covers
25 Pilot's rear view mirrors
26 Student pilot's cockpit canopy
27 Ejection seat headrest
28 Martin-Baker Mk E10 'zero-zero' ejection seat

29 Canopy external latch
30 Engine throttle lever
31 Front seat mounting sloping bulkhead
32 Underfloor control runs
33 Cockpit pressure floor
34 DEFA 30-mm ventral cannon pack
35 Twin Browning 0.5-in (12.7-mm) machine-gun pack (alternative fit)
36 Machine-gun ammunition magazine, 220 rounds per gun
37 Cartridge case ejection chute
38 Battery
39 Cannon ammunition magazine, 130 rounds
40 Nitrogen bottle, emergency undercarriage lowering
41 Rear cockpit pressure floor
42 Rear canopy external latch
43 Rear instrument console
44 Internal windscreen between cockpits
45 Instructor's Martin-Baker Mk E10 ejection seat

46 Instructor's cockpit canopy
47 Starboard outer integral fuel tank, total internal capacity 531 Imp gal/638 US gal (2414 litres); 380 Imp gal/457 US gal (1730 litres) without outboard tanks

48 Starboard stores pylons (3)
49 Machined wing skin/ stringer panel over tank bay
50 Outer wing tank filler cap
51 Formation lighting strip

52 Starboard navigation light
53 Static dischargers
54 Starboard aileron
55 Aileron hydraulic actuator
56 Flap operating link and torque shaft
57 Starboard single-slotted flap

58 UHF antenna
59 Control rod linkages
60 Cockpit sloping rear pressure bulkhead
61 Port air intake
62 Boundary layer diverter
63 Airbrake hydraulic jack
64 Ventral airbrake panel
65 Pressure refuelling connection
66 Air-conditioning pack

67 Wing spar/fuselage bolted attachment joint
68 Front spar attachment fuselage mainframe
69 Fuselage bag-type fuel tank
70 Intake duct structure
71 Boundary layer spill duct
72 Centre/forward fuselage joint frame
73 Tank bay access panel
74 Fuel feed/vent piping

*Although relatively docile in the jet trainer role, the C.101 can pack a punch in the light attack role. The aircraft can be configured with six underwing hardpoints, as illustrated by this **CASA** demonstrator, carrying a wide range of stores including bombs, missiles, rockets and guns. Armed variants are operated by the air arms of Chile, Honduras and Jordan.*

## C.101CC Aviojet

### Dimensions

**Length:** 41 ft (12.50 m)
**Height:** 13 ft 11¼ in (4.25 m)
**Wingspan:** 34 ft 9¼ in (10.60 m)
**Aspect ratio:** 5.6
**Wing area:** 215.29 sq ft (20.00 m²)
**Tailplane span:** 14 ft 2 in (4.32 m)
**Wheel track:** 10 ft 5¼ in (3.18 m)
**Wheel base:** 15 ft 7¾ in (4.77 m)

### Powerplant

One Garrett TFE731-5-1J turbofan rated at 4,300 lb st (19.13 kN) dry normal and 4,700 lb st (20.91 kN) dry with military power reserve

### Weights

**Empty equipped:** 7,716 lb (3500 kg)
**Normal take-off:** 11,023 lb (5000 kg)
**Maximum take-off:** 13,889 lb (6300 kg)

### Fuel and load

**Internal fuel:** 4,017 lb (1822 kg)
**External fuel:** None
**Maximum ordnance:** 4,960 lb (2250 kg)

### Performance

**Never-exceed speed:** 450 kt (518 mph; 834 km/h)
**Maximum level speed 'clean' at 20,000 ft (6095 m):** 435 kt (501 mph; 806 km/h)
**Maximum speed at sea level:** 415 kt (478 mph; 769 km/h)
**Economical cruising speed at 30,000 ft (9145 m):** 354 kt (407 mph; 656 km/h)
**Ferry range:** 2,000 nm (2,303 miles; (3706 km)
**Combat radius:** 280 nm (322 miles; (519 km) on a lo-lo-lo mission with cannon pod and four 551-lb (250-kg) bombs, or 520 nm (599 miles; 964 kg) on a hi-lo-hi photo-reconnaissance mission
**Maximum rate of climb at sea level:** 4,900 ft (1494 m) per minute at normal power and 6,100 ft (1859 m) per minute with military power reserve
**Climb to 25,000 ft (7620 m):** 6 minutes 30 seconds
**Service ceiling:** 42,000 ft (12800 m)
**Take-off run:** 1,835 ft (559 m) at 9,921 lb (4500 kg)
**Take-off distance to 50 ft (15 m):** 2,460 ft (750 m) at 9,921 lb (4500 kg)
**Landing run:** 1,575 ft (480 m) at 10,361 lb (4700 kg)
**g limits:** -3.9 to +7.5 at 10,582 lb (4800 kg) or -1 to +5.5 at 13,889 lb (6300 kg)

### Armament

One 30-mm DEFA fixed forward-firing cannon under the fuselage or two 0.5-in (12.7-mm) Colt-Browning fixed forward-firing machine-guns in the lower-fuselage bay, plus up to 4,056 lb (1840 kg) of disposable stores, including bombs, rockets or missiles, carried on six underwing hardpoints

© 2000 Mike Badrocke

75 Fuselage tank gravity filler
76 Air supply duct to conditioning plant
77 Rear spar attachment fuselage main frame
78 Centre fuselage frame structure
79 Intake plenum
80 ADF antenna
81 Tailplane control rods
82 Ram air intake
83 Engine bleed-air primary heat exchanger
84 Box-section rear fuselage spine structure
85 Finroot fillet
86 Fin spar attachment joint
87 Starboard tailplane
88 Starboard elevator
89 Leading-edge HF antenna
90 Two-spar fin torsion box structure
91 Fin ribs
92 VOR antenna
93 Fintip VHF antenna
94 Anti-collision light
95 ELT antenna
96 Tail navigation light
97 Rudder
98 Honeycomb composite rudder core structure
99 Rudder tab
100 Elevator fixed tab

101 Port elevator honeycomb composite core structure
102 Tailplane ribs
103 Two-spar torsion box tailplane structure
104 Rear formation lighting strip
105 Elevator hinge control
106 Trimming tailplane hinge mounting
107 Rudder hinge control
108 Trimming tailplane sealing plate
109 Tailplane trim control screw jack, electrically operated
110 Engine exhaust nozzle
111 Fan air, cold stream, exhaust duct
112 Core engine, hot stream, exhaust
113 Tail bumper
114 Ventral fin, port and starboard
115 Engine bay cowling panels
116 Accessory equipment gearbox
117 Allied Signal TFE731-5-1J turbofan engine
118 Engine front fan
119 Rear fuselage joint frame
120 Wingroot trailing-edge fillet
121 Lower UHF antenna

122 Flap inboard guide rail
123 Hydraulic reservoir
124 Main undercarriage wheel bay
125 Hydraulic retraction jack
126 Undercarriage mounting auxiliary wing spar
127 Rear spar
128 Wing stringers
129 Flap shroud ribs
130 Port single-slotted flap
131 Flap honeycomb composite core structure
132 Flap outboard guide rail
133 Port aileron hydraulic actuator
134 Fixed aileron tab
135 Port aileron honeycomb composite core structure
136 Composite wingtip fairing
137 Port navigation light
138 Port outer wing tank gravity filler
139 Mk 82 500-lb (227-kg) HE bomb
140 MATRA Magic air-to-air 'self-defence' missile
141 Missile launch rail
142 LAU-3/A rocket launcher, 19 x 2.75-in (70-mm) FFAR

143 Port wing stores pylons (3)
144 Front spar
145 Port outer integral wing tank
146 Main spar
147 Wing rib structure
148 Leading-edge ribs
149 Port mainwheel
150 Trailing-axle suspension
151 Mainwheel leg doors
152 Retractable landing light
153 Main undercarriage leg pivot mounting
154 Wing centre tank gravity filler
155 Centre-section integral fuel tank
156 Extended chord wingroot section
157 Elettronica ELT/555 jamming pod
158 ASM-65A Maverick air-to-surface missile
159 LAU-10 rocket launcher, 4 x 5-in (127-mm) FFAR
160 5-in (127-mm) Zuni rocket
161 2.75-in (70-mm) rocket

# Cessna T-37/A-37 Dragonfly

*The T-37 has been the primary USAF trainer for almost four decades. First scheduled to be replaced by the Fairchild T-46A (cancelled in 1987), the 'Tweet' now awaits replacement by the Raytheon T-6A Texan II, procured jointly under the JPATS scheme with the US Navy.*

## A-37B Dragonfly
### Cutaway key

1 Rudder top hinge and aerodynamic balance
2 VHF communications antenna
3 Pitot head
4 Port elevator
5 Elevator aerodynamic balance
6 Tailplane structure
7 FM homing dipole
8 Elevator trim tab actuator
9 Elevator trim tab (port only)
10 Rudder trim tab actuator
11 Tailfin structure
12 Rudder
13 Rudder trim tab
14 Starboard elevator
15 Tailplane front spar
16 Magnetic detector
17 Rear navigation lights
18 Tail cone
19 Tailplane/fin rear spar attachment
20 Elevator push rod
21 Rudder control bell crank assembly
22 FM homing dipole
23 Tail bumper fairing
24 Rudder/elevator control cables
25 Elevator control quadrant assembly
26 Tailplane fin front spar attachment
27 Tailfin fairing
28 Oxygen cylinders
29 Dorsal UHF TACAN antenna
30 Fuselage frames
31 Avionics bay access door
32 Radio/avionics equipment
33 Low frequency ADI antenna
34 Dorsal IFF antenna
35 Hydraulic reservoir
36 Inverter
37 Fuselage construction
38 Dorsal position light
39 FM communications whip aerial
40 Canopy fairing
41 Fuselage fuel tank, 91 US gal (344 litres)
42 Seat ejection unit
43 Weber ejection seat
44 Harness
45 Headrest
46 Hydraulic power jack canopy actuator
47 Pilot's ejection seat
48 Hinged canopy
49 Retractable landing light
50 Mainwheel leg bay
51 Port flap
52 Flap hydraulic cylinder
53 Port slot lip spoiler
54 Aileron trim tab actuator
55 Aileron trim tab (port only)
56 Wing integral fuel (113 US gal/428 litres each wing)
57 Access/inspection panels
58 Aileron boost tab
59 Port aileron
60 Aileron control quadrant
61 Port wingtip tank (95-US gal/360-litre capacity)
62 Fuel filler cap
63 Outboard pylons (600-lb/272-kg load limit)
64 Wing fuel filler cap
65 Leading-edge tank
66 Inboard pylons (800-lb/363-kg load limit)
67 1,500-round 0.30-in (7.62-mm) SUU-11/A Minigun pod
68 19-tube LAU-3A 2.75-in (69-mm) rocket-launcher
69 100-US gal (377-litre) drop tanks
70 Front spar
71 Inboard leading-edge tank
72 Port mainwheel
73 Curved windshield
74 Chicago Aerial Industries CA-505 non-computing gunsight
75 Inflight-refuelling control panel
76 Port side console
77 Pilot's control column
78 Instrument panel shroud
79 Second pilot's partial instrumentation
80 Fuel line fairing
81 Cockpit air
82 AiResearch air-conditioning pack
83 Batteries
84 Landing-gear emergency air bottle
85 Inverter
86 Auto-spin strake
87 Detachable refuelling probe
88 Gun camera
89 Taxi light
90 Nosewheel door
91 Nosewheel bay
92 Minigun blast tube
93 1,500-round ammunition drum
94 Nosewheel
95 Louvred vent
96 Nosewheel oleo
97 General Electric 0.30-in (7.62-mm) GAU-2B/A Minigun

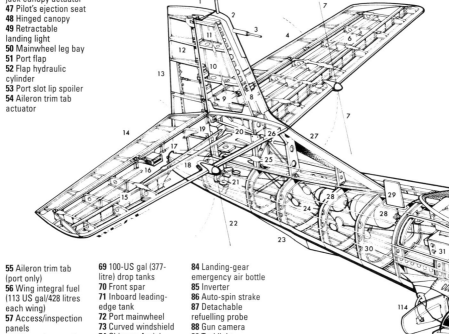

66-7978, a *T-37B-CE*, was typical of the bulk of 'Tweety Bird' production for the *USAF Air Training Command* (*ATC*). A total of 552 *T-37Bs* was built, making it the most numerous Model 318 training variant. The *T-37 powerplant* is the Continental/Teledyne J69 turbojet, a licence-built version of the Turboméca Marboré, the engine used by the Magister. The *T-37B* introduced the uprated (1,025-lb/4.61-kN static thrust) *J69-T-25* in place of the *T-37A's* (920-lb/4.14-kN static thrust) *J69-T-9*.

## SPECIFICATION

### OA-37B Dragonfly

#### Dimensions

**Length excluding probe:** 29 ft 3½ in (8.93 m)
**Height:** 8 ft 10½ in (2.70 m)
**Wingspan with tip tanks:** 35 ft 10½ in (10.93 m)
**Wing area:** 183.90 sq ft (17.09 m²)
**Wing aspect ratio:** 6.2
**Tailplane span:** 13 ft 11¼ in (4.25 m)
**Wheel track:** 14 ft ½ in (4.28 m)
**Wheel track:** 7 ft 10 in (2.39 m)

#### Powerplant

Two General Electric J85-GE-17A turbojets each rated at 2,850 lb st (12.68 kN)

#### Weights

**Basic empty:** 6,211 lb (2817 kg)
**Empty equipped:** 5,843 lb (2650 kg)
**Maximum take-off:** 14,000 lb (6350 kg)

#### Fuel and load

**Internal fuel:** 3,307 lb (1500 kg)
**External fuel:** up to four 100-US gal (378-litre) drop tanks
**Maximum ordnance:** 4,100 lb (1860 kg)

#### Performance

**Never-exceed speed:** 455 kt (524 mph; 843 km/h)
**Maximum level speed at 16,000 ft (4875 m):** 440 kt (507 mph; 816 km/h)
**Maximum cruising speed at 25,000 ft (7620 m):** 425 kt (489 mph; 787 km/h)
**Maximum rate of climb at sea level:** 6,990 ft (2130 m) per minute
**Service ceiling:** 41,765 ft (12730 m)
**Take-off run at maximum take-off weight:** 1,740 ft (531 m)
**Take-off distance to 50 ft (15 m) at maximum take-off weight:** 2,595 ft (791 m)
**Landing run at normal landing weight:** 1,710 ft (521 m)

#### Armament

Up to 4,100 lb (1860 kg) of stores mounted on eight underwing pylons, including unguided bombs and rockets

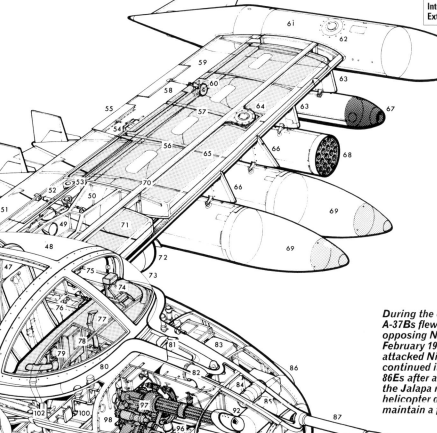

During the civil war in Nicaragua, *Fuerza Aérea Hondureña* (*FAH*) *A-37Bs* flew in support of the *US*-backed Nicaraguan *Contras*, opposing Nicaragua's left-wing Sandinista government. In February 1984, an *FAH A-37B*, supported by five helicopters, attacked Nicaraguan positions. The following year the *FAH* continued its support of the Contras, striking with *A-37Bs* and *F-86Es* after an attack by *Fuerza Aérea Sandinista* Mi-8s and Mi-25s in the Jalapa region in September, when the *FAH* claimed one Mil helicopter destroyed. In early 2000, Honduras continues to maintain a fleet of *A-37B* Dragonflies, principally based at *La Ceiba*.

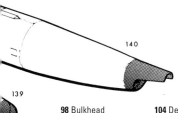

**109** Supplementary intake
**110** Engine rear mount
**111** Tailpipe
**112** Elevator controls
**113** Jet exhaust fairing
**114** Hydraulically-operated thrust attenuator
**115** Wingroot/engine nacelle fairing
**116** Starboard flap
**117** Wheelwell
**118** Front spar
**119** Mainwheel retraction strut
**120** Retractable landing light
**121** Starboard slot lip spoiler

**122** Flap hydraulic cylinder
**123** Mainwheel oleo
**124** Starboard mainwheel
**125** Inboard pylons (see item 66)
**126** Outboard pylons (see item 63)
**127** Leading-edge structure

**128** Fuel filler cap
**129** Wing construction
**130** Access/inspection panels
**131** Rear spar
**132** Starboard aileron
**133** Aileron boost tab
**134** Starboard wingtip tank

**135** Starboard navigation light
**136** Fuel filler cap
**137** Practice-bomb carrier (four 35-lb/16-kg BDU-33 bombs)
**138** 500-lb (227-kg) Mk 82 low-drag bomb
**139** BLU-1/B napalm fire bomb

**140** GPU-2/A 20-mm cannon pod

**98** Bulkhead
**99** Speed brake
**100** Rudder pedals
**101** Fuselage structure
**102** Control column pushrod assembly
**103** Automatically-actuated inlet screen

**104** De-icing inlet lip
**105** Engine forward mount
**106** Front spar attachment points
**107** Engine accessories
**108** General Electric J85-GE-17A engine

233

# Dassault/Dornier Alphajet

*Two French air force Alpha Jets from the advanced training unit at Tours formate with a pair of aircraft from the Moroccan air force equivalent. In addition to their primary role of providing advanced training, the 'Gadgets' of the Ecole de l'Aviation de Chasse 314 are used for fast-jet navigator training. Around 50 French Alpha Jets are being upgraded with 'glass' cockpits to make them more suitable as lead-in trainers for modern fighters such as the Mirage 2000-5F and Rafale.*

### Alpha Jet E

1 Nosecone
2 Nosewheel bay bulkhead
3 Fixed nose strake
4 Nose landing-gear wheel bay
5 Nosewheel door mechanism
6 Temperature probe
7 Fresh air intake
8 Nose landing-gear leg strut
9 Pivoted axle beam
10 Spray suppression nosewheel tyre
11 Pitot tube
12 Nosewheel leg door
13 Nosewheel pivot fixing
14 Oxygen filler point
15 Liquid oxygen container
16 Cockpit front pressure bulkhead
17 Rudder pedals
18 Rudder pedal access panel
19 Footboards
20 Control column linkage
21 Rudder cable run
22 Cockpit coaming
23 Instrument panel shroud
24 Windscreen panels
25 Pilot's head-up display (navigational data display on trainer version)
26 Starboard side console panel
27 Control column
28 Canopy latch
29 Engine throttle levers
30 Front seat boarding step
31 Aileron control rod run

32 Port side console panel
33 Seat/parachute harness
34 Student pilot's Martin Baker AJR1VIA-4 ejection seat
35 Ejection seat headrest
36 Face blind firing handle
37 Canopy breaker arms
38 Forward hinged canopy
39 Canopy operating jack
40 Rear cockpit blast shield
41 Ejection seat launch rails
42 Rear rudder pedal linkages
43 Canopy emergency release handle
44 SFIM 550 inertial platform
45 Rear cockpit elevated floor level
46 Boundary layer splitter plate
47 Port engine air intake
48 Forward avionics equipment bay
49 Intake duct framing
50 Splitter plate honeycomb construction
51 Boarding step
52 Rear throttle levers
53 Boundary layer spill duct
54 Rear canopy latch

55 Rear instrument panel shroud
56 Canopy centre section glazing
57 Fixed canopy arch
58 Rear pilot/instructor's ejector seat
59 Rear hinged canopy cover
60 Ejection seat headrest
61 Cockpit rear bulkhead
62 Canopy hinges
63 Control rod runs
64 Wing leading-edge fairing
65 Wing centre-section carry through
66 Skin panel bolted joint strap
67 Central flap hydraulic jack
68 Electrical cable ducting
69 Dorsal spine fairing
70 UHF aerial
71 Starboard wing panel bolted joint
72 Wing skin panel spanwise joint
73 Starboard wing integral fuel tank. Total internal fuel capacity 418 Imp gal (1900 litres)
74 Compound sweep leading-edge section
75 Inboard pylon hardpoint

76 68-Imp gal (310-litre) auxiliary fuel tank
77 Tank filler cap
78 Outboard tank pylon
79 Leading-edge dog-tooth
80 Fuel system access panels
81 Starboard navigation light
82 Wingtip fairing
83 Starboard aileron
84 Static dischargers
85 Aileron control linkage
86 Hydraulic operating jack
87 Aileron push-pull rod
88 Flap hinge fairings
89 Flap vane
90 Starboard double-slotted tracked flap
91 Inboard flap guide rail

92 Control system mechanical mixer unit
93 Flap operating mechanism
94 Rear spar
95 Rear fuselage fuel tank
96 Fixed trailing-edge fillet
97 Fuel filler cap
98 Air-conditioning plant
99 Dorsal spine access panels

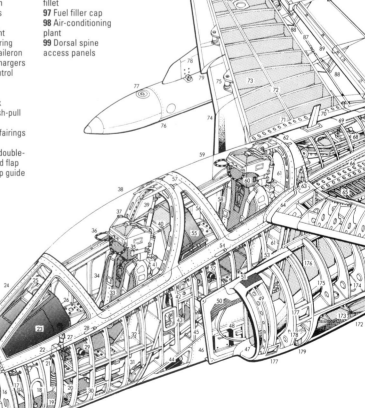

## SPECIFICATION

### Alpha Jet E

#### Dimensions

**Length:** 38 ft 6½ in (11.75 m)
**Height:** 13 ft 9 in (4.19 m)
**Wingspan:** 29 ft 10¾ in (9.11 m)
**Wing area:** 188.37 sq ft (17.50 m²)
**Wing aspect ratio:** 4.8
**Tailplane span:** 14 ft 2½ in (4.33 m)
**Wheel track:** 8 ft 10¾ in (2.71 m)
**Wheelbase:** 15 ft 5¾ in (4.72 m)

#### Powerplant

Two SNECMA/Turboméca Larzac 04-C6 turbofans, each rated at 2,976 lb (13.24 kN) thrust

#### Weights

**Empty equipped:** 7,374 lb (3345 kg)
**Maximum take-off:** 17,637 lb (8000 kg)

#### Fuel and load

**Internal fuel:** 2,976 lb (1350 kg)
**External fuel:** up to four 99-Imp gal (450-litre) or 68-Imp gal (310-litre) drop tanks
**Maximum ordnance:** more than 5,511 lb (2500 kg)

#### Performance

**Maximum level speed at 32,810 ft (10000 m):** 494 kt (569 mph; 916 km/h)

**Maximum level speed at sea level:** 539 kt (621 mph; 1000 km/h)
**Maximum rate of climb at sea level:** 12,008 ft (3660 m) per minute
**Climb to 30,020 ft (9150 m):** less than 7 minutes
**Service ceiling:** 48,000 ft (14630 m)
**Take-off run at normal take-off weight:** 1,215 ft (370 m)
**Landing run at normal landing weight:** 1,640 ft (500 m)
**Ferry range:** more than 2,159 nm (2,486 miles; 4000 km)
**Operational radius:** 361 nm (416 miles; 670 km) on a lo-lo-lo training mission with two drop tanks, or 664 nm (764 miles; 1230 km) on a hi-hi-hi mission
**Endurance on internal fuel:** more than 3 hours 30 minutes at high altitude or 2 hours 30 minutes at low level

#### Armament

Removable centreline pod for one 30-mm DEFA 553 cannon plus 150 rounds (27-mm IWKA-Mauser cannon on Alpha Jet A). Four underwing hardpoints for drop tanks and various unguided munitions, including general-purpose and cluster bombs, MATRA F4 or 155 rocket pods, or Brandt BAT120 retarded bombs

*During the 1991 Gulf War the Alpha Jet received a call-to-alert from a surprising direction. While US and NATO aircraft were assigned directly to the war against Iraq, aircraft from other nations were drafted in to maintain NATO's commitment to defend Turkey. Among the aircraft deployed were the Alpha Jets of 2./JBG 49 (492 Squadron in NATO parlance), seen here at Erhac.*

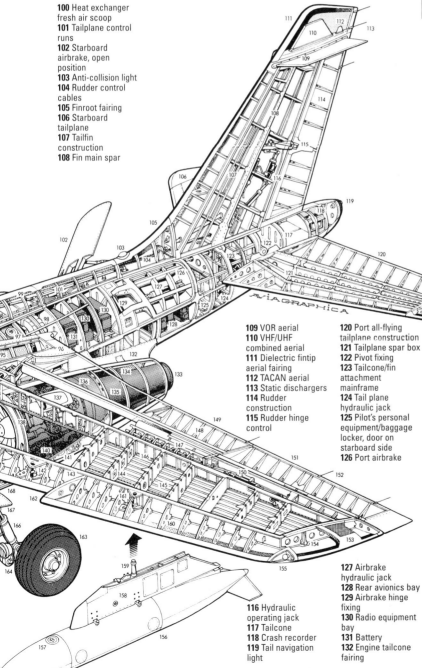

**100** Heat exchanger fresh air scoop
**101** Tailplane control runs
**102** Starboard airbrake, open position
**103** Anti-collision light
**104** Rudder control cables
**105** Finroot fairing
**106** Starboard tailplane
**107** Tailfin construction
**108** Fin main spar

**109** VOR aerial
**110** VHF/UHF combined aerial
**111** Dielectric fintip aerial fairing
**112** TACAN aerial
**113** Static dischargers
**114** Rudder construction
**115** Rudder hinge control
**116** Hydraulic operating jack
**117** Tailcone
**118** Crash recorder
**119** Tail navigation light

**120** Port all-flying tailplane construction
**121** Tailplane spar box
**122** Pivot fixing
**123** Tailcone/fin attachment mainframe
**124** Tail plane hydraulic jack
**125** Pilot's personal equipment/baggage locker, door on starboard side
**126** Port airbrake
**127** Airbrake hydraulic jack
**128** Rear avionics bay
**129** Airbrake hinge fixing
**130** Radio equipment bay
**131** Battery
**132** Engine tailcone fairing

**133** Exhaust nozzle
**134** Fan air duct
**135** Tailpipe, hot stream exhaust
**136** SNECMA/Turboméca Larzac 04-C6 turbofan engine
**137** Engine bay ventilating air scoop
**138** Engine bay bulkhead
**139** Intake compressor face
**140** Engine accessory gearbox
**141** Engine bay access doors
**142** Port wing inboard pylon hardpoint
**143** Front spar
**144** Wing rib construction
**145** Machined wing skin/ stringer panel
**146** Port wing integral fuel tank
**147** Flap shroud fairing
**148** Flap rib construction
**149** Port double-slotted flap
**150** Aileron hydraulic jack

**151** Port aileron construction
**152** Static dischargers
**153** Glassfibre honeycomb wingtip fairing
**154** Wingtip jacking point
**155** Port navigation light
**156** Port 68-Imp gal (310-litre) auxiliary fuel tank
**157** Fuel filler cap
**158** Tank pylon
**159** Pylon attachment spigot
**160** Wing leading-edge rib construction
**161** Outboard pylon hardpoint
**162** Leading-edge dog-tooth
**163** Port mainwheel
**164** Pivoted axle beam
**165** Landing/taxiing lamp
**166** Shock absorber strut
**167** Mainwheel leg door
**168** Ground connections panel, electrical, hydraulic and intercom
**169** Main landing gear leg pivot fixing
**170** Hydraulic retraction jack
**171** Hydraulic downlock strut
**172** Mainwheel door

**173** Main landing wheel bay
**174** Intake duct framing
**175** Intake trunking
**176** Centre fuselage bag-type fuel tank
**177** Rear seat boarding steps
**178** Position of pressure refuelling connection (actually located on starboard side)
**179** Fuselage jacking point

# Transport and
# Tanker Aircraft

# Antonov An-12 'Cub'

*Having demonstrated all the versatility of the Hercules in both transport and 'special' roles, the An-12 is in the twilight of its career with Russian forces. Elsewhere it remains an important type however and is still the subject, in upgraded form, of limited production in China.*

## An-12BP 'Cub-A'

**Cutaway key**

1 Nose compartment glazing
2 Optically flat lower viewing panel
3 Nose radome
4 Weather and navigational radar scanner
5 Chart table
6 Navigator's station
7 Nose compartment entry hatch
8 'Odd Rods' IFF aerials
9 Windscreen panels
10 Windscreen wipers
11 Instrument panel shroud
12 Pilot's instrument panel
13 Control column
14 Rudder pedals
15 Boarding ladder
16 Door mounted retractable taxiing lamp
17 Blade antennas
18 Crew entry door/ escape hatch, open
19 Avionics equipment racks
20 Flight deck floor level
21 Pilot's seat
22 Cockpit eyebrow windows
23 Co-pilot's seat
24 Overhead systems switch panel
25 Aerial lead-in
26 Cockpit roof escape hatch
27 Flight engineer's instrument panels
28 Engineer's swivelling seat
29 Flight deck doorway
30 Cockpit pressure bulkhead
31 Radio operator's station
32 Nose landing gear pivot fixing
33 Pitot head
34 Nosewheel hydraulic steering control unit

35 Twin nosewheels, aft retracting
36 Blade antenna
37 Cargo deck floor level
38 Ventral access hatch
39 Cabin window panels
40 Port side emergency exit window hatch
41 Paratroop seating, 100 troops maximum
42 Central 'back-to-back' seat rows, removable
43 Cabin wall removable troop seat
44 Cabin wall insulating and trim panelling
45 Starboard side emergency exit window hatch
46 D/F loop aerials
47 Fuselage frame and stringer construction
48 Cargo deck floor beams
49 Underfloor bulk stowage compartment
50 Main cargo loading deck
51 Crew/passenger entry door
52 Wing spar/fuselage attachment main frame
53 Engine floodlight
54 Wing root fillet fairings
55 Front spar centre-section carry-through
56 Wing panel bolted root joints
57 Centre section ribs
58 Inboard bag-type fuel tanks (three), total fuel capacity 3058 Imp gal (13901 litres), 3981 Imp gal (18100 litres) with overload tanks
59 Starboard inner engine nacelle

60 Hinged engine cowling panels
61 Ventral oil cooling intake
62 Propeller spinners
63 AV-68 four-bladed fully feathering and reversible, variable pitch propellers
64 Starboard outer engine nacelle
65 Intermediate bag-type fuel tanks (five)
66 Outboard bag-type fuel tanks (three)
67 Outerwing panel joint rib
68 Ventral navigational antennas
69 Anhedral outerwing panel
70 Starboard navigation lights
71 Static dischargers
72 Starboard two-segment aileron
73 Aileron trim tab
74 'Cub-B' electronic intelligence variant (Elint)
75 Variant with maritime surveillance radar
76 'Cub-C' Electronic countermeasures variant (ECM)
77 ASW version with magnetic anomaly detection equipment (MAD)
78 Starboard double-slotted flap, down position
79 Flap guide rails
80 Wing root trailing edge fillet
81 ADF sense aerial, port and starboard
82 Starboard emergency exit window hatch
83 Overhead travelling cargo handling crane
84 Rear cabin roof escape hatches

85 Starboard ramp door, open
86 Fin root fillet
87 Tailfin support structure
88 Two-spar torsion box tailfin construction
89 Starboard tailplane
90 Starboard elevator
91 Fin leading edge thermal de-icing
92 HF aerial cables
93 Short wave ground- control communications antennas

94 Anti-collision light
95 Static dischargers
96 Rudder
97 Rudder trim tabs
98 Tail navigation light
99 Tail warning radar antenna
100 Rear gunner's station
101 Gun turret, two 23-mm NR-23 cannon
102 Elevator tab
103 Port elevator
104 Static dischargers
105 Tailplane leading edge thermal de-icing

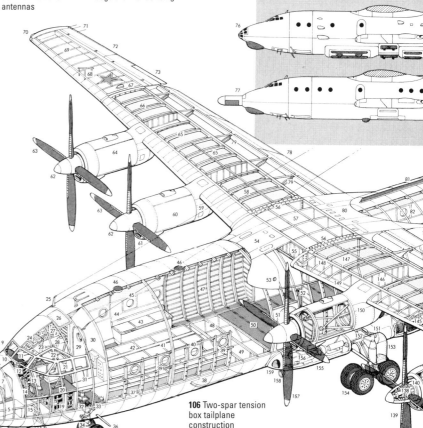

106 Two-spar tension box tailplane construction
107 Ventral radar altimeter antenna

This An-12PS was photographed at Saki in the Crimea during 2000, while on the strength of the Severomorsk Regiment and wearing an unusual polar bear marking. The An-12PS is based on the airframe of the basic An-12B and is believed to have been produced both by conversion and on the production line from 1969. The official line seems to be that the An-12PS was a search and rescue platform, with the initials PS standing for Poiskovo Spasatel'nii. It could reportedly carry and deploy a Type 03473 rescue boat, with a three-man crew. The deployment of the An-12PS suggests that the variant also fulfilled a vital Elint role, for it was frequently encountered shadowing NATO naval forces or monitoring NATO exercises.

## SPECIFICATION

### An-12BP 'Cub-A'

### Dimensions

**Wingspan:** 124 ft 8 in (38 m)
**Wing area:** 1,310.01 sq ft (121.7 m²)
**Length:** 108 ft 7¼ in (33.10 m)
**Height:** 34 ft 6½ in (10.53 m)
**Wing aspect ratio:** 11.85
**Tailplane span:** 40 ft ¼ in (12.20 m)
**Wheel track:** 17 ft 9½ in (5.42 m)
**Wheel base:** 35 ft 6 in (10.82 m)

### Powerplant

Four ZMDB Progress (Ivchyenko) AI-20K turboprops each rated at 4,000 ehp (2983 kW)

### Typical weights

**Empty:** 61,728 lb (2800 kg)
**Normal take-off:** 121,473 lb (55100 kg)
**Maximum take-off:** 134,480 lb (61000 kg)

### Fuel and load

**Internal fuel:** 4,781 US gal (18100 litres)
**Maximum payload:** 44,092 lb (20000 kg)

### Performance

**Maximum level speed 'clean' at optimum altitude:** 482 mph (777 km/h)
**Maximum cruising speed at optimum altitude:** 416 mph (670 km/h)
**Maximum rate of climb at sea level:** 1,969 ft (600 m) per minute
**Service ceiling:** 33,465 ft (10200 m)
**Take-off run at maximum take-off weight:** 2,297 ft (700 m)
**Landing run at normal landing weight:** 1,640 ft (500 m)
**Range with maximum fuel:** 3,542 miles (5700 km )
**Range with maximum payload:** 2,237 miles (3600 km) with maximum payload

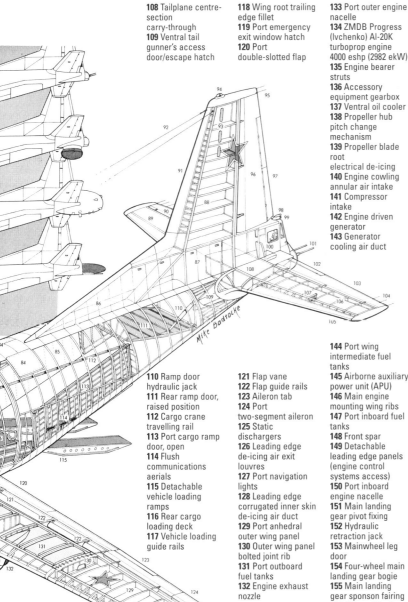

**108** Tailplane centre-section carry-through
**109** Ventral tail gunner's access door/escape hatch
**110** Ramp door hydraulic jack
**111** Rear ramp door, raised position
**112** Cargo crane travelling rail
**113** Port cargo ramp door, open
**114** Flush communications aerials
**115** Detachable vehicle loading ramps
**116** Rear cargo loading deck
**117** Vehicle loading guide rails
**118** Wing root trailing edge fillet
**119** Port emergency exit window hatch
**120** Port double-slotted flap
**121** Flap vane
**122** Flap guide rails
**123** Aileron tab
**124** Port two-segment aileron
**125** Static dischargers
**126** Leading edge de-icing air exit louvres
**127** Port navigation lights
**128** Leading edge corrugated inner skin de-icing air duct
**129** Port anhedral outer wing panel
**130** Outer wing panel bolted joint rib
**131** Port outboard fuel tanks
**132** Engine exhaust nozzle
**133** Port outer engine nacelle
**134** ZMDB Progress (Ivchenko) AI-20K turboprop engine 4000 eshp (2982 ekW)
**135** Engine bearer struts
**136** Accessory equipment gearbox
**137** Ventral oil cooler
**138** Propeller hub pitch change mechanism
**139** Propeller blade root electrical de-icing
**140** Engine cowling annular air intake
**141** Compressor intake
**142** Engine driven generator
**143** Generator cooling air duct
**144** Port wing intermediate fuel tanks
**145** Airborne auxiliary power unit (APU)
**146** Main engine mounting wing ribs
**147** Port inboard fuel tanks
**148** Front spar
**149** Detachable leading edge panels (engine control systems access)
**150** Port inboard engine nacelle
**151** Main landing gear pivot fixing
**152** Hydraulic retraction jack
**153** Mainwheel leg door
**154** Four-wheel main landing gear bogie
**155** Main landing gear sponson fairing
**156** Air conditioning plant
**157** Port AV-68 propellers
**158** Retractable landing lamp, port and starboard
**159** Air conditioning system cooling air ram intake

Replacing the An-12A on the production lines at Tashkent and Voronezh in 1963, the An-12B, as photographed here at Sperenberg in 1992, featured a TG-16 APU with a prominent exhaust in the port undercarriage fairing. This provided an autonomous self-start capability at airfields of up to 3,281 ft (1000 m) in elevation. The rudder trim tab was replaced by a pair of separate tabs, each with its own actuator fairing, which reached higher up the trailing edge of the rudder. The An-12B also lost the provision for the rear pair of external bomb racks.

**2001 Mike Badrocke/**
**Aiagraphica**

# Antonov An-24/26/30/32

*Instantly recognisable by the enlarged nacelles for its Ivchenko AI-40DM engines perched high above the fuselage, this An-32 belongs to the Indian air force (where it is named Sutlej). The good 'hot-and-high' performance of the 'Cline' was well appreciated by the Indians, who chose the aircraft over the G222, DHC-5 and Andover, and the IAF operates six squadrons of the type in 2000.*

## An-24V Series II 'Coke'

**Cutaway key**

1 Radome
2 Weather radar scanner
3 Scanner tracking mechanism
4 Radome hinges
5 ILS glideslope aerial
6 VOR localiser aerial
7 Radar transmitters and receivers
8 Forward pressure bulkhead
9 Nose undercarriage wheel bay
10 Rudder pedals
11 Instrument panel shroud
12 Radar display
13 Curved windscreen panels
14 Windscreen wipers
15 Cockpit eyebrow windows
16 Overhead systems switch panel
17 Co-pilot/ navigator/radio operator's seat
18 Instrument panel
19 Control column
20 Cockpit floor level
21 Nose undercarriage pivot fixing
22 Twin steerable nosewheels, forward retracting
23 Lower electrical equipment bay port and starboard
24 Underfloor control runs
25 Space provision for radio operator
26 Side console panel
27 Pilot's seat
28 Opening (direct vision) side window panel
29 Space provision for flight engineer
30 Circuit breaker panels

31 Aerial lead-in
32 Cockpit roof escape hatch, interchangeable with jettisonable astrodome observation hatch
33 Cockpit doorway
34 Control linkages
35 Cockpit rear bulkhead
36 Radio and electronics equipment racks
37 Baggage compartment
38 Baggage loading shelving

39 Starboard side 'up-and-over' baggage door
40 Crew wardrobe
41 Curtained cabin doorway
42 Passenger cabin front bulkhead
43 Fuselage skin doubler in line with propellers

44 Four-abreast passenger seating, 50-seat all tourist-class layout
45 Cabin window panels
46 Passenger cabin floor panelling
47 VHF aerial
48 Seat mounting rails
49 Emergency exit window hatch
50 Floor beam construction
51 Cabin wall trim panelling
52 Curtained window panels
53 Centre fuselage frame and stringer construction

54 D/F loop aerial
55 Air supply ducting
56 Wingroot fillet
57 Leading-edge de-icing air duct
58 Cabin air supply duct
59 Fuel filler cap
60 Inboard bag-type fuel tanks
61 Leading-edge engine control runs
62 Starboard nacelle
63 Starboard main undercarriage, stowed position
64 Fireproof bulkhead
65 Air-conditioning system, hot air supply
66 Ivchenko AI-24A turboprop engine
67 Engine auxiliary equipment

68 Hot-air de-iced intake lip
69 Propeller hub pitch change mechanism
70 Spinner
71 Propeller blade root electric de-icing
72 AV-72 four-bladed, constant-speed propeller
73 Engine cowling panels
74 Exhaust duct, exhausts on outboard side of nacelle
75 Wing panel joint rib
76 Fuel vent
77 Fuel filler cap
78 Outer wing panel integral fuel tank; total system capacity 1,220 Imp gal (5550 litres)
79 Leading edge de-icing air duct
80 Retractable landing/taxiing lamp
81 Outer wing panel joint rib

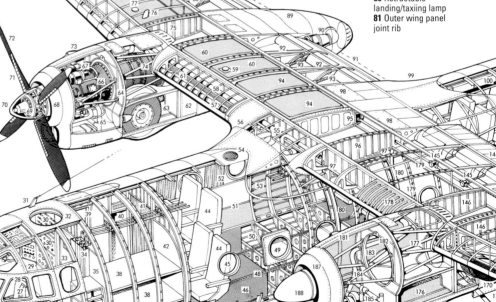

*Russia retained about 120 An-26s after the break-up of the Soviet Union; they remain the principal light transport aircraft in service and there are no current plans to replace them. Variants of the 'Curl' also act as command posts, VIP transport and liaison and SAR/casualty evacuation aircraft.*

## SPECIFICATION

### An-26B 'Curl-A'

### Dimensions
**Length:** 78 ft 1 in (23.80 m)
**Height:** 28 ft 1½ in (8.575 m)
**Wingspan:** 95 ft 9½ in (29.20 m)
**Aspect ratio:** 11:7
**Wing area:** 807.10 sq ft (74.98 m²)
**Tailplane span:** 32 ft 8¾ in (9.97 m)
**Wheel track:** 25 ft 11 in (7.90 m)
**Wheel base:** 25 ft 1¼ in (7.65 m)

### Powerplant
Two ZMDB Progress (Ivchenko) AI-24VT turboprops each rated at 2,820 ehp (2103 kW) and one Soyuz (Tumanskii) RU-19A-300 turbojet rated at 1,765 lb st (7.85 kN)

### Weights
**Empty:** 33,950 lb (15400 kg)
**Normal take-off:** 50,705 lb (23000 kg)
**Maximum take-off:** 53,790 lb (24400 kg)
**Maximum payload:** 12,125 lb (5500 kg)

### Fuel
**Internal fuel:** 12,125 lb (5500 kg)

### Performance
**Maximum level speed at 16,400 ft (5000 m):** 292 kt (336 mph; 540 km/h)
**Maximum level speed at sea level:** 275 kt (317 mph; 510 km/h)
**Cruising speed at 19,685 ft (6000 m):** 237 kt (273 mph; 440 km/h)
**Maximum rate of climb at sea level:** 1,575 ft (480 m) per minute
**Service ceiling:** 24,605 ft (7500 m)
**Take-off run at maximum take-off weight:** 2,559 ft (780 m)
**Landing run at normal landing weight:** 2,395 ft (730 m)

### Range
**With maximum fuel:** 1,376 nm (1,585 miles; 2550 km)
**With maximum payload:** 593 nm (683 miles; 1100 km)

---

82 Anhedral outer wing panel
83 Starboard navigation light
84 Wingtip fairing
85 Starboard two-segment aileron
86 Aileron tabs
87 Outboard double-slotted Fowler-type flap, down position
88 Flap guide rails and screw jacks
89 Nacelle tail fairing
90 TGA 6 turbine starter/generator, starboard side only
91 Inboard double-slotted flap segment, down position
92 Flap guide rails
93 Flap screw jacks
94 Optional long-range fuel tanks (four), capacity 228 Imp gal (1037 litres)

95 Central flap drive electric motor
96 Wing/fuselage attachment main rib
97 Wing attachment joints
98 Control access panels
99 Wingroot trailing-edge fillet
100 Cabin roof lighting panels
101 Overhead light luggage racks

102 Detachable ceiling panels, systems access
103 Cabin warm air ducting
104 Galley/buffet unit
105 Cabin attendant's folding seat
106 Toilet compartment
107 Coat rails
108 Tailplane de-icing air duct
109 Finroot fillet construction
110 HF notch aerial
111 Starboard tailplane
112 Starboard elevator
113 Fin leading-edge de-icing
114 Fin rib and stringer construction

115 HF aerial cable
116 De-icing air exit louvres
117 Static discharger
118 Rudder construction
119 Rudder tabs
120 Tail navigation light
121 Elevator tab
122 Port elevator rib construction
123 Static discharger
124 Tailplane leading-edge de-icing
125 Tailplane rib construction
126 Elevator hinge control
127 Radar altimeters
128 Rudder torque shaft
129 Ventral fin
130 Fin tailplane construction
131 Tailcone construction
132 Tailplane control rods
133 Rear pressure bulkhead
134 Emergency flare chutes, port and starboard
135 Tailcone access door

136 Rear baggage/wardrobe compartment
137 Sliding main entry door, open
138 Folding airstairs
139 Entry doorway
140 Passenger cabin rear bulkhead
141 Cabin fresh air supply duct
142 Cot, port and starboard, infant accommodation
143 Rear cabin passenger seating
144 Port inboard double-slotted Fowler-type flap
145 Flap screw jacks
146 Engine mounting main ribs

147 Control access panels
148 Nacelle tail fairing construction
149 Port outer double-slotted flap
150 Flap shroud ribs
151 Flap rib construction
152 Rear spar
153 Aileron tabs
154 Port two-segment aileron construction
155 Wingtip fairing
156 De-icing air outlet louvres
157 Port navigation light
158 Outerwing panel rib construction
159 Aileron segment interconnection
160 Leading-edge corrugated inner skin panel, de-icing air ducts
161 Front spar
162 Outer wing panel joint rib
163 Port wing integral fuel tank bay
164 Retractable landing/taxiing lamp
165 Wing stringers
166 Wing skin panelling
167 Hydraulic reservoir

168 Main undercarriage pivot fixing
169 Hydraulic retraction jack
170 Port engine exhaust pipe
171 Mainwheel leg doors
172 Main undercarriage leg strut
173 Twin mainwheels, forward retracting
174 Main undercarriage front strut
175 Mainwheel doors, closed after cycling of undercarriage leg
176 Mainwheel bay
177 Engine bearer struts

178 Inboard leading-edge de-icing air ducting
179 Inner wing panel fuel tank bays
180 Wing attachment fuselage main frames
181 Port engine cowling panels
182 Fireproof bulkhead
183 Main engine mounting ring frame
184 Forward engine mounting struts
185 Cabin air system cold air and pressurising supply
186 Oil cooler
187 Engine annular air intake
188 Propeller spinner
189 Oil cooler and air system
190 Intake lip hot air de-icing

# Beech (Raytheon) C-12

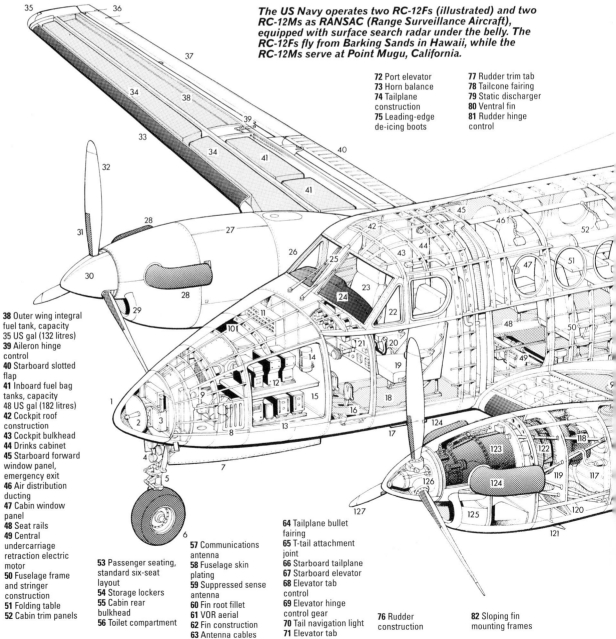

**Super King Air 200**

**Cutaway key**
1 Nosecone
2 Weather radar
3 Radar transmitter
4 Landing and taxiing lamps
5 Nose undercarriage leg strut
6 Nosewheel
7 Nosewheel doors
8 Air louvres
9 Air conditioning plant
10 Nose compartment construction
11 Electrical equipment bay
12 Radio and electronics bay
13 Access door
14 Brake hydraulic reservoir
15 Front pressure bulkhead
16 Rudder pedals
17 Ventral aerials
18 Cockpit floor level
19 Pilot's seat
20 Control column handwheel
21 Instrument panel
22 Opening side window panel
23 Co-pilot's seat
24 Instrument panel shroud
25 Windscreen wipers
26 Electrically heated windscreen panels
27 Starboard engine nacelle cowlings
28 Exhaust stubs
29 Engine intake
30 Propeller spinner
31 Blade root de-icing boots
32 Three-bladed variable-pitch reversible propeller
33 Leading-edge de-icing boots
34 Leading-edge fuel bag tanks, capacity 53 US gal (200 litres)
35 Starboard navigation lights
36 Static discharge wicks
37 Starboard aileron

38 Outer wing integral fuel tank, capacity 35 US gal (132 litres)
39 Aileron hinge control
40 Starboard slotted flap
41 Inboard fuel bag tanks, capacity 48 US gal (182 litres)
42 Cockpit roof construction
43 Cockpit bulkhead
44 Drinks cabinet
45 Starboard forward window panel, emergency exit
46 Air distribution ducting
47 Cabin window panel
48 Seat rails
49 Central undercarriage retraction electric motor
50 Fuselage frame and stringer construction
51 Folding table
52 Cabin trim panels

53 Passenger seating, standard six-seat layout
54 Storage lockers
55 Cabin rear bulkhead
56 Toilet compartment

57 Communications antenna
58 Fuselage skin plating
59 Suppressed sense antenna
60 Fin root fillet
61 VOR aerial
62 Fin construction
63 Antenna cables

64 Tailplane bullet fairing
65 T-tail attachment joint
66 Starboard tailplane
67 Starboard elevator
68 Elevator tab control
69 Elevator hinge control gear
70 Tail navigation light
71 Elevator tab

72 Port elevator
73 Horn balance
74 Tailplane construction
75 Leading-edge de-icing boots

77 Rudder trim tab
78 Tailcone fairing
79 Static discharger
80 Ventral fin
81 Rudder hinge control

76 Rudder construction

82 Sloping fin mounting frames

*The US Navy operates two RC-12Fs (illustrated) and two RC-12Ms as RANSAC (Range Surveillance Aircraft), equipped with surface search radar under the belly. The RC-12Fs fly from Barking Sands in Hawaii, while the RC-12Ms serve at Point Mugu, California.*

*Civilian-model King Air 200s serve in small numbers with a wide variety of nations, mostly employed as light transport/utility types, although a few undertake maritime patrol or training duties. No. 42 Squadron, RNZAF, at Whenuapai flies three leased aircraft on multi-engine training, general transport and VIP duties formerly undertaken by Andovers and Cessna 421s.*

## SPECIFICATION

### King Air B200

**Dimensions**

**Length:** 43 ft 10 in (13.36 m)
**Height:** 14 ft 10 in (4.52 m)
**Wingspan:** 54 ft 6 in (16.61 m)
**Tailplane span:** 18 ft 5 in (5.61 m)
**Wing area:** 303 sq ft (28.15 m²)
**Wheel track:** 17 ft 2 in (5.23 m)
**Wheelbase:** 14 ft 11½ in (4.56 m)
**Passenger cabin volume:** 31,285 cu ft (885.90 m³)

**Powerplant**

Two Pratt & Whitney Canada PT6A-42 turboprops, each rated at 850 shp (634 kW)

**Weights**

**Empty:** 8,192 lb (3716 kg)
**Maximum take-off:** 12,500 lb (5670 kg)
**Maximum ramp weight:** 12,590 lb (5710 kg)

**Fuel and load**

**Fuel capacity:** 544 US gal (453 Imp gal; 2059 litres)
**Maximum fuel load:** 3,645 lb (1653 kg)
**Baggage load:** 550 lb (249 kg)

**Performance**

**Maximum level speed:** 336 mph (541 km/h)
**Service ceiling:** 35,000 ft (10670 m)
**Take-off run:** 1,860 ft (567 m)
**Maximum range:** 2,139 miles (3442 km)

**Accommodation**

Flight deck crew of two, plus up to seven passengers in the cabin

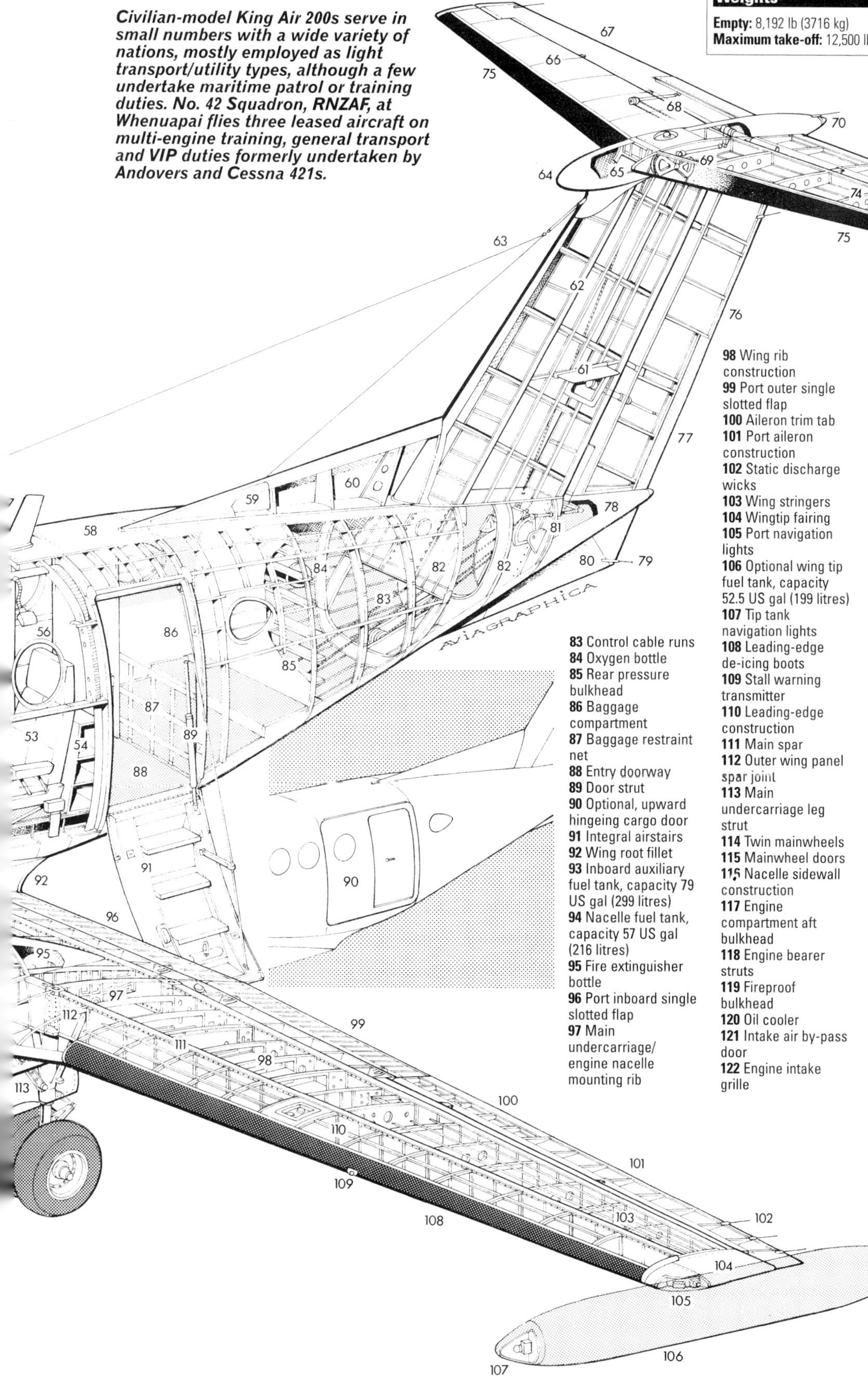

*USAF purchases of the King Air 200 reached 82 aircraft. Forty were C-12Fs, based on the B200C model, and used for general transport duties, although several were reassigned to the US Army in 1995 as C-12F-3s. This example carries the 'ZZ' tailcode of the 18th Wing at Kadena AFB, Okinawa*

98 Wing rib construction
99 Port outer single slotted flap
100 Aileron trim tab
101 Port aileron construction
102 Static discharge wicks
103 Wing stringers
104 Wingtip fairing
105 Port navigation lights
106 Optional wing tip fuel tank, capacity 52.5 US gal (199 litres)
107 Tip tank navigation lights
108 Leading-edge de-icing boots
109 Stall warning transmitter
110 Leading-edge construction
111 Main spar
112 Outer wing panel spar joint
113 Main undercarriage leg strut
114 Twin mainwheels
115 Mainwheel doors
116 Nacelle sidewall construction
117 Engine compartment aft bulkhead
118 Engine bearer struts
119 Fireproof bulkhead
120 Oil cooler
121 Intake air by-pass door
122 Engine intake grille

83 Control cable runs
84 Oxygen bottle
85 Rear pressure bulkhead
86 Baggage compartment
87 Baggage restraint net
88 Entry doorway
89 Door strut
90 Optional, upward hingeing cargo door
91 Integral airstairs
92 Wing root fillet
93 Inboard auxiliary fuel tank, capacity 79 US gal (299 litres)
94 Nacelle fuel tank, capacity 57 US gal (216 litres)
95 Fire extinguisher bottle
96 Port inboard single slotted flap
97 Main undercarriage/engine nacelle mounting rib

123 Pratt & Whitney Canada PT6A-41 turboprop engine
124 Engine exhaust stubs
125 Intake ducting
126 Propeller hub pitch change mechanism
127 Hartzell three-bladed propeller

# Boeing KC-135 Stratotanker

*Playing a major part in the USAF refuelling effort are the 'Weekend Warriors' of the Air Force Reserve and the Air National Guard. AFRes has three squadrons of KC-135Rs and one of Es, while the ANG has 10 KC-135E (with an example from the 190th ARW at Forbes Field, Kansas illustrated) and 13 R units.*

## KC-135R Stratotanker

**Cutaway key**
1 Radome
2 Weather radar scanner
3 ILS glideslope antenna
4 Front pressure bulkhead
5 Underfloor equipment bay
6 Ventral access hatch
7 Rudder pedals
8 Instrument panel
9 Windscreen wipers
10 Instrument panel shroud
11 Windscreen panels
12 Overhead systems switch panel
13 Ditching handholds
14 Cockpit eyebrow windows
15 Co-pilot's seat
16 Pilot's seat
17 Pitot head
18 Nosewheel bay
19 Escape spoiler
20 Entry hatch
21 Twin nosewheels, forward-retracting
22 Boarding ladder
23 Entry/escape hatch
24 Instructor's seat
25 Navigator's station
26 Flight-refuelling receptacle
27 Star tracking windows, celestial navigation system
28 TACAN antenna
29 Cockpit doorway
30 Avionics equipment rack
31 Navigator's stool
32 Supernumerary crew seat

33 Electrical equipment rack
34 Flight deck air supply duct
35 Battery stowage
36 Wash basin
37 Crew toilet
38 Director lighting strip for receiving aircraft, port and starboard
39 Forward underfloor fuel cells (4), capacity 4,830 Imp gal/5,800 US gal (21955 litres)
40 Cargo door latches
41 Door aperture (9 ft 6 in x 6 ft 6 in/2.9 m x 1.98 m)
42 Cargo deck floor structure
43 Tie-down fittings
44 Cargo door hydraulic jacks and hinges
45 Upward-opening cargo door
46 VHF/UHF antenna
47 Door-mounted ADF antennas
48 Conditioned air risers to overhead distribution duct
49 Wing inspection light
50 Front spar attachment fuselage main frame
51 Centre-section fuel tanks (6), capacity 6,084 Imp gal/7,306 US gal (27656 litres)
52 Overwing escape hatches, port and starboard

53 Wing centre-section carry-through structure
54 Floor beam structure
55 Fuselage frame and stringer structure
56 Cabin overhead air distribution duct
57 Inboard integral wing tank, capacity 1,894 Imp gal/2,275 US gal (8612 litres)
58 Tank filler
59 No. 3, starboard inner engine nacelle
60 Nacelle pylon
61 Wing centre main integral tank, capacity 1,717 Imp gal/2,062 US gal (7805 litres)
62 Fuel venting channels
63 Leading-edge flap hydraulic jacks

64 Krüger-type leading-edge flap
65 No. 4, starboard outer engine nacelle
66 Outboard nacelle pylon
67 Outboard reserve integral fuel tank, capacity 361 Imp gal/ 434 US gal (1643 litres)
68 Optional drogue-type refuelling pod, carried by French C-135FR
69 Starboard navigation light
70 Outboard, low-speed aileron

71 Aileron internal balance panels
72 Spoiler interconnection linkage
73 Aileron hinge control linkage

74 Aileron tab
75 Outboard double-slotted Fowler-type flap segment, extended

79 Flap screw jacks
80 Aileron geared tab
81 Inboard, high-speed, aileron
82 Gust damper

83 Aileron actuating linkage
84 Inboard spoiler panels, open
85 Inboard double-slotted Fowler-type flap segment, extended
86 Anti-collision beacon
87 Pressure floor above wheel bay
88 Rear spar attachment fuselage main frame

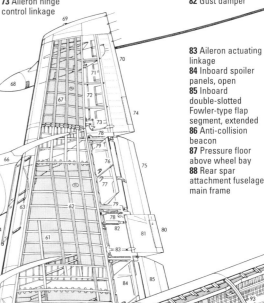

76 Outboard spoiler panels, open
77 Spoiler hydraulic jacks
78 Flap guide rails

## SPECIFICATION

### KC-135A Stratotanker

#### Dimensions

**Length:** 136 ft 3 in (41.53 m)
**Height:** 41 ft 8 in (12.70 m)
**Wing span:** 130 ft 10 in (39.88 m)
**Aspect ratio:** 7.04
**Wing area:** 2,433.00 sq ft (226.03 m²)
**Tailplane span:** 40 ft 3 in (12.27 m)
**Wheel base:** 46 ft 7 in (14.20 m)

#### Powerplant

Four Pratt & Whitney J57-P-59W turbojets, each rated at 13,750 lb st (61.16 kN)

#### Weights

**Operating empty:** 106,306 lb (48220 kg)
**Maximum take-off:** 316,000 lb (143335 kg)

#### Fuel and load

**Internal fuel:** 189,702 lb (86047 kg)
**Maximum payload:** 83,000 lb (37650 kg)

#### Performance

**Maximum level speed at high altitude:** 530 kt (610 mph; 982 km/h)
**Cruising speed at 35,000 ft (10670 m):** 462 kt (532 mph; 856 km/h)
**Operational radius to offload 120,000 lb (54432 kg) of fuel:** 1000 nm (1,151 miles; 1854 km)
**Service ceiling:** 45,000 ft (13715 m)
**Typical take-off run:** 10,700 ft (3261 m) increasing to 14,000 ft (4267 m) under 'hot-and-high' conditions at maximum take-off weight
**Maximum rate of climb at sea level:** 1,290 ft (393 m) per minute

*During Desert Shield, KC-135As refuelled aircraft which were deploying from the USA and Europe to the Persian Gulf, before switching to the delivery of personnel and equipment – a task in which they assisted MAC airlifters. Approximately 200 KC-135s were directly assigned to the theatre, being operated by provisional air refuelling wings, while several hundred other tankers regularly operated between the USA (as seen above) and the Gulf region. Some 15,000 refuelling sorties were flown during the conflict itself, with almost 46,000 aircraft from the USAF, USN, USMC and the Coalition receiving fuel. Though the KC-135s were officially restricted to designated refuelling areas above northern Saudi Arabia, the aircraft sometimes ventured across the Iraqi border to provide fuel for aircraft with critical fuel states.*

Mike Badrocke /97

**109** Trimming tailplane seal
**110** Fin attachment joints
**111** Artificial feel system pressure head
**112** Fin rib structure
**113** VOR antenna
**114** Starboard trimming tailplane
**115** Starboard elevator
**116** Fin leading-edge ribs
**117** Fintip antenna fairing
**118** HF antenna
**119** Starboard refuelling drogue
**120** HF tuner
**121** Refuelling floodlight
**122** Rudder fixed trailing-edge segment
**123** Rudder rib structure
**124** Internal balance panels
**125** Rudder hydraulic actuator
**126** Rudder tab
**127** Trimming tailplane hinge mounting
**128** Tailcone structure
**129** Crash locator beacon
**130** Tail navigation and strobe lights
**131** Refuelling boom, stowed position
**132** Elevator tab
**133** Port elevator structure
**134** Elevator internal balance panels
**135** Port tailplane rib structure
**136** Refuelling boom lifting cable
**137** Alternative central refuelling drogue
**138** Refuelling adaptor
**139** Refuelling boom, fully extended
**140** Ruddervators
**141** Refuelling boom, lowered position
**142** Boom operator's window cover, retracted
**143** Viewing window
**144** Refuelling control panel
**145** Boom operator's pallet
**146** Instructor's pallet
**147** Fuselage lower lobe skin stiffeners

**148** Optional Auxiliary Power Unit (APU)
**149** APU exhaust ducts
**150** Fuselage lower lobe frame and stringer structure
**151** Wingroot trailing-edge fillet
**152** Fillet flap
**153** Flap operating screw jack
**154** Mainwheel doors
**155** Mainwheel leg breaker strut
**156** Hydraulic retraction jack
**157** Wingroot integral fuel tank bay, capacity 1,895 Imp gal/2,275 US gal (8615 litres)
**158** Main undercarriage leg pivot mounting
**159** Shock absorber leg strut
**160** Four-wheel main undercarriage bogie
**161** Port inboard spoiler panels
**162** Inboard double-slotted flap segment
**163** Inboard, high-speed, aileron
**164** Aileron tab
**165** Outboard spoiler panels
**166** Flap rib structure
**167** Outboard double-slotted flap segment
**168** Port aileron hinge control
**169** Aileron tab
**170** Port outboard, low-speed aileron
**171** Static dischargers
**172** Fixed trailing-edge segment rib structure
**173** Port navigation light
**174** Fuel system vent tank
**175** Ventral NACA-type venting intake
**176** Port optional drogue-type refuelling pod
**177** Refuelling pod pylon
**178** Leading-edge skin panelling
**179** Outer-wing panel rib structure
**180** Wing lower skin/stringer panel with access manholes

**181** Leading-edge de-icing air double skin ducting
**182** Outer wing panel joint rib
**183** Engine pylon mounting rib
**184** Port outboard nacelle pylon
**185** Hinged cowling panels, engine access
**186** Engine accessory equipment gearbox
**187** No. 1, port outer engine nacelle
**188** Port leading-edge Krüger-type flaps
**189** Port wing integral fuel tankage
**190** Port wing panel rib structure
**191** Inboard nacelle mounting rib
**192** Nacelle drag strut
**193** Nacelle pylon structure
**194** Core engine, hot-stream exhaust
**195** Fan air, cold-stream exhaust
**196** Engine turbine section
**197** CFM international F108-CF-100 (CFM56-2A2) turbofan engine
**198** Engine fan casing
**199** Long-range oil tank
**200** De-icing air exhaust
**201** Intake lip bleed air de-icing
**202** Engine bleed air ducting
**203** Leading-edge rib structure
**204** Pressure refuelling connection, port and starboard
**205** Main undercarriage mounting rib
**206** Air-conditioning system heat exchanger
**207** Ventral air-conditioning pack
**208** Heat exchanger ram air intake
**209** Landing/taxiing lights

**89** Part main undercarriage wheel bay
**90** Wheel bay bulkhead
**91** Rear underfloor fuel cells (5), capacity 5,311 Imp gal/6,378 US gal (24143 litres)
**92** Single cabin window panel
**93** Centre-facing troop seating, E30-seats
**94** Detachable overhead cargo rail
**95** Cargo sling/winch
**96** Rear cabin cargo-loading deck
**97** Rear escape hatch, starboard only
**98** Troop seating, stowed position
**99** Rear fuselage skin stiffeners
**100** Air supply duct from APU
**101** Access hatch to boom operator's position, port and starboard
**102** Cabin wall insulating blankets
**103** Rear pressure bulkhead
**104** Finroot fillet
**105** Rear upper deck fuel cell, capacity 1,810 Imp gal/2,175 US gal (8230 litres)
**106** Fin spar attachment bulkhead
**107** Trimming tailplane screw jack
**108** Tailplane centre section carry-through

# Lockheed C-141 Starlifter

*Like the USAF's other long-range transport assets, the StarLifter has been expected to perform its appointed roles in all conditions. This Compass Grey C-141B was photographed from a tanker over inhospitable territory during a training mission.*

## C-141B StarLifter

**Cutaway key**
1 Radome
2 Weather radar scanner
3 ILS glideslope aerial
4 Radar tracking mechanism
5 Front pressure bulkhead
6 Windscreen panels
7 Instrument panel shroud
8 Rudder pedals
9 Crew oxygen reservoir
10 Twin nosewheels
11 Nose undercarriage leg strut
12 Flight deck floor level
13 Control column
14 Pilot's seat
15 Direct vision, opening, side window panel
16 Centre console
17 Co-pilot's seat
18 Overhead switch panel
19 Flight engineer's station
20 Navigator's station
21 Folding jump-seat stowage
22 Underfloor radio and electronics racks
23 Nosewheel leg door
24 Crew galley
25 Relief crew rest area seating

26 Cockpit doorway
27 Escape ladder
28 Rest bunks
29 Cockpit roof escape hatch
30 Aerial refuelling director lights
31 Flight refuelling receptacle
32 IFF aerial
33 Fuel delivery piping
34 Troop transport aft facing seating
35 Crew entry door, open
36 Fire extinguisher bottles
37 Wing leading-edge inspection light
38 Cargo loading floor
39 Six-abreast troop seating
40 Cargo hold forward escape hatch
41 Escape ladder stowage
42 UHF (2) aerial
43 Refuelling line fairing
44 Forward fuselage stretch plug section
45 Fuselage skin panelling
46 Cargo hold insulating wall panels
47 Crew walkway

48 Fuselage plug section splice joint
49 Floor beam construction
50 Starboard emergency exit
51 Fuselage frame and stringer construction
52 Cargo floor roller conveyors
53 Port emergency exit
54 463L cargo pallets (13)
55 Wing spar/fuselage main frame
56 Air system vents
57 Ram air intake
58 Wing root leading-edge fairing
59 UHF (1) aerial
60 Air conditioning plant
61 Wing centre-section carry through structure
62 Fuel transfer system piping
63 Starboard wing integral fuel tank bays; total fuel system capacity 23,592 US gal (89305 litres)

64 Engine bleed air ducting
65 Starboard engine nacelles
66 Nacelle pylons
67 Leading edge de-icing air ducts

80 Flap screw jacks
81 VHF (2) aerial
82 Central flap motor
83 Aileron and spoiler drive mechanism

87 Flush ADF sense aerials
88 Starboard side ditching hatch
89 Aft fuselage stretch plug section
90 Air system ducting
91 Recirculation air fan
92 Escape ladder stowage
93 Rear escape hatch
94 Aft fuselage upper decking
95 Cargo ramp pressure door, upward opening

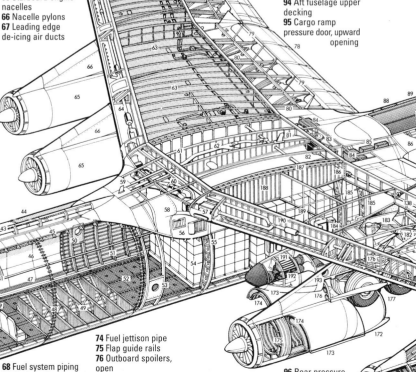

68 Fuel system piping
69 Starboard navigation light
70 Wing tip fairing
71 Static dischargers
72 Starboard aileron
73 Aileron tab

74 Fuel jettison pipe
75 Flap guide rails
76 Outboard spoilers, open
77 Starboard outer flap, down position
78 Starboard inboard flap, down position
79 Inboard spoilers, open

84 Life raft stowage
85 Emergency equipment packs
86 Wing root trailing edge fillet

96 Rear pressure bulkhead
97 Cabin pressurisation outflow valves

## SPECIFICATION

### C-141A StarLifter

**Dimensions**

**Length:** 145 ft (44.2 m)
**Height:** 39 ft 4 in (11.99 m)
**Wingspan:** 160 ft (48.77 m)
**Wing area:** 3,228.1 sq ft (299.901 m²)

**Powerplant**

Four Pratt & Whitney TF33-P-7A turbofans rated at 21,000 lb st (93.4 kN)

**Weights**

**Empty:** 136,900 lb (62097 kg)
**Maximum take-off:** 323,100 lb (146556 kg)

**Performance**

**Maximum speed at 24,000 ft (7440 m):** 565 mph (909 km/h)
**Cruising speed:** 478 mph (769 km/h)
**Initial rate of climb:** 7,925 ft (2416 m) per minute
**Service ceiling:** 51,700 ft (15760 m)
**Range with maximum payload:** 4,155 miles (6685 km)
**Ferry range:** 6,575 miles (10580 km)

**Load**

Five crew and either 138 troops in aft-facing seats, 124 paratroops on side-facing bucket seats, 80 litters and 23 attendants, or a maximum payload of 62,717 lb (28448 kg) of military cargo

### C-141B StarLifter

as for C-141A, except:

**Dimensions**

**Length:** 168 ft 3½ in (51.29 m)

**Weights**

**Empty:** 153,350 lb (69558 kg)

**Performance**

**Initial rate of climb:** 2,990 ft/min (911 m/min)
**Range with maximum payload:** 3,200 miles (5150 km)
**Maximum unrefuelled range without payload:** 6,385 miles (10275-km)

**Load**

Max. payload of 89,152 lb (40439 kg)

*Above: The third StarLifter off the production line was assigned a permament test role throughout its USAF career. Known as an NC-141A, it was latterly employed as an advanced radar testbed, allowing nose-mounted radar sets to be tested in an 'ECM environment'. The aircraft was retired to AMARC in 1997.*

*The SOLL II Special Operations C-141Bs are likely to be among the last StarLifters to be replaced by C-17As when the type is finally retired in 2003.*

*Now in the twilight of its career, the StarLifter is likely to have celebrated 40 years service by the time it is retired.*

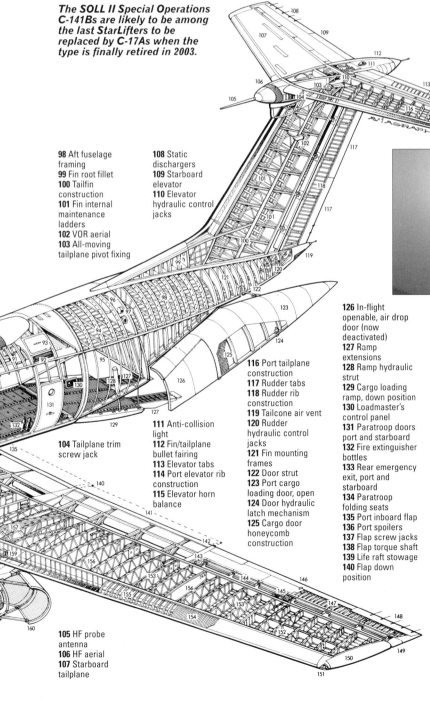

**98** Aft fuselage framing
**99** Fin root fillet
**100** Tailfin construction
**101** Fin internal maintenance ladders
**102** VOR aerial
**103** All-moving tailplane pivot fixing
**104** Tailplane trim screw jack
**105** HF probe antenna
**106** HF aerial
**107** Starboard tailplane
**108** Static dischargers
**109** Starboard elevator
**110** Elevator hydraulic control jacks
**111** Anti-collision light
**112** Fin/tailplane bullet fairing
**113** Elevator tabs
**114** Port elevator rib construction
**115** Elevator horn balance
**116** Port tailplane construction
**117** Rudder tabs
**118** Rudder rib construction
**119** Tailcone air vent
**120** Rudder
**121** Fin mounting frames
**122** Door strut
**123** Port cargo loading door, open
**124** Door hydraulic latch mechanism
**125** Cargo door honeycomb construction
**126** In-flight openable, air drop door (now deactivated)
**127** Ramp extensions
**128** Ramp hydraulic strut
**129** Cargo loading ramp, down position
**130** Loadmaster's control panel
**131** Paratroop doors port and starboard
**132** Fire extinguisher bottles
**133** Rear emergency exit, port and starboard
**134** Paratroop folding seats
**135** Port inboard flap
**136** Port spoilers
**137** Flap screw jacks
**138** Flap torque shaft
**139** Life raft stowage
**140** Flap down position
**141** Port outboard flap
**142** Fuel jettison pipe
**143** Spoiler/aileron interconnection mechanism
**144** Aileron balance weights
**145** Aileron hydraulic control jacks
**146** Port aileron tab
**147** Aileron rib construction
**148** Static dischargers
**149** Aileron horn balance
**150** Wingtip fairing
**151** Port navigation light
**152** Outer wing surge box
**153** Wing lattice rib construction
**154** Corrugated leading-edge inner skin
**155** Leading-edge nose ribs
**156** Port wing integral fuel tank bays
**157** Engine pylon mounting rib
**158** Pylon attachment joint
**159** Engine fire extinguisher bottles
**160** Thrust reverser bucket doors, open
**161** Hot stream exhaust nozzle
**162** Fan air exhaust duct
**163** Pratt & Whitney TF33-P-7 turbofan engine
**164** Nacelle firewall
**165** Engine accessory equipment bay
**166** Front fan casing
**167** Suction relief doors
**168** Inlet guide vanes
**169** Intake centre-body fairing
**170** Engine pylon construction
**171** Cable and pipe ducting
**172** Inboard engine nacelle
**173** Side cowling panels, open
**174** Cowling integral by-pass ducting
**175** Bifurcated fan air duct
**176** Landing/taxiing lamps
**177** Four-wheel main undercarriage bogie
**178** Main undercarriage leg pivot fitting
**179** Mainwheel door
**180** Position of refuelling adaptor on starboard side
**181** Undercarriage side-body fairing construction
**182** Main undercarriage retraction strut
**183** Upper leg door
**184** Hydraulic equipment service centre
**185** Wing/fuselage main frames
**186** Spar attachment joint
**187** Wing panel/centre section bolted joint
**188** Wing root rib
**189** Inboard fuel tank bays
**190** Front spar
**191** APU intake grille
**192** Auxiliary power unit (APU)
**193** APU exhaust

# Lockheed C-130 Hercules

With tensions with China at a high state, Taiwan built up its armed forces during the 1990s. The air force's tactical transport requirements are met by 24 C-130H Hercules aircraft, based at Pingtung North.

## C-130H Hercules
**Cutaway key**
1 Radome
2 Sperry AN/APN-59 radar
3 External interphone connection
4 Nose gear forward door
5 Twin nosewheels
6 Accumulators (port and starboard)
7 Nose landing-gear shock strut
8 External electrical power receptacles
9 Battery compartment
10 Pilot's side console
11 Portable oxygen cylinder
12 Pilot's seat
13 Control column
14 Main instrument console
15 Windshields
16 Co-pilot's seat
17 Systems engineer's seat
18 Navigator's seat
19 Navigator's desk
20 Crew bunks (upper and lower)
21 Forward emergency escape hatch
22 Control runs in bulkhead
23 Fire-extinguisher
24 Crew closet
25 Galley
26 Access steps to flight deck
27 Crew entry well
28 Crew entry door
29 Lower longeron
30 Window ports
31 Cargo floor panels
32 Cargo floor support frames
33 Troop seats (stowed)
34 Overhead emergency equipment stowage

35 Fuselage frames
36 Booster hydraulic system reservoir and accumulator
37 Control runs
38 Starboard main landing-gear access (sealed)
39 Wingroot frame strengthener
40 Fuselage/centre-section join
41 Inboard leading-edge structure
42 Fuel valve inspection access
43 Nacelle panels
44 Starboard auxiliary tanks
45 Tank pylon
46 Fuel filler points
47 Fuel tanks
48 Dry bay
49 Allison T56-A-15 turboprop
50 Reduction gear
51 Four-bladed reversible-pitch Hamilton Standard propeller
52 Engine starter
53 Engine oil tank
54 Limit of wing walkway
55 Starboard navigation lights

56 Starboard aileron
57 Aileron tab
58 Outer wing flap
59 Centre-section flap
60 Centre-section wing box beam structure
61 Flap drive control
62 Internal corrugation
63 Aileron control linkage
64 Port main landing-gear bay

65 Hydraulic actuator motor
66 Fire-extinguisher bottles
67 Main landing gear shock struts
68 Retraction mechanism
69 Air turbine motor (driven by GTC, item 71, to supply electric and hydraulic power)

70 Utility hydraulic system reservoir and accumulator
71 Gas turbine compressor (air supply for engine-starting, ground conditioning and to drive ATM, item 69)
72 Main gear fairing
73 Landing light in outer-door forward section
74 Twin tandem mainwheels
75 Main landing-gear outer door

76 Inner-door section
77 Air deflector door
78 Tank pylon
79 Port auxiliary tank
80 Spinner
81 Chin intake
82 Nacelle structure
83 Engine bearer
84 Exhaust outlet
85 Outboard leading-edge structure
86 Port navigation lights
87 Aileron control bell crank
88 Aileron structure
89 Aileron tab
90 Outer wing box beam structure
91 Flap structure
92 Idler bell crank

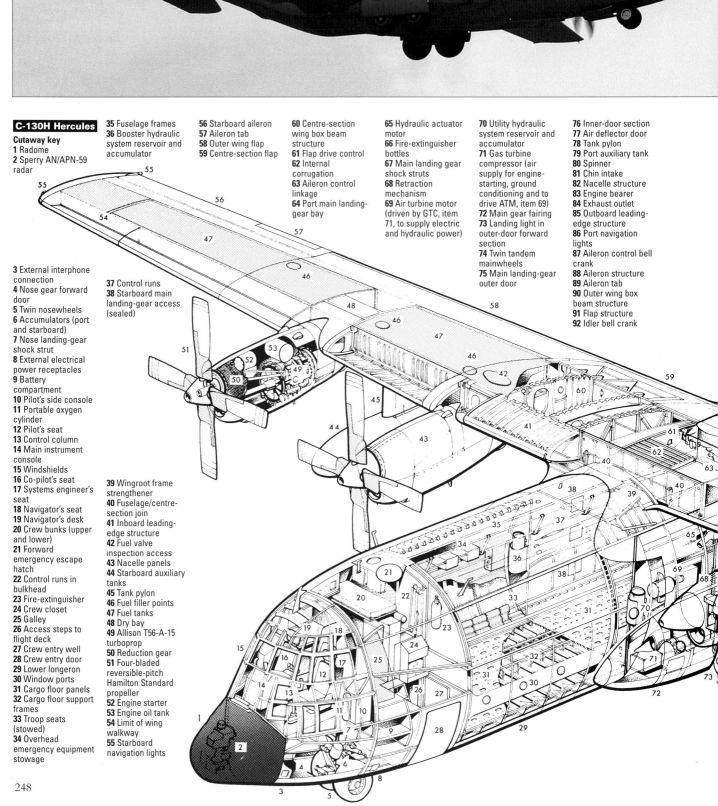

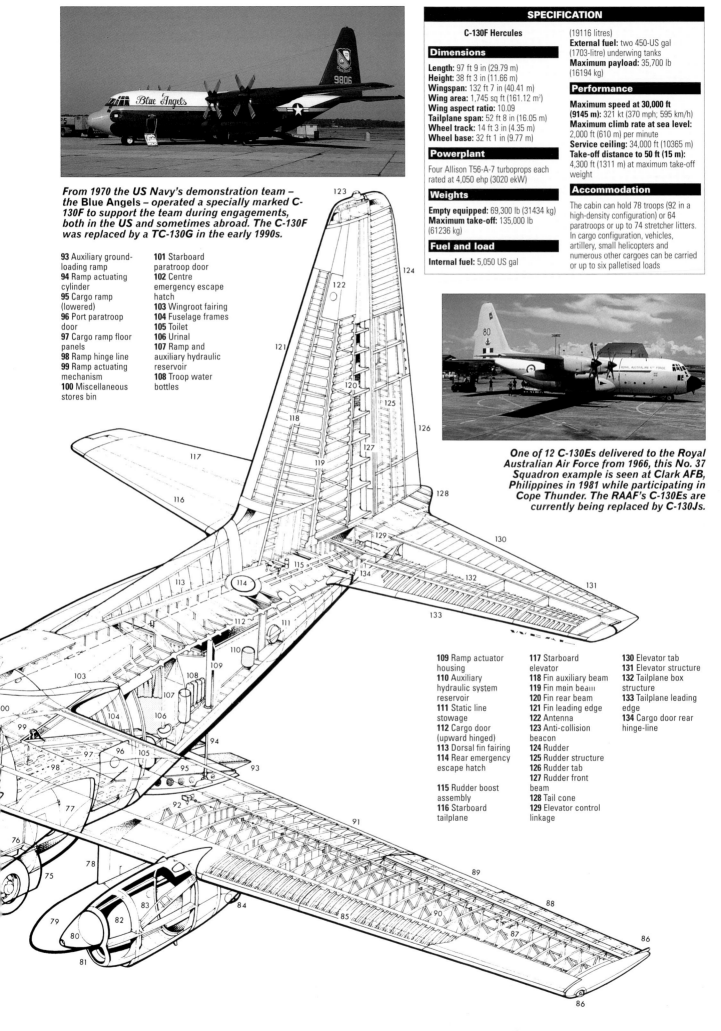

## SPECIFICATION

### C-130F Hercules

#### Dimensions

**Length:** 97 ft 9 in (29.79 m)
**Height:** 38 ft 3 in (11.66 m)
**Wingspan:** 132 ft 7 in (40.41 m)
**Wing area:** 1,745 sq ft (161.12 m²)
**Wing aspect ratio:** 10.09
**Tailplane span:** 52 ft 8 in (16.05 m)
**Wheel track:** 14 ft 3 in (4.35 m)
**Wheel base:** 32 ft 1 in (9.77 m)

#### Powerplant

Four Allison T56-A-7 turboprops each rated at 4,050 ehp (3020 ekW)

#### Weights

**Empty equipped:** 69,300 lb (31434 kg)
**Maximum take-off:** 135,000 lb (61236 kg)

#### Fuel and load

**Internal fuel:** 5,050 US gal

(19116 litres)
**External fuel:** two 450-US gal (1703-litre) underwing tanks
**Maximum payload:** 35,700 lb (16194 kg)

#### Performance

**Maximum speed at 30,000 ft (9145 m):** 321 kt (370 mph; 595 km/h)
**Maximum climb rate at sea level:** 2,000 ft (610 m) per minute
**Service ceiling:** 34,000 ft (10365 m)
**Take-off distance to 50 ft (15 m):** 4,300 ft (1311 m) at maximum take-off weight

#### Accommodation

The cabin can hold 78 troops (92 in a high-density configuration) or 64 paratroops or up to 74 stretcher litters. In cargo configuration, vehicles, artillery, small helicopters and numerous other cargoes can be carried or up to six palletised loads

*From 1970 the US Navy's demonstration team – the Blue Angels – operated a specially marked C-130F to support the team during engagements, both in the US and sometimes abroad. The C-130F was replaced by a TC-130G in the early 1990s.*

93 Auxiliary ground-loading ramp
94 Ramp actuating cylinder
95 Cargo ramp (lowered)
96 Port paratroop door
97 Cargo ramp floor panels
98 Ramp hinge line
99 Ramp actuating mechanism
100 Miscellaneous stores bin
101 Starboard paratroop door
102 Centre emergency escape hatch
103 Wingroot fairing
104 Fuselage frames
105 Toilet
106 Urinal
107 Ramp and auxiliary hydraulic reservoir
108 Troop water bottles

*One of 12 C-130Es delivered to the Royal Australian Air Force from 1966, this No. 37 Squadron example is seen at Clark AFB, Philippines in 1981 while participating in Cope Thunder. The RAAF's C-130Es are currently being replaced by C-130Js.*

109 Ramp actuator housing
110 Auxiliary hydraulic system reservoir
111 Static line stowage
112 Cargo door (upward hinged)
113 Dorsal fin fairing
114 Rear emergency escape hatch

115 Rudder boost assembly
116 Starboard tailplane
117 Starboard elevator
118 Fin auxiliary beam
119 Fin main beam
120 Fin rear beam
121 Fin leading edge
122 Antenna
123 Anti-collision beacon
124 Rudder
125 Rudder structure
126 Rudder tab
127 Rudder front beam
128 Tail cone
129 Elevator control linkage

130 Elevator tab
131 Elevator structure
132 Tailplane box structure
133 Tailplane leading edge
134 Cargo door rear hinge-line

# McDonnell Douglas KC-10 Extender

*During the Allied Force operations over Kosovo in 1999, the USAF assigned 24 KC-10As to the Allied Force tanker fleet, split between Moron in Spain and Rhein-Main in Germany. The example shown here was operated from the latter, as part of the 60th Air Expeditionary Wing.*

## KC-10 Extender

### Cutaway key

1 Radome
2 Weather radar scanner
3 Radar mounting
4 Front pressure bulkhead
5 Radome hinge panel
6 Windscreen wipers
7 Windscreen panels
8 Instrument panel shroud
9 Control column
10 Rudder pedals
11 Underfloor radio and electronics racks
12 Flight deck floor level
13 Pilot's seat
14 Overhead systems control panel
15 Flight engineer's control panel
16 Observer's seat
17 Cockpit doorway
18 Refuelling floodlights
19 Universal air refuelling receptacle (UARSSI)
20 Toilet compartment
21 Crew baggage locker
22 Galley
23 Air conditioning ram air intake duct
24 Entry doorway
25 Air conditioning system access panels
26 Nose landing gear strut
27 Twin nosewheels
28 Nosewheel leg doors
29 Air conditioning plant
30 Passenger seating, six crew and 14 support personnel layout

31 Forward cabin roof trim panels
32 Upper formation light
33 IFF aerial
34 Overhead air conditioning ducting
35 Crew rest bunks (four)
36 Environmental curtain
37 Cargo winch
38 Cargo safety net
39 Powered cargo handling system control box
40 Low voltage formation lighting strip
41 Underfloor oxygen bottle stowage
42 Powered roller cargo handling floor
43 Underfloor water tank
44 Door hydraulic jack
45 Cargo door, 102 in x 140 in (2.59 m x 3.56 m)
46 TACAN aerial
47 VHF aerial
48 Starboard engine nacelle
49 UHF SATCOM aerial, structural provision
50 USAF 463L cargo pallet, 25 pallets in configuration shown
51 Main cabin doorway
52 Forward underfloor fuel cell group, total underfloor cell capacity 18,075 US gal (68420 litres)
53 Fuselage frame and stringer construction
54 Director lights, port and starboard
55 Wing root fillet
56 Runway light

57 Electrical system distribution equipment centre
58 Access ladder to equipment bay
59 Central slat drive unit
60 Wing centre section carry through
61 Single cabin window, port and starboard
62 Centre section fuel tank, aircraft basic fuel system, capacity 238,565lb (108211 kg)
63 Floor beam construction
64 Wing spar/fuselage main frame
65 Overwing integral fuel tank
66 De-activated centre section doors
67 Anti-collision light
68 Starboard wing integral fuel tank
69 Inboard leading edge slat
70 Engine thrust reverser cascades, open
71 Starboard nacelle pylon
72 Outboard slat drive mechanism
73 Pressure refuelling connections

74 Fuel system piping
75 Slat guide rails
76 Outboard leading edge slat segments
77 Starboard navigation light
78 Wing tip formation lights
79 Starboard wing tip strobe light
80 Static dischargers
81 Aileron balance weights
82 Aileron hydraulic jack
83 Outboard low-speed aileron
84 Fuel jettison pipe
85 Outboard spoiler segments (four), open
86 Spoiler hydraulic jacks
87 Flap hydraulic jacks
88 Flap hinge fairings
89 Outboard double slotted flap, down position
90 High-speed aileron
91 Inboard spoiler
92 Inboard double slotted flap, down position
93 Fuselage skin plating

94 UHF aerial
95 Centre fuselage construction
96 Pressure floor above wheel bay
97 Centre landing gearwheel bay
98 Cargo loading floor
99 Roller conveyors
100 Cabin wall trim panels
101 Access ladder to lower deck refuelling station
102 Drogue refuelling hose reel unit
103 Drogue housing
104 Ground emergency exit doorway
105 Rear cabin air conditioning duct
106 HF aerial
107 Centre engine pylon construction
108 Centre engine intake

109 Intake duct construction
110 Intake duct ring frames
111 Tailfin attachment joint
112 Starboard tailplane
113 Starboard elevator
114 Tailfin construction
115 J-band and I-band beacon antennas
116 VOR localiser-1 aerial
117 Fin tip fairing
118 VOR localiser 2 aerial
119 Rudder mass balance
120 Two-segment rudder
121 Rudder hydraulic jacks
122 Fin low

voltage formation lighting strip
123 Centre engine installation

124 Detachable engine cowlings
125 Bleed-air system pre-cooler
126 Engine mounting pylon

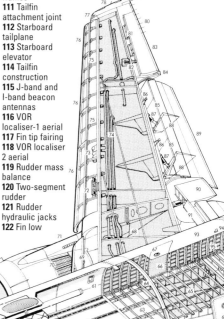

*Above: Crew members from the 2nd Air Refuelling Squadron based at McGuire AFB in New Jersey load up a KC-10A using the upward-hinging cargo door in the forward port fuselage, at NSF Diego Garcia, British Indian Ocean Territory. A total of 60 Extenders was built for the USAF, most of which now carry the all-over charcoal grey colour scheme.*

## SPECIFICATION

### KC-10A Extender

#### Dimensions

**Wingspan:** 155 ft 4 in (47.34 m)
**Wing aspect ratio:** 6.8
**Wing area:** 3,861.00 sq ft (358.69 m²)
**Length:** 181 ft 7 in (55.35 m)
**Height:** 58 ft 1 in (17.70 m)
**Tailplane span:** 71 ft 2 in (21.69 m)
**Wheel track:** 34 ft 8 in (10.57 m)
**Wheel base:** 72 ft 5 in (22.07 m)

#### Powerplant

Three General Electric CF6-50C2 turbofans each rated at 52,500 lb st (233.53 kN)

#### Weights

**Operating empty as a tanker:** 240,065 lb (108891 kg)
**Operating empty as a cargo transport:** 244,630 lb (110962 kg)
**Maximum take-off:** 590,000 lb (267620 kg)

#### Fuel and load

**Basic aircraft fuel system:** 238,236 lb (108062 kg)

**Fuselage bladder fuel cells:** 117,829 lb (53446 kg)
**Total internal fuel:** 356,065 lb (161508 kg)
**Maximum cargo payload:** 169,409 lb (76843 kg)

#### Performance

**Never exceed speed:** Mach 0.95
**Maximum level speed 'clean' at 25,000 ft (7620 m):** 610 mph (982 km/h)
**Maximum cruising speed at 30,000 ft (9145 m):** 564 mph (908 km/h)
**Maximum rate of climb at sea level:** 2,900 ft (884 m) per minute
**Service ceiling:** 33,400 ft (10180 m)
**Nominal range with 100,000 lb (45400 kg) payload:** 6,905 miles (11112 km)
**Maximum range with maximum cargo:** 4,370 miles (7032 km)
**Ferry range:** 11,500 miles (18507 km)
**Take-off balanced field length at maximum take-off weight:** 10,400 ft (3170 m)
**Landing balanced field length at maximum landing weight:** 6,130 ft (1868 m)

---

127 Hot stream exhaust nozzle
128 Fan air exhaust duct
129 Detachable tailcone fairing
130 Centre engine access ladder
131 Inboard elevator section hinged for engine removal
132 Elevator hydraulic jacks
133 Two-segment elevator

134 Flight-refuelling drogue, deployed
135 Port tailplane construction
136 Leading edge nose ribs
137 Refuelling boom, lowered
138 Boom elevator
139 Twin rudders
140 Telescopic refuelling duct
141 Recoil mechanism
142 Accelerometer housing

143 Boom hoist cable and up-lock
144 Auxiliary power unit (APU)
145 Tailplane pivot fixing

150 Fuel feed pipe
151 De-activated doorway
152 Air refuelling officer's (ARO's) control panel
153 Direct vision window

160 Side view mirrors
161 Wing floodlights
162 Mirror fairing
163 Wing root trailing edge fillet
164 Low voltage formation lighting strip
165 Rear underfloor fuel cells
166 Main landing gear bay
167 Centre landing gear hydraulic jack
168 Twin centre wheels
169 Main landing gear leg strut
170 Leg strut pivot fixing
171 Inboard spoiler
172 Port inboard double slotted flap
173 High-speed aileron
174 Outboard double slotted flap

181 Port wing tip formation lights
182 Port navigation light
183 Lower wing skin access panels
184 Aileron hydraulic jack housing
185 Wing ribconstruction
186 Port wing integral fuel tank
187 Front spar
188 Port leading edge slat segments
189 Pressure refuelling connections
190 Leading edge de-icing telescopic air duct
191 Four wheel main landing gear bogie
192 Port engine installation
193 Thrust reverser cascade, closed
194 General Electric CF6-50C2 turbofan engine
195 Fan easing mounted accessory gearbox
196 Engine air intake
197 Nacelle strakes
198 Nacelle pylon construction
199 Pylon attachment joint
200 Wing skin panelling
201 Wing stringers
202 Inboard wing ribs
203 Inboard leading edge slat rib construction
204 Bleed air ducting
205 Slat down position

146 Tailplane centre section carry-through
147 Rear pressure bulkhead
148 Tailplane trim control screwjack
149 Refuelling boom gimballed joints

154 Student's seat
155 ARO's seat
156 Instructor/ observer's seat
157 Direct vision window hatch cover, open
158 Rear vision periscope
159 Periscope mirror

175 Flap down position
176 Port outboard spoilers
177 Rearspar
178 Fuel jettison pipe
179 Port aileron construction
180 Wing tip strobe light

Mike Badrocke

# Transall C-160

*In 1970, the South African Air Force received the first of nine French-built Transalls, the Germans being politically unwilling to deal with the South African government. These were designated C.160Zs, and ordered largely because the US had embargoed further deliveries of Lockheed C-130 Hercules aircraft, which the SAAF had been using up until that time. However, the C.160 proved remarkably successful for the SAAF, and several were returned to service after being withdrawn and stored in 1993.*

## C.160

**Cutaway key**

1 Fixed inflight-refuelling probe
2 Radome
3 Radar tracking mechanism
4 Weather radar scanner
5 Cockpit front pressure bulkhead
6 Battery bay port and starboard
7 Cockpit floor level
8 Rudder pedals
9 Control column
10 Instrument panel
11 Instrument panel shroud
12 Windscreen wipers
13 Windscreen panels
14 Overhead switch panel
15 Co-pilot's seat
16 Centre control pedestal
17 Sliding side window panel
18 Control column handwheel
19 Pilot's seat
20 Chart case
21 Nosewheel bay
22 Twin nosewheels
23 Nosewheel door
24 Boarding steps
25 Door external latch
26 Crew entry door
27 Crew toilet
28 Cockpit steps
29 Cockpit eyebrow windows
30 Radio and electronics racks
31 Navigator's swivelling seat
32 Chart table
33 TACAN aerial
34 Pitot tubes
35 Crew escape hatch
36 Twin rest bunks

37 Cockpit rear bulkhead
38 Main cabin doorway
39 Centre fuselage/cockpit section production joint
40 Main cargo loading deck

41 Floor beam construction
42 Honeycomb floor panels
43 Folding troop seats: up to 93 troops
44 Control rod runs
45 Cabin escape hatch
46 VHF aerial
47 Cabin wall trim panels
48 Soundproofing insulation
49 Starboard sponson air system heat exchanger
50 Water extractor
51 Air conditioning plant
52 Foreign object damage propeller guard skin reinforcing plate
53 Cabin window panel
54 Air system piping
55 HF aerial mast
56 Wing fillet fairing
57 Anti-collision light
58 Wing front spar
59 Strengthened wing centre section construction provision for additional fuel tankage of 1,980 Imp gal (9000 litres)
60 Wing lattice ribs
61 Engine bleed air piping
62 Starboard engine nacelle
63 Engine exhaust duct
64 Rolls-Royce Tyne RTy.20 Mk 22 turboprop engine
65 Engine bearer struts
66 Engine accessory units
67 Oil tank 7½ Imp gal (34 litres)
68 Annular engine air intake
69 Oil cooler air intake
70 Propeller blade root de-icing boots
71 Propeller pitch change mechanism
72 Spinner

73 Four-bladed constant speed propeller
74 Detachable cowling panels
75 Engine bleed air spill duct
76 Engine mounting struts
77 Wing stringers
78 Outer wing panel bolted skin joint
79 Starboard wing integral fuel tanks: normal system capacity 4,190 Imp gal (19050 litres)
80 Fuel filler caps
81 Landing/taxiing lamps
82 Leading edge de-icing boots
83 Starboard navigation light
84 Wing tip fairing
85 VHF aerial
86 Starboard aileron
87 Aileron hydraulic jack
88 Starboard roll control spoiler
89 Perforated airbrake panels upper and lower surfaces
90 Airbrake hydraulic actuators
91 Outboard double-slotted flap segments
92 Flap guide rails
93 Inboard double slotted flap

94 Wing root trailing edge fillet
95 Cabin pressurisation valves
96 Central flap drive motor and gearbox
97 Starboard paratroop door
98 Fuselage skin plating
99 Control rod runs
100 Centre fuselage/tailcone production joint
101 Lower formation light
102 Rear cargo door, open position
103 Cargo door frame construction
104 Tailcone escape hatch (two)
105 Fin root fillet
106 Upper formation light
107 Tailplane leading edge de-icing boot
108 HF aerial cable
109 Starboard tailplane
110 Starboard elevator
111 Fin leading edge de-icing boot
112 Fin rib construction
113 VOR aerial
114 Anti-collision light
115 Rudder construction
116 Rudder hydraulic jack
117 Tailcone
118 Tail navigation light

119 Port elevator construction
120 Fixed tailplane construction
121 Leading edge de-icing boot
122 Elevator hydraulic jack
123 Rudder and elevator control linkages
124 Fin root attachment joint
125 Fin/tailplane attachment main frame
126 Rear cargo door hinge point
127 Cargo door side latches
128 Fuselage lower longeron
129 Tailcone frame construction
130 Detachable vehicle loading ramps
131 Forward cargo door/main loading ramp, lowered position
132 Rear toilet

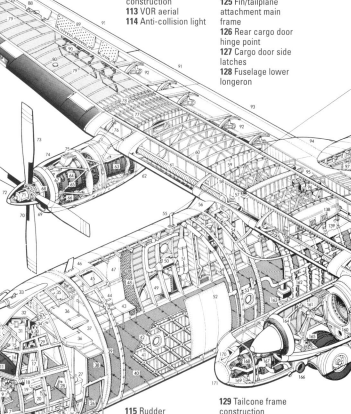

In terms of their general layout the **C-130 Hercules** (background) and **Transall C.160** are very similar. Both have a shoulder-mounted wing leaving the cabin clear of intrusion by the wing spars, a rugged undercarriage with its main units housed in external sponsons and an upswept beaver tail with an in-built loading ramp/door. While the Hercules employs four engines of around 4,050 shp (3020 kW) each, the Transall uses a pair of considerably more powerful Tyne engines. This results in a machine with similar payload capabilities to the US airlifter, but with generally inferior performance, a fact perhaps reflected by l'Armée de l'Air's decision to procure the Hercules as well as the Transall.

## SPECIFICATION

### C.160 (first generation)

#### Dimensions

**Length:** 106 ft 3½ in (32.40 m)
**Height:** 38 ft 5 in (11.65 m)
**Wingspan:** 131 ft 3 in (40.00 m)
**Wing area:** 1,723.36 sq ft (160.10 m²)
**Wing aspect ratio:** 10
**Tailplane span:** 47 ft 7 in (14.50 m)
**Wheel track:** 16 ft 9 in (5.10 m)
**Wheel base:** 34 ft 4½ in (10.48 m)

#### Powerplant

Two Rolls-Royce Tyne RTy.20 Mk 22 each rated at 6,100 ehp (4548 ekW)

#### Weights

**Empty equipped:** 63,400 lb (28758 kg)
**Normal take-off:** 97,443 lb (44200 kg)
**Maximum take-off:** 108,245 lb (49100 kg)

#### Fuel and load

**Internal fuel:** 4,359 US gal (16500 litres)
**Maximum payload:** 35,273 lb (16000 kg)

#### Performance

**Maximum level speed 'clean' at 14,765 ft (4500 m):** 333 mph (536 km/h)
**Maximum cruising speed at 18,045 ft (5500 m):** 319 mph (513 km/h)
**Maximum cruising speed at 26,245 ft (8000 m):** 308 mph (495 km/h)
**Maximum rate of climb at sea level:** 1,444 ft (440 m) per minute
**Service ceiling:** 27,885 ft (8500 m)
**Take-off run at maximum take-off weight:** 2,608 ft (795 m)
**Take-off distance to 35 ft (10.70 m) at maximum take-off weight:** 3,609 ft (1100 m)
**Landing distance from 50 ft (15 m) at normal landing weight:** 2,100 ft (640 m)
**Landing run at normal landing weight:** 1,181 ft (360 m)
**Range with an 8000-kg (17,637-lb) payload:** 2,796 miles (4500 km)
**Range with a 35,273-lb (16000-kg) payload:** 734 miles (1182 km)

*Above: Turkey maintains a tactical transport force similar in constitution to that of France, with **C.160Ds** flying alongside **c-130 Hercules** and **CN-235s**. The Transalls were acquired as 19 secondhand aircraft from West Germany in 1971, and are based at Erkilet with 221 Filo of the Türk Hava Kuvvetleri.*

155 Port wing integral fuel tank bays
156 Fuel filler caps
157 Leading edge nose ribs
158 Mainwheel doors
159 Twin tandem mainwheels
160 Port engine nacelle fireproof bulkhead
161 Main landing gear leg strut mounting
162 Wing attachment fuselage main frame

139 Wing/fuselage attachment bolted joints
140 Centre fuselage frame and string construction
141 Port sponson tail fairing
142 Outer wing skin panel bolted joint
143 Flap vane
144 Port double slotted flaps
145 Airbrake segments
146 Port spoiler
147 Flap rib construction
148 Port aileron construction
149 Aileron hydraulic jack
150 Wing tip fairing
151 Port navigation light

163 Hydraulic system reservoir
164 Port engine cowlings
165 Main landing gear hydraulic retraction/kneeling jack
166 APU exhaust
167 Garrett AiResearch GTCP-85-160A APU
168 APU-driven accessory gearbox
169 Ground power generator
170 APU air intake door
171 Port sponson fairing

compartment water tank
133 Rear toilet
134 Port paratroop door
135 Wing rear spar
136 Flap screw jacks
137 Flap drive shafting
138 Wing/fuselage attachment main rib

152 UHF aerial array
153 Wing leading edge de-icing boot
154 Wing rib construction

*The capability for off-airfield operations is a must for any tactical airlifter. Low-pressure tyres allow the **C.160** to operate from a variety of unprepared surfaces, although operations from autobahns are more demanding of the crew than the aircraft. Provision was made in the Transall design for the installation of underwing booster jets in the 5,250-lb st (23.34-kN) class, for improved take-off and cruise performance, but these have never been used in service.*

# Vickers VC-10

Although the RAF's VC10 fleet is coming to the end of its useful service life, the type is still a vitally important element in the UK's front-line. The VC10s served with distinction during Desert Storm, refuelling US Navy aircraft in addition to RAF machines and have since been active over the Balkans and in support of various UN operations. One K.Mk 2 was initially painted in a grey/green camouflage, but otherwise the hemp scheme has been universal.

### VC10 K.Mk 3
**Cutaway key**
1 Centre refuelling hose and drogue

### VC10 K.Mk 3 fuel system
This diagram of a VC10 K.Mk 3 details the intricate fuel system of the tanker. The K.Mk 3 has the additional fin tank compared to the K.Mk 2, giving a total capacity of 22,925 Imp gal (104217 litres).

### Fin tank
The K.Mk 3 has additional fuel in the fin, this tank filling the inter-spar area. It adds another 1,140 Imp gal (5182 litres).

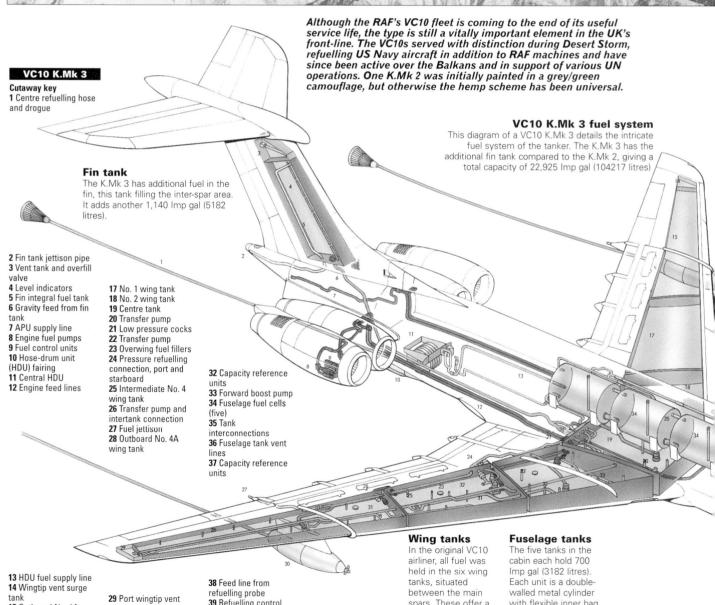

2 Fin tank jettison pipe
3 Vent tank and overfill valve
4 Level indicators
5 Fin integral fuel tank
6 Gravity feed from fin tank
7 APU supply line
8 Engine fuel pumps
9 Fuel control units
10 Hose-drum unit (HDU) fairing
11 Central HDU
12 Engine feed lines

17 No. 1 wing tank
18 No. 2 wing tank
19 Centre tank
20 Transfer pump
21 Low pressure cocks
22 Transfer pump
23 Overwing fuel fillers
24 Pressure refuelling connection, port and starboard
25 Intermediate No. 4 wing tank
26 Transfer pump and intertank connection
27 Fuel jettison
28 Outboard No. 4A wing tank

32 Capacity reference units
33 Forward boost pump
34 Fuselage fuel cells (five)
35 Tank interconnections
36 Fuselage tank vent lines
37 Capacity reference units

13 HDU fuel supply line
14 Wingtip vent surge tank
15 Outboard No. 1A wing tank
16 Flight Refuelling Mk 32 wing pod

29 Port wingtip vent surge tank
30 Starboard Mk 32 refuelling pod
31 Tank vent lines

38 Feed line from refuelling probe
39 Refuelling control panel at flight engineer's station
40 Fixed flight-refuelling probe

### Wing tanks
In the original VC10 airliner, all fuel was held in the six wing tanks, situated between the main spars. These offer a capacity of 17,925 Imp gal (81480 litres).

### Fuselage tanks
The five tanks in the cabin each hold 700 Imp gal (3182 litres). Each unit is a double-walled metal cylinder with flexible inner bag, mounted on two floor beams and restrained by an A-frame structure.

## Extra tanks

The K.Mk 2s and K.Mk 3s have an extra 3,500 Imp gal (15910 litres) of fuel contained in five equal-sized cells in the former passenger cabin. The tanks were installed via the freight doors of the 'Supers' before they were sealed, but the K.Mk 2s had to be cut in half during conversion. The six standard wing tanks in all VC10s hold a total of 17,925 Imp gal (81480 litres), in addition to the optional fin tank and some 20 Imp gal (91 litres) in each of the three refuelling units' reservoirs.

## Hose-drum units

Two types of refueller are used on the VC10. In the lower rear fuselage is a Flight Refuelling Ltd Mk 17B hose-drum unit (HDU) deploying up to 70 ft (21 m) of hose and capable of delivering fuel at up to 4,000 lb (500 Imp gal; 2270 litres) per minute. Outboard, beneath the wings are two FRL Mk 32/2800 pods with a 48-ft (14.60-m) hose length and fuel flow of 2,800 lb (350 Imp gal; 1591 litres) per minute. Normal operating speeds for tanking are between 250-390 mph (400-630 km/h) with either one large aircraft on the centreline or two fighters refuelling from the wing pods. Both Mk 17B and Mk 32 (right) hose-drum units are equipped with signal lights for receiver aircraft and aligning marks. The drogues themselves are equipped with white lights to provide visual cues for night refuelling.

## SPECIFICATION

### VC10 C.Mk 1

### Dimensions

**Wingspan:** 146 ft 2 in 144.55 m)
**Wing area:** 2,932 sq ft (272.38 m²)
**Aspect ratio:** 7.29
**Length (excluding probe):** 158 ft 8 in (48.38 m)
**Height:** 39 ft 6 in (12.04 m)
**Tailplane span:** 43 ft 10 in (13.36 m)
**Wheel track:** 21 ft 5 in (6.53 m)
**Wheel base:** 65 ft 10½ in (20.08 m)

### Powerplant

Four Rolls-Royce Conway RCo.43 Mk 301 turbofans each rated at 21,800 lb st (96.97 kN)

### Weights

**Empty:** 146,000 lb (66224 kg)
**Maximum take-off:** 323,000 lb (146510 kg)
**Maximum take-off (K.Mk 2):** 313,056 lb (142000 kg)
**Maximum take-off (K.Mk 3):** 334,882 lb (151900 kg)
**Maximum take-off (K.Mk 4):** 334,882 lb (151900 kg)

### Fuel and load

**Maximum payload:** 57,400 lb (26037 kg)
**Internal fuel:** 19,365 Imp gal (88032 litres)
**Internal fuel (K.Mk 2):** 21,485 Imp gal (97671 litres)
**Internal fuel (K.Mk 3):** 22,925 Imp gal (104217 litres)
**Internal fuel (K.Mk 4):** 19,425 Imp gal (88306 litres)

### Performance

**Maximum cruising speed at 31,000 ft (9450 m):** 581 mph (935 km/h)
**Economical cruising speed at 30,000 ft (9145 m):** 426 mph (684 km/h)
**Range with maximum payload:** 3,898 miles (6273 km)
**Maximum rate of climb at sea level:** 3,050 ft (930 m) per minute
**Service ceiling:** 42,000 ft (12800 m)
**Take-off distance to 35 ft (10.70 m) at maximum take-off weight:** 8,300 ft (2530 m)
**Balanced landing field length at normal landing weight:** 7,000 ft (2134 m)

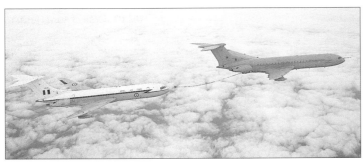

*VC10 C.Mk 1(K) and K.Mk 2 aircraft are being retired as their service life is deemed to expire. A major factor in the case of the C.Mk 1(K) is the cost of deep maintenance and as aircraft become due for their multimillion pound major overhauls, they are being retired. The VC10 tanker/transport fleets are therefore slowing running down, while the demands for their services remain constant – this situation is leading to low morale within the VC10 community. By 2007 the RAF envisages that the VC10's refuelling role will have been put out to a civilian contractor using either Boeing 767- or Airbus A310-based tankers. The practicality of sending civilian aircraft, possibly operated by civilian crews, into a combat environment while laden with fuel has yet to be decided.*

*Above: The VC10 tanker conversion added nose refuelling probes to the aircraft, along with a Turboméca Artouste 520 APU in the tailcone. The 'new' machines received the revised company designations V1112 VC10 and V1164 Super VC10. The latter also had their forward fuselage freight doors sealed.*

*Right: Painted with grey and green disruptive upper surface camouflage, the first K.Mk 2 conversion, ZA141, first flew at Filton on 22 June 1982, piloted by Roy Radford. A structural weakness in the fin resulted in it being fitted with the tail unit of an ex-civil VC10, XX914, which had recently been withdrawn from use as a testbed at RAE, Bedford and, as such, ZA141 was delivered to Boscombe Down on 9 June 1983 for trials by the A&AEE*

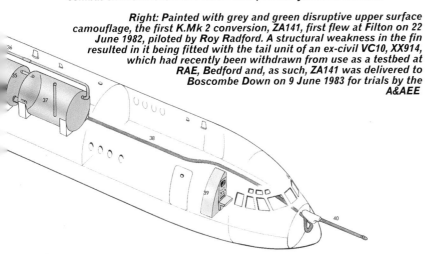

# Index